The Power of Global Performance Indicators

Global performance indicators (GPIs), such as ratings and rankings, permeate nearly every type of human activity, internationally and nationally, across public and private spheres. While some indicators aim to attract media readership or brand the creator's organization, others increasingly seek to influence political practices and policies. *The Power of Global Performance Indicators* goes beyond the basic questions of methodological validity explored by others to launch a fresh debate about power in the modern age, exploring the ultimate questions concerning real world consequences of GPIs, both intended and unintended. From business regulation to terrorism, education to foreign aid, Kelley and Simmons demonstrate how GPIs provoke bureaucracies, shape policy agendas, and influence outputs through their influence on third parties such as donors and market actors and, potentially, even broader global authority structures.

Judith G. Kelley is Terry Sanford Professor of public policy and political science and Dean of the Duke Sanford School of Public Policy. She is the author of *Scorecard Diplomacy: Grading States to Influence Their Reputation and Behavior* (Cambridge University Press) and *Monitoring Democracy: When International Election Observation Works and Why It Often Fails* (Princeton University Press) winner of the Chadwick F. Alger Prize.

Beth A. Simmons is Professor of Law, Political Science and Business Ethics at the University of Pennsylvania and an elected member of the National Academy of Sciences. She is the author of *Mobilizing for Human Rights: International Law in Domestic Politics* (Cambridge University Press) recognized by the American Political Science Association and American Society for International Law, among others, as the best book of 2010.

The Power of Global
Performance Indicators

Edited by
JUDITH G. KELLEY
Duke University

BETH A. SIMMONS
University of Pennsylvania

CAMBRIDGE
UNIVERSITY PRESS

CAMBRIDGE
UNIVERSITY PRESS

University Printing House, Cambridge CB2 8BS, United Kingdom

One Liberty Plaza, 20th Floor, New York, NY 10006, USA

477 Williamstown Road, Port Melbourne, VIC 3207, Australia

314–321, 3rd Floor, Plot 3, Splendor Forum, Jasola District Centre, New Delhi – 110025, India

79 Anson Road, #06-04/06, Singapore 079906

Cambridge University Press is part of the University of Cambridge.

It furthers the University's mission by disseminating knowledge in the pursuit
of education, learning, and research at the highest international levels of excellence.

www.cambridge.org
Information on this title: www.cambridge.org/9781108487207
DOI: 10.1017/9781108763493

First published 2020

Printed in the United Kingdom by TJ International Ltd, Padstow Cornwall

A catalogue record for this publication is available from the British Library.

Library of Congress Cataloging-in-Publication Data
Names: Kelley, Judith Green, editor. | Simmons, Beth A., 1958- editor.
Title: The power of global performance indicators / edited by Judith
Kelley, Duke University, North Carolina, Beth Simmons, University of
Pennsylvania.
Description: New York : Cambridge University Press, 2020. | Includes
bibliographical references and index.
Identifiers: LCCN 2019044097 | ISBN 9781108487207 (Hardback) | ISBN
9781108732741 (eBook)
Subjects: LCSH: Political planning--Evaluation. | Ranking and selection
(Statistics)--Political aspects.
Classification: LCC JF1525.P6 P69 2020 | DDC 320.6--dc23
LC record available at https://lccn.loc.gov/2019044097

ISBN 978-1-108-48720-7 Hardback

Additional resources for this publication at www.cambridge.org.kelleysimmons

Contents

Figures

Tables

Contributors

Joshua Alley
Texas A&M University, USA

James H. Bisbee
New York University, USA

Rush Doshi
Brookings Institution, Washington, DC, USA

James R. Hollyer
University of Minnesota, USA

Dan Honig
Johns Hopkins School of Advanced International Studies, Washington, DC

Hyeran Jo
Texas A&M University, USA

Judith G. Kelley
Duke Sanford School of Public Policy, USA

Rie Kijima
University of Toronto, Canada

Faradj Koliev
Stockholm University, Sweden

Ranjit Lall
London School of Economics, UK

Melissa M. Lee
Princeton University, USA

Phillip Y. Lipscy
University of Toronto, Canada

Aila M. Matanock
University of California, USA

Julia C. Morse
University of California, Santa Barbara

Brian J. Phillips
University of Essex, UK

Jordan Roberts
Duke University, USA

B. Peter Rosendorff
New York University, USA

Beth A. Simmons
University of Pennsylvania, USA

Helena Hede Skagerlind
Stockholm University, Sweden

Thomas Sommerer
Stockholm University, Sweden

Jonas Tallberg
Stockholm University, Sweden

Juan Tellez
Duke University, USA

James Raymond Vreeland
Princeton University, USA

Catherine Weaver
University of Texas at Austin Lyndon B. Johnson School of Public Affairs,
    USA

Preface

The seeds of this volume were planted early in 2011 when we were working on a project about the US efforts to combat human trafficking. That project was focused on the rating system of the US Department of State, which assesses government efforts to combat human trafficking. We wondered, does that "tier" system have any influence on a country's propensity to criminalize human trafficking? Halfway through the project, in the fall of 2011, we were skyping across the Atlantic in a series of intense revision efforts, when we began to realize that we might be onto something larger than this specific example. There was something about the process of rating that went beyond information gathering; it seemed to constitute social pressure, maybe even an effort at governance. While we had worked before on the effects of monitoring and global norms on state behavior and studied causal mechanisms from reputational concerns to domestic mobilization around global norms, this phenomenon seemed to bring together many of these past insights into a unique combination of causal mechanisms.

Soon thereafter, we were both grateful for the opportunity to attend a conference on the construction of performance indices at New York University in 2014 that was organized by Sally Merry and Benedict Kingsbury. The more we started to think about it, the more we were intrigued about the phenomenon of ratings and rankings.

Although a substantial body of work on such ratings and rankings – or indicators as they were often referred to – was developing, much of the work assumed that these indices mattered, and, therefore, they explored their construct validity, deconstructed their methodologies, and debated their normative content. Only a very few studies attempted to assess or theorize effects on state behaviors, and the ones that did typically did not test behavioral outcomes. We made this the goal of our research on the US tier ranking of countries for their efforts to combat human trafficking.

Our research led us to see just how widespread the phenomenon of rating and ranking states was. Indeed, the practice of arraying information to elicit explicit comparisons seemed to be spreading among states, international organizations, and non-state actors. In order to better understand this phenomenon, we conducted interviews in London, Washington, DC, and New York during the summer of 2014, and spoke with over forty individuals from twenty different organizations. These interviews were incredibly rich, allowing us to gain an appreciation for the creators' goals, and for the very intentional strategies to deploy indices to shape not only organizational brands and discourse but also actual policy outcomes. The raters explained how states reacted to being ranked, as well as to specific rankings. It started to appear plausible to us that countries cared about how they compared to others.

Our own analysis of the *Trafficking in Persons Report* revealed that the State Department's rating system had significantly impacted countries' criminalization of human trafficking through multiple causal mechanisms.[1] We were struck by several aspects of the State Department's exercise, which helped us detect and define a broader ranking phenomenon. We felt the flurry of ranking creation and contestation was increasingly going well beyond measurement; it represented a governance struggle that was broadly understood. First, ratings and rankings were *intentional* in their efforts to influence policies, by engaging their targets' sustained attention. This also meant such information had to be *public*. Second, many ratings and rankings schemes were *recurrent*, which appeared to be important for their effectiveness in invoking the enduring reputational concerns that motivated sometimes difficult change over time.

To explore the broader applicability of our ideas, we organized a call for papers for a conference on global performance indices, sponsored by the journal *International Organization*. For focus, we specifically asked that papers examine ratings and rankings as explanatory variables, and examine consequences, for example, on state policies, power relationships, rule-setting, or dominant discourse. We encouraged papers that used a variety of methodological approaches from single-case studies to large N studies, to experiments or statistical analyses. The call elicited nearly 100 proposals. The conference, "Assessment Power in World Politics," was held at the Harvard Weatherhead Center for International Affairs (WCFIA) in May 2016 and was followed in September by a mini-conference at the annual conference of the American Political Science Association (APSA) that same year. These conferences brought together scholars who worked on a wide range of assessments of state qualities (e.g. transparency), state policies (e.g. press freedom), or

---

[1] This work was eventually published as "Politics by Number: Indicators as Social Pressure in International Relations," in the *American Journal of Political Science*, Vol 59(1): 1146–1161, 2015, and as *Scorecard Diplomacy: Grading States to Influence Their Reputation and Behavior*, Cambridge University Press, 2017.

prevalent social practices within a state's jurisdiction (e.g. corruption). Papers contributed theoretical and empirical insights about the use and consequences, or lack thereof, of indicators for domestic politics, transnational and/or international relations. While a subset of the contributions to this volume was published as a symposium with *International Organization*, we are delighted to be able to gather the much broader set of contributions in this edited volume. Together, these contributions present substantial evidence that global performance indicators – ratings and rankings – can influence the behavior of states. They also demonstrate the varied mechanisms of influence, and begin to probe the conditions for their effectiveness. As a set of studies, these chapters make a stronger argument than our sole focus on human trafficking ever could: global performance indicators are a tool of global governance, and rankings often do more than help "brand" organizations. They often alter the normative discourse around a subject, create competition around ranking status, and alter the incentives for specific policies.

We have a lot of people to thank for the overall development of this volume. Sam Chase and Nadia Hajji helped us build the database of indicators on which the introduction is based. We are grateful to the following individuals whom we interviewed during the summer of 2014: Alexandra Gillies (PhD) with the Natural Resource Governance Institute which publishes *The Resource Governance Index* (RGI); Clare Doube with Amnesty International (AI), whom we interviewed about why AI does *not* have an index; Johan Gott, at A. T. Kearney, which publishes the *FDI Confidence Index*; David Roodman, who created the *Commitment to Development Index* for the Center for Global Development; and John Easton, Dan McGrath, and Dana Kelly from the National Center for Education Studies (NCES) who spoke with us about the US interaction with the *PISA Index*. We are grateful to Rita Ramalho, Nadine Shamounki Ghannam, and Betty Mensah at the World Bank, who spoke with us about the *Ease of Doing Business* (EDB), and to Jean-François Arvis and Christina Busch who explained the Bank's *Logistics Performance Index* to us. We are also grateful to Adriana Alberti, Richard Kerby, Zamira Dzhusupova, Anni Haataja, Deniz Susar, and Tyko Dyrksmeyer who helped produce the *E-Governance Index* for the United Nations Department of Economic and Social Affairs, and to Daniel Calingaert who spoke with us about the Freedom House's *Freedom in the World Report*. In addition, we thank the Hudson Institute's Kimberly Russell and Carol Adelman, who created the *Index of Global Philanthropy and Remittances,* and J. J. Messner and Nate Haken at The Fund for Peace, which publishes *The Fragile States Index;* Jeremy Tamanini with Dual Citizen LLC, which creates the *Global Green Economy Index,* and Nathaniel Heller and Hazel Feigenblatt, who help Global Integrity publish the *Global Integrity Index*. At the Heritage Foundation, which produces the *Index of Economic Freedom,* we are thankful to Anthony Kim, Terry Miller, and Kim Holmes. We also thank Klaus von Grebmer who works for the International Food Policy Research Institute and answered our questions about the *Global Hunger Index*; Leon Morse at International Research and Exchanges Board (IREX) who spoke with us about the *Media Sustainability Index*; and at Publish What You Fund, which produces the *Aid Transparency Index*, we thank Rachel Rank, Shreya Basu, and Mark Brough. We are grateful also to Adam Foldes at Transparency International, which produces the *Corruption Perceptions Index*, Milorad Kovacevic with the United Nations Development Program (UNDP) who talked to us about the Human Development Report Office, and Alejandro Ponce and Juan Botero at the World Justice Project, which publishes the *Rule of Law Index*. Finally, we thank Vivek Ramkumar and Michael Castro at the International Budget Partnership, which creates the *Open Budget Survey*, and Nathan Gamester and Novella Bottini at the Legatum Institute, which creates the *Legatum Prosperity Index*.

In addition to the many contributors to this volume, we also thank the other participants at the 2016 conferences at Harvard and APSA: Angelina Fisher, Nancy Green Saraisky, Laura A. Henry, Lisa Sundstrom, Steven Bernstein, David J. Gordon, Matthew Hoffman, Bradley C. Parks, and Takaaki Masaki, for their knowledge on ratings and rankings and their theoretical insights in early discussions. We also thank the paper discussants at these conferences, including Felipe Barrera-Osorio, Daniel Drezner, Martha Finnemore, Jeff Frieden, Thomas Gift, Alicia Harley, Connor Huff, Iain Johnston, Joshua Kertzer, Elise Le, Lucas Linsi, Christopher Lucas, John Marshall, Sally Merry, Richard Nielsen, Solé Prillaman, Karthik Ramanna, Anton Strezhnev, and Dustin Tingley. Robert Keohane and Judith Goldstein also gave us extensive advice on the project.

In addition to the support we received from *International Organization* to hold a 2016 workshop at Harvard, we are grateful to the Weatherhead Center for International Affairs (WCFIA) and to the Institute for Quantitative Social Science, both at Harvard, for supplemental funding. We are also grateful to WCFIA for the staff and logistical support to execute the event smoothly. Thanks also go to APSA for supporting a mini-conference that same year. Several of the contributions in this volume also benefitted from rich reviewer feedback from *International Organization,* and we are grateful to the editors and to the anonymous reviewers. We are grateful to Cambridge University Press for allowing us to include chapters in this volume originally printed in the symposium in *International Organization*, to our Cambridge University Press editor, Robert Dreesen, for shepherding this volume along, and for the production assistance of Jackie Grant at Cambridge University Press.

Beth A. Simmons would like to dedicate this book to her husband, Bruce Jackan. Judith G. Kelley would like to dedicate it to her husband, Michael Kelley.

Introduction

The Power of Global Performance Indicators

Judith G. Kelley and Beth A. Simmons

Political leaders care about their reputations, especially personal reputations relative to their peers. Entrepreneurial actors have seized on this fact as an opportunity for policy influence. They take advantage of the competitive pressures of globalization, the increasing accountability demands flowing from democratization, and the transformative capacities of new information technologies. This all to nudge global governance in important ways by deploying what we call *Global Performance Indicators* (GPIs) – regularized public assessments that rate, rank, and categorize state policies, qualities, and/or performance. Such GPIs aim to (re)define global standards, contrive competition, and provoke action according to specific performance criteria. They exemplify how states, intergovernmental organizations (IGOs), non-governmental organizations (NGOs), and think tanks seek to use modern information politics to invoke reputational concerns and influence policy *through the pressure of comparison.*

Performance assessments and associated indicators permeate human activity, internationally and nationally, across public and private spheres. Some, such as product ratings in *Consumer Reports* or national credit ratings by Standard and Poor's (S&P), have been around for decades; many are intended to inform private decision-making. More recently, agenda-motivated indicators, such as the country ratings of *Freedom in the World* by Freedom House or the *Ease of Doing Business Index* by the World Bank, have appeared.[1] Such indicators overtly and purposively seek to engage actors at the highest levels of government and influence their policies and governance practices.

---

[1] See, respectively, Freedom House *Freedom in the World* ratings at https://freedomhouse.org/report-types/freedom-world and Ease of Doing Business rankings at www.doingbusiness.org/en/rankings.

The rising use of indicators has prompted debates about their construct validity, use, and misuse.[2] Scholarship has flourished about the methodology, reliability, and fairness for a broad range of indicators and has problematized quantification.[3] We build on a range of insights – from sociology to anthropology to political science – and we focus on intentional efforts to use comparative information to influence policy and governance. Why do states and other important actors care about ratings and rankings? Is effective use of GPIs confined to already powerful actors such as the United States, or can GPIs contribute to a diffusion of authority? And if a GPI is effective, does it work primarily through material leverage, or are other mechanisms, such as reputational or social pressure, at work as well?

This volume expands our ability to answer these questions by examining the effects of eleven different GPIs spanning issues such as terrorism, corruption, democracy, business regulation, aid transparency, education, global governance, and labor rights. The chapters present evidence that these GPIs influence discourse, standards, and measurement, but they also examine whether and how GPIs change actions. Do they reverberate in domestic politics, provoke bureaucracies, shape policy agendas, and influence outputs? Do they influence the reactions and responses of donors and market actors? If they alter priorities, do they have *unintended* consequences as well? This volume aims to speak directly to how GPIs might alter politics, policies, and, more speculatively, even broader authority structures.

GLOBAL PERFORMANCE INDICATORS: DEFINITION, SCOPE, AND CONTEXT

Global performance indicators are *a named collection of rank-ordered data that purports to represent the past or projected performance of different units.*[4] While thousands of basic indicators such as Gross Domestic Product (GDP) exist to facilitate research or policymaking, and while all such quantification is normative and contestable,[5] this volume focuses on the consequences of overtly strategic state rating and ranking systems that package and deploy information intentionally for policy advocacy and implementation. Such GPIs assemble selected data – facts and statistics collected together for reference or analysis – to craft "new" information designed and publicized to complement advocacy for specific ends. We focus on GPIs that, in their purest form, meet all the following criteria. They are:

---

[2] Malito, Umbach, and Bhuta 2018.

[3] Arndt and Oman 2006; Ginsburg et al. 2005; Høyland, Moene, and Willumsen 2012; Van de Walle 2006. The World Bank's *Governance Indicators* are a potent example; see Apaza 2009. For a critique of their construct validity see Thomas 2010.

[4] Davis et al. 2012; Davis, Kingsbury, and Merry 2012; Davis, Merry, and Kingsbury 2015; Merry and Conley 2011.

[5] Fioramonti 2013.

- *Public* and easily available;
- *Regular* and published on a predictable schedule;
- *Purposive*, explicitly normative, policy focused;
- Deployed to influence *state-level outcomes*; and
- *Comparative* of the performance of multiple states within a region or more broadly.

Global performance indicators can take several forms. *Indices* or *indicators* use numbers or grades to rate or rank state performance, compressing enormous variance into a simplified scale.[6] *Categorical assessments* use ordinal categories to produce (un)flattering peer groups, while *blacklists* and *watchlists* draw stark distinctions between compliers and offenders. Hybrid systems are also common, as are accompanying country narratives and policy recommendations.

Basic indicators are hardly new – sovereign credit ratings first appeared in 1916 – but nearly all the GPIs that fit our definition were created after 1990.[7] To demonstrate the trend, we systematically gathered a database based on secondary literature, extensive searches of newspapers, magazines, and the wider web, using terms such as ranking, rating, index, blacklist, and watchlist. Each entry was coded, among other things, on launch year, regularity, purpose, creator type, country of origin, issue area(s), and the type of comparison used. To be included, a GPI had to have been created no later than 2015. This search produced 282 entries. Extensive culling[8] left 159 entries that met our criteria, and of these, 133 were still active as of 2018, meaning they had been updated in 2015 or later.[9] These 159 were included in the source data for Figure 1.1.

Global performance indicator growth has been nearly exponential. While it took almost three decades to approach twenty GPIs in the late 1990s, by the next decade the number had roughly quadrupled, and then in the next fifteen years it more than tripled. This proliferation responded to a growing demand for policy-relevant performance data, spurred by a consensus that many past development reforms and governance structures were failing,[10] and facilitated by the fact that information was becoming ever easier to collect, process, and disseminate.

---

[6] Broome and Quirk 2015; Büthe 2012; Davis et al. 2012; Hansen 2012; Karpik 2010.

[7] Löwenheim 2008.

[8] Of the 289, 29 were never reissued, so they failed the regularity criteria. Another 28 were aimed at investors, so they failed the policy purpose. Thirty had no explicit intent stated, so while they might qualify, they fell in a gray zone and for clarity of criteria, we noted them separately. Another 31 were just data (and clearly, we could have found hundreds more that would fit this category). A few others fell in other categories that didn't fit.

[9] The data collection concluded in July 2018.

[10] Arndt 2008; Arndt and Oman 2006. Governance measures are the major theme in the Malito et al. 2018 essay collection.

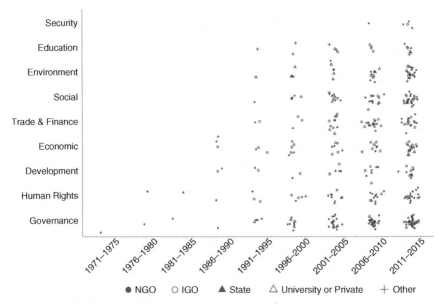

FIGURE I.I. GPI contestation across issues, time, and creators.
Notes: "Environment" covers energy and environment. "Human rights" covers human rights, gender issues and press freedom. "Trade & Finance" covers trade, finance and technology. "Social" covers health and social issues. All other topics are as coded in the dataset in Kelley and Simmons 2019.

As both the demand and supply of indicators grew, various actors began to realize that they could deploy GPIs as policy tools. A host of new GPIs, ranging from Transparency International's *Corruption Perceptions Index* to the Organisation for Economic Co-operation and Development's (OECD's) *Program for International Student Assessment* (PISA) rankings began to flourish. Their labels became more normative and vivid, their content ever more actionable, and their messages increasingly displayed to deliver visual impact. Recent GPIs are relentlessly comparative, suggesting an intention to pressure, shame, or provoke competition among states. Competitive prompts are clear in many GPIs' publicity messages. For example, when releasing the latest PISA rankings, the OECD announced: "Singapore tops latest OECD PISA global education survey."[11] Thus, GPIs are increasingly deployed to stimulate state competition and shape policy agendas; that is, as "technologies of power."[12]

[11] "Singapore Tops Latest OECD PISA Global Education Survey," 6 December 2016, OECD website, <www.oecd.org/education/singapore-tops-latest-oecd-pisa-global-education-survey.htm>, accessed 21 July 2018.
[12] Hansen 2012.

A THEORY OF GPI POWER

Why should governments care about a simple ranking or rating, especially if it merely reformats pre-existing information? We theorize that the power of GPIs is a function of their ability to engage reputations. Ratings and rankings stoke politicians' and bureaucrats' reputational concerns by framing, establishing "standards," and repeatedly engendering public comparisons. The packaging and intentional deployment of comparative information is, thus, an inherently social process that stimulates reputational concerns with how others view the performance of the state elites' competence, effectiveness, and status. These concerns can operate through multiple pathways, depending on local values and institutions.

Sources of GPI Power: Information, Contestation, and the Power to Frame

The social process of GPI influence begins with their ability to frame issues. The GPI promulgators seek to influence targets by designing an attention-grabbing form of political communication. By naming an issue, coining a vocabulary for describing it, and creating categories for its assessment, promulgators hope to affect discourse and, ultimately, policy.[13] This influence is akin to what Davis and colleagues call "knowledge effects"[14] and what Pierre Bourdieu refers to as "symbolic power" – or the power to name and categorize.[15] In some cases, the process begins by collecting new data; in others, existing data are presented in ways that prioritize new objectives. Such efforts shape how the public, organizations, and policymakers think about "what constitutes legitimate social practice."[16]

The GPIs are both products of, and inputs into, active value contestation. Nowhere is this clearer than in the struggle to define, measure, and rate "development" over recent years.[17] The United Nation's (UN) *Human Development Index* was created in 1990, adding lifespan, education, and low fertility to traditional GDP per capita measures to reflect new concerns with the quality of life. A decade later (2000), the new UN *Gender Equality Index* looked at disparities between men's and women's quality of life as the central conceptual issue.[18] The Fraser Institute contested both of these trends with its rival *Index of Human Progress* (2001) that restored weight to high-income

---

[13] Scheufele and Tewksbury 2007.
[14] Davis, Merry, and Kingsbury 2015.
[15] Bourdieu 1989.
[16] Hansen 2012.
[17] For the history of the *Human Development Index*, see Stanton 2007. For the World Bank's Governance Indicators see Kaufmann, Kraay, and Zoido 1999.
[18] United Nations, *Gender Inequality Index*, retrieved from http://hdr.undp.org/en/content/gender-inequality-index-gii.

levels and reflected the institute's interest in supporting competitive markets.[19] In 2006, the Sustainable Society Foundation, an NGO headquartered in the Netherlands, touted its eponymously named index to contest the notion that unbounded growth is desirable.[20] In short, creators of GPIs frame successful performance in preferred directions, often crowding the market with GPIs that jostle for agenda-setting visibility.[21]

Figure 1.1 indicates evidence of contestation across multiple GPI sectors. It shows the gradual uptake of GPIs in various issue areas. A lack of consensus may be one motivation for creating new GPIs and may partly explain the variation in density across issues. For example, while there is likely a greater demand for information about economic and financial performance, which has led to a greater supply by actors keen to dominate such visible issues, it is also likely that the lack of consensus around what constitutes favorable policies and ideal outcomes has contributed to the proliferation. Although we excluded indicators created simply to inform investors, over a third of the GPIs meeting our definition (36%) focused on economic issues with several alternative measures of prosperity and well-being to contest the traditional per capita GDP. Many GPIs are also concerned with various education or social issues (29%), governance (20%), development (20%), and the environment (17%), with several clusters covering hybrids of these issues as well. Many such hybrids represent efforts to contest narrow measures and advocate for broader conceptualizations of policy priorities. This is one reason the classification of GPIs in issue areas results in several that fall in multiple categories. Many are meant precisely to pull traditional conceptions, such as growth, in an unconventional direction, for example, toward justice.

Social Knowledge and Authority

A key source of GPI power is the credibility and authority of its creator.[22] What makes some GPI creators more authoritative than others? The social psychology literature suggests that one source of legitimate authority is trust, which develops out of a perception that an actor is fair, knowledgeable, and/or competent.[23] This may explain why many GPI creators attempt to

---

[19] See Joel Emes and Tony Hahn, "Measuring Development: An Index of Human Progress," Fraser Institute Occasional Paper 36, retrieved from www.fraserinstitute.org/sites/default/files/MeasuringDevelopmentIHP.pdf.

[20] See "Sustainable Society Index – Your Compass to Sustainability," retrieved from www.ssfindex.com/.

[21] Miller 2005.

[22] On private authority in international relations, see Hall and Biersteker 2002.

[23] Espeland and Sauder 2007; Rieh 2002; Wilson 1983. Well-respected raters have accumulative trust over decades, so people may act on this "expert" information, even when it erroneous; see Simonsohn 2011. On the importance of legitimacy for the effectiveness of international organizations see Buchanan and Keohane 2006; Zürn 2004.

bolster their credibility by transparently describing and defending their index's methodology. Just as important, actors who themselves are thought to exemplify specific norms are more likely to be viewed as authoritative in judging them,[24] and to have "normative power," which Manners defines as the ability to shape conceptions of what is "normal."[25]

The GPI creators also gain authority based on their (assumed) competence and expertise,[26] which may be inferred from their tangible power and wealth. The assumption that global competence in governance, economic policy, and human rights, for example, resides in the Western democracies, while contestable, has reinforced their "authority" to rate others in these areas. This may explain why, according to our data, organizations headquartered in the Global North create about 98 percent of the GPIs in existence today.

Social knowledge and authority are also supported by the tangible and intangible advantages of network centrality. Non-state actors with access to decision makers are better able to mine information and deploy it to assert authority.[27] States also have important network resources useful in developing and deploying GPIs. For example, the US Department of State, which creates the *Trafficking in Persons Report* and grades country performance, uses its embassies and NGO contacts around the world to tap into many sources of information. Actors centrally located in a social and political network are better able to set agendas[28] and have an impact on information flows,[29] which facilitates both data collection and GPI dissemination.[30]

Both states and non-state actors can accrue social authority for different reasons. States have advantages that flow from their pre-existing organization, broad resource base, and, in some cases, their political legitimacy. In contrast, non-state actors' authority rests on independence from powerful political actors. An interesting case that Honig and Weaver explore is the *Aid Transparency Index*.[31] They show that a small meagerly resourced NGO used its political independence and first-mover advantage to establish the gold standard for funding transparency. Political independence is plausibly the strength of several GPIs in our database; about half are created by NGOs and the rest are invented by universities, private actors, or a combination of actors. The United States is the only country that has created GPIs that target other states, which is only about 6 percent of the total. Overall, GPIs are largely *not* controlled by individual states or IGOs, although those created by the major IGOs and the United States attract more attention and, on average, may be more influential.

[24] Sikkink 1993.
[25] Manners 2002.
[26] Monks and Ehrenberg 1999.
[27] Hall and Biersteker 2002.
[28] Carpenter 2011 For related "social impact theory," see Latané 1981.
[29] Borgatti and Cross 2003.
[30] Stone 2002.
[31] Honig and Weaver 2019 (this volume).

Judgment and Comparison: Provoking Status Concerns and Competition

Global performance indicators are consequential because they engage the reputation of the people or entities being assessed. A *reputation* refers to a widespread belief that a person or an organization can reliably be characterized in a particular way.[32] *Status* and reputation are related, but status is explicitly comparative: it refers to the *relative* social or professional standing of someone or something in a formal or informal social hierarchy.[33] Both reputation and status are quintessentially social constructs; they are granted or accorded only by a social community. The GPIs confer status, which cannot be credibly claimed or manufactured unilaterally by the target. What makes this form of information deployment potentially powerful is its ability to broadly affect social beliefs about successful states and appropriate policies. It is deployed precisely as a form of social pressure on targets to conform – or suffer the reputational consequences, real or imagined.

Exactly why people value their status and reputation or that of their country is hotly debated. States and their elites likely seek to cultivate reputations as a form of strategic capital[34] to improve their payoffs.[35] Some care about their reputations for reasons having to do with their social role or identity.[36] The massive literature on shaming, for example, is built on the premise that officials want to avoid damaging their personal, professional, or organizational reputations.[37] Bureaucrats, politicians, and their public[38] also care about their own or their country's relative standing, which can be hard to establish in a thinly institutionalized international environment.[39] Status can be parlayed into material benefits and/or be an end in itself.[40] International relations research accords with similar theories in economics,[41] psychology,[42] and sociology[43] in accepting that people are as motivated by status as by power or material goods, with complex consequences for attitudes and behavior.

---

[32] On the reputational impact of comparisons, see Kelley 2017, Chapter 2.

[33] Masaki and Parks 2019 find that policy makers rate comparative assessments as more effective than single country assessments.

[34] Van Ham 2001.

[35] Tingley and Walter 2011.

[36] Dafoe, Renshon, and Huth 2014.

[37] On social pressures, see Checkel 2001; Johnston 2001. On shaming by states or IGOs, see Joachim, Reinalda, and Verbeek 2008; Lebovic and Voeten 2006. By non-governmental actors, see Hendrix and Wong 2013; Murdie and Davis 2012; Risse 1999.

[38] Rosen 2005; Wohlforth 2009.

[39] Dafoe, Renshon, and Huth 2014.

[40] Rege 2008. Some scholarship even suggests that status can propel costly policy choices, even war, see Dafoe, Renshon, and Huth 2014.

[41] Harsanyi 1966.

[42] Blader and Chen 2012.

[43] Ridgeway 2013.

The GPI creators seek to engage this concern with status and reputation by leveraging comparative information among peers.[44] Explicit comparisons create contexts in which judgments are formed and identities are established and reinforced.[45] They foster commensuration, or the comparison of different entities according to a common metric, as a way of making highly simplified sense of the world.[46] Labels like "rule of law," "freedom," "sustainable development," "peacefulness," or "political risk" imply that very different entities are, for the purposes of one concept, *comparable*. Numbers facilitate making standards through the simplest possible means – averaging.[47] The GPIs' recurrent nature incentivizes governments to look to the next iteration of the index and worry about the reputational consequences of their next rating or ranking. The media is particularly fond of reporting relative rankings. In numerous interviews, GPI creators frankly acknowledged that they created such indexes precisely to attract media attention.[48] About two-thirds of the active GPIs we could identify employ explicit top-to-bottom ranking systems, and over a third create clear normative categories or performance tiers, usually in addition to a ranking or rating. These features render GPIs a potent tool for producing social control through the pressure of comparative information.

Pathways to Responses: Domestic Politics, Bureaucratic Responses, and Transnational Pressures

This book explores how comparative rankings influence policy choices through multiple mechanisms.[49] Figure 1.2 illustrates how GPIs reverberate through different levels of politics: domestic, elite, and transnational, and underscores the cyclical nature of iterative assessments.

First, GPIs can provide information that reverberates in domestic politics, especially when amplified by the popular or social media, or circulated in civil society.[50] Important domestic audiences include local advocacy organizations, local

---

[44] In one exceptionally ambitious effort to exercise social control through ranking, China reportedly has pilot programs to rate each and every citizen according to a form of "social credit." See Celia Hatton, "China 'Social Credit': Beijing Sets up Huge System," 26 October 2015, retrieved from <www.bbc.com/news/world-asia-china-34592186>.

[45] Ashmore, Deaux, and McLaughlin-Volpe 2004.

[46] Espeland and Sauder 2007; Espeland and Stevens 1998; Schueth 2011; Sinclair 2008. Processes of commensuration inform global benchmarking, see Broome and Quirk 2015.

[47] Weisband 2000.

[48] This theme was evident in a series of twenty-three interviews conducted by the authors in Washington, DC, August 12–14, 2014.

[49] These processes align with seminal work on information politics, transnational activism, and domestic mobilization including: Davenport, Eccles, and Prusak 1998; Heiss and Kelley 2017; Keck and Sikkink 1998; Ron, Ramos, and Rodgers 2005. In environmental policy, "toteboard diplomacy" has created pressures for change, see Levy 1993. We confirmed similar processes in a series of interviews with GPI creators in Washington, DC, August 2014.

[50] Carpenter 2007; McCombs and Shaw 1972.

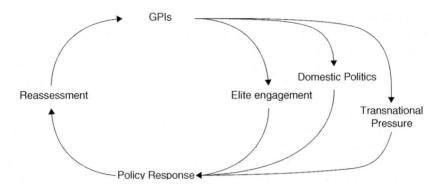

FIGURE 1.2. From GPIs to policy change: pathways, policy response, and reassessment. Adapted from Kelley and Simmons 2015 and Kelley 2017.

businesses, and even popular opinion generally. These groups use the comparative information from GPIs to demand better policy, especially when their country apparently lags behind. The underlying information need not be wholly new, but the assessment of relative performance is. The salience of the new information becomes an opportunity to mobilize in several ways: electorally through the ballot box, by publicizing critiques of performance in the media, engaging in traditional forms of lobbying, or by protesting or engaging in collective action. In responsive political systems, these demands might elicit policy change. At a minimum, officials will have the incentive to claim they are addressing the issue. However, where institutions repress public input and suppress political demands, governments may respond not with reform but by denigrating the GPI or its creator.[51]

Second, many GPIs involve intensive consultations with government bureaucrats during which officials take "expert" advice directly into account in their policymaking.[52] Such monitoring signals the value that the monitor and other actors attach to specific tasks,[53] and can influence targets to internalize monitoring regimes and eventually to self-regulate – a process that may mistakenly lead to underestimating the monitoring effects.[54] Referred to as the "Hawthorne effect," individuals in experimental settings have been found to rearrange their priorities to meet external expectations when they are aware of being observed.[55] This form of *reactivity* – the tendency for people to change their behavior in response to being evaluated – may explain the effect, for example, of *US News & World Report's* best colleges and best grad schools

[51] See Kelley 2017, Chapter 4.
[52] Masaki and Parks 2019 find that GPIs on which bureaucrats are consulted are among the most salient to government officials. On the importance of bureaucrats' reputations, see Chwieroth 2013; Nelson 2017.
[53] Larson and Callahan 1990.
[54] Self-regulation has been found effective in the context of health and safety monitoring by OSHA, see Johnson 2018.
[55] Adair 1984.

rankings on university priorities.[56] When a monitoring regime is applied generally to like units, it eventually gains acceptance by undercutting claims that the monitors have singled out specific targets "unfairly."[57]

Finally, GPIs activate transnational pressures and influence how third parties such as foreign investors, donors, or other states respond to – or are anticipated to respond to – the ratings. Many familiar rating systems leverage social pressure to conform primarily through third parties: universities respond to the *US News & World Report's* rating system because applicants do;[58] hospitals respond because patients do;[59] firms respond to environmental rankings because investors do.[60] Importantly, raters themselves need not control material resources to unleash transnational pressures.

ON SELECTION AND METHODS

Not all GPIs matter all the time. We have chosen contributions to this volume from a pool of about 100 scholar applicants, not based on results, which largely we did not know at the proposal stage, but based on the strength of the proposed methods and an effort to gain a variety of issues and types of GPIs. Still, the initial proposals were more likely to reflect potentially consequential GPIs that scholars were interested in studying. Certainly, we ourselves chose to focus on the *Ease of Doing Business Index* because of its stature. Some GPIs probably never matter, but that's a poor reason to dismiss the phenomenon overall. Furthermore, as with most other efforts to exert influence in international and transnational relations, context matters and, therefore, GPI effects and causal pathways are likely heterogeneous. This makes the mixed methods approaches of this volume and the examination across cases particularly appropriate, as methods that rely purely on testing for an average treatment effect of GPI might otherwise easily overlook important insights.

CONTRIBUTIONS OF THIS BOOK

The contributions in this volume apply an eclectic set of methods to greatly expand our knowledge about how GPIs influence states' policies. Together they explore a range of issues and indicators to describe the empirical terrain and to test for a range of GPA influences.[61] Some find strong support for the proffered framework, while others, such as Ranjit Lall's assessment of state

---

[56] Espeland and Sauder 2007.

[57] Löwenheim 2008.

[58] Luca and Smith 2013; Meredith 2004; Monks and Ehrenberg 1999.

[59] Pope 2009.

[60] Aaron, McMillan, and Cline 2012; Murguia and Lence 2015. Murguia and Lence found that getting one position closer to the top of *Newsweek*'s "Global 100 Green Rankings" increases the value of an average firm in the list by eleven million dollars.

[61] This contrast with the approach in Davis, Merry, and Kingsbury 2015 which relies solely on case studies.

rankings of international organizations, make important amendments.[62] Still others are more circumspect. For example, Melissa Lee and Aila Matanock's[63] analysis of the *Corruptions Perception Index* find no evidence that this GPI influences state reputations much at all. James Bisbee and coauthors uncover unintended consequences to attaching foreign aid to global educational rankings via the UN's Millennium Development Goals.[64]

Although the book is divided into parts, all of the chapters speak to multiple facets of ratings and rankings. Table 1.1 overviews the interwoven mechanisms and features discussed by each contribution.

Chapters 2–4 focus on "Ratings, Rankings, and Regulatory Behavior." Together with Rush we analyze one of the most visible rankings in the world, the World Bank's *Ease of Doing Business (EDB) Index*, which evaluates business regulations worldwide. We explore the history and normative context of the index and its market share among business climate indicators. We then use media analyses and observational data to explore whether the EDB has motivated state regulatory shifts with a specific focus on the bureaucratic channels in play. This analysis is augmented with experimental evidence of the influence of the EDB on business perceptions, and a case study of India to trace domestic channels of EDB influence.

Chapter 3, by Julia Morse, explores the effectiveness of the Financial Action Task Force (FATF), an intergovernmental body that issues a public listing of states and non-binding recommendations about how states should combat money laundering and the financing of terrorism. Morse examines whether information bundled in a list like the FATF is a "global currency" that IGOs can use to create institutional credibility and technical expertise. She examines how FATF designations are used to create transnational market pressure, and asks whether this ultimately can influence the passage of laws that criminalize terrorist financing.

The last chapter in Part I explores the extent and pathways of domestic policy adjustments to the third Millennium Development Goals, which was intended to spur policies that promote gender equality. In this chapter, Helene Skagerlind maps gender policy adoption in fifteen Sub-Saharan African countries over fifteen years. She goes in-depth with case studies of the causal mechanisms of gender policy change in Kenya and Ethiopia to understand the level of true behavioral change. Throughout, she examines an array of causal mechanisms including aid conditionality, social influence, civil-society mobilization, and elite socialization.

Do rating and ranking systems impact normative standards, and if so, with what consequences? Part II of the book, covering Chapters 5–8, tackles such questions. It begins with an examination by Dan Honig and Catherine Weaver of the *Aid*

---

[62] Lall this volume.
[63] Lee and Matanock this volume.
[64] Bisbee, Hollyer, Rosendorf, and Vreeland this volume.

Transparency Index produced by an NGO called Publish What You Fund, which seeks to promote donor transparency. The authors construct an original panel dataset of donor transparency performance before and after their inclusion in the index to examine whether, and which, donors respond to inclusion. Furthermore, they probe the causal mechanisms that explain variations in donor behavior through qualitative research, drawing on over 150 key informant interviews.

In Chapter 6, Rie Kijima and Phillip Lipscy explore the OECD's Program for International Student Assessment (PISA), which is now widely followed as a standard for national educational quality and human capital, and international competitiveness more broadly. In this case, countries opt into assessment voluntarily. The authors study how voluntary participation affects the capacity and motivation of policymakers to implement improvements in education. They rely on an original survey of education officials, as well as personal interviews with officials in target states, assessment agencies, and donor agencies to understand PISA influences at the elite, domestic, and transnational levels.

Chapter 7 shifts the focus to labor rights. Faradj Koliev, Thomas Sommerer, and Jonas Tallberg explore the International Labour Organization's (ILO's) reporting and shaming measure for states who fail to meet basic standards of labor protection. Using statistical analysis, they examine whether ILO reporting has had significant and durable effects on state respect for labor rights, especially in addressing severe cases of non-compliance. They also examine the conditions such as regime type and capacity to address labor issues in the country, and whether it matters whether the ILO merely places countries on the non-compliance list, or whether it must also actively shame them further.

In Chapter 8, Jordan Roberts and Juan Tellez examine the well-known *Freedom in the World* reports published by Freedom House. They explore what they call the "scarlet letter effect," or the idea that being branded "not free" by Freedom House evokes opprobrium by other democratic states. They examine transnational pressures that are consistent with our framework's theory of reputation. The authors assess the independent effect of being designated *not free* by exploiting a discontinuity in the assignment of a country's freedom status, whereby countries on either side of a bright-line receive different statuses, even though their level of political and civil freedom is quite similar.

Non-state actors can be subjected to pressure through ranking and especially blacklisting, as discussed in Part III. In Chapter 9, Hyeran Jo, Brian Phillips, and Joshua Alley look at the US Foreign Terrorist Organization (FTO) list and ask under what conditions it can be an effective counterterrorism tool. They explore the different resource dependencies of a wide range of terrorist organizations, hypothesizing that organizations dependent on private as opposed to state funding will be pressured by designation as an FTO. They examine, therefore, whether the FTO designation can potentially alter financial flows to privately funded organizations enough to ultimately alter terrorist attack patterns.

Whereas many of the indices that have arisen over the past couple of decades are created by intergovernmental organizations (IGOs), in Chapter 10,

TABLE 1.1. *Chapter overview of mechanisms and topics*

Chapter and Author	Creator	GPI	Contestation and Norms	Transnational Pressure	Domestic Politics	Elite Politics	Competition	Status/Reputation	Teaching to the Test	Effects on Targeted policies
2: Doshi, Kelley and Simmons	IGO	Ease of Doing Business Index	x	x	x	x	x	x	x	x
3: Morse	IGO	Financial Action Task Force		x		x		x		x
4: Skagerlind	IGO	MDGs on gender equality	x	x	x	x	x	x		x
5: Honig and Weaver	NGO	Aid Transparency Index	x	x	x	x	x	x	x	x
6: Kijima and Lipscy	IGO	PISA education rankings	x	x	x	x	x	x		x
7: Koliev, Sommerer, and Tallberg	IGO	ILO compliance list		x	x	x		x		x
8: Roberts and Telez	NGO	Freedom in the World Report	x	x						

Chapter and Author	Creator	GPI	Contestation and Norms	Transnational Pressure	Domestic Politics	Elite Politics	Competition	Status/Reputation	Teaching to the Test	Effects on Targeted policies
9: Jo, Phillips, and Alley	United States	Foreign Terrorist Organization (FTO) list	x	x	x	x				x
10: Lall	Countries	Ratings of IO performance	x	x			x	x		
11: Lee and Matanock	NGO	Corruption Perceptions Index		x						
12: Bisbee, Hollyer, Rosendorff, and Vreeland	IGO	MDGs on primary enrollment	x	x	x				x	x

Abbreviations: IGO – Intergovernmental organizations; NGO – Non-governmental organizations; MDG – Millennium Development Goals; PISA – Program for International Student Assessment; IO – Intergovernmental Organization

Ranjit Lall studies an index that is aimed at assessing IGOs themselves. Can a donor ranking of low effectiveness affect financial flows, and if so, are some IGOs more susceptible than others? Lall notes that not all IGOs that have received high performance ratings have been "rewarded" with increased financial contributions. Nor have all IOs that have received low ratings been "punished" with funding cuts or freezes. This study examines the conditions under which IO performance indicators influence resource flows to these institutions.

The last two substantive chapters and the last part of the book reflect the research of skeptical voices. Chapter 11 focuses on a highly visible GPI: Transparency International's *Corruption Perception Index* (CPI). Melissa Lee and Aila Matanock exploit the fact that states rated as the ten most corrupt tend to appear in media reports about corruption while the next ten (though still very corrupt) do not. They use this finding to compare outcomes among states on either side of this "threshold" and explore whether being in the bottom ten of the CPI elicits political pressure or discourages foreign aid. However, whereas other chapters in this book demonstrate that GPIs exercise considerable influence on state behavior, this chapter suggests limits to that influence, which is notable, given that Transparency International's CPI is now one of the highest profile indices.

In Chapter 12, James Bisbee, James Hollyer, Peter Rosendorff, and James Vreeland study a different type of question entirely. While they do find that their index of interest, the Millenium Development Goals regarding primary school education, increases the primary enrollment rate, the effect they are interested in is the secondary one. They reason that, if GPIs induce governments to alter policies in pursuit of given metrics, these indices will alter the equilibrium composition of public goods provision in targeted countries. To explore this possibility, the authors examine how primary and secondary school enrollment rates adjust to the Millennium Declaration across 114 countries with varying levels of transparency and democracy.

All but one of the twelve substantive chapters find that indices alter behaviors of the target, or of transnational or domestic actors, although not always in desired or expected ways. The combined insights about the conditions and mechanisms across chapters is what makes the book valuable. The conclusion overviews the findings and discusses how GPIs that rate and rank their targets have nudged actors, asserted striking degrees of social influence, and thereby changed important aspects of global governance. It also discusses possible scope conditions for their effectiveness. These chapters throw new light on the increasingly common practice of quantitative comparison as a technology of global governance.[65] Just as importantly, they bring attention to new questions ripe for research.

---

[65] Kelley and Simmons, Governance by Other Means: Rankings as Regulatory Systems. *International Theory*, forthcoming.

References

Aaron, Joshua R., Amy McMillan, and Brandon N. Cline. 2012. Investor Reaction to Firm Environmental Management Reputation. *Corporate Reputation Review* 15 (4):304–18.

Adair, John G. 1984. The Hawthorne Effect: A Reconsideration of the Methodological Artifact. *Journal of Applied Psychology* 69 (2):334–45.

Apaza, Carmen R. 2009. Measuring Governance and Corruption through the Worldwide Governance Indicators: Critiques, Responses, and Ongoing Scholarly Discussion. *PS: Political Science & Politics* 42 (1):139–43.

Arndt, Christiane. 2008. The Politics of Governance Ratings. *International Public Management Journal* 11 (3):275–97.

Arndt, Christiane, and Charles Oman. 2006. *Uses and Abuses of Governance Indicators*. Paris: Development Centre of the Organisation for Economic Co-operation and Development.

Ashmore, Richard D., Kay Deaux, and Tracy McLaughlin-Volpe. 2004. An Organizing Framework for Collective Identity: Articulation and Significance of Multidimensionalit. *Psychological Bulletin* 130 (1):80–114.

Blader, Steven L., and Ya-Ru Chen. 2012. Differentiating the Effects of Status and Power: A Justice Perspective. *Journal of Personality and Social Psychology* 102 (5):994–1014.

Borgatti, Stephen P., and Rob Cross. 2003. A Relational View of Information Seeking and Learning in Social Networks. *Management Science* 49 (4):432–45.

Bourdieu, Pierre. 1989. Social Space and Symbolic Power. *Sociological Theory* 7 (1):14–25.

Broome, Andre, and Joel Quirk. 2015. Governing the World At a Distance: The Practice of Global Benchmarking. *Review of International Studies* 41 (Special Issue 5):819–41.

Buchanan, Allen, and Robert O. Keohane. 2006. The Legitimacy of Global Governance Institutions. *Ethics & International Affairs* 20 (4):405–37.

Büthe, Tim. 2012. Beyond Supply and Demand: A Political-Economic Conceptual Model. In *Governance by Indicators: Global Power through Classification and Rankings*, edited by Kevin Davis, Angelina Fisher, Benedict Kingsbury and Sally Engle Merry, 29–51. Oxford: Oxford University Press.

Carpenter, R. Charli. 2007. Setting the Advocacy Agenda: Theorizing Issue Emergence and Nonemergence in Transnational Advocacy Networks. *International Studies Quarterly* 51 (1):99–120.

———. 2011. Vetting the Advocacy Agenda: Network Centrality and the Paradox of Weapons Norms. *International Organization* 65 (1):69–102.

Checkel, Jeffrey T. 2001. Why Comply? Social Learning and European Identity Change. *International Organization* 55 (3):553–88.

Chwieroth, Jeffrey M. 2013. "The Silent Revolution": How the Staff Exercise Informal Governance over IMF Lending. *The Review of International Organizations* 8 (2):265–90.

Dafoe, Allan, Jonathan Renshon, and Paul Huth. 2014. Reputation and Status as Motives for War. *Annual Review of Political Science* 17 (1):371–93.

Davenport, Thomas H., Robert G. Eccles, and Laurence Prusak. 1998. Information Politics. In *The Strategic Management of Intellectual Capital*, edited by David A. Klein, 101–20. Boston, MA: Butterworth-Heinemann.

Davis, Kevin E., Angelina Fisher, Benedict Kingsbury, and Sally Engle Merry, eds. 2012. *Governance by Indicators: Global Power through Classification and Rankings*. Oxford: Oxford University Press.

Davis, Kevin E., Benedict Kingsbury, and Sally Engle Merry. 2012. Indicators as a Technology of Global Governance. *Law & Society Review* 46 (1):71–104.

Davis, Kevin E., Sally Engle Merry, and Benedict Kingsbury. 2015. *The Quiet Power of Indicators: Measuring Governance, Corruption, and the Rule of Law*. Cambridge: Cambridge University Press.

Espeland, Wendy Nelson, and Michael Sauder. 2007. Rankings and Reactivity: How Public Measures Recreate Social Worlds. *American Journal of Sociology* 113 (1):1–40.

Espeland, Wendy Nelson, and Mitchell L. Stevens. 1998. Commensuration as a Social Process. *Annual Review of Sociology* 24 (1):313–43.

Fioramonti, Lorenzo. 2013. *Gross Domestic Problem: The Politics behind the World's Most Powerful Number*. London: Zed Books.

Ginsburg, Alan, Geneise Cooke, Steve Leinwand, Jay Noell, and Elizabeth Pollock. 2005. Reassessing US International Mathematics Performance: New Findings from the 2003 TIMSS and PISA. American Institutes for Research. Available at https://eric.ed.gov/?id=ED491624. Accessed August 24, 2019.

Hall, Rodney Bruce, and Thomas J. Biersteker. 2002. *The Emergence of Private Authority in Global Governance*. New York: Cambridge University Press.

Hansen, Hans Krause. 2012. The Power of Performance Indices in the Global Politics of Anti-Corruption. *Journal of International Relations and Development* 15 (4):506–31.

Harsanyi, John C. 1966. A Bargaining Model for Social Status in Informal Groups and Formal Organizations. *Behavioral Science* 11 (5):357–69.

Heiss, Andrew, and Judith G. Kelley. 2017. From the Trenches: A Global Survey of Anti-TIP NGOs and Their Views of U.S. Efforts. *Journal of Human Trafficking* 3 (3):231–54.

Hendrix, Cullen S., and Wendy H. Wong. 2013. When Is the Pen Truly Mighty? Regime Type and the Efficacy of Naming and Shaming in Curbing Human Rights Abuses. *British Journal of Political Science* 43 (3):651–72.

Honig, D. and C. Weaver. 2019, this volume. A Race to the Top? The Aid Transparency Index and the Social Power of Global Performance Indicators. *International Organization* 73(3): 579–610.

Høyland, Bjørn, Karl Moene, and Fredrik Willumsen. 2012. The Tyranny of International Index Rankings. *Journal of Development Economics* 97 (1):1–14.

Joachim, Jutta M., Bob Reinalda, and Bertjan Verbeek, eds. 2008. *International Organizations and Implementation: Enforcers, Managers, Authorities?* London; New York: Routledge/ECPR.

Johnson, Matthew. 2018. Regulation by Shaming: Deterrence Effects of Publicizing Violations of Workplace Safety and Health Laws. Unpublished manuscript, Duke University. Available at https://drive.google.com/file/d/1 HcKpGXZuFWNNLa1YTl0A4Hte1BiJabT-/view.

Johnston, Alastair Iain. 2001. Treating International Institutions as Social Environments. *International Studies Quarterly* 45 (4):487–516.

Karpik, Lucien. 2010. *Valuing the Unique: The Economics of Singularities.* Princeton, NJ: Princeton University Press.

Kaufmann, Daniel, Aart Kraay, and Pablo Zoido. 1999. Governance Matters. World Bank Policy Research Working Paper No. 2196. Available at SSRN: https://ssrn.com/abstract=188568.

Keck, Margaret E., and Kathryn Sikkink. 1998. *Activists beyond Borders: Advocacy Networks in International Politics.* Ithaca, NY: Cornell University Press.

Kelley, Judith G. 2017. *Scorecard Diplomacy: Grading States to Influence Their Reputation and Behavior.* Cambridge: Cambridge University Press.

Kelley, Judith G., and Beth A. Simmons. Forthcoming. Governance by Other Means: Rankings as Regulatory Systems. *International Theory.*
     2015. Politics by Number: Indicators as Social Pressure in International Relations. *American Journal of Political Science* 59 (1):1146–61.

Lall, R. this volume. Assessing International Organizations: Competition, Collaboration, and Politics of Funding.

Larson, James R., and Christine Callahan. 1990. Performance Monitoring: How It Affects Work Productivity. *Journal of Applied Psychology* 75 (5):530–38.

Latané, Bibb. 1981. The Psychology of Social Impact. *American Psychologist* 36 (4):343–56.

Lebovic, James H., and Erik Voeten. 2006. The Politics of Shame: The Condemnation of Country Human Rights Practices in the UNCHR. *International Studies Quarterly* 50 (4):861–88.

Lee, Melissa M., and Aila M. Matanock. this volume. Third Party Policymakers and the Limits of the Influence of Indicators. Chapter 11 in *The Power of Global Performance Indicators.* Cambridge: Cambridge University Press.

Levy, Marc A. 1993. European Acid Rain: The Power of Tote-Board Diplomacy. In *Institutions for the Earth: Sources of Effective International Environmental Protection*, edited by Peter M. Haas, Robert Owen Keohane and Marc A. Levy, 75–132. Cambridge: MIT Press.

Löwenheim, Oded. 2008. Examining the State: A Foucauldian Perspective on International "Governance Indicators." *Third World Quarterly* 29 (2):255–74.

Luca, Michael, and Jonathan Smith. 2013. Salience in Quality Disclosure: Evidence from the U.S. News College Rankings. *Journal of Economics & Management Strategy* 22 (1):58–77.

Malito, Debora Valentina, Gaby Umbach, and Nehal Bhuta, eds. 2018. *The Palgrave Handbook of Indicators in Global Governance.* Palgrave Macmillan.

Manners, Ian. 2002. Normative Power Europe: A Contradiction in Terms? *JCMS: Journal of Common Market Studies* 40 (2):235–58.

Masaki, Takaaki, and Bradley C. Parks. 2019. When Do Performance Assessments Influence Policy Behavior? Micro-evidence from the 2014 Reform Efforts Survey. *The Review of International Organizations.* doi:10.1007/s11558-018-9342-3.

McCombs, Maxwell E., and Donald L. Shaw. 1972. The Agenda-Setting Function of Mass Media. *Public Opinion Quarterly* 36 (2):176–87.

Meredith, Marc. 2004. Why Do Universities Compete in the Ratings Game? An Empirical Analysis of the Effects of the U.S. News & World Report College Rankings. *Research in Higher Education* 45 (5):443–61.

Merry, Sally Engle, and John M. Conley. 2011. Measuring the World: Indicators, Human Rights, and Global Governance. *Current Anthropology* 52 (S3): S83–95.

Miller, Clark A. 2005. New Civic Epistemologies of Quantification: Making Sense of Indicators of Local and Global Sustainability. *Science, Technology & Human Values* 30 (3):403–32.

Monks, James, and Ronald G. Ehrenberg. 1999. U.S. News & World Report's College Rankings: Why They Do Matter. *Change: The Magazine of Higher Learning* 31 (6):42–51.

Murdie, Amanda M., and David R. Davis. 2012. Shaming and Blaming: Using Events Data to Assess the Impact of Human Rights INGOs. *International Studies Quarterly* 56 (1):1–16.

Murguia, Juan M., and Sergio H. Lence. 2015. Investors' Reaction to Environmental Performance: A Global Perspective of the Newsweek's "Green Rankings." *Environmental and Resource Economics* 60 (4):583–605.

Nelson, Stephen Craig. 2017. *The Currency of Confidence: How Economic Beliefs Shape the IMF's Relationship with Its Borrowers*. Ithaca, NY: Cornell University Press.

Pope, Devin G. 2009. Reacting to Rankings: Evidence from "America's Best Hospitals." *Journal of Health Economics* 28 (6):1154–65.

Rege, Mari. 2008. Why Do People Care about Social Status? *Journal of Economic Behavior & Organization* 66 (2):233–42.

Ridgeway, Cecilia L. 2014. Why Status Matters for Inequality. *American Sociological Review* 79 (1):1–16.

Rieh, Soo Young. 2002. Judgment of Information Quality and Cognitive Authority in the Web. *Journal of the American Society for Information Science and Technology* 53 (2):145–61.

Risse, Thomas. 1999. International Norms and Domestic Change: Arguing and Communicative Behavior in the Human Rights Area. *Politics and Society* 27 (4):529–59.

Ron, James, Howard Ramos, and Kathleen Rodgers. 2005. Transnational Information Politics: NGO Human Rights Reporting, 1986–2000. *International Studies Quarterly* 49 (3):557–87.

Rosen, Stephen Peter. 2005. *War and Human Nature*. Princeton, NJ: Princeton University Press.

Scheufele, Dietram, and David Tewksbury. 2007. Framing, Agenda Setting, and Priming: The Evolution of Three Media Effects Models. *Journal of Communication* 57 (1):9–20.

Schueth, Sam. 2011. Assembling International Competitiveness: The Republic of Georgia, USAID, and the Doing Business Project. *Economic Geography* 87 (1):51–77.

Sikkink, Kathryn. 1993. Human Rights, Principled Issue-Networks, and Sovereignty in Latin America. *International Organization* 47 (3):411–41.

Simonsohn, Uri. 2011. Lessons from an "Oops" at Consumer Reports: Consumers Follow Experts and Ignore Invalid Information. *Journal of Marketing Research* 48 (1):1–12.

Sinclair, Timothy J. 2008. *The New Masters of Capital: American Bond Rating Agencies and the Politics of Creditworthiness.* Ithaca, NY: Cornell University Press.

Stanton, Elizabeth A. 2007. The Human Development Index: A History. PERI Working Paper, 85. Available at https://scholarworks.umass.edu/cgi/viewcontent.cgi?article=1101&context=peri_workingpapers.

Stone, Diane. 2002. Introduction: Global Knowledge and Advocacy Networks. *Global Networks* 2 (1):1–12.

Thomas, Melissa A. 2010. What Do the Worldwide Governance Indicators Measure? *The European Journal of Development Research* 22 (1):31–54.

Tingley, Dustin H., and Barbara F. Walter. 2011. The Effect of Repeated Play on Reputation Building: An Experimental Approach. *International Organization* 65 (2):343–65.

Van de Walle, Steven. 2006. The State of the World's Bureaucracies. *Journal of Comparative Policy Analysis: Research and Practice* 8 (4):437–48.

Van Ham, Peter. 2001. The Rise of the Brand State: The Postmodern Politics of Image and Reputation. *Foreign Affairs* 80 (5):2–6.

Weisband, Edward. 2000. Discursive Multilateralism: Global Benchmarks, Shame, and Learning in the ILO Labor Standards Monitoring Regime. *International Studies Quarterly* 44 (4):643–66.

Wilson, Patrick. 1983. *Second-Hand Knowledge: An Inquiry into Cognitive Authority.* Westport, CT: Greenwood Press.

Wohlforth, William C. 2009. Unipolarity, Status Competition, and Great Power War. *World Politics* 61 (1):28–57.

Zürn, Michael. 2004. Global Governance and Legitimacy Problems. *Government and Opposition* 39 (2):260–87.

PART I

RATINGS, RANKINGS, AND REGULATORY BEHAVIOR

2

The Power of Ranking

The Ease of Doing Business Indicator and Global Regulatory Behavior

Rush Doshi, Judith G. Kelley, and Beth A. Simmons

> The main advantage of showing a single rank: it is easily understood by politicians, journalists, and development experts and therefore created pressure to reform. As in sports, once you start keeping score everyone wants to win.
>
> World Bank Staff Report, 2005[1]

> Stripping the ordinal rankings and "reforming" the report's methodology would have the effect of completely destroying the report's credibility and usefulness as a policy tool.
>
> Steve Hanke, director of the CATO Institute's Troubled Currencies Project, in response to a Chinese-led effort to remove the rankings[2]

The world is increasingly governed not by force but by information that moves markets, affects reputations, and impinges on national security. Global performance indicators (GPIs), especially regimes that rate and rank states against one another, consciously package information to influence the priorities of states, the perceptions of publics, and the decisions of economic actors. As the introduction to this book suggests, GPIs constitute an increasingly important form of social pressure around the world. Their creators promote them to change the information environment of communities that are important to the target to change its behavior. All social pressure is exerted through information: sometimes relying on evidence and rational argument, often using emotive persuasion, and occasionally by making implicit or explicit demands for

---

[1] Djankov et al. 2005. From 2001 to 2005, the Bank did not rank. Data that would eventually form the basis of the rankings were first published in the fall of 2001 on the Bank's website.

[2] Steve H. Hanke, "Singapore Leads the Way in Doing Business," CATO Institute, September 19, 2013, https://www.cato.org/publications/commentary/singapore-leads-way-doing-business.

conformity. This information is intended to affect the views of an audience of importance to the target, anticipating that the target will care about and respond to those views.[3]

That is precisely what GPIs aim to do. Wielding comparative information using simple rankings is designed to alter shared information, affect third-party beliefs and opinions, and ultimately convince targets that their reputation or relative status is at stake, potentially with material and/or social consequences. Social pressure of this kind is evident in the area of business (de)regulation. Since the mid-2000s, the World Bank has used rankings to influence the regulatory policies of countries worldwide. By creating the *Doing Business Report* and the Ease of Doing Business (EDB) Index, the Bank has decisively shaped states' regulatory behavior, especially in emerging markets and developing countries. Even though the EDB is formally a non-coercive reporting exercise and may not always accurately reflect appropriate regulation, its existence has influenced governments around the world to change their economic and regulatory policies to meet the Bank's expectations. By benchmarking, and especially by *ranking*, the Bank intentionally exerts competitive social pressure on states to deregulate.[4] If the World Bank simply wanted to exert traditional *economic pressure*, it has long had the tools at hand, and scarcely needed to construct and propagate such an elaborate way to change the broader informational environment. Instead, the Bank has chosen to innovate by manipulating information that influences official reputations and states' status.

We explore the Bank's intentions in establishing its deregulatory ranking system. We build a prima facie case for the EDB's social influence by demonstrating its salience in the media and on the minds of high government officials. Plausible observational evidence demonstrates an average global correlation between publicizing the rankings, bureaucratic adaptations responding to the rankings, and an acceleration in actual policy reforms. A survey experiment and case study unpack causal mechanisms. By manipulating the information available to an elite panel of investors, we demonstrate that EDB rankings affect assessments of investment opportunities within a controlled experiment involving investors. A case study of India, informed in part by leaked documents, brings the strands of the argument together and provides evidence that politicians see the ranking as affecting domestic politics, altering investor sentiment and engaging bureaucratic reputations. The case demonstrates holistically that altering information allows the World Bank to intensify its influence on states whose national politicians and bureaucrats believe their reputations and ability to attract business are at stake. Consequently, they strive to move

---

[3] Nugent 2013. Unlike much of the socialization and social pressure literature in international relations (relating to human rights, for example), this definition does not take a position on whether social pressure is used for objectively good purposes. Our definition of social pressure can also be used as a synonym for peer pressure.

[4] "Doing Business–About Us," Doing Business 2019, World Bank, http://www.doingbusiness.org/about-us.

up in the rankings. Overall, a broad range of evidence, each source and method tailored to a specific step in the argument, shows that the Bank has intentionally and successfully packaged information to maximize its influence on states to reform business regulations in emerging markets around the world.

COMPARATIVE INFORMATION AND SOCIAL PRESSURE: A THEORY OF THE INFLUENCE OF THE EDB

The World Bank's use of the EDB Index is a prime example of the mechanisms discussed in the this book's introduction.[5] For decades, the Bank has used the traditional tools of loans and technical assistance to influence development strategies. For a number of reasons – including the possibility of growing skepticism about the legitimate role of international organizations in traditional areas of state sovereignty[6] – traditional tools of economic leverage were seen as undesirable and/or ineffective ways to encourage business deregulation. Instead, the Bank intentionally chose a communication device that uses the views of *other actors* to encourage change. Rankings served that purpose. They simplify a complex regulatory reality, compare all states along a set of actionable indicators, and publicize the resulting rankings to media hungry for simple headlines. Investors look for rules of thumb to guide their decisions pay attention. Constituents use the rankings to pass simple judgments on policies and politicians. Knowing this, the Bank sees an opening to use information through these audiences to achieve results. In other words, this is a World Bank-initiated application of social pressure. In anticipation or response, governments alter priorities, make bureaucratic changes, and intensify their engagement with the Bank to improve their rankings. Figure 2.1 illustrates schematically how this process works.

Constructing comparative judgments is crucial in this process.[7] By engaging the right-hand segments of the loop in Figure 2.1, rankings reverberate and magnify whatever direct influence the World Bank may traditionally have had on states. Since the Bank publishes overall and subindex rankings, it could not be easier to sort states by their total number of reforms or a specific reform category.[8] The format is important because broad social engagement is much less likely to be activated by raw data alone than by comparisons.[9]

This is precisely the mechanism that the introduction to this volume theorizes. When the Bank deploys "business climate" information in a simple comparative format such as the EDB Index, it effectively changes the information environment for economic and political groups important to the target state.

---

[5] Kelley and Simmons this volume.
[6] Zürn 2018.
[7] Sinclair 2008.
[8] See "Doing Business – Reform Count," retrieved from http://www.doingbusiness.org/en/reforms/reforms-count.
[9] Hansen and Mühlen-Schulte 2012; Robson 1992.

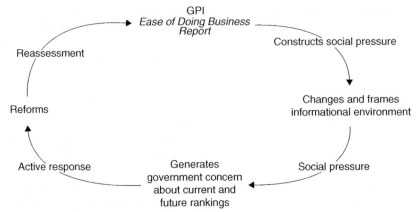

FIGURE 2.1. Theory of the social influence of the Ease of Doing Business ranking.
Notes: By framing good business practices as time and cost reduction, and changing the information environment, in ways that attract attention of investors and domestic groups, the World Bank applies social pressure on its members to reform.
Source: Adapted from Kelley and Simmons, introduction (this volume).

Not only does the Bank staff and the ministry of development (for example) know their rating; they both know that investors know, citizens have gotten wind of the ranking, and other states have become aware, as well. This is the essence of social pressure: it engages the *reputations and status concerns* of relevant bureaucrats and politicians, in some cases fueled by the national pride of domestic publics more generally.[10] When King Abdullah of Saudi Arabia declared in 2006, "I want Saudi Arabia to be among the top ten countries in *Doing Business* [*Report*] in 2010. No Middle Eastern country should have a better investment climate by 2007,"[11] he was displaying a status motivation that has no other metric than his kingdom's relative performance on the Bank's narrowly defined but highly focal scale.

   Social pressure is not a bilateral relationship between the World Bank and a state; our theory stresses that the World Bank alters the informational environment through the EDB ranking which in turn stimulates (often implicit) group pressures on states to reform. Were it not for the anticipated public response, the Bank would not be able to exert *social* pressure of the kind described here (though any economic leverage it may have would remain intact). Governments are likely to care about the beliefs of two groups in particular: domestic constituents (voters, business groups)[12] and international investors. For domestic businesses, the rankings uniquely reveal how much more heavy-handed their government is than its peers. World Bank rankings recalibrate expectations

[10] Kelley 2017; Kelley and Simmons 2015.
[11] World Bank Group 2008.
[12] Dai 2007.

and legitimate demands for a reduction in red tape associated with conducting business. International investors may be influenced by a state's EDB rankings as well.[13] Even more importantly, state regulators *believe* that the rankings influence private investment decisions, and will try proactively to improve their rankings to attract investment.[14] Market actors[15] use the Bank's rankings as a credible shorthand for a competently regulated economy. Perhaps for this reason, EDB rankings correlate with investment flows, consistent with a claim that good ratings attract business.[16] Unfortunately, existing studies do not distinguish between the underlying "business environment" the EDB is meant to reflect and the signal sent by the ratings per se. Methods isolating the influence on investor opinions and beliefs of *information packaged as ratings* are essential to our argument.

But why should bureaucrats – some of whom may collect rents from existing inefficient red tape – care about such information? The EDB rankings also reflect on the personal competence of an individual government minister or that of a department or bureaucracy.[17] Some EDB subindicators are specific enough to implicate the professionalism of business regulators, encouraging policy reform before the next "grading period" to avoid opprobrium. Ongoing EDB monitoring and publicity prompts bureaucracies to develop institutionalized routines and capacities, especially in middle-tier emerging markets where incentives to develop a reputation for a business-friendly environment are strongest.[18]

Finally, governments can use the EDB rankings strategically to gain support for their policies. Global performance indicators can help leaders overcome rent-seeking politicians or competition-fearing monopolies by empowering allies, shaming bureaucrats, mobilizing publics, and promising to attract investment.[19] External validation (or criticism) from a credible institution

---

[13] This claim is tested in the investor survey experiment we describe later.

[14] Jayasuriya 2011. Media analysis speaks directly to this claim. Some scholars argue that states use the EDB rankings specifically as a form of "competitive signaling" to investors and other stakeholders (Appel and Orenstein 2018).

[15] We cast this argument in terms of investors and markets, but for some countries, EDB indicators are more important to access non-market development aid: EDB subindicators are used in awarding Millennium Challenge Corporation (MCC) funding. See "Guide to the Indicators and the Selection Process, FY 2015," Millennium Challenge Corporation, retrieved from https://www.mcc.gov/resources/doc-pdf/report-guide-to-the-indicators-and-the-selection-process-fy-2015. See also "Business Start-Up Indicator," 2007, Millennium Challenge Corporation, retrieved from https://www.mcc.gov/who-we-fund/indicator/business-start-up-indicator. The MCC entered into operation in 2004, before the Bank started ranking.

[16] Corcoran and Gillanders 2015; Klapper, Amit, and Guillén 2010.

[17] Kelley 2017.

[18] Evidence analyzed later on reform committees, bureaucratic statements to the press, and the robust interagency process and subnational competition underway in India's EDB reform effort all suggest that the perception of bureaucratic competency is often at stake.

[19] DeMarzo 1992; Kahler 1994.

can be part of a strategy to bolster a broad domestic coalition for reform.[20] External pressure in the form of rankings is sometimes a politically useful tool to accomplish leaders' objectives in the face of domestic resistance. This possibility is evident in India, where Prime Minister Modi has emulated the World Bank's tactics *intranationally* to intensify social pressure on Indian bureaucrats around the country to improve their performance.

EDB BACKGROUND

Economic Theories and Bank Motives

Over the course of the 1990s, a remarkable development was afoot in one of the most important public investment bureaucracies in the world. The World Bank, whose legal mandate was to promote investment by guaranteeing loans and supplementing private finance, began to turn its attention to what it saw as one underlying reason for underinvestment in the first place: burdensome business regulations.[21] In the spirit of the times, academic and bank researchers began to collect information that would speak to the empirical links between regulatory burdens, investment, and economic outcomes such as growth and development.[22] They developed the concepts and methods underlying the indices on which the rankings were to eventually be based in a widely cited set of academic and policy papers that reflected the deregulatory and pro-investor approaches that were reaching their height at the time.[23]

The EDB Index was "built on the premise that firms are more likely to flourish if they have to abide by fewer, cheaper, and simpler regulations." It seeks to assess "the burden of regulation…as seen from the private firm's point of view," not the net social benefits of regulation, and not net poverty reduction.[24] A ranking that rewards reduced business costs was justified theoretically on the grounds that overregulation stifles business activity, stunting growth and development. In August 2002, the Bank noted its assessments were meant to set standards and to be actionable: "The [EDB] database differs from existing cross-country reports…which…do not identify the nature of regulatory reforms required to improve the investment climate. Doing

---

[20] Kelley 2004.
[21] The Bank's legal mandate is discussed in "IBRD Articles of Agreement: Article I," World Bank, June 27, 2012, http://go.worldbank.org/PK9UNG06S0.
[22] For broader trends see "International Standard Cost Model Manual: Measuring and Reducing Administrative Burdens for Business," 2004, Organisation for Economic Co-operation and Development (OECD), http://www.oecd.org/gov/regulatory-policy/34227698.pdf. For the EU, see Boheim 2006.
[23] See the papers posted on the Doing Business website's methodology page at http://www.doing-business.org/methodology. See especially Djankov et al. 2002, which describes barriers to setting up businesses around the world and has been cited more than 3,000 times.
[24] Independent Evaluation Group 2008.

Business Report aims to provide a new set of objective, quantifiable measures of business regulations and their enforcement."[25]

The decision to rank was a deliberate part of the strategy to affect policy. The EDB's "lively communication style" was designed specifically to establish benchmarks and set states in competition with one another in support of the World Bank's development agenda.[26] To promote its "flagship knowledge product,"[27] the Bank staff carry out a massive media campaign every year when they release the ratings. A separate indicator-based reform team works with countries to target policies effectively.

Market Share

The EDB product line has a robust online presence, including a Wikipedia page and on Chartsbin, Facebook, LinkedIn, Slideshare and in several YouTube videos. Consequently, the EDB Index enjoys tremendous "market share" among the growing list of GPIs that deal with national business environments. To illustrate, we selected seven of the EDB's closest cognate assessments, and searched a database of over fifty thousand online media sources (news organizations, blogs, and other media).[28] The EDB brand dominates the market for easy-to-access comparative rankings of country performance, as Table 2.1 clearly shows. In fact, the EDB had more mentions in the media between 2010 and 2017 than the other seven cognate indicators combined. In 2017, the Doing Business website had nearly 5 million annual visitors, 166 times as many as in 2003 (Figure 2.2).

Contestation

Despite its dominance, the EDB indicator inhabits a contested space and faces criticisms about its accuracy and validity. One critical study compared EDB's de jure measures of regulations with de facto measures from World Bank firm surveys and found significant differences between the two.[29] Some firms in countries with low ranks in categories such as legal requirements for construction permits actually attained permits faster than countries with higher ranks, a pattern that also holds across many other EDB subcategories. The rankings based on formal laws were largely unrelated to actual business practice. The EDB Index has even been assailed for frequent changes in methodology that

[25] "About Doing Business," from the Wayback Machine, World Bank Group, 2002. http://web.archive.org/web/20020806155832/http://rru.worldbank.org/DoingBusiness/AboutDoingBusiness.aspx.
[26] Independent Evaluation Group 2008.
[27] Ibid.
[28] Accessed via the Berkman Center, Harvard University. See "Media Cloud," Berkman Klein Center for Internet and Society, 2019. https://mediacloud.org/.
[29] Hallward-Driemeier and Pritchett 2011.

TABLE 2.1. *Market share of the ease of doing business index*

Cognate Economic Indicators		
Indicator	Hits	Market Share (%)
Ease of Doing Business Index	28,798	65.26
Global Competitiveness Index	7,263	16.46
Heritage Index of Economic Freedom	3,563	8.07
Global Entrepreneurship Monitor	1,901	4.31
Fraser Economic Freedom Index	1,234	2.80
World Competitiveness Rankings	973	2.20
The Enabling Trade Index	272	0.62
Forbes Best Countries for Business	126	0.29

Note: Showing the number and share of hits. Results generated from Harvard Berkman Center, "Media Cloud Database," 2017.

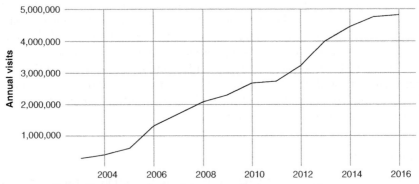

FIGURE 2.2. Doing Business website visits, annually (2003–2016).
Source: World Bank, unpublished data provided to authors.

"had the appearance of being politically motivated."[30] Whether this is true or not, it illustrates disagreement over what the rankings capture.

The ranking criteria face some sharp ideological criticism for their deregulatory biases. Unions and the International Labor Organization (ILO) have criticized the EDB for neglecting the consequences of business deregulation for workers, and the Bank eventually removed labor-related components from

---

[30] Josh Zumbrun and Iain Talley, "World Bank Unfairly Influenced Its Own Competitiveness Rankings," *The Wall Street Journal*, January 12, 2018; "Paul Romer Quits After an Embarrassing Row," *The Economist*, January 25, 2018, retrieved from https://www.economist.com/news/business-and-finance/21735716-world-banks-chief-economist-questioned-integrity-banks-research-his.

the Index.[31] The EDB has likewise been criticized on environmental grounds for downplaying the importance of environmental assessments in favor of a streamlined permits process that could increase the risk of natural disasters.[32] Many have questioned whether restrictions on female participation in business should be included in the ranking. When the Bank's data on "Women and the Law" were included in the rankings, states like Saudi Arabia tumbled downward. These examples suggest that states have reasons to wonder whether competing to ascend the rankings could create new problems or exacerbate existing ones. Unsurprisingly, competitors have developed and deployed alternative measures for states' business environments (Table 2.1). The EDB faces competition from GPIs that prioritize low taxes and limited government (Heritage and Frasier), that include the informal sector (Global Entrepreneurship Monitor), and that include labor (Global Competitiveness Index).

Simplicity, Salience, and Competition: Prima Facie Evidence of the Theory in Practice

Despite questions about its singular deregulatory emphasis and validity, the EDB rankings have become quite salient. Within the first year of publicizing the rankings, leaders from many countries, including Algeria, Burkina Faso, Malawi, Mali, and São Tomé and Príncipe had reportedly requested not general regulatory advice, but specific advice on how to improve their standings. These requests provoked the first epigraph to this chapter, a staff report marveling at the competitive state response, in 2005.[33] The World Bank itself has succinctly summarized our theory of social pressure: decision makers view the EDB Index as a system that compares performance, engages reputations, and incites competition. The Bank explicitly and intentionally designed an assessment system calculated to draw attention to a few very simple criteria that are *plausibly but not unequivocally* associated with a "better" business environment. The index became focal in part because it was one of the first to successfully harness broader intellectual and ideological trends, to link development with a country's business-friendly environment, and thus to ride the crest of the deregulatory wave of the Washington consensus touted by prominent economists. It has also been advocated by arguably the most central development institution in the world, leveraging the World Bank's credibility.

---

[31] See the critique of the International Confederation of Free Trade Unions (ICFTU) by Bakvis 2007.

[32] See, for example, in the case of India, Manju Menon and Kanchi Kohli, "Is Ease of Doing Business Undermining Green Norms?" *DNA India*, November 14, 2017, retrieved from http://www.dnaindia.com/analysis/column-is-ease-of-doing-business-undermining-green-norms-2559752.

[33] Djankov et al. 2005. From 2001 to 2005 the Bank did not rank. Data that would eventually form the basis of the rankings were first published in the fall of 2001 on the Bank's website.

The EDB also benefits from its quantitative clarity. The ranking simply rewards any policy that reduces the *time* or the *cost* of doing business.[34] The Bank chose not to cloud this focal concept with alternative or countervailing values such as fair business, socially responsible business, labor protection, or environmental considerations.[35] The Bank further reinforces the EDB's legitimacy by referring to the rankings themselves as "data" on par with the rest of the world development indicators.[36] As a result, the EDB has survived political pushback from powerful states such as China and Russia, and has become focal enough to significantly influence the behavior of states.

Evidence of our theory in practice can be found in policymakers' own words. Over the past decade, policymakers around the world have spoken and acted as though the EDB mattered greatly. Countries openly publicize their plans to undertake reforms. Georgia – whom some have criticized for gaming the system – announced concerted efforts to rise from one-hundredth to the top twenty in two years.[37] National officials in Yemen,[38] Portugal,[39] Mauritius,[40] El Salvador,[41] and India[42] have also highlighted EDB as motivating reforms.

To test the general plausibility of this claim, we examined a near-comprehensive set of press statements and stories for 2016 in English from the Lexis Nexis database. While hundreds of stories mention the EDB Index, our specific interest was in the fifty-one English language stories covering twenty-six countries that directly cite high-ranking government officials. Illustrating the seriousness with which countries take the EDB Index, 14 percent of the officials cited are heads of state, and another 47 percent are either ministers or deputy ministers, making up over 60 percent of the stories. The remaining stories quoted spokespeople for these offices.

These statements demonstrate the theorized channels of influence. When countries improve, officials highlight this accomplishment: 18 percent brag about progress on the Index. Comparisons are rife: 14 percent of officials compare their countries to others. For example, the undersecretary to Cyprus's

---

[34] For example, days to enforce a contract, and cost of contract enforcement as a share of the total claim. There are just a few exceptions, such as the "quality of judicial processes index" which is a subindicator under "enforcing contracts." See "Doing Business – Enforcing Contracts," World Bank 2019, retrieved from http://www.doingbusiness.org/data/exploretopics/enforcing-contracts#close.

[35] The Bank does maintain a database on labor protections, but does not rank states in this area, and does not combine labor and business regulations for a composite score.

[36] "Ease of Doing Business Index Databank," World Bank, 2018, retrieved from https://data.worldbank.org/indicator/IC.BUS.EASE.XQ.

[37] Schueth 2011.

[38] World Bank Group 2009.

[39] World Bank Group 2008.

[40] World Bank Group 2009.

[41] World Bank Group 2007.

[42] Discussed in detail later, relying only on non-Bank sources.

president, who heads the president's administrative reform unit, noted that Cyprus ranked twenty-fifth of twenty-eight EU states and that "our performance there is not good." Fifteen percent of the stories mention specific bureaucracies tasked with improving the EDB score, potentially amplifying reputational concerns. Most of the stories identify specific policy measures taken and link them to the EDB Index. Indonesia's agrarian and spatial planning minister noted specifically that a "ministerial regulation was made to respond to a survey by the World Bank on the ease of doing business."[43]

Many officials stressed the desire to improve their rankings. For half the countries, official statements – usually by a head of state – publicly commit to a specific target ranking. For example, Indonesian President Jokowi announced "a policy intended to improve Indonesia's position in the World Bank's Ease of Doing Business rankings from 109 to 40." In Bangladesh, a high-level official noted that it was "the prime minister's demand to see Bangladesh among the countries with a double-digit position (10 to 99) in the 'ease of doing business index.' It's an aggressive target, but achievable." In Kazakhstan, Erbolat Dossaev, Minister of National Economy, committed to reach the top thirty, "an objective set by the president of Kazakhstan, Nursultan Nazarbayev." None less than President Vladimir Putin of Russia has gotten into the game. A story reports that "Russia's high positions in the Doing Business ranking were one of the objectives provided in the president's May decrees of 2012. Russia is to go up from the 120th position in 2011 to the 50th in 2015 and to the 20th in 2018."

This evidence shows that high-level government officials make explicit comparative judgments and set goals based on the EDB Index. Some also believe their efforts will be rewarded in a very tangible way – by attracting investment. Serbia's Prime Minister Aleksandar Vucic acknowledged this explicitly, stating that, "Serbia wants to enter the top thirty countries on the World Bank's list. This is very important for the citizens of Serbia because the better positioned we are, the more we will be able to attract foreign and domestic investors." There is ample prima facie evidence that the EDB Index has motivated a wide range of states, especially those with emerging markets, to make policy reforms that will be tallied by the EDB Index.

OBSERVATIONAL EVIDENCE: BUREAUCRATIC
RESTRUCTURING AND POLICY REFORMS

The EDB system has a clear bureaucratic imprint in many states, and new dedicated structures help states ascend the rankings more efficiently. Evidence also suggests that the Bank's strategy of public competition has paid reform

---

[43] A complete file of all the quotes and sources is available online in the appendix on the *International Organization* web page https://www.cambridge.org/core/journals/international-organization/article/power-of-ranking-the-ease-of-doing-business-indicator-and-global-regulatory-behavior/1A1A9602B52185FA0A28F3DFDE2DCF5A#fndtn-supplementary-materials.

dividends: States have responded by reducing costs and time associated with starting a business once the rankings were made public.

Bureaucratic Efforts

Since 2006 when the Bank started tracking, countries have undertaken 3,057 sets of reforms related to the EDB.[44] Many of these reforms appear to be concerted efforts to improve the rankings, as countries initiate collaborations with Bank staff *in response to* the rankings. For example, in 2006, Azerbaijan's president declared the country's ranking "unacceptable," and sent a working group to consult with the Bank to design reforms that moved Azerbaijan up in the rankings.[45] In February 2008, the Albanian government asked the World Bank's Doing Business Reform Unit to review proposed legislation to protect investors and then, one month later, unanimously enacted it.[46] Such consultations are frequent. Between November 2013 and October 2014 alone, the EDB team received over 160 queries from countries, which suggests that bureaucracies are now configured to respond to the Bank's policy advice.[47] More than fifty states have formed or designated "reform committees" that, according to the Bank, "use the Doing Business indicators as one input to inform their programs for improving the business environment."[48]

Table 2.2 lists the reform committees in place as of 2015. Although countries with reform committees resemble those without in terms of relevant factors such as gross domestic product (GDP) growth, World Bank loans, regime type, GDP per capita, or even initial EDB ranking,[49] they differ with respect to their EDB performance over time. Between 2007 and 2014, they undertook many more reforms (a total of 2.7 reforms per year compared to 1.2 reforms for those without committees, a statistically significant difference) and whereas the countries without committees dropped ten spaces in the rankings during this period, the ones with committees rose by nine.[50]

The rankings boost is not merely proportional to the number of reforms for countries with such committees; they systematically get a bigger "ranking bang" for their "reform buck." We coded the annual number of reforms by

---

[44] See World Bank, "Doing Business – Reform Count." In reality, even more reforms occurred because if a country undertook multiple reforms within a given indicator in a given year, it is counted as just one reform.

[45] World Bank Group 2008.

[46] World Bank Group 2009, 55–56.

[47] *Doing Business 2015: Going Beyond Efficiency* 2014.

[48] The appendix on the *International Organization* web page lists the countries by region.

[49] See appendix Table A1, located on the *International Organization* web page.

[50] See Table A3 in the appendix at https://www.cambridge.org/core/journals/international-organization/article/power-of-ranking-the-ease-of-doing-business-indicator-and-global-regulatory-behavior/1A1A9602B52185FA0A28F3DFDE2DCF5A#fndtn-supplementary-materials. Using normalized rankings instead results in a drop of 5 and increase of 10 instead, but the general picture is the same.

TABLE 2.2. *Countries with reform committees directly using the EDB data*

Region	Countries
East and South Asia	Indonesia, the Republic of Korea, Malaysia, the Philippines, and Sri Lanka.
Middle East and North Africa	Algeria, Kuwait, Morocco, Saudi Arabia, and the United Arab Emirates
Europe and Central Asia	Azerbaijan, Croatia, the Czech Republic, Georgia, Kazakhstan, Kosovo, the Kyrgyz Republic, the former Yugoslav Republic of Macedonia, Moldova, Montenegro, Poland, the Russian Federation, Tajikistan, Ukraine, the United Kingdom, and Uzbekistan
Sub-Saharan Africa	Botswana, Burundi, the Central African Republic, the Comoros, the Democratic Republic of Congo, the Republic of Congo, Cote d'Ivoire, Guinea, Kenya, Liberia, Malawi, Mali, Nigeria, Rwanda, Sierra Leone, Togo, and Zambia
Latin America	Chile, Colombia, Costa Rica, the Dominican Republic, Guatemala, Mexico, Panama, and Peru

Notes: No information is available for precise date when committees were formed. These are all reform committees in existence as of 2015.
Source: World Bank.

each subindicator of the Doing Business Index,[51] using a more fine-grained count than the Bank's own data and coding for whether the reforms were positive or negative, based on Bank descriptions.[52] A new variable, TOTAL REFORMS accounts for both positive and negative reforms. This variable has a mean of 1.6 (and a standard deviation of 2.4), suggesting that, on average, countries undertook a net of 1.6 reforms a year. The range is from –6 to 17 (some reforms are negative). It turns out that *per reform*, the countries with designated committees moved up more in the rankings (about 1.03 places) than those without such committees (up about 0.55 places). In other words, countries with committees got nearly double the rankings' reward for each reform effort. In Table 2.3, this TOTAL REFORMS variable is used to predict overall EDB ranking in the subsequent year, using a normal linear regression model and controlling for past ranking as well as year-fixed effects to account for any minor methodological changes over time. Models 1 and 2 demonstrate the separate effects of REFORM COMMITTEE and TOTAL REFORMS, models 3 and 4 illustrate the TOTAL REFORMS for countries with and without reform committees as separate subgroups, and model 5 uses an interaction term between REFORM COMMITTEE and TOTAL REFORMS to demonstrate that the relationship between total reforms and the EDB ranking differs by whether countries have

[51] The indicators and methodology are explained at length online. See "Doing Business – Starting a Business Methodology" at http://www.doingbusiness.org/methodology.
[52] This coding is discussed in the appendix on the *International Organization* web page.

TABLE 2.3. *The efficiency of bureaucratic reforms for ascending the rankings*

	Model 1	Model 2	Model 3	Model 4	Model 5
Countries included in model	All countries	All countries	No Bureaus	Bureaus only	All countries
PUBLISHED RANK, LAG	0.991***	0.988***	0.993***	0.979***	0.989***
	(0.00393)	(0.00376)	(0.00377)	(0.00917)	(0.00389)
REFORM COMMITTEE	-2.924***				0.988
	(0.694)				(0.808)
TOTAL REFORMS, LAG		-0.816***	-0.552***	-1.029***	-0.549***
		(0.0933)	(0.119)	(0.139)	(0.121)
TOTAL REFORMS* REFORM BUREAU, LAG					-0.406**
					(0.172)
Constant	3.965***	4.634***	4.552***	4.253**	4.677***
	(0.819)	(0.842)	(0.849)	(1.987)	(0.85)
Year fixed effects	Yes	Yes	Yes	Yes	Yes
Observations	1,234	1,234	882	352	1,234
Number of countries	188	188	137	51	188

*** $p < 0.01$, ** $p < 0.05$, * $p < 0.10$.

Notes: Dependent variable is EDB Ranking. The coefficients that improve rankings are negative as countries move toward being number 1.

reform committees. The analysis suggests that focused bureaucratic organization produces more strategic responses to the rankings, and not just to global market pressures unrelated to the EDB. As leaders' own commentary in the media suggests, many states undertake *specific* reforms strategically to improve their *rankings*.[53]

Empirical Context: Publicity's Impact

The theory advanced in this volume claims that ranking publicity per se should matter for reform. This is challenging to assess since the World Bank's monitoring, reporting, and public ranking have been introduced gradually. In the late 1990s, several indices around competitiveness were emerging – the Bank was not the first to capture the field. The idea for the EDB report arose with a paper by Djankov and colleagues on "The Regulation of Entry," which has been cited over 3,000 times and was well known before it appeared in print in 2002.[54] The paper ranked regulation on entry procedures derived from 1999 data on eighty-five countries representing a wide array of regimes types and other characteristics. In 2002, the World Bank issued the first data on its website (roughly covering 2001), thus commencing the formal period of monitoring and rating. The early data covered 110 countries, but selection into that sample is not significantly correlated with the outcome variable measuring the regulations.[55] In 2004, a report covering 145 countries was issued for the first time, attracting more attention to the ratings and monitoring, but still without rankings. In 2005, the report included top-twenty and also worst-performer lists, essentially constituting a protoranking. By 2006 (covering 2005 data), a true ranking of all countries debuted. The ranking's introduction was by no means a clean break, which makes it difficult to detect a precise ranking-publicity effect.

Despite the gradual introduction of ratings and rankings, *we hypothesize that the full publication of rankings in 2006 should be associated with*

---

[53] While it is hard to know whether such reforms are more or less appropriate than those made without the Bank's close guidance and without rankings in mind, an analogy to the phenomenon of teaching (and learning) to the test is potentially helpful. The literature is voluminous, especially in the wake of No Child Left Behind policies of the 2000s. See, for example, Jensen et al. 2014; Menken 2006. Much of this literature suggests that overreliance on standardized tests shifts resources and is associated with more superficial learning. While we are agnostic about the quality of EDB-inspired reforms, we use this analogy to understand the *motivation* for making them in the first place. Although we have documented the controversy over the validity of the EDB criteria, assessment of reform quality is beyond our scope here.

[54] "Doing Business – Starting a Business Methodology."

[55] GPD per capita income, GPD growth, democracy, population size, and international or civil conflict rarely correlate significantly with reform and tend not to predict selection into the sample in 2001. Not even the total volume of loans to a country predicts either selection into the original group of rated states or improved business-reform measures. See Table A1 in the appendix on the *International Organization* web page.

TABLE 2.4. *Overview of de jure reform measures (dependent variables)*

Variable Name	Definition	First Year Published Online
Starting a Business Indicators (Entry Regulations)		
CAPITAL	Paid-in minimum capital (% of income per capita) required to start a business	2003
PROCEDURES	Number of procedures required for an entrepreneur to legally operate a business.	2002
DAYS	Number of days required to start a business.	2002
COST	Cost (% of income per capita) of starting a business	2002

Notes: Source is EDB website. Years published covers data from the prior year.

greater efforts to reform and therefore greater reductions in the relevant measures after 2006. The dependent variables are four indicators that were first published for "Starting a Business," the most often referenced component of the index. Larger numbers represent higher costs or longer waits, and so are considered worse from a business perspective. Data were recovered from "the Wayback Machine" internet archive for years prior to publication. Table 2.4 displays the indicators and the years the data collection began.[56]

Average values of these indicators show steady declines, meaning it is easier and cheaper to do business in these countries on average over time. Many more countries have been progressing each year than retrogressing. In 2002, for example, only 13 percent of the countries required fewer than six procedures to start a business. By 2014, half of the countries had come below six procedures. By 2014, in nearly a quarter of countries one could start a business in about a week, something that had been possible in less than 5 percent of countries in 2002. Figures 2.3 and 2.4 show the number of countries over time improving and backsliding on these measures, keeping in mind that countries face a floor effect which at some point makes further reductions difficult or impossible.[57]

[56] To provide a comparable time series for research, the World Bank back calculates to adjust for changes in methodology, but these corrections have been made only since 2003 data (in the 2004 report). Therefore, if the data in 2001 and 2002 were then the biggest, methodology-induced drop will occur between 2002 and 2003, which is a year before rankings existed. This would bias the findings *against* our hypothesis, because it would make a preranking year appear to have large improvements.

[57] It is not suitable to explore similar trends for the other two variables because they are based on GDP and therefore display minor absolute changes even when the country took no action, simply as a result of the change in GDP that inevitably occurs in any given year.

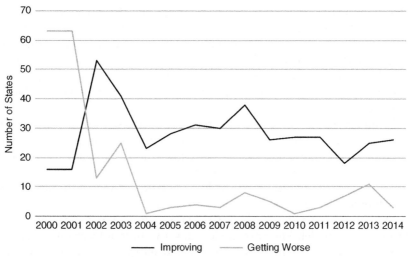

FIGURE 2.3. Days to start a business.
Notes: The number of states improving (dark gray) versus those getting worse (light gray). Source is authors' counting and coding of EDB reforms (detailed in data appendix on the *International Organization* website).

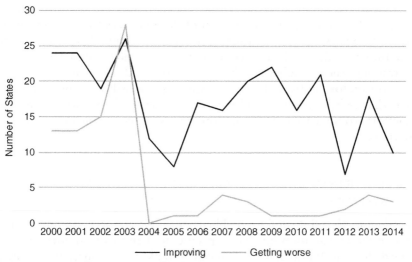

FIGURE 2.4. Procedures to start a business.
Notes: The number of states improving (dark gray) versus those getting worse (light gray). Source is authors' counting and coding of EDB reforms (detailed in data appendix on the *International Organization* website).

To examine the association between ratings and the introduction of rankings, we use a time-series simple regression model that includes controls for the most salient economic indicators: POLITY (as a measure of regime type), GDP, POPULATION, GDP GROWTH, LOANS FROM THE WORLD BANK, as well as a lag of the outcome variable for each of the four sets of models associated with the four subindicators in Table 2.4. The economic and outcome variables are all logged.

The underlying hypothesis is whether 2006 represents a break-point in a trend. This is a hard test because of the gradual introduction in the monitoring, rating, and ranking scheme, and the expectation that policy reactions take some time. The key explanatory variable is RANKED, which equals 1 for all countries in year 2006 and afterwards. Two different specifications were run for each outcome. The first includes RANKED, the control variables, the lagged outcome, and country fixed effects. RANKED is expected to be negative and significant in this model. The next model adds a YEAR trend variable. A negative and significant coefficient on RANKED would indicate greater improvements after the introduction of the rankings.

Table 2.5 displays the results. In Models 6 to 9, which have only country-fixed effects, RANKED is associated with reductions in time, costs, and procedures associated with starting a business, indicating greater improvements after 2006 than before. That 2006 presents a clear break in a trend, is evident for two of the four variables, PROCEDURES and COST, in Models 10 to 13, the set of second models that add a year trend. In all cases, the coefficients are small, suggesting the effects are modest. It is important to interpret these findings in the context of the analysis's findings as a whole. Given the unfavorable conditions for observing any clear break arising from the gradual introduction of the monitoring and rating scheme prior to the ranking, these results, *combined* with the evidence that specific countries are highly motivated by the rankings; plausibly support the argument that publicizing the rankings has contributed to reforms' and that the efforts to improve have been more intense after the introduction of the rankings.

EDB CHANNELS OF INFLUENCE: ALTERING INFORMATION
FOR INVESTORS

Correlations that link ranking publicity to bureaucratic and policy reforms are one thing; causation involving specific mechanisms is another. We have argued that the World Bank promulgates ranking information to pressure states to conform to its favored policies. We have shown that governments pay attention to these rankings, that they have altered their bureaucracies

TABLE 2.5. *The effect of ranking on reductions in time, cost, and procedures for starting a business*

Outcomes:	Model 6 Capital	Model 7 Cost	Model 8 Procedures	Model 9 Days	Model 10 Capital	Model 11 Cost	Model 12 Procedures	Model 13 Days
Explanatory variables								
CAPITAL	0.749***				0.735***			
	(0.0251)				(0.0257)			
COST		0.710***				0.686***		
		(0.0347)				(0.0389)		
PROCEDURES			0.821***				0.805***	
			(0.0189)				(0.0199)	
DAYS				0.755***				0.731***
				(0.0211)				(0.0231)
YEAR					-0.0420***	-0.0218***	-0.00578**	-0.0196***
					(0.014)	(0.00825)	(0.00233)	(0.00597)
RANKED	-0.102*	-0.115***	-0.0356***	-0.0851***	0.000194	-0.0522*	-0.0192*	-0.0327
	(0.0559)	(0.0344)	(0.00931)	(0.0262)	(0.0589)	(0.0283)	(0.0102)	(0.03)
GDP	-0.325*	-0.462***	-0.0831***	-0.251***	0.169	-0.248**	-0.0239	-0.0536
	(0.187)	(0.0793)	(0.0284)	(0.0868)	(0.272)	(0.12)	(0.045)	(0.119)
GDP GROWTH	0.00257	-0.00590***	-0.000857	-0.00478***	-0.000504	-0.00711***	-0.00117	-0.00597***
	(0.00556)	(0.00199)	(0.000746)	(0.00167)	(0.00561)	(0.00194)	(0.000761)	(0.00174)
POLITY	0.0166	-0.0117*	-0.00252	-0.00537	0.0186	-0.0111*	-0.00231	-0.00447
	(0.0181)	(0.00629)	(0.00196)	(0.00469)	(0.00182)	(0.006)	(0.00203)	(0.00508)
WB LOANS	-0.153	-0.197***	-0.0386***	-0.0982**	0.0998	-0.0835	-0.00795	0.00603
	(0.0965)	(0.0396)	(0.0144)	(0.0427)	(0.141)	(0.0631)	(0.0229)	(0.0603)
Country fixed effects	Yes	Yes	Yes	Yes	Yes	Yes	Yes	Yes
Observations	1,551	1,651	1,651	1,651	1,551	1,651	1,651	1,651
Countries	134	134	134	134	134	134	134	134

*** $p < 0.01$, ** $p < 0.05$, * $p < 0.10$.

Notes: All reform variables and economic variables are logged. All explanatory variables except year are lagged one year.

strategically to enhance their performance rankings, and that media coverage suggests that competitive signaling to domestic constituencies and investors is one important reason. But does the *information contained in the ratings themselves* plausibly change important groups' perceptions enough to encourage reform?

Governments have told us – repeatedly and in public – that ascending the EDB rankings will improve their countries' ability to attract business investment. It is therefore tempting simply to run a regression to see whether improvements in the ratings do attract more capital, but this would not help to understand the effect of rankings per se because it is nearly impossible with observational data to separate the ranking effects from the underlying qualities that rankings purport to measure. In fact, economists have run such tests, and have shown that the EDB rankings are, as expected, highly predictive of inward foreign direct investment (FDI) when included in standard models of foreign investment flows. These studies conflate the ranking information with the underlying business environment, and assume they are the same thing. Corcoran and Gillanders, for example, assert that the EDB rankings are "a very objective measure of regulation,"[58] and their study cannot – and was not designed to – separate *ranking pressure* from underlying characteristics of the regulatory environment. The ease-of-starting-a-business component of the rankings has also been used to predict new business start-ups, which is offered as evidence of the positive effects of "good governance" but it could just as well entail a distinct ranking effect. The point is, we cannot distinguish these claims with such correlations.[59] Critical legal research[60] as well as statistical studies[61] have warned against the methodological, substantive, and conceptual problems with relying on the EDB indicators for assessing the business environment. To accept any EDB-investment correlation on face value reinforces the common but potentially fallacious assumption that rankings are meaningful – an assumption that fuels their impact, but which is precisely the relationship scrutinized here.

A better way to explore the causal claim of the power of the ranking per se is with a survey experiment. The goal is to test whether the "false reductionism"[62] of the EDB rankings affect how investors assess investment risks. No study to date – positive or critical – has shown that *the rankings* frame how investors think about risk. To do so we recruited 150 investment professionals and manipulated information about EDB rankings, controlling macroeconomic information for a hypothetical "emerging market economy" (based on India and using Indian macroeconomic information)

---

[58] Corcoran and Gillanders 2015, 105.
[59] Klapper, Amit, and Guillén 2010.
[60] Michaels 2009.
[61] Pinheiro-Alves and Zambujal-Oliveira 2012.
[62] Michaels 2009, 794–95.

and varied the EDB rankings as treatment.[63] We hypothesize that even when controlling for important economic and political conditions, information about EDB rankings will influence the willingness to recommend an investment in the ranked country. By changing investors' information set, we are testing whether the upper right loop of the argument in Figure 2.1 *causally* alters investors' perceptions and therefore *plausibly* provokes the "government concern" in the lower part of the figure within the confines of the experiment.

A perfect approximation of a real-world information environment that informs investment assessment is experimentally unattainable. We do not purport to estimate the EDB's impact on investments in the real world, but rather, show it is plausible that EDB rankings – which may or may not reflect a meaningful reality – prime investment attitudes. In reality, investors confront a more crowded information environment than that in the experiment. But it is also clear that investors depend heavily on a few crucial economic indicators as well as other heuristics when making decisions.[64] We included critical macroeconomic information and alerted investors that the hypothetical country was an "emerging market economy," capturing enough salient features of investor decision making sufficient to glean some insights into EDB's influence on investors' assessments.

The panel of 150 investors was recruited by Qualtrics through a partnership with over twenty Golden Mean certified and actively managed online market research panel providers.[65] Respondents were subjected to comprehension checks, asked to answer free response questions, highly compensated for their time, and directly recruited by Qualtrics – which verified their status as industry professionals. To be clear: we do not claim to have recruited a "globally representative sample of investors" – which we would not begin to know how to define. The sample of portfolio managers are upper-middle-class investment professionals living across the United States. All participants had over five years of experience in the investment industry. About half had over twenty years of experience. Roughly half held high-level positions at their investment firm, such as senior director, managing director, vice president, partner, principal, or president/CEO. Investor strategies varied, with nearly half identifying as value investors and others identifying as macro, stock, bond, long/short, and activist investors. The average respondent was fifty years old; the oldest was seventy-eight and the youngest was twenty-six. Roughly three-quarters of respondents were male.

---

[63] This experiment was preregistered with www.egap.org.

[64] For an in-depth exploration, see Mosley 2000. Sometimes these heuristics are surprisingly unrelated to economic fundamentals. See, for example, Gray 2013.

[65] It was pre-tested on "Mechanical Turk Masters." Treatment effects were present for both experiments, but were stronger and more significant for investors, who are more familiar with investment decision making.

Portfolio managers made up three-quarters of the respondents, while others worked in private equity, venture capital, bank lending, and other investment sectors. Portfolio managers are a hard test for EDB influence. Because they buy and sell securities of foreign firms that are *already* operating in difficult environments, they should be less sensitive to the EDB ranking than direct investors, for whom day-to-day business operations are a primary concern. Portfolio investment is of significant concern to emerging market states since its rapid outflow can precipitate currency and financial crises, which makes the experiment more relevant to emerging economies. Without claiming representativeness, this panel is one of the few in international relations research to recruit relevant professionals rather than draw from students or the general population.

To avoid self-selection bias, recruitment did not involve any discussion of the survey contents. Respondents received a non-trivial incentive for their participation from Qualtrics or its market research partners, and the response rate was 32 percent. The survey asked respondents to consider an investment in an unnamed emerging-market country. To ensure findings are not an artifact of hypothetical conditions, we used India's true (announced) EDB goals and macroeconomic information – the exact information with which investors and the broad public have been "treated" in reality. Respondents were assigned to one of three groups: a control group and two treatment groups. Those in the Control Group (No EDB information) were given four macroeconomic facts about an unnamed country which, unknown to them, was based on India: real GDP growth: 7 percent; inflation rate: 6 percent; unemployment rate: 10 percent; per capita income: $6,000.[66] Those in Treatment Group 1 were given these same four macroeconomic facts, but were also told that the unnamed country had an EDB rank of 30, which in fact is Prime Minister Modi's *target rank* for India. Those in Treatment Group 2 were given the same four macroeconomic facts, but were told that the unnamed country had an EDB rank of 130, which is India's pre-reform rank. Thus, both the panel recruits and the information they were provided are highly realistic, imbuing the survey with as much external validity as is possible in the inherent confines of an experimental setting. To minimize any possible framing effects, all information was presented simultaneously in randomized order in a list so that the EDB indicator received no undue attention.

Respondents were asked, all things equal and based only on the information they were given, how likely they would be to recommend investment in the unnamed country. Answers were scored on a seven-point Likert scale with 7 serving as the highest likelihood of recommending investing and 1 the

---

[66] To check whether people were guessing that this was India, we asked participants to later identify which region they thought the country was in and no clear pattern emerged. This variable was also used as a control.

TABLE 2.6. *Experimental results of ranking differences on investment likelihood*

	OLS	OLS with Controls[a]	Bootstrapped T-Test	Wilcoxon Rank Sums Test
EDB Rank of 30 vs. EDB Rank of 130	1.1273*** (0.3313) $p = 0.0010$	1.1090*** (0.3763) $p = 0.0044$	1.1230*** (0.3372) $p = 0.0008$	W = 789*** $p = 0.0025$
Control vs. EDB Rank of 130 EDB	0.9758*** (0.3020) $p = 0.0017$	0.5920* (0.3512) $p = 0.0962$	0.9774*** (0.3001) $p = 0.0012$	W = 1873*** $p = 0.0024$
EDB Rank 30 vs. Control	0.1515 (0.3645) $p = 0.6790$	0.3956 (0.4046) $p = 0.3320$	0.1503 (0.3632) $p = 0.6790$	W = 1071 $p = 0.7023$

[a] Industry, strategy, title, experience, assumed region.
$^{*}p < 0.1$, $^{**}p < 0.05$, $^{***}p < 0.01$.
Notes: A positive coefficient entails a higher Likert score and a greater willingness to invest in the first group relative to the second.

lowest. Higher scores and positive coefficients reflect an *increase* in likelihood of investment. In addition to ordinary least squares (OLS), three other tests were used: a boot-strapped T-test, a non-parametric Wilcoxon Rank Sum test, and OLS including a series of controls such as investment industry, investment strategy, title, experience, and the respondent's assumption of where the country was located.

The EDB ranking significantly affected investors' expressed intent to recommend investment. Relative to respondents who were told the unnamed country had an EDB rank of 130 (Treatment 2), those told it had a rank of 30 (Treatment 1) said on average that they would be *far likelier to recommend investment* (by more than one full point on a seven-point scale; or roughly 19% more likely). This finding was significant across all four statistical tests at $p < 0.01$ (Table 2.6).

Relative to those told the unnamed country had an EDB rank of 130, those in the control group said they would be much *more likely* to recommend investment (by 0.97 points on a seven-point scale, or roughly 18% more likely).[67] This was significant at $p < 0.01$ across all four tests and suggests politicians may be right to fear that a poor EDB ranking could reduce investment. Within this experiment, a higher EDB rank induced greater investment enthusiasm

---

[67] We also asked respondents what their preferred return would be for this investment. Most respondents complained that this specific question was too difficult to answer. Consequently, answers to these questions exhibited a wide dispersion and no significant differences among groups.

than a lower rank, and low rank significantly depressed willingness to recommend investment relative to no EDB ranking information at all.[68]

In a free-response section after the survey, many respondents who received the EDB rank of 30 noted its influence on their investment recommendation. One respondent wrote: "While real GDP growth is substantial, the high unemployment rate is of some concern... [and] already high inflation could get worse... Ease of doing business certainly helps however." Another thought EDB helped mitigate uncertainty: "while there are risks... it is comparatively easy to do business." One investor even noted that the country was a "great growth opportunity" because of its "low economic barriers" as indicated by the EDB ranking. Conversely, those who received the low ranking of 130 also suggested it guided their decisions negatively. One respondent argued, "While the GDP growth and income numbers suggest potential, the unemployment rate and poor ease of doing business rank indicate some structural issues with the country *and its governance*" (italics added). Finally, the survey also revealed that 40 percent of our sampled investors have consulted EDB rankings or reports, which makes even more plausible the idea that EDB could shape investor behavior.[69]

Finally, those who received an EDB rank of 30 were more likely on a seven-point Likert scale to believe the government was more competent, less corrupt, would attract competing investment, and would not discriminate between foreign and domestic investors compared to those who received a rank of 130. While these results do not quite achieve statistical significance, they tell a consistent story. They also suggest that the EDB may appeal to governments as an "easier" way to attract capital than a far-reaching anticorruption campaign or an expensive infrastructure program, as the case of India shows.

The conclusions drawn from this experiment are significant but limited. Emphatically, they do not prove that high EDB rankings actually increase investment. At least within the experiment, we see that the EDB ranking is an important piece of information that can frame how investors assess investment risk. The framing effect in this experiment illustrates precisely the hypothesized causal mechanism. One might be concerned that surveyed investors are just expressing their own pre-existing belief that rankings represent *genuinely* better business conditions. This may be so, but it is not inconsistent with the proposed mechanism that ranking information influences investor thinking. We are

---

[68] We included one question to ascertain whether the issuer of a hypothetical ranking might affect the willingness of participants to use that ranking. We asked respondents to imagine that four different organizations – the World Bank, the *Economist* magazine, the Heritage Foundation, and the Brookings Institution – all published a fictitious "Global Competitiveness Ranking" (GCR) and then asked which of these organization's GCR they would be most likely to use. We found that 44 percent chose the World Bank's GCR and 33 percent chose the *Economist*'s, with the remainder split by Brookings and Heritage.

[69] We acknowledge that self-reporting bias may inflate this number.

agnostic about what the EDB "really" captures (though we have cited several skeptical studies). Such a belief suggests merely that investors find the rankings useful, perhaps even credible. In the hands of the World Bank, such ratings induce pressure – based on officials' beliefs about investors' beliefs informed by the ranking – to adopt the reforms that will boost their state's rankings.[70]

TRACING INFLUENCE CHANNELS IN MODERN INDIA

Now that we have assembled evidence that the EDB has shaped state behavior and suggested that it can frame the attitudes of investors and other salient groups, our case study explores these mechanisms in the case of India through Indian Hindi- and English-language media, primary sources, and reports on leaked documents related to India's EDB ambitions. It shows that the EDB indicator has created social pressure by encouraging political actors to believe their status is at stake and in competition with other countries and even other Indian states. That competition is heightened because of the perception that investment and political support are at stake. Indian officials seek to improve their EDB rankings because they believe it will win votes, secure investment, and improve official reputations – and they organize major interagency efforts to ascend the rankings. The case ties together much of the preceding evidence, demonstrating that changes in informational framing spark concerns about current and future rankings, and incentivize state reform behavior.

India provides an important – though not an obvious – case to explore these channels. It is significant for its sheer size. If the EDB Index influences policy in the fifth largest economy in the world, the "average" effects described in the observational analysis are even more important. The research is based exclusively on independent (non-World Bank) evidence. It demonstrates that Narendra Modi's reformist government has made climbing the EDB ranks a central feature of his government's agenda. The effort has been mentioned in party platforms, is explicitly coordinated through interagency mechanisms, and is implemented in part through local governments by using subnational

---

[70] In a separate experiment described in the appendix, which can be located on the *International Organization* web page, we found similar ranking effects on the part of the Indian general public, illustrating the potential for a "domestic constituency effect" described in the introduction to this volume. Members of the general public typically have almost no sense of how the business environment at home compares with that elsewhere. The EDB may be one of the few ways these groups can come to learn about whether or not it is reasonable to expect one's own government to do a lot better than it has done to date. In this separate experiment conducted with Indian citizens, information about India's EDB rank of 130 was held constant, but the rank of China – a status competitor for India – was manipulated. A high Chinese ranking was found to stimulate competitive expectations and increase the importance Indians attached to a high EDB ranking and the priority they placed on a better business climate. The experiment offers another plausible way the Bank leverages its ability to apply social pressure to conform. See the appendix for a description of the experiment and findings.

rankings to stimulate competition, embarrass opponents, and reward support-ers. Together, the contextualized Indian evidence strongly suggests that Indian political figures and bureaucrats anticipate and react to the EDB pressures trans-mitted through political, investment, and bureaucratic channels. It also demon-strates strategic behavior on the part of Modi's government, with EDB-related reforms undertaken in large part for their value in lifting India's ranking.

Background

Narendra Modi began to focus on the EDB Index late in his 2013 campaign for prime minister. Emphasizing the business-friendly roots of his political party, the Bharatiya Janata Party (BJP), Modi blamed India's poor rating on the ruling Congress Party and promised to improve the ranking. The BJP implicitly included EDB Index improvement in the 2014 party platform when it promised "making 'doing business' in India easy."[71]

Not long after Modi assumed power with the largest parliamentary majority in decades (2014), he announced the "Make in India" program, a set of policies intended to attract investment and transform India into a manufacturing powerhouse. The EDB Index was central to this new cam-paign. It was linked to manufacturing and investment within the BJP policy platform, and in subsequent official policy. In fact, Modi first formally announced his EDB initiative in a major national speech launching the Make in India Campaign. The effort to improve India's EDB ranking is integral to the country's most visible domestic economic program and is a signature Modi initiative.

Modi has always been clear that his EDB-related reforms were *not* about improving microeconomic incentives but about signaling a welcoming invest-ment climate through a higher EDB ranking. In his speech announcing his EDB effort, Modi declared that "industrialists don't come due to some fancy incentive scheme. One can say you will get this or that we will make this tax free or that tax free. Incentives don't work."[72] Instead, "the investor first wants the security of his investment. Growth and profit come later," Modi argued. For that reason, India needed to send a signal to investors that "your money will not sink." The EDB initiative was part of that signaling effort and Modi committed his entire team in government to improve India's rank-ing from 130 to 50, and then later to 30. While the reforms adopted may well have economic benefits that ordinarily could explain their adoption, they were undertaken for symbolic rather than economic value. The prime minister's words and behavior reveal a belief that *rankings matter more than*

---

[71] "BJP Election Manifesto 2014: Ek Bharat Shreshthah Bharat," from the Wayback Machine, BJP https://web.archive.org/web/20140408115835/http://www.bjp.org/images/pdf_2014/full_manifesto_english_07.04.2014.pdf.
[72] Modi 2014.

economic incentives – they improve India's reputation, and thereby attract investment. This viewpoint also appears in leaked documents related to India's EDB efforts. Two months after Modi was elected, Principal Secretary Nripendra Misra held a high-level meeting to discuss a "concrete strategy for moving up India's rank" on the EDB ranking, with one senior economist later summarizing the meeting in a leaked memo as "focused on the more immediate and quickly doable process improvements."[73] The fact that the EDB effort began by focusing on easier improvements is fully consistent with the argument that countries pursue those reforms that offer the biggest "bang for the buck."

Coordinated Efforts to Improve India's EDB Ranking

Modi followed up his 2014 announcement of an EDB initiative with a wide-ranging interagency coordinated effort to improve the country's ranking. India's most powerful bureaucrat, the cabinet secretary, has called high-profile meetings of senior officials to discuss how to improve India's ranking.[74] These efforts are coordinated not only through the Department of Industrial and Policy Planning (DIPP), which has been tasked with leading Modi's "Make in India" campaign and coordinating state-level reforms. Roughly a month after Modi announced the initiative, DIPP published a report with forty-six policy proposals across several government ministries hewing almost precisely to the Bank's subindicators and intended to improve India's ranking. The Indian government has adopted many of these reforms, including reducing the number of days it takes to register a business from twenty-seven to one; simplifying application forms for industrial licenses; placing license applications online; exempting several business from licensing requirements; extending the validity of licenses; raising FDI caps in several industries; introducing a new regulatory reform law; simplifying import-export documentation; and abolishing the Soviet-style planning commission. At the subnational level, in December 2014, the DIPP sponsored a meeting of central and local governments where state leaders committed to a ninety-eight-point action plan to improve EDB at the local level.[75] DIPP also created

---

[73] Akshay Deshmane, "How Modi and Jaitley Gamed the World Bank's Doing Business Rankings," *Huffington Post India*, November 20, 2018, retrieved from https://www.huffingtonpost.in/2018/11/20/how-modi-and-jaitley-gamed-the-world-banks-doing-business-rankings_a_23594375/.

[74] "DIPP Suggests Steps to Improve Business Climate," *The Hindu Business Line*, October 22, 2014, retrieved from http://www.thehindubusinessline.com/economy/dipp-suggests-steps-to-improve-business-climate/article6526932.ece.

[75] Sai Nidhi, "Ease of Doing Business: Here's All You Need to Know About the Top Ten States," *Daily News and Analysis*, September 16, 2015, retrieved from http://www.dnaindia.com/money/report-ease-of-doing-business-here-s-all-you-need-to-know-about-the-top-10-states-2125690.

a list of 344 recommendations for state-level governments,[76] and organized meetings through which states were to share their best practices.[77] Regardless of whether these reforms have economic benefits, DIPP generally discusses them as ways of improving India's ranking.

The Modi government – convinced of the very EDB influence channels we identify – even chose to reproduce the international EDB competition domestically among Indian states. In concert with the World Bank, the central government created its own state-level EDB indicator to score India's states on their compliance with the ninety-eight-point action plan and publicly praise or criticize them for their performance. In one report, seven Indian states led by the BJP made the top ten, suggesting either party-line cooperation or efforts to reward political allies through the ranking. These rankings were then used as framing devices in domestic politics, instruments to attract state investment, and as proxies for bureaucratic competence. For example, during a visit to BJP-governed Jharkhand, Modi praised its leaders for working hard to improve their EDB ranking.[78] In advance of critical elections in Bihar that would determine the balance of power in India's upper house of parliament, Modi's finance minister attacked Nitish Kumar, the chief minister of Bihar, for his state's low EDB ranking in 2015: "Nitish says let us debate the development issue. What is there to debate? This debate is over. Gujarat [the state Modi previously managed] is number one and Bihar stands at twenty-one [on EDB]. The economy speaks through statistics and not through debate."[79]

Since Modi took office, the World Bank has supported India's attempts to climb the EDB Index, and publicly praised the government for its ambition. The Bank explicitly recognizes that its rankings shape Indian politics. It offered an explanation for why India's ranking ascended so little in Modi's first year that absolved him of responsibility; praised him regularly for his cooperation with the Bank; and even sent the World Bank CEO to attend Modi's celebratory address on India's thirty-place climb and first-ever

[76] "Business Reform Action Plan 2016 for States/UTs," Department of Industrial Policy and Promotion: Ministry of Commerce and Industry, Government of India, 2015, retrieved from http://dipp.nic.in/English/Investor/Ease_DoingBusiness/StateRecommendations_26102015.pdf.

[77] Ruchika Chitravanshi, "States Share Best Ideas to Lift India's Global Ease-of-Doing Business Ranking," *The Economic Times*, October 19, 2015, retrieved from http://economictimes.india-times.com/news/economy/policy/states-share-best-ideas-to-lift-indias-global-ease-of-doing-business-ranking/articleshow/49446000.cms.

[78] Modi 2015b.

[79] "Arun Jaitley Mocks Nitish Kumar on Development; Says Gujarat Number One, Bihar at Twenty-one," *The Economic Times*, September 17, 2015, retrieved from https://economic-times.indiatimes.com/news/politics-and-nation/arun-jaitley-mocks-nitish-kumar-on-development-says-gujarat-number-1-bihar-at-21/articleshow/48998967.cms.

entry into the top one hundred ranks.[80] Attesting to the importance of the rankings, Indian officials have also actively lobbied the World Bank's Doing Business team to improve their scores.[81] As one senior government official involved in those meetings noted, "We listed a host of measures we have taken to cut red tape and improve business environment in the country. We are confident of seeing a substantial improvement in our ranking this year."[82]

EDB Index Channels of Influence

The India case illustrates several of the influence channels described in the introduction to this volume. First, it demonstrates domestic political channels. Indian politicians acted as if they thought the Indian public might be sensitive to the EDB Index's status implications. Indeed, when Modi was an opposition politician, his party used the country's low ranking to shame the incumbent government. Modi himself campaigned on the promise of making improvements. In office, he is making better rankings a priority.[83] Despite criticism, he has doubled down on his commitment to improve India's ranking and has, if anything, scaled up his ambitions by setting a new goal to rank in the top thirty. Importantly, Modi made this commitment credible by promising to achieve a high target rank *before* the next election, allowing voters to punish him for failure. He has hitched his domestic political reputation to the *rankings* – not to a specific growth figure or a poverty-reduction goal. His own public commitments – and the Bank's efforts to avoid embarrassing him – suggest the ranking competition is a significant driver of Indian policy.

Even as India's growth slowed to a three-year low ahead of the next national elections, Modi leaned on India's thirty-place climb in EDB rankings to demonstrate he had improved India's status and its economy.[84] He gave a major address dedicated to India's climb in the rankings and trumpeted India's success relative to other countries: "This year, India's jump in ranking is the

[80] "World Bank 'Ease of Doing Business' Report Doesn't Factor in Modi Government's Reforms: BJP," *The Economic Times*, October 30, 2014, retrieved from http://articles.economictimes.indiatimes.com/2014-10-30/news/55595538_1_modi-government-doing-business-report-world-bank. These actions attest to the Bank's willingness to not only engage in social pressure through rankings but also to engage in related strategies of back patting for favorite pupils as well.

[81] "DIPP Urges World Bank to Upgrade India's Ease of Doing Business Ranking," *The Economic Times*, June 9, 2015, retrieved from http://economictimes.indiatimes.com/news/economy/policy/dipp-urges-world-bank-to-upgrade-indias-ease-of-doing-business-ranking/articleshow/47603975.cms.

[82] Ibid.

[83] Modi 2015a.

[84] Modi 2017.

highest [of all countries]. India has been identified as one of the top reform-ers…[and] may become an example for many other nations." To make EDB even more politically salient, Modi linked it to the "life of a common man" by recasting it as the "Ease of Living Life" indicator. He also leveraged the rating to shame his opposition:

Had these kind of reforms…been carried out during [the opposition's] tenure, then our ranking would have improved much earlier. And the credit for improvement in ranking would have gone to them…they did nothing and have had been raising ques-tions about someone who has been doing something. It's just a coincidence that the World Bank started the process of releasing the ease of doing business ranking in 2004. It's an important year. And all of you know who was in the government [the Congress Party] since then till 2014.[85]

One of India's major newspapers, *The Indian Express,* wrote that India's thirty-rank increase "comes as a shot in the arm for the Narendra Modi gov-ernment amid dissenting voices in certain quarters about implementation of the Goods and Services Tax (GST) as well as demonetization," two policies that had called into question Modi's economic credentials.[86] For that reason, Modi's chief political opponent, Rahul Gandhi, has made attacking Modi's EDB gains a part of his stump speech, stating that Modi's team "listens to outsiders" and should instead ask the Indian people "whether ease of doing business has improved for them…What is spoken abroad is truth for this gov-ernment but what the poor say in India is farce."[87] These statements together demonstrate that India's leading politicians act as if EDB shapes domestic politics and recognize the high ranking as enhancing status for India.

Second, the case demonstrates that political figures in emerging markets act as if they believe the rankings will affect investment levels, which comple-ments the experimental evidence. Modi repeatedly states the belief that EDB affects investment levels. A review of all Modi's foreign addresses establishes that he has broadcast his ambitions on the EDB on virtually every foreign trip for three straight years, including addresses before Davos and the G20 as well as to audiences in capital-rich countries like the United States, China, France, Germany, Japan, Saudi Arabia, South Korea, and the United Kingdom, among

[85] Ibid.

[86] "This Is What Helped India Go Up in World Bank Rankings in 'Ease of Doing Business,'" *The Indian Express,* October 31, 2017, retrieved from http://indianexpress.com/article/business/economy/world-bank-ease-of-doing-business-india-rank-100-arun-jaitley-gst-demonetisation-narendra-modi-4916051/.

[87] "Ease of Doing Business: Rahul Gandhi, Arun Jaitley Take Potshots at Each Other Over India's Ranking," *Hindustan Times,* November 1, 2017, retrieved from https://www.hindustantimes.com/assembly-elections/gst-and-note-ban-have-ruined-ease-of-doing-business-rahul-gandhi-takes-on-govt-day-after-world-bank-report/story-68LlcqSuLmiyTDvfrS7qcP.html.

others.[88] Modi even created a joint "Ease of Doing Business Group" with the United States during the first US-India Strategic and Commercial Dialogue – another signal to the global community that India is a secure and easy place to do business – and has repeatedly declared his belief that EDB efforts have helped attract record investment.[89]

Third, the case demonstrates the importance of bureaucratic channels. Modi embedded the EDB effort in the national bureaucracy, created inter-agency structures to improve the ranking, and tied its success or failure at the national level to specific officials. At the state level, he launched a subnational ranking mechanism and used state EDB rankings to praise reformers and shame laggards, triggering reputational mechanisms among local Indian politicians and bureaucrats. He has publicly acknowledged these mechanisms and declared that under his subnational ranking system states are "often competing with each other in implementing business reforms," which will help the country's overall ranking.[90]

The channels discussed in the introductory chapter are on full display in India. Modi would have been a reformer regardless, but he latched onto the EDB Index as a tool because he believes that domestic political actors, foreign investment communities, and professional bureaucrats care about the Index too. The Index became influential in giving content to his reform ambitions. He even encouraged his subordinates to pursue EDB-tailored reforms. Thus, the EDB Report and rankings are clearly shaping the policy response in one of the world's largest and fastest growing economies.

CONCLUSION

Global performance indicator creators aim not only to call attention to their issue and set standards of appropriate behavior; most hope to change policy outputs and – ultimately – outcomes. By relying on multiple forms of data, we have presented considerable evidence that the World Bank's EDB Index motivates reforms, perhaps even above and beyond those one might expect from consulting with or borrowing from the World Bank alone. One interviewee in the investment consulting industry exclaimed unprompted that the EDB Index was one of the most effective things the World Bank had ever done.[91]

---

[88] For example, see Modi 2015c; "Full Text of Prime Minister Narendra Modi's Speech at the India-China Business Forum in Shanghai," NDTV, May 16, 2015, retrieved from http://www.ndtv.com/india-news/full-text-of-prime-minister-narendra-modis-speech-at-the-india-china-business-forum-in-shanghai-763508.

[89] Modi 2017.

[90] Ibid.

[91] Anonymous interview, August 2014.

The news is good for those who support the contents of the EDB Index and want to use it as a model in other areas.[92] For those who believe the EDB Index is flawed, its influence is cause for concern. Despite episodes of pressure to withdraw the rankings or alter the criteria by countries such as China or organizations such as the ILO, the Bank has continued to rank states because it believes the Index is indeed an effective tool.[93] Both critics of the EDB Index and the Bank's refusal to drop it assume EDB rankings have an effect – for good or for ill – on reform policy. Ours is the first study to systematically document the major influence channels that connect an annually published rank-ordered list of countries with powerful policy trends and consequential shifts in state behavior.

The most important message of this research is what it says about new ways to capture governance spaces and exert social pressure by using ingenious forms of communication. Global performance indicators are communication strategies to draw attention to issues, and to define problems and offer solutions using extreme forms of simplification. As such, they are an international counterpart to "nudge" tactics much touted by behavioral economists and psychologists as ways to shift human behavior in desired ways.[94] Actors who try to create competitive dynamics and other forms of social pressure through ranking systems know that they oversimplify reality, strip concepts of their context and history, and offer a false sense of precision and certainty.[95] But the point of ranking systems is to change behavior, not to faithfully render reality. The ILO has understood this point very well and has been a strong proponent of keeping the labor flexibility measures *out* of the Bank's overall EDB Index, while countries like Saudi Arabia have balked at the recent addition of gender components.

This deep dive into the World Bank indicator has important high-altitude implications for global information politics and governance. It reminds us that information is not neutral but is an important power resource. The World Bank has used the EDB Index to consolidate its authority to address not just development lending but business regulation as well. Arguably, the case of the World Bank's EDB Index suggests that the cumulative effect of widespread comparative quantification is to reinforce global power structures.[96] That said, there is some evidence that alternative power centers – notably China – understand the game. China will soon launch a few new rankings of its own,

[92] Independent Evaluation Group 2008.
[93] In 2013 a formal review which was unhappy with its rankings. The group discussed tensions over the rankings and once again recommended that they be removed. The Bank ignored the recommendation. "Stand Up for 'Doing Business,'" *The Economist*, May 25, 2013, retrieved from https://www.economist.com/leaders/2013/05/25/stand-up-for-doing-business; Independent Evaluation Group 2008.
[94] Thaler and Sunstein 2008.
[95] Merry 2011.
[96] Löwenheim 2008.

and its Asian Infrastructure Investment Bank may eventually be as much an opportunity to offer alternative scorecards for states as it will be a resource for finance.

This study helps explain the influence of rankings in international relations. Combined, the evidence goes beyond the standard scrutiny of the validity of the EDB data to show that rankings stimulate competitive dynamics with policy consequences. These findings invite examination of related questions. For example, is it wise to pursue complex policies of deregulation by deploying simple heuristics, such as ranking systems? Do states regularly game such systems to improve their scores rather than select the most appropriate policies?[97] Who gains "authority" to rank, and why? Is it fair that a few actors worldwide can use first-mover advantage and other strategic positions to set standards over which states are then pressured to compete? How should the use of GPIs as tools of governance themselves be governed – purely by the marketplace of ideas? These and other questions need answers if we are to understand the full range of normative issues associated with the power of assessments in global governance.

ACKNOWLEDGMENTS

This is largely a reprint of our 2019 International Organization paper of the same name, but with minor alterations. We thank Andrew Heiss for outstanding assistance with the empirical analysis and graphics. We also thank all the participants at the May 2016 workshop on Assessment Power in World Politics at Harvard University; participants in colloquia at the Center for Advanced Study, Princeton; International Relations Department, London School of Economics; Legal Studies and Business Ethics Department of the Wharton School of Business; and the Department of Politics and IR, Oxford University. For detailed feedback, special thanks to Indermit Gill, Philip Keefer, Christopher Lucas, Eddy Malesky, Richard Messick, Rita Ramalho, Dani Rodrik, Sylvia Solf, Anton Strezhnev, and Jonas Tallberg. Kate Kelley at the Wharton behavior Lab at the University of Pennsylvania provided advice as well as technical and financial support for the investor survey.

SUPPLEMENTARY MATERIAL

Supplementary material for this chapter is available on the *International Organization* website at https://www.cambridge.org/core/journals/international-organization/article/power-of-ranking-the-ease-of-doing-business-indicator-and-global-regulatory-behavior/1A1A9602B52185FA0A28F3DFDE2DCF5A#fndtn-supplementary-materials.

---

97 While countries often start with easier, more actionable, reforms, we explored gaming in several ways, but found no systematic evidence for it.

References

Appel, Hilary, and Mitchell A. Orenstein. 2018. *From Triumph to Crisis: Neoliberal Economic Reform in Postcommunist Countries.* Cambridge: Cambridge University Press.

Bakvis, Peter. 2007. How the World Bank and IMF Use the Doing Business Report to Promote Labour Market Deregulation in Developing Countries. PB 15-06-06. International Confederation of Free Trade Unions. Available at https://library.fes.de/pdf-files/gurn/00171.pdf. Accessed September 6, 2019.

Boheim, Michael. 2006. *Pilot Project on Administrative Burdens.* Brussels: European Commission.

Corcoran, Adrian, and Robert Gillanders. 2015. Foreign Direct Investment and the Ease of Doing Business. *Review of World Economics* 151 (1):103–26.

Dai, Xinyuan. 2007. *International Institutions and National Policy.* Cambridge: Cambridge University Press.

DeMarzo, Peter. 1992. Coalitions, Leadership, and Social Norms: The Power of Suggestion in Games. *Games and Economic Behavior* 4 (1):72–100.

Djankov, Simeon, Rafael La Porta, Florencio Lopez-de-Silanes, and Andrei Shleifer. 2002. The Regulation of Entry. *Quarterly Journal of Economics* 4 (1):1–37.

Djankov, Simeon, Darshini Manraj, Caralee McLiesh, and Rita Ramalho. 2005. Doing Business Indicators: Why Aggregate and How to Do It. Doing Business Project. World Bank Group. http://siteresources.worldbank.org/EXTAFRSUMAFTPS/Resources/db_indicators.pdf. Accessed September 6, 2019.

Gray, Julia. 2013. *The Company States Keep: International Economic Organization and Sovereign Risk in Emerging Markets.* New York: Cambridge University Press.

Hallward-Driemeier, Mary, and Lant Pritchett. 2011. *How Business is Done and the "Doing Business" Indicators: The Investment Climate When Firms Have Climate Control.* World Bank Policy Research Working Paper Series, no. 5563. Washington, DC: The World Bank.

Hansen, Hans Krause, and Arthur Mühlen-Schulte. 2012. The Power of Numbers in Global Governance. *Journal of International Relations and Development* 15 (4):455–65.

Independent Evaluation Group. 2008. An Independent Evaluation: Taking the Measure of the World Bank IFC Doing Business Indicators. World Bank. Available at http://siteresources.worldbank.org/EXTDOIBUS/Resources/db_evaluation.pdf. Accessed September 6, 2019.

Jayasuriya, Dinuk. 2011. *Improvements in the World Bank's Ease of Doing Business Rankings: Do They Translate into Greater Foreign Direct Investment Inflows?* World Bank Policy Research Working Paper no. 5787. Washington, DC: The World Bank.

Jensen, Jamie L., Mark A. McDaniel, Steven M. Woodard, and Tyler A. Kummer. 2014. Teaching to the Test…or Testing to Teach: Exams Requiring Higher Order Thinking Skills Encourage Greater Conceptual Understanding. *Educational Psychology Review* 26 (2):307–29.

Kahler, Miles. 1994. External Influence, Conditionality, and the Politics of Adjustment. In *Voting for Reform: Democracy, Political Liberalization, and Economic Adjustment*, edited by Stephan Haggard and Steven Benjamin Webb, 89–136. Oxford: Oxford University Press.

Kelley, Judith G. 2004. *Ethnic Politics in Europe: The Power of Norms and Incentives*. Princeton, NJ: Princeton University Press.

———. 2017. *Scorecard Diplomacy: Grades States to Influence Their Reputation and Behavior*. Cambridge: Cambridge University Press.

Kelley, Judith G., and Beth A. Simmons. 2015. Politics by Number: Indicators as Social Pressure in International Relations. *American Journal of Political Science* 59 (1):1146–61.

———. this volume. Global Assessment Power in the Twenty-First Century. *International Organization* 73 (3).

Klapper, Leora, Raphael Amit, and Mauro F. Guillén. 2010. Entrepreneurship and Firm Formation Across Countries. In *International Differences in Entrepreneurship*, edited by Joshua Lerner and Antoinette Schoar, 129–58. Chicago, IL: University of Chicago Press.

Löwenheim, Oded. 2008. Examining the State: A Foucauldian Perspective on International "Governance Indicators." *Third World Quarterly* 29 (2):255–74.

Menken, Kate. 2006. Teaching to the Test: How No Child Left Behind Impacts Language Policy, Curriculum, and Instruction for English Language Learners. *Bilingual Research Journal* 30 (2):521–46.

Merry, Sally Engle. 2011. Measuring the World: Indicators, Human Rights, and Global Governance: With CA Comment by John M. Conley. *Current Anthropology* 52 (3):83–95.

Michaels, Ralf. 2009. Legal Origins Thesis, Doing Business Reports, and the Silence of Traditional Comparative Law. *American Journal of Comparative Law* 57 (4):765–95.

Modi, Narendra. 2014. Text of Prime Minister Shri Narendra Modi's Address at the Launch of "Make in India" Global Initiative. Narendramodi. In 25 September. Available at http://www.narendramodi.in/text-of-prime-minister-shri-narendra-modis-address-at-the-launch-of-make-in-india-global-initiative-2867.

———. 2015a. Text of PM's Letter to the People on Economic Issues. Bharatiya Janata Party. Available at http://www.bjp.org/en/shri-narendra-modi-feed/text-of-pm-s-letter-to-the-people-on-economic-issues. Accessed March 3, 2017.

———. 2015b. Through Mudra Yojana We Want to Accelerate Development Process in India: PM at Inauguration of Mega Credit Camp in Jharkhand. Bharatiya Janata Party. Available at http://www.bjp.org/en/shri-narendra-modi-feed/through-mudra-yojana-we-want-to-accelerate-development-process-in-india-pm-at-inauguration-of-mega-credit-camp-in-jharkhand.

———. 2015c. Text of PM's Statement at India-Republic of Korea CEOs Forum. Bharatiya Janata Party. 19 May. Available at http://www.bjp.org/en/shri-narendra-modi-feed/text-of-pm-s-statement-at-india-republic-of-korea-ceos-forum.

2017. PM Modi Attends Programme on "Ease of Doing Business."
New Delhi. 4 November. Available at https://www.narendramodi.in/
pm-modi-attends-programme-on-ease-of-doing-business--537653.

Mosley, Layna. 2000. Room to Move: International Financial Markets and
National Welfare States. *International Organization* 54 (4):737–73.

Nugent, Pam. 2013. Social Pressure. *Psychology Dictionary*. April 13.
Available at https://psychologydictionary.org/social-pressure/.

Pinheiro-Alves, Ricardo, and João Zambujal-Oliveira. 2012. The Ease of
Doing Business Index as a Tool for Investment Location Decisions.
Economic Letters 117 (1):66–70.

Robson, Keith. 1992. Accounting Numbers as "Inscription": Action
at a Distance and the Development of Accounting. *Accounting,
Organizations, and Society* 17 (7):685–708.

Schueth, Sam. 2011. Assembling International Competitiveness: The
Republic of Georgia, USAID, and the Doing Business Project. *Economic
Geography* 87 (1):51–77.

Sinclair, Timothy J. 2008. *The New Masters of Capital: American Bond
Rating Agencies and the Politics of Creditworthiness*. Ithaca, NY:
Cornell University Press.

Thaler, Richard H., and Cass R. Sunstein. 2008. *Nudge: Improving Decisions
about Health, Wealth, and Happiness*. New Haven, CT: Yale University
Press.

World Bank Group. 2007. *Celebrating Reform 2007: Doing Business Case
Studies*. Washington, DC: World Bank.

2008. *Celebrating Reform 2008: Doing Business Case Studies*. Washington,
DC: World Bank.

2009. *Celebrating Reform 2009: Doing Business Case Studies*. Washington,
DC: World Bank.

2014. *Doing Business 2015: Going Beyond Efficiency*. Washington, DC:
The World Bank.

Zürn, Michael. 2018. *A Theory of Global Governance: Authority,
Legitimacy, and Contestation*. New York: Oxford University Press.

3

Blacklists, Market Enforcement, and the Global Regime to Combat Terrorist Financing

Julia C. Morse*

INTRODUCTION

Over the last twenty years, intergovernmental organizations (IGOs) have increasingly relied on global performance indicators (GPIs) to disseminate information about state policies. In this volume, Kelly and Simmons suggest GPIs influence policy outcomes in states through three pathways: changes in domestic politics, shifts in elite preferences, and transnational pressure.[1] Bisbee and colleagues show that the Millennium Development Goals encourage greater domestic attention to evaluated policy objectives,[2] while Kelley, Simmons, and Doshi suggest the World Bank's Ease-of-Doing-Business index provokes domestic awareness and pressures bureaucrats to change business regulation.[3] Honig and Weaver reveal how the Aid Transparency Index alters the behavior of development aid donors by diffusing professional norms and affecting organizational learning.[4] In contrast to these works, I focus on the third causal pathway – transnational market pressure – and highlight how such forces led to deep and widespread policy change on how states combat terrorist financing. Following the 9/11 terrorist attacks, several international institutions, most notably the UN Security Council, adopted resolutions calling

* I am grateful to numerous government, IO, and financial industry professionals for agreeing to be interviewed and for sharing their expertise. I also thank Ryan Brutger, Christina Davis, Kosuke Imai, Jeffry Frieden, Julia Gray, Roy Hwang, Judith Kelley, Amanda Kennard, Robert Keohane, Christoph Mikulaschek, Helen Milner, Duane Morse, Tyler Pratt, Beth Simmons, the Imai Research Group, and participants in the Global Assessment Power project conferences for valuable feedback and guidance on this project.
[1] Kelley and Simmons 2019.
[2] Bisbee et al. this volume.
[3] Kelley, Simmons, and Doshi 2019.
[4] Honig and Weaver 2019.

for the worldwide adoption of domestic laws criminalizing terrorist financing. A decade later, most countries had laws that were weak and ineffective. Since 2010, however, a non-binding regulatory institution has used a GPI – in this case, a public non-complier list – to reverse this trend. Today, more than 100 countries have adopted comprehensive laws on terrorist financing, making it significantly more difficult for terrorists to use the international financial system.

One small institution achieved such an effect by harnessing the power of GPIs to outsource enforcement to market actors. Existing scholarship has highlighted how civil society can pressure governments to comply with international agreements.[5] In such models, domestic actors draw attention to instances of non-compliance in their own states. I argue that GPIs can lead transnational market actors to serve as outside enforcers, punishing foreign countries that fail to comply with multilateral rules. Every day, market actors make decisions about how to allocate their capital under conditions of uncertainty. Banks decide whether individuals from countries with a high risk of money laundering can open savings accounts, while investment firms decide whether to buy debt from emerging economies. In such cases, market actors must evaluate potential risks based on limited information.

Intergovernmental organizations can use GPIs to fill this informational gap and stabilize market expectations. Because of their multilateral nature, many IGOs have high credibility as monitors, and are able to leverage their bureaucratic authority, technical expertise, and access to government policy to provide unique, detailed insight into policy issues in different countries. When GPIs provide credible information about the domestic policies of states, they are more likely to influence the actions of outside audiences. GPIs are particularly likely to lead to market enforcement when they provide information about country risk and serve as heuristics. Under these conditions, IGO-produced GPIs can be influential in determining how market actors invest, loan money, or make purchasing decisions.

I illustrate this argument by analyzing global policy change on combating terrorist financing and highlighting the role of the Financial Action Task Force (FATF). The FATF is an intergovernmental body that makes recommendations about how states should combat money laundering and terrorist financing; it has been instrumental in driving global compliance on this issue. The FATF is a relatively weak international institution; although it issues global recommendations, it has no permanent charter and only thirty-eight members. Lacking legally binding authority, the FATF relies in part on a non-complier list to generate policy change in states. This list has been remarkably effective: more than 90 percent of listed countries had adopted FATF-compliant laws on terrorist financing as of 2015, compared to only about 50 percent of

---

[5] See, for example, Dai 2007; Johns 2012; Mansfield and Milner 2012; Simmons 2009.

non-listed countries. This is a stark reversal in trends from 2009, when not one soon-to-be-listed country had a compliant law. Using a new dataset that compiles information about the laws of 179 states, I employ a cox proportional hazards model to show that the FATF non-complier list makes states significantly more likely to adopt FATF-compliant laws on terrorist financing in a given period.

Additional tests highlight market enforcement as a core causal mechanism for this process. Although the list drives policy change across states, it has the strongest effect on compliance in countries that are highly integrated into the global economy. In an analysis of how the FATF list affects cross-border bank-to-bank lending, I show that listed countries experience on average a 16 percent decrease in lending, compared to when they are not listed. I illustrate the underlying causal process through a case study of Thailand, where market actors played an integral role in pushing for policy change following FATF listing in 2010.

IGO-PRODUCED GPIs AND MARKET ENFORCEMENT

Intergovernmental organizations are credible sources of information about government policy thanks to institutional advantages like bureaucratic authority, technical expertise, and access to monitored states. The authority of a GPI's creator is likely to boost the GPI's perceived legitimacy and salience.[6] Because of their bureaucratic nature, IGOs tend to be particularly authoritative evaluators of policy success. As Barnett and Finnemore point out, bureaucracies "embody a form of authority, rational-legal authority, that modernity views as particularly legitimate and good."[7] The IGO bureaucracies are also a source of significant technocratic expertise, which bureaucrats can draw upon as they assemble GPIs and which may intensify the impact of GPIs on monitored states through the diffusion of professional norms[8] and specific standards.[9] Indeed, states often delegate monitoring responsibilities to IOs in order to develop technical expertise.[10] When IGOs assess state compliance with specific standards, this process can lead to extra scrutiny of specific policies and encourage greater domestic political attention to specific criteria.[11]

Authoritative and technical monitoring can come from many sources, but IGOs may have a third comparative advantage: access. While non-governmental organizations provide policy information through on-the-ground informants, reporting on economic or security issues often requires

---

[6] Kelley and Simmons 2019.
[7] Barnett and Finnemore 1999, 707.
[8] Honig and Weaver 2019.
[9] Kelley, Simmons and Doshi 2019.
[10] Hawkins et al. 2006.
[11] Bisbee et al. this volume.

direct access to governments. The IGOs have significant advantages in this regard – as long-standing organizations, they can draw on established relationships to extract information from the evaluated countries. Indeed, because monitoring is so common across IGOs, governments may be less likely to resist IGO monitoring. Government bureaucrats are used to responding to IGO requests for information, meeting with IGO officials, and receiving IGO-provided technical assistance. Many IGOs rely on interactive evaluation systems, where monitoring procedures include a combination of government reporting, direct evaluation, and final written assessments. The Organization for Economic Cooperation and Development's (OECD) monitoring process, for example, includes a detailed country questionnaire, two staff team visits to the country, and several draft reports, with a final report adopted in the OECD plenary. The entire process "is motivated by peer review and peer pressure."[12] This type of participatory approach not only enhances the legitimacy of the reporting but may also make GPIs more effective at driving policy change.[13]

GPIs and Markets

Kelley and Simmons 2019 suggest that GPIs influence the conduct of states through three pathways: domestic, elite, and transnational politics. Although many IGO-produced GPIs affect elite interests and mobilize domestic audiences, I focus on the third, less common but perhaps more powerful mechanism: transnational market pressure. When IGO-produced GPIs are credible, they can lead to a process of "market enforcement," whereby financial actors reallocate resources away from poorly performing countries.[14] Market enforcement is most likely to occur when market actors are dividing finite resources among states, leading to intergovernmental competition. Under this condition, market actors are likely to seek out new information about foreign governments. Global performance indicators fill such informational gaps when they reduce uncertainty about country risk and serve as heuristics that shape expectations about market sentiments.

The GPIs are most likely to lead to market enforcement when market actors are dividing finite resources among states, not among substate units. For these types of financial decisions, governments, rather than firms, are in competition with each other. When a government issues a new sovereign bond, for example, investors evaluate not just the specific government and its likeliness of repaying the debt, but also the larger economic climate and alternative options for investment.[15] Similarly, when a bank decides whether to establish

[12] Schäfer 2006, 74.
[13] Parks and Masaki 2017.
[14] For previous work on the link between market pressures and government policy, see Buthe and Milner 2008; Elkins, Guzman and Simmons 2006; Mosley 2003; Simmons 2000 among others.
[15] See Baldacci, Gupta and Mati 2011; Hilscher and Nosbusch 2010; Longstaff et al. 2011.

a cross-border banking relationship with a bank in another country, it weighs the profits and costs of working in a particular country against other possible relationships that might be established.[16] In such cases, governments have incentives to make their countries as attractive as possible to foreign market actors, even by withholding negative information. Market actors, meanwhile, have incentives to seek out the best possible information to reduce uncertainty about the profitability and risk of different opportunities.

Global performance indicators are also more likely to lead to market enforcement when they reduce uncertainty about the quality of a government or characteristics of an investment environment.[17] As long as IGOs are credible providers of information, GPIs by their very nature are likely to lead to "uncertainty absorption."[18] Although an IGO may have assembled an index from a large body of evidence, the GPI communicates only the IGO's inferences, not the original data. In financial markets, as Bruce Carruthers explains, "rather than founder on the fact that probabilities are truly unknown, decision-makers instead try to gather more information, estimate probabilities and simply proceed with estimates."[19] GPIs, particularly rankings or blacklists, are ideal inputs into this process because they "rely on the magic of numbers" to render evaluations more certain and objective.[20]

By absorbing uncertainty and coordinating market expectations, GPIs act as a type of heuristic for market participants. Recent work in political science highlights the degree to which market actors like investors may use cognitive shortcuts to make financial decisions.[21] Ozturk suggests that credit rating agencies use the Worldwide Governance Indicators to assess the credit worthiness of governments, despite known problems with the data.[22] While existing arguments focus on investors and sovereign debt, a similar logic applies to banks and other financial institutions that make investment and business decisions based in part on country risk.

Market actors may also use GPIs as heuristics for understanding how *other* banks or investors will evaluate the risk of doing business with a country. In many types of market activity, the profitability of an investment depends on

---

[16] Bank for International Settlements 2016.

[17] Lee and Matanock 2019 highlight the importance of this scope condition. In this volume, they show that while Transparency International's Corruption Perception Index attracts media attention, it does not influence the allocation of foreign aid, perhaps because policymakers are already aware of the information contained in the index.

[18] March and Simon 1958.

[19] Carruthers 2013, 526.

[20] Merry 2011, S84.

[21] See Tomz 2007 on investor beliefs about a government's "type," Gray 2013 on investors using a country's IO membership as a heuristic, and Brooks, Cunha and Mosley 2014 on investors comparing countries to their peers.

[22] Ozturk 2016.

how other market participants judge its quality.[23] Investors consider not only the true value of a commodity or bond, but also conventional wisdom surrounding a particular acquisition.[24] For banks, heuristics about country risk may affect loan rates. Banks may charge high-risk countries higher loan rates because they expect fewer competitors will offer good rates, or because they assume that the high-risk label will lead other market actors to cut off access to capital (thus decreasing the likelihood of repayment).

From Market Enforcement to Policy Change

When IO monitoring leads to market enforcement, it can create new advocates for compliance. In particular, banks, investors, or companies that are hurt by the market enforcement process are likely to push the government to change its policies. Countries will vary in how responsive they are to these processes; domestic institutions and politics are likely to influence how leaders allocate resources among competing policy priorities.[25] However, one of the strengths of market enforcement is that international banks and investors typically have direct access to the leader's "winning coalition," that is, those people whose support is essential to maintaining power.[26] The domestic banking community and the central bank are part of the winning coalition in many countries, which makes them persuasive advocates for policy change. In countries where market integration is high, domestic banks are likely to be an influential part of the economy and to have significant pull with the government. Market integration thus intensifies reputational effects and incentivizes compliance.

REGULATING GLOBAL FINANCE

To examine how GPIs can lead to market enforcement, I analyze international cooperation on "financial integrity" – efforts to keep illicit money out of the financial system. The organization at the heart of this endeavor is the Financial Action Task Force (FATF). The FATF is an informal intergovernmental body that was created in 1989 to set global standards and promote the implementation of policies to combat money laundering.[27] Founding members included the G-7 countries, the European Commission, and eight other European states.[28] Over the past three decades, the FATF has broadened its

---

[23] See, for example, arguments by Amato, Morris and Shin 2002 about the Central Bank or Shiller 2015 about the role of the media in driving major market movements.

[24] Abdelal and Blyth 2015.

[25] Milner 1997; Moravcsik 1997; Rickard 2010.

[26] Bueno de Mesquita et al. 2003.

[27] The FATF does not have a standing charter; instead, member states periodically extend its mandate (the current one runs through 2020).

[28] Australia, Austria, Belgium, Italy, Luxembourg, Netherlands, Spain, and Switzerland.

mission to include combating terrorist financing and proliferation financing, and expanded its reach. Today, it has 38 members (36 countries and two regional organizations) and nine associated regional bodies that assess compliance in more than 190 countries.[29]

FATF Rules and Monitoring

The FATF issues recommendations on how states should combat the problems of money laundering and terrorist financing through legal and regulatory action. Recommendations include legal changes, preventive measures on how banks evaluate customer risk and keep records, and improved international cooperation. The FATF's formulation of global standards has been crucial for fighting money laundering and terrorist financing. For many years, legal differences across jurisdictions created significant problems for the bureaucratic offices' anti-money laundering enforcement. Rule conflicts also provided opportunities for jurisdictional arbitrage, whereby criminals could take advantage of multiple rules and conflicting agreements.[30] By formulating global standards, the FATF has helped states coordinate definitions of money laundering and terrorist financing, producing greater legal harmonization and facilitating policy implementation.

The FATF also has an impact on state policy through its monitoring and evaluation system, which evaluates compliance in more than 190 countries. Each FATF assessment is conducted by a small team of evaluators made up of legal and financial experts from peer countries, FATF Secretariat officials, and often bureaucrats from the International Monetary Fund (IMF) or the World Bank. This team of assessors rates a country's level of compliance on each recommendation based on the following scale: compliant, largely compliant, partially compliant, non-compliant, or not applicable.[31] The evaluation process is lengthy, often taking more than a year, and technical; each country is fully assessed approximately once per decade. Between full evaluations, the FATF and its regional bodies conduct shorter, more targeted evaluations of specific problem areas.

Final FATF reports are adopted in tri-annual plenary meetings. During these sessions, evaluated countries may argue against portions of the draft report, advocating for rating changes.[32] Such rating upgrades are difficult to achieve because the FATF operates by consensus decision-making: an evaluated country must convince all other member countries to support a rating upgrade on a specific recommendation. This is a difficult task; reports are

---

[29] A full list of FATF members and the nine regional bodies is available in Appendix A.
[30] Unger and Busuioc 2007.
[31] FATF-GAFI 2009c.
[32] Nakagawa 2011.

usually adopted over some objections from the evaluated states.[33,34] Even G-7 countries like the United States, Japan, and Canada receive non-compliant ratings.[35]

FATF Technical Expertise and Credibility

Market actors, governments, and even other IOs rely on the FATF for information about states' financial integrity policies because of the highly technical nature of this issue area. Governments require significant legal and administrative expertise to implement the FATF's recommendations. Without FATF guidance and substantive expertise, many countries would struggle to meet these requirements.[36] The FATF issues detailed working papers that highlight best practices for governments and for private sector actors. It also connects bureaucrats across countries, building a network of technical experts. The FATF draws on this network when it evaluates countries. Because the FATF Secretariat is small, evaluation teams always include bureaucratic officials from peer countries. Chip Poncy, former head of the US delegation to FATF, described this network structure as essential to the FATF's success. "For FATF, the shareholder countries are the managers and also do the work, together with the Secretariat. The minute you hire more people into the Secretariat, there's daylight between what managers are deciding and what shareholders are implementing."[37]

The FATF's credibility as a monitor is also a result of its reputation as a highly technocratic, apolitical organization. Rather than high-level political actors, government bureaucrats staff FATF plenary meetings. FATF monitoring reports are drafted primarily by the evaluation team, with only a limited discussion in the plenary session. When countries discuss specific ratings for reports during the plenary session, they are encouraged to provide technical justifications for their support or dissent.[38] Former FATF President Antonio Gustavo Rodrigues described the FATF by highlighting this technocratic nature, saying "FATF is a unique organization. Of course, in any organization with human beings, you have politics. But in the FATF, politics is a secondary aspect."[39]

---

[33] Interview of FATF regional body official, January 7, 2015; Participant-Observation, September 2016 and May 2017.

[34] I conducted more than twenty interviews over the course of this project but due to the sensitive nature of this issue area, most people were unwilling to speak for direct attribution. Additional details on the interview process and a list of interviews are available in Appendix C.

[35] In the third round of mutual evaluations, the US was rated noncompliant on four recommendations (FATF-GAFI 2006), while Japan and Canada were rated non-compliant on ten and eleven recommendations respectively (FATF-GAFI 2008b, 2008c).

[36] Indeed, even a long-standing FATF member like Germany received failing ratings on 20 of the FATF recommendations (FATF-GAFI 2010).

[37] Author interview, February 7, 2018.

[38] This statement is based on the author's participant-observation experience at two FATF regional body meetings.

[39] Author interview, March 29, 2017.

The Non-Complier List

A few years into the FATF's third round of mutual evaluations, FATF and regional affiliate member states began to call for more consistent procedures for dealing with non-compliant countries.[40] In June 2009, the FATF adopted new, systematic procedures whereby all countries that received failing scores on ten or more of the FATF's sixteen most important recommendations[41] would be eligible for inclusion on a "non-complier list."[42] Under this process, the FATF has publicly identified fifty-seven countries since February 2010.[43] To select countries for the list, the FATF uses the results of mutual evaluation reports, reviewing all countries that fail on ten or more recommendations. Figure 3.1 shows the results of the FATF's third round of mutual evaluations, comparing the number of non-listed (grey, bottom of stacked bars) and listed (black, top of stacked bars) countries by the number of failing recommendations.[44]

Once countries are eligible for listing, the FATF gives governments up to a year to undertake policy improvements before deciding whether to list them. Governments work with the FATF to develop and implement action plans to

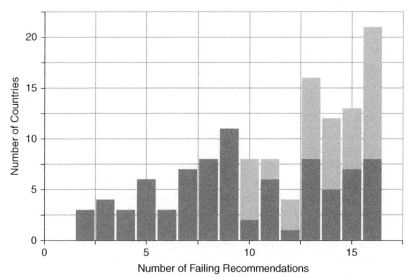

FIGURE 3.1. The figure shows the number of non-listed countries (dark grey, bottom of stacked bars) and listed countries (light grey, top of stacked bars) by the total number of failing ratings.

[40] FATF-GAFI 2009a.
[41] See Appendix B.
[42] The FATF "non-complier list" is formally known as the International Cooperation Review Group (ICRG) process. The FATF adopted new procedures for this process in June 2009 (FATF-GAFI 2009b) and issued its first announcement in February 2010.
[43] See Appendix D for countries listed through June 2016.
[44] Data is limited to countries included in subsequent empirical analyses.

address deficiencies; countries that are slow to implement their action plans are more likely to be listed. In addition to considering political will, the FATF makes listing decisions using a "risk-based approach," whereby countries with larger financial sectors or greater risks of money laundering or terrorist financing are more likely to be listed.[45] Other considerations include a country's legal framework, its responses to requests for international cooperation, and whether it is involved in a follow-up process.[46]

The FATF noncomplier list is an important source of information about the financial integrity policies of other countries. Prior to the list's creation, an observer interested in learning about a state's anti-money laundering policies had to read through its most recent mutual evaluation report. The report would likely be several years old and more than 200 pages in length, and would not include any comparable summary judgment of the country's policies. But the FATF noncomplier list is based on new, up-to-date information and the list consolidates risk into an easily interpretable metric. As a result, the noncomplier list is a straightforward way for observers to clearly identify the highest-risk countries.

Listing and Market Enforcement

The FATF noncomplier list is a powerful driver of policy change because market actors use the list to allocate resources away from noncompliant states. The FATF itself is responsible for some of this market behavior. One of the FATF's most important recommendations requires banks, corporate service providers, remittance services, and lawyers to maintain "customer due diligence procedures," taking measures to verify customer identities using a risk-based approach. In effect, this recommendation requires market actors to assess the risk of money laundering and terrorist financing emanating from different jurisdictions, creating a perfect audience for the noncomplier list. Although some FATF members, like the United States and the United Kingdom, might have adopted such regulations independently, the FATF has encouraged worldwide policy diffusion.[47]

Banks have clear regulatory incentives to reallocate resources on the basis of the noncomplier list. Because of the diffusion of customer due diligence regulations, most banks have standardized procedures for determining whether customers are high risk for money laundering and terrorist financing, based in part on countries of origin. Banks typically subject customers from high-risk jurisdictions to longer screening and administrative procedures. In some cases, banks might even opt to forgo all business with high-risk countries.[48] Countries like the

---

[45] FATF-GAFI 2009b.
[46] Ibid.
[47] Sharman 2008.
[48] Collin, Cook and Soramaki 2016.

United States follow up regulation with government enforcement, ensuring that banks are adequately complying with the law. The financial penalties for such a violation can be enormous. In 2012, for example, the US Government fined HSBC, a British financial services holding company, 1.256 billion US dollars for "failing to maintain an effective anti-money laundering program."[49]

Banks also need information on money laundering and terrorist financing risk because they are likely to suffer significant reputational damage if they are involved in a financial integrity scandal. Reputational damage can lead to financial costs. The US government's discovery that Riggs Banks was helping several dictators launder money resulted in relatively small financial penalties, but led to the bank's demise.[50] As a compliance executive from one of the biggest banks in the United States described, "no firm wants the reputational damage of having been used as a vehicle for criminal activity, or worse, as a channel for financing terrorism."[51] Indeed, damage to reputation is often used as a way to sell risk management systems to financial institutions.[52]

For both regulatory and reputational reasons, banks face a Herculean task: to evaluate and assess customer risk under conditions of high uncertainty. The FATF noncomplier list offers an easy way for banks to quantify this risk. Prior to the list, banks were stuck trying to interpret the results of 200-page monitoring reports and making independent judgments about which types of noncompliance posed the biggest threats. Such information was often several years old. Chip Poncy, former head of the US delegation to FATF, noted the challenge for market actors of digesting the lengthy FATF monitoring reports. "When you publish 300-page mutual evaluation reports that no one in the market really understands how to read and there are no cumulative ratings, markets don't know how to react. There's not enough depth, understanding, or expertise in the market yet to understand and react to these technical issues absent country lists for material noncompliance."[53] With the advent of the noncomplier list, the FATF now provides more recent information and points banks toward the highest-risk countries.

Reputation

This process of market enforcement interacts with and intensifies GPIs' reputational effects. The FATF list damages a country's international reputation not just through a "peer effect"[54] but through something like a

[49] US Department of Justice 2012.
[50] Jamieson 2006.
[51] Author interview, August 28, 2015.
[52] Author interview with Jeff Soloman, Financial and Risk Sales Specialist, Thomson Reuters, September 28, 2015.
[53] Author interview, February 7, 2018.
[54] Brooks, Cunha and Mosley 2014.

"lowest-common-denominator effect," where countries are judged by the worst of the group. After Antigua and Barbuda were listed in February 2010, for example, the leading opposition leader criticized the ruling party for the fact that Antigua and Barbuda were on a list with Nigeria, Sudan, Ukraine, and Myanmar. This lowest-common-denominator effect is compounded by media coverage where news outlets often ignore the nuances of listing.[55]

Enforcement by market actors intensifies the FATF list's reputational effects. Daniel Glaser, the former US Assistant Secretary for Terrorist Financing and Financial Crimes, noted that part of the power of the FATF list is that "it creates dynamics that you don't fully control, where small actions have systemic resonance. Once FATF lists a country, FATF does not control how the market responds."[56] The perception that listing leads to market enforcement increases reputational costs. If a government fails to prevent its country from being listed, this policy failure signals to outside observers that the listed government is unable or unwilling to tackle money laundering and terrorist financing. In some countries, reputational concerns may be more important than specific financial consequences. An official from one formerly listed country reported, "As far as markets, I'm not saying we're unaware of the side effects, but at least from my perspective, that's not the main motivation. We just wanted a clean reputation internationally."[57]

The FATF Noncomplier List: Testable Hypotheses

My theory suggests that the FATF noncomplier list stigmatizes states directly and that market pressure intensifies this effect. As a result, being listed should incentivize improved FATF compliance. Gordon Hook, the Executive Secretary of the Asia/Pacific Group on Money Laundering, described this impact. "The list has had a phenomenal effect on policymakers. If they are listed, they work extremely hard and fast to get off the list. At the government level, we always saw high levels of commitment from the executive but that would slow down once parliament was involved. Now countries move at a much faster pace."[58]

> H1. (Reputation Hypothesis): Countries that are listed by the FATF
>   should adopt FATF-compliant laws on terrorist financing more
>   quickly than nonlisted countries.

The actual process of market enforcement can occur along several pathways. In some cases, banks simply exercise enhanced due diligence, subjecting

---

[55] The FATF non-complier list is composed of several different lists, colloquially referred to as the "grey" list, the "dark grey" list, the "black" list, and the counter measures list; however, this differentiation is often lost in media reporting. See, for example, Rubenfeld 2011.

[56] Author interview, February 12, 2018.

[57] Author interview, February 9, 2016.

[58] Author interview, June 30, 2016.

customers in listed countries to greater scrutiny or longer waiting times. In other cases, banks have refused to allow any transactions from listed countries. In May 2014, for example, banks in the United States, Europe, Germany, and Turkey stopped dealing with certain Afghan commercial banks.[59] By June, the cost of money transfers had gone up 80 percent.[60]

One likely moderator for the effect of the noncomplier list on compliance is a country's integration into international markets. Countries that are more open to transnational financial flows should be particularly responsive to the noncomplier list. I proxy market integration with cross-border bank liabilities, which indicate the amount of money that domestic banks in a particular country owe to international banks. Bank-to-bank financial transactions are a key part of the global economy, and facilitate trade finance, short-term borrowing, and foreign investment. If the FATF list leads banks to reallocate resources away from noncompliant countries, countries with higher levels of bank-to-bank lending should be particularly affected by the process.

> H2. *(Market Enforcement Hypothesis): Listed countries that are highly integrated into global markets should adopt FATF-compliant laws on terrorist financing more quickly than less-integrated listed countries.*

Market enforcement by banks is likely to lead to significant financial consequences for listed countries. Banks integrate the FATF noncomplier list directly into their risk models; these models, in turn, drive bank procedures for verifying customer identities and monitoring potential anti-money laundering transactions. Individuals and companies in listed countries may experience delays in transferring money or conducting business abroad. Over the last five years, international banks have increasingly opted to pull out of high-risk financial jurisdictions. Although bank enforcement against listed countries could take a variety of forms, the consequences of such action are straightforward – banks and customers in listed countries should find it harder to access international capital.

> H3. *(Bank-to-Bank Lending Hypothesis): Banks in developed economies should be less willing to loan money to banks in listed countries, compared to when these countries are not listed.*

EMPIRICAL APPROACH

My primary analysis examines how the FATF noncomplier list affects state behavior. I focus on a key indicator of compliance with the FATF standards – the criminalization of terrorist financing (FATF Special Recommendation II) – and analyze how being included on the noncomplier list has affected the length of time that it takes for a country to criminalize terrorist financing in

---

[59] Donati 2014.
[60] Carberry 2014.

line with FATF standards. I begin the analysis in February 2010 because that is start of the current noncomplier list, and my data goes through December 2015. Data on country listing status is collected from FATF noncomplier list announcements (published online in February, June, and October every year).

I test my theory using a Cox Proportional Hazards model, which analyzes how variables affect the length of time in months it takes for a country to criminalize terrorist financing in line with the FATF recommendation. This model is appropriate given the unidirectional nature of the data – once a country has fully criminalized terrorist financing, it is unlikely to repeal its law. As a result of this approach, however, countries that criminalized terrorist financing in line with FATF guidelines prior to February 2010 are excluded from the analysis. In analyses where the proportional hazard assumption does not hold, I follow the advice of Box-Steffensmeier and Zorn, who suggest including a log-time interaction for variables with substantial evidence of nonproportionality.[61]

Selection into listing poses potential challenges for the empirical analysis. If the FATF is more likely to list countries that are also more likely to criminalize terrorist financing, failing to account for the selection process could inflate my findings. Conversely, if the FATF is more likely to list the most reluctant compliers, failing to account for selection could attenuate the results. I address these concerns through sample construction and the addition of covariates. I construct a full sample of 132 countries that had not criminalized terrorism in line with FATF standards as of February 2010. This sample includes forty-six of the fifty-seven countries listed as part of the noncomplier list. As I add covariates, the sample drops to 120 countries (37 listed) in Model 2, 96 countries (32 listed) in Model 3, and 87 countries (30 listed) in Model 4.[62]

Second, I establish a universe of potential listed countries through matching. Ho and colleagues suggest that preprocessing data through matching produces more accurate and less model-dependent causal inferences.[63] To compare countries with similar probabilities of being listed, I use nearest-neighbor matching to create a set of twelve listed and twelve nonlisted countries that are similar in terms of diffusion, alliance with the United States, private sector credit, capacity, level of democracy, and risk of terrorism. More specifically, I subset the data to the first period of the analysis (February 2010) and assemble a matched data set of twenty-four countries based on variable

---

[61] Box-Steffensmeier and Zorn 2001. I include a log-time interaction for the variable *US Ally*, although results are robust to not including this interaction term. See Appendix G, which replicates Table 3.1 without the log-time interaction term.

[62] This reduction in the sample is primarily due to the addition of the variable "Risk of Terrorism," which comes from the *International Country Risk Guide* and is only available for a subset of countries. Appendix E lists the countries that are included in each model. The results are robust to imputing missing data (Appendix F).

[63] Ho et al. 2007.

values in this period. I then assemble panel data for this set of twenty-four countries for the full time period (2010–2015).[64] Matching improves the balance of the sample on the majority of variables included in the model.[65]

Finally, I construct a dataset of all non-FATF member countries that were eligible for listing based on FATF bureaucratic criteria as of February 2010. When FATF member states set the new listing eligibility threshold of ten failing recommendations in June 2009, the FATF and its regional bodies had already completed close to 100 evaluations of members of the FATF global network. Most of these countries were not members of FATF regional bodies, rather than the FATF itself, and were therefore uninvolved in setting the new listing threshold. Instead, these countries found themselves suddenly under consideration for a new listing process, with no ability to change their listing eligibility. I examine how listing affects compliance outcomes within this set of sixty-eight countries, fifteen of which were listed by the FATF.

My unit of observation is country-month. In the simplest model for the full sample, this equates to 7308 observations and seventy-two events (instances where a country criminalizes terrorist financing in line with FATF guidelines). In the simplest model in the matched sample, there are 1104 observations and seventeen events. Finally, in the simplest model in the sample of countries eligible for listing, there are 3420 observations, and thirty-six events.

Dependent Variable: Criminalization of Terrorist Financing

Although the FATF issues forty recommendations,[66] this paper focuses on one specific indicator of compliance: the criminalization of terrorist financing. The FATF considers the criminalization of terrorist financing to be a top priority. Compliance with this recommendation is also a clear indication of policy change. The FATF did not adopt the criminalization of terrorist financing as a recommendation until 2001, and prior to that time, only a handful of states had laws criminalizing terrorist financing.[67]

---

[64] A standard matching approach would use the entire data set to assemble a matched sample; however, because I run a hazard model, countries drop out of the sample as they criminalize terrorist financing in line with FATF standards. For this reason, I assemble a group of comparable countries based only on 2010 values, and then expand the sample to include data on this select group of countries from the complete time period.

[65] See Appendix J for more details.

[66] This study covers the FATF's third round of mutual evaluations, during which the FATF actually issued forty-nine recommendations. For its fourth round of evaluations (currently ongoing), the FATF consolidated its recommendations to forty.

[67] This variable is, at best, a partial measure of compliance, as demonstrated by Findley, Nielson and Sharman 2014. Legal compliance and even policy implementation cannot prove that the institution has reduced money laundering or terrorist financing. While these are important issues, they are outside the scope of this study.

The FATF requirement to criminalize terrorist financing is broad and far reaching. States must criminalize terrorist financing beyond what is required in the Terrorist Financing Convention, extending the terrorist financing offense to any person who provides or collects funds with the intention that they be used to carry out a terrorist act, by a terrorist organization, or by an individual terrorist. Laws must define "funds" as including assets of any kind from both legitimate and illegitimate sources. According to FATF guidelines, laws should stipulate that funds provided to terrorists do not actually have to be linked to any specific terrorist act.

I collected data on the month and year in which each country adopted legislation that fulfilled all of the FATF requirements on criminalizing terrorist financing. I coded this variable based on information contained in FATF mutual evaluation reports and follow-up reports, announcements about the noncomplier list, and the FATF's Terrorist Financing Fact-Finding Initiative. For a law to be considered FATF-compliant, it has to extend to any person who willfully provides or collects funds with the intention or knowledge that they are to be used to carry out a terrorist attack, by a terrorist organization, or by an individual terrorist.[68] Figure 3.2 shows the distribution of this variable over time, separated by whether a country is eventually listed (dashed line) or is never listed (solid line). As of late 2008, most countries had not

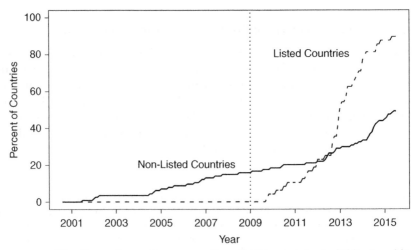

FIGURE 3.2. The figure shows the percent of nonlisted countries (solid line) and listed post-2009 countries (dashed line) that have adopted FATF-compliant laws on terrorist financing. The dotted vertical line indicates the 2009 announcement of the revamped FATF noncomplier process that issued its first noncomplier list in February 2010.

[68] FATF Interpretive Note to Recommendation 5 (Terrorist Financing Offence); FATF Methodology, 2012.

adopted FATF-compliant laws on terrorist financing. Instead, many countries had partial laws that criminalized terrorist financing only when linked to a terrorist act.[69] Such gaps are quite meaningful – funds are fungible, and while terrorist organizations need relatively little money to mount an attack, they require significant resources to sustain recruitment, propaganda, and legitimation activities.[70] Noncompliance may also arise when countries adopt a too-narrow definition of terrorism.

Since the FATF adopted new noncomplier list procedures in 2009, countries have been significantly more likely to adopt laws on terrorist financing that meet FATF standards. As of 2015, close to 90 percent of listed and formerly listed countries had FATF-compliant laws, whereas only about 50 percent of nonlisted countries had similarly compliant laws. This significant policy change by listed countries is the reason that the FATF has removed so many countries from listing – as of 2016, forty-six of fifty-seven listed countries had "graduated" from the noncomplier list following major improvements in their laws.[71]

Explanatory Variables

The primary variable of interest is whether, at a given point in time, a country is on the noncomplier list. I create a dichotomous variable *Listing*, which indicates whether a country is on the noncomplier list at any time. In the largest version of the data, approximately 17 percent of observations are coded as 1s.[72]

To test the market enforcement hypothesis, I include in my sample the variable *Market Integration*. This variable is a continuous measure of a country's aggregate cross-border liabilities in 2008, and proxies for a country's level of market integration prior to the FATF's new noncomplier list procedures.[73]

Data on cross-border bank-to-bank liabilities comes from the Bank for International Settlements (BIS) locational banking statistics. This data set provides information about outstanding claims and liabilities as reported by internationally active banks that are located in the forty-four reporting countries. Because these banks report international cross-border flows, the data covers banking relationships in more than 200 countries, capturing about 95 percent of all cross-border interbank business. For the countries included in

---

[69] FATF-GAFI 2015.
[70] FATF-GAFI 2008a.
[71] See Appendix D for more information.
[72] I also create an ordinal variable *List Level*, which disaggregates listing into different levels. See Appendix I.
[73] I use this early time period to indicate market integration *prior* to the creation of the noncomplier list. I estimate the conditional marginal effect of listing moderated by market enforcement through an interaction term, following guidelines set forth in Brambor, Clark and Golder 2006 and Hainmueller, Mummolo and Xu Forthcoming. Appendix H provides support for the linearity assumption.

the data set, this variable ranges from an average quarterly liabilities of USD 7 million for Dominica to USD 1.7 trillion for Germany. Because the data are highly skewed, I transform the variable by logging it.

A country's direct ties to the FATF may also affect how quickly it meets FATF standards on the criminalization of terrorist financing. In the full sample, I include the variable *FATF Member* to account for whether a country is a member of the FATF in a given year.[74]

Countries may also be influenced by the policies of neighbors or regional partners through processes of policy diffusion.[75] Jason Sharman argues that diffusion has affected the adoption of anti-money laundering policies throughout the developing world.[76] I include the variable *Diffusion*, which ranges from 0 to 1 and for each country, represents the proportion of member states in the country's FATF regional affiliate that have adopted FATF-compliant laws on terrorist financing.[77]

Government capacity is also likely to affect the time to policy change; following previous studies,[78] I control for *Capacity* using gross domestic product (GDP) per capita.[79] Countries that face a higher threat of terrorism might also be faster to comply with the FATF recommendation on terrorist financing. I include the variable *Terrorism Risk*, which ranges from 0 (lowest risk) to 3 (highest risk).[80] The literature also suggests that a country's political system may impact its ability or willingness to fulfill international commitments.[81] I include *Democracy*, drawn from Polity IV data.[82]

Confounders

In the FATF guidelines, the FATF considers a country's legislative history on terrorist financing when making listing decisions. Prior to 2010, many

---

[74] This variable is excluded from the matched sample analysis and the eligible country analysis because these samples include no FATF members.

[75] Elkins, Guzman and Simmons 2006; Gleditsch and Ward 2006; Simmons and Elkins 2004.

[76] Sharman 2008.

[77] For comparability across institutions, the variable is scaled by rounding to nearest 0.1 value in the regression.

[78] Guzman and Simmons 2005; Horn, Mavroidis and Nordström 1999.

[79] This variable is drawn from the World Bank World Development Indicators, and is standardized in 2010 US dollars. Due to the skewed distribution and for ease of interpretability, I transform the variable by adding 1 and taking the log.

[80] Drawn from the *International Country Risk Guide*. Variable scales from 1 (highest risk) to 4 (lowest risk). For ease of interpretability, I have inverted the variable and set the minimum value at 0.

[81] See Helfer and Slaughter 1997; Martin 2000; Raustiala and Victor 1998; or Mansfield, Milner and Rosendorff 2002, among others.

[82] Polity IV codes a country's political system on a scale of −10 to 10, where higher values equate to more democratic countries. This data is supplemented with data from Gleditsch 2013. Due to data availability issues for smaller countries, I omit this variable from the matched sample and the eligible-for-listing sample analyses.

countries had criminalized terrorist financing, but most of these laws were weak and not in keeping with FATF standards. I include the variable *Previous Terrorist Fin Law*, which indicates whether a country had some type of non-FATF-compliant law on terrorist financing as of the end of 2009 (two months before the start of the noncomplier list). Of the 141 countries included in the full sample, 96 (68 percent) had adopted some type of non-FATF-compliant law on terrorist financing by the end of 2009.

The FATF builds a pool of potential listed countries based on all countries that receive failing scores on ten or more of the sixteen most important recommendations in their third-round mutual evaluation reports. I include the variable *Eligible for Listing*, which is a dichotomous indicator of whether a country receives ten or more failing scores on the FATF's most important recommendations. The FATF and its regional bodies only evaluate a country once per cycle, so for most countries, the number of failing recommendations does not change across the data set.[83]

Another important listing determinant is the size of a country's financial sector.[84] As a proxy for this factor, I include *Private Sector Credit*, which indicates the amount of financial resources provided to the private sector by financial corporations. Such resources may be provided through loans, purchases of non-equity securities, trade credits, or other accounts receivable that establish a claim for repayment. This variable is drawn from the World Bank, based on its "Domestic credit to private sector (% of GDP)" and is standardized in 2010 US dollars.

Plausible Alternative: US Power

The most plausible alternative explanation is the possibility that the United States is directly or indirectly responsible for policy change. The FATF's regulatory agenda aligns closely with US foreign policy objectives.[85] Scholars have also argued that US economic power has contributed to the diffusion of US regulatory standards in other areas of global finance.[86] The US government devotes significant resources to providing technical assistance that promotes the worldwide adoption of financial integrity standards; it also monitors other countries' policies.

The US may affect a country's willingness or ability to criminalize terrorist financing through measures of influence and coercion. I include the variable *US Ally*, which is drawn from the Correlates of War project and indicates whether a country has a defense pact, entente, or neutrality agreement with

---

[83] This variable is omitted from the analysis of the eligible-for-listing sample since sample only includes countries that had ten or more failing recommendations.

[84] FATF-GAFI 2009b.

[85] Jakobi 2013, 2018.

[86] Drezner 2007; Posner 2009; Simmons 2001.

the United States in a given year.[87] To further account for US influence, I also rerun my main analysis with four additional controls. I account for US trade ties with the variable *Trade with US*, which is drawn from the IMF and reflects a country's total volume of trade with the United States as a percent of GDP. In a second model, I include *US Foreign Aid*, which is drawn from the United States Agency for International Development (USAID) and indicates the amount of foreign aid disbursed to a particular country in a given year.

A third model controls for the possibility that the United States might use economic sanctions to pressure countries to change its policies. Since 2001, the US Secretary of Treasury has had the authority to designate foreign jurisdictions and institutions as "primary money laundering concerns" under Section 311 of the USA Patriot Act. US financial institutions and agencies are required to take special measures against designated entities. As of June 2017, the US Treasury had listed twenty banks and five countries under this process. I include the dichotomous variable *311 Sanctions List* to indicate if a country's financial institution or the country itself was on the 311 Special Measures list in a given month. Approximately 2 percent of observations are coded as 1s in the dataset.

A final model controls for US bilateral pressure. The US State Department could raise FATF compliance during bilateral meetings, or encourage foreign partners to seek technical assistance. I proxy US bilateral pressure with data from the State Department's annual International Narcotics Control Strategy Report (INCSR), which summarizes money laundering and terrorist financing policies across most countries. It prioritizes countries using a three-tier classification system, where "Jurisdictions of Primary Concern" are major money laundering countries where financial institutions "engage in transactions involving significant amounts of proceeds from all serious crimes" or where financial institutions are vulnerable because of weak supervisory or enforcement regimes.[88] I create an ordinal variable *US State Dept List* that indicates each country's assigned INCSR tier, where 1 indicates a country is of low concern and 3 indicates a country is categorized as a "Jurisdiction of Primary Concern" in a given year. In the data, approximately 32 percent of observations are coded as 3s.

FINDINGS: LISTING INCREASES COMPLIANCE THROUGH MARKETS

Hypotheses 1 and 2: Time to Criminalization

The results provide strong support for hypotheses 1 and 2. Countries on the FATF noncomplier list adopt FATF-compliant laws on terrorist financing more quickly than their nonlisted counterparts and market integration appears to intensify this effect. Table 3.1 shows the effect of listing on the time

[87] Gibler 2009.
[88] See: https://www.state.gov/j/inl/rls/nrcrpt/2016 /vol2/2533 67.htm.

TABLE 3.1. *Listing, market enforcement, and criminalization: Cox proportional hazards models for full sample – Hazards ratios for cox proportional hazards models*

	Dependent Variable: Time to Criminalization			
	(1)	(2)	(3)	(4)
Listing	9.029***	8.156***	5.849***	8.429***
	(0.336)	(0.455)	(0.526)	(0.567)
Market Integration		1.006	1.003	1.026
		(0.067)	(0.096)	(0.106)
Listing* Market Integration		1.207**	1.314**	1.345**
		(0.108)	(0.142)	(0.149)
FATF Member	1.013	0.623	0.672	0.929
	(0.409)	(0.612)	(0.629)	(0.737)
Previous Terrorist Fin Law	1.370	1.067	0.934	0.877
	(0.286)	(0.357)	(0.402)	(0.448)
Diffusion	1.059**	1.061**	1.073**	1.079**
	(0.013)	(0.017)	(0.020)	(0.021)
Eligible for Listing	0.827	1.147	1.103	0.950
	(0.380)	(0.557)	(0.611)	(0.615)
US Ally	3.825	1.831	1.942	1.960
	(1.390)	(1.719)	(1.753)	(1.825)
Private Sector Credit		1.020	0.935	1.130
		(0.183)	(0.237)	(0.260)
Capacity		1.144	1.174	0.822
		(0.296)	(0.321)	(0.375)
Terrorism			1.071	1.435
			(0.256)	(0.314)
Democracy				0.945
				(0.039)
Observations	7308	5850	4635	4114
Countries	132	120	96	87
Events	72	52	43	39

*$p < 0.1$; **$p < 0.05$; ***$p < 0.01$.

Notes: Values over 1 indicate a positive effect; values below 1 indicate a negative effect. Standard errors are clustered by country and shown in parentheses. All models include log-time interaction for US ally.

it takes for a country to criminalize terrorist financing in line with FATF standards for the full sample. Model 1 serves as a baseline for the effect of listing without controlling for any financial considerations. Model 2 tests the effect of listing and market integration, adding controls for private sector credit and capacity. Model 3 adds a control for terrorism, while Model 4 adds a control for democracy. Across all four models, listing has a positive and statistically significant effect on compliance. In model 4, listed countries are eight times as likely to criminalize terrorist financing in a given period. Policy diffusion also has a strong effect, suggesting that as more states within an organization criminalize terrorist financing, other states are increasingly likely to adopt new laws in line with FATF standards.

Market integration appears to intensify the effect of listing in a consistently positive and significant manner. In model 4, a 50 percent increase in cross-border liabilities is associated with an 11 percent increase in the probability of criminalizing terrorist financing.[89] While a 50 percent increase in a country's cross-border liabilities may seem like a large change, consider that between 2002 and 2009, at least seven countries in Europe had increases larger than this amount.[90]

Figure 3.3 shows the effect of market integration on the cumulative probability that a listed country criminalizes terrorist financing. The plot suggests that market integration has its largest effect on criminalization in the first year of listing.

I replicate my main analyses on the matched sample and the sample of countries eligible for listing. Within these samples, listing has an even stronger effect on compliance, and market integration continues to moderate this effect.[91] Table 3.2 shows these results. In the matched sample, listed countries are 13.3 times more likely to criminalize terrorist financing in a given period, while in the sample of eligible-for-listing countries, the estimated effect is even stronger (18.5 in the full model). The sizable increase in the coefficients for listing reflects separation in the data – almost all countries that change their laws are listed by the FATF. In model 1, for example, fifteen of the seventeen countries that comply with FATF standards are listed countries. In model 3, thirty-one of the thirty-six countries that eventually comply with FATF standards are listed countries. Such skewed results suggest that the estimates in the full sample are attenuated, and underestimate the full effect of listing. An additional possibility is that the FATF listing process is driving countries toward the extremes of compliance – listed countries become more likely than before to change their policies, while nonlisted countries become less likely (since they know that they've avoided the list).

---

[89] Data on cross-border liabilities is logged and therefore the coefficient cannot be interpreted directly. To calculate this estimate, I use the following formula: $e^{(ln(1.3) \times ln(1.5))}$.

[90] These countries are the United Kingdom, Denmark, the Netherlands, Norway, Sweden, Finland, and Ireland Allen et al. 2011.

[91] Although the interaction term in model 4 of Table 3.2 is not significant, it has a p-value of 0.11.

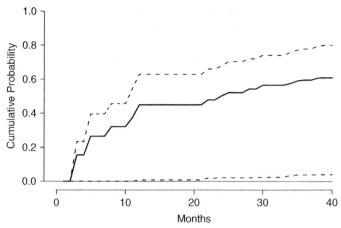

FIGURE 3.3. The figure shows the change in the cumulative probability of criminalizing terrorist financing in line with FATF guidelines, comparing listed countries with high market integration (one standard deviation above the mean) with listed countries with low market integration (one standard deviation below the mean). First difference calculations estimated using the results of a cox proportional hazards model (Model 4 in Table 3.1). Dotted lines show the 95 percent confidence interval, calculated using a Monte Carlo simulation sampling over 500 iterations.

Hypotheses 1 and 2: Robustness

US pressure is the most plausible alternative explanation for why countries criminalize terrorist financing in line with FATF standards. I replicate model 4 in Table 3.1, adding different indicators to proxy for US power or coercion. Table 3.3 displays these results. Model 1 includes a control for a country's level of trade dependence on the United States. Model 2 adds a control for annual US foreign aid to each country. Model 3 controls for whether a country is on the US Department of Treasury's 311 Sanctions List, which pertains specifically to high-risk money laundering countries. Model 4 controls for US bilateral pressure, proxied with an ordinal indicator of whether the US State Department considers the country to be a high-risk money laundering jurisdiction in a given year.

FATF listing continues to have a strong, positive effect on compliance, while variables proxying for US pressure have insignificant or negative effects. Both trade dependence and US foreign aid have weak, insignificant effects, while US government listing has a negative effect. Countries included on either the US Department of Treasury's 311 Sanctions List or the US Department of State's list of high-risk money laundering jurisdictions are less likely to comply with FATF standards in a given period. The most likely explanation for this finding is the difference in the type of countries listed. The US government uses the 311 list only against the most reluctant compliers because listing requires market actors to stop all business with a listed country or bank.

TABLE 3.2. *Listing, market enforcement, and criminalization:* Cox proportional hazards models for matched sample and eligible-for-listing sample – Hazards ratios for cox proportional hazards models

	Dependent Variable: Time to Criminalization			
	Matched Sample		Eligible-for-Listing Sample	
	(1)	(2)	(3)	(4)
Listing	11.467***	13.250*	17.067***	18.491***
	(0.891)	(1.093)	(0.501)	(0.879)
Market Integration		1.251		1.011
		(0.281)		(0.218)
Listing* Market Integration		1.608*		1.589
		(0.396)		(0.287)
Previous Terrorist Fin Law	2.035	2.020	1.292	1.048
	(0.791)	(1.040)	(0.363)	(0.583)
Diffusion	1.076	1.144*	1.050***	1.058***
	(0.041)	(0.060)	(0.017)	(0.028)
Eligible for Listing	0.932	1.138		
	(0.943)	(1.267)		
US Ally	0.457	1.010	5.090	0.955
	(4.576)	(5.688)	(1.689)	(2.979)
Private Sector Credit		0.390*		1.109
		(0.716)		(0.328)
Capacity		2.713		0.867
		(0.924)		(0.528)
Polity IV		0.893		0.933
		(0.078)		(0.056)
Terrorism Risk		0.531		2.091
		(1.698)		(0.517)
Weights	0.001***	0.00000**		
	(3.072)	(9.160)		
Observations	1104	1018	3420	1675
Countries	24	24	66	39
Events	17	16	36	20

*$p < 0.1$; **$p < 0.05$; ***$p < 0.01$.

Notes: Values over 1 indicate a positive effect; values below 1 indicate a negative effect. Standard errors are clustered by country and shown in parentheses. All models include log-time interaction for US ally.

TABLE 3.3. *Listing, market enforcement, and criminalization: Cox proportional hazards models for US power alternatives – Hazards ratios for cox proportional hazards models*

	Dependent Variable: Time to Criminalization			
	(1)	(2)	(3)	(4)
Listing	8.372***	8.230***	8.618***	8.462***
	(0.568)	(0.559)	(0.564)	(0.555)
Market Integration	1.028	1.022	1.050	0.969
	(0.107)	(0.106)	(0.108)	(0.110)
Listing* Market	1.339**	1.364***	1.340**	1.306**
Integration	(0.149)	(0.149)	(0.149)	(0.151)
FATF Member	0.872	1.137	0.851	1.248
	(0.779)	(0.758)	(0.736)	(0.761)
Previous Terrorist	0.889	0.877	0.888	0.809
Fin Law	(0.452)	(0.448)	(0.446)	(0.456)
Diffusion	1.078***	1.075***	1.084***	1.074***
	(0.021)	(0.021)	(0.021)	(0.021)
Eligible for Listing	0.981	1.018	0.966	0.879
	(0.630)	(0.611)	(0.607)	(0.600)
US Ally	1.990	1.773	2.204	1.742
	(1.828)	(1.831)	(1.830)	(1.819)
Private Sector Credit	1.145	1.179	1.236	1.194
	(0.268)	(0.259)	(0.271)	(0.259)
Capacity	0.821	0.908	0.673	0.755
	(0.378)	(0.385)	(0.414)	(0.377)
Democracy	0.946	0.936	0.942	0.926*
	(0.039)	(0.040)	(0.039)	(0.041)
Terrorism Risk	1.431	1.514	1.453	1.516
	(0.315)	(0.319)	(0.317)	(0.314)
Trade with US	0.956			
(Percent GDP)	(0.196)			
US Foreign Aid		1.128		
		(0.125)		
US – 311 Sanctions			0.301**	
List			(1.136)	
US – AML List				0.612*
				(0.312)
Observations	4103	4114	4114	4090
Countries	88	88	88	88
Events	41	41	41	41

*$p < 0.1$; **$p < 0.05$; ***$p < 0.01$.

Notes: Values over 1 indicate a positive effect; values below 1 indicate a negative effect. Standard errors are clustered by country and shown in parentheses. All models include log-time interaction for US ally.

The State Department list, on the other hand, focuses on countries with high volumes of money laundering, and therefore includes most large financial centers (including the United States). As a result, the list is unlikely to lead to any significant material consequences for identified countries.

An additional way to probe the robustness of these results might be to conduct a placebo test for the period prior to the creation of the FATF noncomplier list. Between 2005 and 2007, the FATF evaluated more than sixty countries, fifty-six of which had not criminalized terrorist financing in line with FATF standards. Many of these countries would subsequently be eligible for listing after the FATF created its new listing procedures in 2009. If the FATF noncomplier list is really driving policy change, then we should see no significant improvements in compliance in 2008 and 2009 for countries evaluated during this earlier period. Descriptive statistics confirm this trend. Of the fifty-six noncompliant countries evaluated between 2005 and 2007, only two countries adopted FATF-compliant laws on terrorist financing prior to 2010.[92]

Hypothesis 3: Bank Lending and Market Enforcement

If international market actors like multinational banks allocate resources differently based on FATF noncomplier list announcements, then international banks should be less willing to do business with banks, companies, and individuals in listed countries. I test this causal mechanism by examining how listing affects cross-border liabilities, i.e. the money that banks in a given country owe international banks. Data on cross-border liabilities comes from BIS and is available on a quarterly basis. Cross-border liabilities for the period of 2010–2015 range from 0 to 3.9 trillion. Because the distribution is highly skewed, I add 1 to all values and take the log.[93]

To analyze the effect of listing on cross-border liabilities, I build an economic model that takes into account a country's underlying economic structure and macroeconomic fluctuations that are likely to affect bank-to-bank flows. Core economic factors that are likely to influence banking relationships include *GDP Growth* and *Inflation*. The rate of economic growth in a country could affect its demand for bank-to-bank lending, while higher inflation might limit the supply of credit. GDP data comes from the World Bank, while inflation data comes from the IMF's International Financial Statistics (IFS) database. I also include the *Real Exchange Rate*, which comes from IFS and is computed using nominal exchange rate data and the ratio of the US Consumer Price Index (CPI) to the local CPI in a given year. Bruno and Shin link bank leverage and monetary policy, finding that a contradictory shock

---

[92] Liechtenstein and Georgia.
[93] Following Herrmann and Mihaljek 2010, my dependent variable does not consider changes in liabilities but rather reveals changes in lending and borrowing.

to US monetary policy leads to a decrease in the cross-border capital flows of the banking sector.[94]

A country's level of debt (private sector and government) is also likely to affect the willingness of banks to do business with a jurisdiction. Specifically, the local banking sector's leverage ratio, that is, the relationship between its core capital and total assets, is likely to affect bank-to-bank transfers across borders. Following Bruno and Shin, I include the variable *Credit-to-GDP Ratio*, which proxies for the leverage of local banks using the ratio of bank assets to capital from the World Bank World Development Indicators (WDI) dataset.[95] I also include *Debt-to-GDP Ratio*, drawn from IFS. Debt-to-GDP ratio is a commonly used measure of a country's economic health, particularly for emerging economies. Higher levels of external debt should make borrowers more vulnerable, which may reduce an international bank's willingness to lend money.[96]

I include *Interest Spread* to account for the difference between the local lending rate and the US Fed Fund rate, which may affect the price determinants of local demand for cross-border credit. Interest rate data comes from the World Bank WDI dataset, but are only available for a subset of countries. As a result, I include this variable in two of the four models. I also include the variable *Money Supply* (from the World Bank WDI) in the latter two models. Local borrowers may borrow in US dollars and then deposit the local currency proceeds into the domestic banking system, which would lead banking inflows to be associated with increases in M2.[97]

I evaluate the effect of listing on cross-border liabilities between March 2010 and December 2015, where the unit of observation is country-quarter (producing four observations per year). I use an ordinary least squares regression with country-fixed effects; as a result, the unit of comparison is within country over time. In all models, I lag explanatory variables by one year and cluster standard errors. Models 2 and 4 also include a time polynomial. In the simplest model, I analyze the effect of listing on cross-border liabilities for fifty countries, twelve of which were listed by the FATF. As I add variables, the sample drops to thirty-nine countries, ten of which were listed by the FATF.[98]

Table 3.4 shows the estimated effect of listing on cross-border liabilities. In line with the theory, listing leads to a statistically significant and

---

[94] Bruno and Shin 2015b. The results are robust to including trade balance in the model instead of the real exchange rate. See Appendix K.

[95] Bruno and Shin 2015a.

[96] Takáts and Avdjiev 2014.

[97] For a more detailed explanation of this link, see Bruno and Shin 2015a, 21.

[98] I restrict my analysis to the 141 countries that were included in the previous regression analysis of how listing affects the probability of criminalization. Economic data is not available for many of the smaller countries included in that analysis, which is why the sample size decreases significantly in this test.

TABLE 3.4. *The effect of listing on cross-border liabilities – Dependent variable is logged cross-border liabilities*

	Dependent Variable: Cross-Border Liabilities (log)			
	(1)	(2)	(3)	(4)
Listing	−0.158*** 0.157*** (0.045)	−0.149*** (0.045)	−0.167*** (0.045)	– (0.045)
Inflation	0.008*** 0.010*** (0.002)	0.009*** (0.002)	0.008*** (0.002)	(0.003)
GDP Growth (Percent Change)	−0.002 (0.005)	0.0001 (0.005)	−0.002 (0.005)	0.002 (0.005)
Real Exchange Rate	−0.00001 (0.00002)	−0.00001 (0.00002)	0.00001 (0.00002)	−0.00001 (0.00002)
Credit-to-GDP Ratio	−0.005*** (0.002)	−0.005*** (0.002)	−0.005*** (0.002)	−0.004*** (0.002)
Debt-to-GDP Ratio	−0.005*** (0.002)	−0.006*** (0.002)	−0.005*** (0.002)	−0.008*** (0.002)
Money Supply			0.001 (0.001)	0.001 (0.001)
Interest Rate Spread			−0.014** (0.006)	−0.006 (0.006)
Observations	828	828	656	656
Countries	50	50	39	39
Country Fixed Effects	Y	Y	Y	Y
Time Polynomial	N	Y	N	Y

$*p < 0.1$; $**p < 0.05$; $***p < 0.01$.

Notes: OLS regression with country-fixed effects, with robust clustered standard errors shown in parentheses. Quarterly observations for 2010–2015.

substantively large decrease in cross-border liabilities across all four models. In Model 4, listing leads to a 16 percent decrease in liabilities. To provide context for this number, consider a country like the Philippines, which was listed from 2010 to 2013. In 2010, the Philippines' average cross-border liabilities per quarter were USD 11.5 billion. Based on the estimate in this model, listing should lead to a decline of USD 1.84 billion in cross-border liabilities. And indeed, by 2012, the average quarterly cross-border liabilities in the Philippines had declined significantly to 8.7 billion, and rebounded to pre-listing levels only in 2014.

Hypothesis 3: Robustness

I probe the robustness of these results with a placebo test that analyzes the effect of post-2009 listing on cross-border liabilities in an earlier period. If the FATF noncomplier list is truly driving the change in cross-border liabilities, then being listed in subsequent years (2010 and on) should have no effect on cross-border liabilities in previous years. In contrast, if listing is proxying for an underlying state-specific characteristic, then this omitted variable could have an effect on outcomes even in the period prior to the creation of the non-complier list. I replicate the previous analysis for the period of 2006–2008, matching each country's listing status in the years 2010–2012.[99] In the placebo time period, listing has no effect on cross-border liabilities. These results are available in Appendix L.

CASE STUDY OF THAILAND

Thailand's experience with the noncomplier list shows how the reputational consequences of listing combine with market enforcement to generate policy change. When the FATF listed Thailand in February 2010, the country was in compliance with very few FATF recommendations. The Thai government viewed anti-money laundering and combating terrorist financing as low priorities. The FATF noncomplier list's impact on markets, however, reoriented government interests as the banking community and private sector actors began to advocate for compliance. Over the course of a few years, Thailand significantly improved its policies and was subsequently removed from the list.

Thailand and the Noncomplier List

Although Thailand is highly integrated into the global economy, and also susceptible to money laundering and terrorist financing, the Thai government did not prioritize compliance with the FATF recommendations in the early 2000s.[100] The Asia/Pacific Group on Money Laundering's 2007 mutual evaluation report rated Thailand fully compliant with only two of the FATF's forty-nine recommendations. At the time, the FATF had very few tools in place to deal with noncompliant jurisdictions. The repercussions of non-compliance were minimal; Thailand had only to submit follow-up reports. In 2009, however, the FATF revitalized its process for dealing with noncompliant jurisdictions. When the FATF issued its first noncomplier list in February 2010,

---

[99] For example, if a country was listed in 2010 but not 2011 or 2012, it will be listed in the placebo test in 2006 but not 2007 or 2008.
[100] IMF 2007.

Thailand was one of twenty countries listed at the lowest level. In its first statement, the FATF called on Thailand to criminalize terrorist financing, establish and implement procedures to freeze terrorist assets, and strengthen its supervision of relevant laws.

Thailand's Anti-Money Laundering Office (AMLO) responded immediately to listing, but its actions had little effect on the Thai parliament's willingness to adopt reforms.[101] Although the AMLO launched a big public information campaign to convince the Thai National Assembly to adopt new laws, the response from the rest of the government was sluggish.[102] According to a senior Thai banking official, while the AMLO recognized the significance of listing and the possible financial repercussions, the National Assembly was slow to understand the possible consequences.[103] As a result, by the end of 2010, Thailand had approved a national anti-money laundering and combating the financing of terrorism strategy and drafted proposed legislation,[104] but made no other improvements.

In this first year, the market response was negligible. Since the list was so new, it received very little media attention; indeed, *The Wall Street Journal* did not publish a single article about the FATF list in the six months following its creation.[105] Additionally, because the noncomplier list included several different lists, it was difficult for outside observers like banks, investors, or even other countries to know how to interpret the meaning of a country's inclusion on one of the lists. For this reason, market actors were slow to integrate the list into decision-making practices.

By February 2011, however, the FATF had issued three listing announcements, each of which described ongoing compliance problems in listed countries. As such, third-party observers like banks and investors began to realize that many countries would require significant legal change before the FATF would remove them from the list. Market actors began to adjust risk appraisals accordingly. For Thailand, a country with an economy heavily dependent on trade and investment, the response from markets was crucial for driving policy change. It became more difficult for Thai banks to do business abroad, as foreign banks began to ask more questions about anti-money laundering rules and regulations.[106] Despite these costs, Thailand failed to make significant changes

---

[101] The AMLO is a Thai government bureaucratic unit that supervises how the financial sector implements financial integrity policy.
[102] Author interview with Thai government official, February 14, 2016.
[103] Author interview, March 9, 2017.
[104] US Department of State 2011.
[105] This lack of media attention is notable compared to 2014 and 2015, when *The Wall Street Journal* published approximately 5–6 articles per year mentioning the FATF non-complier list.
[106] Author interview with Thai banking official, March 9, 2017.

to its legal framework in 2011, partly because of domestic political unrest.[107] In October 2011, the FATF placed Thailand on a list of countries not making enough progress. In February 2012, Thailand was bumped up to the so-called "black" list.

The higher listing level intensified the costs to Thailand's financial sector and increased pressure on the government to change its laws. In an interview, a Thai government official reported that "the impact (of the "black" list) was considerably more acute...Financial institutions reported unexpected difficulties in obtaining permits to open branches in EU countries. A bank in (the) EU even contemplated scrapping a deal to lend money to Thai banks."[108] The AMLO suddenly had new allies, as the Board of Trade, the Federation of Thai Industries, the Thai Bankers Association, and the Federation of Capital Markets Association began joint action with the AMLO and the Attorney General's office to push for new laws on money laundering and terrorist financing.[109] Less than a month later, in May 2012, Deputy Prime Minister Kittiratt Na-Ranong promised Thailand would amend its Anti-Money Laundering Act by the end of the year. In a public statement, Na-Ranong linked anticipated policy changes directly to the FATF list.[110] The Thai government followed through on its promises, passing new laws on money laundering and terrorist financing weeks before the February 2013 FATF plenary. Following an on-site visit to confirm progress, the FATF removed Thailand from the noncomplier list in June 2013.

Financial Costs of Listing

Quantifying the full impact of the noncomplier list on Thailand's economy is difficult because the list affected financial flows in diverse ways. There is, however, at least correlational evidence that the noncomplier list impacted cross-border liabilities. Figure 3.4 shows cross-border liabilities (money that Thai banks owe to international banks) between 2009 and 2015. When the FATF listed Thailand in February 2010, cross-border liabilities stayed relatively stable; however, after the FATF bumped Thailand up to a higher listing level in February 2012, cross-border liabilities declined significantly. Specifically, cross-border liabilities declined from USD 1.7 billion to USD 1.4 billion, a decrease of 17.6 percent. This number is remarkably close to the

---

[107] According to a State Department assessment "Political and civil unrest in Thailand in mid-2010, followed by catastrophic flooding, the dissolution of Parliament and subsequent general election in July 2011, have impeded Thailand's implementation of its AML/CFT action plan" US Department of State 2012, 171.

[108] Author interview, February 14, 2016.

[109] *Private sector pressures for solution on FATF blacklist – The Nation* 2012.

[110] Fernquest 2012.

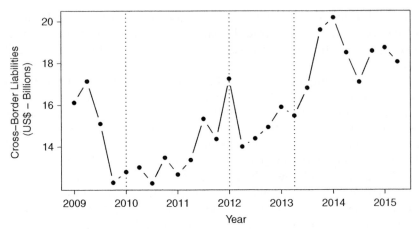

FIGURE 3.4. The figure shows cross-border liabilities (billions of US dollars) from 2009 to 2015. The FATF listed Thailand in February 2010 and in February 2012, placed Thailand on its "black" list for failing to improve its laws in a timely fashion. Following significant legal changes, the FATF removed Thailand from its monitoring process in June 2013.

estimate obtained from the regression analysis of the effect of listing on cross-border liabilities (Table 3.4, which suggested that listed countries experience a 16 percent decline in liabilities). In the case of Thailand, however, the country almost immediately began to modify its policies, and cross-border flows began to increase.

Since Thailand was removed from the FATF list in June 2013, the Thai government has continued to improve its compliance with FATF standards, albeit at a slower pace. The AMLO has taken a much more active role in regulating the banking sector, clarifying bank reporting obligations and promoting information sharing on this issue.[111] The FATF's 2017 evaluation of Thailand notes that there is "strong political support for recent AML/CFT reforms" and highlights how "institutional arrangements have developed significantly since the 2007 mutual evaluation report."[112]

GPIs IN A GLOBALIZED WORLD

In today's globalized world, institutionalized cooperation is essential for addressing transnational threats. While most international institutions continue to lack formal enforcement power, this gap should not suggest that such

[111] Author interview with Thai banking official, March 9, 2017.
[112] FATF-GAFI 2017, 3.

institutions are weak or ineffective. Instead, the same processes of interdependence that generate new threats also expand opportunities for institutions to drive policy change. The IGOs can use GPIs to harness institutional advantages like credibility and technical expertise into informational power. The FATF case suggests that GPIs are particularly effective drivers of policy change when they are used by market actors like banks and investors to shift resources away from noncompliant states. Markets are natural audiences for financial GPIs because such measures convert uncertainty into risk. By stabilizing market expectations, GPIs can engender market pressure to create new incentives for policy change.

References

Abdelal, Rawi, and Mark Blyth. 2015. Just Who Put You in Charge? We Did: CRAs and the Politics of Ratings. In *Ranking the World: Grading States as a Tool of Global Governance*, edited by Alexander Cooley and Jack Snyder. New York: Cambridge University Press.

Allen, Franklin, Thorsten Beck, Elena Carletti, Philip R. Lane, Dirk Schoenmaker, and Wolf Wagner. 2011. *Cross-Border Banking in Europe: Implications for Financial Stability and Macroeconomic Policies.* London: Centre for Economic Policy Research.

Amato, Jeffery D., Stephen Morris, and Hyun Song Shin. 2002. Communication and Monetary Policy. *Oxford Review of Economic Policy* 18 (4):495–503.

Baldacci, Emanuele, Sanjeev Gupta, and Amine Mati. 2011. Political and Fiscal Risk Determinants of Sovereign Spreads in Emerging Markets. *Review of Development Economics* 15 (2):251–63.

Bank for International Settlements. 2016. Correspondent Banking. Technical Report.

Barnett, Michael N., and Martha Finnemore. 1999. The Politics, Power, and Pathologies of International Organizations. *International Organization* 53 (4):699–732.

Bisbee, James H., James R. Hollyer, B. Peter Rosendorff, and James Raymond Vreeland. this volume. The Millennium Development Goals and Education: Accountability and Substitution in Global Indicators. In *The Power of Global Performance Indicators*, edited by Judith Kelley and Beth A. Simmons. New York: Cambridge University Press.

Box-Steffensmeier, Janet M., and Christopher J. W. Zorn. 2001. Duration Models and Proportional Hazards in Political Science. *American Journal of Political Science* 45 (4):972–88.

Brambor, Thomas, William Roberts Clark, and Matt Golder. 2006. Understanding Interaction Models: Improving Empirical Analyses. *Political Analysis* 14:63–82.

Brooks, Sarah M., Raphael Cunha, and Layna Mosley. 2014. Categories, Creditworthiness, and Contagion: How Investors' Shortcuts Affect Sovereign Debt Markets. *International Studies Quarterly* 59 (3):587–601.

Bruno, Valentina, and Hyun Song Shin. 2015a. Cross-Border Banking and
    Global Liquidity. *The Review of Economic Studies* 82 (2):535–64.
    2015b. Capital Flows and the Risk-Taking Channel of Monetary Policy.
    Journal of Monetary Economics 71:119–32.
Bueno de Mesquita, Bruce, Alastair Smith, Randolph M. Siverson, and James D.
    Morrow. 2003. *The Logic of Political Survival.* Cambridge, MA: MIT Press.
Buthe, Tim, and Helen V. Milner. 2008. The Politics of Foreign Direct
    Investment into Developing Countries: Increasing FDI through
    International Trade Agreements? *American Journal of Political Science*
    52 (4):741–62.
Carberry, Sean. 2014. Afghans Must Pass Anti-Money Laundering Law or
    Face Blacklist. Available at http://www.npr.org/2014/06/05/319030334/
    afghans-must-pass-anti-money-laundering-law-or-face-blacklist. Accessed
    January 15, 2016.
Carruthers, Bruce G. 2013. From Uncertainty Toward Risk: The Case of
    Credit Ratings. *Socio-Economic Review* 11 (3):525–51.
Collin, Matthew, Samantha Cook, and Kimmo Soramaki. 2016. The Impact
    of Anti-Money Laundering Regulation on Payment Flows: Evidence from
    SWIFT Data. Technical Report 445.
Dai, Xinyuan. 2007. *International Institutions and National Policies.*
    Cambridge: Cambridge University Press.
Donati, Jessica. 2014. Exclusive: Afghanistan Suffers Trade Blow as China
    Halts Dollar Deals with Its Banks. *Reuters.*
Drezner, Daniel W. 2007. *All Politics Is Global: Explaining International
    Regulatory Regimes.* Princeton, NJ: Princeton University Press.
Elkins, Zachary, Andrew T. Guzman, and Beth A. Simmons. 2006.
    Competing for Capital: The Diffusion of Bilateral Investment Treaties,
    1960–2000. *International Organization* 60 (4):811–46.
FATF-GAFI. 2006. Third Mutual Evaluation Report on Anti-Money
    Laundering and Combating the Financing of Terrorism. Technical Report.
    2008a. Terrorist Financing. Technical Report.
    2008b. Third Mutual Evaluation on Anti-Money Laundering and
    Combating the Financing of Terrorism. Technical Report.
    2008c. Third Mutual Evaluation Report: Japan. Technical Report.
    2009a. FATF Annual Report: 2008–2009. Technical Report.
    2009b. ICRG Co-Chairs' Report. Technical Report.
    2009c. *Methodology for Assessing Compliance with the FATF 40
    Recommendations and the FATF 9 Special Recommendations.* February
    27, 2004 (Updated February 2009) Paris: FATF/OECD.
    2010. Mutual Evaluation Report: Germany. Technical Report.
    2015. Results of the Terrorist Financing Fact-Finding Initiative – FATF
    Members. Technical Report FATF/PLEN(2015)30.
    2017. Mutual Evaluation Report: Thailand. Technical Report.
Fernquest, Jon. 2012. Anti-Money Laundering Blacklist Spells Trouble. Available
    at http://www.bangkokpost.com/learning/learning-from-news/294602/
    anti-money-laundering-blacklist-spells-trouble.
Findley, Michael G., Daniel L. Nielson, and J. C.Sharman. 2014. Causes
    of Noncompliance with International Law: A Field Experiment on
    Anonymous Incorporation. *American Journal of Political Science*
    59 (1):146–61.

Gibler, Douglas M. 2009. *International Military Alliances, 1648–2008*. Washington, DC: Congressional Quarterly Press.

Gleditsch, Kristian Skrede. 2013. Modified Polity P4 and P4D Data, Version 4.0. Available at http://www.ksgleditsch.com/polity.html. Accessed August 27, 2019.

Gleditsch, Kristian Skrede, and Michael D. Ward. 2006. Diffusion and the International Context of Democratization. *International Organization* 60 (4):911–33.

Gray, Julia. 2013. *The Company States Keep: International Economic Organizations and Investor Perceptions*. New York: Cambridge University Press.

Guzman, Andrew T., and Beth A. Simmons. 2005. Power Plays and Capacity Constraints: The Selection of Defendants in World Trade Organization Disputes. *The Journal of Legal Studies* 34 (2):557–98.

Hainmueller, Jens, Jonathan Mummolo, and Yiqing Xu. Forthcoming. How Much Should We Trust Estimates from Multiplicative Interaction Models? Simple Tools to Improve Empirical Practice. *Political Analysis* 27:163–92.

Hawkins, Darren G., David A. Lake, Daniel L. Nielson, and Michael J. Tierney. 2006. *Delegation and Agency in International Organizations*. Cambridge: Cambridge University Press.

Helfer, Laurence R., and Anne-Marie Slaughter. 1997. Toward a Theory of Effective Supranational Adjudication. *The Yale Law Journal* 107 (2):273–391.

Herrmann, Sabine, and Dubravko Mihaljek. 2010. The Determinants of Cross-Border Bank Flows to Emerging Markets: New Empirical Evidence on the Spread of Financial Crises. *BIS Working Paper* No. 315, pp. 1–42. Retrieved from https://www.bis.org/publ/work315.htm. Accessed August 27, 2019.

Hilscher, Jens, and Yves Nosbusch. 2010. Determinants of Soverign Risk: Macroeconomic Fundamentals and the Pricing of Sovereign Debt. *Review of Finance* 14 (2):235–62.

Ho, Daniel E., Kosuke Imai, Gary King, and Elizabeth A. Stuart. 2007. Matching as Nonparametric Preprocessing for Reducing Model Dependence in Parametric Causal Inference. *Political Analysis* 15 (3):199–236.

Honig, Dan, and Catherine Weaver. 2019. A Race to the Top? The Aid Transparency Index and the Normative Power of Global Performance Assessments. In *The Power of Global Performance Indicators*, edited by Judith Kelley and Beth A. Simmons. New York: Cambridge University Press.

Horn, Henrik, Petros C. Mavroidis, and Håkan Nordström. 1999. Is the Use of the WTO Dispute Settlement System Biased? CEPR Discussion Papers.

IMF. 2007. Thailand: Detailed Assessment Report on Anti-Money Laundering and Combating the Financing of Terrorism. Technical Report.

Jakobi, Anja P. 2013. *Common Goods and Evils? The Formation of Global Crime Governance*. Oxford: Oxford University Press.

———. 2018. Governing Illicit Finance in Transnational Security Spaces: The FATF and Anti-Money Laundering. *Crime, Law and Social Change* 69:173–90.

Jamieson, Craig. 2006. Reputation Damage: The Price Riggs Paid. Technical Report.

Johns, Leslie. 2012. Courts as Coordinators: Endogenous Enforcement and Jurisdiction in International Adjudication. *Journal of Conflict Resolution* 56 (2):257–89.

Kelley, Judith G., and Beth A. Simmons. 2019. Introduction: The Power of
    Global Performance Indicators. In *The Power of Global Performance
    Indicators*, edited by Judith Kelley and Beth A. Simmons. New York:
    Cambridge University Press.
Kelley, Judith G., Beth A. Simmons, and Rush Doshi. 2019. The Power of
    Ranking: The Ease of Doing Business Report as a form of Social Pressure.
Lee, Melissa, and Aila M. Matanock. 2019. Third Party Policymakers
    and the Limits of the Influence of Indicators. In *The Power of Global
    Performance Indicators*, edited by Judith Kelley and Beth A.Simmons.
    New York: Cambridge University Press.
Longstaff, Francis A., Jun Pan, Lasse Heje Pedersen, and Kenneth J. Singleton.
    2011. How Sovereign Is Sovereign Credit Risk? *American Economic
    Journal Macroeconomics* 3 (2):75–103.
Mansfield, Edward D., and Helen V. Milner. 2012. *Votes, Vetoes, and the
    Political Economy of International Trade Agreements*. Princeton, NJ:
    Princeton University Press.
Mansfield, Edward D., Helen V. Milner, and B. Peter Rosendorff. 2002. Why
    Democracies Cooperate More: Electoral Control and International Trade
    Agreements. *International Organization* 56 (3):477–513.
March, James G., and Herbert W. Simon. 1958. *Organizations*. New York:
    Wiley.
Martin, Lisa L. 2000. *Democratic Commitments: Legislatures and
    International Cooperation*. Princeton, NJ: Princeton University Press.
Merry, Sally Engle. 2011. Measuring the World. *Current Anthropology*
    52(S3):S83–95.
Milner, Helen V. 1997. *Interests, Institutions, and Information: Domestic
    Politics and International Relations*. Princeton, NJ: Princeton University
    Press.
Moravcsik, Andrew. 1997. Taking Preferences Seriously: A Liberal Theory of
    International Politics. *International Organization* 51 (4):513–53.
Mosley, Layna. 2003. *Global Capital and National Governments*. New York:
    Cambridge University Press.
Nakagawa, Junji. 2011. *International Harmonization of Economic
    Regulation*. New York: Oxford University Press.
Ozturk, Huseyin. 2016. Reliance of Sovereign Credit Ratings on Governance
    Indicators. *The European Journal of Development Research* 28
    (2):184–212.
Parks, Bradley C., and Takaaki Masaki. 2017. When Do Performance
    Assessments Influence Policy Behavior? Micro-Evidence from the 2014
    Reform Efforts Survey. *Working Paper.* http://docs.aiddata.org/ad4/pdfs/
    wps40_when_do_government_performance_assessments_influence_
    policy_behavior.pdf. Accessed August 27, 2019.
Posner, Elliot. 2009. Making Rules for Global Finance: Transatlantic
    Regulatory Cooperation at the Turn of the Millennium. *International
    Organization* 63 (4):665–99.
Private Sector Pressures for Solution on FATF Blacklist – The Nation. 2012.
Raustiala, Kal, and David G. Victor. 1998. Conclusions. In *The
    Implementation and Effectiveness of International Environmental
    Commitments*, edited by David G. Victor, Kal Raustiala and Eugene B.
    Skolnikoff, 659–707. Cambridge, MA: MIT Press.

Rickard, Stephanie J. 2010. Democratic Differences: Electoral Institutions and Compliance with GATT/WTO Agreements. *European Journal of International Relations* 16 (4):711–29.

Rubenfeld, Samuel. 2011. FATF Removes Ukraine from Blacklist, Updates on Argentina. *The Wall Street Journal.* Blog post. Retrieved from https://blogs.wsj.com/corruption-currents/2011/11/01/fatf-removes-ukraine-from-blacklist-updates-on-argentina/. Accessed January 15, 2016.

Schä fer, Armin. 2006. A New Form of Governance? Comparing the Open Method of Co-ordination to Multilateral Surveillance by the IMF and the OECD. *Journal of European Public Policy* 13 (1):70–88.

Sharman, J. C. 2008. Power and Discourse in Policy Diffusion: Anti-Money Laundering in Developing States. *International Studies Quarterly* 52 (3):635–56.

Shiller, Robert J. 2015. *Irrational Exuberance,* 3rd ed. Princeton, NJ: Princeton University Press.

Simmons, Beth A. 2000. The Legalization of International Monetary Affairs. *International Organization* 54 (3):573–602.

2001. The International Politics of Harmonization: The Case of Capital Market Regulation. *International Organization* 55 (3):589–620.

2009. *Mobilizing for Human Rights: International Law in Domestic Politics.* New York: Cambridge University Press.

Simmons, Beth A., and Zachary Elkins. 2004. The Globalization of Liberalization: Policy Diffusion in the International Political Economy. *American Political Science Review* 98 (1):171–89.

Takáts, Elod, and Stefan Avdjiev. 2014. Cross-Border Bank Lending during the Taper Tantrum: The Role of Emerging Market Fundamentals. *BIS Quarterly Review (September 2014):*1–12.

Tomz, Michael. 2007. *Reputation and International Cooperation: Sovereign Debt Across Three Centuries.* Princeton, NJ: Princeton University Press.

Unger, B. Brigitte, and Madalina Busuioc. 2007. *The Scale and Impacts of Money Laundering.* Northampton, MA: Edward Elgar.

US Department of Justice. 2012. HSBC Holdings Plc. and HSBC Bank USA N.A. Admit to Anti-Money Laundering and Sanctions Violations, Forfeit 1.256 Billion in Deferred Prosecution Agreement.

US Department of State. 2011. Money Laundering and Financial Crimes Country Database. Washington, DC: US Department of State. pp. 1–383.

2012. International Narcotics Control Strategy Report. Technical Report. Washington, DC: US Department of State.

4

The Power of Indicators in Global Development Policy

The Millennium Development Goals

Helena Hede Skagerlind

Increasing demands for accountability coupled with a growing supply of performance accounts, collected and mediated through new forms of information technology, have led to the proliferation of global performance indicators (GPIs) as a means to influence policy.[1] As a case in point, the Millennium Development Goals (MDGs) introduced a set of quantitative targets and indicators against which to measure and compare the development performance of countries. As the MDGs reached their deadline in December 2015, a new set of goals and targets – the Sustainable Development Goals (SDGs) – stood ready to replace them. This implies that indicator-based development governance will continue at least until 2030. The MDGs, convincingly referred to as the world's biggest promise,[2] entailed a significant shift from the structural adjustment development recipe of liberalization and privatization of the 1980s and 1990s. The agenda quickly became a new poverty eradication "supernorm,"[3] consisting of a number of specific and interrelated sub-norms related to particular dimensions of poverty, such as education, health, and gender equality. Over their 15 years of implementation, the MDGs gained unparalleled levels of international consensus and political commitment. However, the questions of the extent to which and how the MDGs influenced national policy remain inadequately addressed.[4]

The MDG literature is broad, spanning different disciplines, theoretical points of departure, and empirical focus areas. A large share of MDG research has focused on the normative effects of the content of the goals,[5]

---

[1] Kelley and Simmons, Chapter 1, 2.
[2] Hulme 2009.
[3] Fukuda-Parr and Hulme 2011: 18; Manning 2010, 10.
[4] Lucci, Khan and Hoy 2015, 6.
[5] E.g. Alston 2005; Barton 2005; Clemens et al. 2007; Langford 2010.

the consequences of narrow, quantitative international development agendas,[6] or on their outcomes in terms of goal achievement in developing countries.[7] Accordingly, this literature has thoroughly and competently answered questions regarding, for instance, the MDGs' normative origins and effects on development discourse and narratives; their reductionist consequences in terms of overlooked or marginalized targets; and their effects on development outcomes and public sector investments within different sectors.[8] A few studies have explored the relationship between the MDGs and national development policy, pointing to a rhetorical commitment to the MDGs that exceeds further levels of implementation, such as action plans[9] or budgetary allocations.[10] Moreover, studies have pointed to a variation in the degrees of domestic commitment to the different MDG priorities, gender equality being among the most neglected.[11] The reasons for this variation, however, remain unaccounted for. Despite the valuable insights generated by this research, the relationship between global and domestic development target-setting remains unclear since studies have not explored policy change over time, throughout the MDG period, or – more crucially – the causal mechanisms of adjustment. Due to the persistence of GPI-based development governance – as a result of SDG adoption – the effectiveness and implications of global development target-setting arguably need to be more thoroughly and explicitly studied through the lens of the GPI framework.

This chapter addresses the gap in the existing literature by exploring the extent to which and how the MDGs led to domestic policy adjustment. It does so by studying policy adjustment to MDG 3, aimed at furthering development through the promotion of gender equality and the empowerment of women, in Sub-Saharan Africa. The study employs a mixed-methods design, where the extent of policy adjustment is explored through a comprehensive mapping of MDG 3-related policy output in Poverty Reduction Strategy Papers (PRSPs) in 15 Sub-Saharan African countries[12] over 15 years (2000–2015). The pathways to policy adjustment are explored through two case studies, where process-tracing[13] is used to establish the causal mechanisms of gender policy change in Kenya and Ethiopia. The study uses primary data comprising interview material, collected through field studies in Kenya and Ethiopia, and policy documents. The decision to study Sub-Saharan Africa was made based on the fact that the MDG anti-poverty agenda mainly targeted this region, implying that

---

[6] E.g. Fukuda-Parr 2014, 2017.

[7] E.g. Bruns et al. 2003; United Nations 2014, 2015. See also Bisbee et al. this volume.

[8] See for example Bisbee et al. this volume; Cohen 2014; Díaz-Martínez and Gibbons 2014; Fukuda-Parr 2014; Sen and Mukherjee 2014; Unterhalter 2014.

[9] Fukuda-Parr 2008.

[10] Seyedsayamdost 2017.

[11] Fukuda-Parr 2008; Harrison et al. 2003; Seyedsayamdost 2017.

[12] See the list of countries and PRSPs included in the study in online Appendix I, Table A1.

[13] Bennett and Checkel 2015; Beach and Pedersen 2013.

the pressure for behavioral change directed at Sub-Saharan African countries is likely to have been the greatest.

The chapter makes three principal contributions. First, it explores domestic policy adjustment to a GPI at multiple levels. By capturing MDG effects on different *dimensions* of policy (policy goals and implementation plans), corresponding to different degrees of implementation, the study enables the assessment of the depth of domestic GPI-related change. Second, it theorizes three causal mechanisms of domestic GPI adjustment: aid conditionality, social influence, and civil society mobilization. While working through different pathways, including transnational, elite, and domestic politics,[14] these mechanisms are theorized as complementary in stimulating GPI adjustment. Third, empirically, the chapter examines domestic policy adjustment through a specific focus on gender with the help of a mixed-methods design. Notwithstanding an expanding human rights regime, gender inequality continues to be among the most pervasive forms of discrimination globally.[15] This suggests that gender equality change faces a particularly high level of resistance at the national level. Considering the proliferation of GPIs and the fact that the MDGs was the first international agreement to spell out quantitative targets along with timeframes for gender equality, studying the extent and mechanisms of domestic MDG 3 influence contributes with valuable insights regarding GPI effectiveness in general and gender equality behavioral change in particular. The combination of a quantitative mapping of policy adoption across 15 countries over 15 years and in-depth process-tracing of the policy adjustment processes in two different cases allows for conclusions concerning the extent to which as well as how development GPIs may influence state behavior.

The chapter presents three central findings. First, it demonstrates significant policy adjustment to MDG 3 in Sub-Saharan Africa, pointing to the effectiveness of development GPIs in leading to domestic policy adjustment. By the year 2013, 11 out of the 15 countries explored had adopted all seven policy goals associated with MDG 3, related to enhancing gender equality in education, employment and political participation. Overall, there was an increase in the average adoption of all policy goals and implementation plan features between 2000 and 2015. Second, while effects on policy goal-setting were substantial, the adoption of implementation plans, i.e. quantitative targets, timeframes and budgets, to address the goals was much more limited. In other words, while the MDG 3 indicators were embraced as national policy commitments, behavioral change in terms of programming and budgeting was moderate. Thus, I demonstrate a significant and lasting gap between GPI commitments and implementation. Third, process-tracing of the Kenyan and Ethiopian policy processes indicates that behavioral change was induced by the interaction of mechanisms working through the pathways of transnational

---

[14] Kelley and Simmons, Chapter 1, 12.
[15] Kabeer 2003, 50; World Bank 2012.

pressure, direct elite responses and domestic politics. The mechanisms include aid conditionality tied to MDG policy adjustment, social influence by means of praise and shame through MDG performance reporting, and – to a lesser extent – the empowerment and mobilization of domestic actors promoting change. The finding of these predominantly incentive-based mechanisms as the principal causal pathways to domestic change, and of the limited socialization of government actors, enhances the understanding of why gender policy implementation processes have been characterized by continued resistance and contestation. The case studies further illustrate the non-linear character of gender equality behavioral change, typically underplayed in diffusion as well as socialization research. The chapter's final section elaborates the broader implications of these findings in terms of development governance, gender equality change and the nature of global power relations.

THE MDGs AS A DEVELOPMENT GPI

The MDGs stemmed from the commitments of the Millennium Declaration,[16] adopted by the UN General Assembly in 2000 following a decade of UN development conferences.[17] In order to track progress related to the declaration, 8 specific goals, with 21 associated quantitative and time-bound targets and 60 indicators, were specified. This means of development governance, which the UNICEF's Progress of Nations Reports and the UNDP's Human Development Reports paved the way for in the 1990s, effectively created a dominant global agenda for development. The MDGs were accompanied by new data collection practices and a comprehensive regularized monitoring framework. State performance in relation to each indicator was tracked continuously through reporting at three different levels – global, regional, and national. The global reports,[18] published annually from 2005 onwards, focused on comparing progress in nine different world regions[19] but also included cross-country comparisons. The regional MDG reports were issued by the UN Regional Commissions and from 2010 onwards, regional MDG progress reports for Africa were published annually until the year 2015.[20]

[16] UNGA 2001.
[17] Fukuda-Parr and Hulme 2011, 19.
[18] These were coordinated and published by the Statistics Division of the United Nations Department of Economic and Social Affairs, see http://www.un.org/millenniumgoals/reports.shtml.
[19] The regions include the Caribbean, Caucasus and Central Asia, Eastern Asia, Europe, Oceania, Southern Asia, South-Eastern Asia, Northern Africa and Sub-Saharan Africa.
[20] The regional Africa reports were the joint products of the African Union Commission (AUC), the Economic Commission for Africa (ECA) of the UN, the African Development Bank (AfDB) and the United Nations Development Programme-Regional Bureau for Africa (UNDP-RBA) in consultation with stakeholders and African policymakers. See http://www.undp.org/content/undp/en/home/librarypage/mdg/mdg-reports/africa-collection.html.

These reports used data from the United Nations Statistics Division (UNSD), the World Bank and the Organisation for Economic Co-operation and Development (OECD) to directly compare and rank MDG progress in African countries. In relation to MDG 3, for instance, the reports typically displayed cross-country performance – from worst to best performer – in terms of the gender parity index in primary, secondary, and tertiary education, the share of women in wage employment and the share of women in parliament at different points in time from 1990 onwards. These rankings were accompanied by narrative reporting, bringing attention to "best performing" and "worst performing" countries with regard to particular indicators.[21] At the national level, country MDG reports, published at three to five year intervals in conjunction with communications strategies and advocacy campaigns,[22] tracked national progress in relation to each goal. The purpose of the country reports was "to engage political leaders and top decision-makers as well as to mobilise civil society, communities, the general public, parliamentarians and the media in a debate about human development."[23] In other words, they were designed to trigger political commitment, accountability, and action to stimulate MDG progress domestically through public information dissemination and social mobilization.[24]

In addition to these three levels of MDG reporting, various web-based platforms, such as the World Bank's "MDG Progress Status" website[25] and the MDG Monitor,[26] which tracked MDG indicator trends for developing countries, were set up to facilitate cross-country performance assessment. Hence, the MDGs and their monitoring frameworks were intended to pressure policymakers by means of strategic public dissemination of country performance and through the reputational concerns of policymakers to shape domestic policy agendas. The pathways of this influence were intended to be multiple, as reporting was explicitly designed to mobilize civil society, media, and the public to push policymakers to strengthen their efforts toward MDG fulfillment. The MDG country reports, which outlined progress as well as specific policy, legislative, or institutional changes furthering MDG implementation,[27] were designed to be used as leverage in aid negotiations to hold policymakers to account for their MDG efforts. Thus, MDG performance assessment enabled three pathways of GPI influence – domestic politics, elite politics, and transnational politics.

---

[21] UNDP 2010, 32.
[22] United Nations Development Group (UNDG) 2003, 5.
[23] UNDG 2003, 2.
[24] https://undg.org/wp-content/uploads/2014/12/Item-3c-2nd-Guidance-Note-on-Country-Reporting-on-the-MDGs.pdf.
[25] http://datatopics.worldbank.org/mdgs/index.html.
[26] http://www.mdgmonitor.org/millennium-development-goals/.
[27] UNDG 2003, 5.

MAPPING ADJUSTMENT TO THE MDGs

The MDGs had a great impact on global development discourse. Yet, the agenda's effectiveness must ultimately be judged based on its effects on domestic development policy since this constitutes the causal link between global development indicators and domestic development outcomes. Hence, this mapping of MDG 3-related policy adjustment explores domestic policy output, or the policies spelled out by governments, in national PRSPs. The Poverty Reduction Strategy approach, initiated in 1999 and finalized in 2014, was introduced to serve as a basis for debt relief within the Heavily Indebted Poor Countries (HIPC) initiative. A PRSP outlines a country's structural, macroeconomic and social policy commitments and programs for a period of three or more years and has the overarching aim to reduce poverty and promote economic growth. PRSPs were prepared by governments through participatory processes involving the World Bank, the IMF, development partners and domestic stakeholders.[28] PRSPs are deemed suitable for the study of MDG policy adoption as they constituted crucial vehicles for poverty reduction, outlining national priorities, policies and action plans. As such, they should reflect a government's intention to implement the MDGs.[29] Moreover, the lower-income countries that were instructed to adopt PRSPs were also the central targets of the MDGs' anti-poverty agenda, which implies that a focus on PRSP-producing countries is sensible. In addition, the study of PRSPs ensures policy document comparability.

Regarding the selection of countries, I chose to limit the sample to the countries in Sub-Saharan Africa that fulfilled the two criteria of having produced their first PRSP by the year 2000 and having released at least four PRSPs between 2000 and 2015. The selection of this sample allows me to observe policy developments throughout the studied period – from the year *before* the MDGs were introduced and until the MDG period – rather than at just two or three points in time. Since this study concerns not merely the end results, or final degrees, of MDG adjustment, but also the patterns of adjustment of different policy dimensions in countries over time, the inclusion of several instances of policy revision (i.e. new PRSPs) is crucial. Thus, out of the 34 Sub-Saharan African countries that adopted PRSPs, I selected all 15 countries that fulfilled these two criteria. Importantly, the selected sample includes countries that vary with regard to variables that are theorized to influence the operation of the causal mechanisms of policy change. These include existing policy environment (initial degree of policy adoption), regime type and the associated degree of civil society strength and independence, income group and aid dependence.[30] Yet, since the sample only

[28] See https://www.imf.org/external/np/prsp/prsp.aspx.
[29] Fukuda-Parr 2008, 5.
[30] See the list of countries and associated characteristics online in Appendix I, Table A2.

includes PRSP-producing, i.e. lower-income countries that may be seen as particularly sensitive to the policy influence of external actors, the results with regard to MDG policy influence are not considered representative of countries in general, or even of African countries, but rather of this particular group of aid-dependent countries.

MDG 3 aimed to promote gender equality by decreasing gender disparities in education, wage employment, and political representation.[31] The mapping of MDG 3 adjustment focuses on two different dimensions of policy output – *policy goals* and *implementation plans*[32] – related to MDG 3 achievement. This enables the assessment of policy effects at different levels of implementation. Altogether, seven policy goals and three different features of implementation plans were coded.[33] In a first step, I map the formulation of policy goals, or commitments, related to the MDG 3 target and indicators. In a second step, I map the formulation of quantitative targets, budgets, and timeframes; here conceptualized as implementation plans, in relation to the three broader categories of policy goals. The adoption of a policy goal demands less of a government than the adoption of an implementation plan feature, as it only constitutes a statement of intention, typically precedes the adoption of other policy dimensions and, in itself, has no associated cost or specificity in terms of how or when it should be achieved. Thus, countries are expected to have converged more around the adoption of MDG 3-related policy goals than implementation plan features.

Figure 4.1 illustrates the average degree of adoption of the seven policy goals associated with MDG 3. By the year 2013, all except four countries – Mali,

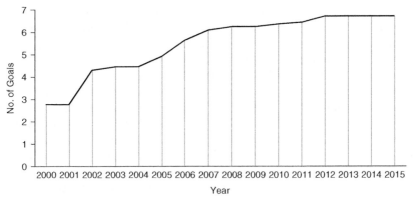

FIGURE 4.1. MDG 3 policy goal adoption, mean for 15 countries.

[31] See the precise formulation of the MDG 3 target and indicators online in Appendix II.
[32] See Dolowitz and Marsh 2000.
[33] The coded variables are listed online in Appendix II.

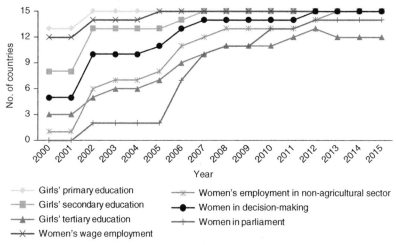

FIGURE 4.2. MDG 3 policy goal adoption, by goal.

Mozambique, Niger and Rwanda – had incorporated all seven policy goals in their PRSPs, implying a significant adjustment to MDG 3 in terms of policy goal-setting.

Figure 4.2 illustrates the policy goal adoption patterns across countries for each separate goal.

While the adoption of the different policy goals follows similar patterns, with incremental increases in the number of adopters and all except two policy goals reaching the highest possible adoption rates by 2013, the goals have varying initial adoption rates. This may reflect divergent degrees of fit with prior local norms[34] of the different goals, e.g. that the goal of increasing women's representation in decision-making has faced more normative contestation than that of increasing girls' educational opportunities. The figure further illustrates that the adoption of more general, or less ambitious, goals exceeds or precedes the adoption of more specific or ambitious goals. For example, the adoption of the goal to increase the share of girls in primary education precedes that of increasing the share of girls in secondary education. Comparing the adoption patterns of different countries (see online Figure A1, Appendix III), Kenya stands out as an early adopter of policy goals. Conversely, Zambia, followed by Benin, Ethiopia, Mali, Senegal and Tanzania experienced the greatest increases in policy goal adoption, starting at low levels while reaching high adoption rates by 2015.

Turning to the adoption of implementation plans across countries, Figures 4.3–4.5 illustrate the extent to which the three general goals of increasing women's wage employment, girls' education, and women's political representation were accompanied by quantitative targets, budgets and timeframes over the MDG period.

[34] Acharya 2004; Cortell and Davis 1996, 2005.

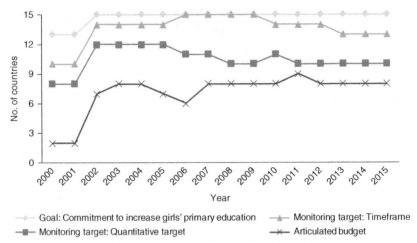

FIGURE 4.3. Adoption of implementation plans, girls' education.

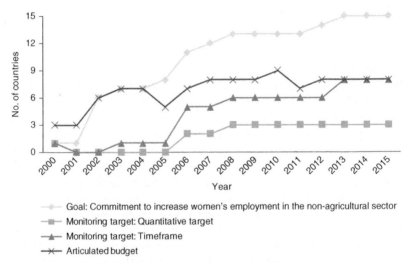

FIGURE 4.4. Adoption of implementation plans, women's wage employment.

   In addition to the three features of implementation plans, the figures display the adoption of one of the policy goals within each policy area in order to enable the comparison of adoption patterns across these two policy dimensions. The mapping demonstrates that the degree of adoption of policy goals is higher than that of implementation plans in all three policy areas, implying that commitments to goals precedes, or is favored over, the articulation of budgets, quantitative targets and timeframes for their

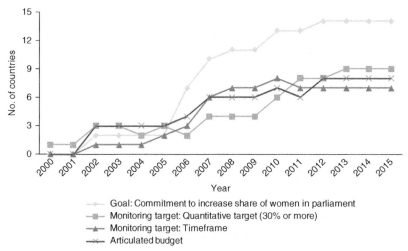

FIGURE 4.5. Adoption of implementation plans, women's political participation.

implementation. This resonates with Fukuda-Parr and Hulme's conclusion that while the MDGs were institutionalized at the level of national policy statements, actual behavioral change in terms of the articulation of budgets and practical actions for MDG achievement was more limited.[35] Figure 4.6, which displays the average adoption rates of policy goals and implementation plans across countries over time, clearly illustrates this discrepancy between MDG 3-related commitments and implementation frameworks in PRSPs.

Notwithstanding the divergence between the adoption of policy goals and implementation plans, it is clear that the overall articulation of MDG 3-related targets, timeframes, and budgets increased over time. As a case in point, in 2000, only one country – Kenya – had adopted the quantitative target of achieving at least 30 percent female representation in parliament, while in 2015, 9 (or 60 percent) of the 15 countries had formulated such a target. In sum, there has been a noteworthy adjustment to MDG 3 across both policy dimensions. Comparing the initial and final implementation plan adoption rates of the different countries (see Figure A2, Appendix III), we see that while all countries except Mozambique and Gambia adopted an increasing number of MDG 3-related implementation plan features between 2000 and 2015, the *degree* of behavioral change varies considerably. While a few countries, notably Zambia, Malawi, Niger and Ethiopia, changed significantly between 2000 and 2015, others, particularly Benin, Tanzania, Rwanda, and Guinea, progressed marginally. Kenya, again, stands out as an early adopter.

---

[35] Fukuda-Parr and Hulme 2009, 4.

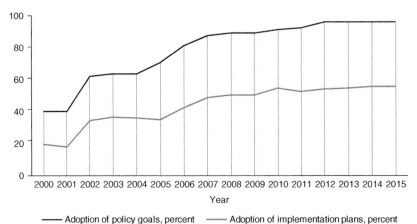

——— Adoption of policy goals, percent   ——— Adoption of implementation plans, percent

FIGURE 4.6. Adoption of policy goals and implementation plans, mean for 15 countries.

In conclusion, the mapping of domestic policy adjustment to MDG 3 has led to three main findings. First, the MDGs were generally effective in engendering gender policy output in PRSPs in Sub-Saharan Africa. Second, MDG 3 affected the adoption of different policy dimensions to different extents. While countries reached close to full convergence in terms of the adoption of MDG 3-related policy goals, they converged less around the adoption of implementation plans. This may indicate that countries were uncommitted to the *implementation* of goals and therefore only rhetorically adjusted by endorsing goals without taking further action. Alternatively, it could signify that countries were *unable* to tie goals to concrete targets, budgets, or timeframes, e.g. due to resource or capacity constraints. Third, the mapping demonstrates significant variations across countries with regard to the degrees and patterns of policy adoption. These findings actualize the question of how domestic MDG 3 policy adjustment may be explained.

EXPLAINING GPI INFLUENCE: THREE CAUSAL MECHANISMS

The chapter argues that development GPIs like the MDGs may constitute effective means of influencing domestic policy. They are argued to be particularly effective in engendering adjustment when they trigger a combination of influence mechanisms and resonate with the policy preferences of, and hence manage to engage, international *and* domestic actors. More specifically, when GPIs evoke mechanisms that work through all three pathways outlined by Kelley and Simmons,[36] including *transnational pressure, elite engagement* and *domestic politics*, GPI-related policy change is likely to be significant and occur swiftly. Importantly, GPIs are primarily likely to be effective in generating behavioral

---

[36] Kelley and Simmons, Chapter 1, 12.

change in target states when the reporting of performance triggers direct material or social rewards or punishments. Typically, materially powerful and authoritative actors, such as IOs or wealthy states, determine rating criteria and perform the rating while poorer states constitute the rated.[37] Consequently, the raters tend to possess the power to inflict significant economic and/or reputational penalties or rewards on the assessed based on GPI performance. Thus, development GPIs may introduce significant social as well as material incentives for behavioral change, thereby manipulating the utility calculations[38] of policymakers in aid-dependent countries to induce behavioral change. Below, three specific causal mechanisms through which this may occur are theorized.

Aid Conditionality

The quintessential incentive-based influence strategy, and one commonly used by the World Bank and the IMF in aid negotiations,[39] is *aid conditionality*. This mechanism works through the pathway of transnational politics and exploits power asymmetries between economically powerful actors promoting certain policies, e.g. IOs or states, and economically weaker target states. The leverage of the more powerful increases with the target's degree of aid dependence, i.e. material and social vulnerability.[40] As suggested by Kelley and Simmons, GPIs may be used as a form of eligibility criteria for aid allocation.[41] By bringing attention to the relative performance of countries and tying aid allotment to this, GPIs may pressure economically weaker states to adjust their behavior.

Since the main organizations promoting and assessing MDG performance – the various UN agencies – also constitute the major contributors of economic assistance to developing countries, the allocation of aid was since the inception of the MDGs largely allocated or tied (directly or indirectly) to MDG-related interventions. Moreover, as bilateral donors also had an interest in displaying their MDG-related efforts, and could utilize MDG reporting to pressure states, their aid was to varying extents also tied to conditions of MDG adjustment in recipient countries. In total, this amounted to large amounts of material benefits being tied to national MDG adjustment efforts. Consequently, it is likely that transnational and third party pressure, leveraged through aid conditionality, generated significant pressure on developing countries to adjust policy frameworks to the MDGs. This leads to the following expectation:

> *H1: The conditioning of aid on GPI-related behavioral change is likely to influence domestic GPI-related policy adjustment positively.*

---

[37] Kelley and Simmons, Chapter 1, 8.
[38] Börzel and Risse 2012, 6.
[39] Ibid., 7; Kelley 2004, 434.
[40] Risse et al. 2013, 14.
[41] Kelley and Simmons 2015, 60.

Social Influence

In addition to the material pressure that performance assessment may generate, GPIs are through their regularized and public monitoring and reporting
practices likely to evoke social pressure for policy change through the mechanism of social influence. This mechanism works through elite politics and the
active promotion of change through peer criticism and reputational effects.
Specific strategies may include praise or status markers that induce actors
with a sense of well-being, belonging or status, or punishments, including
shaming, exclusion or status devaluation.[42] GPIs typically target policy areas
for which certain government departments and officials are responsible. To
evade social disapproval as a result of poor performance, government actors
are expected to adjust their behavior, though initially primarily by engaging
in rhetorical maneuvers without conforming to new rules.[43] In this process,
however, they become "rhetorically entrapped" by their own use of arguments
and, hence, pressured to live up to their commitments. This influence mechanism is likely to generate "public conformity without private acceptance."[44]
Social influence relies on social pressure, and can work independently of the
rater's material power, and may stimulate behavioral change without persuasion or direct internalization,[45] just like aid conditionality.

In the MDG case, this mechanism of influence is likely to have been facilitated
through the intense MDG performance monitoring and reporting. In particular,
the regional MDG progress reports, which displayed MDG fulfillment across
countries and brought attention to "best performing" and "worst performing"
countries, may have triggered the social influence mechanism. Moreover, the
country reports were explicitly designed to engage the public and media in order
to pressure decision-makers by means of information dissemination.[46]

> H2: *The exercise of social influence through GPI reporting is likely to
> influence domestic GPI-related policy adjustment positively.*

Civil Society Mobilization

Development GPIs may also trigger the activation of domestic politics and
influence mechanisms, especially if performance monitoring attracts public
attention and civil society has sufficient capacity to mobilize. Crucially, GPIs
contribute to the generation and dissemination of new information, which may
affect public opinion and enable civil society organizations (CSOs) to hold the

---

[42] Schimmelfennig 2003, 218.
[43] Schimmelfennig 2003, 220.
[44] Schimmelfennig 2003, 222.
[45] Johnston 2008, 24–25.
[46] https://undg.org/wp-content/uploads/2014/12/Item-3c-2nd-Guidance-Note-on-Country-Reporting-on-the-MDGs.pdf.

government to account for its performance, thereby pushing for policy change or implementation.[47] As part of their influence strategies, multilateral and bilateral donors may work to reinforce this domestic pressure by empowering nationally based CSOs to push for change through organizational capacity-building and/or economic support. Thus, this influence mechanism may successfully be combined with aid conditionality and social influence to pressure target states through different channels. In countries where civil society is generally weak, suppressed or inadequately organized, however, GPI influence through the domestic pathway is likely to be circumscribed.

In the case of MDG adjustment, domestic CSOs could utilize the cross-country comparisons to bring public attention to domestic MDG performance and advocate for further policy adjustment, especially in cases of poor performance. Moreover, domestic CSOs were typically directly involved in MDG performance monitoring through the writing and dissemination of shadow progress reports and participation at MDG conferences. Such activities imply reputational effects for governments.

H3: Civil society mobilization in favor of GPI standards is likely to influence domestic GPI-related policy adjustment positively.

When it comes to the status of these hypothesized causal mechanisms in relation to each other, they are expected to be complementary rather than mutually exclusive. Independently, the relevance of each mechanism depends on different scope conditions, e.g. the level of aid dependence in the case of aid conditionality, state actors' concern for their reputation in the case of social influence and civil society strength in the case of civil society mobilization.

Observable Implications

In order to systematically examine the argument related to the operation of the three causal mechanisms of MDG 3 adjustment, I outline a number of observable implications for each mechanism. The observable implications relate to the same set of questions for all mechanisms. The presence of these observable implications are then examined in the accounts of the Kenyan and Ethiopian MDG 3 implementation processes. The questions were selected based on what is deemed crucial to observe empirically in order to establish the operation of each mechanism.

What is most central here is the establishment of *direct pressure* exerted on government actors. First, demonstrating the operation of aid conditionality demands evidence that MDG monitoring led to the conditioning of aid on MDG policy adjustment and of government actors responding to this. Second, establishing the operation of social influence requires evidence of the use of shame or

[47] Kelley and Simmons, Chapter 1, 13.

praise in relation to MDG 3 performance/rankings to exert social pressure on policymakers and of government actors responding to this. Third, demonstrating the operation of civil society mobilization and influence demands evidence of such strategies, e.g. advocacy campaigns targeting government performance or policies, and of government actors responding to these.

The empirical material, i.e. interview material, policy documents etc., should further reveal the relevant actor's attempt at *driving, steering, or influencing* MDG 3 policy adjustment. To establish the operation of aid conditionality, there should be evidence of active and successful efforts on the part of development partners to drive and steer MDG 3 implementation. To establish that the mechanism of social influence has been operational, accounts should indicate that the donor community and/or domestic elites have been active in influencing MDG 3 implementation. To provide support for the relevance of the mechanism of civil society mobilization, accounts should point to the significance of domestic actors – civil society, the media etc. – in steering implementation processes.

Evidence related to the *timing* of policy change could also indicate the operation of a certain causal mechanism. If policy adoption coincides with or follows bilateral or multilateral loan agreements or negotiations, this suggests that aid conditionality may have been relevant in incentivizing change. If policy adoption follows public statements or reports, e.g. shaming a country for inaction in relation to the issue in question, this suggests that social influence may have been at work. In cases where policy change coincides with civil society advocacy campaigns or public debate related to an issue, this could indicate the operation of the causal mechanism of civil society mobilization.

The *motivation* for policy adoption could also constitute an observable implication of the operation of a causal mechanism. If accounts motivate change with reference to material pressure from donors, this points to the relevance of aid conditionality as a driving force for MDG 3-related policy adjustment. If accounts suggest that political elites and decision-makers motivated policy changes with reference to social pressure, e.g. through attention to poor performance, from donors, this may be viewed as evidence of successful social influence strategies. If change is motivated with reference to pressure from domestic actors and public opinion, this suggests that civil society mobilization may have operated.

Finally, the overall *level* and *characteristics* of MDG 3 implementation may indicate the operation of particular causal mechanisms. In contrast to processes of socialization or learning, the three proposed mechanisms rely on change processes that are driven by external actors through social and/or material pressure, i.e. incentives. When policy prescriptions associated with GPIs do not resonate with prior domestic preferences or policy frameworks, but generate swift initial policy adjustment due to material and social rewards, the risks of resistance, contestation, and negotiation during the implementation phase are inherent. This may lead to a gap between policy adoption and implementation in the short term (Table 4.1).

TABLE 4.1. *Observable implications of causal mechanisms*

Questions	Aid Conditionality	Social Influence	Civil Society Mobilization
Was there external direct pressure for MDG 3 implementation?	Yes – evidence of direct pressure exerted through material incentives (aid or loans) and of policymakers responding to this	Yes – evidence of direct pressure exerted through social incentives (shame or praise) and of policymakers responding to this	Yes – evidence of direct pressure exerted through social pressure (civil society advocacy campaigns, media attention etc.) and of policymakers responding to this
Who drove/steered early MDG 3 implementation?	The donor community (through material incentives)	The donor community (through social incentives) and domestic elites (status and reputational concerns)	Civil society, the media, domestic public opinion/ debate (through advocacy)
What was the timing of MDG 3 alignment/policy adoption/ implementation?	Coincided with bilateral or multilateral aid or loan agreements or negotiations?	Coincided with conferences/ public statements or reports shaming, praising or comparing MDG 3 performance	Coincided with civil society advocacy campaigns/media attention/public debate
How was policy adoption motivated?	With reference to pressure (material incentives) from donors	With reference to pressure (social incentives) from donors	With reference to pressure (civil society mobilization, advocacy) from domestic CSOs, media, public opinion
What was the level and characteristics of MDG 3 implementation?	In line with MDG 3/donor prescriptions	In line with MDG 3/donor prescriptions	In line with civil society preferences, advocacy campaigns

Alternative Explanations

The proposed causal mechanisms of MDG 3 adjustment all rely on the public monitoring and reporting aspects of the MDGs. Yet, the observed pattern of domestic MDG 3 alignment could potentially be explained by altogether different factors or processes. Below, I list three alternative explanations for domestic MDG 3-related behavioral change, the first based on incentives, the second on normative change and socialization, and the third based on processes of learning.

First, adjustment to MDG 3 could potentially have occurred independent of the MDG agenda and instead reflect general progress in terms of gender equality policy and legislation. Gender equality progress could, for instance, have occurred in response to external incentives for change, such as aid conditionality tied to gender equality interventions but unrelated to the MDGs or its GPI aspects. If this explained MDG 3 adjustment, policy change should coincide with aid being conditioned on gender equality reforms, rather than MDG or MDG 3 progress specifically. Moreover, change should be unrelated to performance monitoring.

Second, a global normative change related to gender equality and women's rights, and the socialization of government actors around these norms, could explain domestic policy change. Socialization processes involve not only behavioral change, but shifts in interests and identities as new norms become internalized and taken for granted.[48] Since the adoption of the Convention on the Elimination of all forms of Discrimination Against Women (CEDAW) in 1979, and the UN World Conferences on Women between 1975 and 1995, gender equality norms have been in development and focus internationally and have influenced policymaking in many countries. If this explained MDG 3-related policy adoption, we should observe policy adjustment over a longer period of time, including the decades preceding the adoption of the MDG agenda. Moreover, successful socialization should be reflected in real efforts to implement adopted policies.

A third possible explanation for increasing gender policy adoption across countries is processes of rational learning. According to this mechanism, governments learn or draw conclusions based on data generated through observations of policy experiences elsewhere, which may be channeled through IOs like the UN or the World Bank.[49] In this particular case, the new knowledge could relate to the economic gains associated with gender equality policies, such as increasing girls' education or women's participation in the labor force. If this were a relevant explanation for MDG 3-related policy adoption, efforts to implement gender policies should be evident, since gains only accrue following implementation.

---

[48] Johnston 2001.
[49] Dobbin et al. 2007, 462.

THE CAUSAL MECHANISMS AT WORK: KENYA AND ETHIOPIA

This section illustrates the workings of the theorized causal mechanisms and probes the alternative explanations of domestic gender policy change in line with MDG 3 in Kenya and Ethiopia. The accounts are based on empirical material comprising interview data, collected through field studies in Kenya and Ethiopia in 2014 and 2015, and policy documents. Altogether, 41 interviews were carried out with government officials and representatives of bilateral donor agencies, the IMF, the World Bank, UN agencies, academia and international and domestic civil society organizations (CSOs) operating in the two countries.[50] The case studies complement and build on the mapping of policy output by illustrating *how* MDG 3 influenced gender equality policymaking in the two countries. Specifically, process-tracing is employed to identify the causal mechanisms[51] that connect the emergence of the MDG norm and domestic policy change. The cases demonstrate the operation of the causal mechanisms of aid conditionality and social influence, both leveraged through concentrated MDG monitoring and reporting by donors, coupled with the social pressure exerted by domestic civil society. The finding of these mechanisms as the primary causal pathways to domestic behavioral change explains why early adjustment remained primarily rhetorical, aimed at accommodating conditions of aid and evading social disapproval, shaming and negative public opinion as a result of poor MDG performance.

Kenya and Ethiopia were selected as cases from the sample of 15 countries included in the mapping of policy output based on case selection guidelines suited to process-tracing studies. First, in theory-centric process-tracing, cases where X and Y are present, along with the relevant scope conditions, should be selected.[52] Since the aim here is to study the causal process whereby GPIs (the cause) produce domestic policy adjustment (the outcome), only positive cases of MDG 3 influence – i.e. where policy adjustment has occurred – are relevant to consider. Clearly, in this study, the presence of the outcome is a matter of degree rather than something that has occurred in full or not at all. Nevertheless, based on the mapping, Kenya and Ethiopia are both considered clearly positive cases of GPI influence since significant MDG 3 adjustment can be observed in the two countries.

Second, if it is possible to conduct two process-tracing analyses in a single study, the selection of diverse cases, which capture significant variation along the dimensions of interest within the population, is advised as this enables the assessment of how the causal mechanisms play out for different starting conditions.[53] Due to the variance introduced, the diverse-case strategy has a

---

[50] See the full list of interviewees online in Appendix IV.
[51] Beach and Pedersen 2011; Checkel 2006.
[52] Beach and Pedersen 2013, 147.
[53] Schimmelfennig 2014, 105; Seawright 2006, 99.

strong claim to representativeness within the specified context and thereby maximizes the external validity of the causal inferences.[54] Since process-tracing does not assess the magnitude of the causal effects of different independent variables, but the explanatory relevance of causal mechanisms and their scope conditions, this variation should concern the hypothesized scope conditions. Hence, the selection of cases where the scope conditions are satisfied, but to different extents, enables the assessment and refinement of their effects on the hypothesized causal mechanisms.

Kenya and Ethiopia are considered diverse cases in a number of respects. First, they vary in terms of their initial gender policy adoption rates, i.e. existing policy environments, which may signal divergent normative contexts with regard to gender equality. While the two countries, as established, both reached high levels of MDG 3 policy adoption by 2015, Kenya had a relatively ambitious gender policy agenda at the outset, in 2000, while Ethiopia had among the lowest levels of gender policy adoption at this time. Second, the two cases display differences with respect to regime type, where Kenya is categorized as "partly free" while Ethiopia is considered "not free."[55] Ethiopia's autocratic regime is, moreover, associated with a higher degree of CSO containment and exclusion of civil society from the policy processes.[56] These differences have implications for the degree of reputational concerns, and thus GPI responsiveness, among government elites and the potential for civil society mobilization. Fourth, Kenya is a lower-middle-income country while Ethiopia is a low-income country. Finally, the countries' levels of aid dependence differ, signalling divergent incentives to respond to economic conditionality.[57] If the same causal mechanisms are found to explain the relationship between the cause and the outcome in two such diverse cases within the studied population, their relevance and explanatory power are deemed stronger than otherwise.

The Kenyan Process of Gender Policy Change

The following analysis of the Kenyan gender policy process between 2000 and 2015 illustrates the operation of the causal mechanisms of aid conditionality, social influence and CSO capacity-building and mobilization for domestic change. Incentivized by the promise of aid, the hope of praise, and the fear of shame in policy performance monitoring reports, Kenya adopted MDG 3 policy goals and implementation plan features early on compared to other countries in the region. However, efforts to implement these remained minimal for years, weakening the likelihood of socialization or learning mechanisms.

---

[54] Schimmelfennig 2014, 105; Seawright 2006, 99.
[55] Freedom House 2017.
[56] Bertelsmann Stiftung 2016.
[57] Table A2 in online Appendix 1 lists income group, regime type, levels of aid dependence and colonial background for all 15 countries included in the study.

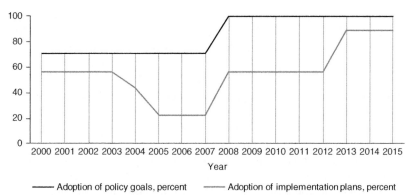

FIGURE 4.7. Adoption of policy goals and implementation plans, Kenya.

As illustrated in Figure 4.7, the gap between policy output and implementation grew initially as policy commitments increased while actual interventions were stalled and gender budgeting was withdrawn. Moreover, the gender machineries set up to ensure implementation were effectively paralyzed due to persistent understaffing, inadequate financing, and a lack of prioritization of gender concerns. As gender equality became increasingly prioritized by the donor community, however, the pressure on the Kenyan government mounted due to two factors. First, gender equality-focused aid increased, creating growing incentives for its accommodation in the form of a more comprehensive policy framework. Second, the failures of the Kenyan government with regard to MDG 3 indicators were increasingly emphasized in public donor reports and statements. Domestically, the Kenyan women's movement gained leverage in relation to the government through growing donor support and increasing public debate surrounding MDG performance. Due to the continued exertion of pressure, implementation progressed. However, though the contestation around gender policy may have become internalized within the government apparatus, MDG 3 socialization must be seen as limited.

The initial Kenyan policy adaptation in line with the MDGs was facilitated and fast-tracked by the PRSP process, involving intense and frequent interaction between domestic policymakers and the IMF and the World Bank. The Kenyan PRSP process was launched in 2000. The broader MDG implementation process was initiated in September 2002 with a stakeholders' workshop held to enhance the understanding of the MDGs, their links to the national planning frameworks, and the mode and frequency of country-level reporting.[58] Together with development partners, the Kibaki government then undertook an MDG needs assessment, which concluded that "…the government needed to stop the usual business and embark on a well thought-out planning process aimed at putting the country on track towards realizing

[58] Republic of Kenya 2005.

the goals."[59] Hence, the Kenyan government made a commitment to create a national policy framework conducive to the achievement of the MDGs. In 2004, with assistance from the Government of Finland and the United Nations Developent Programme (UNDP), the MDGs Project Implementation Unit was set up within the government to track MDG progress and prepare MDG status reports biennially, as demanded by the UNDP. With the set-up of this institution, comprehensive MDG data collection and performance monitoring was initiated, thus triggering social pressure on the government to initiate the policy alignment process.

Kenyan policy adjustment to the MDGs was at an early stage promoted through the mechanism of aid conditionality. The PRSP process created substantial economic incentives for MDG alignment since aid decisions were made based on the World Bank and the IMF staff's judgement of the soundness of PRSPs, made public in its Joint Staff Assessments (JSAs) shortly after the release of each PRSP.[60] Since the spelled-out objective of PRSPs was to create links between national policy, donor support, and MDG implementation,[61] a sound PRSP was MDG-aligned. Therefore, the Kenyan government, along with all other PRSP-producing governments, was exerted to direct pressure to adhere to the policy prescriptions of these institutions. Country "ownership" of development agendas came to be increasingly emphasized following the adoption of the Paris Declaration on Aid Effectiveness in 2005. Nevertheless, early PRSPs largely worked according to the logic of the structural adjustment regime of the 1980s and 1990s, characterized by a high level of policy influence of the UN's financial institutions and their conditionality.[62]

To spur gender equality improvements in fragile states, which displayed particularly bad performance with regard to the MDG 3 indicators, the amount of gender equality-focused aid from OECD countries to fragile states increased fourfold over the MDG period.[63] In Kenya, the promise of increased budget support conditioned on the adoption of policies conducive to MDG 3 progress clearly contributed to the introduction of economic incentives for policy adjustment.[64] According to an official at the Kenyan Ministry of Health, "the government sort of aligns their priorities based on where the money goes, rather than the opposite,"[65] implying that donors strongly influence government priorities

---

[59] Republic of Kenya 2005, 5.
[60] From 2005 onwards, the IMF and World Bank staff released Joint Staff Advisory Notes (JSANs) rather than JSAs. Unlike the JSAs, JSANs did not make statements regarding whether PRSPs "qualified" as bases for concessional assistance.
[61] See https://www.imf.org/external/np/exr/facts/prsp.htm.
[62] Interview 10.
[63] OECD DAC 2015.
[64] Interview 6, Interview 17.
[65] Interview 6.

through aid allocation. Several reports documenting government-donor inter-actions during this period reveal the donor community's dissatisfaction with Kenya's performance with regard to the MDGs and the conditioning of aid to the Kenyan government on MDG and MDG 3 implementation. The Summary Report[66] of the 2005 Donor Consultative Group meeting, for example, prom-ised the unlocking of budget support following the introduction of programs aimed at achieving the MDGs. In the Joint Staff Advisory Note (JSAN) com-menting on the PRSP from 2005,[67] World Bank and IMF staff emphasized the need for a more comprehensive monitoring and evaluation framework, disaggregated by gender and based on the MDGs as benchmarks, along with a timeframe for the achievement of each goal.[68] While the Kenyan govern-ment was both praised and shamed for its efforts, it was recommended further MDG adjustment in order to receive the full economic support of partners. In response to the donors' Summary Report, the Kenyan government issued a Cabinet memo directing all ministries, departments, and agencies to main-stream the MDGs in all development processes. This suggests that the condi-tioning of aid on MDG-related policy adaptation was effective in generating prescribed change. Hence, there is evidence both of the introduction of aid conditionality, based on Kenya's poor MDG performance, for further MDG alignment and of the government responding to these conditions through pol-icy adjustment.

In addition to allowing for the conditioning of aid on MDG policy adjust-ment, the PRSP process demanded the inclusion of women's rights CSOs in the policymaking process. Even though this amounted to little more than the commenting on policy drafts, this channel of influence, along with the direct economic support allocated to these organizations by UN women and other donors,[69] worked to strengthen CSO capacity to advocate for MDG implementation. Their increasing strength and influence played an important role for progressive legal and policy reform within the area of gender equal-ity, starting with the Sexual Offenses Act from 2006 and culminating in the gender-sensitive constitution of 2010. As suggested by several interviewees,[70] civil society was a crucial driver of gender equality progress in Kenya both prior to and following MDG adoption. However, the accountability, moni-toring, and cross-country comparison that the MDGs enabled greatly facili-tated the exertion of social pressure on government actors. Kenyan women's rights CSOs typically receive a large share of their budgets from international donors, who, in turn, channel aid through like-minded CSO. Thus, develop-ment partners have further enabled the exertion of domestic mobilization and

[66] The World Bank 2005.
[67] Republic of Kenya 2005.
[68] IMF 2005, 1–5.
[69] Interview 6, Interview 15, Interview 16.
[70] E.g. Interview 1, Interview 2, Interview 3, Interview 14, Interview 15, Interview 16.

pressure for gender equality change. In addition to commenting on the PRSPs, Kenyan women's rights organizations also wrote and disseminated shadow MDG[71] reports, holding the government to account for its performance. This further triggered the mechanism of social influence. Hence, the MDG framework provided Kenyan CSOs with a stronger stake in organizing to demand progressive change.

The Kenyan MDG monitoring and reporting was extensive and included the biennial national MDG reports, prepared by the government and UNDP Kenya, the annual regional MDG reports that ranked progress across African countries, and the various NGO reports that evaluated progress related to specific goals. This comprehensive reporting framework entailed a very direct accountability pressure on the Kenyan government, making it an easy target of social influence. Several respondents referred to this mechanism as crucial for MDG and MDG 3 implementation in Kenya. For example, a staff member at the Kenyan Gender Directorate stated that "we have a report developed every year on the implementation of the MDGs in the country ... and then reporting to Parliament every six months ... So when you're reporting to parliament, that means you have no option but to implement the MDGs."[72] In the same vein, a staff member at the National Gender and Equality Commission (NGEC), which oversees the implementation of gender equality policy and legislation, contended that since the MDGs constituted a an explicit commitment and performance monitoring, " ... the different governments that have come on board have had no choice but to really ensure that we comply. ... "[73] Similarly, the USAID representative argued that " ... there is performance-contracting within government and gender is one requirement. So within government, there is [progress] because of the pressure from development partners and the annual review, that pressure has helped."[74] This alludes to the rhetorical entrapment that the public commitment to an agenda entails,[75] in line with Simmons' findings concerning the significance of accountability mechanisms triggered by CEDAW reporting requirements.[76]

Hence, due to the pressure exerted on Kenyan policymakers, national development targets were swiftly pegged on the MDGs. Despite this early policy alignment, however, accounts of the relationship between the government rhetoric and action in relation to MDG 3 point to a lack of commitment to its achievement. Illustrating this, the Social Development Adviser at the

---

[71] NGOs wrote and disseminated shadow MDG reports in the early phase of MDG implementation but later provided input on the government MDG reports, Interview 4.

[72] Interview 3.

[73] Interview 1.

[74] Interview 13.

[75] Schimmelfennig 2003, 222.

[76] Simmons 2009, 212.

British Department for International Development (DfID), explained that " ... we see a disconnect between the government rhetoric, the commitments, and again the action."[77] Confirming this rhetorical adaptation, a women's rights CSO representative stated that:

Kenya has always had some very good technocrats and because the UN is here and the World Bank has a regional office here, part of what they've been doing is make sure that we come up with some very good policies to buy the goodwill of the UN and of the rest of the world. At least on the rhetorical level, they want to look progressive.[78]

In the same vein, an official at the Ministry of Health contended that "the MDGs are good because people have to do something to meet the international obligations because there will be a report and we don't want to look bad."[79] These quotes all point to social influence, triggered by performance monitoring and public reporting, as a decisive force for MDG policy alignment and to the irrelevance of MDG-based socialization or learning among government actors. Accounts suggest that the Kenyan government, at least initially, engaged in rhetorical maneuvers in order to evade social disapproval as a result of non-compliance. But while the policy framework became increasingly aligned with the MDG 3 indicators, implementation failed to keep pace, as confirmed by the mapping of policy adjustment.

In 2007, Kenya's development partners became increasingly vocal in their critique of the government's failure with regard to MDG 3 implementation. With the launch of the donors' common development strategy – the Kenya Joint Assistance Strategy (KJAS) – gender equality became a donor priority. Meanwhile, Kenya was shamed for its MDG 3 performance, which had been slow in all areas, particularly in terms of women's political representation.[80] The document further noted that the gender institutions were severely understaffed and underfunded and suffered from low status within the government structure, a view shared by several respondents.[81] The donor policy hence gave impetus to several initiatives to address gender equality, further pressuring the Kenyan government to create a policy framework that could accommodate donor investments in gender equality and enhance MDG 3 performance. In response, the long-term national development framework launched the following year – the Vision 2030 – addressed MDG 3 in a more comprehensive manner than previous policies, e.g. introducing affirmative action for women's representation in parliament. Kenya had previously been shamed for its poor performance with regard to women's political representation in the KJAS as well as in the regional MDG report. These reforms may hence be interpreted

[77] Interview 12.
[78] Interview 17.
[79] Interview 6.
[80] HAC Donor Working Group 2007, 10.
[81] E.g. Interview 9, Interview 17.

as responses to the critique expressed by donors and the bad ranking in relation to other African countries. Vision 2030 explicitly framed MDG interventions as conditioned on additional donor support,[82] while the donors in
the Summary Report from the Donor Consultative Group meeting promised
the unlocking of budget support following the introduction of MDG-related
reforms. This illustrates the degree to which MDG 3 adjustment was promoted through social influence, channeled through performance monitoring
and reporting, combined with aid negotiation and mutual conditionality.

The concern for gender equality became partly institutionalized in Kenya
through its inclusion in the constitution, gender mainstreaming and the introduction of a Gender Directorate and an independent commission with the
mandate to oversee implementation. But while MDG 3-related concerns were
internalized to some extent, interview respondents complained of a persistent
lack of understanding of gender equality beyond the measurement of gender disparities and of the underfunding and neglect of gender machineries. Regarding
MDG internalization, the Ministry of Health Officer concluded that:

We never domesticated it. We signed it, report on it and work towards the targets … We
should have had a conversation around the specific targets and translated them to the
national context. We never have conversations until we have to send the reports. Now,
as 2015 is approaching, there's a meeting every week on the MDGs … But last year,
we were doing other things … Kenya has been doing it to be politically correct. … [83]

The demonstrated lack of commitment to and internalization of MDG 3,
and the resulting continued resistance and contestation around its implementation, are indications of failed socialization and a lack of MDG-based
learning. The evidence suggests that the different Kenyan governments in
power during the 15 years of MDG implementation contributed to MDG 3
implementation when this was compatible with the development ambitions
of the government or associated with significant social and/or material
pressure. Specifically, behavioral change was promoted through the causal
mechanisms of aid conditionality, social influence, and the capacity-building
and mobilization of domestic CSOs promoting change, confirming hypotheses 1–3. While rhetorical commitment and policy adjustment to MDG 3
came about rather swiftly, actual gender equality progress was slow and
irregular. This implies that incentive-based mechanisms of influence may
be more effective in generating rhetorical adaptation than actual behavioral
change, at least initially, when they fail to socialize government actors, i.e.
alter preferences. This may cause a lasting gap between policy adoption and
implementation.

---

[82] Republic of Kenya 2008a, 15.
[83] Interview 6.

The Ethiopian Process of Gender Policy Change

Process-tracing of the Ethiopian MDG 3 policy process illustrates the prominent role played by the donor community in domestic MDG adjustment processes. As in Kenya, the exertion of social influence through comprehensive MDG performance assessment coupled with the conditioning of large quantities of aid on MDG 3 implementation were the central drivers of policy adjustment in Ethiopia. These mechanisms worked through the pathways of direct elite responses, inducing government officials and ministries with accountability for MDG progress, and transnational pressure, evoking aid conditionality tied to MDG performance. The implementation process was further triggered through the pathway of domestic politics and the mechanism of civil society mobilization. Yet, while the Kenyan women's movement grew stronger over the MDG period, the leverage of Ethiopia's civil society was partly quenched in 2009 due to a law banning foreign-funded NGOs to work with human rights-related issues. Overall, despite the diversity of the two cases, both the Ethiopian and Kenyan MDG 3 adjustment processes were characterized by swift policy adjustment followed by slow implementation, as evident in Figure 4.8. This reflects the non-prioritization of, or in some cases outright resistance to, gender equality implementation.

When it comes to initial steps toward MDG 3 policy adoption, the Ethiopian government prepared its first five-year National Action Plan on Gender Equality (NAP-GE) with support from donors in 2001.[84] Though aligned with MDG 3, the plan's lack of targets, monitoring and evaluation procedures, budgets, and translations to local languages meant that it contributed faintly to action on gender equality, signaling a lack of government commitment to its implementation.[85] Moreover, due to the failure to integrate

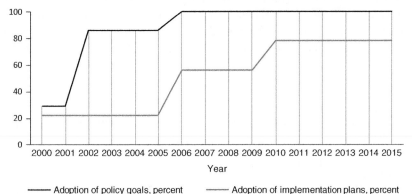

FIGURE 4.8. Adoption of policy goals and implementation plans, Ethiopia.

---

[84] African development Bank 2004, 9; Demessie and Yitbark 2008, 99.
[85] Demessie and Yitbark 2008, 100.

the plan in the 2002 PRSP, "the NAP-GE (2002–2006) became like any other paper which was not popularized enough amongst policy makers, implementers and stakeholders."[86] Though Ethiopia was one of only four[87] out of the 15 countries explored to reference the MDGs in its PRSP as early as in 2000, the gender equality dimension were in the first two PRSPs subsumed under the education goal. This meant that the economic and political dimensions of gender equality were completely disregarded.[88] Thus, the characteristics of early gender policy adoption points to rhetorical adjustment to what was perceived as appropriate by international actors rather than the government's conviction of its salience.

In 2001, the donors established two new institutions – the Development Assistance Group (DAG) and the Donor Consortium on the PRSP, made up of more than 20 bilateral and 25 multilateral donors – as forums for donor coordination to enhance their leverage on Ethiopian policymaking.[89] The consortium established a pooled fund, which amounted to more than one third of Ethiopia's public expenditure, that became a tool for influencing Ethiopian development policy through the conditioning of aid on the adoption of prescribed policies, such as the MDGs.[90] As the Ethiopian UN Country Team[91] (UNCT) observed the PRSP consultations gain momentum, it seized the opportunity to advocate for harmonizing the PRSP with the long-term objectives of the MDGs and for preparations for the writing of the first national MDG report.[92] Meanwhile, in June 2002, Africa's first MDG Campaigning for Action Forum was held in Addis Ababa, further raising the profile of the MDGs in the country. In the words of UNDP, "increased awareness of the MDGs…and the prospect of additional aid helped to motivate the Government to address the goals."[93] This reveals the importance of the mechanism of aid conditionality in incentivizing the Ethiopian government to align its policy agenda with the MDGs.

When it comes specifically to MDG 3, the first UN Development Assistance Framework (UNDAF)[94] – the policy document guiding all UN activities in Ethiopia – for the period 2002–2004 prioritized gender equality due to Ethiopia's particularly poor ranking with regard to the three MDG

---

[86] Demessie and Yitbark 2008, 113.
[87] The other three countries to refer to the MDGs in their interim PRSPs were Benin, Gambia, and Rwanda.
[88] Federal Democratic Republic of Ethiopia 2000, 24–26.
[89] Feyissa 2011, 788; UNDP 2005, 7.
[90] UNDP 2005, 7.
[91] UNCT in Ethiopia is composed of representatives of 26 UN funds and programs, specialized agencies and other UN entities accredited to Ethiopia as well as representatives of the Bretton Woods institutions.
[92] UNDP 2005, 7.
[93] UNDP 2005, 7.
[94] See http://web.undp.org/execbrd/pdf/UNDAF%20for%20Ethiopia.pdf.

3 indicators. Thus, UN institutions clearly used MDG performance data as a basis for action. This pressured the government to incorporate gender concerns in its development agenda. Consequently, the MDGs and MDG 3 (though mainly its education target) were relatively well-integrated into the first PRSP.[95] In preparation for the writing of the first MDG report, the government established the MDG Task Force, made up of government and UN agency representatives. The task force initiated MDG advocacy work to raise the status of the MDGs among Ethiopian policymakers.[96] Despite the public display of commitment to the MDGs, successfully persuading the government to link the PRSP more concretely to the specific MDGs required "sustained, concerted effort by the UN and partners,"[97] according to the UNDP. Thus, the MDG implementation process, particularly that pertaining to the gender equality indicators, continued to be driven by the development partners through the exertion of social and material pressure. Confirming this, the Ethiopian scholar interviewed contended that "when it comes to the driving forces for gender equality, I would say that especially the donors have pushed for change."[98] This clearly contradicts the assumptions of learning mechanisms, which theorize a self-driven willingness to change, spurred by new information, as well as domestic socialization.

Having succeeded in creating a shared government-donor agenda for development through the first PRSP process, the donors pledged US$ 3.6 billion in aid for the three-year period of the PRSP, which was more than expected.[99] In response, however, the donors would come to expect MDG-related progress. In 2003, MDG tracking and reporting mechanisms were set up as the government and donors established quarterly high-level forums and a computerized aid management system, and the Donor Consortium assisted the government in policy review and program implementation.[100] This created additional social pressure and accountability on government actors, whose MDG performance thereafter was thoroughly evaluated and analyzed together with donors, who invested heavily in Ethiopia's MDG efforts. Motivated by this pressure and the prospect of debt relief, the government followed donor prescriptions and reported meticulously on MDG progress in its first PRSP progress report, issued in 2003.[101] As a result, "the report helped Ethiopia to qualify under the enhanced Highly Indebted Poor Country (HIPC) initiative for US$ 3.3 billion in additional relief."[102] Thus, policy adjustment to the MDGs generated

95   The Federal Democratic Republic of Ethiopia 2002.
96   UNDP 2005, 9.
97   UNDP 2005, 9.
98   Interview 41.
99   UNDP 2005, 10.
100 UNDP 2005, 10.
101 UNDP 2005, 11.
102 UNDP 2005, 11.

substantial aid allocations directed at MDG-related interventions to the Ethiopian government, confirming the operation aid conditionality.

Despite the progress in MDG alignment, the PRSP still lacked specified, scaled-up actions to achieve the MDGs by 2015.[103] The first MDG report, released in 2004, focused on clearly illustrating the gaps between PRSP and MDG targets, triggering the mechanism of social influence by exposing the government to external criticism and shaming for poor MDG performance.[104] The report concluded that MDG 3 was the least integrated of all MDGs and criticized the lack of specific and timebound MDG 3 targets.[105] Though expressing optimism regarding the narrowing gender gap in primary and secondary education, the report articulated deep concern over the slow progress in terms of female literacy, representation in parliament, and participation in productive activities.[106] In sum, the government was shamed for the overall status of gender equality in the country and for its inaction in relation to MDG 3. In 2004, the donors scaled up MDG performance monitoring in Ethiopia by funding the installation of new MDG monitoring software to enable targeted policies and programs and MDG data availability to non-technical audiences.[107] This further triggered the mechanism of social influence. The combined effects of the allocation of aid conditioned on stronger efforts toward MDG implementation and the social influence exerted on policymakers through thorough MDG monitoring and reporting resulted in an escalation in the government's MDG-related action.[108] This points to the effectiveness of the two causal mechanisms of influence.

Further reinforcing the international and domestic salience of the MDGs, two high-level events – a conference on the hunger MDG in Africa and an OECD conference on MDG implementation – were held in Addis Ababa in 2004. According to the UNDP, "both events indicated the value of the MDGs in attracting international attention to Ethiopia and as a means for directing increased aid."[109] This reinforces the idea that Ethiopia's embrace of the MDGs was associated with international praise and status as well as the prospect of increased aid. In addition to being targeted by a coordinated donor community operating in the country, Ethiopia – among the worst performers in the world in terms of poverty rates and gender equality at the time[110] – was selected as one of eight "pilot countries" for the Millennium Project.[111]

103 UNDP 2005, 11.
104 Federal Democratic Republic of Ethiopia and UNCT Ethiopia 2004, 41–42.
105 Federal Democratic Republic of Ethiopia and UNCT Ethiopia 2004, ii, viii–ix.
106 MoFED and UNCT 2004, 22.
107 UNDP 2005, 12.
108 UNDP 2005, 12.
109 UNDP 2005, 12.
110 In 2000, Ethiopia was the poorest country in the world and ranked 141 out of 143 in UNDP's gender development index (GDI), see UNDP 2000, 149–154.
111 See http://www.millennium-project.org/.

This entailed additional support to the Ethiopian government and the UNCT for the integration of MDG targets and timeframes in ongoing policy processes.[112] It moreover increased MDG monitoring, adding pressure on the government to proceed with MDG-related policy adjustment.

In 2004, the Millennium Project, the World Bank, and the UNCT supported the government in a major needs assessments for MDG implementation.[113] Hence, each government ministry was instructed to spell out targets, timelines, and budgets for MDG achievement in the PRSP.[114] This ensured a higher degree of direct responsibility and accountability for MDG performance at the ministry level, reinforcing the behavioral change pathway of direct elite responses. Despite some recent legal developments furthering women's rights,[115] MDG 3 progress still lagged behind other countries and the domestic advances made in relation to other goals. Consequently, the Women's Affairs Office was instructed to prepare a second National Action Plan for Gender Equality.[116] Thus, the performance monitoring, made public through MDG progress reports, had a significant impact on behavioral change at this early stage of MDG implementation.

In response to the criticism of the lack of MDG 3 integration in the PRSP, the 2005 PRSP Progress Report stated that "the government has moved decisively to advance the agenda on gender dimensions of poverty in the past year, and a significant number of initiatives are underway,"[117] revealing the Ethiopian government's response to the donors' criticism. As discussed, there was a sharp increase in gender equality-focused aid to fragile states during the MDG period.[118] Over the period 2012–2013, Ethiopia – among the poorest MDG 3 performers – received the second largest share of this category of aid, amounting to US\$ 721 million (or 49 percent of its total aid). This budget support targeted toward gender equality policy and interventions, coupled with the social pressure exerted on Ethiopian policymakers in interactions with development partners, generated a significant push for further MDG 3 implementation.

The PRSP process also demanded the inclusion of women's rights CSOs in the policymaking process. As in the Kenyan case, this channel of influence, coupled with the donors' economic support to CSOs,[119] strengthened civil society's policy influence through enhanced capacity and resources. As opposed to in Kenya, however, the Ethiopian civil society's political influence was significantly curtailed from 2009 onwards due to the Charities and

---

[112] UN Millennium Project 2005, 195.

[113] UNDP 2005, 13–14; UN Millennium Project 2005, 207.

[114] UNDP 2005, 13.

[115] E.g. the 2004 Family Code and the 2005 Criminal Code, Oxfam Canada 2012, 6–8.

[116] Demessie and Yitbark 2008, 113; UNDP 2005, 13.

[117] MoFED 2005, 49.

[118] OECD/DAC 2015.

[119] Interview 27, Interview 30, Interview 40.

Societies Proclamation. The law prohibits organizations that receive more than 10 percent of their funding from foreign sources to work with human rights, including the promotion of women's rights.[120] Importantly, this also prohibits CSOs from monitoring and reporting on women's rights violations and from holding the government to account for gender equality performance. Thus, domestic pressure for MDG adjustment was limited between 2009 and 2015.

Despite the circumscription of the domestic pathway, the Ethiopian institutions for MDG monitoring and reporting established by the donors and the Ethiopian government ensured a high level of government accountability in relation to MDG performance. The government's concern for its reputation and, hence, vulnerability to social influence strategies is illustrated in the following statement by a UNICEF representative:

> [I]f you look at the definition of famine in the *Oxford Dictionary*, it still says Ethiopia, you know. So they want to remove that completely ... And one of the ways they can do that is to show their obtainment of the MDGs because then they can stand up and say to the other African nations and the rest of the world – we've achieved MDG 4, we've achieved MDG 7. We're no longer that country that you thought we were in the 1980s.[121]

Though the period 2000–2005 witnessed a noteworthy policy adjustment to the MDGs, the gap between gender policy adoption and implementation had remained.[122] In 2006, as a baseline for the new gender policy – the second NAP-GE[123] – the new Ministry of Women's Affairs summarized the current situation with regard to gender equality in the country. This amounted to a scathing critique of government inaction.[124] The alleged institutional incapacity was confirmed by many of the interview respondents.[125] In order to get to grips with the government's failure to act, the new gender action plan mandated gender mainstreaming and gender-budgeting in all ministries. Disconcertingly, a 2008 review of the government's efforts concluded that " ... there is no clear evidence as to what has been achieved owing to the introduction of the women's policy and the action plans."[126]

In response to the public shaming of the Ethiopian Government for gender equality inaction, the new Ministry of Women, Children and Youth Affairs and six UN agencies together initiated the Joint Programme for Gender Equality and Women's Empowerment (JP GEWE) in 2011. The program aimed to enhance the pressure on the government for, and aid allocation to, MDG 3 implementation.[127] However, a program evaluation revealed major limitations

---

[120] Amnesty International 2011, 4.
[121] Interview 24.
[122] Interview 29, Interview 35, Interview 40, Interview 41.
[123] MoWA 2006.
[124] MoWA 2006.
[125] Interview 25, Interview 28, Interview 30, Interview 33, Interview 34, Interview 36, Interview 39, Interview 41.
[126] Demessie and Yitbark 2008, 117.
[127] UN One 2013, iv.

in terms of budgets and documentation practices and discrepancies between a strong conceptual program design and weak implementation.[128] Commenting on the overall performance of the Ministry, the USAID representative echoed this inconsistency between vision and practice:

[T]here is a commitment at the Ministry. Still, when it comes to the actual work and the implementation, this is mainly pushed by donors. So there is a lot of push within the gender equality area from the international community. ... So there are good policy frameworks but the challenge is implementation.[129]

Regarding the institutionalization of MDG 3 concerns, a 2012 review by the Ethiopian government and the UN concluded that the implementation of gender mainstreaming and budgeting thus far had failed.[130] Consequently, despite the development of a formal institutional context for gender equality, " ...the institutionalization of gender equality has not met objectives, due to inadequate staffing, equipment and training."[131] According to the Ethiopian human rights scholar interviewed "there is a problem with implementation of policy, which derives from a lack of commitment to gender equality at the higher level. ... So the machineries are there but they are not empowered, not capacitated. A gender awareness is severely lacking"[132] In line with this, the EU Delegation representative commented that "it's the same in the whole administrative structure – horizontally and vertically in all the women's machineries... When you meet people on the ground, they say we lack trainings, we lack budgets, and so on."[133]

Hence, despite the MDGs' creation of an enabling environment for the promotion of gender equality in Ethiopia,[134] the failure to implement adopted gender policies slowed the pace of MDG 3 progress. The empirical evidence suggests that the government's lack of sufficient political will was an important factor in explaining gender equality inertia,[135] signaling the failure of MDG 3-related socialization or learning. The relationship between MDG 3 policy and action in Ethiopia toward the end of the MDG period was summarized by a representative of the Finnish International Development Agency in the following way:

I still see that there is much of a gap really. It's being said in words [but] in practice with respect to gender issues, not much has been done I can say ... There are the gender officers ... the gender focal points and things like that. But in real terms, I cannot say that really those things have been addressed ... Sometimes, there are more political [statements] than [action] in practical terms.[136]

---

[128] UN One 2013, viii.
[129] Interview 35.
[130] UNICEF Ethiopia 2012, 23–24.
[131] Oxfam Canada 2012, 3.
[132] Interview 41.
[133] Interview 23.
[134] Demessie and Yitbark 2008, 114.
[135] Demessie and Yitbark 2008, 119.
[136] Interview 29.

In conclusion, the analysis of the Ethiopian MDG 3 implementation process has shown that policy adjustment mainly was promoted through the donors' aid conditionality and social influence strategies and – to a lesser extent – domestic pressure for change. Hence, hypotheses 1–3 are deemed strengthened, though the inability of domestic civil society to mobilize and conduct advocacy work following 2009 largely incapacitated this mechanism of influence. Thus, even though the domestic pathway generated additional pressure for policy adjustment throughout the MDG period in the Kenyan case, the externally driven incentive-based influence mechanisms were the primary triggers of change in both cases. As a consequence of their operation, some progress in terms of gender equality policy frameworks was achieved in Ethiopia during the MDG period. Nevertheless, much like in the Kenyan case, the incapacity of government gender institutions and the slow progress in policy implementation reflect an insistent lack of political will within this policy area during the studied period. Depending on the new government's course of action, sustained gender equality progress during the SDG period may depend on the continued exertion of external pressure within the gender equality area.

CONCLUSIONS

The MDGs entailed the introduction of a comprehensive set of GPIs within the area of international development. Despite a broad MDG literature, the domestic effects and influence mechanisms of development GPIs have remained unclear. By mapping the extent of policy adjustment to MDG 3 in 15 Sub-Saharan African countries and exploring the causal mechanisms of gender policy change in two cases, this chapter has arrived at three main findings. First, it has demonstrated that the MDGs had a decisive effect on gender equality policy commitments in Sub-Saharan Africa, indicating the effectiveness of development GPIs in influencing domestic policy. Second, it has shown that despite the considerable effects on policy goal-setting, the adoption of implementation plans to address the goals was much more modest. This suggests that commitments and rhetorical adjustments to the MDGs exceeded actual behavioral change in terms of MDG-based programming, at least within the contested area of gender equality. Third, process-tracing of the Kenyan and Ethiopian policy processes has revealed that policy adoption and implementation processes were primarily activated through the interaction of mechanisms working through transnational pressure, direct elite responses, and domestic politics. Specifically, the donor-driven causal mechanisms of aid conditionality and social influence, complemented by the mobilization and empowerment of domestic CSOs promoting change, explain MDG adjustment in the two cases. Though some government officials may have internalized the normative content of MDG 3 during the policy processes, the evidence has pointed to a lack of socialization and learning on the part of government actors in both cases. This is reflected in the continued negotiation and resistance characterizing the different stages of MDG 3 implementation. Moreover, the case studies have illustrated the non-linear and contested character of gender equality behavioral change, typically underplayed in diffusion and socialization research.

Beyond pointing to the overall effectiveness of development GPIs, and illustrating the particular pathways of domestic GPI influence, the conclusions of this study have three broader implications. First, development GPIs may effectively stimulate domestic GPI-related commitments when they trigger transnational as well as domestic pressure and mechanisms for behavioral change. Second, while incentive-based causal mechanisms may prompt domestic policy change, reforms may ultimately be superficial and unsustainable as policy is likely to be realtered as new targets or priorities are introduced. In the case of gender policy, where progress typically occurs slowly due to normative contestation at the national level, deeper GPI-related behavioral change will then ultimately depend on the continued exertion of pressure until desired outcomes have been achieved. Third, the MDGs did little to change the power structures of development cooperation despite the agenda's ambition to do so. While donors now may stress terms like ownership and partnership, and are more reluctant to talk about their conditions of support as aid conditionality, the practice of international development cooperation suggests that little has changed since the SAP era. Development GPIs like the MDGs seem to be associated with similar top-down influence strategies as preceding periods. Yet, the domestic resistance to GPI influence that the MDG 3 process points to may contradict those who have warned of the risks, associated with the proliferation of GPIs, of governing at a distance through overly rigid, externally imposed standards.[137] The SDG agenda's emphasis on countries' rights to themselves prioritize among the globally set targets in order to accommodate national and local agendas and needs could potentially contribute to more sustainable development outcomes and the true dispersion of agenda-setting power.

References

Acharya, Amitav. 2004. How Ideas Spread: Whose Norms Matter? Norm Localization and Institutional Change in Asian Regionalism. *International Organization* 58 (2):239–75.

African Development Bank. 2004. Ethiopia. Multi-Sector Country Gender Profile. Available at http://www.afdb.org/fileadmin/uploads/afdb/Documents/Project-and-Operations/ADBGenderEthiopia.pdf. Accessed March 29, 2016.

Alston, Philip. 2005. Ships Passing in the Night: The Current State of the Human Rights and Development Debate Seen through the Lens of the Millennium Development Goals. *Human Rights Quarterly* 27 (3):755–829.

---

[137] See e.g. Merry 2016; Rosga and Satterthwaie 2009.

Amnesty International. 2011. Ethiopia Briefing to the UN Committee on the Elimination of Discrimination against Women, 49th session, July 2011. London: Amnesty International Publications.

Barton, Carol. 2005. Where to for Women's Movements and the MDGs? *Gender & Development* 13 (1):25–34.

Beach, Derek, and Rasmus Brun Pedersen. 2013. *Process-Tracing Methods: Foundations and Guidelines*. Ann Arbor, MI: University of Michigan Press.

Bertelsmann Stiftung. 2016. *Civil Society Participation, Bertelsmann Transformation Index*. Available at https://www.bti-project.org/en/reports/downloads/bti-2016/. Accessed March 1, 2019.

Bisbee, James H., James R. Hollyer, B. Peter Rosendorff, and James Raymond Vreeland. this volume. The Millennium Development Goals and Education: Accountability and Substitution in Global Indicators. In *The Power of Global Performance Indicators*, edited by Judith Kelley and Beth A. Simmons. New York: Cambridge University Press.

Börzel, Tanja A., and Thomas Risse. 2012. From Europeanisation to Diffusion: Introduction. *West European Politics* 35 (1):1–19.

Bruns, Barbara, Alain Mingat, and Ramahatra Rakotomalala. 2003. *Achieving Universal Primary Education by 2015: A Chance for Every Child*. Washington, DC: World Bank.

Checkel, Jeffrey T. 2015. Mechanisms, Process, and the Study of International Institutions. In *Process Tracing: From Metaphor to Analytic Tool*, edited by Andrew Bennett and Jeffrey T. Checkel, 74–97. Cambridge: Cambridge University Press.

Clemens, Michael A., Charles J. Kenny, and Todd J. Moss. 2007. The Trouble with the MDGs: Confronting Expectations of Aid and Development Success. *World Development* 35 (5):735–51.

Cortell, Andrew P., and James W. Davis. 1996. How Do International Institutions Matter? The Domestic Impact of International Rules and Norms. *International Studies Quarterly* 40 (4):451–78.

——— 2005. When Norms Clash: International Norms, Domestic Practices, and Japan's Internalisation of the GATT/WTO. *Review of International Studies* 31 (1):3–25.

Demessie, Sosena, and Tsahai Yitbark. 2008. A Review of National Policy on Ethiopian Women. In *Digest of Ethiopia's National Policies, Strategies and Programs*, edited by Taye Assefa, 93–126. Addis Ababa: African Books Collective.

The Federal Democratic Republic of Ethiopia. 2000. *Interim Poverty Reduction Strategy Paper 2000/01–2002/03*. Addis Ababa: Federal Democratic Republic of Ethiopia.

——— 2002. *Ethiopia: Sustainable Development and Poverty Reduction Program*. Addis Ababa: Federal Democratic Republic of Ethiopia.

Federal Democratic Republic of Ethiopia and UNCT Ethiopia. 2004. *Millennium Development Goals Report: Challenges and Prospects for Ethiopia*. Addis Ababa, Ethiopia: Ministry of Finance and Economic Development (MoFED), Federal Democratic Republic of Ethiopia and the United Nations Country Team in Ethiopia.

Feyissa, Dereje. 2011. Aid Negotiation: The Uneasy "Partnership" between EPRDF and the Donors. *Journal of Eastern African Studies* 5 (4):788–817.

Freedom House. 2017. *Freedom in the World 2017: Populists and Autocrats. The Dual Threat to Global Democracy.* New York: Freedom House.

Fukuda-Parr, Sakiko. 2008. Are the MDGs Priority in Development Strategies and Aid Programmes? Only Few Are!, Working Paper, International Poverty Centre, No. 48.

2014. Global Goals as a Policy Tool: Intended and Unintended Consequences. *Journal of Human Development and Capabilities* 15 (2–3):118–31.

2017. *Millennium Development Goals: Ideas, Interests and Influence.* New York: Routledge.

Fukuda-Parr, Sakiko, and David Hulme. 2011. International Norm Dynamics and the "End of Poverty": Understanding the Millennium Development Goals. *Global Governance: A Review of Multilateralism and International Organizations* 17 (1):17–36.

Harmonization, Alignment and Coordination (HAC) Donor Working Group. 2007. *Kenya Joint Assistance Strategy 2007–2012.* Nairobi: HAC Donor Working Group.

Holzinger, Katharina, and Cristoph Knill. 2008. Theoretical Framework: Causal Factors and Convergence Expectations. In *Environmental Policy Convergence in Europe: The Impact of International Institutions and Trade,* edited by Katharina Holzinger, Christoph Knill, Bas Arts, 30–63. Cambridge: Cambridge University Press.

Hulme, David. 2009. The Millennium Development Goals (MDGs): A Short History of the World's Biggest Promise. BWPI Working Paper 100. Available at http://papers.ssrn.com/sol3/papers.cfm?abstract_id=1544271. Accessed March 29, 2016.

International Monetary Fund (IMF). 2005. *Kenya: Joint Staff Assessment of the Poverty Reduction Strategy Paper.* Washington, DC: IMF.

2010. *Kenya: Joint Staff Advisory Note of the Poverty Reduction Strategy Paper.* Washington, DC: IMF.

2011. *The Federal Democratic Republic of Ethiopia: Joint Staff Advisory Note on the Growth and Transformation Plan 2010/11–2014/15.* Washington, DC: IMF.

Johnston, Alistair Iain. 2001. Treating International Institutions as Social Environments. *International Studies Quarterly* 45 (4):487–515.

Kabeer, Naila. 2003. *Gender Mainstreaming in Poverty Eradication and the Millennium Development Goals: A Handbook for Policy-Makers and Other Stakeholders.* London: The Commonwealth Secretariat.

Kelley, Judith. 2004. International Actors on the Domestic Scene: Membership Conditionality and Socialization by International Institutions. *International Organization* 58 (3):425–57.

Kelley, Judith G., and Beth A. Simmons. 2015. Politics by Number: Indicators as Social Pressure in International Relations. *American Journal of Political Science* 59 (1):55–70.

2019. Introduction: The Power of Global Performance Indicators.

Langford, Malcolm. 2010. A Poverty of Rights: Six Ways to Fix the MDGs. *IDS Bulletin* 41 (1):83–91.

Lucci, Paula, Amina Khan, and Chris Hoy. 2015. Piecing together the MDG Puzzle: Domestic Policy, Government Spending and Performance. ODI Working Paper 426.

Manning, Richard. 2010. The Impact and Design of the MDGs: Some Reflections. *IDS Bulletin* 41 (1):7–14.

Merry, Sally Engle. 2016. *The Seductions of Quantification: Measuring Human Rights, Gender Violence, and Sex Trafficking.* Chicago, IL: The University of Chicago Press.

Ministry of Finance and Economic Development (MoFED). 2005. *Ethiopia: Sustainable Development and Poverty Reduction Program (SDPRP). Annual Progress Report (2003/04).* Addis Ababa: Federal Democratic Republic of Ethiopia.

Ministry of Women's Affairs (MoWA). 2006. *National Action Plan for Gender Equality (NAP-GE).* Addis Ababa: Federal Democratic Republic of Ethiopia.

National Planning Commission and the United Nations in Ethiopia. 2015. *Millennium Development Goals Report 2014 Ethiopia. Assessment of Ethiopia's Progress towards the MDGs.* Addis Ababa: The United Nations.

OECD. 2015. *States of Fragility 2015: Meeting Post-2015 Ambitions.* Paris: OECD Publishing.

OECD/DAC. 2015. Financing UN Security Council Resolution 1325: Aid in Support of Gender Equality and Women's Rights in Fragile Contexts – OECD. Available at http://www.oecd.org/dac/gender-development/ Financing%20UN%20Security%20Council%20resolution%201325% 20FINAL.pdf. Accessed August 27, 2019.

Oxfam Canada. 2012. Country Profile: Ethiopia. Available at https:// www.itacaddis.org/docs/2013_09_24_08_07_10_Country%20Profile_ Ethiopia%20Oxfam%202012.pdf. Accessed August 27, 2019.

Puddington, Arch, and Tyler Roylance. 2017. *Freedom in the World 2017: Populists and Autocrats. The Dual Threat to Global Democracy.* Freedom House. Available at https://freedomhouse.org/report/freedom-world/ freedom-world-2017. Accessed August 27, 2019.

Republic of Kenya. 2007. *Gender Mainstreaming Implementation Plan of Action for the National Policy on Gender and Development. Draft Report.* Nairobi: Ministry of Gender, Sports, Culture and Social Services.

2008a. *Kenya Vision 2030.* Nairobi: Ministry of Planning, National Development and Vision 2030.

2008b. *Kenya Vision 2030: First Medium Term Plan 2008–2012.* Nairobi: Ministry of Planning, National Development and Vision 2030.

2013. *Kenya Vision 2030: Second Medium Term Plan 2013–2017.* Nairobi: Ministry of Devolution and Planning.

Republic of Kenya and the International Monetary Fund (IMF). 2005. *Kenya: Poverty Reduction Strategy Paper.* Washington, DC: IMF.

Risse, Thomas, Stephen C. Ropp, and Kathryn Sikkink, eds. 2013. *The Persistent Power of Human Rights: From Commitment to Compliance.* New York: Cambridge University Press.

Rosga, AnnJanette, and Margaret L. Satterthwaie. 2009. The Trust in Indicators: Measuring Human Rights. *Berkeley Journal of International Law* 27 (2):253–315.

Sakiko Fukuda-Parr, and Hulme, David. 2009. International Norm Dynamics and "the End of Poverty": Understanding the Millennium Development Goals (MDGs), Brooks World Poverty Institute Working Paper 96. Available at http://sakikofukudaparr.net/wp-content/uploads/2013/01/InternationalNormDynamics2009.pdf. Accessed March 29, 2016.

Schimmelfennig, Frank. 2003. *The EU, NATO and the Integration of Europe: Rules and Rhetoric*. Cambridge: Cambridge University Press.

Scott, Andrew, and Paula Lucci. 2015. Universality and Ambition in the Post-2015 Development Agenda: A Comparison of Global and National Targets. *Journal of International Development* 27 (6):752–75.

Simmons, Beth A. 2009. *Mobilizing for Human Rights: International Law in Domestic Politics*. Cambridge: Cambridge University Press.

Transitional Government of Ethiopia, Office of the Prime Minister. 1993. *National Policy on Ethiopian Women*. Addis Ababa: Transitional Government of Ethiopia.

UNICEF Ethiopia. 2012. *Investing in Boys and Girls in Ethiopia: Past, Present and Future*. Addis Ababa: UNICEF.

United Nations. 2001. *Road Map towards the Implementation of the United Nations Millennium Declaration: Report of the Secretary-General*. Available at http://bases.bireme.br/cgi-bin/wxislind.exe/iah/online/?IsisScript=iah/iah.xis &src=google&base=REPIDISCA&lang=p&nextAction=lnk&exprSearch= 10830&indexSearch=ID.

    2014. *The Millennium Development Goals Report 2014*. New York: United Nations.

    2015. *The Millennium Development Goals Report 2015*. New York: United Nations.

United Nations Development Program (UNDP). 2000. *Human Development Report 2000*. New York: Oxford University Press.

    2005. Linking the National Poverty Reduction Strategy to the MDGs: A Case Study of Ethiopia. Available at http://unpan1.un.org/intradoc/groups/public/documents/un/unpan032503.pdf. Accessed March 29, 2016.

United Nations General Assembly (UNGA). 2001. United Nations Millennium Declaration. Available at http://www.un.org/millennium/declaration/ares552e.htm. Accessed March 29, 2016.

UN Millennium Project. 2005. *Investing in Development. A Practical Plan to Achieve the Millennium Development Goals*. London: Earthscan.

UN One. 2013. *Ethiopia Joint Flagship Programme on Gender Equality and Women's Empowerment (JP GEWE) End-Evaluation of Phase 1. Final Report*. Addis Ababa: United Nations.

UN Population Division, Department of Economic and Social Affairs. 2015. Population in 1999 and 2000: All Countries. Available at http://www.un.org/popin/popdiv/pop1999-00.pdf. Accessed March 29, 2016.

The World Bank. 2005. Summary Report, Kenya Consultative Group Meeting, Nairobi, April 11–12, 2005. Available at http://siteresources.worldbank.org/INTKENYA/Resources/summary_report.pdf. Accessed March 24, 2016.

    2012. *World Development Report 2012: Gender Equality and Development*. Washington, DC: The World Bank.

PART II

THE NORMATIVE INFLUENCE OF RATINGS AND RANKINGS

5

A Race to the Top? The Aid Transparency Index and the Social Power of Global Performance Indicators

Dan Honig and Catherine Weaver

One of the more striking examples of the power that global performance indicators exercise in world politics is the case of the Aid Transparency Index (ATI), an annual rating and ranking of international development assistance donor agencies by Publish What You Fund (PWYF).[1] PWYF was established as a nongovernmental organization (NGO) in 2008 to monitor the progress of international donors by disclosing where they spend their aid funds, on whom, and for what. PWYF is small, with nine staff members and a 2017 budget of less than £600,000.[2] Housed in a modest one-room office above an Italian restaurant on London's South Bank, PWYF has no direct material power with which to coerce change in the behavior of these large multilateral and bilateral donors.

Nonetheless, the ATI has contributed greatly to global aid transparency. The ATI has attained and exercised significant symbolic and normative power by defining clear indicators and benchmarks for donor transparency.[3] Its authority derives from its independence and its process of working with donors and external reviewers to construct and validate the annual ratings and rankings. The ATI catalyzes behavior change by publicly comparing and categorizing donors as "very good," "good," "fair," "poor," and "very poor" performers, thus invoking peer reputation and status concerns and mobilizing pressure for donor reforms.

---

[1] UK Charity Registration #1158362. In the interests of full disclosure, both authors have a prior relationship with the organization. Weaver worked as an external reviewer for the ATI's 2016 and 2018 indices. Honig has a long-standing friendship with PWYF's CEO at the time this study was conducted, Rupert Simons. Neither Simons nor PWYF have had any influence over the research questions asked or results discussed here, though PWYF has commented on drafts of the paper for errors of fact regarding PWYF's activities.

[2] Publish What You Fund Annual Report 2017.

[3] This is consistent with the theory articulated in this volume's introduction, Kelley and Simmons 2019.

This is important. Since the first High-Level Forum on Aid Effectiveness in Rome in 2003, a cascade of initiatives and organizations have sought to pry open the spigot of information on donor agencies' projects and programs.[4] The principles of transparency and open data are centrally embedded in the 2030 Sustainable Development Goals and the UN's "Data Revolution,"[5] in hopes of centralizing information and improving donor coordination, country-level development planning, and management.[6] Advocates also claim that transparency empowers the poor by providing opportunities for citizen voice and feedback. For example, in January 2018, two Ebola survivors from Sierra Leone sued their government, alleging that it had misdirected millions of dollars of foreign aid marked for the Ebola crisis.[7] Transparency, simply put, promises to make aid more inclusive, accountable, and effective. The notion that transparency is coincident with public disclosure of greater information is not limited to the ATI. For example, Hollyer, Rosendorff, and Vreeland have taken greater public disclosure to be a key element of transparency in a series of scholarly publications.[8]

However, to an aid industry long subject to public scrutiny, the push for transparency presents a double-edged sword. On the one hand, the transparency agenda promises to assuage NGOs, civil society organizations (CSOs), and national parliaments who have long demanded enhanced access to donor information as a tool for accountability. On the other, as our interviews with donor staff and management suggest, transparency also threatens to lift the veil on internal processes that might disrupt donors' relationships with borrowers, introduce onerous reporting burdens, and invite further interrogation from parties disaffected by aid programs. Not all donor agency staff agree that the ATI's thirty-nine indicators represent the "right path" toward transparency. PWYF's efforts to promote convergence on the ATI's particular standards are not simply a matter of pushing on an open door. The ATI constitutes a critical case study that can address key questions regarding under what conditions and through what mechanisms an NGO-produced Global Performance Indicator (GPI)

---

[4] For reviews of transparency and accountability initiatives in global development, including campaigns and initiatives focused on aid transparency, see Carothers and Brechenmacher 2014; Darby 2010; Gaventa and McGee 2013.

[5] See "Guiding Principles of Data Reporting and Data Sharing for the Global Monitoring of the 2030 Agenda for Sustainable Development," https://unstats.un.org/sdgs/files/meetings/iaeg-sdgs-meeting-06/2017-10-04_CCSA%20Guiding%20Principles%20data%20flows.pdf.

[6] Interviews with Owen Barder, Center for Global Development [June 26, 2011]; and with Tony German, Development Initiatives, January 11, 2017. See also Barder 2016; Carothers and Brechenmacher 2014; Collin, Zubairi, Nielson and Barder 2009; Florini 2007; Herrling 2015; Mulley 2010; Publish What You Fund 2009.

[7] Cooper Inveen, "Ebola Survivors Sue Government of Sierra Leone Over Missing Millions," *The Guardian*, January 5, 2018. Retrieved from https://amp.theguardian.com/global-development/2018/jan/05/ebola-survivors-sue-sierra-leone-government-over-missing-ebola-millions?CMP=share_btn_tw&__twitter_impression=true, January 13, 2018.

[8] Hollyer, Rosendorff, and Vreeland 2011, 2014, 2015, 2018a, 2018b.

can influence powerful actors to do what they otherwise might not do on their own volition. Bisbee et al.; Doshi et al.; and Skagerlind's contributions to this volume demonstrate the impact of GPIs propogated in part by international donors (the Millennium Development Goals and Ease of Doing Business indicators, respectively) on the behavior of countries.[9] We explore whether the donor community is also itself influenced by GPIs. We find that the ATI does affect donors' transparency practices, but not evenly. Agencies that have aid distribution as their primary operational mandate (e.g. the US Agency for International Development) are much more likely to respond to the ATI than donors for whom the provision of official development assistance is secondary to their core mandate (e.g. the US Department of Defense). When agencies respond to the ATI, they do so because of the ATI's influence on policy *elites*. The ATI diffuses via networks of elite actors, consistent with Morse's findings in her analysis of the Financial Action Task Force (FATF) in this volume.[10]

Similarly to the findings in Kijima and Lipscy, Koliev et al. and Roberts and Tellez' contributions to this volume the ATI operates via normative pressure, which in the ATI's case operates through professional networks.[11] Elites worry about their status in their peer group of aid professionals and are susceptible to socialization around new norms. The very process of being closely monitored and regularly interacting with the PWYF team produces inter- and intra-organizational learning and norm diffusion, and professionalizes aid staff and management around ATI's standards. Secondarily, the ATI enhances domestic *political pressure* by equipping transparency reform proponents (particularly those with some material power over aid agencies) with critical information and clear standards to guide policy change.

In what follows, we provide a brief overview of the international aid transparency movement to provide context for our study of the ATI. We use quantitative analysis to understand variation in donor performance on, and donor response to, the ATI. Then we further examine mechanisms using qualitative interview evidence.[12] This qualitative research enables us to dig deeper into how the channels of influence work. Together, our quantitative and qualitative evidence informs our conclusion that the ATI does in fact influence donors, and does so primarily through elite channels of influence and secondarily through its indirect influence via political pressure of donors' principals.

---

[9] Bisbee et al. this volume; Doshi et al. 2019; Skagerlind 2019.

[10] Morse 2019.

[11] Kijima and Weaver 2019; Koliev et al. 2019; Roberts and Tellez 2019.

[12] Specifically, as part of a broader project on aid transparency between 2010 and 2017, Weaver personally interviewed or sent trained graduate research assistants to conduct 465 interviews in eight countries, with a concentrated focus on members of the development community based in the US (DC and New York), the United Kingdom, Kenya, Uganda, Malawi, and Nepal. These interviews are listed in the online appendix and discussed further later.

THE INTERNATIONAL AID TRANSPARENCY
MOVEMENT AND THE ATI

The transparency movement represents a sea change for international aid. Ten years ago, if you wanted to find out how much development assistance was going to Kenya, to whom, and for what, you would have needed high-bandwidth access to the Organisation for Economic Co-operation and Development's (OECD) creditor reporting system and the ability to decipher the complex accounting jargon of elaborate spreadsheets. Even then, only highly aggregated data were available. Actual project documents, which might or might not have contained information on the subnational locations of aid activities, implementing partners, and details on project objectives, could be attained only in hardcopy and for a fee, through a few select donors' public information centers. Borrower governments themselves had scant knowledge of where the aid was in their country. As one Malawian Deputy Minister of Finance told us in 2010, "We don't really know where the aid is in our country, what [it] is doing, and who is doing it. How can we plan to properly spend government money to build schools, hire doctors, or provide services when we don't know if our donor partners are already doing this?"[13]

By 2017, the aid information landscape had dramatically changed. It is easy now to go directly to the World Bank's website to find full project documents. Most major donors have created public dashboards, with infographics and interactive maps. The International Aid Transparency Initiative, established in 2008, is rapidly moving toward a common, publicly accessible database with standardized information on the precise geographical locations of aid, budget data, and activity-level project details. While significant challenges remain, the past decade has been nothing short of a revolution in aid data.[14] Achieving this transparency in the multibillion dollar global aid industry has not been an easy task. Donor agencies have enjoyed relative opacity for most of their existence. Past efforts to enact fundamental changes in national freedom of information acts and organizational information disclosure policies have been met with resistance and persistent delays.[15] Numerous published analyses and interviews point out pervasive problems of organizational inertia, staff's cultural fears surrounding transparency, and a myriad of technological and economic barriers to change.[16]

PWYF was established in 2008 by International Aid Transparency Initiative (IATI) advocates, including founding CEO Karin Christiansen, with funding from the Hewlett Foundation and Open Society Foundation. Three short years later, at the Fourth High Level Forum on Aid Effectiveness in Busan, South Korea, in November 2011, most major donor countries and

---

[13] Interview with Deputy Minister of Finance, government of Malawi, Nairobi, Kenya, December 2010.
[14] Lee 2016.
[15] Carothers and Brechenmacher 2014; Florini 2007; Ingram 2015; Nelson 2001.
[16] Bent 2015; Weaver and Peratsakis 2014.

agencies – including many from the global south – committed themselves to reporting their aid information to a common standard.[17] A rich set of supranational initiatives (such as the EU Aid Transparency Guarantee and the Global Partnership for Effective Development Cooperation), national-level policies, open data systems,[18] and international non-governmental organizations and networks have since been created to advocate for open aid data.[19] PWYF's ATI plays a specific role in this advocacy movement by translating the broad goals of transparency into measurable standards of performance and using ratings and rankings to monitor and enforce donor agencies' compliance with these international commitments.

The ATI works explicitly through engagement with donors and independent experts to collate annual data. Publish What You Fund publishes the evaluation criteria for a given year's index and engages in a three-month dialogue with every aid agency prior to the finalization of annual ATI scores. There were annual releases of the ATI from 2011 to 2016.[20] While the methodology of the ATI has been modified slightly over time, the ATI has always focused on publishing specific data regarding aid flows at the activity level – that is, the details regarding particular interventions and projects. While the ATI is primarily disseminated to the public via hierarchical rankings of agencies into

---

[17] The standard combined three complementary systems: the Organisation for Economic Co-operation and Development (OECD) Development Assistance Committee (DAC) Creditor Reporting System (CRS++), the OECD DAC Forward Spending Survey (FSS), and the International Aid Transparency Initiative (IATI). See https://stats.oecd.org/Index.aspx?DataSetCode=CRS1, https://stats.oecd.org/Index.aspx?DataSetCode=FSS, and http://www.aidtransparency.net for more on each of the three systems.

[18] For example, many countries – especially lead countries such as Sweden, Britain, Denmark, and the US – adopted national transparency guarantees with specific references to aid (Sweden, Britain), integrated aid transparency commitments within their Open Government Partnership National Action Plans, and similar open aid data strategies and policy papers. In the US case, see Obama's executive order on open government (Obama 2009) and the Office of Management and Budget's open government directive (Orszag 2009). For examples of aid transparency systems, see the UK Department for International Development's DevTracker, Sweden's openaid.se, Denmark's Danida Open Aid USAID's Global Aid Explorer, and the US Government's Foreign Assistance Dashboard. See also Clare, Verhust, and Young 2016; Speech by the Secretary of State for International Development, Justine Greening, MP, at an event hosted by PWYF, BOND, and UK Aid Network, 2012, on file with authors.

[19] See, for example, AidData, Aidwatch, aidinfo, Development Gateway, DevInfo, Development Initiatives, Data2X, Interaction, Modernizing Foreign Assistance Network, Open Aid Partnership, Oxfam International, and many others.

[20] In that time there were five full waves of the ATI: 2011, 2012, 2013, 2014, and 2016, In 2015, PWYF conducted a mid-term review covering only EU and US agencies. The 2011 data were called a "pilot index"; there was also a 2010 assessment, but at a country level and based on perceptions surveys. While annual through 2016 (the last data included in this paper), the ATI has now transitioned to an eighteen-month cycle. (E-mail from Elise Dufief, PWYF Research Manager, November 21, 2017), and there is no 2017 ATI. The 2018 index was launched in June 2018, after conditional acceptance of this paper. We therefore do not consider the 2018 data, with data through 2016 included in the analysis.

categories (good, fair, poor, etc.), these rankings draw from a continuous scale drawn from a series of indicators. There are currently thirty-nine indicators in the ATI, which cover information such as project title, description, budget, and objectives of interventions. Table 5.1 provides greater detail.

The comprehensive index largely evaluates national government agencies and international organizations, as well as a few foundations (e.g. Hewlett and Gates). The primary focus is bilateral aid agencies (e.g. the US Agency for International Development or the UK Department for International Development) and major multilateral aid-focused organizations (e.g. the UN Development Program or the World Bank), who together account for the vast majority of official development assistance (ODA). The index also includes agencies that disburse significant amounts of foreign aid, even though development assistance is not their primary mandate. For example, the 2016 index includes six US government agencies, only three of whom have ODA as a primary mandate.[21]

WHEN AND HOW DOES THE ATI INFLUENCE AID DONORS?

A recent survey of staff within US development agencies revealed that over 75 percent of respondents thought the ATI had a "very positive impact" on their own agency's transparency efforts.[22] To what extent does observable agency behavior support this claim? If indeed the ATI influences organizational practices, under what conditions do we observe this impact? How exactly does the ATI influence targeted donors? Key informants and our examination of agency-level documents suggest that not all donors are equally concerned about, or responsive to, the ATI's assessment of their agencies' performance.[23] One key mediating factor appears to shape agencies' reaction to the ATI: whether their primary mandate is to provide ODA.

In the introduction to this volume Kelley and Simmons suggest there are several possible channels of influence for GPIs.[24] In the case of the ATI, our

[21] The three agencies with aid as a primary mandate are the US Agency for International Development (USAID), the Millennium Challenge Corporation (MCC), and the President's Emergency Plan for AIDS Relief (PEPFAR). The other three US agencies are the US Department of Defense, the US Department of State, and the US Department of the Treasury. While the US has the greatest number of evaluated agencies in 2016 (and 2014, the year with the broadest coverage), it is not alone in having multiple units evaluated. In 2014, five UK, three German, and three French agencies were evaluated. Among multilaterals, four European Commission (EC) and three United Nations (UN) agencies were evaluated. The online appendix provides a complete listing of all covered agencies and their inclusion in the various waves of the ATI.

[22] Friends of Publish What You Fund 2016, 10.

[23] Interview with Sally Paxton (Publish What You Fund, October 2015), George Ingram (Brookings Institution, October 2015), Nilmini Gunaratne Rubin (US Foreign Affairs Committee, September 2014), and two senior staff at USAID (September 2014).

[24] Kelley and Simmons 2019.

TABLE 5.1. *2016 ATI indicators and weights*

ATI Total Score out of 100%

1. **Commitment to Aid Transparency (10%)**
   - Quality of FOIA Legislation (3.33%)
   - Implementation Schedule (for IATI Common Standard) (3.33%)
   - Accessibility of Aid Information through donor portals, databases, etc. (3.33%)

2. **Organizational-Level Publications (25%)**
   - Planning: Strategy Documents (2.5%)
   - Planning: Annual Report (2.5%)
   - Planning: Allocation Policy by Themes or Countries (2.5%)
   - Planning: Procurement Policy (2.5%)
   - Planning: Strategy Documents – Country Level (2.5%)
   - Financial: Total Organization Budget (three year forward spending) (4.17%)
   - Financial: Disaggregated Budget (4.17%)
   - Financial: Audits (4.17%)

3. **Activity-Level Publications (65%)**
   - Basic Activity Information: Implementer (1.63%)
   - Basic Activity Information: Unique ID (1.63%)
   - Basic Activity Information: Title (1.63%)
   - Basic Activity Information: Description of Activity (1.63%)
   - Basic Activity Information: Planned Dates (1.63%)
   - Basic Activity Information: Actual Dates (1.63%)
   - Basic Activity Information: Current Status (1.63%)
   - Basic Activity Information: Contact Details (1.63%)
   - Classifications: Collaboration Types (1.86%)
   - Classifications: Flow Type (1.86%)
   - Classifications: Aid Type (1.86%)
   - Classifications: Finance Type (1.86%)
   - Classifications: Sectors (1.86%)
   - Classifications: Sub-National Location (1.86%)
   - Classifications: Tied Aid Status (1.86%)
   - Related Documents: Memorandum of Understanding (2.17%)
   - Related Documents: Evaluations (2.17%)
   - Related Documents: Objectives (2.17%)
   - Related Documents: Budget Documents – Activity Level (2.17%)
   - Related Documents: Contracts (2.17%)
   - Related Documents: Tenders (2.17%)
   - Financial: Budget – Annual/Quarterly; total activity commitments (3.25%)
   - Financial: Commitments (3.25%)
   - Financial: Disbursements & Expenditures (3.25%)
   - Financial: Budget ID (3.25%)
   - Performance: Results (4.33%)
   - Performance: Impact Appraisals (4.33%)
   - Performance: Conditions (4.33%)

Source: Publish What You Fund. 2016a. *2016 Aid Transparency Index.*

interviews indicate that two channels are at play.[25] First, the ATI influences donors by inciting external political pressure, particularly by providing critical information to key domestic stakeholders who may then use the ATI's scores to monitor, sanction, and reward aid agencies. Second, the ATI plays a direct role in shaping the interests and behavior of elites within aid organizations by translating broad political mandates and commitments regarding transparency into distinct operational policies that can be enacted through internal reforms.

Donors act as the agents of principals, notably national legislatures (in the case of bilateral agencies, such as USAID or the US Department of Defense) or multinational executive boards (in the case of multilateral agencies, for example, the World Bank, or foundations such as the Hewlett Foundation). In this relationship, principals (member states or national parliaments) can exercise oversight and control over agents (donor agencies) through mechanisms such as mandated audits or threats of changes to financial appropriations. Here, as principal-agent theory hypothesizes,[26] the ATI reduces critical information asymmetries and provides clear assessments of agents' relative performance. With such information, principals can more easily detect and sanction agents' deviant behavior. This is consistent with previous scholarship, which has shown that aid agencies are sensitive to demonstrating success to principals, with some agencies much more concerned with appearing successful to principals than others.[27] The mere presence of the ATI incites agencies to be more proactive in transparency reforms, often in *anticipation* of increased principal oversight and control even when principals do not actually make overt gestures to this end.[28]

Our interviews also suggest that the ATI shapes what transparency means to the elite professionals who staff aid agencies. This channel focuses on aid professionals' logic of appropriateness rather than the more traditional payoffs that might accrue to organizational reputational changes, such as greater funding, access to markets, or private investment. Scholars often frame donor organizations, in our view correctly, as part of an "aid industry."[29] Professionals in that industry see themselves as part of a broader community of peers. By influencing the meaning of what it is to be a "good" aid agency and thus "good" aid professional, the ATI influences aid professionals' actions.

---

[25] These observations were offered by several senior staff at USAID, US Congress House Foreign Affairs Committee and Senate Foreign Relations Committee, think tanks, and NGOs. See the online appendix.

[26] On PA models, see Hawkins et al. 2006.

[27] Buntaine 2016; Honig 2018, 2019.

[28] This observation was offered by a senior staff member of the US House Foreign Affairs Committee (interview, September 2014) and confirmed by several senior officials working on transparency reforms at USAID, MCC, and the World Bank (interviews in Washington, DC, September 2014, February 2015, and October 2015).

[29] Engel 2014; Gulrajani 2011; Hanlon, Barrientos, and Hulme 2010.

Both the political pressure and direct elite response channels imply a scope condition for the ATI's influence. We hypothesize that when aid is an agency's primary mandate (versus a secondary mandate or goal), the agency will be more sensitive to the delegitimizing effect of poor ATI scores. Agencies that do not primarily provide aid are less likely to be staffed by individuals who see themselves as part of a broader professional aid community, nor are these agencies' political principals likely to express concern over agencies' level of aid transparency.

We hypothesize that both channels – political pressure and direct elite response – are operative, yet we remain agnostic about which of the two channels is more influential. We construct a quantitative test for which of these is the more influential mechanism. We believe leveraging variation in agency insulation from the pressure to respond to principals, or (as we call it) an agency's relative independence, is a way of getting purchase on which of these channels is the dominant means through which the ATI influences agencies. We hypothesize that the political pressure and direct elite response channels have conflicting implications for whether more or less independent agency will be more responsive.

If political pressure is the stronger channel, then less independent agencies – agencies that are more susceptible to political pressure – should be more responsive to the ATI, as measured via their yearly net change on the ATI ratings and rankings. This channel rests on the ATI enabling the materially weak PWYF and its key allies in the aid transparency movement to capture principals' "power of the purse" and executive or legislative authority over donor agencies. Consequently, if principals are indeed paying attention to and taking action on the ATI's information, then aid agencies with higher degrees of dependence on principals' financial contributions should be especially sensitive to the ATI's effects.

However, if direct elite response is the stronger channel, then agencies that have more relative independence to engage in needed reforms are likely to be more responsive to the ATI. This is because more independent agencies can react faster to emerging standards around transparency policies and to the ATI's professional norm diffusion and socialization effects. Less independent agencies may hold more limited capacity to enact wide-sweeping operational reforms around transparency and data reporting without the consent and resources of their principals.

To restate our argument: we hypothesize that the ATI influence's donor agencies, prompting them to alter their information disclosure practices. The ATI achieves this both via reducing information asymmetries for political principals (*political pressure*) and by constructing meaning and inducing competition not tied to direct payoffs for the professionals who staff donor agencies (*direct elite effects*).

We explore these hypotheses using a mixed-methods approach. We employ regression analysis using a panel data set of ATI scores with the unit of observation as the agency-year. In addition to each agency's overall and indicator-by-indicator score from 2011 to 2016, our data set includes independent data on aid agency disclosure and transparency practices from 2006 to 2013 compiled by AidData at our request.[30] The AidData data allow us to model the presence of the ATI as a treatment, examining whether (and which) agencies are responding to the ATI.

Then we utilize 465 semistructured key informant interviews between 2010 and 2017, primarily in the US, UK, Malawi, Uganda, Kenya, Nepal, and Honduras. These interviews were conducted with staff and management of donor organizations' headquarters and mission offices, national parliamentary and US Congressional staff, relevant think tanks, civil society groups, and international non-governmental organizations. In addition, we analyzed a wide array of primary and secondary materials, including donor organization press releases, policy documents, parliamentary and congressional hearings and legislation, and the research and advocacy materials of NGOs, CSOs and think tanks.

QUANTITATIVE RESULTS: DOES THE ATI ALTER DONOR BEHAVIOR?

To present evidence on whether the ATI has systematically affected donor practices, and for whom, we include agency independence in regression models to provide suggestive evidence that the elite channel of influence is more important than the political pressure channel in explaining the ATI's effects. To explore differing organizational response to "treatment" by the ATI, we build a panel at the agency-year of ATI scores (and thus ATI coverage), complementing this with historic data on agency transparency practices. We also include a calculation of agency independence and an indicator for whether the aid agency's primary purpose involves giving foreign aid (e.g. USAID) or not (e.g. the US Department of Defense) in the data set. These agencies are hereafter referred to as "aid" and "non-aid" agencies to signal their primary mandate. Forty-five of the eighty-four agencies that appear in the ATI at some time between 2011 and 2016 are coded as aid agencies.[31] Online appendix

---

[30] AidData is a "stand-alone development research and innovation lab at the College of William and Mary" http://aiddata.org/about. For a given country-year AidData uses the best, most complete data source available. Over the period in question (2006–2013) the primary source is agencies' official reporting to the OECD Development Assistance Committee's Creditor Reporting System, but the source is sometimes agencies' annual reports and public websites. AidData source choice represents a determination by arguably the organization most concerned with finding high-quality historic aid data of what source provides the best available data for a given country-year. The source of data is never the IATI data on which the ATI most directly contracts. This does not mean that, for example, the data reported to OECD and that reported to IATI in a given year are independent, of course. This is not a concern, inasmuch as our focus (and what the alternative scale drawn from AidData's data measures) is changes in the quality of the best data disclosed regardless of the forum where that disclosure occurs, whether it is via the IATI or not.

[31] At the time of writing, the 2018 ATI had not yet been released so is excluded from our study.

TABLE 5.2. *Summary statistics of selected variables*

Variable	Obs	Mean	Std. Dev.	Min	Max
ATI Score	333	40.448	24.009	0	93.3
Net Change in ATI Score Over Coverage Period	77	10.15	18.772	−39.3	75.7
Agency Independence (using Gilardi scheme)	84	0.435	0.154	0	1
Aidagency Status Dummy	84	0.536	0.502	0	1
AidData Activity Scale	367	90.784	14.941	25	100

Table A1 lists every covered agency, their country, their years of ATI coverage, and our assignment of the indicator for whether giving foreign aid is the agency's primary mandate.

Table 5.2 provides summary statistics of key variables.

To calculate agency independence, we build on Gilardi's work on Western European regulatory agencies.[32] The Gilardi Index is explicitly focused on agencies' relative independence from political authorizers' control and influence. Gilardi developed the index to allow cross-national calculation of formal agency independence from politicians for a variety of agencies. Independence is coded as a time-invariant measure based on the best available data. We were able to find consistent information for just four of Gilardi's twenty-one indicators of agency independence: agency head's term of office, source of budget, whether independence is formally stated, and whether the head of the agency is of cabinet rank.[33] Each of these four measures is scored between 0 and 1 using Gilardi's coding scheme. For example, agencies whose head has a fixed term of office receive one point, agencies whose term of office is six to eight years receive eight points, and so on. While this opens up possible measurement error regarding changes in independence within organizations over time, we expect this measurement error should be orthogonal to the primary analysis and thus add noise (reducing power) rather than lead to spurious inferences. The measure constructed using the Gilardi method is broad, incorporating both aid and non-aid agencies. The online appendix details the full coding scheme.

---

[32] Gilardi 2002. Gilardi develops a scale of twenty-one indicators, unique in its attempt to compare the independence of a variety of agencies focusing on different issue areas from a range of countries. In collaboration with research assistants, we applied Gilardi's scheme to all agencies covered by the ATI using those indicators we were able to consistently code.

[33] While our results apply this scale to multilaterals and foundations – that is, organizations without cabinet rank by definition, and for whom the scale was not intended by Gilardi – the results are robust to restricting the sample to bilateral agencies.

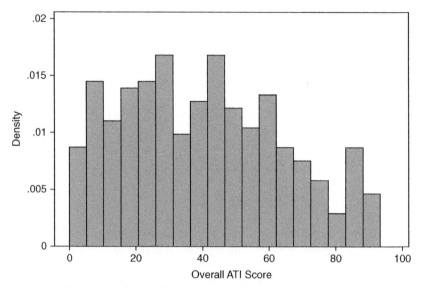

FIGURE 5.1. Histogram of overall ATI scores, 2011–2016.

A visual examination of ATI scores and changes over time underscores the heterogeneity of agency response to the ATI. The wide differences in donors' behavior are demonstrated in Figure 5.1, which shows the variation in realized scores, and Figure 5.2, which compares each agency's score in its most recent year of ATI coverage to the agency's score in its first first year of ATI coverage.

Table 5.3 uses the ATI overall score data to examine differential performance on the ATI with and without country, year, and country-year fixed effects, allowing us to examine intra-country differences in ATI performance. The results are quite stable with and without these fixed effects. Agencies whose primary purpose is to give foreign aid perform better in the ATI ratings than those for whom foreign aid is a secondary task. This is true looking both across all agencies and within a given country's set of covered agencies.[34]

Table 5.3 suggests that for non-aid agencies, greater independence has no association with higher ATI scores. For aid organizations, however, the picture is quite different. More independent aid organizations score better on the ATI than less independent aid organizations from the same country.

Of course, differential performance on the ATI by aid agencies of varying independence does not mean that it is the ATI that has affected aid agencies' disclosure and transparency practices. Aid agencies, particularly those with

[34] Substantive findings in Table 5.3 are unchanged when running these models using the Hainmueller, Mummolo, and Xu 2019 interflex test for multiplicative interactions. That is, use of linear estimates of multiplicative interactions does not yield misleading conclusions.

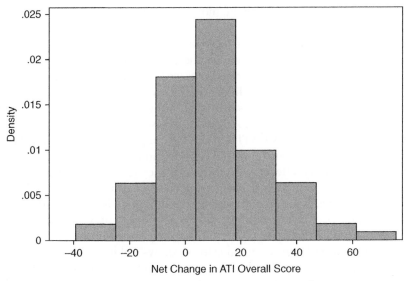

FIGURE 5.2. Net change by agency on ATI over coverage period.

TABLE 5.3. *Performance on the ATI*

DV: Overall ATI Score, 2011–2016	(1)	(2)	(3)	(4)
Aid Agency Dummy	19.00***	16.16***	−17.11***	−28.89*
	(0.954)	(1.934)	(2.596)	(12.02)
Independence (Gilardi)			−29.57***	−5.376
			(6.119)	(19.92)
Ind*Aid Agency			85.64***	129.9***
			(4.560)	(24.66)
Constant	21.79***	27.82***	36.53***	34.28**
	(0.592)	(4.493)	(3.040)	(11.35)
Year FEs	Y	Y	Y	Y
Country FEs	N	Y	N	Y
R^2	0.262	0.724	0.332	0.756
Observations	333	333	333	333

*$p < 0.10$, **$p < 0.05$, ***$p < 0.01$.
OLS, Ordinary Least Squares; Standard errors in parentheses, clustered by year.

more independence, may simply be more apt to disclose information, regardless of the ATI's influence.

Our primary econometric test exploits intertemporal variation in ATI coverage across agencies. The ATI covers the vast majority of consequential aid agencies – that is, those that provide between 84 and 94 percent of global official development assistance between 2011 and 2016.[35] Of the eighty-four agencies in our sample to *ever* be included in the ATI, fifty-eight are included in the first full year of the ATI (2011). In 2012, seventy-two are covered. In 2013, sixty-seven agencies receive ATI scores. The empirical strategy in Table 5.4 exploits this within-organization and across-time variation, including both agency and year fixed effects in examining agency responsiveness to the ATI.

Table 5.4 shifts to modeling inclusion in the ATI in a given year as a binary treatment variable. If an agency exists in the ATI in a given year, this variable takes the value of 1. Alternatively, if an agency is not covered by the ATI in a given year it takes the value of 0.[36] Intra-agency variation in coverage years, when combined with agency fixed effects, allows Table 5.4 to better identify whether inclusion changes within-agency transparency practices.

Since ATI scores exist only in years where an agency is covered by the ATI, we draw on disclosure quality measures from AidData's historic aid flow reporting data described earlier to separately measure transparency practices.[37] These data commence in 2006, five years prior to the ATI's first year of coverage and two years prior to the launch of PWYF. They run through 2013, thus overlapping with the first three waves of the ATI (in 2011, 2012, and 2013).[38]

To construct the dependent variable in Table 5.4, we use a subset of the AidData historic data. This is quite similar in thrust to the ATI's "Activity

---

[35] Authors' calculations. This is the proportion of Official Development Assistance (ODA) reported to the OECD Development Assistance Committee's Creditor Reporting System (CRS) at www.stats.oecd.org represented by those agencies included in both the ATI and the CRS. This necessarily underestimates the actual aid provided by agencies included in the ATI, inasmuch as some agencies (e.g. Chinese development aid, the European Bank for Reconstruction and Development, the Hewlett Foundation, the European Investment Bank) are covered by the ATI but do not report to CRS. This calculation uses the year of reporting and net disbursements when possible. For example, the 2011 statistic is the proportion of 2011 net disbursements accounted for by agencies covered by the 2011 ATI. The broad coverage also unfortunately precludes matching strategies of included agencies to agencies never included in the ATI, as there are few, if any, plausible untreated agencies with which to match those covered by the ATI.

[36] This treatment variable is not lagged because agencies do respond to the ATI in the same year as they are covered. Indeed, PWYF's process is explicitly designed to induce agencies to do so. PWYF staff engage in a three-month dialogue with covered agencies prior to the generation of an ATI rating for a given agency in a given year. As such, agencies are clearly aware of whether and when they will be covered and thus have the ability to alter their practices accordingly. PWYF frames this dialogue and the ability of agencies to improve scores in response to knowledge of ATI coverage as a critical part of the ATI's method.

[37] AidData generously provided these data to us on request. See footnote 31 for more information.

[38] Table 5.4 thus cannot speak to how the ATI has come to influence donors in the past few years if the pattern of influence has changed.

TABLE 5.4. *ATI as treatment*[39]

DV: AidData Activity Scale	All Agencies (1)	All Agencies (2)	All Agencies (3)	All Agencies (4)	Non-Aid Only (5)	Non-Aid Only (6)	Aid Only (7)	Aid Only (8)
Covered by ATI in Year (Treatment)	9.059*** (1.988)	3.289 (1.890)	5.960** (1.942)	0.229 (2.566)	-1.830 (3.337)	-7.7852*** (3.071)	-5.467 (4.528)	-9.038*** (3.639)
Treatment*Aid Agency			4.697** (1.573)	4.852*** (1.253)				
Treatment*Independence (Gilardi)					16.85 (10.18)	17.15 (11.15)	39.16*** (9.933)	37.97*** (10.46)
Constant	90.60*** (1.238)	98.08*** (1.709)	90.14*** (1.420)	97.77*** (1.775)	87.81*** (5.874)	91.41*** (7.217)	91.39*** (1.484)	97.51*** (1.650)
R^2	0.593	0.623	0.597	0.627	0.594	0.623	0.607	0.640
Observations	367	367	367	367	152	152	215	215

* $p < 0.10$, ** $p < 0.05$, *** $p < 0.01$.
Standard errors in parentheses

[39] Specifications 3–6 have interaction terms but no "base" term for independence (calculated using the Gilardi scale) as independence does not vary within organization and is thus absorbed in the organization fixed effect. This is also why specifications 1–2 do not have a "base" term for aid agency dummy. As with Table 5.3, all findings are consistent with running these models using the Hainmueller, Mummolo, and Xu (2019) interflex test for multiplicative interactions.

Level" component (see Table 5.1), which focus on the completeness of individual aid activity reporting. We also employ AidData's measures of the percent of projects for a given donor in a given year that provide a project title, a project description, report the source of the project's funding, and describe the type of flow (e.g. a grant as opposed to a loan). We take the simple average of these four measures, and call this the AidData Activity Scale.[40]

The AidData Activity Scale is a distinct measure of a subset of items on which the ATI focuses.[41] It begins before the ATI and is available even when agencies are not covered by the ATI (and thus in agency-years when the binary ATI treatment variable takes a value of 0). We can thus examine whether inclusion on the ATI is in fact associated with a change in a covered agency's disclosure behavior, leveraging the variation in agency years of coverage we discussed earlier. In models with both year and agency fixed effects, Table 5.4's analysis indicates whether within-agency performance rose in years where the agency was covered by the ATI (over and above secular time trends).

Table 5.4 strongly suggests that inclusion in the ATI changes aid agencies' behavior. Models 3 and 4 indicate that the quality of covered agencies' reporting at the "activity level" – the level of individual projects and interventions – improves when agencies are covered by the ATI. This finding is robust in the case of only dedicated aid agencies, however. When year fixed effects are included, the disclosure practices of aid agencies are positively correlated with coverage by ATI assessments, but there is no evidence that this holds for non-aid agencies.

This relationship is further conditional on agency independence. Models 5 through 8 of Table 5.4 examine the role of agency independence for aid and non-aid agencies. While there is no evidence of a relationship between independence and response for non-aid agencies, for aid agencies, greater independence is associated with greater improvement on the AidData scale, *ceteris paribus*. Indeed, for the median aid agency on the independence scale (independence = 0.375), there is no statistically significant effect of ATI inclusion. For a firm at the seventy-fifth percentile, however (independence = 0.5), there is a

---

[40] Table 5.2's summary statistics provide fuller information on the measure's distribution. The AidData Activity Scale is calculable in at least one year for fifty-six of the eighty-four agencies to ever be included in the ATI. Appendix Table A1 provides information on which agencies have AidData Activity Scale scores.

[41] This does not mean that the AidData Activity Scale (with its four items) is well correlated with a donor's overall ATI score in the same year. Indeed, the two are slightly negatively correlated in practice (–.145). This is not terribly troubling, inasmuch as the ATI's much broader scale covers many, many other elements of transparency. A given donor could, for example, improve on the components of the ATI measure related to activity level transparency in a given year, yet still decline on the ATI scale overall.

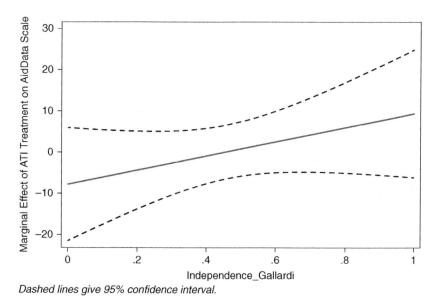

Dashed lines give 95% confidence interval.

FIGURE 5.3. Marginal effect of treatment by independence for non-aid agencies.

ten-point treatment effect statistically distinguishable from 0.[42] This ten-point effect would raise the median aid agency (score = 89.1) to a near-perfect 99.1.[43]

Figures 5.3 and 5.4 graphically represent the role of independence for aid and non-aid agencies respectively (Table 5.4, models 4 and 6), demonstrating the importance of agency independence for aid but not non-aid agencies.

The AidData Activity Scale captures the completeness of the information donors disclose about projects (titles, descriptions, financing agency names, and flow types) in percentage-point terms. A one scale point is the equivalent of a one percentage-point shift in performance on the underlying measures. The ten-point treatment effect for an aid agency at the seventy-fifth percentile of independence is equivalent to a shift from non-disclosure to full disclosure of ten percentage points of a given agency's projects. For example, in 2012 USAID had USD 17 billion of total disbursements and over 8,500 activities.[44] This means an increase of ten percentage points of transparency for

[42] Drawn from model 6, Table 5.4. Net treatment effect is the sum of the beta on the interaction term (37.97) and the beta on the effect of ATI coverage (–9.038).

[43] The maximum possible score on the AidData Activity Scale is 100 (full disclosure of all information fields for all projects, in percentage-point terms). This ceiling effect means the test in Table 5.4 may in fact understate the effect of ATI inclusion on covered agencies.

[44] Data drawn from USAID's "Foreign Aid Explorer," retrieved from explorer.usaid.gov. The explorer covers all US government assistance; these are the USAID – only 2012 disbursement statistics reported as of December 30, 2017.

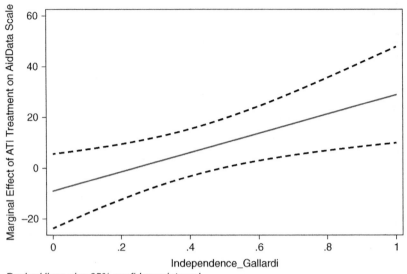

FIGURE 5.4. Marginal effect of treatment by independence for aid agencies.

USAID would cover about USD 1.7 billion of aid flows and 850 activities. For these 850 activities, observers could now know what USAID's programs were doing, where, and who was financing them. Individuals and civil society organizations in recipient countries could access information that would help them hold foreign donors and their own governments accountable. Individuals and politicians in the US could better understand where their tax dollars are going. Other donors could better understand what 1.7 billion dollars of USAID funding was doing, allowing for better coordination and planning.

The independence scale itself is a patchy measure – a mere echo of the original Gilardi measure on agency independence. As such, these econometrics provide strong evidence that ATI coverage is associated with changes in the disclosure practices of (some) covered agencies. However, this analysis can only be suggestive about the mechanisms underlying any ATI coverage effect. In sum, donors included in the ATI are more transparent, especially if they are more independent and designated aid agencies. The finding that greater aid agency independence is associated with greater change in response to ATI coverage suggests the ATI primarily works through aid agency elites: if agencies primarily responded to pressure from their principal(s), then more dependent (less independent) agencies should perform better on the ATI. But this does not mean that direct elite influence is the only channel of influence. To further explore how the ATI drives donors to change, we turn to a closer examination of the nature of the ATI's power and its key mechanisms of influence over donor agencies.

HOW DOES THE ATI AFFECT DONORS? QUALITATIVE EVIDENCE ON MECHANISMS AND CHANNELS OF INFLUENCE

Between 2010 and 2016, we conducted 465 open-ended and semi-structured interviews[45] with aid donors, governments, NGOs and CSOs, academics, and other subject matter experts. We conducted these interviews primarily in seven countries: the United States, the United Kingdom, Malawi, Uganda, Kenya, Nepal, and Honduras (see Table 5.2 and the online appendix). Many of these interviews broadly focused on aid transparency in donor agencies, with some focused on specific sectors (such as climate change, agriculture, and education). In most cases, to avoid leading questions, we did not ask directly about the ATI or its effects. Instead, we asked about general pressures for donor-level transparency, general data needs and uses in resource allocation decisions, and awareness and use of open aid data at the agency or country level. Some interviewees referred to the ATI explicitly. In other cases, interviewees referred to the "index" associated with the International Aid Transparency Initiative or Publish What You Fund. We subsequently coded all the interviews to assess both awareness of the ATI and, where awareness existed, the overall perceptions regarding the ATI's influence over donors' transparency behavior.

As Table 5.5 indicates, 186 (40 percent) of all interviewees indicated they were familiar with the ATI. Of these, 125 thought the ATI had a positive influence in shaping donor agencies' transparency behavior, whereas sixty-one reported that they did not think the ATI had any influence or simply expressed that they had no opinion. Ninety-three of these 125 who reported a positive influence for the ATI were based in Washington, DC, London, or another major donor country where donor aid agencies are headquartered.

General awareness of the ATI was largely confined to interviewees who worked in donor headquarters (e.g. Washington, DC, London, Stockholm, Brussels) or who with NGOs, think tanks, and academic research programs that pay explicit attention to aid transparency issues. ATI awareness was significantly lower among government and donor staff in borrowing countries. In these instances, respondents were more aware of domestic donor aid transparency initiatives, such as their respective aid management platforms. In a few cases, respondents conflated aid transparency with general government transparency.[46] The handful of respondents in aid-receiving countries that

---

[45] All interviews conducted on the record are listed in the online appendix. Interviews who requested partial anonymity are listed according to institutional affiliation. Interview subjects who requested full anonymity, or were exempt from attribution in our IRB protocols, are not listed.

[46] This became evident when interviewees discussed the ATI in the context of Transparency International's transparency ratings or other international transparency indices such as the Open Budget Index or the Open Government Partnership.

TABLE 5.5. Perceptions of ATI influence on donor transparency behavior

Country	Interview Dates	Interviewee Role	Total # of Interviews	Awareness of ATI***			
				Yes – Positive Influence	Yes – Negative Influence	Yes – No Influence / No Opinion	Not Aware of ATI / Did Not Mention ATI
United States	2/2011; 6/2013; 9/2014; 2/2015; 10/2015; 1-2/2016; 9/2016; 2/2017	Government	12	10	0	0	2
		Donor Agency	21	15	3	1	5
		Other**	34	31	2	1	2
United Kingdom	7/2013; 5/2014; 12/2015	Government	2	2	0	0	0
		Donor Agency	6	6	0	0	0
		Other**	17	17	0	0	0
Malawi	12/2010; 1/2013; 12/2014	Government	22	0	0	2	20
		Donor Agency	35	0	0	2	33
		Other**	9	0	0	0	9
Uganda	6/2014; 3/2015	Government	6	0	0	2	4
		Donor Agency	30	1	3	5	24
		Other**	28	4	0	1	23
Kenya	12/2010; 6/2017	Government	9	1	0	1	7
		Donor Agency	23	2	0	2	19
		Other**	13	2	0	2	9

Country	Interview Dates	Interviewee Role	Total # of Interviews	Awareness of ATI***			
				Yes – Positive Influence	Yes – Negative Influence	Yes – No Influence / No Opinion	Not Aware of ATI / Did Not Mention ATI
Nepal	12/2014; 3/2015	Government	8	1	0	3	4
		Donor Agency	34	3	1	16	15
		Other**	11	2	0	7	2
Honduras	3/2016; 6–8/2016	Government	36	2	0	1	33
		Donor Agency	20	1		6	13
		Other**	28	0	0	0	28
AMP Workshop Delegates	Nairobi 2010 and Nepal 2014	Government	38	10	0	5	23
		Donors	0	0	0	0	0
		Other**	11	3	0	4	4
Remote Correspondence	2013–2017	Government	0	0	0	0	0
		Donor Agency	7	7	0	0	0
		Other**	5	5	0	0	0
TOTAL			465	125 (26.9%)	9 (1.9%)	61 (13.1%)	279 (60%)

Notes:

* Includes interviews that were conducted under agreement of non-attribution or deep background (off the record only), per IRB protocol. In these instances, the names are not listed in the online appendix.

** Other includes international and national non-governmental organizations, civil society groups, think tank and academic subject matter experts.

*** ATI awareness includes explicit reference or implicit reference (for example, the "index used by" the International Aid Transparency Initiative or Publish What You Fund). (see the online appendix for interview list).

signaled awareness of the ATI were individuals in government or donor agencies that were explicitly involved in reporting to domestic aid information management platforms or those who worked with domestic aid-transparency advocacy groups that had connections to transnational aid-transparency-advocacy groups (such as Development Initiatives).

Direct Elite Response to the ATI's Social Power

Donor agencies clearly care about their reputation and perceived legitimacy, even when such status is not explicitly linked to material rewards or sanctions. In interviews at donor headquarters and in official organizational documents, management and staff nearly universally report that their agencies use ATI ratings and rankings to draw positive attention to themselves, direct negative attention to others, or signal their own good intentions and commitments. Landing in the "very good" category grants bragging rights, and large legitimacy gains, which organizations value independently from any direct link to financial sanctions or rewards.[47] Consistent with GPIs more broadly, the very act of the ATI's regularized monitoring triggers reactivity, with target actors changing their behavior (if not their underlying interests) in reaction to being evaluated, observed, and measured.[48]

The ATI's ability to incite status and reputational concerns has two effects on organizations. The ATI's peer rankings serve to motivate poorly performing donor organizations to communicate renewed commitments and refocus organizational resources on transparency reforms.[49] At the same time, the ATI peer rankings and release of annual reports provide opportunities for well-performing organizations to signal to external constituents that they have made good on transparency promises and, in some instances, achieved compliance with international commitments and open data standards. According to fifteen interviews with donor agencies and NGOs in the US and UK, a fair amount of institutional rivalry reinforces organizations' desire for status and positive reputations. This appears to especially resonate in countries with

---

[47] Interviews with World Bank (Elizabeth Dodds, Johannes Kiess, Carolyn Antsey, Jeffrey Gutman), USAID (Augusta Abrahamse, Jeremiah Crew, Kim Smith, Tom Zearley), MCC (Sheila Herrling), SIDA-Nepal (Pramila Shrestha), DFID (John Adams) and DANIDA staff. See Clare, Verhust and Young 2016, 4 (Sweden's SIDA); George 2012 (World Bank IDA); Greening speech (UK DFID).

[48] Kelley and Simmons 2019; Saunder and Espeland 2009.

[49] Interviews with PWYF staff (David Hall Matthews, Catalina Reyes, Mark Brough, and Nicholas Dorward, Elise Dufief London 2014 and 2016, plus e-mail correspondence 2017–2018), CRS and GAO staff (Tom Melito from the GAO, Marion Lawson from CRS in DC, October 2015), and senior officials at USAID (Kim Smith and Joan Atherton in DC), UNDP (Danila Boneva in New York), World Bank (Jakob Fredensborg-Rasmussen in Uganda), SIDA (Pramila Shrestha in Nepal), GIZ (Nora Rohner in London), and DFID (John Adams in London; Andy Murray in Nepal). Various dates; see the online appendix.

multiple aid agencies that jostle for favorable positions in the eyes of the same political authorizers.[50] This is clearest in the case of the US. In our observations and interviews with donor staff and external aid experts in DC, there is a palpable rivalry between the Millennium Challenge Corporation (MCC) and the US Agency for International Development (USAID), both of whom have mandates that focus solely on official development assistance and "vie for the top spot in the ATI."[51]

The peer pressure invoked by the ATI motivates key reforms in US agencies that have performed poorly in past rankings, particularly at USAID and the US Department of State. In the first months after then-Secretary of State Hillary Clinton announced that the US would become a signatory to IATI in November 2011, these agencies (especially State) argued "vigorously through back channels" against an aggressive timeline and benchmarks for implementation.[52] They argued this was because of the anticipated high costs of required changes in underlying data technology systems. Agencies also argued they needed time to build capacity and buy-in from staff to report to new standards and dashboards, including the newly established US Foreign Assistance Dashboard. Interviews with approximately a dozen actors within US aid agencies, the US General Accounting Office, and US Congress reveal that much of the rationale behind this argument fell by the wayside when the Millennium Challenge Corporation quickly enacted an ambitious transparency agenda and vaulted to number one on the ATI in 2013.

Policy and behavior change in response to the ATI need not emerge solely from shifts in professional status. As Kelley and Simmons note, GPI processes can alter identity and professional norms through knowledge production and socialization.[53] The ATI shapes how the concept of aid transparency is collectively understood and acted upon.[54] Our interview with Publish What You Fund's Sally Paxton and public comments made by donor representatives at annual ATI launches suggest that circulation of elite staff between organizations and the sharing of "best practices"

---

[50] Interviews with George Ingram, Brookings Institute, and senior officials, USAID. This sentiment was reiterated by other senior staff and management at MCC (Sheila Herrling), USAID (Kim Smith), DFID (John Adams), UNDP (Danila Boneva), and UNICEF (Carey McCormack in Uganda). In addition to the US, three other countries have at least two agencies assessed by the ATI, including France (MINEFI and MAEDI), Japan (JICA and MOFA), and Germany (BMZ-GIZ and BMZ-KfW). Four multilateral groups also have multiple agencies in the ATI: United Nations (UN DP, UNICEF, UN OCHA), the World Bank (IFC and IDA) and the European Communities (EBRD, EIB, DG-NEAR, DG-DEVCO, DG ECHO and DG Enlargement).

[51] This rivalry became evident in interviews with senior staff at USAID and MCC (various dates). Such rivalry was also noted by senior staff in the US House Foreign Affairs Committee.

[52] Interview with senior USAID official.

[53] Kelley and Simmons 2019.

[54] Interview with Sally Paxton from Friends of Publish What You Fund, February 2015.

spurred by the ATI's annual rankings, publications, and public discussions foster interorganizational learning and diffusion of new policies.[55] For example, Sheila Herrling, Vice President for the MCC, declared that the MCC learned directly from the transparency initiatives of other donors, including PLAN USA.[56]

Annual ATI releases also diffuse learning by providing critical information on the experiences of peer institutions in building organizational cultures around transparency reforms, overcoming technological barriers, and building staff capacity in needed areas. This is done through donor-level narrative reviews, press releases, and open discussion forums. For example, interviews with Department for International Development (DFID) staff in London and USAID staff in DC affirm that the ATI has helped to "prove" that organizational change in possible, and PWYF's donor-level reports have provided key insights into how to approach difficult organizational reform.[57] This is an effect quite synergistic, but distinct, from that of peer naming and shaming. In the words of Brookings scholar George Ingram, such interorganizational learning helps organizations to "stop hugging data" and to release more of the information they gather.[58] The success of the IDA (World Bank), MCC, DFID (United Kingdom), and UNDP in scoring very highly on the ATI led other agencies such as USAID, IFC (World Bank), Swedish International Development Cooperation Agency (SIDA), and German Corporation for International Cooperation (GIZ), to adopt disclosure policies on sensitive areas such as procurement and finance that they previously had been reluctant to pursue. These first movers tend to be more independent agencies on the Gilardi independence scale. This is also true for within country measures. For example, in the US, the MCC scores higher on the independence scale than USAID does, and was the "first mover" on improved transparency practices. In sum, some agencies performing well on the ATI are able to demonstrate to other organizations that implementing seeming "costly" or "risky" transparency reforms are, contrary to expectations, neither costly nor risky.[59]

Similarly, the process of constructing the annual ATI itself is critical to understanding its social power and influence over elites within donor agencies. The inclusive nature of the ATI review process, which provides opportunities for target organizations to participate in the collection of data and

[55] Ibid. We observed several general comments to this effect at the ATI launches in both Washington, DC, and London. Panelists often offered these comments in direct response to questions posed by panel moderators or audience members regarding how organizations do – or can – learn from the successes of other donor agencies that have performed well on the ATI.

[56] Herrling 2015.

[57] PWYF 2015a, 2015b.

[58] Interview with George Ingram, Brookings Institution, January 2016.

[59] Interviews with Sheila Herrling (MCC), Kim Smith (USAID), John Adams (DFID), Sally Paxton (PWYF), Aleem Walji (World Bank). See also Clare, Verhust and Young 2016, 10; Hansen and Marschner 2015.

validation of results, lends considerable authority to Publish What You Fund and the ATI. Because donors are directly involved in reporting to the index, and have opportunities to review the data before the index is finalized, the results are rarely openly contested.[60]

Nearly two dozen interviews with the staff of PWYF and donor staff based in their agency's headquarters revealed that the process of collating the ATI results every year provides further opportunities for organizational learning and diffusion of transparency norms. During the review process, which takes several months and involves repeated interaction with PWYF, donors provide their own assessment of their performance on the ATI's indicators. When these donor-generated assessments conflict with scores generated by PWYF staff and independent reviewers, PWYF and the donor discuss what exactly is expected to achieve a full score on each of the ATI's indicators and how the donor may achieve such scores via full compliance with reporting standards.[61] Thus, according to PWYF staff in both London and DC, donors are compelled to reflect on their progress toward transparency. Because the ATI grants some points in donors' overall score for organizational commitments and implementation plans even in the absence of actual policy changes, the review period becomes an opportune time to double down on public statements in support of transparency reforms.[62] According to George Ingram, Brookings Institution senior fellow and co-lead of the Modernizing Foreign Assistance Network, the cost of inattention to this process is a stagnant or bad score for the agency, which leaves agencies' stakeholders and peers within the aid community with a lingering sense of "what have you done lately?"[63]

The period of review also enhances the reactivity effects of the ATI's monitoring.[64] A donor agency may report that they are fully compliant with the ATI's expectations regarding information disclosure policies (i.e. they will argue they deserve a score of 100 on that measure). However, two sets of independent reviews plus PWYF's assessment can catch where such policies are weak – for example, if the disclosure policy provides few appeals mechanisms or puts limitations on the acceptance of third-party information. Among the

---

[60] Interview with Sally Paxton, February 2015, This is similar to the repeated social interaction learning affect, discussed in Kelley 2017, Chapters 3 and 6.

[61] Weaver made this observation several times while participating as an external reviewer for the 2016 and 2018 ATI. This observation is also based upon conversations with the PWYF staff who compile the ATI scores.

[62] This is based upon impressions provided by three senior staff officials at USAID (Kim Smith, Joan Atherton, and Jeremiah Carew), one senior staff official at DFID (Alasdair Wardhaugh), one senior staff official at DANIDA (nonattribution), and two staff members of Publish What You Found (David Hall-Matthews and Sally Paxton). See also Clare, Verhust, and Young 2016, 9; Hansen and Marschner 2015; UK DFID 2015.

[63] Interview with George Ingram, Brookings Institution, January 2016.

[64] As observed through Weaver's participant role as an external reviewer in the 2016 and 2018 ATI review.

USAID and PWYF staff we interviewed, the process reifies the sense that the annual review is deep and rigorous, with layers of independent analysis from subject matter experts to serve as a check against agencies' self-assessments.[65] In the case of USAID, staff reported that this prompted the organization to steer away from rhetorical commitments that might otherwise be used to "game" the assessment process (a form of shallow behavioral change), instead focusing on meaningful policy and operational changes.

The ATI also empowers elites to mobilize support for reforms by clearly defining what transparency looks like and setting specific benchmarks for success. According to John Adams, staff member at DFID and chair of the IATI Technical Secretariat, references to the ATI help champions of transparency reforms to persuade reticent staff of the merits of policy change.[66] Specifically, according to staff in charge of transparency reforms at USAID, the MCC, and GIZ, the ATI's detailed set of indicators reduces uncertainty on the part of agency leaders in terms of identifying precisely what policies and practices need to change to meet expectations set in international commitments and national law. Some donors' transparency strategies are, in fact, directly oriented around the standards in the ATI.[67] For example, the Millennium Challenge Corporation (ranked first in the 2014 ATI), states that "through the Aid Transparency Index process, Publish What You Fund and other advocacy groups have made specific recommendations to MCC in the interest of moving the field of aid transparency forward, particularly regarding how to prioritize improvements to IATI data."[68] The ATI, in essence, became the MCC's "blueprint for reform." This dynamic shows up in other interviews and in internal and published organizational strategy papers and operational policies at USAID and SIDA. Notably, we see it even when there continues to be disagreement within organizations on the importance or fit of the ATI's ideals and standards with the organization's overall transparency agenda and core values.[69]

USAID's response to the ATI illustrates the central role that elite channels play. In July 2015, after struggling in prior years in the ATI rankings, USAID published a strategy paper on open data depicted as the agency's "roadmap" to transparency.[70] The strategy paper, also known as the IATI Implementation Cost Management Plan (CMP – Phase 2), explicitly stated that one of the strategy's four central goals was to increase USAID's ATI score.[71] A month later, Alex Thier,

[65] Interview with two senior USAID officials and Sally Paxton, September 2016.
[66] Interview with John Adams, DFID, September 2014.
[67] Ibid. See Clare, Verhust, and Young 2016 on Sweden's aid transparency strategy.
[68] Hansen and Marschner 2015. For similar statements by the Canadian International Development Agency, see Bhushan and Bond 2013.
[69] See also Koeberle 2016.
[70] Hamilton 2015; see also Thier and Crumbly 2015.
[71] USAID 2015.

then-chief for the Bureau of Policy, Planning, and Learning at USAID, stated "after we implemented Phase One of the CMP, our Publish What You Fund Aid Transparency Index...increased more than twenty points and moved USAID from 'Fair' to 'Good.' This was an exciting, tangible way to demonstrate our progress, and this success raised awareness around the Agency on these important efforts."[72] This internally driven, elite-led reform effort is consistent with the quantitative evidence we presented earlier regarding agency independence.

The ATI's Power via Political Pressure

While nearly 80 percent of our interviewees discussed direct elite responses to the ATI, approximately 65 percent of those who perceived the ATI as positive also noted that the ATI reduces information asymmetries and induces greater principal attention to donor organizations' disclosure practices. The ATI creates awareness and support among political principals for aid transparency via lobbying and advocacy campaigns of PWYF and like-minded members of the epistemic community. As such, the ATI is a useful tool for resolving information asymmetries that hinder principal oversight and control. In providing detailed, regular data on agencies' transparency performance, the ATI essentially acts as an information intermediary for politicians who may have neither the capacity nor inclination to closely monitor agent behavior.[73] According to one senior staff member in the US House Foreign Affairs Committee, the ATI is "great for letting us know when there's a problem [with US aid agencies]... We don't have time to follow that stuff that closely."[74] We also found that principals use the ATI's detailed information on where donors lag in transparency performance to inform specific policies within national legislation on open data standards. National "aid transparency guarantees" in the UK and Sweden and the 2016 US Foreign Aid Transparency Act make specific recommendations that align with the indicators and goals of the ATI.

In other instances, it is quite apparent that the ATI is empowering third-party actors. In the US, for example, a thriving group of think tanks, academics, and NGOs pays close attention to the ATI.[75] The rankings and ratings inform their analytical reports, lobbying, and activism.[76] Interviews with senior congressional staff in the US House Foreign Affairs Committee and the US Senate Foreign

---

[72] Quoted in Hamilton 2015.

[73] Interviews with staff in the US House Foreign Affairs Committee and Senate Foreign Relations Committee (nonattribution), George Ingram (Brookings Institution), Ben Leo (Center for Global Development), Lori Rowley (Lugar Center), Joe Powell (Open Government Partnership [OGP]).

[74] Interview with senior staff member, USHFAC, February 2015 (nonattribution).

[75] See the online appendix for the list of thirty-four interviewees that fall into this category, including the Modernizing Foreign Assistance Network, Center for Global Development, and Oxfam International.

[76] USAID 2015.

Relations Committee reveal that a great deal of their information on the transparency performance of US aid agencies comes from this epistemic community, with frequent reference to the ATI as a primary source of evidence.

Some of the competitive pressure between agencies we described has links to political pressure. According to three interviews with Congressional staff, the US Senate has also brought attention and importance to the ATI. The MCC's success, and the need for other US agencies to "catch up," has been prominently discussed in congressional hearings. For example, this was noted in the very first question asked to Dana Hyde in her 2013 confirmation hearing as MCC CEO, by Senator Markey (D-MA). As Markey put it, MCC's success on the ATI was "a very impressive record" and she asked "how do we keep it going, and how do we transfer that transparency to all of these other venerable institutions [e.g. USAID]?"[77] While only two interviewees admitted that the MCC's success was an official reason for the significant shift in USAID's approach to a more aggressive IATI implementation plan shortly thereafter, nearly all of the USAID, US State Department, and other US government interviews (20 out of 25) remarked that this competition had a lot to do with getting the attention of top USAID management and putting data transparency reforms "on the front burner."[78]

Consistent with our hypotheses, political pressure appears to play a stronger role with respect to less independent aid agencies. For example, close observers of the US system note that staff from USAID, which has relatively little financial autonomy vis-à-vis Congress, fear that the ATI's score may influence the way their political masters decide to appropriate funds.[79] By contrast, interviews on the evolution of the transparency initiative at the World Bank, whose funds come from a more diverse set of sources (including trust funds and profits from non-concessional lending and bonds) make no mention of the shadow of appropriations, even when asked directly.[80] The World Bank has consistently placed in the top ten of all donors and in the "very good" category of the ATI. Our interviews also reveal that staff in less independent agencies do not always wait for clear threats or actual principal exercise of oversight and control. Instead, they can act *in anticipation* of principals' possible greater oversight and control, exhibiting a desire to "get ahead of the game" by taking proactive steps to implement data reporting standards that would be fully compliant with IATI and aligned to the metrics in the ATI.[81]

[77] Senate Foreign Relations Committee 2013.

[78] Interviews with Kim Smith and USAID staff who requested nonattribution, October 2014.

[79] Interviews with staff in the US Congressional Research Service (Marion Lawson), US General Accounting Office (Tom Melito), and USAID (nonattribution).

[80] Interviews with World Bank staff, February 2011, June 2013, February 2017 (Aleem Walji, Jeff Chelsky, Jeffrey Gutman, Carolyn Anstey and a few that requested nonattribution).

[81] Interviews with staff at the US General Accounting Office (Tom Melito), Congressional Research Service (Marion Lawson), and USAID (Kim Smith). See also Marks 2012.

CONCLUSION: THE ATI'S SOCIAL POWER AND INFLUENCE

The qualitative and quantitative empirics jointly suggest that both political pressure and direct elite channels play a role in the ATI's influence. The elite channel appears to be the more influential of the two. The ATI provides information to political principals; it also provides information to elite bureaucrats inside donor agencies. These elites are the primary drivers of agency changes as the ATI has created a clear standard of what it means to be "transparent," invoking normative and reputational power for these policy elites.

GPIs can enable weak actors to influence powerful actors in world politics. The ATI is a remarkable case in point. Created nearly ten years ago by a small NGO with no direct material power, the ATI now sets best practices in aid transparency. The ATI exercises influence via political pressure and elite channels to invoke important socialization, learning, and peer pressure effects that discernibly shape many donors' transparency policies. Agencies with aid as their primary mandate are more responsive to the ATI's assessments, particularly when those agencies are relatively independent and thus more able to act in response to a change in aid professionals' priorities and understandings. The ATI thus demonstrates that a GPI creator (in this case, Publish What You Fund) can substantially alter behavior within a relatively tightly knit professional community.

The case of the ATI suggests that there may be advantages to focusing on elite channels and construction of meaning in professional communities. At the same time, this case also suggests that a GPI that operates via social pressure will be unlikely to influence those who overtly reject the importance of the goal (such as China or the United Arab Emirates) or are not part of the community in which social pressure operates. In this case of the ATI, organizations that are primarily focused on other matters and only incidentally disburse aid are not part of the professional community. The ATI's efforts to affect change in these agencies may be of limited usefulness.

In sum, the ATI has drawn critical attention to donors' aid transparency commitments and performance. It is now an industry leader in assessing aid transparency and setting donor accountability standards. The ATI alters what transparency means in practice, even as it encourages greater disclosure. It does more than merely assess transparency practices: it defines norms of transparency.

At the same time, the ATI's influence is not always viewed in a positive light, even when it pushes donor agencies toward transparency. For example, when asked if the ATI presented any concerns or risks, five interviewees in the US (in donor agencies and NGOs) pointed out that the systems put in place in response to the ATI did not always represent the quickest or most efficient route to full transparency for their organization.[82] It is interesting

---

[82] Interviews with senior staff at USAID, World Bank, GIZ, UNICEF, Japan International Cooperation Agency (JICA), Norwegian Agency for Development Cooperation (NORAD) (various dates; see the online appendix, nonattribution).

that conformity around the ATI's transparency norms has taken hold, despite emerging reservations about the appropriateness of its assessment criteria and specific indicators. This qualitative observation may portend a varying level of normative power over time as the ATI ages. Contestation over the operationalization of "transparency" may lead to some discrediting or distancing from the ATI. It might also create pressure to alter the index to include other indicators and weights, or perhaps even enable the rise of GPI competitors that reflect changing norms regarding the structure and goals of aid transparency.[83]

What is clear today is that the ATI has been a key part of the transparency revolution in international development aid. PWYF's indicators have helped to set a clear standard for the over 600 governmental and non-governmental signatories of the International Aid Transparency Initiative. For an NGO that still occupies just one room, it shows that GPI creators do not necessarily need material power to influence the behavior of the powerful. David may move Goliath with a well-aimed slingshot fired in conflict. But David can also induce Goliath to change by orienting Goliath's attention toward the behavior David wishes to alter.

ACKNOWLEGMENTS

This is largely a reprint of our 2019 *International Organization* paper of the same name, but with minor alterations. The online appendix associated with this article can be accessed at https://dataverse.harvard.edu/dataset.xhtml? persistentId=doi:10.7910/DVN/3GQTYA. Many thanks to Rucheta Singh, Grace Chao, Susannah Horton, and particularly Yunhui Lin for research assistance. We are also thankful to Publish What You Fund for their time and clarification; AidData, and particularly Brooke Russell and Brad Parks, for assistance in generating critical additional data; Dennis Vega and Jessica Klein of the US Department of State's Office of US Foreign Assistance Resources; Sally Paxton at Friends of Publish What You Fund; and numerous officials from aid agencies, parliaments, think tanks, and NGOs that graciously agreed to interviews. Many thanks to Sam Asher, James Bisbee, Stephen Chaudoin, Laura Henry, George Ingram, Judith Kelley, Eddy Malesky, John Marshall, Beth Simmons, the *IO*

[83] At the Fourth High-Level Forum on Aid Effectiveness in Busan, South Korea in November 2011, the Global Partnership on Effective Development Cooperation was created and mandated to monitor donor progress toward the Busan agreement, including commitments to transparency. The first Global Monitoring Report 2014 was released just prior to the 2015 Fifth High Forum on Aid Effectiveness in Mexico. The monitoring framework thus far appears to depend upon voluntary reporting by participating countries and organizations and a vague methodology and set of indicators. As such, it does not appear to be emerging yet as a viable competitor to the ATI. However, the clear overlap in the indices' purposive goals may indicate some movement in the competitive landscape, with yet unknown consequences for its power and influence of the ATI.

reviewers and editors, and participants in the May 2016 and September 2016 APSA Assessment Power in World Politics conferences as well as the 2017 Political Economy of International Organizations conference for valuable comments and guidance. Last but far from least, many thanks to the editorial team and professional staff at *International Organization* for their time and efforts, and to anonymous reviewers for their helpful comments in improving this manuscript.

SUPPLEMENTARY MATERIAL

Supplementary material for this article is available at https://dataverse.harvard.edu/dataset.xhtml?persistentId=doi:10.7910/DVN/3GQTYA.

References

Barder, Owen. 2016. Aid Transparency: Are We Nearly There? *Center for Global Development*, April 13, 2016. Available at www.cgdev.org/blog/aid-transparency-are-we-nearly-there.

Bent, Rodney. 2015. A Sad State of Affairs: Is Transparency a Solution? *Publish What You Fund* blog, September 23. Available at http://www.publishwhatyoufund.org/updates/by-country/us/state-transparency-solution/. Accessed January 13, 2018.

Bisbee, James H., James R. Hollyer, B. Peter Rosendorff, and James Raymond Vreeland. this volume. The Millennium Development Goals and Education: Accountability and Substitution in Global Indicators. *The Power of Global Performance Indicators*, New York: Cambridge University Press.

Bhushan, Aniket, and Rebekka Bond. 2013. Open Data, Transparency and International Development. Summary Report for the North-South Institute, November. Available at http://www.nsi-ins.ca/wp-content/uploads/2013/11/2013-Open-Data-Summary-Report.pdf. Accessed January 13, 2018.

Buntaine, Mark T. 2016. *Giving Aid Effectively*. New York: Oxford University Press.

Carothers, Thomas, and Saskia Brechenmacher. 2014. *Accountability, Transparency, Participation and Inclusion: A New Development Consensus?* Washington, DC: Carnegie Endowment for International Peace. Available at http://carnegieendowment.org/files/new_development_consensus.pdf. Accessed September 1, 2015.

Clare, Ali, Stefaan Verhulst, and Andrew Young. 2016. OpenAid in Sweden: Enhanced Transparency and Accountability in Development Cooperation. Report for the GovLab, in collaboration with the Omidyar Network. Available at http://odimpact.org/case-openaid-in-sweden.html. Accessed February 9, 2016.

Collin, Matt, Asma Zubairi, Daniel Nielson and Owen Barder. 2009. The Costs and Benefits of Aid Transparency: A Draft Analytical Framework. Avalable at https://iatistandard.org/documents/482/1140-100407-Framework-for-Costs-and-Benefits-of-transparency-with-Annexes.pdf.

Darby, Sefton. 2010. *Natural Resource Governance: New Frontiers in Transparency and Accountability*. London, UK: Transparency and Accountability Initiative, Open Society Foundation. Available at http://www.transparency-initiative.org/uncategorized/613/natural-resource-governance-new-frontiers-in-transparency-and-accountability/. Accessed January 13, 2018.

Doshi, Rush, Judith G. Kelley, and Best A. Simmons. 2019. The Power of Ranking: The Ease of Doing Business Indicator as a form of Social Pressure. *The Power of Global Performance Indicators*, New York: Cambridge University Press.

Engel, Susan. 2014. The Not-So-Great Aid Debate. *Third World Quarterly* 35 (8):1374–89.

Espeland, Wendy Nelson, and Michael Sauder. 2007. Rankings and Reactivity: How Public Measures Recreate Social Worlds. *American Journal of Sociology* 113 (1):1–40.

Florini, Ann. 2007. *The Right to Know: Transparency for an Open World*. New York: Columbia University Press.

Friends of Publish What You Fund. 2016. *How Can Data Revolutionize Development? Putting Data at the Center of US Global Development: An Assessment of US Foreign Aid Transparency*. Available at http://media.wix.com/ugd/9a0ffd_2ce18150803b48989905acabf9bb91d6.pdf. Accessed January 13, 2018.

Gaventa, John, and Rosemary McGee. 2013. The Impact of Transparency and Accountability Initiatives. *Development Policy Review* 31 (S1):S3–28.

George, Hannah. 2012. Raising the Bar on Transparency, Accountability and Openness. *World Bank's Inside the Web*. (Blog.) February 16. Available at http://blogs.worldbank.org/insidetheweb/raising-the-bar-on-transparency-accountability-and-openness. Accessed January 13, 2018.

Gilardi, Fabrizio. 2002. Policy Credibility and Delegation to Independent Regulatory Agencies: A Comparative Empirical Analysis. *Journal of European Public Policy* 9 (6):873–93.

Gulrajani, Nilima. 2011. Transcending the Great Foreign Aid Debate: Managerialism, Radicalism and the Search for Aid Effectiveness. *Third World Quarterly* 32 (2):199–216.

Hamilton, Joni. 2015. USAID's Strategic Approach to Improving IATI Compliance. August 13. Available at http://www.aidtransparency.net/news/usaids-strategic-approach-to-improving-iati-compliance. Accessed February 9, 2016.

Hainmueller, Jens, Jonathan Mummolo, and Yiqing Xu. 2019. How Much Should We Trust Estimates from Multiplicative Interaction Models? Simple Tools to Improve Empirical Practice. *Political Analysis* (Forthcoming).

Hanlon, Joseph, Armando Barrientos, and David Hulme. 2010. *Just Give Money to the Poor: The Development Revolution from the Global South*. Sterling, VA: Kumarian Press.

Hansen, Heather, and Catherine Marschner. *Millennium Challenge Corporation: Principles into Practice*. Washington, DC: Millennium Challenge Corporation. Available at https://assets.mcc.gov/content/uploads/2017/05/paper-2015001163301-principles-transparency.pdf. Accessed February 27, 2019.

Hawkins, Darren, David A. Lake, Daniel L. Nielson, and Michael J. Tierney, eds. 2006. *Delegation Under Anarchy: States, International Organizations and Principal-Agent Theory.* Cambridge: Cambridge University Press.

Herrling, Sheila. 2015. The Business Proposition of Open Aid Data: Why Every US Agency Should Default to Transparency. *Publish What You Fund* (blog). Available at http://www.publishwhatyoufund.org/updates/by-country/us/business-proposition-open-aid-data-why-every-u-s-agency-should-default-transparency/. Accessed January 13, 2018.

Hollyer, James R., B. Peter Rosendorff, and James Raymond Vreeland. 2011. Democracy and Transparency. *Journal of Politics* 73 (4):1191–205.

2014. Measuring Transparency. *Political Analysis* 22 (4):413–34.

2015. Transparency, Protest, and Autocratic Instability. *American Political Science Review* 109 (4):764–84.

2018a. *Information, Democracy, and Autocracy: Economic Transparency and Political (In)Stability.* Cambridge: Cambridge University Press.

2018b. Transparency, Protest and Democratic Stability. *British Journal of Political Science* 1–27.

Honig, Dan. 2018. *Navigation by Judgment: Why and When Top-Down Control of Foreign Aid Doesn't Work.* New York: Oxford University Press.

2019. When Reporting Undermines Performance: The Costs of Politically Constrained Autonomy in Foreign Aid Implementation. *International Organization* 73 (1):171–201.

Ingram, George. 2015. Making Aid Transparency a Reality. https://www.brookings.edu/blog/up-front/2015/02/11/making-aid-transparency-a-reality/. Accessed February 27, 2019.

Kelley, Judith G., and Beth A. Simmons. 2014. Politics by Number: Indicators as Social Pressure in International Relations. *American Journal of Political Science* 59 (1):55–70.

2019. Introduction: The Power of Global Performance Indicators. *The Power of Global Performance Indicators.* New York: Cambridge University Press.

Kelley, Judith G. 2017. *Scorecard Diplomacy: Grading States to Influence Their Reputation and Behavior.* Cambridge: Cambridge University Press.

Kijima, Rie and Phillip Lipscy. 2019. The Politics of International Testing. *The Power of Global Performance Indicators.* New York: Cambridge University Press.

Koeberle, Stefan. 2016. The World Bank Is Again in the Top Ten of the Aid Transparency Index. *The World Bank Data Blog.* March 3. Available at https://blogs.worldbank.org/opendata/world-bank-again-topo-aid-transparency-index.

Koliev, Faradj, Thomas Sommerer, and Jonas Tallberg. 2019. Reporting Matters: Performance Assessment and Compliance in the ILO. *The Power of Global Performance Indicators.* New York: Cambridge University Press.

Lee, Sung. 2016. The Data Revolution That's Reshaping American Foreign Assistance. *US Global Leadership Coalition.* (Blog). May 11. Available at http://www.usglc.org/blog/the-data-revolution-thats-reshaping-american-foreign-assistance/.

Marks, Joseph. 2012. USAID Plans to Map All Its Spending Data in Some
    Countries. January 19. Available at http://www.nextgov.com/technology-
    news/2012/01/usaid-plans-to-map-all-its-spending-data-in-some-countries/
    50481/. Accessed January 13, 2018.
Morse, Julia. 2019. Blacklists, Market Enforcement, and the Global Regime to
    Combat Terrorist Financing. *International Organization* 73 (3).
Mulley, Sarah. 2010. Donor Aid: New Frontiers in Transparency and
    Accountability. Transparency and Accountability Initiative. Available
    at http://www.transparency-initiative.org/archive/wp-content/
    uploads/2011/05/donor_aid_final1.pdf. Accessed February 27, 2019.
Nelson, Paul J. 2001. Transparency Mechanisms at the Multilateral
    Development Banks. *World Development* 29 (11):1835–47.
Obama, Barack. 2009. Transparency and Open Government. Memorandum
    for the Heads of Executive Departments and Agencies. Available at
    https://www.whitehouse.gov/sites/whitehouse.gov/files/omb/
    memoranda/2009/m09-12.pdf. Accessed February 27, 2019.
Orszag, Peter. 2009. Open Government Directive. Memorandum for the
    Heads of Executive Departments and Agencies. Available at
    https://www.treasury.gov/open/Documents/m10-06.pdf. Accessed
    February 27, 2019.
Publish What You Fund. 2009. Briefing Paper 1: Why Aid Transparency
    Matters, and the Global Movement for Aid Transparency.
    (2011–2016). Aid Transparency Indices: 2011–2016. Available at
    http://ati.publishwhatyoufund.org/. Accessed January 13, 2018.
    2015a. 2015 EU Aid Transparency Review. Available at
    http://ati.publishwhatyoufund.org/. Accessed January 13, 2018.
    2015b. 2015 US Aid Transparency Review. Available at
    http://ati.publishwhatyoufund.org/. Accessed January 13, 2018.
    Annual Reports of the Aid Transparency Index, 2011–2017. *London:
    Publish What You Fund.* Available at http://ati.publishwhatyoufund.org/.
    Accessed January 13, 2018.
    Publish What You Fund Annual Report 2017. *London: Publish What You
    Fund.* Available at https://www.publishwhatyoufund.org/
    download/11964/. Accessed February 27, 2019.
Roberts, Jordan and Juan Tellez. 2019. Freedom House's Scarlet Letter:
    Assessment Power Through Transnational Pressure. *The Power of Global
    Performance Indicators*, New York: Cambridge University Press.
Saunder, Michael, and Wendy Nelson Espeland. 2009. The Discipline of
    Rankings: Tight Coupling and Organizational Change. *American
    Sociological Review* 74 (1):63–82.
Senate Foreign Relations Committee. 2013. Full Committee Hearing:
    Nomination. November 19. Available at https://www.foreign.senate.gov/
    hearings/2013/11/19/nomination. Accessed February 15, 2018.
Skagerlind, Helena Hede. 2019. Power in Global Development Policy: The
    Millennium Development Goals. *The Power of Global Performance
    Indicators*, New York: Cambridge University Press.
Thier, Alex, and Angelique Crumbly. 2015. It's Clear: Transparency Works.
    USAID Blogs, July 2. Available at https://blog.usaid.gov/2015/07/
    its-clear-transparency-works/. Accessed January 13, 2018.

United Kingdom Department for International Development. 2015. Key
Topics in Transparency. Memo of the International Development Sector
Transparency Panel, 5 March. Available at https://www.gov.uk/
government/uploads/attachment_data/file/441699/Key_topics_in_
transparency_-_Paper_5_March_2015.pdf. Accessed 13 January 2018.
United States Agency for International Development. 2015. *International Aid
Transparency Initiative (IATI) Cost Management Plan.* Washington,
DC: USAID. Available at https://www.usaid.gov/sites/default/files/
documents/1870/IATI%20Cost%20Management%20Plan_u_14July2015.pdf.
Accessed February 9, 2016.
Weaver, Catherine, and Christian Peratsakis. 2014. Engineering Policy Norm
Implementation: The World Bank's Transparency Transformation. In
*Implementation and World Politics: How International Norms Change
Practice,* edited by Alexander Betts and Phil Orchard, eds., 179–94.
Oxford: Oxford University Press.

6

International Assessments and Education Policy

Evidence from an Elite Survey

Rie Kijima[1] and Phillip Y. Lipscy

In recent years, an increasing number of countries have participated in cross-national assessments (CNAs) in education, but their impact remains underexplored. We argue that CNA participation increases the capacity and motivation of policymakers to implement improvements in education through mechanisms at the elite, domestic, and transnational levels. We find evidence consistent with our propositions using an original survey of 77 education officials directly responsible for the planning and implementation of CNAs in 46 countries and personal interviews with 48 officials in target states, assessment agencies, and donor agencies.

The number of countries participating in CNAs in education has grown rapidly over the last 50 years. Countries are increasingly willing to use assessments to measure and disseminate the state of their education. This represents

[1] Rie Kijima (University of Toronto) is Assistant Professor, Munk School of Global Affairs and Public Policy, and Phillip Y. Lipscy (University of Toronto) is Associate Professor of Political Science and Chair in Japanese Politics & Global Affairs. We would like to thank Felipe Barrera-Osorio, Eric Bettinger, Patricia Bromley, Martin Carnoy, Judith Goldstein, Elena Tej Grewal, Edward Haertel, Judith Kelley, David Laitin, Aila Matanock, John Meyer, Lambrina Mileva-Kless, Sonal Pandya, Francisco Ramirez, Kenneth Schultz, Beth Simmons, Michael Tomz, Catherine Weaver, Imeh Williams, and conference participants at APSA 2016, Harvard, Stanford, and U.C. Berkeley for their valuable feedback. Jane Leer, Idalia Rodriguez Morales, and Trevor Incerti provided excellent research assistance. We thank all individuals who responded favorably to requests for interviews, survey completion, and documents collected over a period of three years. We also thank Dr. Hans Wagemaker, former Director of International Association for the Evaluation of Educational Achievement (IEA), and Dr. Dirk Hastedt, current Director of IEA for their unwavering support of this study. This research was supported by the Stanford Global Development and Poverty Initiative, Stanford Graduate School of Education, Education International's Mary Futrell Scholarship Fund, the Freeman Spogli Institute for International Studies at Stanford University, the Center of East Asian Studies at Stanford University, and Stanford Center on Philanthropy and Civil Society.

a stark departure from the traditional politics of education, in which information about student performance was largely contained within the borders of nation-states.[2] Assessment results from CNAs such as Trends in International Mathematics and Science Study (TIMSS) and the Program for International Student Assessment (PISA) are now widely followed as indicators for national educational quality and, more broadly, human capital and international competitiveness.[3] More than 60 countries now regularly participate in CNAs, a fivefold increase from 1959. Participation among developed countries is now nearly universal, and about half of participants are developing countries.[4]

CNAs are an important substantive topic of inquiry for several reasons. First, by allowing countries to benchmark their progress over time and against their peers, CNAs can improve education performance and economic outcomes. Education policy directly affects the prospects of over 1.8 billion school-age children in the world today, with more to come.[5] In addition, education quality has been widely recognized as an important source of economic development.[6]

Second, CNAs have been the subject of considerable controversy and value contestation. At their best, CNAs bring transparency to policymaking by offering a standard metric for cross-national comparison. They can help international and domestic audiences hold political leaders accountable for education quality and performance.[7] However, test scores can be misinterpreted, leading to misleading conclusions.[8] CNA critics have argued that other indices focusing on national innovation or creativity better account for the ultimate consequences of education outcomes.[9] Others have condemned CNAs as "educational colonialism,"[10] which imposes Western values and shifts the focus of education toward "teaching to the test"[11] rather than less quantifiable goals such as personal and moral development.[12]

Finally, the impact of CNAs on policy remains understudied. Existing research has predominantly focused on the role of global norms and culture

[2] Anderson 2006.

[3] Among others, see "Testing Education: Pisa Envy," *The Economist*, January 19, 2013.

[4] Based on data from TIMSS. We use the World Bank classification of economies to define developing countries, which are low-income, lower-middle income, and upper middle income countries.

[5] World Bank Group 2011.

[6] Hanushek and Kimko 2000; Hanushek and Woessmann 2008, 2012; Rodrik 1995.

[7] Benveniste 1999; Carnoy 2014.

[8] Koretz 2009; Loveless 2012.

[9] Valerie Strauss, "Three Global Indexes Show that U.S. Public Schools Must Be Doing Something Right," *Washington Post*, February 13, 2017.

[10] "OECD and Pisa tests are damaging education worldwide – academics," *The Guardian*, May 6, 2014, https://www.theguardian.com/education/2014/may/06/oecd-pisa-tests-damaging-education-academics.

[11] Jennings and Bearak 2014; Sutton 2004; Volante 2004.

[12] Meyer and Benavot 2013.

institutionalized by Western countries and multilateral agencies,[13] which have compelled developing countries to participate in CNAs.[14] Although this is a useful framework for explaining the general proliferation of CNAs, it is less useful for explaining their consequences. Studies that consider the influence of CNAs on policymaking have largely focused on case studies.[15]

In this chapter, we will consider the "assessment power"[16] of CNAs. Do CNAs affect education policy, and if so, how?[17] We argue that CNAs increase both the capacity and motivation of policymakers to implement improvements in education. CNAs exert a particularly strong influence at the elite level.[18] Because administering a CNA requires extensive elite interaction with authoritative agencies and experts, there is considerable scope for technical transfers, learning, and socialization. CNAs also generate detailed information about the shortcomings of a country's education system, which can inform reforms. In addition, the clear, transparent, and comparative rankings produced by CNAs invoke strong status concerns among elite policymakers that serve as a motivation for improvements in education policy. We expect domestic and transnational pressures for reform to be conditional: public pressure generated by poor rankings is an important motivation for education reforms among more democratic states, and international pressure, particularly from donor agencies, is an important impetus for aid-dependent developing countries.

Many of the pathways of influence associated with our proposed causal mechanisms are either difficult to observe or quantify: e.g. the relative status perceptions of policymakers; learning and knowledge transfers. To address this challenge, we conducted an elite survey of 77 education officials directly involved in the planning and implementation of CNAs in their countries. The survey allows us to examine the perceived importance of specific pathways of influence that would otherwise be difficult to observe. In addition, we personally interviewed 48 policymakers in both target states and assessment agencies to qualitatively examine the assessment power of CNAs. The evidence is consistent with our proposition that CNA participation has a substantial impact on education policymaking, particularly at the elite level.

[13] Ramirez, Meyer, and Lerch 2015; Smith 2016.
[14] Kamens and McNeely 2010.
[15] Abdul-Hamid, Abu-Lebdeh, and Patrinos 2011; Addey 2015; Grek 2009; Takayama 2008.
[16] Kelley and Simmons this volume.
[17] We evaluate the impact of CNAs on education *outcomes* in related work (Kijima and Lipscy 2018) using a panel dataset covering all CNAs to date. The empirical analysis suggests CNA participation has important effects on policy outcomes – education reforms, foreign aid to education, and secondary enrollment – even after accounting for selection effects.
[18] In this chapter, elites are policymakers involved in the formulation and implementation of education policy in a given country. We focus primarily on public officials in education bureaucracies, but elites may also include politicians and experts involved in the formulation of education policy.

THE RISE OF CROSS-NATIONAL ASSESSMENTS IN EDUCATION

The first CNA, the Pilot Twelve-Country Study, was administered in 1959. Western countries were riveted by the launch of Sputnik and attributed the success of the Soviet space program to high-quality science education.[19] Educational researchers expressed concerns about their inability to judge the quality of education cross-nationally. Driven by a strong desire to demonstrate educational progress empirically, a group of mostly Western industrialized countries joined the effort to create an "internationally valid standard."[20] The Twelve-Country Study consisted of 120 test items that covered reading, math, science, and geography.[21]

CNAs encompass both global assessments and regional assessments. Global assessments, like TIMSS and PISA, are universalistic in spirit. Although participation is voluntary, and hence universality has not been achieved, global assessments place few restrictions on participation based on country-specific factors.[22] Regional assessments are administered in countries from a particular region, such as Africa or Latin America. Examples of regional assessments are the Southern and Eastern Africa Consortium for Monitoring Educational Quality (SACMEQ) in Africa and the Second Regional Comparative and Explanatory Study (SERCE) in Latin America.

Today, over 60 countries and economies regularly participate in global international assessments like PISA, TIMSS, and the Program in International Reading Literacy Study (PIRLS) conducted by the IEA. Figure 6.1 traces participation in CNAs since 1959. CNAs primarily attracted a handful of economically advanced nations from 1959 through the 1980s. Participation expanded sharply since the 1990s, particularly among less developed countries.[23] In 2015, 72 countries and economies participated in PISA.[24] With each round, international assessments in education have attracted more participants from around the world.

---

[19] Husén 1979, 374.

[20] Ibid.

[21] Husén 1979.

[22] Countries need to implement the assessments themselves in cooperation with assessment agencies, and CNAs generally involve a membership/participation fee. However, financial and technical assistance is usually available from donor or assessment agencies even for less economically developed countries. As a reference, the cost associated with TIMSS Grade 8 assessment is approximately 40,000 USD per year, excluding costs associated with analysis and dissemination Greaney and Kellaghan 2008, vol. 1, 75. OECD has a fee structure that corresponds with the country's economic development (author interview with an education expert at OECD 2012).

[23] There is a jump in the number of countries participating in CNAs in 1990, which falls on a year when three CNAs were administered at the same time. These three tests are: International Assessment of Educational Progress, Reading Literacy Study, and Pacific Islands Literacy Level.

[24] OECD, "About PISA," https://www.oecd.org/pisa/aboutpisa/.

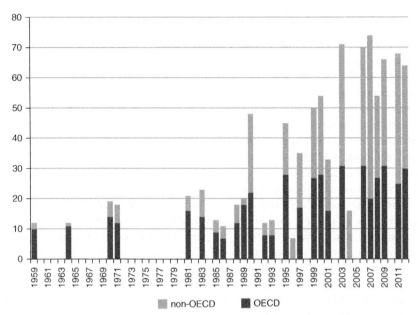

FIGURE 6.1. The number of participants in cross-national assessments in education (1959–2012).

THE POLICY IMPACT OF CROSS-NATIONAL
ASSESSMENTS IN EDUCATION

While the proliferation and increasing visibility of CNAs is unmistakable, very little scholarship has systematically examined how CNAs affect policymaking. Our central argument is that CNA participation increases the capacity and motivation of education policymakers to pursue improvements in education quality. CNA participation improves the capacity of education officials to implement effective reforms by increasing access to technical expertise, training, and information about shortcomings in their education systems. In addition, CNA participation increases the motivation of policymakers to pursue improvements in education quality by generating status competition, socialization, and domestic and international pressure for reform. In this section, we will discuss the specific features of CNAs and how they affect education policymaking.

It is helpful to place CNAs within the broader context of global performance indicators (GPIs), "a named collection of rank-ordered data that purports to represent the past or projected performance of different units."[25] CNAs clearly fit the criteria for a GPI. The results of CNAs are generally public and presented openly, clearly, and simply, resulting in transparency

---

[25] Kelley and Simmons this volume.

and wide dissemination.[26] Major CNAs are conducted on a regular and predictable cycle.[27] CNAs are inclusive and explicitly comparative in nature, seeking to rank countries based on student performance in subject areas such as reading, math, and science. Assessment agencies conduct CNAs in a purposive manner, linking test results to improvements in education policy.[28] Participation in a CNA thus publicly reveals information about a country's education performance and its relative standing in international comparison.

CNAs generally involve extensive interaction and feedback between education policy elites in the target country and authoritative assessment agencies. This makes elite mechanisms a particularly important source of assessment power. Unlike GPIs that rely primarily on existing data sources,[29] CNAs generate new data through the active participation of students, teachers, school administrators, and government officials in the target country. Hence, CNAs are typically conducted by countries in close cooperation with assessment agencies, which provide direct and extensive assistance with development of test items, planning, sampling, field trials, and analysis.[30] Other organizations, such as bilateral and multilateral donor agencies, often assist with funding and administration of the assessment and policy design in response to the findings.[31] It is also common for governments to involve domestic and international academics and education policy experts to provide technical support at all stages. Education policymakers from participant countries also attend conferences and receive extensive information about successful reforms implemented in other countries.[32] Hence, CNAs provide significant opportunities for capacity building of education policy elites through interaction with assessment agencies, international organizations, foreign counterparts, and technical experts.[33]

---

[26] There is some variation in transparency regarding specific data associated with CNAs. For example, while the headline national test scores are disseminated widely, and data by gender, socio-economic status, and performance variance are readily available, some potentially useful data to conduct longitudinal analysis are not released to the public (e.g. https://www.oecd.org/pisa/aboutpisa/pisafaq.htm).

[27] E.g. PISA is conducted every three years, and TIMSS every four years.

[28] E.g. the IEA website's overview of TIMSS notes that "Assessing fourth grade students can provide an early warning for necessary curricular reforms, and the effectiveness of these reforms can be further monitored at the eighth grade" (http://www.iea.nl/timss); OECD similarly highlights how PISA shapes education reform, noting that "countries such as Germany and Brazil have been able to improve their student performance in PISA and make their education systems more inclusive" (http://www.oecd.org/pisa/aboutpisa/).

[29] E.g. the Aid Transparency Index is produced without significant consultation with target governments as discussed by Honig 2016; Weaver 2016.

[30] Henry et al. 2001; Lockheed 2012.

[31] Kijima 2010.

[32] E.g. "5th IEA International Research Conference," June 26–28, 2013, Conference Program.

[33] Lockheed 2012.

CNA participation is not just an exercise in capacity building. Government interaction and learning surrounding CNAs involves authoritative counterparties with strong reputations and technical capabilities.[34] OECD, the administrator of PISA, draws on its prestige as a club of the most advanced economies in the world as well as its research and technical capabilities.[35] Similarly, IEA draws on its expertise as a pioneer in international assessments and nearly 60-year history of conducting CNAs worldwide.[36] Since the end of WWII, international aid agencies have played a central role in setting the agenda on global governance in education.[37] These organizations construct "shared ideologies of an 'imagined' world order through process of negotiation, diffusion, and sometimes contestation."[38] Assessment and aid agencies leverage their authority and access to education policy elites to motivate changes in policies consistent with global values such as "education for all," gender equality, and an emphasis on economically important skills such as reading, math, and science.[39]

CNA participation also motivates education policy elites by generating status competition. CNAs reveal, for all to see, quantitative information about a country's education performance and relative standing in international comparison. Education is a fundamental policy issue that touches upon essentially all citizens, and it is also naturally associated with status competition as the first institutionalized setting that subjects children to evaluation and relative comparison. For some countries, education performance is deeply tied to a sense of identity and self-worth, while for others, it is perceived as a proxy for broader economic or geopolitical competition.[40] Assessment agencies also reinforce status competition by sponsoring conferences that routinize personal, cross-national interaction among education policy elites of participant countries.[41] We thus expect CNA participation to facilitate status competition and strengthen the motivation of policy elites to make improvements to their education systems.

Compared to other GPIs, we expect transnational pressure to be somewhat less salient and conditional for CNAs. In contrast to GPIs such as terrorist designations by the US government,[42] assessment agencies do not explicitly link CNAs to formal rewards or punishments: there is no direct

---

[34] For analogous arguments about the World Bank and International Labour Organization, see Kelley, Simmons, and Doshi 2016; Koliev, Sommerer, and Tallberg 2019.

[35] Meyer and Benavot 2013.

[36] Mullis and Martin 2007, 9.

[37] Mundy 1999; Mundy and Manion 2014.

[38] Mundy 1999, 28.

[39] Martens and Niemann 2013.

[40] Ibid.

[41] See Chabbott 2003 for an analysis of Education for All Conferences.

[42] Jo, Phillips, and Alley 2016; Morse 2016.

channel for international pressure. However, CNAs provide reliable data on the status and progress of a country's education system. Hence, international donor agencies may be more willing to disburse aid to CNA-participating countries, where the scores can serve as benchmarks for the monitoring and evaluation of projects. In addition, CNA scores may also serve as a proxy for quality of human capital, influencing decisions by private investors. Insofar as these informal transnational pressures exist, we expect them to be particularly salient for developing countries that are dependent on foreign aid and investment flows.

We also expect the observed impact of domestic political pressures to be somewhat weaker and conditional for CNAs compared to other GPIs. Low CNA performance can trigger public criticism and upheaval, facilitating education reforms.[43] However, several factors limit the impact of domestic political mechanisms. First, domestic political pressure is more likely to matter in democratic states, where leaders face electoral repercussions from poor performance. In autocratic states, which are participating in CNAs in greater numbers, leaders may be better able to ignore or suppress domestic pressures. Second, specific education reforms are often highly politicized – e.g. charter schools, higher salaries for teachers – which may limit the ability for domestic groups to rally around a coherent objective.[44] More broadly, unlike GPIs that target government policies or activities,[45] which can be reformed directly by executive or legislative action, governments exercise only indirect control over the academic performance of schoolchildren.[46] This is not to say that education outcomes are immovable: evidence from impact evaluations indicate that there are many practical policy interventions available to policymakers that rapidly and cheaply move salient education outcomes, such as student and teacher absenteeism.[47] Third, participation in CNAs is largely voluntary. The voluntary nature of participation raises the potential problem of self-selection. Specifically, leaders who particularly fear the domestic political repercussions of publicizing the state of their education systems may opt out, limiting the capacity of CNAs to shape the policies of the most problematic countries.[48] This is not always a problem: as we will discuss, leaders sometimes opt for participation despite low expected performance, and some countries participate in CNAs due to external mandates.

---

[43] Takayama 2010.

[44] E.g. Ladd 2002.

[45] Some GPIs explicitly target actions directly under government control, e.g. the Aid Transparency Index (Honig 2016; Weaver 2016) and subnational performance indicators focusing on administrative procedures (Le and Malesky 2016).

[46] Analogously, governments may find it difficult to reduce corruption even when they seek to do so (Lee and Matanock this volume).

[47] Benhassine et al. 2013; Duflo, Hanna, and Ryan 2012; Kremer, Brannen, and Glennerster 2013; Miguel and Kremer 2004.

[48] Kijima 2013.

In summary, we expect that CNA participation will have tangible effects on education policymaking and facilitate improvements in education quality. Concerning mechanisms, we expect *elite politics* to be particularly important for CNAs. Relative to other GPIs, CNAs inherently involve extensive interaction between target states on the one hand and assessment agencies, assessment experts, and aid agencies on the other hand. This suggests that CNAs are highly likely to provide significant opportunities for policy change through elite mechanisms such as learning, socialization, and status concerns. We expect the role of *transnational politics* to be conditional, as CNAs are not associated with explicit rewards or sanctions. However, informal rewards, such as increases in foreign aid or investment, are likely to be an important consideration for policymakers in less developed countries. The importance of *domestic politics* as a mechanism is also likely to be conditional. The simplicity, transparency, and comparability of test scores provide ample opportunity for the mobilization of public opinion and civil society groups around education reform. However, the domestic political channel is likely to be limited in less democratic societies. In addition, the observable efficacy of the domestic political channel may be mitigated due to politicization of education reforms and self-selection: political leaders particularly concerned about domestic repercussions may opt out ex ante.

SURVEY DATA ON INTERNATIONAL ASSESSMENTS

One common challenge in international relations research is the difficulty of analyzing causal mechanisms. This is no different in the study of GPIs. Many of the proposed pathways of influence associated with assessment power are difficult to measure or quantify – e.g. reputational and status concerns – or difficult to observe – e.g. informal interaction between an assessment agency and a target state. In this chapter, we address this empirical challenge by utilizing a survey of elite education officials responsible for the planning and administration of CNAs in their countries.

Unlike many other GPIs, CNAs are conducted with the direct involvement of education officials in the target country. We were able to participate in two international conferences that involved these officials from all countries participating in two major global assessments, TIMSS and PIRLS. Because the survey respondents are education policy elites directly responsible for the planning and administration of CNAs, they are intimately familiar with the context of CNAs and education policy in their countries. More importantly, they are important subjects in their own right, as they are the relevant policy elites hypothesized to serve as conduits of assessment power. In the exposition below, we will also draw on in-depth interviews conducted with 48 officials from target countries, assessment agencies, and donor agencies (Supporting Information Table 6.A1).

Survey Description

We collected data at two international conferences in 2011 and 2012 sponsored by the IEA, the organization responsible for TIMMS and several other CNAs. The conferences provided us with direct access to country delegates who were involved in high-level education policy discussions on topics such as participation, administration, and usage of international assessments. The number of countries participating in these international conferences was at a historical peak in 2012 due to increasing participation and the simultaneous administration of two major CNAs, TIMSS and PIRLS. The conferences involved the participation of 150 delegates[49] from 67 countries[50] responsible for the administration and post-implementation analysis of CNAs in their countries (Supporting Information Table 6.A2). We received responses from 77 delegates representing 46 countries.[51] Due to potential bias that could result from non-response, we checked to see if there were statistically significant differences in several characteristics between countries that responded to the survey and those that did not. We ran bivariate comparisons on several variables: GDP/capita, net secondary enrollment rate, polity score, and on global dataset on education quality in reading, mathematics and science at the secondary level (Supporting Information Table 6.A3). There were no statistically significant differences between the two subgroups.

This survey data is useful for three purposes. First, it sheds light on the mechanisms through which CNAs affect education policy across contexts. When administering assessments, are education officials concerned about rankings, technical transfers, international status, domestic political repercussions, or pressure from third parties such as international organizations? These are questions that are difficult to address with country-level data. Second, the survey and interviews shed light on the policy discourse and contestation surrounding CNAs across a large number of countries. Third, the analysis reinforces the plausibility of our central claim that CNA participation affects education policy and outcomes. It would be troubling for our theoretical propositions if most education officials indicated that CNAs have no meaningful effect on policy. However, the findings in this section reinforce

---

[49] These delegates are representatives sent by their respective ministries or departments of education and responsible for the administration of cross-national assessments and post-implementation analysis through their respective ministries or departments of education.

[50] For the purposes of our analysis, we treat several "partner economies" as countries as they have substantially greater autonomy over policies within their jurisdictions than typical subnational governments. These are Chinese Taipei (Taiwan), Hong Kong, and the Palestinian Authority (West Bank and Gaza).

[51] There are more respondents than number of countries/economies because more than one delegate represented each country and every participant received an individual survey link.

our related work on cross-national education policy outcomes[52] by illustrating that education officials do in fact generally perceive a meaningful impact of assessments on education policy outcomes.

Cross-National Assessments and Education Reforms

We begin with a basic question: what is the perceived association between CNAs and domestic education policies? Our survey respondents are well positioned to answer this question, as they are policy elites not only responsible for planning and implementing CNAs, but also part of and intimately familiar with their countries' education policymaking establishment. We should note that the survey respondents are not advocates for assessments, but generally education bureaucrats on rotation within their ministries who happened to be working on assessments when we conducted the survey. The conference at which we conducted the survey was largely technical, focusing on how to administer assessments rather than discussing their broader impact. As such, we do not have a strong prima facie basis to believe that our respondents would exhibit a positive bias regarding the impact of assessments. However, these findings should be interpreted with appropriate caution, as they reflect the subjective assessments of policy officials.

The survey asked respondents to answer an open-ended question about how CNAs impacted their country's education policy. Several of the respondents answered that their country had only recently initiated participation in CNAs, and therefore it was too early to determine their impact. Omitting these responses, about 22 percent of respondents answered that CNAs had no impact on their country's education policies. Seventy percent of respondents provided examples of how CNAs had affected the substance of their country's education policy or curriculum, and 7 percent mentioned other impacts such as the development of greater national assessment capacity, increases in the education budget, or greater participation in other CNAs.[53]

Many respondents drew specific, direct connections between CNAs and the substantive content of education reform in their countries. For example, a representative from Hungary noted that "PISA and PIRLS reading results led to the extension of reading and math skill-improving classes beyond grade 4,

---

[52] In Kijima and Lipscy 2018, we use a panel dataset covering all CNAs and countries and a difference-in-difference specification to show that CNA participation is associated with meaningful changes in education policy and outcomes as well as foreign aid inflows to education. These findings are robust to a variety of model specifications and accounting for self-selection by limiting the analysis to countries where CNA participation occurred due to an external mandate.

[53] The numbers were similar when using countries rather than individual respondents as the unit of analysis: 21 percent no impact, 74 percent impact on education policy or curriculum, and 5 percent other impact.

in grades 5 and 6."[54] A representative from New Zealand similarly noted that "The impact of the early cycles of TIMSS was quite significant as a driver for math educational policy, with the establishment of a math and science taskforce and then the numeracy strategy."[55] Similarly, in Malta, "the new science education strategy was based on the findings from TIMSS."[56] In Botswana, the 2003 TIMSS led to "changes in the curriculum for [grades] 1 to 3 ... [and] introduction of a programme called SMASSE [Strengthening of Math and Science in Secondary Education]."[57] In Iran, "policy-makers changed the content of textbooks in Science and Reading ... and adapted our curriculum to the framework of TIMSS and PIRLS."[58] In South Korea, "PISA 2006 results showed the drop of science literacy ranking in Korea. Due to this drop, educational policy of science education for helping female students was implemented."[59]

It is important to note that many of the policy changes mentioned by our respondents were reforms based on information first revealed by CNAs or which directly incorporated expertise gained by participation. The presence of these types of CNA-dependent reforms strengthens the case that CNAs likely play an important role in education policymaking: such reforms are highly unlikely to have occurred in the counterfactual case where countries had opted out of participation. Our findings reinforce existing, mostly qualitative work that identifies a link between CNA participation and education reforms.[60]

To provide additional support for our proposition that CNA participation tends to accelerate education reforms, we collected data on education reforms for all countries that initiated participation in CNAs after 1980. Education reforms are difficult to quantify systemically due to differences in policy contexts (e.g. legislation vs. administrative measures; centralized vs. decentralized education systems), differences in information availability (e.g. developed vs. developing countries), and subjective judgments about what actually constitutes an education reform. These caveats notwithstanding, we identified education reforms based on World Bank and UNESCO documents[61]

---

[54] Answer to survey question.

[55] Ibid.

[56] Author interview with the Director of Assessments from Malta, Vienna, Austria, December 2011.

[57] Author interview with the Director of Assessments and three education officers from Botswana, Singapore, March 2013.

[58] Author interview with an education officer from Iran, in Singapore, March 2013.

[59] Answer to survey question.

[60] Abdul-Hamid, Abu-Lebdeh, and Patrinos 2011; Addey 2015; Breakspear 2012; Grek 2009; Takayama 2008.

[61] For the sake of consistency, we used two primary sources for all countries: (i) World Bank Project Appraisal Documents, and (ii) UNESCO IBE National Reports/database. The World Bank is the largest multilateral aid agency that finances education projects around the world. Whenever the country develops a program, the World Bank publishes a Project Appraisal Document (PAD). The PAD describes the country context, strategic objectives in

and examined a 10-year window around each country's first-time participation in a CNA. Based on this data, countries implemented an average of 0.4 education reforms per year in the 5 years prior to CNA participation, and this accelerated to 0.8 education reforms per year in the 5 years after participation. We performed the same comparison using an independently collected dataset covering education reforms in developed European countries for a different time period (1929–2000),[62] and the results were analogous: there were 0.1 education reforms per year in the 5 years before first-time CNA participation, and this accelerated to 0.3 reforms per year in the 5 years after (in years prior to the 10-year window, the rate was also 0.1 education reforms per year).

Elite Politics

Our survey generally showed agreement with questions associated with elite politics mechanisms. Survey respondents were unanimous that a primary motivation for participating in international assessments is "to compare our education quality with other countries or economies." It is striking that no other survey item received unanimous support from respondents, including, "to measure and understand the current state of educational quality of my country/economy." The raison d'être of CNAs unquestionably stems from its comparative function, i.e. the ability of countries to place themselves within a global ranking of education quality. Our interviews tell a similar picture: officials repeatedly pointed to the comparative aspect as a core rationale for CNAs. An official from Jordan noted, "When you participate in international studies, you know whether you are performing well or worse compared to others."[63]

We asked survey respondents to identify the specific countries against which they compare their own scores. Broadly, respondents split into three groups: (1) those that tend to compare their scores against the highest performers (e.g. Finland, South Korea, Singapore); (2) those that situate themselves within a regional or linguistic grouping (e.g. Arab countries, English-language countries), and (3) those that compare their results to countries at a similar level of economic development (e.g. developing countries, OECD countries).

---

the education sector, and identifies education reforms. These documents are translated into English and are available online via their website. We also consulted UNESCO's IBE database for a more comprehensive data collection of reforms developed by both the individual countries as well as projects supported by international entities. Within the documents, we looked for keywords such as reforms, projects, and education goals under the subsection of each country's "Major Reforms in Education." The year in which the country participated in an international assessment was coded as post-assessment (omitting this year does not have a large bearing on the findings). This process was conducted for a list of countries for a time span of 10 years (–5 years pre and +5 years post first time participation in an international assessment).

[62] Braga, Checchi, and Meschi 2013.

[63] Author interview with an education officer from Jordan, Austria, Vienna, December 2011.

Interestingly, countries that place themselves in the first group are not necessarily those with the highest scores themselves. By providing clear, comparative rankings of educational performance, CNAs establish an international status hierarchy and compel countries to either accept their position within a plausible peer group or aspire to higher status.

Fifty-six percent of respondents agreed that CNA participation "improves our reputation/status in the international community," even though our sample included a large number of developing countries that typically have low scores. Officials saw CNAs as a way to increase their country's international profile by associating with high-performance countries and adopting their assessment standards. An official from Ghana noted that CNA participation created an " ... opportunity to be on the map. It projected us in the international community."[64] Trinidad and Tobago participates in CNAs in order to, " ... position ourselves as the hub in the Caribbean for international communication. We want to be seen as the Caribbean leader."[65]

Survey respondents frequently noted that CNAs facilitate learning through interaction with assessment agencies and foreign counterparts. Eighty-four percent of respondents agreed that CNA participation "improves our capacity to conduct and evaluate our own assessments," and 73 percent agree that participation "facilitates exchange of information between countries/economies." A Chilean official emphasized that participation in PISA involved sending a large delegation to OECD for consultations, information exchange, and training, "a very, very impressive experience ... it was very important to have progress in our capabilities."[66] A delegate from Trinidad and Tobago indicated that CNAs allowed them to "interact with IEA to learn about best practices ... and to validate our own standard system."[67] In Botswana, the main benefit of CNA participation " ... is to improve our research skills."[68] By participating in CNAs, countries are able to acquire valuable technical expertise to evaluate and improve the substance of their domestic education policy.

Several of our subjects went further and noted that CNA participation had a deeper impact on the discourse and norms surrounding education in their countries by shifting attention toward the goals, metrics, and standards supported by international assessment agencies.[69] A representative from Kuwait commented that, "Once our country was exposed to international meetings that talked about international assessments, the revolution of education began.

---

[64] Author interview with an education officer from Ghana, Singapore, March 2013.
[65] Author interview with an education officer from Trinidad and Tobago, Singapore, March 2013.
[66] Author interview with a government officer at the Ministry of Education in Chile, videoconference, May 2013.
[67] Author interview with an education officer from Trinidad and Tobago, Singapore, March 2013.
[68] Author interview with the Director of Assessments and three education officers from Botswana, Austria, December 2011.
[69] Martens and Niemann 2013.

We started many awareness campaigns to also educate the mass[es]."[70] Similarly, a delegate from Honduras noted that CNAs have shaped a "big debate about what quality of education means" by focusing attention on "very valid and reliable instruments" promulgated by international assessment agencies, which tend to focus on skills such as math and reading.[71]

We also found evidence that political leaders view CNA participation as a mechanism to motivate education officials and improve standards. In Brazil, President Cardoso supported joining PISA despite predicting that his country would "come out at the bottom," because he saw participation as a mechanism to improve domestic education performance.[72] Similarly, in Vietnam, an important turning point was the personal involvement of then Deputy Prime Minister Nguyen Thiên Nhân, who staked his personal reputation on PISA participation. In 2011, Nguyen signed a letter confirming his country's participation in PISA despite the fact that "lower-level ministry staff was unsure of what participation in PISA [meant] for Vietnam."[73] Nguyen saw assessments as a way to signal educational and economic competitiveness as well as train and motivate education policymakers to maintain high standards.[74]

In short, our survey results and interviews indicate that elite politics is a major source of influence for CNAs. The nature of CNAs, which require extensive interaction and consultation with assessment agencies, provides ample opportunities for learning, professionalization, and norm diffusion. By quantifying education quality and explicitly ranking countries, CNAs also trigger status concerns, creating an impetus for policy change.

Domestic Politics

Our survey respondents provided mixed views regarding the importance of domestic political considerations in the administration of CNAs. Sixty-two percent of our respondents agreed that CNAs "improve our accountability with our citizens," and 43 percent agreed that "Negative [test] results could result in public upheaval." However, our respondents may have been relatively insulated from public pressures associated with CNAs, as they were education officials rather than elected politicians. In addition, as we discuss below, our sample includes both democratic and autocratic states, and officials from the latter may be relatively less concerned about public pressures.

Several delegates we interviewed noted that their country's relative ranking can shape the domestic education policy discourse and accelerate reforms.

---

[70] Author interview with an education officer from Kuwait, Singapore, June 2013.
[71] Author interview with an education officer from Honduras, Vienna, December 2011.
[72] Author interview with the Director of Education at OECD, teleconference, February 2012.
[73] Author interview with an education officer at the World Bank, Hanoi, Vietnam, June 2011.
[74] Author interview with an official in the Ministry of Education and Training in the Government of Vietnam, Hanoi, Vietnam, June 2011.

For example, a US delegate noted that "TIMSS results and PISA results provided data to justify the sweeping reforms of the No Child Left Behind Act," though the impact was primarily "rhetorical justification" rather than shaping the content of legislation.[75] Japan's declining rankings in international assessments built political momentum in favor of abandoning *yutori kyoiku*, which emphasized creativity under a relaxed curriculum, to one that emphasized more traditional rote and academic rigor.[76] Poor Hungarian PISA performance since 2006 ignited protests, calls for the resignation of government ministers, and reforms such as the centralization of authority over the education system.[77]

Chile provides an informative case of how CNAs can alter the public discourse surrounding education and increase public accountability. After the fall of Pinochet's authoritarian regime, the newly established democratic government sought to differentiate itself by placing a strong emphasis on transparency, equity, and efficiency. As such, the government committed to participating in CNAs and making the results publically available. This contrasted with the previous regime, which did not disclose results from national assessments.[78] As a Chilean official noted, "in that context, to have an international, cross-national examination that…shows your relative position as these tests developed, announces to you and your population if you are advancing or not, or if you are going back in terms of results, it's of extreme importance."[79]

In Chile, CNAs provide a language and framework through which key stakeholders, such as teachers, parents, and students, articulate their concerns and frustrations. During the *Pingüino* Movement of 2006, college students criticized Chile's poor relative CNA performance compared to other OECD countries. Protesters expressed their concerns and used the results of CNAs to argue that the Chilean government must do more to improve the quality of education.[80] Chile's decision to drop out of TIMSS 2007 illustrates the potential salience of domestic political mechanisms. Although the Chilean government explained that it intended to focus on PISA and ongoing national assessments in lieu of TIMSS, it came under intense criticism for the decision: "[the opposition party and media] accused the government of skipping TIMSS because the results of the reform were so poor that we were hiding…Politically, it was a disaster. From there onwards, there's no major international assessment that Chile skips."[81]

---

[75] Answer to survey question.
[76] Takayama 2008.
[77] Blanka Zoldi, "Poor PISA Looms over Hungarian Education Reform," *IntelliNews*, January 6, 2017.
[78] Kijima and Leer 2016.
[79] Author interview with the Director of Evaluation and Curriculum at the Ministry of Education in Chile, videoconference, May 2013.
[80] Kijima and Leer 2016.
[81] Author interview with the Director of Evaluation and Curriculum at the Ministry of Education in Chile, videoconference, May 2013.

In sum, both survey and case study evidence suggest that the domestic political channel can be an important source of assessment power for CNAs, though the impact may be limited to democratic or democratizing states. The Chilean case demonstrates that parties newly in power may seek CNA participation as a means of demonstrating their commitment to transparency and reform. Teachers, students, and opposition politicians have used the results of CNAs to voice their discontent with the status quo. In effect, participation in CNAs has the potential to mobilize civic participation and intensify domestic demands for education policy reform.

Transnational Politics

According to our survey respondents, the role of transnational pressure as a pathway of influence for CNAs is somewhat limited. Only 22 percent of respondents agreed that CNA participation "attracts investors" to their country, and an even lower share of respondents, 12 percent, agreed that CNAs lead to "more resources/foreign aid to education by donors who credit our effort." However, it is important to note that our survey includes a large share of advanced industrialized countries, which may be less responsive to transnational economic pressure compared to developing countries.[82]

In some developing countries, officials believe that CNA participation facilitates foreign investment. According to two officers at the Ministry of Education in Malaysia, "The Prime Minister goes to other countries to promote us. [But] investors went to China, because it's cheap labor. After the [TIMSS] test results, however, investors started coming back to Malaysia, because we have intellectual human capital...The test results directly impact investors' decisions."[83] Furthermore, assessments provide countries with an indicator of the quality of their human capital. In Botswana, assessments are used to "build a profile of competitiveness. These indexes are indicators of economic growth."[84] In these countries, the perception that CNA results are tied to foreign investment flows or economic growth appear to provide an additional motivation to implement education quality improvements.

Among developing countries, multilateral and bilateral aid agencies can be an important source of third-party influence. Donors occasionally step in to ease the financial burden on countries that require resources to implement CNAs: e.g. in Colombia, the Inter-American Development Bank provides supplementary funding to cover costs associated with analyzing TIMSS

---

[82] When limiting the sample to countries with GDP/capita below 20,000 USD (PPP), affirmative answers were somewhat higher, at 32 percent for each question.

[83] Author interview with a Director of Assessment and an education officer from the Ministry of Education in Malaysia, Singapore, June 2012.

[84] Author interview with a Director of Assessment and three other education officers from the Ministry of Education in Botswana, Vienna, Austria, December 2011.

results.[85] Furthermore, aid agencies value CNAs as a tool to monitor progress in the education sector. A Jordanian government officer indicated, "Most of our programs are funded by other agencies, like [the] World Bank, UNDP, Arab organizations, and EU. They want to have access to indicators [to measure the progress] of the reform."[86] A Yemeni official similarly observed that donor agencies look favorably upon CNA participation, as they are "interested to see the results of their support for countries."[87] Hence, CNAs give donor agencies a point of leverage to influence national education policies and the quantitative data necessary to monitor and evaluate the progress of education projects.

ORDERED PROBIT ANALYSIS OF SURVEY DATA

In this section, we consider variation in the pathways of influence associated with CNAs using ordered probit models. CNAs will not necessarily impact policymaking in the same way in Finland and Kazakhstan and Botswana. In this section, we will consider how country-specific factors might affect the mechanisms through which CNAs exert influence.

In order to examine variation in causal mechanisms, we break out questions associated with specific pathways of influence from our survey. Using responses to these questions as dependent variables, we examine what country-specific covariates affect the likelihood of respondents answering in the affirmative. Specifically, for *Elite Response*, we use responses related to questions about reputation/status in the international community (ER1), leadership in the world (ER2), risk perceptions about low rankings (ER3), concern about the participation of economic competitors (ER4), and desire for technical support and expertise (ER5).[88] For *Domestic Politics*, we use responses related to questions about the potential for domestic public upheaval from poor performance (DP1), improving accountability with citizens (DP2), and

---

[85] Answer from survey question.

[86] Author interview with the Director of Evaluation from Jordan, Vienna, Austria, December 2012.

[87] Author interview with officers in charge of basic education from Yemen, Vienna, Austria, December 2011.

[88] The specific survey questions were: ER1: "What are the benefits associated with your country/economy's participation in global international assessments like PISA, TIMSS and/or PIRLS? Improves our reputation/status in the international community." ER2: "What are the main reasons why your country/economy participates in cross-national assessments? To be a leader in the world." ER3: "What are the main challenges associated with your country/economy's participation in global international assessments like PISA, TIMSS and/or PIRLS? Ranking low on the international scale is a risk." ER4: "What are the main reasons why your country/economy participates in cross-national assessments? Because our economic competitors are participating." ER5: "What are the main reasons why your country/economy participates in cross-national assessments? To obtain technical support and expertise to improve our own capacity for conducting assessments."

citizen pressure (DP3).[89] For *Transnational Pressure*, we use responses related to questions about CNAs as attracting investors (TP1), CNA participation in response to requests from donor agencies (TP2), and CNAs as a condition for aid disbursement (TP3).[90] Each of these survey questions touches on a somewhat different causal mechanism within the broader pathways of elite response, domestic politics, and transnational pressure.

We use independent variables that proxy for factors that might make countries particularly susceptible to influence through distinct mechanisms: (1) GDP per capita (PPP) is included to account for varying levels of economic development. The scope for policy change through learning and interaction with international assessment agencies is presumably greater for economically less-developed countries that lack the resources and knowhow of more developed peers. Less developed countries may also be more susceptible to transnational pressure from markets and aid agencies; (2) Net secondary enrollment (%) is a proxy for the quality of the domestic education system;[91] (3) Gender Equality: because CNAs typically break out performance according to the student gender, officials from countries with large gender disparities in education may be sensitive to reputational consequences. We use the Global Gender Gap Index, in which high scores indicate higher levels of gender equality; (4) Polity score: ceteris paribus, officials of more democratic countries are likely to be more receptive to domestic pathways of influence such as demands from civil society and citizens; (5) Country membership in international non-governmental organizations (NGOs): a high concentration of NGOs may also increase the salience of domestic pathways of influence. As data on general NGO density is not readily available,[92] we use membership in international human rights NGOs. This is a somewhat crude proxy, as human rights NGOs are often concerned about a variety of issues aside from the right to education. However, the number of such NGOs is a plausible proxy for the

---

[89] The specific questions were: DP1: "What are the main challenges associated with your country/economy's participation in global international assessments like PISA, TIMSS and/ or PIRLS? Negative results could result in public upheaval." DP2: "What are the benefits associated with your country/economy's participation in global international assessments like PISA, TIMSS and/or PIRLS? Improves our accountability with our citizens." DP3: "What are the main reasons why your country/economy participates in cross-national assessments? Pressures from citizens about showing results in the education sector."

[90] The specific questions were: TP1: "What are the benefits associated with your country/ economy's participation in global international assessments like PISA, TIMSS and/or PIRLS? Attracts Investors." TP2: "What are the main reasons why your country/economy participates in cross-national assessments? Requests from donor agencies." TP3: "What are the main reasons why your country/economy participates in cross-national assessments? Participation in assessment is a conditionality for aid disbursement"

[91] We also tried substituting actual test scores in lieu of secondary enrollment. As several countries in our survey did not yet have test scores available, this results in fewer observations and less precision in our estimates. However, the substantive results were generally similar using test scores.

[92] Boulding 2014, 16.

strength of domestic civil society and the potential for NGOs to shape the domestic policymaking process[93]; (6) Intergovernmental organization (IGO) memberships: governments with dense ties to IGOs may be more open to or susceptible to external influence or pressure. Some IGOs mandate CNAs as a condition for membership or aid. Even where this is not the case, IGOs are often directly involved in the implementation and analysis of CNAs; (7) Inward Foreign Direct Investment/GDP: countries that receive large inward FDI flows may be more responsive to the consequences of CNAs on investor behavior. Participating in CNAs and performing well can send a signal to potential investors about the high quality of a country's labor force, facilitating greater investment flows; (8) Net official development assistance received per capita: dependence on foreign aid will likely make countries more susceptible to pressure by international aid agencies and bilateral donors.

As all of our dependent variables are measured as scales, with high numbers indicating agreement with the question and low numbers indicating disagreement, we use ordered probit for all specifications. Standard errors are clustered by country to account for multiple responses received from delegates representing the same country.

The results associated with elite politics are presented in Table 6.1. The dependent variable in column 1 is respondent agreement with the notion that CNAs improve their country's reputation/status in the international community. The results suggest that representatives of relatively democratic states with low NGO density and high aid dependence view CNAs as enhancing their reputations. The substantive effects associated with these variables are quite large. For example, holding all other variables to their mean values, the predicted probability of a delegate from an autocratic country with the minimum polity score of −10 (e.g. Qatar) agreeing or strongly agreeing with the reputation question was respectively 0.13 and 0.02,[94] while the same for a democratic country with the maximum polity score of 10 (e.g. Norway) was respectively 0.46 and 0.33.[95] The tendency for democracy and NGO density to cut in opposite directions is interesting, and we will return to this point below.

Column 2 indicates that representatives of economically developed countries are more likely to agree with the idea that CNAs allow their country to be a "world leader," suggesting that distinct reputational mechanisms may at be at work for different types of countries. Column 3 indicates that developed countries are less likely to view low rankings as a risk. Interestingly, our proxy for education quality – secondary school enrollment – is not a meaningful predictor of responses to these questions or any of the others in

---

[93] Keck and Sikkink 1998, vol. 35; Mundy and Murphy 2001; Suárez, Ramirez, and Koo 2009.

[94] Ninety-five percent confidence intervals respectively [0.00,0.45] and [0.00,0.18].

[95] Ninety-five percent confidence intervals respectively [0.30,0.62] and [0.15,0.57].

TABLE 6.1. *Survey analysis – Elite response (Ordered probit)*

Indep/Dep Variables	Improves Reputation/ Status	To be a World Leader	Low Ranking Is a Risk	Economic Competitors Participate	Obtain Technical Support & Expertise
GDP/capita	0.009	0.012*	−0.012*	0.006	−0.015*
	(0.008)	(0.005)	(0.003)	(0.004)	(0.003)
Secondary	0.032	0.011	−0.017	0.008	0.006
Enrollment	(0.019)	(0.010)	(0.011)	(0.014)	(0.013)
Gender	−3.079	−1.968	2.073	−1.540	1.705
Equality	(4.458)	(3.086)	(2.883)	(3.175)	(3.200)
Democracy	0.108*	0.058	−0.013	−0.002	0.004
(Polity)	(0.051)	(0.034)	(0.022)	(0.029)	(0.028)
NGO	−1.491*	−0.249	−0.156	0.853*	−1.312*
	(0.447)	(0.576)	(0.304)	(0.374)	(0.406)
IGO	0.014	−0.018	−0.013	−0.025	0.033
	(0.017)	(0.020)	(0.015)	(0.015)	(0.019)
FDI/GDP	−0.053	−0.011	0.016	0.039*	0.013
	(0.030)	(0.025)	(0.014)	(0.020)	(0.015)
ODA/capita	0.006*	0.002	0.002	0.005*	−0.003
	(0.002)	(0.003)	(0.002)	(0.002)	(0.002)
n	53	67	53	67	67

* Denotes a coefficient at least two standard errors removed from zero.
Note: Numbers in parenthesis are country-clustered standard errors.

this table. Furthermore, we tried substituting actual CNA scores in lieu of secondary enrollment, and the results were substantially similar. Absolute CNA test scores per se do not appear to play a meaningful role in how education officials view their own countries' participation in CNAs. There are several reasons why this might be the case. For one, depending on their policy views, education officials may view low rankings as a net positive, for example if they lead to education reforms or larger education budgets. It may also be that low-ranking countries are able to justify their weak absolute performance by comparing themselves to other low-ranking countries in their region or other peer group.

As one might expect, column 4 shows that delegates were more likely to agree that the status of their economic competitors matters in their decision-making about CNAs if their country is a relatively large recipient of inward FDI and foreign aid. High NGO density also appears to be associated with concern about economic competitors. Column 5 indicates that relatively poor countries with low NGO density tend to see the technical support and expertise obtained from participation in CNAs as an important benefit of participation. These are countries like Ghana and Yemen, which do not have strong domestic capacity in education.

TABLE 6.2. *Survey analysis – Domestic politics (Ordered probit)*

Indep/Dep Variables	Fear of Public Upheaval	Accountability with Citizens	Pressure from Citizens
GDP/capita	0.001	0.009	0.016*
	(0.007)	(0.006)	(0.007)
Secondary Enrollment	−0.006	0.008	−0.012
	(0.012)	(0.015)	(0.016)
Gender Equality	−9.902*	−9.868*	−6.170
	(2.651)	(4.330)	(4.605)
Democracy (Polity)	0.127*	0.106*	0.131*
	(0.035)	(0.041)	(0.045)
NGO	−0.894*	−0.587	−0.701
	(0.378)	(0.520)	(0.399)
IGO	0.039*	0.006	0.026
	(0.018)	(0.018)	(0.019)
FDI/GDP	0.037	−0.048	−0.060
	(0.022)	(0.027)	(0.049)
ODA/capita	0.001	−0.003	0.004
	(0.003)	(0.002)	(0.003)
n	53	53	56

* Denotes a coefficient at least two standard errors removed from zero.
Note: Numbers in parenthesis are country-clustered standard errors.

Turning to Table 6.2, across all three of the dependent variables, more democratic states tend to exhibit greater concern regarding the domestic political implications of CNAs. This is consistent with our theoretical predictions, though NGO density again generally enters with a negative sign. Countries with stronger gender equality tend to be less concerned about public upheaval associated with CNA results and are less likely to cite public accountability as a reason for participation.

Table 6.3 presents results associated with transnational politics. As predicted, high aid-dependence is associated with respondents agreeing that donor requests and conditionality are important. IGO membership is also associated with affirmative responses for donor conditionality. The results for "attracting investors" are more puzzling. Inward FDI is not a meaningful predictor of agreement with this question. Instead, expressed concern with attracting investors is higher in democratic countries with low NGO density, low secondary school enrollment, and low gender equality.

The tendency for democracy and NGO density to cut in opposite directions in several of our empirical models is somewhat puzzling. In our dataset, there are several democratic states with low NGO density, such as Botswana, Ghana, Honduras, Lithuania, and Trinidad and Tobago. Democratic governments with weak civil society face some distinct challenges of governance that may be contributing to these results. An active civil society tends

TABLE 6.3. *Survey analysis – Transnational pressure (Ordered probit)*

Indep/Dep Variables	Attracting Investors	Donor Agency Request	Aid Conditionality
GDP/capita	0.007	−0.029	−0.028
	(0.005)	(0.028)	(0.015)
Secondary Enrollment	−0.029*	0.007	−0.015
	(0.013)	(0.025)	(0.024)
Gender Equality	−14.454*	−9.064*	−7.204
	(4.047)	(6.494)	(5.406)
Democracy (Polity)	0.128*	0.314*	−0.058
	(0.030)	(0.153)	(0.061)
NGO	−1.122*	0.079	0.669
	(0.460)	(0.505)	(0.659)
IGO	0.046	0.036	0.054*
	(0.025)	(0.023)	(0.024)
FDI/GDP	0.027	−0.195*	−0.052
	(0.038)	(0.073)	(0.035)
ODA/capita	0.001	0.031*	0.012*
	(0.002)	(0.010)	(0.005)
n	53	53	56

* Denotes a coefficient at least two standard errors removed from zero.
Note: Numbers in parenthesis are country-clustered standard errors.

to aggregate information about citizen preferences and facilitate predictable patterns of political interaction.[96] In the absence of strong civil society, policymakers may become more reliant on external assessments to convey information about competence and responsiveness to citizen needs. CNAs may thus play a particularly important informational role in democratic countries with weak civil society.

The findings in this section are largely consistent with our expectations: respondents in democratic countries are more likely to agree with survey questions associated with domestic political mechanisms, and respondents in aid-dependent countries are more likely to agree that receiving foreign aid is an important benefit of CNA participation. However, the results also reveal some surprising patterns that may be worthy of further exploration, such as the tendency for democracy and NGO density cut in the opposite direction and the weak relationship between FDI exposure and respondent perceptions that CNA participation attracts private investors.[97]

[96] Molutsi and Holm 1990.
[97] This is broadly consistent with the findings from Kijima and Lipscy 2018, which shows using a panel dataset that CNA participation is not associated with an increase in FDI inflows.

CONCLUSION

We have argued that cross-national assessments in education increasingly play an important role in the determination of education policymaking. CNAs have proliferated rapidly over the past three decades, bringing comparability, transparency, and accountability to education policy. CNA participation can increase the capacity of education officials and provide incentives to facilitate improvements in education quality. We found evidence consistent with our theory based on survey data and personal interviews with education policymaking elites.

The nature of CNAs makes *elite politics* a powerful pathway of influence. CNAs inherently involve close coordination between target states and authoritative organizations (i.e. assessment and donor agencies), providing opportunities for learning, professionalization, and norm diffusion. The comparative and transparent nature of CNAs also evokes reputational and status concerns, motivating policymakers to improve education performance and climb international ranking tables.

The observable impact of *domestic political pressures* may be somewhat limited for CNAs due to politicization of education reforms and self-selection, i.e. non-participation of leaders particularly concerned about domestic backlash. Nonetheless, we found qualitative evidence of mobilization around CNAs by citizens and political parties, particularly in democracies and democratizing states. Our survey also suggests that education officials in more democratic states tend to be more cognizant of the domestic political consequences of CNAs.

Our results suggest that *transnational pressure* is most relevant vis-à-vis aid-dependent developing countries, which are sensitive to the economic implications of CNA participation. Donor agencies see CNAs as a method to better evaluate education development projects and therefore improve education outcomes. Officials in some developing countries see CNAs as a way to signal high labor quality to potential investors.

The rapid growth in the number of CNAs and participants represents an important shift in global education policymaking. Assessment agencies and international organizations play an increasingly influential role in how countries discuss, design, and evaluate education policy. The rapid adoption of CNAs worldwide has coincided with the evolution of education from a national to a global issue[98] and an increasing recognition that education is a basic human right and global public good.[99] Although CNAs have not been without critics, this chapter illustrates how participation can positively impact education. In related work, we show that CNA participation is associated

---

[98] Steiner-Khamsi 2003.

[99] Meyer, Bromley, and Ramirez 2010; Ramirez, Suárez, and Meyer 2007; Tsutsui and Wotipka 2004.

with tangible policy outcomes such as more frequent education reforms, greater foreign aid to education, and higher secondary enrollment rates.[100] CNA participation enhances domestic and international accountability and provides policymakers with tools necessary to make informed decisions about the effective allocation of educational resources.

Nonetheless, we should not be dismissive of critics who see CNAs as "educational colonialism" and an exertion of power by unaccountable, mostly Western technocrats.[101] Our findings show non-trivial norm contestation surrounding CNAs, such as concerns in developing countries that assessments do not adequately reflect cross-national variation in cultural, ethnic, or linguistic diversity.[102] Several interviewees specifically mentioned such challenges: a Kuwaiti official noted that "Translations are not done properly and are not culturally adaptable."[103] However, Western norms may benefit students underserved by conventional approaches to education rooted in local traditions, such as girls and ethnic minority students.

Healthy criticism and norm contestation surrounding CNAs can be ultimately helpful for education outcomes. Participation in CNAs may reflect some degree of "gaming,"[104] in which governments invest efforts to prepare students for assessments while sacrificing other educational goals such as ethical and personal development or artistic expression. The debate over CNAs has highlighted various methodological flaws in assessment administration, which can be remedied to make the results more credible.[105] US critics of CNAs have recently sought to "fight the index with an index" by arguing that alternative GPIs focusing on national innovation or creativity better capture the long-term consequences of education.[106] These indices are flawed as education performance measures – e.g. the US ranks high in the Global Creativity Index partly because it attracts talented individuals educated abroad.[107] However, this debate may ultimately lead to the creation of more targeted GPIs that capture aspects of education traditionally neglected by CNAs. In the meantime, we would caution that it is important for governments not to focus solely on rankings but to use CNAs as one of many inputs to improve the overall quality of education.

---

[100] Kijima and Lipscy 2018.

[101] Meyer and Zahedi 2014.

[102] Fifty-seven percent of developing country respondents to our survey agreed that "Test items and surveys do not accurately reflect our country/economy's cultural or ethnic diversity" compared to 14 percent for developed-country delegates. The percentages were identical to a similar question about linguistic diversity.

[103] Author interview with an education officer from Kuwait, Singapore, June 2013.

[104] See Bisbee et al. 2017.

[105] E.g. Gary Sand, "Are The PISA Education Results Rigged?" *Forbes*, January 4, 2017.

[106] Valerie Strauss, "Three Global Indexes Show that U.S. Public Schools must be Doing Something Right," *Washington Post*, February 13, 2017.

[107] "The Global Creativity Index 2015," Marin Prosperity Institute, Toronto, Canada.

References

Abdul-Hamid, Husein, Khattab M. Abu-Lebdeh, and Harry A. Patrinos. 2011. Assessment Testing Can Be Used to Inform Policy Decisions: The Case of Jordan. World Bank Policy Research Working Paper no. 5890, Washington, DC: The World Bank.

Addey, Camilla. 2015. Participating in International Literacy Assessments in Lao PDR and Mongolia: A Global Ritual of Belonging. In *Literacy as Numbers: Researching the Politics and Practices of International Literacy Assessment*, edited by Mary Hamilton, Bryan Maddox and Camilla Addey, 147–64. Cambridge: Cambridge University Press.

Anderson, Benedict. 2006. *Imagined Communities: Reflections on the Origin and Spread of Nationalism*. London: Verso Books.

Angrist, Noam, Harry A. Patrinos, and Martin Schlotter. 2013. An Expansion of a Global Data Set on Educational Quality: A Focus on Achievement in Developing Countries. World Bank Policy Research Working Paper (6536).

Benhassine, Najy, Florencia Devoto, Esther Duflo, Pascaline Dupas, and Victor Pouliquen. 2013. Turning a Shove into a Nudge? A "Labeled Cash Transfer" for Education. National Bureau of Economic Research.

Benveniste, Luis. 1999. *The Politics of Student Testing: A Comparative Analysis of National Assessment Systems in Southern Cone Countries*. Doctoral dissertation, Stanford: Stanford University.

Bisbee, James H., James R. Hollyer, B. Peter Rosendorff, and James Raymond Vreeland. 2017. The Millennium Development Goals and Education: Accountability and Substitution in Global Assessment.

Boulding, Carew. 2014. *NGOs, Political Protest, and Civil Society*. Cambridge: Cambridge University Press.

Braga, Michela, Daniele Checchi, and Elena Meschi. 2013. Educational Policies in a Long-Run Perspective. *Economic Policy* 28 (73):45–100.

Breakspear, Simon. 2012. *The Policy Impact of PISA*. OECD Education Working Papers. Paris: Organisation for Economic Co-operation and Development. Available from http://www.oecd-ilibrary.org/content/workingpaper/5k9fdfqffr28-en. Accessed April 14, 2017.

Carnoy, Martin. 2014. Globalization, Educational Change, and the National State. In *Globalization and Education: Integration and Contestation Across Cultures*, edited by Nelly P. Stromquist and Karen Monkman, 21–38, Maryland: Rowman & Littlefield Education, 2014.

Chabbott, Colette. 2003. *Constructing Educational Development: International Development Organizations and the World Conference on Education for All*. New York: Routledge.

Duflo, Esther, Rema Hanna, and Stephen P. Ryan. 2012. Incentives Work: Getting Teachers to Come to School. *The American Economic Review* 102 (4):1241–78.

Greaney, Vincent, and Thomas Kellaghan. 2008. Assessing National Achievement Levels in Education. Vol. 1. World Bank Publications.

Grek, Sotiria. 2009. Governing by Numbers: The PISA "Effect" in Europe. *Journal of Education Policy* 24 (1):23–37.

Hanushek, Eric A., and Dennis D. Kimko. 2000. Schooling, Labor-Force Quality, and the Growth of Nations. *American Economic Review* 90 (5):1184–208.

Hanushek, Eric A., and Ludger Woessmann. 2008. The Role of Cognitive Skills in Economic Development. *Journal of Economic Literature* 46 (3):607–68.
    2012. Do Better Schools Lead to More Growth? Cognitive Skills, Economic Outcomes, and Causation. *Journal of Economic Growth* 17 (4):267–321.
Henry, Miriam, Bob Lingard, Fazal Rizvi, and Sandra Taylor. 2001. *The OECD, Globalisation and Education Policy*. Published for IAU Press, Pergamon.
Honig, Dan. 2016. Seeing is Believing: The Normative Drivers of Agency Response to the Aid Transparency Index. Unpublished manuscript.
Husén, Torsten. 1979. An International Research Venture in Retrospect: The IEA Surveys. *Comparative Education Review* 23 (3):371–85.
Jennings, Jennifer L., and Jonathan Marc Bearak. 2014. "Teaching to the Test" in the NCLB Era How Test Predictability Affects Our Understanding of Student Performance. *Educational Researcher*:0013189X14554449.
Jo, Hyeran, Brian Phillips, and Joshua Alley. 2016. One Man's Terrorist: When Does Blacklisting Reduce Terrorism? Unpublished manuscript.
Kamens, David H., and Connie L. McNeely. 2010. Globalization and the growth of international educational testing and national assessment. *Comparative Education Review* 54 (1):5–25.
Keck, Margaret E., and Kathryn Sikkink. 1998. *Activists beyond Borders: Advocacy Networks in International Politics*. Vol. 35. Cambridge University Press.
Kelley, Judith G., and Beth A. Simmons. this volume. Introduction: The Power of Global Performance Indicators. Chapter 1 in *The Power of Global Performance Indicators*.
Kelley, Judith G., Beth A. Simmons, and Rush Doshi. 2016. The Power of Ranking: The East of Doing Business Indicator as a Form of Social Pressure. This Volume.
Kijima, Rie. 2010. Why Participate? Cross-National Assessments and Foreign Aid to Education. In *The Impact of International Achievement Studies on National Education Policymaking*, 13: Vol. 13. International Perspectives on Education and Society Series. Emerald Group Publishing.
    2013. The Politics of Cross-National Assessments: Global Trends and National Interests. Stanford University, Ph. D. Dissertation.
Kijima, Rie, and Jane Leer. 2016. Legitimacy, State-building, and Contestation in Education Policy Development: Chile's Involvement in Cross-national Assessments. In *The Global Testing Culture: Shaping Education Policy, Perceptions, and Practice*, edited by William Smith, 43–62. Oxford: Symposium Book.
Kijima, Rie, and Phillip Lipscy. 2018. The Politics of International Testing. Stanford University, Working Paper.
Koliev, Faradj, Thomas Sommerer, and Jonas Tallberg. 2019. Reporting Matters: Performance Assessment and Compliance in the ILO.The Power of Global Performance Indicators. New York: Cambridge University Press.
Koretz, Daniel M. 2009. *Measuring Up: What Educational Testing Really Tells Us*. Cambridge, MA: Harvard University Press.
Kremer, Michael, Conner Brannen, and Rachel Glennerster. 2013. The Challenge of Education and Learning in the Developing World. *Science* 340 (6130):297–300.
Ladd, Helen F. 2002. School Vouchers: A Critical View. *The Journal of Economic Perspectives* 16 (4):3–24.

Le, Anh, and Edmund Malesky. 2016. Do Subnational Governance Indices Lead to Improved Governance? Evidence from Field Experiment in Vietnam. Unpublished manuscript.

Lee, Melissa M., and Aila M. Matanock. this volume. Third Party Policymakers and the Limits of the Influence of Indicators. Chapter 11 in *The Power of Global Performance Indicators*.

Lockheed, Marlaine. 2012. Policies, Performance and Panaceas: The Role of International Large-Scale Assessments in Developing Countries. *Compare: A Journal of Comparative and International Education* 42 (3):512–18.

Loveless, Tom. 2012. *Misinterpreting International Test Scores: In 2012 Brown Center Report on American Education.* Washington, DC: Brookings Institution Press.

Martens, Kerstin, and Dennis Niemann. 2013. When Do Numbers Count? The Differential Impact of the PISA Rating and Ranking on Education Policy in Germany and the US. *German Politics* 22 (3):314–32.

Meyer, Heinz-Dieter, and Aaron Benavot. 2013. *PISA, Power, and Policy: The Emergence of Global Educational Governance.* Oxford: Symposium Books Ltd.

Meyer, John, Patricia Bromley, and Francisco Ramirez. 2010. Human Rights in Social Science Textbooks Cross-national Analyses, 1970–2008. *Sociology of Education* 83 (2):111–34.

Meyer, Heinz-Dieter and Katie Zahedi. 2014. An Open Letter: To Andreas Schleicher, OECD, Paris. *GDM-Mitteilungen* 97: 31–36.

Miguel, Edward, and Michael Kremer. 2004. Worms: Identifying Impacts on Education and Health in the Presence of Treatment Externalities. *Econometrica* 72 (1):159–217.

Molutsi, Patrick P., and John D. Holm. 1990. Developing Democracy When Civil Society Is Weak: The Case of Botswana. *African Affairs* 89 (356):323–40.

Morse, Julia. 2016. Pathways to Policy Change: Blacklists and Market Enforcement in the Regime to Combat Terrorist Financing. In *Assessment Power in World Politics Conference.* Cambridge: Harvard University.

Mullis, Ina, and Michael Martin. 2007. TIMSS in Perspective: Lessons Learned from IEA's Four Decade of International Mathematics Assessments. In *Lessons Learned: What International Assessments Tell Us about Math Achievement.* International Perspectives on Education and Society Series. Brookings Institution Press.

Mundy, Karen. 1999. Educational multilateralism and world (dis) order. *Comparative Education Review* 42 (4):448–78.

Mundy, Karen, and Caroline Manion. 2014. Globalization and Global Governance in Education. In *Globalization and Education*, edited by Nelly P. Stromquist and Karen Monkman, 39–54, Maryland: Rowman & Littlefield Education.

Mundy, Karen, and Lynn Murphy. 2001. Transnational Advocacy, Global Civil Society? Emerging Evidence from the Field of Education. *Comparative education review* 45 (1):85–126.

Ramirez, Francisco O., John W. Meyer, and Julia Lerch. 2015. World Society and the Globalization of Educational Policy. In *The Handbook of Global Policies and Policy-Making in Education*, edited by Karen Mundy, Andy Green, Bob Lingard, and Antoni Verger, 43–63. Sussex: Wiley-Blackwell Publisher.

Ramirez, Francisco O., David Suárez, and John W. Meyer. 2007. The Worldwide
    Rise of Human Rights Education. In *School Knowledge in Comparative and
    International Perspectives*, edited by Aaron Benavot and Cecilia Braslavsky,
    35–52. the Netherlands: Springer.
Rodrik, Dani. 1995. Getting Interventions Right: How South Korea and
    Taiwan Grew Rich. *Economic Policy* 10 (20):53–107.
Smith, William. 2016. Introduction. In *The Global Testing Culture:
    Shaping Education Policy, Perceptions, and Practice, Oxford Studies
    in Comparative Education*, edited by William Smith, 43–62. Oxford:
    Symposium Books.
Steiner-Khamsi, Gita. 2003. The Politics of League Tables. *Journal of Social
    Science Education* 2 (1). Available from http://www.jsse.org/index.php/
    jsse/article/view/470. Accessed April 14, 2017.
Suárez, David F., Francisco O. Ramirez, and Jeong-Woo Koo. 2009. UNESCO
    and the Associated Schools Project: Symbolic Affirmation of World
    Community, International Understanding, and Human Rights. *Sociology
    of Education* 82 (3):197–216.
Sutton, Rosemary E. 2004. Teaching under High-Stakes Testing Dilemmas
    and Decisions of a Teacher Educator. *Journal of Teacher Education*
    55 (5):463–75.
Takayama, Keita. 2008. The Politics of International League Tables: PISA
    in Japan's Achievement Crisis Debate. *Comparative Education*
    44 (4):387–407.
    2010. Politics of Externalization in Reflexive Times: Reinventing Japanese
    Education Reform Discourses through "Finnish PISA Success."
    Comparative Education Review 54 (1):51–75.
Tsutsui, Kiyoteru, and Christine Min Wotipka. 2004. Global Civil Society
    and the International Human Rights Movement: Citizen Participation
    in Human Rights International Nongovernmental Organizations. *Social
    Forces* 83 (2):587–620.
Volante, Louis. 2004. Teaching to the Test: What Every Educator and Policy-
    Maker Should Know. *Canadian Journal of Educational Administration
    and Policy*, 35.
Weaver, Catherine. 2016. The Power and Politics of Aid Transparency
    Rankings and Ratings. Unpublished manuscript.
World Bank Group. 2011. Learning for All: Investing in People's Knowledge
    and Skills to Promote Development. The World Bank. Available at http://
    siteresources.worldbank.org/EDUCATION/Resources/ESSU/Education_
    Strategy_4_12_2011.pdf. Accessed May 8, 2013.

7

Reporting Matters

Performance Indicators and Compliance in the
International Labor Organization (ILO)

Faradj Koliev, Thomas Sommerer, and Jonas Tallberg

Recent decades have witnessed a rise in the use and forms of global performance indicators (GPIs) in world politics.[1] GPIs are regularized, publicized
reporting routines that states, international organizations (IOs), non-
governmental organizations (NGOs), or other actors use to attract attention
to the relative performance of countries or other organizations.[2] GPIs are
intentional exercises of power, ultimately designed to influence actor behavior through information, comparison, and social pressure. Yet, to date, we
have little systematic knowledge about their effects, as research so far has
focused mainly on documenting and understanding their proliferation. Do
GPIs systematically impact behavior or are they a governance fad with few
observable consequences? If GPIs have an impact, are those effects long-
lasting or temporary? How do the effects of GPIs compare to those of other
factors shaping actor behavior? What are the conditions under which GPIs
have stronger or weaker effects?

In this article, we address the effects of GPIs through a specific focus
on IOs' reporting on state compliance with international rules and norms.
Reporting is an integral part of IOs' systems for monitoring compliance. By
collecting and presenting information on the conformance of state behavior
to agreed standards, IOs attempt to deter states from violations and compel
states into compliance if violations nevertheless occur. Like other GPIs, compliance reporting is public, regular, inclusive, purposive, and comparative.[3]
In the terminology of this volume, IOs' reporting on state compliance qualifies as a type of watchlist, whereby states identified as violators are implicitly

---

[1] Cooley and Snyder 2015; Davis et al. 2012; Kelley and Simmons 2015, 2019.
[2] Kelley and Simmons 2019, 5.
[3] Kelley and Simmons 2019, 6.

compared to the compliant parties not included on the list.[4] Sometimes, reporting is linked to threats of enforcement through legal coercion and material sanctions, if states are found guilty of violating international law. However, in many IOs, reporting operates on its own, raising important questions about the effects of non-coercive performance indicator on state behavior.

We focus empirically on the International Labour Organization (ILO), which in many respects presents an ideal and unique context for our purposes. The ILO has for many decades engaged in regularized and publicized reporting on member state compliance with international labor standards.[5] These reports are not linked to a threat of enforcement, making it possible to isolate the effect of performance indicator on states' correction of their behavior once identified as violators of ILO conventions. In addition, the case of the ILO offers a rare opportunity to evaluate if the effects of compliance reporting vary depending on characteristics of the target countries and characteristics of the reporting process. Specifically, the article analyzes behavioral adjustments of states to compliance reporting in the ILO over the time period 1989 to 2011, based on a novel dataset.

Our central findings can be summarized in three points. First, reporting by the ILO has positive and durable effects on state respect for international labor standards, especially when targeting severe restrictions in labor rights. Second, reporting has fairly immediate effects on state behavior, but can also lead to improvements when repeated over longer periods of time. Third, reporting has stronger effects on improvements in labor rights when the target states are democratic and have the resource capacity to correct violations. By contrast, it does not matter whether states have a strong presence of labor NGOs or are highly economically dependent on the outside world. Neither does it strengthen the general effect of reporting if it is combined with active shaming of non-compliant states. Robustness tests demonstrate that these positive findings on the effects of reporting are not the result of ILO selection strategies or secular trends in targeted countries.

The findings from the ILO suggest that IO reporting is a consequential form of performance indicator in world politics. They also demonstrate how an appreciation of indicator power can require a reevaluation of an organization's effectiveness. It is widely assumed that the ILO is ineffective since it lacks an enforcement mechanism. The organization has varyingly been described as a "toothless tiger" and "the 90-pound weakling of UN agencies."[6] Such descriptions fail to recognize what this article demonstrates: even IOs whose monitoring systems rely exclusively on reporting can impact the behavior of states in positive ways. While hard enforcement may still matter, it is not the

---

[4] Kelley and Simmons 2019, 6. See also Jo, Philips, and Alley 2017.
[5] For earlier studies, see Helfer 2008; Thomann 2011; Weisband 2000.
[6] Elliot and Freeman 2003, 102 and 95. See also Cooney 1999; Douglas et al. 2004.

exclusive path to compliance in international cooperation. In the conclusion, we expand on the implications of the ILO case for our understanding of GPIs and the effectiveness of IO reporting on state compliance.

The article proceeds as follows. In the next section, we develop our argument about reporting's impact on state behavior, and derive hypotheses about general and conditional effects. The second section characterizes ILO monitoring as performance indicator, and describes how reporting is organized and carried out in the ILO. The third section outlines the research design and reports the results of the empirical analysis. We conclude by discussing the broader implications of our findings.

THE ARGUMENT

Performance indicator is a central component of IOs' systems for monitoring state compliance with international rules. When routinely collecting, systematizing, and publishing comparable information on state compliance, IOs engage in performance indicator. We suggest that reporting may affect state compliance, even in the absence of enforcement, by activating reputational and status concerns among state elites, mobilizing domestic societal interests, and generating transnational normative pressure. In the following, we describe these pathways of influence, and identify conditions that may shape the effects of reporting on compliance. Our argument is formulated in generic terms, since we expect reporting to have effects in other domains than labor rights as well, even if we test this argument in the context of the ILO.

IO Reporting and State Compliance

The framing article of this volume identifies three pathways through which GPIs may affect actor behavior: elite politics, domestic politics, and transnational politics.[7] Our argument suggests that all three are relevant channels for reporting's effects on state compliance.

At the elite level, reporting influences state compliance by activating government elites' concerns with reputation and status. Elites include both politicians and senior officials with responsibility for the policies of a state in a particular domain. Reporting involves public exposure of violations of joint rules, and creates social pressure on elites to rectify non-compliant behavior. Elites are responsive to such pressure because of its implications for their own professional standing, the standing of the organization they direct, and the standing of the country they represent.[8] This expectation is theoretically anchored in a growing literature on social pressure, reputation, and status in world politics.[9]

---

7 Kelley and Simmons 2019, 25ff.
8 Kelley and Simmons 2019, 28–30. See also Johnston 2001.
9 E.g. Checkel 2001; Hafner-Burton 2008; Johnston 2001, 2008; Kelley and Simmons 2015; Schimmelfennig 2001.

More specifically, elites adjust to public exposure because it generates social rewards and punishments that officials appreciate and fear.[10] "Rewards might include psychological well-being, status, a sense of belonging, and a sense of well-being derived from conformity with role expectations. Punishments might include shaming, shunning, exclusion, and demeaning, or dissonance derived from actions inconsistent with role and identity."[11] Hence, when states are publicly exposed as violators of jointly agreed rules, this generates social and psychological discomfort that state elites are anxious to avoid.

At the domestic level, reporting influences state compliance by equipping political interests with the information and moral leverage to challenge government practices in violation of international rules. Domestic interests include non-profit and for-profit actors with an ambition to influence government policy. To begin with, IO reporting increases the information on state practices available to domestic interests.[12] While domestic interests themselves sometimes are the best sources of information on state non-compliance, IOs in other cases have comparative advantages as "police patrols" engaging in systematic collection of comparable data. Reporting makes this information publicly available and actionable, opening up possibilities for domestic interests to mobilize public opinion and pressure policy-makers. A principal contribution of compliance reporting by IOs, like GPIs in general, is thus the new information it generates.[13]

In addition, IO reporting on non-compliance boosts the moral leverage of domestic interests by coming from an authoritative source and exposing a government's wrongdoings in relation to the performance of other states. This makes it particularly useful for reformists.[14] Even for domestic interests who have known and complained about violations, having an IO pronounce on the government's failings is an entirely different thing. IOs are typically seen as more impartial and credible than partisan interests, making their information more useful for persuasive purposes. In addition, IO reporting places a government's practices next to those of other states, giving reformists the additional fire power of comparison and embarrassment.

Transnationally, reporting influences state compliance by activating pressures from external actors. Transnational pressure is dependent on external actors caring about and responding to IO reporting on state compliance. Those external actors may be other states that are committed to the normative principles in question or generally value partners that stick to their commitments. International Organization reporting brings violations to the attention of other states, which may exert pressure through public criticism or material

---

[10] Checkel 2001; Johnston 2001; Risse et al. 2013.
[11] Johnston 2001, 499.
[12] Dai 2007; Simmons 2009.
[13] Kelley and Simmons 2019, 11–12.
[14] Kelley and Simmons 2019, 25–26.

punishment.[15] Reporting by international organization (IO) also threatens the reputation of target states, which may carry social and material costs.[16] If exposed as violators, other states may be less likely to engage in cooperation with them in the future, resulting in a loss of gains.

Transnational pressure may also come through non-state actors in other countries. Transnational NGO campaigns targeting states seen as violating international rules are common, exemplified by mobilization against Israeli settlements in the West Bank, Turkish violations of human rights, and Hungarian restrictions on press freedom and judicial independence.[17] But transnational pressure may also consist of, for instance, firms mobilizing against the protectionist practices of states whose markets they want to enter. In either case, IOs publicly identifying a state as violator of international rules is likely to facilitate transnational mobilization and influence, much like it strengthens the hand of domestic interests against their government. International organizations authoritatively proclaiming a state to be in violation offers a focal point for mobilization and lends legitimacy to transnational efforts aimed at changing its behavior.

Elite, domestic, and transnational politics are useful for understanding the different ways in which compliance reporting by IOs can affect state behavior. We do not theorize or assess the relative prominence of these channels. Instead, we consider them as complementary pathways for the effects of reporting on state behavior. To begin with, they generate the combined expectation that public exposure of violations through reporting has positive effects on state compliance.

H1: Reporting makes it more likely that states correct non-compliant behavior.

As a second step, we theorize the conditions under which reporting by IOs is likely to be particularly effective in producing compliance. We focus on two categories of factors: characteristics of the target countries and characteristics of the reporting process. The factors we privilege are theoretically linked to the pathways of elite, domestic, and transnational politics. We begin with four conditions at the country level that could make states more or less responsive to reporting.

First, democracies may be more receptive than autocracies to international reporting of illegitimate behavior. According to Risse and Ropp, public exposure should be particularly effective with regard to stable democratic regimes, especially in the area of human rights where such regimes are normatively committed to the content of these rules.[18] In democracies, gaps between

---

[15] Lebovic and Voeten 2009.
[16] Guzman 2008; Keohane 1984; Tomz 2007. For an overview, see Brewster 2013.
[17] E.g. Della Porta and Tarrow 2005; Keck and Sikkink 1998; Khagram, Riker, and Sikkink 2002.
[18] Risse and Ropp 2013, 17.

commitments and actual behavior are more likely to create political and legal pressure from below. In addition, democratic states are more likely to care about public exposure of their wrongdoings, because they usually aspire to belong to the civilized community of states that respect international law. This expectation ties in with a broader literature on democratic states in world politics, which shows that democracies behave systematically different from autocracies in terms of military conflict, trade liberalization, human rights protection, and international cooperation.[19] At the same time, a number of studies in the human rights field have been unable to establish a positive effect of democracy on the effectiveness of public exposure.[20] Hendrix and Wong even found that naming and shaming by NGOs is more effective in relation to autocracies than democracies.[21]

Second, states that are more economically dependent on the outside world may be more sensitive to public reporting of non-compliant behavior. Exposure as a violator may lead to partners cutting back on economic cooperation, or at least to fears that they might. The more dependent a state is on external partners, the more likely it is that such concerns influence responses to reporting. This theoretical expectation features prominently in existing research, which varyingly emphasizes dependence on bilateral aid, foreign direct investments, and international trade.[22] Available empirical results from the area of human rights both support and challenge this proposition. While one study finds a significant conditional effect of states' economic dependence on the effectiveness of public exposure, other studies are unable to corroborate this finding.[23]

Third, states with a more vibrant civil society may be more responsive to reporting by IOs. Public exposure can lead to pressure from below, from domestic interests advocating and defending the principles in question. The importance of NGO mobilization for state compliance with international rules and norms has been theorized in a range of influential works.[24] In addition, there is a large body of qualitative and quantitative work suggesting that NGO pressure has some effect on state compliance.[25] However, we know of no study that assesses whether domestic NGO presence affects the impact of IO reporting. Some studies evaluate the simultaneous influence of both IO and NGO exposure of violations.[26]

---

[19] E.g. Mansfield et al. 2000; Pevehouse and Russett 2006; Simmons and Danner 2010; Tallberg et al. 2016.
[20] Hafner-Burton 2008; Murdie and Davis 2012.
[21] Hendrix and Wong 2013.
[22] DeMeritt 2015; Franklin 2008; Keck and Sikkink 1998; Lebovic and Voeten 2009; Murdie and Davis 2012; Risse and Ropp 2013; Risse and Sikkink 1999; Sharman 2009.
[23] Franklin 2008; Krain 2012; Murdie and Davis 2012.
[24] Dai 2007; Keck and Sikkink 1998; Risse and Sikkink 1999; Risse et al. 2013; Simmons 2009.
[25] E.g. Hafner-Burton and Tsutsui 2005; Hendrix and Wong 2013; Murdie and Davis 2012; Murdie 2014.
[26] Franklin 2008; Krain 2012.

Fourth, states with fewer capacity constraints may be better positioned to adjust their behavior in line with international rules. It is a long-standing insight in research on compliance that economic, technological, and political capacity constraints partly explain cross-national differences in compliance.[27] Carrying the costs of adjustment to demanding environmental standards, compensating losers from free-trade, investing in training of public bureaucracies, and other measures required to comply with international rules are often costly, at least in a short-term perspective. Among states exposed as violators, those with greater capacity constraints should therefore have a tougher job correcting non-compliance. Conversely, states with fewer capacity constraints should have a greater ability to correct their behavior in line with international expectations.

These factors generate four hypotheses about the effects of target country characteristics on state responsiveness to reporting:

H2a: Reporting is more effective in correcting non-compliant behavior among more democratic states.

H2b: Reporting is more effective in correcting non-compliant behavior among states more economically dependent on the outside world.

H2c: Reporting is more effective in correcting non-compliant behavior among states with a higher domestic NGO presence.

H2d: Reporting and shaming are more effective in correcting non-compliant behavior among states with fewer capacity constraints.

In addition to country characteristics, we expect characteristics of the reporting process to shape the effects. Specifically, we find it plausible that reporting may be more effective when combined with explicit shaming of non-compliant states. Shaming builds on reporting, but adds a strong evaluative component of explicit condemnation of the illegitimate behavior.[28] In shaming, IOs do not content themselves with identifying non-compliant states in a report, but subject them to social opprobrium through active and public blame. It sends a strong signal of disapproval to the violating state and the broader community. Assuming that state elites care about reputation and status, this mobilization of blame should increase the social costs of non-compliance and make reporting more likely to produce behavioral adjustment. In addition, IO reporting supplemented with shaming should give additional leverage to domestic interests and transnational actors that mobilize for change in a country.

---

[27] E.g. Börzel et al. 2010; Chayes and Chayes 1995; Jacobson and Weiss 1998; Simmons 2009, ch. 8; Tallberg 2002.

[28] Adler-Nissen 2014; Franklin 2008; Johnston 2001; Lebovic and Voeten 2006; Murdie and Davis 2012; Risse and Sikkink 1999. This distinction between reporting and shaming shares analytical affinities with the distinction between naming and shaming, where the first involves public identification of a norm-violating target and the second a public condemnation of the same target. See Friman 2015a; Hafner-Burton 2008; Krain 2012.

The specific ways in which reporting and shaming are combined can vary. In some cases, reporting and shaming are performed simultaneously, as when states listed by Human Rights Watch are condemned for violating human rights. In other cases, the two processes are sequential, as in the case of the International Narcotics Control Board, where reporting precedes shaming in a process designed to gradually ramp up the pressure on non-compliant states.[29] We hypothesize:

> H2e: *Reporting is more effective in correcting non-compliant behavior when combined with shaming.*

Alternative Expectation: Enforcement Required

The argument we advance suggests why reporting should be effective in pushing non-compliant states to correct their behavior, and when those effects are likely to be more or less prominent. However, this positive interpretation does not stand unchallenged. Some scholars are more skeptical, arguing that reputational and status concerns do little to move state behavior, and that enforcement through legal coercion and material sanctions ultimately is the only effective instrument.[30] Unless states face a credible threat of enforcement, they will violate international rules and norms if it is in their interest to do so.

In this vein, Downs et al. argue that aggressive enforcement practices are necessary to counter non-compliance, especially where international rules and norms require significant and costly adjustments in state behavior.[31] More information about state behavior will have little effect, unless linked to material sanctions if violations are detected.[32] Similarly, Goldsmith and Posner explicitly challenge the idea that compliance with international law could derive from non-instrumental values, such as a sense of obligation, concern with the regard of others, and the legitimacy of the law.[33] Instead, their basic premise is that states only keep promises when their interests tell them otherwise in order to avoid retaliation.

Others conceive of enforcement as central in interaction with public exposure. Ostrom suggests that compliance systems work best when first using monitoring to induce behavioral changes, and then applying sanctions against the tough cheaters.[34] Tallberg argues that compliance systems which rely on a combination of management and enforcement tend to be particularly effective, while those that only rely on one of the strategies often suffer in identifiable ways.[35]

---

[29] Friman 2015b.
[30] For an overview of research on coercive enforcement of international law, see Thompson 2013.
[31] Downs et al. 1996.
[32] Downs et al. 1996, 396–97.
[33] Goldsmith and Posner 2005.
[34] Ostrom 1990.
[35] Tallberg 2002.

Demonstrating that reporting has an effect on state behavior that is independent of enforcement requires a research design that controls for this alternative explanation. We follow a strategy with three components in the remainder of this article: showing that an institutional environment presents opportunities for reporting; showing that state behavior changes in conformance with expectations after public exposure; and showing that threats of enforcement were not part of the decision to conform.[36]

PERFORMANCE INDICATOR IN THE ILO

Global performance indicators are "regularized, publicized reporting routines that states, IGOs, NGOs, or private actors use to attract attention to the performance of countries or other organizations in a given policy or performance area."[37] In this section, we explain why the ILO's reporting on state compliance with international labor standards constitutes an example of performance indicator, and how the specific construction of this system makes it possible to isolate effects of reporting, but also the consequences of combining reporting with shaming.

ILO Monitoring as Performance Indicator

Since 1919, the ILO has been the main organization to develop and monitor international labor standards. The core of the ILO's regulatory function is its eight fundamental conventions. These conventions have been drawn up by representatives of governments, employers, and workers in the ILO's unique tripartite governance structure. The conventions cover areas considered as fundamental to worker rights: freedom of association, elimination of forced labor, abolition of child labor, and eradication of discrimination. The ILO's efforts to promote these fundamental conventions come in two steps: first, by encouraging ratification of the conventions among its member states, and second, by monitoring compliance with the conventions once they have been ratified. The ILO does not have effective recourse to enforcement through legal or material sanctions against states that fail to respect labor rights.[38] To date, the combined ratification rate in the ILO membership (186 states) is about 86 percent (ILO 2016a). The responsibility to monitor compliance with the fundamental conventions rests with two supervisory bodies: Committee of Experts on the Application of Conventions and Recommendations (CEACR) and Committee on the Application of Standards (CAS).

---

[36] Johnston 2001, 510.
[37] Kelley and Simmons 2019, 5.
[38] The ILO lacks centralized sanctioning mechanisms, but it can recommend decentralized sanctions under Article 33. It is then up to member states to decide whether they want to impose sanctions or not. In the history of the ILO, this article has only been used once, against Burma in 2000 with regard to convention 29. Moreover, the International Court of Justice may issue interpretations over state compliance with ILO conventions. However, this has never happened.

The ILO's monitoring system qualifies as global performance indicator by being public, regular, inclusive, purposive, and comparative.[39] The monitoring bodies systematically collect and publish information on member state compliance with the fundamental conventions of the ILO for the explicit purpose of promoting respect for international labor standards. In terms of types of GPIs, the ILO's reporting system best conforms to that of a watchlist.[40] States are either on the list because of identified non-compliant behavior or off the list because of conformance to agreed standards. There is no internal ranking on the list. In addition, this system distinguishes itself among GPIs by involving: social punishments and rewards; the consent of the assessed; elite interaction with the assessed; direct involvement of domestic and transnational interests in the process; the creation of new compliance data; actionable policies for the targeted states; and extensive authority for the creator of the list.

Global performance indicators are associated with different pathways of influence: elite politics, domestic politics, and transnational politics.[41] Reporting by the ILO may affect state behavior through all three pathways. It generates social pressure on elites required to explain the actions of their government in front of their peers in the ILO's monitoring bodies. It spurs domestic mobilization and criticism by labor unions and other civil society groups. And it leads to transnational normative pressures when governments, labor unions, and other actors in third party join in efforts to name and shame a state violating labor rights.

What makes the ILO's monitoring system uniquely well suited for an indicator of the effectiveness of compliance reporting as a GPI is the absence of enforcement and the clear-cut separation of reporting from shaming in its construction. While reporting is the central activity of the CEACR and the principal instrument of monitoring in the ILO, shaming is the exclusive task of the CAS and is used in select cases to complement reporting.

The members of the CEACR are eminent jurists, such as supreme court judges and law professors, appointed by the governing body of the ILO. They do not represent their governments or organizations, but serve on the CEACR in a personal capacity. The CEACR meets once a year in Geneva. Its meetings are closed and its documents confidential. The principal task of the CEACR is to examine the extent to which domestic law and practice in the member states conform to the ratified conventions:

Its function is to determine whether the requirements of a given Convention are being met, whatever the economic and social conditions existing in a given country. Subject only to any derogations, which are expressly permitted by the Convention itself, these requirements remain constant and uniform for all countries. In carrying out this

[39] Kelley and Simmons 2019, 6.
[40] Kelley and Simmons 2019, 6.
[41] Kelley and Simmons 2019, 25ff.

work, the Committee is guided by the standards laid down in the Convention alone, mindful, however, of the fact that the modes of their implementation may be different in different States.[42]

The CEACR's indicators of state conformance with the ratified conventions are published annually. When the CEACR establishes that a state is not in compliance, it issues an "observation" in the annual report. This is tantamount to the inclusion of the state on a compliance watchlist, since observations exclusively target serious violations. As the ILO Handbook states: "[O]bservations are generally used in more serious or long-standing cases of failure to fulfill obligations."[43] If a member state rectifies its behavior after inclusion on the list, the CEACR removes the state from the observation list.[44]

The CEACR makes its assessments based on documentation submitted by the governments and social partners. Governments are obliged to send a copy to employers' and workers' organizations, which may comment on the report. Social partners also have the option to communicate directly with the ILO. This possibility guarantees the independence of social partners from their governments and allows for a better assessment of states' national legislation and practice with regard to international labor standards. In addition, other ILO bodies may submit information to the CEACR. For the fundamental conventions, the normal reporting cycle is two years. However, the CEACR may request additional reports beyond the normal cycle if necessary.

Due to its composition and the nature of its indicators, some regard the CEACR as a quasi-judicial body.[45] Its main task is of a legal nature and its comments typically relate to the need for introducing new legislation to bring states into conformity with international labor standards. However, its indicators are not those of a tribunal. Rather, the CEACR attempts to nudge states into compliance by way of exposure and comparison. Through its indicators, the CEACR makes clear that the labor practices of states are monitored and compared in the international community. These reports exert pressure on states to conform to international labor norms through evidence of worker rights violations and anticipation of labor rights improvements.

Most member states of the ILO have been put on the observation list by the CEACR. Over the time period 1989 to 2011, only five of the 154 states in our dataset were not listed as non-compliant in a CEACR report. All other states were put on the list at least once. The CEACR is persistent: if non-compliance with labor standards is detected, it will continue listing a state until change

---

[42] ILO 1977, 10–11.
[43] ILO 2012, 36. In contrast, "direct requests" relate to matters of secondary importance, such as technical questions of implementation.
[44] In addition, it may take note of this explicitly by issuing a "satisfaction note" in the next report. This implies that a government has taken measures considered sufficient for the CEACR to end the public exposure in the annual report.
[45] Thomann 2011.

has been achieved. There are instances where the CEACR has listed states for years while receiving no or very little response. For example, from 1996 to 2011, the CEACR listed Azerbaijan in all reports because of an ongoing violation of workers' right to strike. While the government of Azerbaijan replied to the observations, it did not change its legislation. Instead, it defended its restrictions on collective action by underlining that strikes only are forbidden when they create threats to people's lives and health – an argument the CEACR rejected.[46]

In other cases, CEACR reporting has been more effective, and we include two episodes as illustrations. In 1994, the CEACR, after receiving information from the government of Greece and the General Confederation of Greek Workers, noted in the annual report that Greece violated convention 98 by intervening in the free collective bargaining process.[47] In its observation, the CEACR regretted that the government had taken legislative measures to set the maximum wage levels for employees in the public sector.[48] The CEACR urged the government of Greece to stop intervening in the collective bargaining process and to "keep the Committee informed of any development." A year later, in 1995, the CEACR noted with "satisfaction" that the government of Greece had suspended the implementation of the problematic decree, thus creating conditions for free collective bargaining.[49]

In the second case, the CEACR targeted Guatemala because of violations of conventions 87 and 98. In three consecutive reports, from 1989 to 1991, the CEACR stressed the need for Guatemala to bring its national labor laws into conformity with the conventions' principles. For instance, the CEACR urged the Guatemalan government to cease its strict supervision of trade union activities, make it possible for unions to take part in politics, and introduce dissuasive sanctions against employers prohibiting workers from joining trade unions. In 1993, the government of Guatemala removed the provisions in the Labor Code that prohibited unions to take part in politics, and increased the sanctions against employers prohibiting union enrollment.[50] Yet, despite these improvements, lasting progress has been difficult to achieve because of corruption and an ineffective legal system.[51]

In contrast to the CEACR, the CAS is a political body comprised of government, worker, and employer representatives. The composition reflects the ILO's unique tripartite structure. Its main task is to examine CEACR reports and select cases for "discussion" – a euphemism for public shaming. The cases selected for shaming typically involve violations of a more serious

---

[46] ILO 1998.
[47] ILO 1994a, 1994b.
[48] ILO 1994b, 1994c.
[49] ILO 1996.
[50] ILO 1993a, 1993b.
[51] US State Department 1996.

nature. In the ILO, then, reporting and shaming are sequential processes: reporting always comes first and only sometimes is it complemented by shaming. The CAS meets once a year in association with the International Labour Conference (ILC) and is open to all delegates. Representatives of the governments targeted by the CAS are invited to respond before the committee. The CAS usually draws up conclusions that recommend a government to adopt a particular measure or to welcome an ILO mission. The discussions and conclusions are summarized in the annual report of the CAS. Given the discomfort of this procedure to non-compliant states, the shaming practices of the CAS have for a long time been a controversial issue within the ILO.[52] Shaming of states by the CAS is much less common than countries being listed as non-compliant in CEACR reports. The CAS has shamed 70 of the 154 states in the dataset at least once during time period 1989–2011.

EMPIRICAL ANALYSIS

We examine the effects of ILO reporting on states' worker rights improvement through a multivariate regression analysis. We begin by briefly describing operationalizations and models, before turning to the results.

Dependent Variable

Our dependent variable is *worker rights improvement,* capturing whether states improve the protection of labor rights by passing and enforcing laws. This variable is based on data from Cingranelli-Richards' (CIRI) dataset on human rights. The CIRI worker rights variable has an ordinal scale and is coded for each country year. The variable ranges from 0 to 2, where 0 indicates "severely restricted" worker rights, 1 "somewhat restricted" worker rights, and 2 "fully protected" worker rights (see Table 7.1). The level of labor protection in the CIRI dataset depends on workers' right to free association and collective bargaining.[53] These rights are regulated in two fundamental ILO conventions, number 87 (freedom of association) and 98 (collective bargaining).[54] The dataset includes the years 1989–2011 and the 154 countries that have ratified either one of these two conventions.

The CIRI coding of worker rights is based exclusively on the US State Department's country reports on human rights practices. The initial drafts of the State Department's reports are prepared by embassy staff in each country on the basis of information from government officials, opposition parties, human rights activists, academics, and others actors.[55] These drafts are then

---

[52] Thomann 2011, 146–47.
[53] Cingranelli and Richards 2014, 65–70.
[54] Freedom of Association and Protection of the Right to Organize Convention, 1948 (No. 87); Right to Organize and Collective Bargaining Convention, 1949 (No. 98).
[55] Mosley 2011, 2.

TABLE 7.1. *CIRI worker rights coding*

Score	Label	Description
0	Severely restricted	Right of association and right to organize and bargain collectively are systematically violated
1	Somewhat restricted	Government generally protects these rights, but there are occasional violations and other problems, e.g. no right to strike for public employees; child labor; forced labor; discrimination at work; no minimum wage
2	Fully protected	Government consistently protects these rights; no mentions of violations of other worker rights

reviewed by staff at the State Department's Bureau of Democracy, Human Rights, and Labor, with further input from other staff at the State Department and outside experts. The ILO reports are not a systematic source of information in this broad process of consultation.[56] We can therefore expect the CIRI worker rights score to provide an autonomous measure of state respect for worker rights. This distinguishes the CIRI data from alternative measures of labor rights protection, which use ILO reports as a principal or partial component.[57]

To test the effects of ILO reporting, we transform the CIRI score into a dichotomous variable that captures *worker rights improvements* by coding all positive annual changes for each state-year.[58] For the full time period and all included countries, we count a total of 368 improvements in worker rights. Of these 368 cases, 196 are improvements of worker rights from "severely restricted" to "somewhat restricted," while 158 are improvements from "somewhat restricted" to "fully protected."[59] The distinction between improvements from 0 to 1 and from 1 to 2 enables us to control for the effect of the initial level of workers' rights. Although our theoretical expectations focus on improvements, the dataset also includes an almost equal amount of decreases in the CIRI score of worker rights. We use these data to construct a measure of CIRI score decreases as a robustness check. Finally, the volatility

---

[56] Which is why some composite indices of collective labor rights (e.g. Mosley 2011) include ILO reports as an additional source, next to CIRI data.

[57] Kuchera and Sari 2016; Mosley 2011.

[58] See, e.g. Kim 2012.

[59] Due to the low number of cases in this category (n = 13), improvements from "severely restricted" to "fully protected" are not analyzed in a separate category.

of CIRI scores is quite high for many countries. To control for the possibility that an increase is followed by a decrease, we introduce an additional version of the dependent variable. We assess the effect of reporting on long-lasting or sustainable improvements of worker rights, where the binary improvement variable gets a score of "1" only if no decrease of the CIRI score occurs within the following five years (44.6 percent of all improvements).

Explanatory Variables

Our main explanatory variable captures ILO performance indicator. *Reporting* is coded "1" if the CEACR includes a country in its report in a given year with regard to conventions 87 and 98, and "0" otherwise.[60] The data for this variable were gathered from the ILO's NORMLEX database and annual documents from the CEACR.[61]

There is strong consensus in the naming and shaming literature that explanatory variables must be lagged to account for the time it takes for countries to comply.[62] While a one-year time lag is the minimum to avoid problems of endogeneity, previous scholarship on social influence in international cooperation has shown that even longer time lags have to be considered.[63] Due to the two-year reporting cycle for basic ILO conventions, we opt for a two-year time lag for the *reporting* variable. The two-year lag also makes sense in view of the time it takes to adjust policies in response to international criticism.

On average, each of the 154 countries in our dataset were subject to about 12 CEACR observations (*reporting*) between 1989 and 2011, and shamed 1.8 times over the same time period. Single observations on non-compliance in just one year are the exception. More common is the recurrent listing of a country in successive CEACR reports, with an empirical range of 1–20 years during our observation period. As part of our test of H1, we assess if an effect of *reporting* on workers' rights is linked to the length of the listing period. For this purpose, we create three additional versions of the *reporting* variable that represent different lengths of the listing period: one to four years, five to ten years, and a category for more than 10 years of iterated observations.

A particularity of the ILO's reporting process is the possibility of combining reporting with shaming of non-compliant states by another body, the CAS (H2e). We build a *shaming* variable that is coded "1" if the CAS has included a country on its shaming list, and "0" otherwise. The data for this variable were also gathered from the ILO's NORMLEX database and annual

---

[60] We control for the effects of individual conventions as well.
[61] ILO 2016b, 2016c.
[62] Hill et al. 2013; Hillebrecht 2014; Krain 2012.
[63] E.g. Bearce and Bondanella 2007, 716.

documents from the CAS.[64] While it is logically impossible that a country is shamed without first having been reported, only some report listings lead to shaming. As a consequence, the statistical correlation between *reporting* and *shaming* is relatively low (r = 0.26). Whereas some countries, like Colombia (18 shaming events/22 reporting events), Myanmar (17/21), and Turkey (14/22) have almost as many shaming events as reporting events, other countries with similar numbers of reporting events have not been subject to a single shaming event, among them Trinidad (22 reporting events), Portugal (16), Libya (16), and Austria (13). To minimize the overlap between the *reporting* and *shaming* variables, we build an additional version of *reporting* that is sensitive to parallel action by CAS and thus allows us to test if shaming matters.

In the theory section, we identified a number of conditions under which reporting is expected to be more or less effective (H2a–d). Studies have shown that democracies tend to have better labor protection.[65] To control for regime type, we include the variable *polity* based on Polity IV data.[66] The variable ranges from −10 to +10. Second, the variable *trade dependence* represents the degree of economic dependence and is measured in trade as share of GDP.[67] To capture pressures from domestic and transnational civil society, we use a labor rights NGO variable from Peksen and Blanton, which expresses the number of pro-labor rights organizations with international ties in a country in a given year.[68] Fourth, we use the level of economic development as a proxy for a country's capacity constraints, measured as *GDP per capita*.[69] We add a few additional control variables that often are invoked in the quantitative study of labor rights, such as the number of ratified fundamental *ILO conventions* and *GDP growth*.[70] We also use the initial value of the worker rights variable as a proxy for the history of the protection level (*past worker rights*).[71] Finally, we account for time-dependent effects by considering the number of years since the last improvement in the CIRI worker score (*time since last improvement*).[72]

Model Specification

We use logistic regression models due to the nature of our dependent variable.[73] The use of a measure of change as the dependent variable decreases

[64] ILO 2016b, 2016d.
[65] Mosley and Uno 2007.
[66] Marshall et al. 2014.
[67] World Bank 2016.
[68] Peksen and Blanton 2016.
[69] World Bank 2016. See Norris 2015, ch. 7, for a similar use of GDP per capita as measure of capacity.
[70] Kim 2012.
[71] Peksen and Blanton 2016, 9.
[72] Kim 2012, 709.
[73] The nature of changes in the CIRI score with repeated increases speaks against the use of an event history model.

the problem of autocorrelation, but we control for time dependence through the three variables time, time^2, and time^3.[74] With the exception of *reporting*, we enter all time-variant independent variables with a lag of one year. We cluster the data by countries and calculate robust standard errors. We begin the empirical analysis with a logit estimation of the effects of reporting and analyze the effects using different specifications of the dependent variable (Table 7.2). In a second step, we assess the effects of different lengths of the period that states are reported as non-compliant (Table 7.3). Finally, we test the potential impact of conditioning factors on the effects of *reporting* on *improvements in worker rights* (Table 7.4).

Results

The analysis reveals an effect reporting by the ILO, supporting the general expectation from H1 (Table 7.2). *Reporting* has a positive and significant effect on *improvements in worker rights* (Model 1). The results also hold if we estimate ILO convention 87 and 98 separately (Model 2).

Models 3 and 4 present the results for alternative versions of the dependent variable. Model 3 demonstrates that H1 is confirmed for changes from severely restricted (0) to somewhat restricted worker rights (1), whereas ILO reporting has no significant effect on shifts toward full protection of worker rights (2).[75] This suggests that compliance review through CEACR reporting is effective in improving the worst cases of non-compliance, but not in getting fairly compliant states to fully comply with international labor standards.

As mentioned earlier, some countries show frequent increases and decreases in their CIRI scores over time. To test if *reporting* has long-lasting effects, we compare sustainable CIRI improvements that were not followed by decreases within the next five years (Model 5) with cases of less sustainable improvements (Model 6). Our analysis shows that *reporting* indeed leads to sustainable improvements, whereas it does not have an effect on unsustainable improvements. The finding that performance indicator has durable effects on state behavior differs from results in some earlier research on naming and shaming.[76] Finally, additional support for H1 comes from a placebo test in Model 7, where we assess if *reporting* also can explain decreases in the CIRI score. The results show it cannot, strengthening our confidence that the effects of ILO reporting on improvements in labor standards are robust.

Next to *reporting, labor NGOs,* and *trade dependence* have positive effects on improvements in worker rights. The effect of labor NGOs is robust and significant except for CIRI changes from 1 to 2 (Model 4). The coefficient

---

[74] Carter and Signorino 2010.
[75] A regression of the few cases of changes from "0" to "2" does not yield positive results either.
[76] Hafner-Burton 2008.

TABLE 7.2. Logistic regression of CIRI improvements, 1991–2011

	1	2	3	4	5	6	7
	CIRI Score, Improvement		CIRI Score, Improvement from 0 to 1	CIRI Score, Improvement from 1 to 2	CIRI Score, Sustainable Improvement	CIRI Score, Non-Sustainable Improvement	CIRI Score, Decrease
ILO reporting	0.303 [0.135]**		0.513 [0.182]***	-0.037 [0.195]	0.449 [0.171]***	-0.063 [0.199]	-0.062 [0.122]
Convention 87 only		0.284 [0.159]*					
Convention 98 only		0.321 [0.178]*					
Polity	-0.037 [0.012]***	-0.030 [0.016]*	-0.068 [0.019]***	0.022 [0.020]	-0.022 [0.015]	-0.053 [0.016]***	0.002 [0.010]
Trade dependence (log)	0.162 [0.079]**	0.113 [0.098]	0.170 [0.128]	0.149 [0.127]	0.092 [0.097]	0.245 [0.107]**	0.057 [0.058]
Labor NGOs	0.479 [0.142]***	0.520 [0.159]***	0.569 [0.204]***	0.308 [0.246]	0.397 [0.178]**	0.538 [0.218]**	0.250 [0.145]*
GDP per capita (log)	-0.137 [0.063]**	-0.170 [0.084]**	-0.095 [0.103]	-0.250 [0.096]***	-0.079 [0.082]	-0.211 [0.087]**	-0.076 [0.055]
GDP growth rate (log)	0.046 [0.068]	0.063 [0.080]	0.005 [0.081]	0.101 [0.114]	0.018 [0.078]	0.093 [0.105]	0.029 [0.061]
ILO conventions	0.010 [0.043]	0.068 [0.087]	0.048 [0.068]	-0.060 [0.065]	0.022 [0.068]	0.002 [0.065]	-0.045 [0.037]
Past worker rights	-0.096 [0.077]	-0.115 [0.094]	-0.418 [0.115]***	0.379 [0.138]***	-0.188 [0.111]*	-0.034 [0.119]	0.091 [0.071]
Time since last improvement	0.013 [0.015]	0.021 [0.019]	0.023 [0.019]	-0.005 [0.022]	0.034 [0.018]*	-0.029 [0.026]	-0.208 [0.028]***

	1	2	3	4	5	6	7
	CIRI Score, Improvement	CIRI Score, Improvement	CIRI Score, Improvement from 0 to 1	CIRI Score, Improvement from 1 to 2	CIRI Score, Sustainable Improvement	CIRI Score, Non-Sustainable Improvement	CIRI Score, Decrease
Time	0.353	0.341	0.129	0.781	0.415	0.191	0.105
	[0.130]***	[0.154]**	[0.155]	[0.235]***	[0.146]***	[0.143]	[0.114]
$Time^2$	-0.048	-0.049	-0.030	-0.076	-0.055	-0.026	-0.007
	[0.013]***	[0.015]***	[0.015]**	[0.022]***	[0.014]***	[0.015]*	[0.010]
$Time^3$	0.001	0.002	0.001	0.002	0.002	0.001	0.000
	[0.000]***	[0.000]***	[0.000]***	[0.001]***	[0.000]***	[0.000]*	[0.000]
Constant	-4.207	-4.217	-4.621	-5.796	-4.644	-5.101	-2.224
	[1.015]***	[1.262]***	[1.477]***	[2.061]***	[1.196]***	[1.458]***	[0.962]**
Wald	86.63	66.86	86.84	71.78	48.08	64.20	76.23
AIC	1677.4	1293.5	1075.8	909.47	1241.51	913.37	1670.76
N	2,376	1,917	2,376	2,376	2,454	2,454	2,376

*$p < 0.1$; **$p < 0.05$; ***$p < 0.01$.
Logit regression with STATA 14.1. Estimation clustered by panel identifier (country). Robust standard errors in parentheses.

TABLE 7.3. Logistic regression of CIRI improvements, length of reporting, 1991–2011

	8	9	10	11	12
	Varying Length of CEACR Reporting Episode	Control for Democratization	Control for GDP Growth	Control for NGO Increase	Control for Trade Growth
ILO reporting, 1–4 years	0.336 [0.175]*	0.376 [0.157]**	0.396 [0.157]**	0.428 [0.166]**	0.334 [0.159]**
ILO reporting, 5–10 years	-0.048 [0.149]	-0.011 [0.152]	0.029 [0.139]	0.002 [0.139]	-0.050 [0.137]
ILO reporting, >10 years	0.257 [0.132]*	0.184 [0.110]*	0.319 [0.109]***	0.290 [0.102]***	0.251 [0.105]**
Polity IV	-0.036 [0.012]***	-0.039 [0.012]***	-0.037 [0.012]***	-0.039 [0.012]***	-0.036 [0.012]***
Trade dependence (log)	0.167 [0.080]**	0.163 [0.080]**	0.192 [0.082]**	0.186 [0.081]**	0.139 [0.081]*
Labor NGOs	0.457 [0.144]***	0.494 [0.138]***	0.462 [0.141]***	0.481 [0.140]***	0.465 [0.142]***
GDP per capita (log)	-0.150 [0.064]**	-0.148 [0.065]**	-0.171 [0.065]***	-0.146 [0.066]**	-0.160 [0.067]**
GDP growth rate (log)	0.046 [0.069]	0.045 [0.068]	0.050 [0.069]	0.045 [0.068]	0.046 [0.069]
ILO conventions	0.007 [0.042]	0.001 [0.043]	0.000 [0.043]	0.009 [0.044]	0.002 [0.043]
Past worker rights	-0.081 [0.077]	-0.092 [0.077]	-0.078 [0.077]	-0.084 [0.077]	-0.086 [0.078]
Time since last improvement	0.012 [0.015]	0.011 [0.015]	0.014 [0.015]	0.014 [0.015]	0.012 [0.015]

	8	9	10	11	12
	Varying Length of CEACR Reporting Episode	Control for Democratization	Control for GDP Growth	Control for NGO Increase	Control for Trade Growth
Time	0.351 [0.125]***	0.353 [0.125]***	0.340 [0.125]***	0.347 [0.126]***	0.351 [0.124]***
Time^2	-0.047 [0.012]***	-0.047 [0.012]***	-0.046 [0.012]***	-0.047 [0.012]***	-0.047 [0.012]***
Time^3	0.001 [0.000]***	0.001 [0.000]***	0.001 [0.000]***	0.001 [0.000]***	0.001 [0.000]***
Constant	-4.076 [1.017]***	-4.095 [1.029]***	-4.163 [1.035]***	-4.321 [1.048]***	-3.782 [1.016]***
Wald	100.33	102.07	109.30	107.23	103.27
AIC	1,697.97	1697.06	1692.68	1692.76	1696.03
N	2,401	2,401	2,401	2,401	2,401

*$p < 0.1$; **$p < 0.05$; ***$p < 0.01$.
Logit regression with STATA 14.1. Estimation clustered by panel identifier (country). Robust standard errors in parentheses.
Abbreviation: NGO: non-governmental organizations.

TABLE 7.4. *Logistic regression of CIRI improvements, interaction effects, 1991–2011*

	13	14	15	16	17	18	19	20	21
ILO reporting	0.194 [0.141]	2.029 [1.123]*	0.235 [0.250]	-1.670 [0.882]*					
ILO reporting, no shaming					0.301 [0.146]**	0.301 [0.147]**	0.294 [0.146]**	0.295 [0.146]**	0.301 [0.146]**
ILO reporting*Polity	0.039 [0.019]**								
ILO reporting*Trade		-0.238 [0.152]							
ILO reporting*NGO			0.004 [0.011]						
ILO reporting*GDP				0.278 [0.123]**					
ILO shaming					0.327 [0.268]	0.206 [0.292]	4.160 [1.276]***	-3.765 [1.911]**	0.415 [2.253]
ILO shaming*Polity						0.034 [0.042]			
ILO shaming*Trade							-0.568 [0.193]***		
ILO shaming*NGO								1.317 [0.622]**	
ILO shaming*GDP									-0.012 [0.317]

	13	14	15	16	17	18	19	20	21
Polity IV	-0.061 [0.018]***	-0.038 [0.012]***	-0.037 [0.012]***	-0.037 [0.012]***	-0.036 [0.013]***	-0.040 [0.014]***	-0.039 [0.014]***	-0.040 [0.014]***	-0.036 [0.013]***
Trade dependence (log)	0.167 [0.080]**	0.325 [0.137]**	0.162 [0.079]**	0.163 [0.080]**	0.175 [0.083]**	0.183 [0.083]**	0.263 [0.092]***	0.192 [0.083]**	0.175 [0.082]**
Labor NGOs	0.502 [0.145]***	0.487 [0.143]***	0.447 [0.166]***	0.501 [0.146]***	0.524 [0.150]***	0.528 [0.150]***	0.544 [0.154]***	0.481 [0.151]***	0.523 [0.150]***
GDP per capita (log)	-0.130 [0.064]**	-0.140 [0.064]**	-0.137 [0.063]**	-0.291 [0.096]***	-0.137 [0.069]**	-0.135 [0.069]*	-0.152 [0.071]**	-0.133 [0.069]*	-0.136 [0.072]*
GDP growth rate (log)	0.050 [0.068]	0.045 [0.068]	0.047 [0.068]	0.050 [0.068]	0.082 [0.078]	0.082 [0.078]	0.090 [0.081]	0.079 [0.080]	0.082 [0.078]
ILO conventions	0.013 [0.043]	0.012 [0.043]	0.010 [0.043]	0.016 [0.043]	-0.025 [0.060]	-0.023 [0.060]	-0.011 [0.062]	-0.017 [0.060]	-0.025 [0.060]
Past worker rights	-0.110 [0.077]	-0.097 [0.078]	-0.097 [0.077]	-0.100 [0.077]	-0.119 [0.084]	-0.118 [0.084]	-0.118 [0.087]	-0.122 [0.084]	-0.119 [0.084]
Time since last improvement	0.014 [0.015]	0.013 [0.015]	0.013 [0.015]	0.013 [0.016]	0.005 [0.017]	0.006 [0.017]	0.003 [0.017]	0.006 [0.017]	0.005 [0.017]

(continued)

TABLE 7.4 *(continued)*

	13	14	15	16	17	18	19	20	21
Time	0.370	0.354	0.354	0.365	0.340	0.348	0.337	0.358	0.340
	[0.131]***	[0.130]***	[0.130]***	[0.130]***	[0.138]**	[0.138]**	[0.138]**	[0.139]***	[0.138]**
Time^2	-0.049	-0.048	-0.048	-0.049	-0.047	-0.048	-0.047	-0.049	-0.047
	[0.013]***	[0.013]***	[0.013]***	[0.013]***	[0.013]***	[0.013]***	[0.013]***	[0.013]***	[0.013]***
Time^3	0.002	0.001	0.001	0.001	0.001	0.002	0.001	0.002	0.001
	[0.000]***	[0.000]***	[0.000]***	[0.000]***	[0.000]***	[0.000]***	[0.000]***	[0.000]***	[0.000]***
Constant	0.502	0.487	0.447	0.501	0.524	0.528	0.544	0.481	0.523
	[0.145]***	[0.143]***	[0.166]***	[0.146]***	[0.150]***	[0.150]***	[0.154]***	[0.151]***	[0.150]***
Wald	85.76	91.28	86.84	84.32	87.30	87.03	103.47	89.85	89.23
AIC	1675.79	1677.06	1679.28	1675.04	1497.81	1498.97	1493.95	1495.20	1499.81
N	2,376	2,376	2,376	2,376	2,164	2,164	2,164	2,164	2,164

*$p < 0.1$; ** $p < 0.05$; *** $p < 0.01$.
Logit regression with STATA 14.1. Estimatiowvdard errors in parentheses.
Abbreviation: NGO: non-governmental organizations.

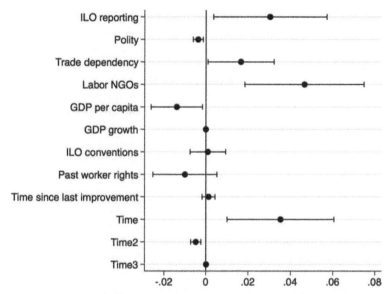

FIGURE 7.1. Marginal effects on CIRI improvements (Model 1).

for trade is only significant in Models 1 and 5, suggesting that improvements driven by the vulnerability of the domestic economy do not lead to persistent improvements in workers' rights. Conversely, the effect of *polity* and *GDP per capita* is strongly negative and significant. Many of the improvements at the lower end of the scale take place in poor countries with low democracy scores. Moreover, 80 percent of all countries categorized in the highest category of the CIRI score are democracies. While the ratification of *ILO conventions* and the *GDP growth rate* do not reveal significant results, we find that the level of *past worker rights*, as could be expected, has a negative effect on improvements from "severely restricted" to "somewhat restricted" (Model 3), and a positive effect on shifts to the highest level of "fully protected" rights (Model 4).

If we compare the marginal effect of our main explanatory variable to the effects of other significant variables on all improvements (Model 1), it is clear that reporting by the ILO has a weaker effect than the strength of labor NGOs, but a stronger effect than all other covariates, including the political regime, trade dependence, and implementation capacity of a country (Figure 7.1).

The next step after establishing the existence of a general positive effect of ILO reporting is to assess if this effect varies depending on the number of consecutive times a state is listed as non-compliant (Table 7.3). Does reporting have fairly immediate effects, indicating that ILO member states are very responsive to listing, or does it take a long time for reporting to affect behavior?

The analysis reveals that reporting both has immediate effects and can affect behavior when repeated over long time periods (Model 8). The coefficient for *reporting* between one and four years is positive and significant. It represents cases like Slovakia, where employer and worker organizations in 1997 were excluded from the wage negotiations process due to a proposal by the Slovakian government to enact wage regulations.[77] The CEACR included the country in the report, criticizing the practice and requesting the government to respect Convention 98.[78] In 1999, the government decided to reenter the tripartite negotiations.[79] We also find support for a positive effect of more than ten years of iterated reporting (Model 8). A case in point is Morocco, which for a long period, beginning in the early 1990s, was included in the reported because of its lack of legislation protecting workers from acts of anti-union discrimination. The reports brought up serious allegations of frequent dismissals of workers based on trade union membership and activities.[80] During this period, the CEACR requested the government to take legislative steps to protect trade unions. In 2002, the government of Morocco finally introduced legislation prohibiting discrimination against workers based on trade union membership or activities.[81]

We also control for the possibility that our main results could be affected by the presence of ceiling or floor effects. We re-estimate Models 1, 3, and 4 (Table 7.2) by excluding all countries that are stuck at the top (2) or bottom (0) of the CIRI score. For these countries, it is logically impossible to expect an increase (decrease) of the CIRI score. Table A.1 presents the results without ceiling and floor effects (Model A.13–A.15) and without ceiling effects only (Models A.16–A.18). We find that our main results are robust to the exclusion of these cases, while the control for a ceiling effect in Model 1 (Model A.13) leads to a somewhat weaker, yet still significant, effect of *reporting*.[82]

Our results so far indicate that ILO reporting has a positive and durable effect on state respect for labor rights. Yet might it be that these findings are the result of a secular trend? It is possible that improvements in worker rights are the result of structural changes in a country occurring in parallel to ILO reporting, such as societal modernization or regime transformation? We undertook a number of measures that together suggest this to be an unlikely explanation of our findings.

First, we have included a set of variables intended to control for the possibility of a secular trend: *past worker rights*, *time since last improvement*, ratified *ILO conventions*, and *GDP growth rate* (Table 7.2). These variables did

---

[77] US State Department 1998.
[78] ILO 1997.
[79] US State Department 2000.
[80] ILO 1999.
[81] ILO 2002.
[82] It is important to note that 88 percent of the 494 ceiling cases (country years) that we exclude in Table A.3 correspond to the same score for the *past worker rights variable* based on CIRI scores before the beginning of the observation period.

not have any significant impact on CIRI improvements. Second, the positive finding for an immediate effect in Model 8 minimizes the likelihood that processes of domestic structural change drive the results for reporting. Substantial changes in economic development or civil society strength can be expected to take longer than the one to four years of repeated reporting captured by this variable. Third, we explicitly control for the presence of such domestic structural changes by assessing if the effects of reporting still hold when paralleled by strong increases in democracy scores, income levels, civil society strength, and trade openness. For this purpose, new versions of the ILO *reporting* variable were created that are sensitive to disproportional changes in these four control variables.[83] For instance, CEACR reporting on Indonesia on convention 98 from the beginning of the 1990s to the end of the observation period is excluded from Model 9, since the country has undergone a process of democratization from a polity score of −7 in 1990 to +8 in 2011. The results from Models 9–12 in Table 7.3 suggest that the previously established effect of ILO reporting is robust to this test. The immediate effects (1–4 years) of reporting are quite stable or even stronger. The only visible difference is the effect of repeated reporting over longer time periods (more than 10 years), which becomes slightly weaker when we control for parallel processes of domestic democratization (Model 9).

As a third step of our analysis, we test the conditions under which *reporting* affects worker protection (H2a–e). We find that some of the conditions expected to shape the effects of reporting are relevant in the ILO. As Table 7.4 indicates, we observe two significant interaction effects that support H2a and H2d. To begin with, the effect of reporting observed in Table 7.3 mainly holds for democracies. The interaction of *reporting* and *polity* is significant, while the coefficient for *reporting* becomes weaker and loses its significance (Model 13).[84] The interaction effect for *reporting* and *polity* is visualized in Figure 7.2. It highlights the difference in the marginal effect of *polity* on positive changes in the CIRI score when we add *reporting*.

The same positive interaction is observed for *GDP per capita*, our proxy for a country's capacity to implement improvements of worker rights (Model 16 and Figure 7.2). Here, the *reporting* variable even shows a negative coefficient when we add this interaction term. We get an even stronger result for this interaction for the version of the dependent variable that only captures improvements from "somehow restricted" to "fully protected" (Model A8 in Table A.2). These positive interaction results from Models 13 and 16 contrast with the negative independent effects of *GDP per capita* and *polity* on labor

[83] Disproportional change is defined by the 75 percent percentile for changes in the polity score, GDP per capita, labor NGOs and trade openness during our observation period. If the change on one of these variables during a reporting episode is higher than the 75 percent percentile (this corresponds, e.g. to an increase of more than 2 points on the polity score), the ILO variable is zeroed.

[84] The same effect occurs if we substitute the polity variable by a democracy dummy (with a Polity score of "6" as the threshold).

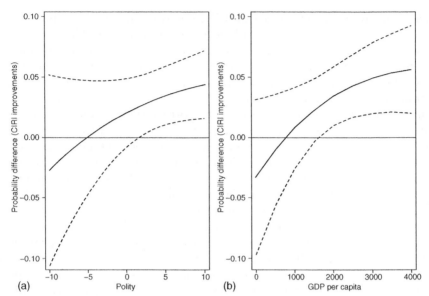

FIGURE 7.2. Conditional marginal effects of ILO reporting. (a) Democracy and (b) Capacity.

rights improvements. Whereas autocracies and poorer countries in general have a higher likelihood of improving the protection of labor rights, mainly due to the lower initial level of worker rights protection, we find that ILO reporting is more effective for richer and more democratic countries.[85]

Considering that reporting mainly has effects in cases of poor labor protection, it is reasonable to wonder what richer democracies, if any, actually conform to this profile. The data reveal several interesting cases. The UK was classified as having "severely restricted" labor rights from 1991 to 1998, when it was reclassified as having improved to "partly restricted" rights. In 2000, it was finally considered to have "fully protected" rights. Similarly, Israel belonged to the category of "severely restricted" labor rights from 1992 to 1993, Greece from 1994 to 1995, Chile from 2003 to 2004, and Brazil from 2009 to 2010.

Models 14 and 15 in Table 7.4 show that there is no support for the other two theorized conditions – economic vulnerability to foreign trade flows (H2b) and the presence of labor NGOs (H2c). This is surprising, given that existing literature typically assumes that more vulnerable states are more receptive to

[85] Since democracy and wealth are known to be correlated ($r = 0.35$ in our sample), we go one step further and test if one and the same mechanism drives this result. We create dummy variables for the combinations of poor democracies and rich autocracies, but none of the coefficients shows significant interaction terms with reporting, supporting the presence of two different explanations.

naming and shaming, and that public exposure often has an effect on state behavior by mobilizing domestic or transnational civil society.[86]

We also ran additional models to see if the conditional effects of reporting observed in Models 13 and 16 vary depending on the different lengths of reporting episodes. We do not find any significant interaction effect, with one minor exception (Models A9–A12, Table A.3). Hence, there is nothing to indicate that the previously observed effect of shorter periods of iterated reporting (Model 8) would be limited to more developed or democratic countries, or that the effect of longer reporting episodes would pertain specifically to authoritarian regimes with lower capacities.

In the theory section, we also hypothesized that reporting might have stronger effects if combined with active shaming of non-compliant states (H2e). Some countries listed as non-compliant by the CEACR in a given year are also actively and publicly shamed by CAS, while others are not. To test the expectation that shaming matters for the likelihood of improvements, we compare the effect of CEACR reporting with and without associated shaming by the CAS (Models 17–21; Table 7.4). We separate the effect of mere *reporting* from CAS *shaming* by manipulating the *reporting* variable in such a way that it scores "0" if shaming took place in the same year. The *shaming* variable represents all cases where reporting and shaming occurred in parallel, since the CAS never takes action unless a country is also listed as non-compliant in a CEACR report. While reporting is still robust in these models, the results do not indicate that shaming brings additional effects, with two exceptions. First, we find that the combination of *shaming* and strong *labor NGOs* has a positive effect (Model 20), suggesting that international shaming of a country results in particular effects when there is a strong domestic and transnational labor NGO community that can use this criticism to pressure the government.[87] Second, we find a negative effect when *shaming* is interacted with *trade dependence* (Model 19). Contrary to our expectations, it appears that the less a country depends on foreign trade, the more likely it is to correct its behavior following shaming by the ILO. The lack of a general effect of shaming may be explained by the political character of the CAS, which is considered less credible and impartial than the CEACR.[88]

Finally, we want to rule out the possibility that our positive results on reporting are affected by selection bias in the ILO's choice of what states to target. Does the ILO target states with poor worker rights protection or does it strategically target easy-to-influence states with less severe worker rights violations? Table 7.5 shows the results of a logistic regression predicting targeting by the

---

[86] E.g. Franklin 2008; Krain 2012; Risse and Ropp 2013.

[87] This result lends support to studies suggesting that the effects of shaming are conditional on the presence of NGO communities. See, e.g. Murdie and Davis 2012.

[88] Thomann 2011, 146.

TABLE 7.5. *Logistic regression of ILO targeting*

	22	23	24	25	26	27
		CEACR Reporting			CAS Shaming	
		Conv. 87	Conv. 98		Conv. 87	Conv. 98
CIRI worker rights "severely restricted"	0.718*** [0.193]	0.601*** [0.190]	0.957*** [0.229]	1.838*** [0.427]	1.878*** [0.473]	1.636*** [0.489]
CIRI worker rights "somewhat restricted"	0.252 [0.169]	0.284 [0.177]	0.373* [0.197]	1.185*** [0.345]	1.127*** [0.436]	1.583*** [0.440]
Polity IV	-0.008 [0.016]	-0.033** [0.016]	0.012 [0.017]	-0.015 [0.033]	-0.032 [0.036]	-0.005 [0.050]
Trade dependence (log)	-0.216** [0.097]	-0.102 [0.108]	-0.263*** [0.089]	-0.317*** [0.120]	-0.330** [0.147]	-0.265* [0.160]
Labor NGOs	0.483*** [0.183]	0.507*** [0.188]	0.017 [0.215]	0.535* [0.312]	0.433 [0.314]	0.354 [0.453]
GDP per capita (log)	-0.028 [0.093]	-0.131 [0.107]	0.163 [0.117]	0.722*** [0.188]	0.665*** [0.209]	0.875*** [0.235]
Left government	-0.292** [0.147]	-0.321** [0.146]	-0.271 [0.169]	-1.124*** [0.296]	-0.944*** [0.289]	-1.363*** [0.504]
Population (log)	-0.076 [0.070]	0.022 [0.085]	-0.047 [0.087]	0.135 [0.119]	0.128 [0.132]	0.247 [0.168]

	22	23	24	25	26	27
		CEACR Reporting			CAS Shaming	
		Conv. 87	Conv. 98		Conv. 87	Conv. 98
Time	0.295***	0.132	0.216***	0.135	0.093	0.080
	[0.074]	[0.085]	[0.080]	[0.157]	[0.194]	[0.201]
Time^2	−0.015**	−0.004	−0.013	−0.027*	−0.024	−0.025
	[0.007]	[0.008]	[0.008]	[0.015]	[0.018]	[0.024]
Time^3	0.0002	−0.00002	0.0003	0.001**	0.001*	0.001
	[0.0002]	[0.0002]	[0.0002]	[0.0004]	[0.001]	[0.001]
Constant	0.449	−0.914	−0.631	−9.129***	−8.221***	−12.980***
	[1.549]	[2.106]	[1.786]	[2.333]	[2.752]	[4.363]
Chi2	171.278***	129.151***	188.240***	180.532***	136.632***	85.027***
N	2,586	2,215	2,487	1,564	1,403	1,505

* $p < 0.1$; ** $p < 0.05$; *** $p < 0.01$.
Logit regression with STATA 14.1. Estimation clustered by panel identifier (country). Robust standard errors in parentheses.

CEACR (Model 22–24) and the CAS (Model 25–27).[89] Models 22–24 show a positive effect for "severely restricted worker rights" and no significant coefficient for "somewhat restricted worker rights." This means that states' actual violations of worker rights matter when the CEACR decides what countries to include on its list. The results are robust when assessing each convention separately. States are also more likely to be listed in a report if they have a higher presence of labor NGOs, while states that are left-leaning and trade more are less likely to be included. The measures for country size – GDP per capita and population – and the level of democracy, do not predict reporting. The results for shaming (Models 25–27, Table 7.5) are similar, except that the CAS also is more likely to shame states with better worker rights protection and higher GDP per capita. In short, we find no evidence that the ILO does not target states based on their actual violations of worker rights.

To summarize, our statistical analysis shows that performance indicator by the ILO indeed affects state compliance. The effects of reporting survive several critical robustness tests; importantly, they are not the product of biased targeting by the ILO or a secular trend resulting from domestic structural changes. Reporting mainly has an effect on democracies and countries with higher capacity, and mainly leads to improvements where the initial respect for worker rights is poor. Supplementing reporting with active shaming of a non-compliant state only improves respect for worker rights under specific conditions. Reporting tends to affect state behavior quite immediately, but there is also evidence of reporting leading to improvements after longer periods of repeated observations. Finally, and importantly, the effects of reporting are durable.

CONCLUSION

Global performance indicators are proliferating, but so far we have little systematic knowledge about their effects. In this article, we have sought to evaluate the effect of performance indicators in the shape of IO reporting on state compliance. We have done so through an in-depth study of the ILO, which has a long history of monitoring international labor standards, allowing us to control for the potential impact of enforcement on compliance, making it possible to evaluate if reporting's effects vary depending on characteristics of target countries and the reporting process. We summarize our principal findings and discuss their broader implications in terms of three conclusions.

First, reporting works. In the ILO, regularized and publicized reporting on state compliance has significant, positive effects, particularly when dealing with severe violations of international labor standards. Reporting's effects are quite immediate; already after one or a few listings as non-compliant do states take measures to improve their labor rights records. But reporting can also work

---

[89] In Models 4 to 6, we use a sample that is limited to years for which countries have been reported by the CEACR, which is the relevant sample for CAS targeting.

through repeated listing over extended time periods. Reporting's effects are long-lasting and not just temporary adjustments to momentarily please international partners or domestic interests. It is also notable that reporting (naming) need not involve shaming to be effective; in fact, combining reporting with shaming only contributes to further improvements under very specific circumstances.

These findings on the effects of reporting are particularly important in light of some other considerations. They likely underestimate the full consequences of performance indicators, since they only capture the compellence effect of monitoring – being pushed to comply when revealed to be a violator – but not the deterrence effect – abstaining from violations because of the risk of exposure. In addition, they were obtained without simultaneous threats of enforcement, which often are considered a necessary condition for international monitoring to work. While striking, these effects of IO reporting may not be surprising in the context of GPIs, where we would expect the most significant consequences when the GPI is promulgated by a highly respected authority, data are gathered by monitoring, and the GPI facilitates explicit comparisons.[90]

Second, reporting does not work equally well for all countries. Reporting is a tool that primarily works for the liberal world of democratic and wealthy states with strong commitments to international norms and sufficient capacity to do something about violations. For this group of states, public exposure as rights violators is highly uncomfortable, internationally and domestically, leading them to take immediate and sustainable action. By contrast, autocratic and poor states lack both the domestic political pressures and resources to respond to international criticism with measures that bring about real improvements in labor rights. Other cross-country differences – whether countries have a strong NGO presence or are highly trade dependent – do not appear to matter systematically for reporting's effects on state behavior, contrary to expectations in some earlier literature.

Third, the effects of ILO reporting are good news for compliance. Our evidence suggests that labor rights are promoted through a broader set of measures than often assumed. Earlier literature has demonstrated how ratification of ILO conventions has positive results on respect for labor rights, as do participation in preferential trade agreements and the presence of domestic NGOs.[91] We join others in arguing that the ILO's monitoring system is an additional source of compliance with international labor law, for which the ILO seldom gets enough credit.[92] While the ILO might lack teeth, its procedures for monitoring, assessing, and comparing the performance of ILO member states are effective in ways that deserve greater attention.

More broadly, the ILO represents a type of monitoring system that is common in world politics, yet often dismissed as ineffective because of its absence

[90] Kelley and Simmons 2019, 37.
[91] Clark 2013; Kim 2010, 2012; Rodrik 1996.
[92] Helfer 2008; Weisband 2000.

of enforcement through legal coercion and material sanctions. Our findings suggest that existing research has underestimated the potential of monitoring systems based on reporting to generate compliance with international rules and norms.[93] For sure, enforcement measures could have stronger effects. But this option is not always available because of sovereignty concerns and collective-action problems. Indeed, the UN's Agenda 2030 for sustainable development and the Paris Agreement on climate change suggest that the international community is putting growing faith in performance indicators without teeth. Knowing that reporting, on its own, can nudge states toward compliance is comforting against this backdrop.

References

Adler-Nissen, Rebecca. 2014. Stigma Management in International Relations: Transgressive Identities, Norms, and Order in International Society. *International Organization* 68 (1):143–76.

Bearce, David, and Stacy Bondanella. 2007. Intergovernmental Organizations, Socialization, and Member-State Interest Convergence. *International Organization* 61 (4):703–33.

Börzel, Tanja, Tobias Hofmann, Diana Panke, and Carina Sprungk. 2010. Obstinate and Inefficient: Why Member States Do Not Comply with European Law. *Comparative Political Studies* 43 (11):1363–90.

Brewster, Rachel. 2013. Reputation in International Relations and International Law Theory. In *Interdisciplinary Perspectives on International Law and International Relations*, edited by Jeffrey L. Dunoff and Mark A. Pollack, 524–43. Cambridge: Cambridge University Press.

Carter, David, and Curtis Signorino. 2010. Back to the Future: Modeling Time Dependence in Binary Data. *Political Analysis* 18 (3):271–92.

Chayes, Abram, and Antonia Handler Chayes. 1995. *The New Sovereignty: Compliance with International Regulatory Agreements*. Cambridge, MA: Harvard University Press.

Checkel, Jeffrey T. 2001. Why Comply? Social Learning and European Identity Change. *International Organization* 55 (3):553–88.

Cingranelli, David, and David Richards. 2014. The Cingranelli-Richards (CIRI) Human Rights Data Project Coding Manual Version 5.20.14. Available at http://www.humanrightsdata.com/p/data-documentation.html.

Clark, Ann Marie. 2013. The Normative Context of Human Rights Criticism: Treaty Ratification and UN Mechanisms. In *The Persistent Power of Human Rights: From Commitment to Compliance*, edited by Thomas Risse, Stephen C. Ropp, and Kathryn Sikkink, 125–44. Cambridge: Cambridge University Press.

Cooley, Alexander, and Jack Snyder, eds. 2015. *Ranking the World*. Cambridge: Cambridge University Press.

Cooney, Sean. 1999. Testing Times for the ILO: Institutional Reform for the New International Political Economy. *Comparative Labor Law and Policy Journal* 20 (3):365–400.

---

[93] For an overview, see Simmons 2012.

Dai, Xinyuan. 2007. *International Institutions and National Policies.* Cambridge: Cambridge University Press.

Davis, Kevin, Angelina Fisher, Benedict Kingsbury, and Sally Engle Merry, eds. 2012. *Governance by Indicators: Global Power through Classification and Rankings.* Oxford: Oxford University Press.

Della Porta, Donnatella, and Sidney Tarrow, eds. 2005. *Transnational Protest and Global Activism.* Lanham, MD: Rowman & Littlefield.

DeMeritt, Jacqueline H.R. 2015. Delegating Death: Military Intervention and Government Killing. *Journal of Conflict Resolution* 59 (3):428–54.

Douglas, William A., John-Paul Ferguson, and Erin Klett. 2004. An Effective Confluence of Forces in Support of Workers' Rights: ILO Standards, US Trade Laws, Unions, and NGOs. *Human Rights Quarterly* 26 (2):273–99.

Downs, George W., David M. Rocke, and Peter N. Barsoom. 1996. Is the Good News about Compliance Good News about Cooperation? *International Organization* 50 (3):379–406.

Elliott, Kimberly Ann, and Richard B. Freeman. 2003. *Can Labor Standards Improve under Globalization?* Washington, DC: Peterson Institute Press.

Franklin, James C. 2008. Shame on You: The Impact of Human Rights Criticism on Political Repression in Latin America. *International Studies Quarterly* 52 (1):187–211.

Friman, H. Richard, ed. 2015a. *The Politics of Leverage in International Relations.* Basingstoke: Palgrave Macmillan.

Friman, H. Richard. 2015b. Behind the Curtain: Naming and Shaming in International Drug Control. In *The Politics of Leverage in International Relations*, edited by H. Richard Friman, 143–64. Basingstoke: Palgrave Macmillan.

Goldsmith, Jack L., and Eric A. Posner. 2005 *The Limits of International Law.* Oxford: Oxford University Press.

Guzman, Andrew T. 2008. *How International Law Works: A Rational Choice Theory.* Oxford: Oxford University Press.

Hafner-Burton, Emilie M. 2008. Sticks and Stones: Naming and Shaming the Human Rights Enforcement Problem. *International Organization* 62 (4):689–716.

Hafner-Burton, Emilie M., and Kiyoteru Tsutsui. 2005. Human Rights in a Globalizing World: The Paradox of Empty Promises. *American Journal of Sociology* 110 (5):1373–411.

Helfer, Laurence R. 2008. Monitoring Compliance with Unratified Treaties: The ILO Experience. *Law and Contemporary Problems* 71 (1):193–217.

Hendrix, Cullen S., and Wendy H. Wong. 2013. When Is the Pen Truly Mighty? Regime Type and the Efficacy of Naming and Shaming in Curbing Human Rights Abuses. *British Journal of Political Science* 43 (3):651–72.

Hill, Daniel W., Will H. Moore, and Bumba Mukherjee. 2013. Information Politics versus Organizational Incentives: When Are Amnesty International's "Naming and Shaming" Reports Biased? *International Studies Quarterly* 57 (2):219–32.

Hillebrecht, Courtney. 2014. *Domestic Politics and International Human Rights Tribunals: The Problem of Compliance.* Cambridge: Cambridge University Press.

ILO. 1977. Report of the CEACR. 63rd Session 1977. Report III. part 4A, p. 10–11. International Labour Office, Geneva, Switzerland.

1993a. Observation (CEACR) – adopted 1993, published 80th ILC session. Available at http://www.ilo.org/dyn/normlex/en/f?p=1000:13100:0::NO: 13100:P13100_COMMENT_ID:2112822. Accessed April 11, 2016.

1993b. Observation (CEACR) – adopted 1993, published 80th ILC session. Available at http://www.ilo.org/dyn/normlex/en/f?p=1000:13100:0::NO: 13100:P13100_COMMENT_ID:2127318. Accessed April 11, 2016.

1994a. Observation (CEACR) – adopted 1994, published 81st ILC session. Available at http://www.ilo.org/dyn/normlex/en/f?p=1000:13100:0::NO: 13100:P13100_COMMENT_ID:2127304. Accessed April 11, 2016.

1994b. Observation (CEACR) – adopted 1994, published 81st ILC session. Available at http://www.ilo.org/dyn/normlex/en/f?p=1000:13100:0::NO: 13100:P13100_COMMENT_ID:2127318. Accessed April 11, 2016.

1994c. Report of the CEACR. International Labour Office, Geneva, Switzerland. Available at http://www.ilo.org/public/libdoc/ilo/ P/09661/09661%281994-81-1-2-3%29.pdf. Accessed April 11, 2016.

1996. Report of the CEACR. International Labour Office, Geneva, Switzerland. Available at http://www.ilo.org/dyn/normlex/en/f?p=1000: 13100:0::NO:13100:P13100_COMMENT_ID, P11110_COUNTRY_ID, P11110_COUNTRY_NAME, P11110_COMMENT_YEAR:2147837,102 658,Greece,1995. Accessed April 11, 2016.

1997. Direct Request (CEACR) – Adopted 1996, Published 85th ILC Session (1997). Freedom of Association and Protection of the Right to Organise Convention, 1948 (No. 87) – Slovakia. Available at http://www.ilo.org/ dyn/normlex/en/f?p=1000:13100:0::NO:13100:P13100_COMMENT_ ID:2154742. Accessed April 11, 2016.

1998. Report of the CEACR. International Labour Office, Geneva, Switzerland. Available at http://www.ilo.org/public/libdoc/ilo/ P/09661/09661%281998-86%29.pdf. Accessed April 11, 2016.

1999. Observation (CEACR) – Adopted 1998, Published 87th ILC Session (1999). Right to Organise and Collective Bargaining Convention, 1949 (No. 98) – Morocco. Available at http://www.ilo.org/dyn/normlex/en/f?p =1000:13100:0::NO:13100:P13100_COMMENT_ID:2173009. Accessed April 11, 2016.

2002. Observation (CEACR) – Adopted 2011, Published 90th ILC Session (2002). Right to Organise and Collective Bargaining Convention, 1949 (No. 98) – Morocco. Available at http://www.ilo.org/dyn/normlex/en/f?p =1000:13100:0::NO:13100:P13100_COMMENT_ID:2202143. Accessed April 11, 2016.

2012. *Handbook of Procedures relating to International Labour Conventions and Recommendations*. Geneva, Switzerland: International Labour Office.

2016a. Conventions and Protocols. Available at http://www.ilo.org/global/ standards/introduction-to-international-labour-standards/conventions- and-recommendations/lang--en/index.htm. Accessed April 11, 2016.

2016b. NORMLEX: Information System on International Labour Standards. Available at http://www.ilo.org/dyn/normlex/ en/f?p=NORMLEXPUB:1:0::NO:::. Accessed April 11, 2017.

2016c. Information and Reports on the Application of Conventions and Recommendations. Available at http://www.ilo.org/public/libdoc/ ilo/P/09661/. Accessed April 11, 2017.

2016d. Reports of the Conference Committee on the Application of Standards. Available at http://www.ilo.org/global/standards/information-resources- and-publications/publications/WCMS_190528/lang--en/index.htm. Accessed April 11, 2017.

Jacobson, Harold, and Edith Brown Weiss, eds. 1998. *Engaging Countries: Strengthening Compliance with International Environmental Accords.* Cambridge, MA: MIT Press.

Jo, Hyeran, Brian Philipps, and Joshua Alley. 2017. One Man's Terrorist: When Does Blacklisting Reduce Terrorism? This volume.

Johnston, Alastair I. 2001. Treating International Institutions as Social Environments. *International Studies Quarterly* 45 (4):487–516.

2008. *Social States: China in International Institutions, 1980–2000.* Princeton, NJ: Princeton University Press.

Keck, Margaret E., and Kathryn Sikkink. 1998. *Activists beyond Borders: Advocacy Networks in International Politics.* Ithaca, NY: Cornell University Press.

Kelley, Judith G., and Beth A. Simmons. 2015. Politics by Number: Indicators as Social Pressure in International Relations. *American Journal of Political Science* 59 (1):55–70.

2019. Introduction: The Power of Global Performance Indicators. This volume.

Keohane, Robert O. 1984. *After Hegemony: Cooperation and Discord in the World Political Economy.* Princeton, NJ: Princeton University Press.

Khagram, Sanjeev, James V. Riker, and Kathryn Sikkink, eds. 2002. *Restructuring World Politics: Transnational Social Movements, Networks, and Norms.* Minneapolis, MN: University of Minnesota Press.

Kim, Moonhawk. 2012. Ex Ante Due Diligence: Formation of PTAs and Protection of Labor Rights. *International Studies Quarterly* 56 (4):704–19.

Kim, Wonik. 2010. The Ratification of ILO Conventions and the Provision of Unemployment Benefits: An Empirical Analysis. *International Social Security Review* 63 (1):37–55.

Krain, Matthew. 2012. J'accuse! Does Naming and Shaming Perpetrators Reduce the Severity of Genocides or Politicides? *International Studies Quarterly* 56 (3):574–89.

Kuchera, David, and Dora Sari. 2016. New "Labour Rights Indicators": Method and Results. Unpublished paper.

Lebovic, James H., and Erik Voeten. 2006. The Politics of Shame: The Condemnation of Country Human Rights Practices in the UNCHR. *International Studies Quarterly* 50 (4):861–88.

2009. The Cost of Shame: International Organizations and Foreign Aid in the Punishing of Human Rights Violators. *Journal of Peace Research* 46 (1):79–97.

Mansfield, Edward D., Helen V. Milner, and B. Peter Rosendorff. 2000. Free to Trade: Democracies, Autocracies, and International trade. *American Political Science Review* 94 (2):305–21.

Marshall, Monty G., Ted Gurr, and Keith Jaggers. 2014. *Polity IV Project. Center for Systemic Peace.* Available at www.systemicpeace.org.

Mosley, Layna. 2011. Collective Labor Rights Dataset Codebook. Available at
    https://dataverse.harvard.edu/file.xhtml?fileId=2288282&version=1.0.
Mosley, Layna, and Saika Uno. 2007. Racing to the Bottom or Climbing to the
    Top? Economic Globalization and Collective Labor Rights. *Comparative
    Political Studies* 40 (8):923–48.
Murdie, Amanda. 2014. *Help or Harm? The Human Security Effects of
    International NGOs.* Stanford, CA: Stanford University Press.
Murdie, Amanda M., and David R. Davis. 2012. Shaming and Blaming: Using
    Events Data to Assess the Impact of Human Rights INGOs. *International
    Studies Quarterly* 56 (1):1–16.
Peksen, Dursun, and Robert Blanton. 2016. The Impact of ILO Conventions
    on Worker Rights: Are Empty Promises Worse than No Promises? *Review
    of International Organization*, Online First.
Pevehouse, Jon, and Bruce Russett. 2006. Democratic International
    Governmental Organizations Promote Peace. *International Organization*
    60 (4):969–1000.
Risse, Thomas, and Kathryn Sikkink. 1999. The Socialization of International
    Human Rights Norms into Domestic Practices: Introduction. In *The
    Power of Human Rights: International Norms and Domestic Change*,
    edited by Thomas Risse, Stephen C. Ropp, and Kathryn Sikkink, 1–38.
    Cambridge: Cambridge University Press.
Risse, Thomas and Stephen C. Ropp. 2013. Introduction and Overview. In *The
    Persistent Power of Human Rights: From Commitment to Compliance*,
    edited by Thomas Risse, Stephen C. Ropp, and Kathryn Sikkink, 3–25.
    Cambridge: Cambridge University Press.
Risse, Thomas, Stephen Ropp, and Kathryn Sikkink, eds. 2013. *From
    Commitment to Compliance. The Persistent Power of Human Rights.*
    Cambridge: Cambridge University Press.
Rodrik, Dani. 1996. Labor Standards in International Trade: Do they Matter
    and What Do We Do about Them? In *Emerging Agenda for Global
    Trade: High Stakes for Developing Countries*, edited by Robert Lawrence,
    Dani Rodrik, and John Whalley. Washington, DC: Overseas Development
    Council.
Schimmelfennig, Frank. 2001. The Community Trap: Liberal Norms,
    Rhetorical Action, and the Eastern Enlargement of the European Union.
    International Organization 55 (1):47–80.
Sharman, Jason C. 2009. The Bark is the Bite: International Organization and
    Blacklisting. *Review of International Political Economy* 16 (4):573–96.
Simmons, Beth A. 2009. *Mobilizing for Human Rights: International Law in
    Domestic Politics.* Cambridge: Cambridge University Press.
    2012. International Law. In *Handbook of International Relations*, 2nd
    ed., edited by Walter Carlsnaes, Thomas Risse, and Beth A. Simmons.
    London: Sage.
Simmons, Beth A., and Allison Danner. 2010. Credible Commitments and the
    International Criminal Court. *International Organization* 64 (2):225–56.
Tallberg, Jonas. 2002. Paths to Compliance: Enforcement, Management, and
    the European Union. *International Organization* 56 (3):609–43.
Tallberg, Jonas, Thomas Sommerer, and Theresa Squatrito. 2016. Democratic
    Memberships in International Organizations: Sources of Institutional
    Design. *Review of International Organizations* 11 (1):59–87.

Thomann, Lars. 2011. *Steps to Compliance with International Labour Standards: The International Labour Organization and the Abolition of Forced Labour*. Wiesbaden: vs Verlag fur Sozialwissenschaften.

Thompson, Alexander. 2013. Coercive Enforcement of International Law. In *Interdisciplinary Perspectives on International Law and International Relations*, edited by Jeffrey L. Dunoff and Mark A. Pollack, 502–23. Cambridge: Cambridge University Press.

Tomz, Michael. 2007. *Reputation and International Cooperation: Sovereign Debt across Three Centuries*. Princeton, NJ: Princeton University Press.

US State Department. 1996. Country Reports on Human Rights Practices. Guatemala. Available at http://dosfan.lib.uic.edu/ERC/democracy/1995_hrp_report/95hrp_report_ara/Guatemala.html. Accessed April 11, 2016.

———. 1998. Slovak Republic Country Report on Human Rights Practices for 1997. Available at http://www.state.gov/www/global/human_rights/1997_hrp_report/slovakre.html. Accessed April 11, 2016.

———. 2000. 1999 Country Reports on Human Rights Practices: Slovak Republic. Available at http://www.state.gov/www/global/human_rights/1999_hrp_report/slovakre.html. Accessed April 11, 2016.

Weisband, Edward. 2000. Discursive Multilateralism: Global Benchmarks, Shame and Learning in the ILO Labor Standards Monitoring Regime. *International Studies Quarterly* 44 (4):643–66.

World Bank. 2016. World Bank Development Indicators. Available at http://data.worldbank.org/data-catalog/world-development-indicators. Accessed April 11, 2017.

8

Freedom House's Scarlet Letter

Assessment Power through Transnational Pressure

Jordan Roberts and Juan Tellez

The ease with which information is constructed, packaged, and disseminated in the twenty-first century has dramatically transformed the way in which states are held accountable to both domestic and international audiences. Global performance indicators (GPIs) are at the forefront of such information-based tools of accountability and have drawn intense interest from scholars, both for their potential to affect meaningful policy change in the international arena and for the "assessment power" their deployment entails (Kelley and Simmons this volume). Research into the effects of GPIs is still a new and growing field in the study of international relations and many substantive and methodological questions remain to be explored.

Substantively, while scholars have examined whether the states (or other entities) ranked by GPIs alter their own behavior in response to being assessed (including Honig and Weaver this volume; Kelley, Simmons, and Doshi this volume; Kijima and Lipscy this volume; Le and Malesky this volume; Morse this volume), we know very little about how the international community responds to a state's assessment.[1] When a state's performance along some dimension is assessed by a GPI, do other states in the international community respond? And if so, how? For policymakers and activists seeking meaningful political change in a foreign country these are crucial questions, as one of the main strategies these actors rely on to promote change is to petition their *own* government to pressure poorly performing states to change their ways (Keck and Sikkink 1998). If governments are generally unresponsive to the poor assessments received by other states, activists may be lobbying their governments in vain. If, on the other hand, governments are responsive to the poor assessments of other states, transnational pressure is a significant mechanism through which GPIs assert influence (Kelley and Simmons this volume).

[1] See Lee and Matanock in this volume for a more skeptical take on this issue.

Methodologically, scholars and policymakers interested in the potential for GPIs to serve as policy levers face the problem of properly identifying the effects they theorize (Kelley and Simmons this volume). A country rated poorly by a credit-rating agency might also experience a large decrease in foreign direct investment. Was the reduction in foreign investment *caused* by the negative assessment itself? Or, were both the reduction in investment and poor assessment the result of a significant change in the country's underlying suitability for investment? This example highlights the perils of trying to measure the effect of an indicator *itself* on state behavior by comparing low and high-ranking states along an index.

In this paper, we contribute both substantively and methodologically to the current understanding of GPIs and their role in the international system. We specifically focus on one of the longest-running and most prominent GPIs in world politics: Freedom House's annual *Freedom in the World* report. We overcome the identification problems inherent to measuring the impact of GPIs by exploiting a discontinuity in Freedom House's rating scheme, where two states with substantively similar levels of freedom are given different qualitative labels. By only looking at countries right above and below the sharp cutoff between states branded "Not Free" and those labeled "Partly Free," we can more convincingly evaluate the effect of GPI labeling on state behavior. We use this methodology to explore the questions of whether, how, when, and by whom states are treated differently as a result of their assessed level of freedom according to Freedom House.

We demonstrate that the international community responds to GPIs by worsening diplomatic relations with states that are branded with a negative label, a phenomenon we term the "Scarlet Letter effect." This deterioration in diplomatic relations is not limited to comments about the illiberal governance of the state labeled as "Not Free" by Freedom House. Moreover, we find that not all states respond to Freedom House's negative assessments in the same way. Only liberal, democratic countries increase their number of conflictual verbal statements targeting poorly assessed states, a finding that reflects previous literature concerning democracies and the enforcement of international norms.[2] Additionally, we explore the temporal effects of the *Freedom in the World* report's release and find evidence that the effect is strongest in the month following the annual release of the report, dissipating over time as

---

[2] These results have implications for existing and future research on the enforcement of international norms. While a substantial literature has centered on the role of various international organizations as plausible vehicles for norm enforcement in the international system (Donno 2010; Hafner-Burton 2005; Pevehouse 2002), the present study suggests that at least the use of "soft" diplomatic sanctioning by democracies can be triggered by GPI assessment power. This dynamic has implications both for broadening theory about how democratic norms are enforced and perpetuated in the international system, as well as for the function that GPIs serve in international politics.

the publicity and attention devoted to the report diminishes. We also find, however, that these effects to not extend beyond diplomacy to economic or military policy.

In the following sections we (1) discuss global performance indicators broadly, (2) present the format and content of Freedom House's annual *Freedom in the World* report, (3) outline the definition, measurement, and observable implications of the Scarlet Letter effect, (4) discuss our data and methods used in the testing of the observable implications outlined in the previous section, (5) present and interpret our empirical results, and (6) briefly conclude with potential avenues for future research.

GLOBAL PERFORMANCE INDICATORS

Global performance indicators (GPIs) are a form of intentionally deployed information whose impact on the behavior of policymakers is just beginning to be understood (Davis et al. 2012; Kelley and Simmons 2015). Global performance assessments are regular and publicly reported measures of some like entities' performance in a given domain. GPIs are the subset of these assessments with the highest level of comparability between assessed units established by the use of numerical grades or rankings to relate the relative performance of assessed units (Kelley and Simmons this volume). Examples of GPIs include the World Bank's *World Governance Indicators* and Transparency International's *Corruption Perception Index* (*CPI*). While there are more than 150 composite GPIs assessing country performance across a wide range of domains (Bandura 2008), all GPI's are similar in that they simplify, condense, define, and quantify complex social hierarchies (Davis et al. 2012; Hansen and Mühlen-Schulte 2012). Two especially notable characteristics of GPIs are that they are presented in a rank-order structure and simplify a complex phenomenon (Davis, Kingsbury, and Merry 2012). The rank-order structure places the assessed states in an ordinal hierarchy which enables comparison and ranking in a way that non-ordinal blacklists or narrative assessments could not. The simplification is the primary source of appeal and impact of GPIs. Simplification makes GPIs convenient and easy to interpret, but also abstracts away from the unique context of each case and the underlying uncertainty this introduces into the assessment process. Fundamentally, GPIs seeks to simplify a world with many shades of gray into a world of black and white.

GPIs constitute a form of social power and affect how policymakers think and behave (Kelley and Simmons 2015). They are especially attractive to policymakers because they can be presented as objective, impartial, and supported by scientific authority. For example, author interviews with Millennium Challenge Corporation (MCC) officials revealed a strong interest on the part of the organization to use indicators in their partner selection process. Indicator-producers outside the US government can be seen as objective evaluators and allow the organization to deflect criticisms of bias in their aid decisions.[3] GPIs hold additional value to policymakers in that reliance on an extant GPI reduces the burden of collecting, processing, and evaluating data, allowing organizations to conserve resources for other tasks (Davis, Kingsbury, and Merry 2012). Furthermore, GPIs are constructed to facilitate comparison across units and establish standards to which different units can be compared (Kelley and Simmons 2015).

One of the primary ways in which GPIs are used is in shaming or drawing attention to states assigned a low ranking. This negative labeling is a particularly powerful tool in the arsenal of indicator producers, since it signifies which states are preforming poorly and serves to "name and shame" them via the production and dissemination of the indicator (Kelley and Simmons 2015). Naming and shaming is a powerful mechanism for enforcing political norms in the international system (Keck and Sikkink 1998; Ropp and Sikkink 1999). The reputation of states has the potential to alter their treatment by other states in a number of domains, including security, trade, development funding, and other areas that state leaders inherently care about (Weisiger and Yarhi-Milo 2015). Other states, international organizations, and domestic political actors frequently seek to capitalize on the importance of international reputation by publicly criticizing the offending behavior of a target state–shifting international discourse against the offender. Capitalizing on this opportunity need not be purely instrumental or cynical on the part of the shaming actor; international actors can be intrinsically motivated to pursue a number of policy objectives. International relations scholars have highlighted democracy, for example, as a constellation of norms that can determine a number of dimensions of interstate behavior (Caprioli 2003; Peterson and Graham 2011; Sobek, Abouharb, and Ingram 2006). A large literature has argued that shaming, particularly via the use of indicators, produces substantive changes in the target state's behavior along a number of dimensions, including the protection of political freedoms, human rights, and improvements in human trafficking laws (Franklin 2008; Hafner-Burton 2008; Kelley and Simmons 2015). Others have focused on how and why states are selected for shaming in the international community, arguing that there is substantial variation in who international actors choose to shame and when they choose to do so, often not in accordance with how grievous the behavior of the targeted state actually is (Hafner-Burton 2008). Scholars have highlighted a number of factors, such as the presence of domestic human rights institutions and other national-level characteristics, as determinants for which states are shamed (Hafner-Burton 2008; Meernik et al. 2012; Ramos, Ron, and Thoms 2007).

Many studies of indicators posit that assessed states alter their behavior in response to observed or expected changes in their relationship with other

[3] Interview by Juan Tellez with senior MCC officials, August 18, 2016.

actors in their international community.[4] State leaders, for example, may seek
to alter their economic policies if they receive a poor assessment from a GPI
producer evaluating domestic economic conditions, possibly due to fears that
the unfavorable assessment will have negative repercussions for trade relations
with other states. However, little research has sought to capture and quantify whether the international community does in fact respond to indicators
and treat negatively assessed states differently. Relatedly, no prior research
has explained or empirically tested whether all states are equally compelled
by indicators to shame norm-violators, or whether there is variation in which
states respond to the labeling effect of indicators. This paper seeks to fill that
gap in the literature by explicitly focusing on how negatively assessed states are
treated by the international community. We explore questions about why and
how states in the international system respond to the assessment of their peers
by testing the effect of one of the longest-running indicators in international
politics: the *Freedom in the World* reports. In the following section we describe
the history of the reports and the unique empirical opportunity they present.

THE *FREEDOM IN THE* WORLD REPORT

Freedom House was first established in 1941 as an American research and
advocacy non-governmental organization with the stated goal of promoting
democratization and human rights around the world. Its founding members
were primarily concerned with the rising threat of National Socialism in
Europe and sought to encourage American support for military involvement in
World War II (Freedom House 2016). Later they would channel their research
and advocacy against what they saw as other great obstacles to the expression
of freedom in the world, including the spread of Communism in the developing world and the growth of McCarthyism domestically (Bradley 2015).
Freedom House's research on the state of freedom in the world eventually led
the organization, under the direction of social scientist Raymond D. Gastil, to
create a systematic measurement of freedom at the country level (Gastil 1985,
1990). These measurements were released as yearly reports starting in 1973
and were meant to capture changes in the state of freedom in the world, giving policymakers and advocates an easily digestible metric with which to craft
and influence policy.

The *Freedom in the World* (*FitW*) report quickly became the organization's flagship publication. Changes in methodology eventually coalesced into
a coherent system for scoring countries based on their observance of freedom,
as understood by Freedom House. Two broad categories – Political Rights
(PR) and Civil Liberties (CL) – serve as the foundation of a country's overall

---

[4] For example, see contributions from the following in this volume: Kelley, Simmons, and
Doshi; Kijima and Lipscy; Le and Malesky; Morse.

freedom score, or Freedom Rating (Gastil 1990). To rank countries along these two dimensions, experts are asked to score countries on scales ranging from 0 (lowest degree of freedom) to 4 (highest degree of freedom) for 10 PR indicators and 15 CL indicators.[5] Scores are then aggregated and, based on specific cut-points, countries are separately rated in their protection of both PR and CL from 1 (most free) to 7 (least free). The average of a country's score along these two dimensions constitutes their Freedom Rating, which is then used to place states into Free (1.0 to 2.5), Partly Free (3.0 to 5.0) and Not Free categories (5.5 to 7.0). Although the rankings countries receive in PR and CL are highlighted in the reports, the final Freedom Rating is typically highlighted as the most important outcome in the *FitW* report, evidenced in part by the iconic color-coded mapping of the world based on Freedom Ratings that is highlighted in every annual report.

The *FitW* Freedom Rating has been widely used by both policymakers and academics. At the same time, its claim to measure concepts related to freedom and democracy are highly contested on both ideological and methodological grounds (Giannone 2010; Høyland, Moene, and Willumsen 2012). Such contestation is not uncommon for GPIs: in proposing a definition and operational measurement of a specific concept, GPIs often provoke contestation in the form of criticism of concepts and measures, the formulation of competing indicators, and calls for greater access or transparency to the GPI's construction (Davis et al. 2012). In terms of conceptual and ideological contestation, the reports have been criticized for a free-market and pro-Western bias in its definition of freedom (Bollen and Paxton 2000; Giannone 2010). Here, we focus on methodological concerns with the Freedom Rating, which have bearing on our empirical strategy.

On methodological terms, even if one grants that the Freedom Rating captures traits broadly related to freedom and democracy in an individual country (Diamond 1999), the ability of the rating to capture small changes in a country's freedom status from year to year or small differences between countries with very similar levels of freedom is less clear. Using Bayesian factor analysis, Armstrong (2011) finds that "a number of countries that are classified as different regime-types are not significantly different from each other" once within-class uncertainty is taken into account. According to Armstrong's analysis, this uncertainty is much larger in countries classified in adjacent categories, whereas countries two or more categories apart have a large probability of being substantively different. Similarly, Høyland, Moene, and Willumsen (2012) find that while the *FitW* accurately captures large differences between

---

[5] Some examples of indicators that experts use to score countries include the relative freedom of travel in and out of the country, how secure property ownership rights are within the country, the relative freedom of operating a private business, and gender equality. The experts providing this scoring are generally academics, researchers, or policy advisors, and a list of these experts is made available by Freedom House each year.

countries, small differences such as those along the border between Partly Free and Not Free are much more fraught with uncertainty.

Part of the difficulty *FitW* has in capturing small differences between similar states arises from the fact that the reports do not incorporate any kind of "scoring uncertainty" into their methodology. Country experts may disagree about particular scores, and while these disagreements may in fact reflect some of the underlying uncertainty inherent in estimating a country's "true" score; Freedom House's prioritization of a single number for each category obscures this uncertainty. Interviews with a senior official at Freedom House confirm that disagreements between country experts over specific scores are common.[6] The result is that some countries may appear more dissimilar based on their scores and ratings – particularly in adjacent Freedom Rating categories – than they would otherwise if expert discordance was captured in the reports (Armstrong 2011).

Another important source of uncertainty in adjudicating small differences between states or within a state over time arises in the score aggregation process, where absolute changes can move countries across Freedom Rating categories in a seemingly arbitrary way. For example, in 2014 Burundi had an aggregated PR score of 12/40 and an aggregated CL score of 22/40, giving it PR and CL ratings of 5 and 5 and a Freedom Rating of 5.0 (Partly Free). In 2015, however, Burundi received an aggregated PR score of 11/40 and an aggregated CL score of 21/40, giving it a PR and CL rating of 6 and 5 for a combined Freedom Rating of 5.5 (Not Free). With an unsubstantial difference of one point in PR, Burundi went from being a PF state to a NF state in the matter of a year. The near-arbitrary nature of this difference is made clearer when one considers that Burundi could have instead lost up to 4 points in CL and still maintained its status as Partly Free. The concerns with the cutoffs across multiple levels of aggregation are compounded when one considers cross-country comparisons, as countries' scores are based off of their own scores from the previous year. This makes for more consistent scoring of individual countries across time, but renders cross-country comparison more difficult as each country has a different reference point from which its scores are based.

Despite these methodological issues, the *FitW* reports have had substantial consequences for international politics. A recent article in *Foreign Policy* called the reports "a crucial tool for pro-democracy activists. They drive dictators crazy. And, perhaps most important of all, they get worldwide attention" (Lozovsky 2016). Pro-democracy activists, either within their own countries or internationally, use the *FitW* reports to demand change in illiberal regimes. Government actors also make use of the reports in similar ways in order to shape policy. For example, multiple departments within the American federal

---

[6] Interview by Roberts and Tellez with Sarah Repucci, Senior Director for Global Publications at Freedom House, June 29, 2016.

government, US lawmakers, and aid agencies are all briefed on the scores. These organizations consider the ratings as part of their decision-making process to varying degrees. USAID, for example, uses the scores as a "first stop" in the democratic assessment of potential and existing aid recipients.[7] Additionally, the Millennium Challenge Corporation incorporates minimum Political Rights and Civil Liberties score requirements in the scorecard used to evaluate potential partners.[8] The *FitW* report can even matter for subnational policymaking in the US, such as when the state governments of California and Wisconsin considered investing their massive pension funds into countries based partly on their Freedom Rating (Bradley 2015).

The importance of Freedom House is driven in part by the organization's long history as well as its own efforts to promote the release of the *FitW* reports, particularly among Western democratic states. Major roll-out events in Washington, Brussels, and other regional offices around the world take place immediately following the annual release. The European Parliament, External Action Service, and foreign aid agencies in countries such as Canada and Australia are also briefed about the report release by Freedom House.[9] These efforts ensure that states, and particularly those states in the West most likely to apply pressure for enhancing political and civil liberties abroad, are aware of the reports and the information contained within them.

State actors from countries singled out by *FitW* for bad behavior also take notice of the reports. Interviews with Freedom House officials revealed numerous examples of state representatives contacting the organization to discuss their scores. Public official from Côte d'Ivoire have held twice-yearly meetings with Freedom House and dedicated a department to the improvement of the country's annual scores, spurred in part by rivalries with neighboring Liberia and Sierra Leone. Taiwanese officials have similarly held meetings with Freedom House over concerns of the country's performance in the reports. More generally, Freedom House officials assert that states that value their international image tend to care about their scores in the annual reports, resulting in an established pattern of state representatives contacting Freedom House in the months or weeks leading up to the release of the reports.[10] As further evidence of *FitW*'s impact, the 2016 Governance Data Alliance Snap Poll of public, private, and civil society leaders in low- and middle-income countries found that among individuals working in the "governance domain" familiar with the *FitW* reports, 79 percent found the reports to be *important*

---

[7] Interview by Tellez with USAID officials Neil Levine, David Black, and Nick Higgins, July 19, 2016.
[8] Interview by Tellez with senior MCC official, August 18, 2016.
[9] Interview by Roberts and Tellez with Mark Lagon, Freedom House President and Vukasin Petrovic, Senior Director for Program Strategy, Development and Learning, June 3, 2016.
[10] Interview by Roberts and Tellez with Mark Lagon, Freedom House President and Vukasin Petrovic, Senior Director for Program Strategy, Development and Learning, June 3, 2016.

or *essential* to their work (Masaki, Sethi, and Custer 2016). The *FitW* reports represent an ideal GPI for our study. The prestige and long tenure of the publication gives us assurance that this is a GPI that states care about and are likely to respond to. Furthermore, the *FitW* indicator makes explicit cross-country comparisons and allows assessed government to participate in the assessment process (by discussing how their scores could be improved, providing information to Freedom House about reforms made, etc.), the two assessment features shown by Parks and Masaki (2016) to increase the policy influence an assessment has on individual policymakers.

Although the reports capture broad differences between states accurately, the difficulty in correctly estimating small differences in levels of freedom can be exploited to identify the effect of the reports on international politics. Since small, plausibly random differences in rankings can produce different categorical assessments for otherwise similar countries, identifying the effect from the assessment *itself* becomes possible.

THE SCARLET LETTER EFFECT

Previous research on the effect of indicators on targeted countries have focused on the behavior of changes in the behavior of the target state. For example, Kelley and Simmons (2015) find that countries that are placed on the blacklist or watchlist of the US *Trafficking in Persons* report are more likely to criminalize human trafficking than countries not on those lists. Our interest is not in explaining the behavior of the monitored state, but rather in exploring the international community's behavior toward the monitored state. This requires a slightly different framework, one we find a literary inspiration for. In Nathaniel Hawthorne's classic novel, *The Scarlet Letter*, the protagonist Hester Prynne is sentenced to wear a scarlet letter "A" on her person after being convicted of adultery, signifying her as an adulterer to be scorned by her community (Hawthorne 1850). Similarly to Prynne, states which get labeled as "Not Free" by the annual *FitW* report wear their scarlet "NF," signifying their particularly illiberal and undemocratic governance. When Freedom House brands a country as "Not Free," certain states in the international community listen, and they condemn, scorn, and punish that country accordingly in what we term the Scarlet Letter effect (SLE). In the Hawthorne effect, the subject being monitored acts differently due to the monitoring; in the Scarlet Letter effect, the subject is *treated* differently due to the monitoring. Kelley and Simmons (2015, this volume) outline three mechanisms through which GPIs affect the behavior of target states: domestic politics, direct elite responses, and third party pressure. The last of these is related, but not identical, to the SLE. Kelley and Simmons are primarily concerned with third parties pressuring target states to perform better *specifically* in the domain assessed by the GPI. Third parties use the information contained in the indicator to monitor and pressure states, either materially (by granting or withholding aid, for example) or verbally through condemnations and criticism. Lee and Matanock (this volume) explicitly test this mechanism in the case of Transparency International's Corruption Perception Index (CPI), finding that neither material or verbal pressure is affected by a country's performance on the CPI.

The SLE, however, occurs when poor-performing states are stigmatized *generally*. These states are treated worse on the whole, not simply within the domain they received a negative rating. General stigmatization is distinct from targeted shaming in that general stigmatization need not specifically criticize the target for their norm-violations. Many of the negative verbal interactions received by a poorly assessed actor experiencing the Scarlet Letter effect may not be explicitly about their poor performance. However, these condemnations and threats about seemingly unrelated issues, such as trade or territorial claims, are still expected to come more frequently after a state has been labeled as a norm violator. When a state's reputation is damaged, the inhibitions restraining other states from criticism and insult are lowered, resulting in the country on the receiving end of the SLE experiencing heightened levels of negative verbal interaction across the board – not just on issues that directly resulted in them initially receiving the Scarlet Letter. Those states who get branded as poorly performing in an area of great importance (such as protections of freedom) are perceived to have a different level of status in the international community than they would have absent their negative assessment. Policymakers in other states internalize these unflattering images of the negatively assessed states, and subtly alter their behavior toward the "offender," for example, by generally increasing public criticism and disapproval. Additionally, negative assessment could provide the cover for condemnations that were already motived by wider geopolitical issues. In this sense, we follow Dolan (2017) in believing that both cognitive and strategic mechanisms are meaningful when looking at the impact of indicators.

Very few GPIs have the degree of comparability, level of creator authority, amount of public exposure, frequency of assessment, and scope of the domain assessed to create such wide-ranging stigmatization.[11] One GPI that does manage to meet all of these criteria is Freedom House's *Freedom in the World* report. The *FitW* report is also an excellent test case for the SLE because of its target audience. While many GPIs are produced in a fashion that targets the assessed state, the numerous materials produced each year by Freedom House seem to clearly target certain actors in the international community: democratic states who value political and civil liberties, transnational activists, and

---

[11] When we consider the scope of domain assessed, we mean that evaluations of the level of democracy in a country are likely to affect how that country is viewed *overall*. This is not the case for more targeted assessments. For example, poor ratings in primary school mathematics education is unlikely to substantially reshape how a country is viewed by the international community.

the media. In effect, the goal of Freedom House is not just to directly instigate change by shaming regimes about their illiberal policies, but also to prompt a response from free states and international activists.

IDENTIFYING THE SLE

What effect does a state being labeled "Not Free" in Freedom House's reports have on how that state gets treated by other states in the international community? The difficulty in answering this question is that states may receive a "Not Free" rating for reasons that could engender criticism unrelated to the release of the report itself. For example, states that openly violate human rights norms are likely to receive both admonishment from the international community as well as Freedom House's "Scarlet Letter." In this example, the international community's criticisms could have occurred *independently* of the *FitW* reports, posing a serious threat to casual inference.

To overcome this threat to inference, we exploit the fact that Freedom House's *categorical assessment* of states as "Not Free," "Partly Free," and "Free" are built upon numeric *ratings*.[12] The point at which a country's numeric rating pushes it from one category to the next (in our case, from "Partly Free" to "Not Free") is ultimately the result of an arbitrary decision. As discussed above, small differences in ratings can often put otherwise very similar countries in different categories (Armstrong 2011). Indicators commonly rank states in a hierarchical fashion even when there is no meaningful distinction between them once the underlying uncertainty in the ranking process is taken into account (Davis, Kingsbury, and Merry 2012). This uncertainty is effectively masked from the consumers of an indicator who do not delve deeply into the weighting decisions and methodology of the indicator's construction. This is certainly true in the case of Freedom House's indicator, which tends to emphasize differences even when similarity is the dominant feature. Høyland, Moene, and Willumsen (2012) reestimate the freedom scores for 2008 with a method that captures the uncertainty in their assignment. They find that the 95 percent confidence interval for each country heavily overlaps with countries near it, showing that Freedom House cannot claim with a great deal of confidence that a country is indeed a 5.5 instead of a 5.0 or 6.0. For the edge cases where a change of just 0.5 on the indicator determines if a country gets labeled as "Partly Free" or "Not Free" this is particularly relevant. In 2008, there were 14 countries near the PF–NF distinction that could not be sorted into one category or the other with at least 75 percent confidence. Given that 27 countries were assigned the score of 5.0 or 5.5 in 2008, this means that *more than half* of these borderline cases could not be clearly

---

[12] For another example of a discontinuity approach to measuring the effect of indicators, see Lee and Matanock in this volume.

classified as either "Partly Free" or "Not Free." This produces a *discontinuity* between the freedom scores of 5.0 and 5.5 where the underlying levels of freedom in countries on either side are not meaningfully different, but the label assigned to the country is.

We exploit this discontinuity to test the presence of the SLE. If countries who are assigned a freedom score of 5.5 are treated systematically worse that countries who are assigned 5.0, we can reasonably conclude that this difference is due to the variation in Freedom House's label, and not a difference in the underlying level of freedom within a country.[13]

One possible concern with respect to the existence of a discontinuity in the Freedom House rating scheme is that countries may strategically sort themselves into one of the two categories through improved performance or lobbying. While it is impossible to rule this possibility out completely, Freedom House's methodology and author interviews with the organization suggest this is unlikely.[14] First, Freedom House expressed that country ratings are "driven from the bottom up," that is, via the 25 dimensions on which countries are scored. Freedom Ratings only emerge after scoring has taken place and any unusual or unexpected ratings are noted in country narratives, rendering the kind of retroactive scoring necessary for selection to occur difficult. These unexpected Freedom Ratings are interesting to readers and consumers of the reports, providing incentives for the organization to resist shaping ratings to expectation. Second, while arguably the most likely sorting mechanism would suggest countries actively try to sort into the preferable "Partly Free" category to avoid incurring reputation costs, our data actually shows more countries are in the "Not Free" category during the 2001 to 2014 period used in our analysis. This is also true along the bright-line between the two categories, as there are consistently more countries ranked as 5.5 than 5.0. In fact, as Figure 8.2c in the Data and Methods section will illustrate, there are more countries who receive a 5.5 rating than a 5.0 rating in every year of our sample.

HYPOTHESES

The existence of a Scarlet Letter effect that characterizes the differential treatment of target states by users in the international community has a number of testable implications. First and foremost, if the SLE is actually operational in the case of the *FitW* reports, then we should expect to see that states labeled "Not Free" will be treated systematically worse by the international community than

---

[13] In addition to the previous arguments, we test the balance of covariates that may influence assignment to treatment (receiving a freedom score of 5.5) across the proposed discontinuity and employ propensity score matching to improve balance in control and treatment groups (Ho et al. 2007). Results of this additional analysis are included in the online appendix, and further details are given in the results below.

[14] Interview by Roberts and Tellez with Sarah Repucci, Senior Director for Global Publications at Freedom House, June 29, 2016.

their counterparts. We expect that the international community will internalize the information presented in the *FitW* report releases and alter their behavior accordingly by worsening diplomatic relations with the negatively assessed state through increasing verbal conflict. By verbal conflict, we mean public announcements, declarations, or statements on the part of state leaders that are meant to condemn, criticize, or accuse the negatively assessed state's leadership. These types of verbal, conflictual actions punish poorly performing states, even when they are not explicitly related to the target's illiberal governance.

> *Hypothesis 1*: States barely labeled "Not Free" (5.5) in the *FitW* report will receive higher levels of verbal conflict than states barely labeled "Partly Free" (5.0).

However, we do not believe that all states will respond equally to the call of the Scarlet Letter. Only states with strong normative investments in the concepts of political and civil liberty will respond to Freedom House's assessment. That states pursue foreign policy goals in line with normative beliefs is a central claim in international relations Acharya 2004; Björkdahl 2002; Russett 1994), and so we may expect that democratic states will criticize states who have been branded violators of democratic norms. More specifically, the *FitW* reports' assessments have greater authority among actors who have a high ideological affinity with Freedom House as an organization, and the ideas embedded in their indicators in particular (Bush 2017).

> *Hypothesis 2a*: States barely labeled Not Free (5.5) in the *FitW* report will receive higher levels of verbal conflict *from democracies* than states barely labeled Partly Free (5.0).

Conversely, we do not hold the same expectations for states that disregard the values Freedom House evaluates. Regimes that do not invest in the dual norms of personal and civil liberty will be unlikely to treat "Not Free" states differently than other states for many of the same reasons we've outlined above. Contrary to the logic driving the behavior of democratic states, illiberal states will not be motivated by liberal norms to increase their condemnation of norm-violators. More intuitively, it would be strange for illiberal states to criticize target states for receiving a "Not Free" rating from Freedom House, since illiberal states are, by definition, likely to be rated poorly in their respect of personal freedoms and civil liberties.

> *Hypothesis 2b*: States barely labeled Not Free (5.5) in the *FitW* report will *not* receive higher levels of verbal conflict *from non-democracies* than states barely labeled Partly Free (5.0).

DATA AND METHODS

Data

As is likely expected, the data for the key casual variable comes directly from Freedom House's *FitW* reports (Freedom House 2015). We also use Freedom House to determine which event senders are democracies. Those states receiving a "Free" rating are classified as democracies; those receiving either a "Partly Free" or "Not Free" rating are considered non-democracies. Operationalizing the degree of verbal conflict a state receives from other states is not as straightforward. This variable is constructed from information in the Integrated Crisis Early Warning System (ICEWS) event-level data collected by the US government (Boschee et al. 2015; O'Brien 2010). The ICEWS data consists of machine-coded news reports from hundreds of sources, such as newspapers and news magazines. These news reports are coded by the automated information extraction system SERIF, which has been shown to outperform similar algorithms designed for the same task (Boschee, Natarajan, and Weischedel 2013). The reports are coded based on the categorical coding scheme developed by the Conflict and Mediation Event Observation (CAMEO) program (Gerner, Schrodt, and Omur 2009; Schrodt 2012). The ICEWS data is considered the current gold standard for event data (D'Orazio, Yonamine, and Schrodt 2011), and has been used to assess conflictual behavior in opposition networks (Metternich et al. 2013), irregular leadership change (Beger, Dorff, and Ward 2014), cooperation and conflict between political parties in Europe (Weschle forthcoming), and the role of politically excluded ethnic groups in conflict contagion (Metternich, Minhas, and Ward 2015).

For each of the 68 million events recorded in ICEWS, the source (sender of the event), target (receiver of the event), date, and type of event are recorded. As an example of what this data looks like, on February 22, 2005, the Reuters News Agency reported on a statement made by then-US President George W. Bush, in which he criticized Vladimir Putin and his administration for failing to implement democratic reforms during his tenure. The statement was made in reference to upcoming talks between the two countries that same week. The news report on the President's public criticism of Russia is treated as a singular event whose properties are categorized according to the CAMEO typology. This news report was parsed and machine coded for a variety of important information related to the event in question, including: the date (in this case, 2005-02-22), the name of the actor whose action initiated the event (George W. Bush), the type for this actor (government actor), the country the actor represents (United States of America), the same information for the target who received the action (Vladimir Putin; government actor; Russia), and the type of action taken by source ("criticize or denounce"). In addition, the news source from which the event was created is also captured, as well as the publication date, the headline for that news story, and the body of the text.

For the purpose of measuring the SLE, we use the subset of ICEWS events that correspond to a country (source) sending an event to an edge case country (target) within one month of the release of a *Freedom in the World* report for issues 2000/2001 through 2014.[15,16] We specifically focus on *conflitual verbal* events (Duval and Thompson 1980) as our measure of the SLE. Such events include condemnations, demands, accusations, expressions of disapproval, and threats. We further disaggregate events by the *FitW* category of their source, separating conflictual verbal events sent by democracies from those sent by non-democracies.

Figure 8.1 displays the frequency of conflictual verbal events sent by democracies according to CAMEO typology.[17] As is evident, criticisms, denouncements, accusations, and rejections of diplomatic activity make up the bulk of the verbally conflictual events that democracies are sending states at the discontinuity. As expected, these are relatively low-level, low-cost actions taken by democratic states to punish countries branded with the Scarlet Letter. Stronger actions, such as making threats or giving ultimatums are relatively rare.

Methods

As previously discussed, our strategy for overcoming the identification challenge inherent in any study of GPIs is to exploit a discontinuity in Freedom House's rating scheme around the "Partly Free," "Not Free" bright-line. Discontinuity-based approaches have a long history going back to Thistlethwaite and Campbell (1960), and are the closest researchers can

---

[15] To remove duplicate news stories covering the same event, we remove any instance of an event with the same sender, receiver, date, and event type that is not the first with that set of properties.

[16] When we talk about actions taken by a "country," we are using actions taking by an actor whose CAMEO Primary Role code is either GOV (Government, including the executive, governing parties, coalitions partners, and executive divisions) or MIL (Military, including troops, soldiers, and all state-military personnel and equipment) (Schrodt 2012). In practice, the verbal conflict events recorded in the ICEWS data are primarily from chief executives, foreign minister equivalents, or other significant national political figures. As an example, in the verbal conflict events sent from the United States to countries assigned 5.0 or 5.5 Freedom Ratings during 2000–2012, three of the five most frequent event sources represented the US President (George W. Bush, Barack Obama, and "Executive Office of the President"), while the other two represented the Secretary of State (Condoleeza Rice and Hillary Clinton). Other frequent sources are nationally significant politicians (such as Senator John McCain) or other major figures in the US foreign policy (such as CIA Director Robert M. Gates). These actors account for the vast majority of events from the United States.

[17] For definitions and examples of each of these broad event categories, see the CAMEO codebook (Schrodt 2012).

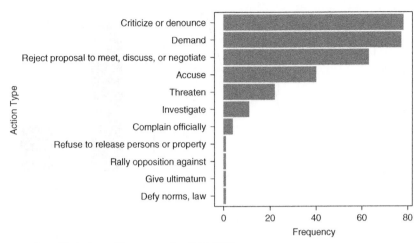

FIGURE 8.1. Verbal conflict events by CAMEO category.

get to a randomized control trail in non-experimental settings (Linden and Adams 2012). Discontinuities constitute a type of natural experiment in which assignment to treatment for the units of interest is determined wholly or in part by the value of a forcing variable (in this case, the Freedom Rating between 1.0 and 7.0) being on one side or the other of an exogenous threshold (Hahn, Todd, and Van der Klaauw 2001; Imbens and Lemieux 2008). Well-identified discontinuities provide compelling evidence that exposure to treatment in close proximity to the threshold is exogenous or approximately random and thus not dependent on potentially confounding variables (Angrist and Pischke 2008). The existence of the discontinuity allows us to identify and accurately estimate the SLE for states located close to the "Not Free" bright-line.

Figure 8.2a shows the apparent discontinuity in the relationship between the forcing variable (Freedom House's Freedom Rating) and the outcome of interest (the amount of incoming verbal conflict from democratic states, averaged for each Freedom Rating). As can be seen, the relationship between the two variables is relatively smooth until we reach the point of discontinuity: the score of 5.5 at which a country becomes "Not Free." At this point there is a significant jump in the volume of incoming negative verbal events from democratic states that is unlikely to be due to objective differences in underlying levels of freedom. Figure 8.2b depicts only the edge cases (Freedom Rating of 5.0 or 5.5) and shows that there is a substantial difference in the effect of this threshold on the behavior of democratic and non-democratic states toward the assessed countries. Democratic states are much more likely than

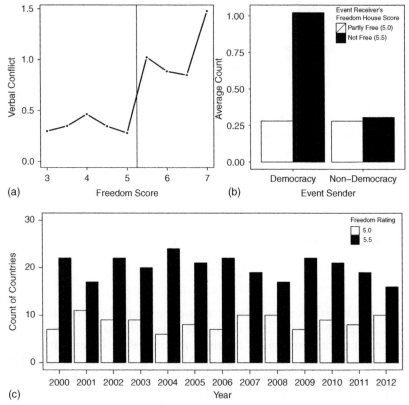

FIGURE 8.2. The Freedom House classification discontinuity. (a) Discontinuity: Freedom score and average verbal conflict from democracies, (b) edge cases: Verbal conflict from democracies and non-democracies, and (c) distribution of edge cases over time.

non-democratic states to criticize a negatively labeled country. Non-democratic states, on the other hand, do not appear to treat "Not Free" states any differently from "Partly Free" states. These observations are explicitly tested in the following section.[18] Figure 8.2c shows the distribution of 5.0s and 5.5s across

---

[18] As can be seen from the raw event count on the y-axis of Figure 8.2b, most countries receive a small number of verbal conflict events in a single month. States labeled with either a 5.0 or 5.5 Freedom Score receive about 0.25 verbal conflict events from democracies in the average month. Nearly the same number of verbal conflict events from non-democracies is received by 5.5 states. However, states barely labeled as "Not Free" receive nearly four times as many verbal conflict events from democracies in the month after the Freedom House *FitW* is issued. While this difference is large in relative size, it is important to note that the absolute number of negative verbal events (approximately one) is still small. Outright combative verbal language from democracies remains rare, but significantly more likely for states labeled "Not Free."

all years in our sample. The consistently higher count of 5.5s reduces concern about a sorting effect at the discontinuity.[19]

We do not carry out a standard regression discontinuity design, since observations on either side of the threshold are highly binned. Our forcing variable is ordinal instead of continuous, and the theoretically appropriate bandwidth is one *category* on either side of the discontinuity (5.0 on the "Partly Free" side and 5.5 on the "Not Free" side). This heavily simplifies our design, as all treated units have the same value on the forcing variable, as do all non-treated units. While the intuition is identical to that in the standard regression discontinuity design, our execution is much more streamlined: we limit our universe of observations to those within our theoretically derived bandwidth (states assigned a 5.0 or 5.5 Freedom Rating), and assign those on the "Not Free" side of the discontinuity (Freedom Rating = 5.5) to the treatment group. Those on the "Partly Free" side (Freedom Rating = 5.0) are the control group. Since our dependent variable is the *count* of conflictual verbal events received by a given borderline state in the month after the release of a *FitW* report, we fit negative binomial models to our data in our primary results below.

RESULTS

The results from the negative binomial models confirm each of the hypotheses presented above and provide strong empirical evidence that Freedom House does indeed create a Scarlet Letter effect that stigmatizes countries they brand as "Not Free." Figure 8.3 presents bivariate results assessing the claims made regarding the general effect of the SLE and its specific impact on events originating from free, democratic states and non-democratic states.[20] The first model (Total Verbal Conflict) looks at how receiving a score of 5.5 instead of 5.0 affects the number of verbal conflict events received by a given state in the thirty days after the release of the report. As can be seen, receiving the harsher rating from Freedom House significantly affects the count of incoming verbal conflict events a country experiences, such that they are treated worse than their 5.0 counterparts. This supports the expectation described in *Hypothesis 1*.

The second and third models separate incoming verbal conflict by its sources: the second model looks at verbal conflict from democracies and the

---

[19] Specifically, this distribution provides *some* empirical evidence against the idea that some countries are consistently "gaming the system" to get over the discontinuity in a way that weakens our argument for as-if random assignment. If this phenomenon was occurring, we would expect a distribution of cases such as 5.0s regularly outnumber 5.5s, since there would be some subset of cases which are not sorted randomly, but who are selecting themselves into the 5.0 classification. Instead, we observe the opposite distribution, which reduces concern about the existence of such a sorting effect.

[20] For the standard regression table see Table 8.A1–8.A9 in the appendix.

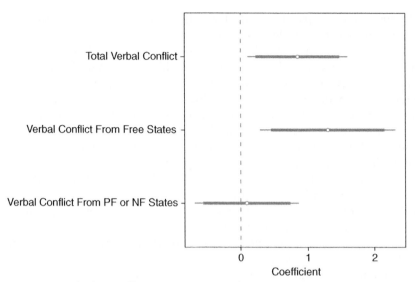

FIGURE 8.3. Scarlet letter effect across sources of verbal conflict.

third model looks at verbal conflict from non-democracies. Together, these models show that the level of verbal conflict from democracies is increased for countries who get branded as "Not Free," while the level of verbal conflict from non-democracies does not change, in accordance with *Hypotheses 2a* and *2b*. Together, the models in Figure 8.3 are strong indicators that the SLE is at work, as both the general increase in punishment and the type of states doing the punishing are consistent with what would be expected from a Scarlet Letter effect.[21]

Scope Conditions and Robustness Tests

While the evidence in Figure 8.3 shows a difference between states assigned a 5.0 and labeled "Partly Free" and states assigned a 5.5 and labeled "Not Free," three concerns remain: (1) How long does this effect persist? (2) Is this effect unique to the states at the discontinuity, or is it present at other locations along Freedom House's scale? and (3) How robust is this empirical relationship?

---

[21] While additional analysis was planned to look at the effect of moving across the discontinuity from one annual report the next, too few states made this transition during our timeframe for such an analysis to be meaningful. Simple t-tests on this small sample indicated that a state may see increased verbal conflict if they move from 5.0 to 5.5, but that moving from 5.5 to 5.0 was unlikely to produce the inverse effect.

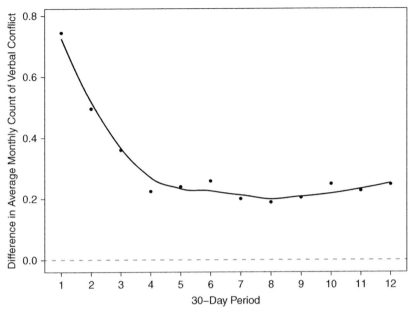

FIGURE 8.4. Temporal decay of the Scarlet Letter effect.

Each of the models in Figure 8.3 looks at events that occur within thirty days of a report's release, but how much does the SLE decay over time? Figure 8.4 shows the difference between the average number of verbal conflict events from democracies received by countries assigned a 5.5 and those assigned a 5.0 by the *FitW* over time, calculating the number of events for each thirty-day period out. The first dots for each group represent the number of events within thirty days of the report's release, the second dots for the first sixty days, and so on. As can be seen, the difference between a country scored 5.0 and a country scored 5.5 is the highest in the thirty days proceeding the release of the report. This difference then steeply declines over the 120-day period after the release of the report before flattening out for the remainder of the year. This shows that while the effect of Freedom House's report persists until the release of the subsequent report (the difference never decreases to zero), that effect is much stronger in the months immediately after the report's release. This is powerful evidence of the Scarlet Letter effect at work. While possible, it seems highly unlikely that 5.5s receive a larger number of conflictual verbal events from democracies than 5.0s in the late January through early February period due to some seasonal effect not associated with the release of the *FitW* immediately preceding this period.

The standard approach for evaluating if an effect is unique to a point of discontinuity, and not present at multiple values of the forcing variable, is

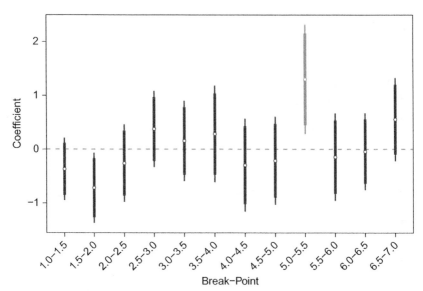

FIGURE 8.5. Placebo tests for the Scarlet Letter effect.

to conduct placebo tests, which we do in Figure 8.5. The analysis of verbal conflict from democracies was rerun for every adjacent values along Freedom House's 1–7 scale. The coefficient estimates for each of these models are shown, ranging from the 1.0–1.5 pairing to the 6.5–7.0 pairing. As can be seen, the 5.0–5.5 pairing stands out among the rest. Ten out of eleven of the other pairings do not see a statistically significant difference in the number of verbal conflict events received by the countries with the slightly worse score, and the point estimates on the coefficients are all notably closer to zero than the estimate on the 5.0–5.5 pairing. Even the one significant placebo pairing is just barely so, and the coefficient is much smaller than the point estimate for the 5.0–5.5 pairing.

In order to verify that our key findings are robust, and not merely obtained due to chance or minor modeling decisions, we specified a variety of additional models. These models consistently indicate the presence of the Scarlet Letter effect. In our first set of robustness tests, we removed all events sent by the United States. Given that Freedom House in based in the US capital and partially funded by the US State Department, we were concerned our results could be driven by the fact that the United States was especially sensitive to Freedom House's reports. Models with the US-sent events removed still show a statically significant increase in the number of verbal conflict events sent from democracies to states falling on the "Not Free" side of the discontinuity, although the magnitude of the effect is noticeably reduced. This indicates that while the United States is probably more sensitive to how a state is scored by

Freedom House than other democratic states, other democracies still respond with increased condemnation of poor performers.[22]

The second set of robustness tests includes country-level fixed effects. The results are consistent with the main results above and show that verbal conflict from democracies is higher for states assigned a score of 5.5 than those states assigned a score of 5.0.[23] The third set of robustness tests specifies zero-inflated negative binomial models instead of standard negative binomial models, and also produces results similar to those obtained above.[24] The fourth set of robustness tests looks at bandwidth sizes of more than one category (wider than just looking at 5.0s and 5.5s), which actually constitutes an easier test of our hypotheses, and once again provide the expected results.[25]

CONCLUSION

Freedom House's annual *Freedom in the World* report matters – not only because it informs governments and activists around the globe, but because it affects one of the most fundamental aspects of international relations: how states treat each other. A state branded by Freedom House's Scarlet Letter experiences increased verbal conflict with democracies, especially in the months immediately following the annual release of the report. We show this by exploiting a discontinuity inherent in how Freedom House assigns countries the labels "Partly Free" or "Not Free." By inviting the international community to ostracize and punish states that do not meet a specific conceptualization of democracy, Freedom House plays a subtle but important role in shaping which states face consequences of norm-defying behavior. This effect is largely contained to verbal interactions and does not appear to extend *directly* to economic or military policy. However, this does not diminish the importance of the Scarlet Letter effect, as conflict rarely escalates to material conflict without verbal conflict preceding it, and the vast majority of what constitutes "international relations" are the trading of verbal and written statements between actors – statements which ultimately accumulate into a relationship between the actors.

As with other cases of assessment power, there are concerns as to where organizations like Freedom House derive their authority and influence. Kelley and Simmons this volume note that the bulk of GPIs have been produced in

---

[22] The full results from these models removing US-sent events is available upon request.

[23] The full results from these models including fixed-effects are available upon request. Only verbal conflict from democratic states is significant in these tests. Verbal conflict from non-democracies, as well as verbal conflict from both types of senders, is not statistically significant. These results indicate the SLE produces within-country changes in the level of verbal conflict received.

[24] The full results from these zero-inflated models are available upon request. As expected, the SLE primarily operates on the degree (count) of verbal conflict, not on the presence (binary) of verbal conflict.

[25] The full results from these extended bandwidth models are available upon request.

the West, and it is reasonable to expect that receiving financial support from Western states is going to influence the biases that GPI-creators bring to the table when they assess states. In the case of Freedom House, its close relationship to the United States and institutional belief in free-market principles influence the vision of freedom and democracy that it uses to guide its assessment of states (Giannone 2010). These ideological foundations might have a number of implications. If democracy-promoting GPIs like Freedom House help shape *which* states receive negative attention, then norm-enforcement through shaming or other channels might well depend on how these GPIs define what democracy means (Hafner-Burton 2008; Pevehouse 2002). Responses to democratic assessment are also likely to depend on how GPIs define democracy. Elites in poorly performing states may criticize the assumed definition of democracy presented by a given GPI, or encourage contestation from competing GPIs. More broadly, the ideological foundations of GPIs and the consequences those foundations have for assessment power demand further study.

The paper also raises additional questions that warrant future attention. First, is the Scarlet Letter effect unique the Freedom House's report, or do other actors have sufficient assessment power to produce similar effects of their own? Freedom House has a long history that has earned it a place of trust and established its authority, making the institution well positioned to have a large impact on how the entities it assesses are treated. Do other established GPIs have similar effects? If so, what features of an indicator determine if it has a SLE associated with it? Parks and Masaki (2016) show that explicit cross-country comparisons and involving assessed states in the assessment process increases a measure's impact, but what other features affect the effectiveness of performance indicators? It may be that the scope, duration, legitimacy of producer, or a variety of other factors are systematically related to if a given performance indicator produces backlash against poorly rated actors.

Second, democracy-promoting GPIs like Freedom House could be influencing the behavior of actors other than states. Global or regional institutions, such as the Organization for American States, may respond to one of their own receiving the Scarlet Letter. At the domestic level, major media outlets may respond to the labeling of their host state or other states (particularly if there are historical ties or similarities between those states). An avenue for future research could examine whether other domestic or international actors respond to Freedom House's Scarlet Letter in the same way that democratic states do.

Finally, future research on the effects of GPIs should exploit opportunities for cleaner identification that the structure of the GPIs themselves may provide. Particularly for GPIs that rely on numerical ratings or rankings, the uncertainty inherent in attempting to quantify small differences between units may lead very similar units to receive drastically different treatments. In the absence of true counterfactuals, these opportunities provide the most promising opportunity to test the assessment effects on both assessed units and the audience responding to indicators.

References

Acharya, Amitav. 2004. How Ideas Spread: Whose Norms Matter? Norm Localization and Institutional Change in Asian Regionalism. *International Organization* 58 (2):239–75.

Angrist, Joshua D., and Jörn-Steffen Pischke. 2008. *Mostly Harmless Econometrics: An Empiricist's Companion.* Princeton, NJ: Princeton University Press.

Armstrong, David A. 2011. Stability and Change in the Freedom House Political Rights and Civil Liberties Measures. *Journal of Peace Research* 48(5):653–62.

Bandura, Romina. 2008. A Survey of Composite Indices Measuring Country Performance: 2008 Update. *Office of Development Studies.* New York: United Nations Development Programme.

Beger, Andreas, Cassy L. Dorff, and Michael D. Ward. 2014. Ensemble Forecasting of Irregular Leadership Change. *Research & Politics* 1(3):2053168014557511.

Björkdahl, Annika. 2002. Norms in International Relations: Some Conceptual and Methodological Reflections. *Cambridge Review of International Affairs* 15(1):9–23.

Bollen, Kenneth A., and Pamela Paxton. 2000. Subjective Measures of Liberal Democracy. *Comparative Political Studies* 33 (1):58–86.

Boschee, Elizabeth, Jennifer Lautenschlager, Sean OBrien, Steve Shellman, James Starz, and Michael Ward. 2015. ICEWS Coded Event Data. *Harvard Dataverse Network [Distributor]*, 1.

Boschee, Elizabeth, Premkumar Natarajan, and Ralph Weischedel. 2013. Automatic Extraction of Events from Open Source Text for Predictive Forecasting. In V. S. Subrahmanian, editor, *Handbook of Computational Approaches to Counterterrorism*, 51–67. Dordrecht, the Netherlands: Springer.

Bradley, Christopher. 2015. International Organizations and the Production of Indicators: The Case of Freedom House. In Sally Engle Merry, Kevin E. Davis, and Benedict Kingsbury, editors, *The Quiet Power of Indicators: Measuring Governance, Corruption, and the Rule of Law.* Cambridge: Cambridge University Press.

Bush, Sarah Sunn. 2017. The Politics of Rating Freedom: Ideological Affinity, Private Authority, and the Freedom in the World Ratings. *Perspectives on Politics* 15 (3):711–31.

Caprioli, Mary. 2003. Gender Equality and State Aggression: The Impact of Domestic Gender Equality on State First Use of Force. *International Interactions* 29 (3):195–214.

Davis, Kevin E., Angelina Fisher, Benedict Kingsbury, and Sally Engle Merry. 2012. *Governance by Indicators: Global Power through Classification and Rankings.* Oxford: Oxford University Press.

Davis, Kevin E., Benedict Kingsbury, and Sally Engle Merry. 2012. Introduction: Global Governance by Indicators. In Kevin E. Davis, Angelina Fisher, Benedict Kingsbury, and Sally Engle Merry, editors, *Governance by Indicators: Global Power through Quantification and Rankings*, 3–28. New York: Oxford University Press.

Diamond, Larry. 1999. *Developing Democracy: Towards Democratic Consolidation*. Baltimore, MD: John Hopkins University Press.

Dolan, Lindsay R. 2017. Labeling Laggards and Leaders: International Organizations and the Politics of Defining Development. Available at www.peio.me/wp-content/uploads/2018/01/PEIO11_paper_16.pdf

Donno, Daniela. 2010. Who Is Punished? Regional Intergovernmental Organizations and the Enforcement of Democratic Norms. *International Organization* 64 (4):593–625.

D'Orazio, Vito, James E. Yonamine, and Philip A. Schrodt. 2011. Predicting Intra-State Conflict Onset: An Event Data Approach Using Euclidean and Levenshtein Distance Measures. In *69th Annual Meeting of the Midwest Political Science Association*, Chicago, IL.

Duval, Robert D., and William R. Thompson. 1980. Reconsidering the Aggregate Relationship between Size, Economic Development, and Some Types of Foreign Policy Behavior. *American Journal of Political Science*, 511–25.

Franklin, James C. 2008. Shame on You: The Impact of Human Rights Criticism on Political Repression in Latin America. *International Studies Quarterly* 52 (1):187–211.

Freedom House. 2015. *Freedom in the World 2015: The Annual Survey of Political Rights and Civil Liberties*. New York: Rowman & Littlefield. 2016. Our history.

Gastil, Raymond Duncan. 1985. The Past, Present and Future of Democracy. *Journal of International Affairs* 38 (2):161–79.
        1990. The Comparative Survey of Freedom: Experiences and Suggestions. *Studies in Comparative International Development* 25 (1):25–50.

Gerner, Deborah J., Philip A. Schrodt, and Yilmaz Omur. 2009. Conflict and Mediation Event Observations (CAMEO): An Event Data Framework for a Post-Cold War World. In *International Conflict Mediation: New Approaches and Findings*, edited by Jacob Bercovitcch and Scott Sigmund Gartner, 287–304. New York: Routledge.

Giannone, Diego. 2010. Political and Ideological Aspects in the Measurement of Democracy: The Freedom House Case. *Democratization* 17 (1):68–97.

Hafner-Burton, Emilie M. 2005. Trading Human Rights: How Preferential Trade Agreements Influence Government Repression. *International Organization* 59 (3):593–629.
        2008. Sticks and Stones: Naming and Shaming the Human Rights Enforcement Problem. *International Organization* 62 (4):689–716.

Hahn, Jinyong, Petra Todd, and Wilbert Van der Klaauw. 2001. Identification and Estimation of Treatment Effects with a Regression-Discontinuity Design. *Econometrica* 69 (1):201–09.

Hansen, Hans Krause and Arthur Mühlen-Schulte. 2012. The Power of Numbers in Global Governance. *Journal of International Relations and Development* 15 (4):455–65.

Hawthorne, Nathaniel. 1850. *The Scarlet Letter*. Boston, MA: Ticknor, Reed & Fields.

Ho, Daniel E., Kosuke Imai, Gary King, and Elizabeth A. Stuart. 2007. Matching as Nonparametric Preprocessing for Reducing Model Dependence in Parametric Causal Inference. *Political Analysis* 15 (3):199–236.

Honig, Dan and Catherine Weaver. this volume. A Race to the Top?: The Aid Transparency Index and the Normative Power of Global Performance Assessments. *Annual Meeting of the American Political Science Association.*

Høyland, Bjørn, Karl Moene, and Fredrik Willumsen. 2012. The Tyranny of International Index Rankings. *Journal of Development Economics* 97 (1):1–14.

Imbens, Guido W., and Thomas Lemieux. 2008. Regression Discontinuity Designs: A Guide to Practice. *Journal of Econometrics* 142 (2):615–35.

Keck, Margaret E., and Kathryn Sikkink. 1998. *Activists Beyond Borders: Advocacy Networks in International Politics*, volume 6. Ithaca, NY: Cambridge University Press.

Kelley, Judith G., and Beth A. Simmons. 2015. Politics by Number: Indicators as Social Pressure in International Relations. *American Journal of Political Science* 59 (1):55–70.

this volume. Introduction: The Power of Global Performance Indicators. Chapter 1 in *The Power of Global Performance Indicators.*

Kelley, Judith G., Beth A. Simmons, and Rush Doshi. this volume. The Power of Ranking: The Ease of Doing Business and Global Regulatory Behavior. Chapter 2 in *The Power of Global Performance Indicators.*

Kijima, Rie and Phillip Y. Lipscy. this volume. International Assessments and Education Policy: Evidence from an Elite Survey. Chapter 6 in *The Power of Global Performance Indicators.*

Le, Ahn, and Edmund Malesky. this volume. Do Subnational Performance Assessments (SPAs) Lead to Improved Governance?: Evidence from Field Experiment in Vietnam. *Annual Meeting of the American Political Science Association.*

Lee, Melissa M., and Aila M. Matanock. this volume. Third Party Policymakers and the Limits of the Influence of Indicators. Chapter 11 in *The Power of Global Performance Indicators.*

Linden, Ariel and John L. Adams. 2012. Combining the Regression Discontinuity Design and Propensity Score-Based Weighting to Improve Causal Inference in Program Evaluation. *Journal of Evaluation in Clinical Practice* 18 (2):317–25.

Lozovsky, Ilya. 2016. Freedom by the numbers. *Foreign Policy.* Available at https://foreignpolicy.com/2016/01/29/freedom-by-the-numbers-freedom-house-in-the-world/.

Masaki, Takaaki, Tanya Sethi, and Samantha Custer. 2016. In the Eye of the Beholder: When is governance data good enough? AidData at the College of William & Mary and the Governance Data Alliance.

Meernik, James, Rosa Aloisi, Marsha Sowell, and Angela Nichols. 2012. The Impact of Human Rights Organizations on Naming and Shaming Campaigns. *Journal of Conflict Resolution* 56 (2):233–56.

Metternich, Nils W., Cassy Dorff, Max Gallop, Simon Weschle, and Michael D Ward. 2013. Antigovernment Networks in Civil Conflicts: How Network Structures Affect Conflictual Behavior. *American Journal of Political Science* 57 (4):892–911.

Metternich, Nils W., Shahryar Minhas, and Michael D. Ward. 2015. Firewall?
    or Wall on Fire? a Unified Framework of Conflict Contagion and the Role
    of Ethnic Exclusion. *Journal of Conflict Resolution* 0022002715603452.
Morse, Julia C. 2016. Blacklists, Market Enforcement, and the Global Regime
    to Combat Terrorist Financing. *Annual Meeting of the American Political
    Science Association.*
O'Brien, Sean P. 2010. Crisis Early Warning and Decision Support:
    Contemporary Approaches and Thoughts on Future Research.
    International Studies Review 12 (1):87–104.
Parks, Bradley G., and Takaaki Masaki. 2016. Do Performance Assessment
    Influence Policy Behavior? Micro-Evidence from the 2014 Reform Efforts
    Survey. Paper presented at the 112th Annual Meeting of the American
    Political Science Association.
Peterson, Timothy M., and Leah Graham. 2011. Shared Human Rights Norms
    and Military Conflict. *Journal of Conflict Resolution* 55 (2):248–73.
Pevehouse, Jon C. 2002. Democracy from the Outside-In? International
    Organizations and Democratization. *International Organization* 56
    (3):515–49.
Ramos, Howard, James Ron, and Oskar N.T. Thoms. 2007. Shaping the
    Northern Media's Human Rights Coverage, 1986–2000. *Journal of Peace
    Research* 44 (4):385–406.
Ropp, Stephen C., and Kathryn Sikkink. 1999. *The Power of Human Rights:
    International Norms and Domestic Change*, volume 66. Cambridge:
    Cambridge University Press.
Russett, Bruce. 1994. *Grasping the Democratic Peace: Principles for a Post-
    Cold War World*. Princeton, NJ: Princeton University Press.
Schrodt, Philip A. 2012. CAMEO: Conflict and Mediation Event Observations
    Event and Actor Codebook. *Event Data Project, Department of Political
    Science*, Pennsylvania State University.
Sobek, David, M. Rodwan Abouharb, and Christopher G. Ingram. 2006. The
    Human Rights Peace: How the Respect for Human Rights at Home Leads
    to Peace Abroad. *Journal of Politics* 68 (3):519–29.
Thistlethwaite, Donald L., and Donald T. Campbell. 1960. Regression-
    Discontinuity Analysis: An Alternative to the Ex Post Facto Experiment.
    Journal of Educational psychology 51 (6):309.
Weisiger, Alex and Keren Yarhi-Milo. 2015. Revisiting Reputation: How Past
    Actions Matter in International Politics. *International Organization*
    69 (2):473–95.
Weschle, Simon. The Impact of Economic Crises on Political Representation in
    Public Communication: Evidence from the Eurozone. *British Journal of
    Political Science*, forthcoming.

PART III

BEYOND AND WITHIN STATE

Influences and Impacts on Non-State Actors

9

Can Blacklisting Reduce Terrorist Attacks?

The Case of the US Foreign Terrorist Organization (FTO) List

Hyeran Jo, Brian J. Phillips, and Joshua Alley

Blacklisting defines social and political relations between designators and designees.[1] In the realm of international security, the United States Foreign Terrorist Organization (FTO) list is a salient blacklist. As one of the centerpieces of US counterterrorism policy,[2] the FTO list proscribes groups as terrorist organizations which threaten the United States. The FTO list comes with legal, political, and economic consequences. Designated organizations face financial and travel restrictions. Financial sanctions include freezing of assets by the Treasury Department.[3] Travel restrictions include no entry into the United States or deportation for individuals associated with the group, which could be especially detrimental to groups that lobby in the United States to procure funds.

As a global performance indicator (GPI) that defines who is terrorist group and who is not, the FTO list has political consequences in global security. Who is affected by the terrorist list and what are the associated political processes? Using the framework of GPIs as outlined in Chapter 1 by Kelley and Simmons, this chapter examines how FTO designation affects

---

[1] Social science research in political science, psychology, sociology, and criminology, all emphasize the importance of labels. See for example, Becker 1997; Bernburg et al. 2006; Feldman 1977; Link et al. 1989; Paternoster and Bachman 2012.

[2] The Bureau of Counterterrorism within the State Department reports "FTO designations play a critical role in our fight against terrorism and are an effective means of curtailing support for terrorist activities and pressuring groups to get out of the terrorism business." See US State Department, Bureau of Counterterrorism, "Foreign Terrorist Organizations," http://www.state.gov/j/ct/rls/other/des/123085.htm.

[3] For example, USD 13.5 million in cash flow to al-Qaeda was blocked as of 2013 in the wake of FTO designation of the group in 1999 (Treasury Department 2014).

the behavior of listed groups. We argue and demonstrate that the impact of FTO listing depends on the characteristics of listed terrorist groups. Groups with private funding sources, such as diaspora population, are vulnerable to stigmatization and sanctions from the FTO list. By contrast, groups with less observable funding sources, such as terrorist networks, are unaffected by listing and may even increase attacks. Our finding generates a general lesson: understanding differences between targets is essential to evaluating the impact of GPIs.[4]

The FTO list could reduce terrorism by generating political responses from relevant political actors. The list is determined by the US State Department and serves as a guide for the US bureaucracy, other countries' listing, and counterterrorism actions taken by the United Nations. The blacklist triggers international cooperation, especially from ally countries of the United States, and creates fear of being branded as terrorists among vulnerable populations like diaspora or humanitarian communities. In this way, blacklisting affects the reputations of listed groups, essentially naming and shaming them. In addition to such social sanctions, blacklisting exposes listed groups and their supporters to political and financial sanctions, particularly when the countries hosting terrorist organizations employ such domestic measures. Consequently, terrorist groups that rely on political and material support from those who are subject to scrutiny by the blacklist will be affected by the FTO list. Groups with less public sources of support will be relatively less impacted by the force of blacklist.

We test our predictions about the conditional impact of the FTO list using new data on terrorist group funding sources. We find that designation is only associated with reductions in attacks of terrorist groups that depend on private funding. This highly conditional finding suggests that GPIs have a limited impact in this example of global security. We also provide case evidence that some terrorist groups alter their financing strategies after designation. By restricting private support, for example, listing may lead terrorist groups to rely more on criminal activities. In this fashion, blacklisting has a potential to produce unintended consequences in the long-run.[5]

We start this chapter with background on the FTO list and the designation process, and then explain why blacklisting is only likely to affect groups that depend on private funding sources. Empirical tests on terrorist groups between 1970 and 2014 provide some evidence that the FTO blacklist had some intended effects of reducing terrorist groups' attacks, but only under limited scope conditions. Case study evidence then illustrates potential unintended consequences as some terrorist organizations shifted their resource base

---

[4] Also see Chapter 7 by Koliev et al. in this volume.
[5] See further Chapter 11 by Lee and Matanock and Chapter 12 by Bisbee et al. in this volume.

in response to the blacklisting and regulatory pressure. We conclude with a discussion of the implications for scholarship and policy.

FTO BLACKLISTING IN GLOBAL SECURITY

Relative to other issue areas such as human rights, business, environment, or education, global security has few GPIs.[6] The dearth of security indicators may be due to the nature of high politics where countries refrain from provoking others, or the security risks associated with the information. For instance, policymakers were concerned that the issuance of Nuclear Threat Initiative's (NTI) Sabotage Index might be used by terrorists to exploit the vulnerability of countries that are weak on nuclear security.[7]

The FTO list is clearly a global performance indicator (GPI) where an "assessment" exercise creates an "indicator." The list is a regularized policy "assessment" based on the performance and status of violent non-state actors across a common set of criteria, namely their use of terrorism and threats to US national security. The list has been updated almost annually since 1997, adding several groups each year, making 67 groups total on the list at the beginning of 2019.[8] The assessments of foreign terrorist organization essentially produces binary indicator that brands some groups as terrorists but others not. The designation then becomes public as the list is announced by the federal registrar and delivered to Congress through State Department public release. Although the list currently includes a disproportionate number of Middle Eastern groups, it has always contained groups from around the world, giving the indicator global coverage.

Blacklisting is essential to the FTO process as the list labels some non-state actors as dangerous deviants. The FTO designation creates a stark distinction, leading to GPI dynamics that are different from other rankings, ratings and benchmarks. This branding usually comes from more powerful, established actors with more authority and social acceptance. Blacklisting clearly marks the boundary between acceptable and unacceptable behavior. The FTO case thus embodies authority relationships in world politics where powerful actors create structure and weaker actors operate within that structure. Published by the United States as the power wielder and indicator creator, the FTO list helps define unacceptable political violence vis-à-vis the superpower.[9]

---

[6] Examples include the sabotage/threat ranking (Nuclear Threat Initiative), PowerIndex (Bonn International Center), European Foreign Policy Scorecard (European Council on Foreign Relations), Global Peace Index (Vision of Humanity), and PowerIndex (GlobalFirepower).

[7] We owe Matt Fuhrmann on this point.

[8] GAO 2015. See Murphy 2003 for general background of FTO listing. Also see Cronin 2003; Cronin et al. 2004. The current list is available here: https://www.state.gov/j/ct/rls/other/des/123085.htm.

[9] Other examples of blacklists, in association with US counterterrorism policy, such as State Sponsors of Terrorism, or Specially Designated Global Terrorist List, would have similar political dynamics we highlight with respect to the FTO blacklist.

Such framing alters the security policies of other states as well as international organizations, including the United Nations and the Financial Action Task Force (FATF).[10]

By making what was previously unofficially legitimate as officially illegitimate, the blacklist's reframing also configures the perceptions and actions of support networks of a target. It changes the political, legal, and social landscapes for national governments, international organizations, and beyond. This enabling power of blacklisting is activated when the target is hit by the erosion of its political support, ultimately impacting its operations and possibly survival. Blacklisting in the context of FTO designation undermines some terrorist groups' financial base and that in turn will influence their capacity to undertake violence. FTO listing will not always achieve its intended effect, however. Some terrorist groups adapt to new regulatory frameworks by shifting their resource base.

CONTESTATION AND LISTING POLITICS

The famous adage "one man's terrorist is another man's freedom fighter" encapsulates potential contestation surrounding the validity of the FTO list.[11] Designation of terrorist organizations is a debated issue in policy circles. Cronin sums up this contestation over the FTO list: "there are hundreds of groups that meet the criteria for the Foreign Terrorist Organization (FTO) list but do not get added."[12] To be listed as FTO, a militant group must be a foreign organization that engages in terrorist activity[13] and threatens US national security.[14] Threat perception is always subject to debate, as are national security interests.

---

[10] The designation of terrorist groups by other countries closely follows the US list, although differences exist given security circumstances of each country. See the discussion in Freedman 2010. Also, the United Nations sanctions dates closely follow the actions of the US Treasury. See the dates in Treasury 2016. On the FATF, see Chapter 3 by Morse in this volume.

[11] See Jarvis and Legrand 2018 and its associated special issue on what they call "proscription regimes."

[12] Cronin 2012.

[13] US Code § 2656 f (d) (2) defines terrorist activity as "premeditated, politically motivated violence perpetuated against noncombatant targets by subnational groups or clandestine agents." While there is no universal definition of terrorism, studies on political violence define terrorism as political acts to invoke physical or psychological pain on civilians. Terrorist organizations are groups that exercise terrorist acts and prescribe to terrorism. The terrorist label is not a neutral term, but carries negative connotations about social exclusion and unacceptable behavior.

[14] Section 219 of the Immigration and Nationality Act (INA) (8 U.S.C. 1101 et seq.) as amended under the Antiterrorism and Effective Death Penalty Act of 1996 (AEDPA) (P.L. 104–32).

Who is listed and who is not,[15] whether the process of listing meets statutory requirements,[16] and whether listing has human rights implications[17] are all controversial.[18] Proponents of designation want to declare a group illegitimate and deny the access to funds. Those who are *against* designation of a certain group raise concerns over the human rights and humanitarian implications of the listing.[19]

Cross-national differences between terrorist lists reveal the presence of contestation. Some overlap exists between the US list and those of Australia, Canada, the EU and the UN, but there is little overlap with India's and Russia's lists.[20] The fact that there is substantial overlap with most of the lists suggests the US list is influential, and that the FTO list, like other GPI instruments, alters other political actors' responses and labeling.

Besides listing itself, the efficacy of FTO list is also disputed. In an interview with the *Washington Post*, a White House official said that the designation is "all theatrics," and merely "symbolic."[21] Others describe it as a "meaningless political tool"[22] or playing only a "modest role"[23] in counterterrorism. On the other hand, Hillary Clinton placed the designation of the Haqqani network as a foreign terrorist organization within "our robust campaign of diplomatic, military, and intelligence pressure on the network, demonstrating the United States' resolve to degrade the organization's ability to execute violent attacks."[24] Given these divergent views on the policy utility of FTO listing, we believe social science theory and methods can inform the policy debate. In this study, we demonstrate that any impact of FTO listing on terrorist activity depends on the characteristics of the target.

[15] Just a few examples: see discussion on Haqqani network in Afghanistan (Cronin 2011), weighing on Muslim Brotherhood FTO designation (Baker 2017), or controversy over the delisting of the Communist Party of the Philippines-New People's Army (CPP-NPA) in Gagalac 2017.

[16] See United States Court of Appeals for the District of Columbia Circuit, No. 12-1118 (*MeK v. State Department*, 2012).

[17] Head 2016.

[18] See Crenshaw and LaFree 2017; Phillips 2015.

[19] See Ranstorp and Wilkinson 2013; *Holder v. Humanitarian Law Project,* 561 U.S. 1, 130 S.Ct. 2705.

[20] India and Russia focus their terrorist organization lists on domestic opponents. In our dataset, the correlation between US FTO list and other countries' lists is as follows: Canada 0.81, Australia 0.53, EU 0.61, UK 0.53, UN 0.40, Russia 0.22, and India 0.07. On the comparison among terrorist lists, see also Freedman 2010 and Beck and Miner 2013.

[21] DeYoung 2012. More recently, the former US Director of National Intelligence, James Clapper, said "for whatever reason it seemed as though our listing a group had an impact. People noticed and the rest of the world cared, but as far as impact on us in intelligence, it really didn't have any." (Legrand 2018).

[22] Lobe and Ramsey 2012.

[23] Hufbauer and Moll 2007.

[24] BBC. 2012. "U.S. to designate Haqqani network as terror group," September 7, 2012. Available at https://www.bbc.com/news/world-asia-19521773.

A POLITICAL ECONOMY THEORY OF BLACKLISTING

To develop an explanation for the effects of the FTO blacklist, we study political, economic, and social connections between terrorist groups and their supporters (targets of the GPI) and the United States government (issuer of the GPI). We provide a typology of the financial bases of terrorist groups, examine terrorism supporters' reactions to the FTO listing, and attempt to predict the ultimate impact on terrorist groups' activities.

In sociology and criminology, blacklisting is hypothesized to have two divergent effects: positive and negative.[25] On one the one hand, deterring deviant behaviors using blacklist could reduce terrorism. On the other hand, blacklisting can trigger negative responses from the target, creating more nonconformist actions.[26] This logic produces an expectation that the FTO designation can galvanize groups to carry out more attacks. Adjudicating between these divergent expectations, we develop a political economy explanation of how the FTO list affects terrorist attacks. We argue that listing generates less terrorist activity when the target is vulnerable to political processes triggered by designation. Conversely, we would expect the terrorist list will have no impact or has a potential to create more terrorist activity when the target is less vulnerable to the regulatory pressure ensued by the FTO process.

Vulnerability depends on the structure of funding base for each terrorist group. Some funding is easier to monitor and disrupt, and terrorist groups with such funding sources will be more likely to be affected by FTO designation. Private funding, such as donations and diaspora support, is especially vulnerable to sanctions and social stigma. Terrorist groups that depend on private funding are likely impacted by blacklists, as supporters suffer legal, financial, and social consequences. In contrast, funding sources that are more difficult to detect and provide greater autonomy to terrorist groups – like criminal activities – are unlikely to be impacted by FTO listing. In some cases, blacklisting these groups may even contribute to increased attacks when terrorists adapt and gain notoriety.

The effect of blacklisting depends on the financial support of targeted groups for several reasons. The financial support network of the blacklisted target gives us clues about the vulnerability of the target, responses of supporters, and regulatory issues for the US. If the support network is clandestine, blacklisting will

---

[25] See the review of literature in Paternoster and Bachman 2012.
[26] The two competing theories – "labeling theory" and "deterrence theory" – help theorize the potential effect of FTO listing. Labeling theory in criminology proposes that criminals react negatively to negative labeling, which leads to *more* crimes, not less. Labeling theory therefore would predict that FTO listing would lead to *more* terrorism. On the other hand, deterrence theory would point out the legal and economic consequences for the terrorist groups as well as the likelihood of them being affected by the designation. Deterrent theory therefore would predict that blacklisting leads to *fewer crimes*. Our theory seeks to reconcile the two views.

not shame and stigmatize supporters of the terrorist organization. As a result, the target organization will not change its behavior. In contrast, if a support network is open and subject to shaming, blacklisting could change how the target operates, by eroding its support network. Consequently, the target would be weakened and blacklisting will reduce terrorist attacks. Terrorist groups might not necessarily be shamed by the FTO list, but their supporters might be shamed, which can impact how terrorist groups operate. This line of argument highlights how target heterogeneity elicits different responses to the blacklisting. Terrorist groups that rely on one type of open funding may behave differently from those that rely on other clandestine funding types. We now explore the resulting sensitivity to blacklisting of different funding sources in more depth.

VARIETIES OF TERRORISM FUNDING

Financing is essential to many terrorist groups, as it provides resources to support members and fund operations. Although lone wolves do not require funding systems, most terrorist organizations actively manage their funds to pay members and to maintain operational cells.[27] Most importantly, funding has consequences for terror acts. Some attacks have few costs, but others such as coordinated hijacking or military actions require sustained hierarchical operations.[28] Disruption of their financial and support network reduces terrorists' capability over time by reducing their capacity to pay recruits, launch attacks, and build political capacity.

We identify and classify four primary ways for terrorist groups to fund their activities: (1) private funding, (2) state sponsorship, (3) terrorist networks, and (4) criminal activities.[29] The four funding types differ in "financial vulnerability," social pressures on supporters from blacklisting, as well as how adaptable terrorist groups could be in securing new types of funds.

Private funding includes money from private actors – business, charities, or individuals. Examples include money from private donors, charities,[30] or diaspora populations.[31] Private donors and charities are directly hit by the material support ban that follows FTO designation. These actors face fines or have their operations shut down if they are deemed to support terrorist groups. Banks, businesses, and other organizations are also affected by the FTO designation. If they are branded as entities that provide "material support" for terrorist organizations, they could be sanctioned. The attention given to the

---

[27] Shapiro 2013; Vittori 2011. Recent research shows that AQI and ISIS dispersed funding to maintain recruits and to augment their attack capacity (Johnston et al. 2016).

[28] For example, the 2004 Madrid train bombings cost an estimated USD 10,000, and the 2002 Bali bombings an estimated USD 50,000 (FATF 2008, pp. 7–8).

[29] On the types of terrorism financing, see FATF 2008; Vittori 2011.

[30] See the list of charities in Treasury Department 2016.

[31] See Hess 2007 for nexus between diaspora and terrorism.

Holy Land Foundation, a Hamas charity, is one example of a material support ban triggered by the FTO designation.[32] A US Supreme Court case, *Holder v. Humanitarian Law Project*, also shows how the FTO list has created new restrictions on how international humanitarian organizations engage with non-state conflict actors.[33]

Private donations are relatively easy for governments to monitor, especially for larger groups with extensive financial flows. Also, some private actors could potentially face the shame and stigmatization of blacklisting along with sanctions. The reaction of the Tamil Tigers diaspora population is a case in point. The Tamil diaspora helped fund the Liberation Tigers of Tamil Eelam (LTTE) in Sri Lanka, but FTO designation restricted the flow of resources. Following the American lead, Canada and UK raised barriers for charities channeling funds to the LTTE for fear of being branded as supporting terrorism.[34] Before the FTO listing of LTTE, some members of the Tamil diaspora in Europe and North America often contributed financially to the "freedom fighters,"[35] but opinions changed when the LTTE was branded as "terrorists." The diaspora withdrew their support after FTO designation, not just because of the threat of legal punishment but also because of shame and stigmatization.[36] Stigmatization was likely at work eliciting responses from donor community and ultimately affecting LTTE operations.[37]

State sponsors are another source of funds for terrorist groups.[38] Libya, Syria, Iran, Pakistan, and Iraq, among others, have provided sanctuaries or given weapons to terrorist groups to advance their geopolitical interests. State sponsorship subjects terrorist groups to the political whims of their sponsors.[39] Depending on changes in the domestic coalition of the sponsor country or shifting geopolitical tides, terrorist groups expose themselves to the risks of fluctuating funding, so many organizations tend to seek self-sufficiency.[40] For the implementation of the FTO list, sanctioning state sponsorship is complicated

---

[32] See Levitt 2004 for more examples involving charities and terrorism.

[33] 561 U.S. 1, 130 S.Ct. 2705. Also see Modirzadeh, Lewis and Bruderlein 2011; Said 2015.

[34] See International Crisis Group 2010.

[35] Considered the claim of five defendants of Tamil diaspora that LTTE is not a terrorist organization, but a liberation movement, in the Hague district court in 2011 LTTE case (as discussed in Wellens 2015, pp. 88–91).

[36] LTTE was said to have affected by the FTO designation due to the dwindling funding from diaspora offices in Canada and UK, but its demise was eventually caused by battle losses against the Sri Lankan government. See Roberts 2012.

[37] We however recognize that some private funders may be immune to the FTO listing if they have particular religious or geopolitical interests. See Burr and Collins 2006 for the case of Islamic charities. Even in these cases, charities are subject to monitoring by national authorities and therefore are more observable than criminal activities 73.

[38] Byman 2005; Carter 2012.

[39] Salehyan et al. 2014.

[40] Johnston et al. 2016.

by potential issue linkages. Efforts to sanction states for sponsoring terrorism may be hindered by other foreign policy concerns. For instance, the United States has struggled to address Pakistan's relationship with Islamic militants, including several groups on the FTO list. Furthermore, state sponsors are unlikely to change their behavior in response to FTO designation. Countries view sponsoring armed groups as means of advancing their geopolitical interests, making FTO designation comparatively unimportant.[41] So, even though the FTO list signals to state sponsors of terrorism, designation alone will not impact state support.

Terrorist networks, or alliances among terrorist organizations, are the third source of financial and logistical support to facilitate attacks.[42] Heavily networked terrorist organizations can survive longer by reducing mobilization concerns.[43] As well, network provides a valuable support for many groups especially if they operate under restrictive environments. Consider ties between al-Qaeda and al-Qaeda in the Arabian Peninsula (Yemen), al-Qaeda in the Islamic Maghreb (AQIM in Mali), and al-Shabaab (Somalia). Ideological affinity, shared training, and operating reach give the groups more power. We expect that groups relying on terrorist networks are less vulnerable to FTO designation, as they already operate beyond the reach of sanctions and monitoring.

Criminal activities are an essential source of funding for many terrorist organizations.[44] Terrorist groups fund their groups from the profits of criminal activities, such as kidnapping, ransom, extortions, illicit trade, and drug trafficking.[45] Involvement in crime contributes to organizational longevity.[46] Criminal activities, compared to other funding sources, are low on financial vulnerability. The clandestine nature of criminal activities makes them difficult to trace and sanction. Local criminal activities such as extracting forced donations from local business or civilian population are especially difficult to observe. International criminal activities are relatively more detectable than domestic/local extortion activities. Even then, sanctions are hard to enforce when trade occurs in black markets or international buyers engage in sanction-busting activities.[47] In addition, terrorist groups relying on criminal activities are often immune from

---

[41] This is in line with the finding in Phillips 2019 that the FTO effects differ between US allies and non-allies.
[42] Asal and Rethemeyer 2008; Bacon 2018; Karmon 2005.
[43] Phillips 2014.
[44] Shelley 2014.
[45] For example, Hezbollah, despite its service provision, exhibit the characteristics of crime syndicates, engaged in illicit trades. See Leuprecht et al. 2015.
[46] Piazza and Piazza 2017.
[47] Early 2015.

blacklisting, because their funding is autonomous. Low financial vulnerability in criminal activities is reinforced by shifts from one criminal source to the other. For example, Al-Shabaab moved from black market charcoal to extortion and ivory trading, making their funding versatile and adaptable.[48] As a result of funding autonomy and adaptability, groups that fund their operations through criminal activities are unlikely to be affected by FTO designation.

RESPONSES BY THE USA, OTHER STATES, AND
INTERNATIONAL ORGANIZATIONS

The FTO list can impact a proscribed group via various domestic and international political channels. In the domestic arena, FTO designation triggers interagency cooperation for proper implementation among the Departments of State, Justice, Homeland Security, and the Treasury.[49] Agencies implement financial sanctions, immigration bans, and oversee the legality of sanctions. Abroad, the US government uses the FTO list as a foreign policy signal to terrorist-hosting governments. According to the State Department, FTO listing "signals to other governments our concern about named organizations."[50] In advocating the listing of Haqqani network, a terrorism expert on South Asia said in a congressional testimony: "Pakistani officials repeatedly questioned why they should take military action against the Haqqanis if the US was seeking a negotiated settlement. With this terrorist designation, the US leaves no doubt on where it stands on the issue and thus removes a Pakistani excuse for failing to take military action."[51]

The FTO designation spurs host governments to take action against proscribed groups.[52] Listing a group sometimes leads to US military and diplomatic support for host governments.[53] Such aid helps US allies in their

---

[48] Radtke and Jo 2018.
[49] Cronin 2003, 3; Decker 2014 also writes that the FTO designation "provides a clear focal point for interagency cooperation."
[50] Fact Sheet: Secretary of State designates Foreign Terrorist Organizations (FTOs); office of the Spokesman, Washington, DC, October 5, 2001. http://fas.org/irp/news/2001/10/fr100501.html.
[51] Curtis 2012.
[52] Note the principal-agent relationship between the host government and the United States (See Bapat 2011 for the analysis of moral hazard problem in the context of US counterterrorism effort.). Not all states share the preferences of the United States. The government might not necessarily fight the terrorist organization absent military aid. The government might have an understanding with terrorist groups, or the government might want to rely on aid relationships and prefer that that conflict continue to secure further aid. As an agent, then, a resident government might have a diverging preference from the United States.
[53] Increased foreign aid to Uganda after the designation of the Lord's Resistance Army as an FTO in December 2011 is one such example (Mills 2015, p. 138 in particular; also see Finnström 2008).

counterterrorism efforts, which can be guided by the FTO list.[54] The terrorist list also produces elite responses within the host governments of FTO groups.[55] According to Julia Morse's data on counterterrorism financing (2006–2014), a larger number of FTO-host countries have instituted new laws compared to non-FTO host countries to tackle terrorism financing after FTO designation of their residing terrorist groups.[56] Among the 71 countries that created counterterrorism financing domestic regulations, 24 countries have FTOs in their territory. This includes almost all states with FTO-listed groups. In one example, around the time several Pakistani groups were listed as FTOs, the Pakistani government established the Financial Monitoring Unit at Ministry of Finance, amended Anti-Terrorism Act of 1997, and subsequently enacted an Anti-Money Laundering Act in 2010.[57]

A specific way FTO designation affects designated groups, is by influencing other countries' lists. The United States seems to be an important agenda-setter regarding which groups are counterterrorism priorities.[58] After the US list was created in 1997, the United Kingdom created its own list using similar policies in 2000. The European Union, and countries beyond Europe, took similar steps after the September 11, 2001, terrorist attacks.[59] The United States listing seems to influence other countries' designation decisions, multiplying impact on listed groups.

Governments with terrorist groups in their countries often exploit FTO status to stigmatize domestic enemies and use it as an opportunity for repression. For example, the Sri Lankan government used LTTE's FTO status to justify their actions and bolster domestic political support for military campaigns. As a counterterrorism tool, the FTO list triggers military and political responses that would not otherwise be possible for host governments. FTO designation

---

[54] See Boutton and Carter 2014. The United States appears to increase military aid to FTO-resident countries after FTO designation. We examined the increase amount after 2001 to FTO-holding countries. For example, the Philippines received about 1 million ($1,330,744) in Year 1999 but 15 million ($55,127,153) in Year 2002 for the category of "Foreign Military Financing (FMF)" Program. Those are grants for the acquisition of US defense equipment, services, and training, which is essential for "building partner nation capacity and helping allies defend themselves." Such dramatic increases are not observed in other non-FTO resident countries. See "Foreign Military Financing Program" House Appropriations Committee Reports, 112th Congress (2011–2012) House Report 112–494: State, Foreign Operations, and Related Programs Appropriations Bill, 2013. http://thomas.loc.gov/cgi-bin/cpquery/?&sid=cp112WcH61&r_n=hr494.112&dbname=cp112&&sel=TOC_218118. On how the effects of FTO status seem to be more powerful in US allied countries, see Phillips 2018.

[55] Here we use the term "host" in the general sense to include countries with FTOs in their territory, regardless of whether the state authorizes the groups' actions or existence.

[56] Chapter 3 by Morse, in this volume.

[57] Zahid 2015.

[58] Beck and Miner (2013, pp. 852–53) find prior US designation is associated with subsequent UK or EU designation.

[59] Jarvis and LeGrand 2018.

by the United States became a powerful policy tool for elites within host countries, especially after 9/11. Elites facing internal opposition can use FTO designations to clamp down on long-time foes.

The long-running conflict in the Philippines illustrates this impact of the US FTO designation. The Philippine government has faced an insurgency in the Mindanao region for over three decades and the FTO designation of Abu Sayyaf provided the government political and military tools to fight this group and other insurgents. More recently, the Duterte administration opposed the United States attempt to remove the Communist Party of the Philippines from the FTO list.[60] The case demonstrates how the FTO designation becomes a political and policy-framing tool on the part of domestic elites in the United States and host countries.

Beyond the United States and host government politics, the FTO list impacts transnational political processes, with consequences for terrorists' attack capacity. UN Designation of FTO-linked charity organizations closely follow the United States, usually with five to ten days' delay.[61] Also, charities and banks that operate internationally must ensure money does not flow to terrorist organizations for the fear of being tagged as "material supporters" of terrorism.

HOW TERRORIST GROUPS REACT TO BLACKLISTING

Like governments and international organizations, terrorist groups respond to FTO designation. Their reactions to blacklisting are diverse. Some contest the listing. Mujahadeen-e-Khalq (MeK), for example, demanded the revocation of its designation for years and finally achieved it in 2012.[62] Others have responded to designation with defiance. The al-Aqsa Martyrs' Brigades, an extremist group in Palestine under Fatah control, responded to the designation decision with a statement resolving to "continue until we vanquish the occupation."[63] The third category of terrorist groups attempt to evade the legal reach of FTO designation. Harkat ul-Mujahedin has frequently changed its name to avoid sanctions and disguised itself as a charity organization.[64] Other terrorist groups engage in public relations as a counter to FTO listing. Al-Qaeda in the

---

[60] Gagalac 2017.

[61] Treasury Department 2016. It is no coincidence that al-Qaeda related entities were designated as UN-terrorist list only a few days after the US FTO designation.

[62] In petitioning against its designation, the MeK noted that "A FTO designation results in 'dire consequences' for an organization, its members and other supporters." (*MeK v. State Department*, 2012: 3).

[63] Levitt 2002. Analysts noted that the designation also signaled to Fatah that they could be next, as many members of the al-Aqsa Martyrs' Brigades were associated with Fatah's military wing. This again demonstrates that the message of blacklisting via FTO designation gets to the target terrorist group as well as other terrorist groups.

[64] State Department 2014, "Amendments to, and Maintenance of, the Terrorist Designations of Harakat ul-Mujahidin" Media Note, Office of the Spokesperson, Washington, DC, August 7, 2014. http://www.state.gov/r/pa/prs/ps/2014/230373.htm.

Arabian Peninsula (AQAP) in Yemen started publishing its online magazine, *Inspire*, in July 2010, shortly after its FTO designation in January 2010, reacting to the designation by enhancing its social status to draw recruits.[65]

Part of these reactions is a function of from where these groups draw support. Terrorist groups' financial bases are important for determining how much FTO designation will penetrate their operations and how they react to the blacklist. Terrorist groups that have relied on criminal activities will retain freedom of action. In contrast, groups that have relied on private funding are more vulnerable to the consequences of FTO listing, either because the sponsor was shamed (as in Tamil diaspora) or subject to domestic or international sanctions on the money trail (with the help of Financial Action Task Force). From the perspective of the monitor (US authorities), reliance on private funding would result in relatively high visibility in tracking down the flow of funds.[66] Additionally, other countries with terrorist groups, especially US allies, would mobilize their own resources to catalyze their anti-terrorism efforts. The high detectability allows for sanctions to be implemented, and some private supporters will also face stigmatization. These domestic and international political and social processes lead to our main hypothesis, which we test in the next section.

Hypothesis: If a terrorist group relies on private funding and is subject to FTO designation, the group is more likely to reduce attacks, compared to FTO-designated groups that rely on other types of funding.

STATISTICAL ANALYSIS OF FTO LISTING IMPACT

To test our hypothesis, we built a dataset on terrorist groups between 1970 and 2014, by extending the dataset by Gaibulloev and Sandler (2013) that covers the period between 1970 and 2007.[67] The unit of analysis is terrorist

---

[65] "Al Qaeda Organization in the Arabian Peninsula" Global Security. Available at http:// www.globalsecurity.org/military/world/para/al-qaida-arabia.htm.

[66] This is not to say that private funding is easy to detect. Charities are sometimes difficult to detect because of their global reach, name changes, and shell companies. We argue that private funding is *comparatively* easier to monitor than say, the terrorist funding based on criminal activities. The relative easiness is the key. We recognize the difficulty of tracking down overseas remittances for example. In many cases, even if the funds are tracked down, linking them to material support for a certain terrorist group is uncertain.

[67] In extending the dataset up to 2014, we focused on constructing reasonable comparison sets – terrorist groups that are comparable to the Gaibulloev and Sandler (2013) data. We used the list of groups from the Global Terrorism Database (GTD) and then we excluded lone wolves and amorphous groups. Individual terrorists (i.e. lone wolves) do not fit the "group" standard, and other GTD "groups" include actors who are at best suspected of one attack, or primarily engage in other forms of contentious politics. We also removed actors that are coded as groups by the GTD, but have a group name of "Jihadists" or "Leftists," suggesting that the perpetrators were not necessarily part of a formal organization, but that GTD coders attached a name indicating what they knew about them. These criteria are consistent with Gaibulloev and Sandler's coding, and with other terrorist group databases, as in Cronin 2009.

group-year, as we analyze the pattern of terrorist attacks in response to the FTO listing. Our dataset includes 412 terrorist groups.[68] A terrorist group enters the data when it is first formed, which is often made clear by its first claimed attacks, and exits the data when it is no longer operational for more than five years or is disbanded. Since FTO listing started in 1997, we have 27 years of data before the FTO listing and 17 years after the FTO listing.[69] Given that the FTO list started in 1997, some terrorist groups are designated years after their formation. For example, al-Qaeda formed in 1988, but it was only listed as a FTO in 1999 after a threat assessment based on the 1998 bombings of the US embassies in Kenya and Tanzania.

In our dataset, a terrorist group is a subnational political organization that uses terrorism,[70] where terrorism is defined as "the use of politically motivated violence against non-combatants to cause intimidation or fear among a target audience."[71] Based on these definitions of terrorist organizations and terrorism, our dataset includes various non-state armed groups, such as those often called rebel groups or paramilitaries – as long as they use terrorist tactics. Our dataset excludes peaceful movements or violent non-state actors that do not use terror tactics. This general definition produces different set of terrorist organizations from what the United States brands as "foreign terrorist organizations." This difference between regular scholarly terrorist group lists and the FTO list highlights the highly political nature of the FTO designation.

Our dependent variable is the number of terrorist attacks associated with each group in a year.[72] Terrorist attacks are an important outcome of interest because they are the main output of groups and reflect organizational capacity.[73] In our dataset, terrorist attacks include both domestic and transnational

---

[68] The number of groups used is consistent with some other global analyses of terrorist groups, which include several hundred organizations. Blomberg, Gaibulloev, and Sandler 2011 include 367 groups in their analysis, and Cronin 2009 includes 450. Neither author, however, tried to find organizational information as specific as ours, regarding funding sources. Other missing data issues, including how the groups used in the sample are comparable with FTOs, are discussed below.

[69] The mean duration for terrorist groups is 12 years, with a minimum of 1 year and a maximum of 45 years (our observation window of 1970–2014). About 50 percent of groups dissolve after 8 years.

[70] Phillips 2015. This is consistent with other studies, such as Carter 2012; Hoffman 2006; Jones and Libicki 2008.

[71] Jones and Libicki 2008: p. 3.

[72] We draw attacks data from the Global Terrorism Database. We could have opted for other dependent variables such as group survival (whether a group survives or not, as in Gaibulloev and Sandler 2014) or fate (ending in negotiation, military defeat or victory as in Carter 2012). We chose to analyze attacks first because survival and fates require distinct theorizing (e.g. why terrorist groups want to negotiate) and the FTO effect might have less of a long-term effect (on survival) than a short-term effect (on attack patterns).

[73] For these reasons, other studies use terrorist attacks as the dependent variable (e.g. Li 2005; Nemeth, Mauslein, and Stapley 2014).

terrorism, as some domestic attacks in other countries might also affect US global security interests.[74] The mean of the dependent variable is approximately seven annual attacks, but ranges from 0 to 1032.

The first set of key independent variables includes our measures of funding sources. We classify terrorist funding into four binary variables: private funding, state sponsorship, terrorist network, and criminal activities. For each type, we construct an indicator[75] to denote if a particular group has a particular type of funding.

Private funding (82 groups) included financing for terrorist organizations from members, charitable donations, and other miscellaneous sources. State sponsorship (85 groups) was coded based on information which clarified whether a group was funded in part or in whole by a state entity. Terrorist network (57 groups) was coded 1 if a group received resources from other terrorist organizations. Criminal activities (101 groups) were coded based on illicit funding such as bank robberies, kidnapping for ransom, extortion, or the drug trade. To collect the funding data, the research team utilized official or reliable academic sources, mostly based on the group profiles from the Mapping Terrorism Project at Stanford as well as data from the START (Study of Terrorism and Responses to Terrorism) Center at University of Maryland.

We were unable to code data for 230 obscure groups due to a lack of adequate data. This restricts our analysis to a smaller sample than desired (about 500 groups out of 1000). But we are confident to proceed with our analysis because the missing values mainly come from groups that are too small to be placed on the FTO list. Most groups with missing funding data have few recorded attacks and members.[76]

The second key independent variable is FTO designation of a group. The *FTO* is a binary measure indicating whether a group is on the FTO list in a particular year. A total of 49 groups are on the FTO list at some point. Some groups are delisted, switching the FTO indicator from one to zero. We interact

---

[74] One of the criteria for the FTO designation was the threat to US national security. In the analysis reported in this chapter, we did not count transnational attacks after 2007 but mainly incorporated domestic attacks. The results before 2007 with both transnational and domestic attacks do not substantively change compared to the whole sample.

[75] The ideal measure for us would be a measure of funding employing the concept of portfolio – reflecting the share of revenue for each funding type. This would give us a more valid measure for terrorist groups' financial vulnerability. Such information is present for some prominent groups that receive sufficient attention. For example, ISIL is funded by oil (38.7 percent), contracting work (37.9 percent), spoils (19.7 percent), real estate (2.8 percent) and miscellaneous 0.9 percent) activities, with little few private donations or foreign state sponsorship. AQIM acquired funds mostly from sales of spoils with geographic and temporal variations (Shapiro et al. 2016). But for many terrorist groups, even rough data do not exist. Currently, we are missing 40 percent of our funding data (4427 available out of 7397 total observations). This means that in most cases, funding information is not easy to track down, let alone the exact share of revenues.

[76] This claim is based on a logit analysis of missing observations in the funding variables.

the FTO variable with dummy indicators of funding type in our statistical analysis to examine the differential effects of FTO effect across funding types.

We also controlled for other correlates of terrorist attacks and FTO designation. *Group size* is a variable that measures the size of a terrorist group. It is a logarithm of a group's membership at its peak.[77] *Religious group* indicates if a group is characterized by religious motivations, rather than left-wing, right-wing, nationalist, or others.[78] *Political regime type* is the democracy score for the country the group is primarily based in, ranging from 0 to 10 indicating most autocratic to most democratic. It comes from the Quality of Government project.[79] Democratic countries often experience more terrorism.[80] We control for *GDP per capita* and *population* as economic development and country size might influence occurrence of terrorist attacks.[81]

Models include two variables that account for time trend and temporal patterns of terrorist attacks, as the capability to launch attacks is likely to change slowly. *Year trend* – a time counter for each year – accounts for global trends in terrorist attacks. To account for autocorrelation of terrorist attacks over time, we included *Attacks (lag)* – the number of terrorist attacks by a group in the previous year. Including the lagged dependent variable means our model is equivalent to estimating changes in attacks.

Since our dependent variable is a count, we employed a count model that accounts for between-subject heterogeneity as well as the over-dispersion of the data.[82] About two-thirds of the observations are zero for the dependent variable, and the occurrence of zeroes is probably non-random. To address this, we use zero-inflated negative binomial regression, a two-stage model where the first stage estimates the likelihood of a zero, and the second stage is a negative binomial regression.[83] The first stage includes all the independent variables of the count models except the interaction terms. It includes the variables that are likely to contribute to the generation of zeros in our dependent variable.

Table 9.1 reports our main results. Model 1 provides baseline estimates, and Models 2–5 include interaction terms to estimate FTO effects conditional on funding types. Interestingly, in Model 1 the coefficient on FTO

[77] Gaibulloev and Sandler 2013.
[78] Ibid.
[79] Dahlberg et al. 2017. The variable is primarily based on Freedom House, but uses the Polity2 variable to impute missing Freedom House data.
[80] Chenoweth 2013; Li 2005.
[81] Gaibulloev and Sandler 2013.
[82] The mean of our dependent variable, number of terrorist attacks, is 6.578 and the standard deviation is 29.917, indicating the overdispersion of the data.
[83] See Cameron and Trivedi 2013; Long and Freese 2014. A Vuong test suggests the zero-inflated model is preferable to regular negative binomial models, but we also report the results of negative binomial models in supplemental document because both types of models are commonly used in terrorist studies.

TABLE 9.1. *Statistical analysis of terrorist attacks and FTO designation*

	Model 1 No Interactions	Model 2 Private Funding	Model 3 State Sponsor	Model 4 Terrorist Networks	Model 5 Criminal Activities
FTO	0.425***	0.791***	0.409**	0.351**	0.461*
	(0.159)	(0.217)	(0.187)	(0.159)	(0.268)
Private funding		0.370**			
		(0.151)			
FTO * Private funding		−0.685***			
		(0.233)			
State sponsor			0.207		
			(0.156)		
FTO * State sponsor			−0.042		
			(0.245)		
Terrorist network				0.129	
				(0.216)	
FTO * Terrorist network				0.185	
				(0.303)	
Criminal activities					0.516***
					(0.142)
FTO * Criminal activities					−0.229
					(0.274)
Attacks (lag)	0.025***	0.025***	0.025***	0.025***	0.024***
	(0.005)	(0.005)	(0.005)	(0.005)	(0.005)
Group size (log)	0.208***	0.187***	0.202***	0.206***	0.164***
	(0.045)	(0.043)	(0.046)	(0.045)	(0.043)
Religious group	0.264	0.175	0.275	0.193	0.361*
	(0.214)	(0.215)	(0.217)	(0.238)	(0.211)
Regime type	0.026	0.024	0.029	0.026	0.017
	(0.029)	(0.029)	(0.029)	(0.030)	(0.031)
GDP per capita (log)	0.017	−0.042	0.037	0.009	0.035
	(0.089)	(0.086)	(0.093)	(0.092)	(0.095)
Population (log)	−0.066	−0.086	−0.051	−0.061	−0.105**
	(0.056)	(0.056)	(0.057)	(0.057)	(0.053)
Year trend	−0.027***	−0.028***	−0.026***	−0.027***	−0.024***
	(0.008)	(0.008)	(0.008)	(0.008)	(0.008)
N (groups)	4,758	4,758	4,758	4,758	4,758
	(412)	(412)	(412)	(412)	(412)

***$p < 0.01$, **$p < 0.05$, *$p < 0.1$.
Note: Dependent variable is the number of yearly terrorist attacks. Estimates are from zero-inflated negative binomial count models. Second stages of zero-inflated models are shown. Constants are not reported to save space. Robust standard errors in parentheses, clustered by terrorist group.

is statistically significant and positively signed suggesting that FTO status is correlated with increased terrorist attacks. However, this is an unconditional effect that does not take into consideration the heterogeneity of funding types. Model 2 includes the interaction of FTO status and private funding, and this interaction term is negative and statistically significant. This suggests that terrorist groups that use private funding are less likely to undertake attacks with FTO designation.[84] Private funding is positively correlated with attacks in the absence of FTO designation. None of the other funding types has a statistically significant interaction effect with FTO status.

Figure 9.1 reports the substantive effects of FTO status conditional upon funding types. The estimated impact of FTO status on a terrorist group that does not receive private funding such as donations is about five more attacks per year, with other variables held at their means. By contrast, the impact of FTO status is not conditional upon any of the other funding types. In the case

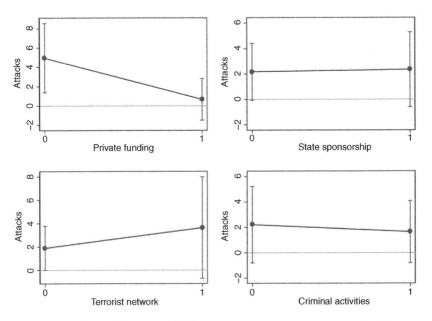

FIGURE 9.1. Estimated impact of FTO status on group terrorist attacks. Estimates from Model 5 in Table 9.1, with other variables at their means.

[84] We also conducted separate analysis with different types of terrorism, such as kidnapping and suicide bombing. The key result for Model 2 in relation to privately funded groups and FTO holds for kidnapping, but not suicide bombing. This is consistent with our theory that funding types will affect expensive operations such as large scale terrorist attacks or kidnapping, but do not travel to smaller scale terror operations such as suicide bombing. Results on file with authors.

of groups with terrorist networks or criminal activities, FTO appears to be associated with a slight increase in attacks, compared to groups without such funding. This provides some support for the idea that terrorist groups that use private funding are especially vulnerable to FTO designation.

For the approximately 75 percent of terrorist groups that do not receive private funding, FTO designation is associated with more attacks. However, there is no such association for the terrorist groups that use private funding. FTO designation appears to limit the momentum of privately funded groups that might otherwise have launched additional attacks.

Regarding control variables, some results are consistent with the literature. The lagged dependent variable is statistically significant and positively signed, suggesting groups' attacks the previous year are associated the current year's value. Larger groups are likely to wage more attacks, which is consistent with other studies. The coefficient on *Religious* groups is positively signed, but is usually statistically significant. This is consistent with mixed results in other studies. The coefficients on the state-level independent variables are mostly insignificant. This is perhaps because group-level variables are more important for explaining group behavior. Note that other studies of terrorist *group* attacks or lethality often do not find associations between these factors and, for example, regime type.[85] The results are robust to changes in estimator, such as regular negative binomial regression,[86] and also consistent to the inclusion of other control variables, such as other terrorist organization lists from Australia, Canada, EU, India, Russia, and UK.

We further checked whether non-random selection into the FTO list affects our results. The process of designation may influence the estimates for the FTO effects on terrorist attacks, so we examined whether that blacklisting process affects our inferences regarding FTO designation and terrorist attacks. Certain groups are likely to be designated as FTO groups in the first place. FTOs are large in size; they have a history of substantial and damaging terrorist attacks. Some anecdotal evidence suggests that US allies are actively involved in the FTO listing process. FTO list also includes a disproportionate number of Islamic groups.

More critically, the United States might strategically select easy targets such as terrorist groups with private funding. Taking stock of these correlates of FTO selection (group size, US ally,[87] past history of attacks, religious group, private funding dummy), we use coarsened exact matching (CEM) to match listed and

---

[85] e.g. Asal and Rethemyer 2008.

[86] Results on file with the authors.

[87] US Ally variable is a binary indicator of whether a host country has one of the military pacts: alliance treaty, defense pact, non-aggression pact, or entente. The data source is the Correlates of War Alliances database. Gibler 2009. International Military Alliances, 1648–2012.

not listed observations across different funding types, taking into account the FTO selection process.[88] CEM coarsens the data by placing bins and strata to create treatment and control groups (e.g. creating 43 matched strata out of selection covariates), finds exact matches (e.g. a large group in control reservoir, matched to a large group in treatment reservoir), and ultimately produces comparable matches between FTO and non-FTO observations. After implementing CEM, we estimate the zero-inflated negative binomial regression models with the weights created by CEM. The results are analogous to the ones reported in Table 9.1, except that the significance of the interactive term in Model 2 (private funding) is somewhat attenuated for a two-tailed hypothesis test. This check lends support for our conclusion about the differential impacts of blacklisting depending on the heterogeneity of funding among terrorist groups.

Finally, since FTO designation usually comes with the sanctioning tools such as travel bans or asset freezes, it is important to distinguish the effect of listing from sanctioning. Although we cannot cleanly parse out the effect of sanctions from listing, we can at least systematically test whether the listing effect holds when sanctioning is weak. We exploit the fact that sanctioning was weak before 9/11 and that increased dramatically after 9/11. If we are correct about the listing effect, we should still see the hypothesized private funding effect even for pre-9/11 sample. We report the results for pre- and post-9/11 in Table 9.2. It is essentially the same model reported in Table 9.1, Model 2 with two subsamples. We see that listing effect still exists pre-9/11 when sanctioning regime was weak, and that the FTO effect is relatively pronounced after 9/11 In light of this evidence, we conclude that listing effect is not ignorable and is fortified by sanctioning measures.

A few examples illustrate how our expectations work. We give examples of al-Qaeda, MeK, and the FARC to highlight the mechanisms we outline in this chapter, with regard to funding types, FTO designation, and responses by the terrorist organization.

The example of al-Qaeda demonstrates how terrorist organizations adapt. Al-Qaeda depended on opium trade before 1999.[89] With the support from the private donors from Saudi Arabia, the al-Qaeda central managed to carry out the September 11 attacks, even after designation as FTO in 1998. After the funds dried up with the augmented sanctions after the 9/11, the group transformed itself to be heavily linked to other terrorist groups and formed a broader network. FTO designation had little impact on al-Qaeda because their funding was hard to monitor and sanction after al-Qaeda adapted itself to new regulatory environment.[90]

Mujahedin-e-Khalq (MeK), in contrast, exclusively relied on US political support and diaspora networks in Europe. The legal actions by MeK challenging the

---

[88] Iacus et al. 2012. Results on file with the authors.

[89] UNSCR 1267.

[90] Stern and Modi 2008 highlight the importance of studying terrorist groups' adaptability.

TABLE 9.2. *Listing vs. sanctioning effect Analysis of Pre and Post-9/11 Subsamples*

	Model 1 Pre 9/11	Model 2 Post 9/11
FTO	0.433**	1.078***
	(0.181)	(0.357)
Private funding	0.367**	0.676**
	(0.169)	(0.304)
FTO * Private funding	−0.397*	−1.178**
	(0.235)	(0.457)
Attacks (lag)	0.0224***	0.0535***
	(0.00527)	(0.0156)
Group size (log)	0.189***	0.114
	(0.0477)	(0.0707)
Religious group	−0.104	0.465
	(0.268)	(0.287)
Regime type	0.0104	0.0435
	(0.0325)	(0.0521)
GDP per capita (log)	0.0203	−0.232
	(0.102)	(0.143)
Population (log)	−0.0548	−0.118
	(0.0697)	(0.0860)
Year trend	−0.0174*	0.0106
	(0.00907)	(0.0435)
N (groups)	3,349	1,219
	(315)	(256)

*** $p < 0.01$, ** $p < 0.05$, * $p < 0.1$.

Note: Dependent variable is the number of yearly terrorist attacks. Robust standard errors in parentheses, clustered by terrorist group.

FTO process as well as its renewed political lobbying after their FTO designation in 1997 are one indication that FTO listing indeed affected the terrorist organization's operations. Their dependency on private funding and donations seems to have made FTO listing more effective for this group than it was for others.

The example of the Revolutionary Armed Forces of Colombia (FARC) presents a different degree of vulnerability compared to MeK. The FARC once received support from Cuba, but mainly depended on drug trafficking and criminal activities. Criminal activities are difficult to monitor and punish through the sanctions imposition on the groups, and the stigmatization effect would be almost absent. Our political economy theory of blacklisting would predict that FARC would be less affected by the direct blacklisting or associated sanctions. The indirect path of US support for the Colombian government in the war on drugs had the later effect of reducing FARC's attack capability. This was not a direct consequence of the FTO designation, but associated ally support and consequence of designation politics.

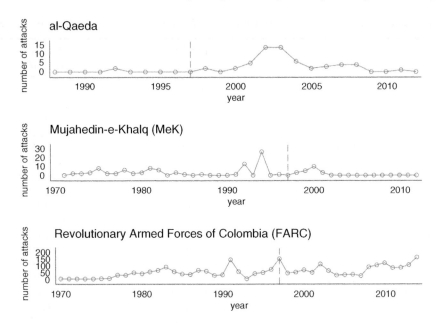

FIGURE 9.2. Terrorist attacks and funding types. Al-Qaeda, MeK, and FARC. Vertical dashed line indicates the year of FTO designation. Of the three groups, only MeK was heavily and singularly dependent on private funding such as donations.

The diverging attack series of the three groups in Figure 9.2 match our expectations about funding vulnerability and FTO designation.[91] All three groups were FTO-listed in 1997, but their attack patterns diverge: al-Qaeda attacks increased, MeK eventually reduced attacks, while FARC retained the same level of activity and even increased attacks, although eventually reducing attacks at the end of the series due to Plan Colombia and other pressures. The only group to show a substantial and sustained decrease in its attacks was MeK, which depended exclusively on private funding and was therefore more vulnerable to blacklisting. These examples serve as a reminder that funding heterogeneity might matter in understanding how the target responds to the blacklist. The examples indicate the variety of terrorist groups in terms of financing, and they suggest that recognizing heterogeneity is one of the key aspects to policy responses.

CONCLUSION

The power of GPIs, such as blacklisting, depends on the nature of the target. Blacklisting can change a target's behavior when the target is especially vulnerable to the erosion of its support base. We focused on terrorist groups' funding structure and vulnerability in assessing the potential impact of the

---

[91] For al-Qaeda series, we took al-Qaeda central as well as other associated/affiliated groups that have alleged alliance with the al-Qaeda central.

blacklisting. The target's vulnerability to blacklisting depends on terrorist groups' social, political, and economic relations. Terrorists themselves may not be shamed by the blacklist, but some of their social circles or supporters might feel shamed and vulnerable to changing regulations.

The importance of target heterogeneity has broader implications for the exercise of power in world politics. Not all targets of attempts at influence are equally vulnerable. In the case of terrorist groups, funding sources play a key role. Our findings also address the literature on naming and shaming. Consistent with the literature that finds both effective and ineffective tools,[92] we find that naming and shaming could contribute to the reduction of terrorist attacks in some groups that rely on private funding. But in other cases where terrorists can adapt to new funding sources, naming and shaming using blacklist could have no discernible impact or even unintended consequences.

Any effect of blacklisting will be attenuated when terrorist groups adapt and reinvent themselves. These potentially unintended consequences of backlash or setbacks should be considered and carefully monitored by policymakers. Combatting more adaptive groups will require other policy responses beyond blacklisting. Therefore, future policies should address target heterogeneity and the possibility that blacklisting may have intended and unintended consequences. The conditional effectiveness of blacklisting can be extended to other naming and shaming settings, especially the aspects of the heterogeneity of funding reliance on the side of target.

The analysis of the FTO list echoes the main theme of this volume on GPIs. Blacklisting triggers political and social mobilization of domestic and international actors. By re-framing the debate and boundary between legitimate and illegitimate activities globally, FTO designation engages, enables, and empowers networks of domestic and international stakeholders. In this respect, our chapter matches other chapters in this volume in terms of global indicators' social ramifications, and ensuing political changes. The key differences, though, are to bring in the role of non-state actors and to highlight the theoretical and empirical implications of target heterogeneity and vulnerability that can produce divergent global indicators' effects.

We also chart a number of paths for future research. One is the adaptability of terrorist organizations. Our data did not measure shifting resources of terrorist organizations because it is difficult to track down transformations in funding types over the years for most groups. But how terrorists adapt and innovate to regulations and blacklisting should be examined more.[93]

---

[92] Both DeMeritt 2012 and Krain 2012 find naming and shaming by international organizations reduces atrocities; Hafner-Burton 2008 however finds perverse effects of human rights naming and shaming where some governments ramp up violations.

[93] For example, al-Qaeda turned to kidnapping after a drop in donations (Braun 2011), which might have consequences for their attack patterns. Experts also note the adaptability of terrorist groups' war economy and decreasing use of philanthropic organizations for funding (Lake 2016). This may hint at terrorist groups' substitution strategy in response to FTO designation targeting private charities mainly.

Most importantly, the dynamics of blacklisting and how the target fully adapts to new regulatory environments was not fully explored in this chapter, as our focus was to show the link between terrorist groups' funding dependency and the FTO blacklisting effect. Group vulnerabilities generate divergent consequences for non-state actors such as rebel groups, terrorist organizations, or criminal gangs, regarding leadership targeting, government negotiations, and other interactions. A second point concerns how counterterrorism policies cohere. We focused on the impact of blacklisting, but the combination of sanctions and military interventions, for instance, likely generates different effects on the attack capacity of terrorist organizations. Future research could examine the joint impact of various counterterrorism efforts.

References

Asal, Victor, and R. Karl Rethemeyer. 2008. The Nature of the Beast: Organizational Structures and the Lethality of Terrorist Attacks. *Journal of Politics* 70 (2):437–49.

Bacon, Tricia. 2018. *Why Terrorist Groups Form International Alliances.* Philadelphia, PA: University of Pennsylvania Press.

Baker, Peter. 2017. White House Weighs Terrorist Designation for Muslim Brotherhood. *New York Times.* February 7. Available at https://www.nytimes.com/2017/02/07/world/middleeast/muslim-brotherhood-terrorism-trump.html?_r=0.

Bapat, Navin. 2011. Transnational Terrorism, US Military Aid, and the Incentive to Misrepresent. *Journal of Peace Research* 48 (3):303–18.

Beck, Colin, and Emily Miner. 2013. Who Gets Designated a Terrorist and Why? *Social Forces* 91(3):837–72.

Becker, Howard. 1997. *Outsiders: Studies in the Sociology of Deviance.* London: Free Press.

Bernburg, Jon Gunnar, Marvin Krohn, and Craig Rivera. 2006. Official Labeling, Criminal Embeddedness, and Subsequent Delinquency: A Longitudinal Test of Labeling Theory. *Journal of Research in Crime and Delinquency* 43(1):67–88.

Bisbee, James H., James R. Hollyer, B. Peter Rosendorff,and James Raymond Vreeland. this volume. The Millennium Development Goals and Education: Accountability and Substitution in Global Indicators. In *The Power of Global Performance Indicators,* edited by Judith Kelley and Beth A. Simmons. New York: Cambridge University Press.

Blomberg, S. Brock, Khusrav Gaibulloev, and Todd Sandler. 2011. Terrorist Group Survival: Ideology, Tactics, and Base of Operations. *Public Choice* 149: 441–463.

Boutton, Andrew, and David Carter. 2014. Fair Weather Allies: Terrorism and the Allocation of United States Foreign Aid. *Journal of Conflict Resolution* 58(7):1144–73.

Braun, Stephen. 2011. Al-Qaida Turns to Kidnappings as Donations Drop. *NBC News.* Available at http://www.nbcnews.com/id/43457579/ns/world_news-south_and_central_asia/t/al-qaida-turns-kidnappings-donations-drop/. Accessed March 20, 2016.

Burr, Millard, and Robert Collins. 2006. *Alms for Jihad: Charity and Terrorism in the Islamic World.* Cambridge: Cambridge University Press.

Byman, Daniel. 2005. *Deadly Connections: States That Sponsor Terrorism.* Cambridge: Cambridge University Press.

Cameron, Colin, and Prvain Trivedi. 2013. *Regression Analysis of Count Data.* Cambridge: Cambridge University Press.

Carter, David. 2012. A Blessing or a Curse? State Support for Terrorist Groups. *International Organization* 66(1):129–51.

Chenoweth, Erica. 2013. Terrorism and Democracy. *Annual Review of Political Science* 16:355–78.

Crenshaw, Martha and Gary LaFree. 2017. *Countering Terrorism.* Washington, DC: Brookings Institution.

Cronin, Audrey. 2009. *How Terrorism Ends: Understanding the Decline and Demise of Terrorist Campaigns.* Princeton, NJ: Princeton University Press.

——— 2011. Why the Haqqani Network Is Not on the Foreign Terrorist Organizations List: The Politics of Naming and Shaming. *Foreign Affairs,* December 21, 2011. Available at https://www.foreignaffairs.com/articles/ 2011-12-21/why-haqqani-network-not-foreign-terrorist-organizations-list. Accessed December 27, 2015.

——— 2012. Politics, Strategy, and the Haqqani Network. *Small Wars Journal,* September 6. Available at http://smallwarsjournal.com/author/ audrey-kurth-cronin.

Cronin, Audrey Kurth. 2003. The "FTO List" and Congress: Sanctioning Designated Foreign Terrorist Organizations, Congressional Research Service (CRS) Report RL32120. Available at http://fas.org/irp/crs/ RL32120.pdf. Accessed December 27, 2015.

Cronin, Audrey Kurth, Huda Aden, Adam Frost, and Benjamin Jones. 2004. Foreign Terrorist Organizations. *Congressional Research Service (CRS) Report* RL32223. Available at https://fas.org/irp/crs/RL32223.pdf. Accessed December 27, 2015.

Curtis, Lisa. 2012. Combating the Haqqani Terrorist Network. Testimony before the Committee on Foreign Affairs, Subcommittee on Terrorism, Nonproliferation, and Trade, United States House of Representatives, September 13, 2012.

Dahlberg, Stefan, Sören Holmberg, Bo Rothstein, Anna Khomenko, and Richard Svensson. 2017. The Quality of Government Basic Dataset, version Jan17. University of Gothenburg: The Quality of Government Institute. Available at http://www.qog.pol.gu.se.

Decker, Eileen. 2014. The Enemies List: The Foreign Terrorist Organization List and Its Role in Defining Terrorism. Master's Thesis in Security Studies (Homeland Defense and Security). Naval Postgraduate School. Available at https://www.hsdl.org/?view&did=753810. Accessed December 29, 2015.

DeMeritt, Jacqueline. 2012. International Organizations and Government Killing: Does Naming and Shaming Save Lives? *International Interactions* 38 (5):597–621.

DeYoung, Karen. 2012. Haqqani Network to be Designated a Terrorist Group. *Washington Post,* September 7, 2012. Available at https:// www.washingtonpost.com/world/national-security/haqqani-network- to-be-designated-a-terrorist-group-obama-officials-say/2012/09/07/e6576aco- f8f6-11e1-a073-78d05495927c_story.html. Accessed February 4, 2016.

Early, Brian. 2015. *Busted Sanctions: Explaining Why Economic Sanctions Fail*. Stanford, CA: Stanford University Press.

Feldman, Philip. 1977. *Criminal Behavior: A Psychological Analysis*. London: John Wiley & Sons.

Financial Action Task Force. 2008. Terrorist Financing. FATF/OECD, February 29, 2008.

Finnström, Sverker. 2008. *Living with Bad Surroundings: War, History, and Everyday Moments in Northern Uganda*. Durham, NC: Duke University Press.

Freedman, Benjamin. 2010. Officially Blacklisted Extremist/Terrorist (Support) Organizations: A Comparison of Lists from Six Countries and Two International Organizations. *Perspectives on Terrorism* 4 (2):46–52.

Gaibulloev, Khusrav, and Todd Sandler. 2013. Determinants of the Demise of Terrorist Organizations. *Southern Economic Journal* 79 (4):774–92.

2014. An Empirical Analysis of Alternative Ways that Terrorist Groups End. *Public Choice* 160 (1–2):25–44.

Gagalac, Ron. 2017. CPP-NPA Is Still a Terrorist Group, US Says. *ABS-CBN News*, February 3, 2017. Available at http://news.abs-cbn.com/news/02/02/17/cpp-npa-is-still-a-terrorist-group-us-says.

GAO. 2015. Combating Terrorism: Foreign Terrorist Organization Designation Process and U.S. Agency Enforcement Actions. United States Government Accountability Office. June 2015. GAO-15-629. Available at http://www.gao.gov/assets/680/671028.pdf. Accessed January 21, 2016.

Gibler, Douglas. 2009. *International Military Alliances, 1648–2008*. Washington, DC: CQ Press.

Hafner-Burton, Emilie M. 2008. Sticks and Stones: Naming and Shaming the Human Rights Enforcement Problem. *International Organization* 62 (4):689–716.

Head, Michael. 2016. Global Governance Implications of Terrorism: Using UN Resolutions to Justify Abuse of Basic Rights. In *Transnational Governance: Emerging Models of Global Legal Regulation*, edited by Mann, Scott, 179–212. London: Routledge.

Hess, Michel. 2007. Substantiating the Nexus between Diaspora Groups and the Financing of Terrorism. In *Terronomics*, edited by Sean Costigan and David Gold, 49–63. Aldershot: Ashgate.

Hoffman, Bruce. 2006. *Inside Terrorism*. New York: Columbia University Press.

Hufbauer, Gary, and Thomas Moll. 2007. Using Sanctions to Fight Terrorism. In *Terronomics*, edited by Sean Costigan and David Gold, 179–94. Aldershot: Ashgate.

Iacus, Stefano, Gary King, and Giuseppe Porro. 2012. Causal Inference without Balance Checking: Coarsened Exact Matching. *Political Analysis* 20 (1):1–24.

International Crisis Group. 2010. The Sri Lankan Tamil Diaspora after the LTTE. Crisis Group Asia Report N°186, February 23, 2010.

Jarvis, Lee, and Tim Legrand. 2018. The Proscription or Listing of Terrorist Organizations: Understanding, Assessment, and International Comparisons. *Terrorism and Political Violence* 30 (2):199–215.

Johnston, Patrick, Jacob Shapiro, Howard J. Shatz, Benjamin Bahney, Danielle F. Jung, Patrick Ryan, and Jonathan Wallace. 2016. *Foundations of the Islamic State: Management, Money, and Terror in Iraq, 2005–2010*. Santa Monica, CA: RAND Corporation.

Jones, Seth, and Martin Libicki. 2008. *How Terrorist Groups End: Lessons for Countering al Qaida.* Santa Monica, CA: RAND Corporation.

Karmon, Eli. 2005. *Coalitions Between Terrorist Organizations: Revolutionaries, Nationalists, and Islamists.* Leiden: Brill Academic Publishers.

Koliev, Faraj, Thomas Sommerer,and Jonas Tallberg. this volume. Reporting Matters: Performance Assessment and Compliance in the ILO. *The Power of Global Performance Indicators.* New York: Cambridge University Press.

Krain, Matthew. 2012. J'accuse! Does Naming and Shaming Perpetrators Reduce the Severity of Genocides or Politicides? *International Studies Quarterly* 56 (3):574–89.

Lake, Eli. 2016. US Stopped Blacklisting Domestic Terror Charities under Obama. *Bloomberg,* May 12, 2016. Available at https://www.bloomberg.com/view/articles/2016-05-12/u-s-stopped-blacklisting-domestic-terror-charities-under-obama.

Lee, Melissa M., and Aila M. Matanock. this volume. Third Party Policymakers and the Limits of the Influence of Indicators. Chapter 11 in *The Power of Global Performance Indicators.* Cambridge: Cambridge University Press.

Legrand, Tim. 2018. More Symbolic—More Political—Than Substantive: An Interview with James R. Clapper on the U.S. Designation of Foreign Terrorist Organizations. *Terrorism and Political Violence* 30:356–72.

Leuprecht, Christian, Olivier Walther, David B. Skillicorn, and Hillary Ryde-Collins. 2015. Hezbollah's Global Tentacles: A Relational Approach to Convergence with Transnational Organised Crime. *Terrorism and Political Violence.* doi:10.1080/09546553.2015.1089863.

Levitt, Matthew. 2002. Designating the al-Aqsa Martyrs Brigades. *PolicyWatch* 371. *Washington Institute,* March 25, 2002. Available at http://www.washingtoninstitute.org/policy-analysis/view/designating-the-al-aqsa-martyrs-brigades.

———. 2004. Charitable Organizations and Terrorist Financing: A War on Terror Status-Check. Washington Institute for Near East Policy, March 19. Available at http://www.washingtoninstitute.org/policy-analysis/view/charitable-organizations-and-terrorist-financing-a-war-on-terror-status-che.

Li, Quan. 2005. Does Democracy Promote or Reduce Transnational Terrorist Incidents? *Journal of Conflict Resolution* 49 (2):278–97.

Link, Bruce, Francis Cullen, Elmer Struening, Patrick Shrout, and BruceDohernwend. 1989. A Modified Labeling Theory Approach to Mental Disorders: An Empirical Assessment. *American Sociological Review* 54 (3):400–23.

Lobe, Jim, and Jasmin Ramsey. 2012. U.S. to Take Iran Anti-Regime Group Off Terrorism List. *Inter Press Service News Agency,* September 22. Available at http://www.ipsnews.net/2012/09/u-s-to-take-iran-anti-regime-group-off-terrorism-list/.

Long, Scott, and Jeremy Freese. 2014. *Regression Models for Categorical Dependent Variables Using Stata.* College Station, TX: Stata Press.

Mills, Kurt. 2015. *International Responses to Mass Atrocities in Africa.* Philadelphia, PA: Pennsylvania University Press.

Modirzadeh, Naz, Dustin Lewis, and Claude Bruderlein. 2011. Humanitarian Engagement under Counter-Terrorism: A Conflict of Norms and the Emerging Policy Landscape. *International Review of the Red Cross* 93 (883):623–47.

Morse, Julia C. this volume. Blacklists, Market Enforcement, and the Global
    Regime to Combat Terrorist Financing. *Annual Meeting of the American
    Political Science Association.*
Murphy, Sean. 2003. *United States Practice in International Law: Volume 1,
    1999–2001.* Cambridge: Cambridge University Press.
National Consortium for the Study of Terrorism and Responses to Terrorism.
    2009. *Global Terrorism Database (GTD) (CD-ROM).* College Park,
    MD: University of Maryland.
Nemeth, Stephen, Jacob Mauslein, and Craig Stapley. 2014. The Primacy of
    the Local: Identifying Terrorist Hot Spots Using Geographic Information
    Systems. *Journal of Politics* 76 (2): 304–17.
Paternoster, Raymond, and Ronet Bachman. 2012. Labeling Theory. In
    Oxford Bibliographies in Criminology, edited by Richard Wright.
    Oxford: Oxford University Press.
Phillips, Brian J. 2014. Terrorist Group Cooperation and Longevity.
    International Studies Quarterly 58 (2):336–47.
    2015. What Is a Terrorist Group? Conceptual Issues and Empirical
    Implications. *Terrorism and Political Violence* 27 (2):225–42.
    2019. Foreign Terrorist Organization Designation, International
    Cooperation, and Terrorism. *International Interactions* 45 (2): 316–43.
Piazza, James A., and Scott Piazza. 2017. Crime Pays: Terrorist Group
    Engagement in Crime and Survival. *Terrorism and Political Violence,*
    OnlineFirst.
Radtke, Mitchell, and Hyeran Jo. 2018. Fighting the Hydra: United Nations
    Sanctions and Rebel Groups. *Journal of Peace Research* 55 (6):759–73.
RAND. 2012. *RAND Database of Worldwide Terrorism Incidents.* Available
    at http://www.rand.org/nsrd/projects/terrorism-incidents.html. Accessed
    August 3, 2012.
Ranstorp, Magnus and Paul Wilkinson. 2013. *Terrorism and Human Rights.*
    London: Routledge.
Roberts, Adam. 2012. *Democracy, Sovereignty and Terror.* London: I.B.Tauris.
Said, Wadie. 2015. *Crimes of Terror: The Legal and Political Implications of
    Federal Terrorism Prosecutions.* New York: Oxford University Press.
Salehyan, Idean, David Sirosky, and Reed Wood. 2014. Delegation and
    Civilian Abuse: A Principle-Agent Analysis of Wartime Atrocities.
    International Organization 68 (3):633–61.
Shapiro, Jacob. 2013. *The Terrorist's Dilemma: Managing Violent Covert
    Organizations.* Princeton, NJ: Princeton University Press.
Shapiro, Jacob, Patrick Johnston, Howard J. Shatz, Benjamin Bahney, Danielle
    F. Jung, Patrick K. Ryan, and Jonathan Wallace. 2016. *Foundations of the
    Islamic State: Management, Money, and Terror in Iraq.* Santa Monica,
    CA: RAND Corporation.
Shelley, Louise I. 2014. *Dirty Entanglements: Corruption, Crime, and
    Terrorism.* New York: Cambridge University Press.
State Department. 1997. Designation of Foreign Terrorist Organizations.
    Office of the Coordinator for Counterterrorism. Federal Register. 52650.
    Vol. 62, No. 195. Wednesday October 8.
    2014. Amendments to, and Maintenance of, the Terrorist Designations of Harakat
    ul-Mujahidin. Media Note, Office of the Spokesperson, Washington, DC,
    August 7. Available at http://www.state.gov/r/pa/prs/ps/2014/230373.htm.

Stern, Jessica, and Amit Modi. 2008. Producing Terror: Organizational Dynamics of Survival. In *Countering the Financing of Terrorism*, edited by Thomas Biersteker and Sue Eckert. London: Routledge.

Treasury Department. 2014. Terrorist Assets Report. Twenty-second Annual Report to the Congress on Assets in the United States Relating to Terrorist Countries and International Terrorism Program Designees. Office of Foreign Assets Control. US Department of the Treasury. Available at https://www.treasury.gov/resource-center/sanctions/Programs/ Documents/tar2013.pdf. Accessed January 21, 2016.

———. 2016. US Department of the Treasury. "Designated Charities and Potential Fundraising Front Organizations for FTOs" Protecting Charitable Organizations under Terrorism and Illicit Finance, Treasury Department Resource Center. Available at https://www.treasury.gov/resource-center/ terrorist-illicit-finance/Pages/protecting-fto.aspx. Accessed May 4, 2016.

Vittori, Jodi. 2011. *Terrorist Financing and Resourcing*. New York: Palgrave MacMillan.

Wellens, Karel. 2015. *International Law in Silver Perspective: Challenges Ahead*. Leiden: Brill.

Zahid, Farhan. 2015. Islamist Charity Organizations: Avenues of Terrorism Financing in Pakistan. *Foreign Analysis* No. 30. Centre Francais de Recherche sur le Renseignement.

Assessing International Organizations

Competition, Collaboration, and Politics of Funding

Ranjit Lall*

INTRODUCTION

During the past decade, states have initiated a striking trend in global governance: the development and promulgation of indicators of the performance of international organizations (IOs). These assessments possess all of the defining characteristics of global performance indicators (GPIs) outlined by Kelley and Simmons in the introduction to this volume. They are available to citizens of any country free of charge (*publicity*); they cover multiple IOs, including all those that regularly receive substantial funding from the government in question (*inclusiveness*); they rate IOs on a common numerical or ordinal scale (*comparativeness*); and they are typically updated on a consistent multiyear basis (*regularity*). Perhaps most importantly from an analytical perspective, the assessments are *purposive*: they were created to help policymakers make more efficient use of their multilateral funding in the context of budgetary pressures induced by the global economic crisis. In other words, they were conceived with the explicit intention of influencing financial resource flows to IOs.

A cursory examination of funding patterns since the emergence of the indicators, however, reveals an intriguing puzzle: only resource flows to *some* assessed IOs show signs of responsiveness to performance ratings. That is, for one subset of assessed IOs, there is a strong positive relationship between ratings and resource flows: high ratings have been met with a sizable increase in financial contributions, whereas low ratings have been followed by funding

* For valuable feedback on earlier drafts of this chapter, I am indebted to Daniel Drezner, Jeffry Frieden, Hyeran Jo, Judith Kelley, Christopher Lucas, Walter Mattli, Beth Simmons, Anton Strezhnev, and participants in the 2016 Conference on Assessment Power at Harvard University and the Mini-conference on Global Assessment Power at the 2016 Annual Meeting of the American Political Science Association. Supplementary materials can be accessed at the following link: https://scholar.harvard.edu/files/ranjitlall/files/online_appendix_lall_ch10_pgpi.pdf.

cuts or freezes. For instance, while the strongly rated Office of the United Nations High Commissioner for Refugees (UNHCR) has seen its annual contributions rise by more than 50 percent since the release of its first set of ratings, the poorly rated Joint United Nations Programme on HIV/AIDS (UNAIDS) has seen them fall by almost one fifth. For another subset of assessed IOs, by contrast, there is no clear relationship between ratings and resource flows, with high-rated institutions seeing no financial "reward" and low-rated ones avoiding any "punishment." Despite receiving similar ratings to UNHCR, for example, the European Development Fund (EDF) has suffered a decline in contributions comparable to that of UNAIDS. Conversely, despite receiving similar ratings to UNAIDS, the United Nations Environment Programme (UNEP) has enjoyed an increase in funding comparable to that of UNHCR.

These surprising differences pose a challenge to the few existing theories of the determinants of IO funding. Traditional analyses of the budgetary process in IOs draw attention to how procedural rules and practices constrain the ability of states to alter the size and composition of the budget, resulting in a high degree of stability in funding levels over time.[1] Yet as the above examples suggest, resource flows to many IOs have exhibited significant change since the release of the performance indicators. The more recent literature on the concept of delegation to IOs highlights the tendency of "state principals" to use the budget as an instrument for deterring and sanctioning opportunistic behavior by "IO agents," implying that they will respond to performance indicators by increasing funding for IOs with strong ratings and reducing funding for IOs with weak ratings.[2] Once again, however, this prediction is not consistent with the pattern described earlier: only some high-rated institutions have received additional contributions, while only some low-rated ones have been subject to cuts. This pattern suggests the need for a more nuanced analysis of the factors affecting whether states and other donors are responsive to ratings. In other words, it calls for an answer to the question: *Under what conditions do IO performance indicators influence resource flows to these institutions?*

Analyzing ratings as a form of social knowledge that draws attention and gives meaning to institutional performance, I develop an argument that highlights how different aspects of the *relationship* between IOs and other actors within their policy space mediate the financial effects of such knowledge. Two aspects are particularly important. The first is the degree of competition IOs face from institutions performing similar functions to them. When competition is intense – which is most likely in policy spaces characterized by low barriers to entry and diseconomies of

---

[1] Ackrill and Kay 2006; Hoole, Handley, and Ostrom 1979; Hoole, Job, and Tucker 1976; Singer 1961.

[2] As one influential study of delegation states, "Agents that are perceived as succeeding in their missions are rewarded with larger budgets, allowing individuals to perform their jobs more easily or supervise larger staffs with compensatory benefits. Agents that are perceived as failing are punished with smaller budgets, and may even be eliminated entirely." Hawkins et al. 2006, 30. Also see Nielson and Tierney 2003; Pollack 1997.

scale in the provision of goods – donors act on material and social incentives to respond to ratings because IOs have a large number of substitutes to which they can reallocate resources. When competition is limited, however, IOs have few or no substitutes, deterring donors from either sanctioning low-rated IOs or rewarding high-rated ones. The second aspect is the robustness of governance partnerships between IOs and non-state actors – both domestic and transnational – who possess complementary skills and resources and can thus enhance their capacity to achieve organizational objectives. I argue that robust partnerships render resource flows more responsive to ratings by incentivizing partners to assist high-rated IOs in mobilizing additional funds but – perhaps surprisingly – to weaken or exit partnerships with low-rated IOs, exacerbating the reputational damage suffered by such institutions and raising fears that they may perform even worse in the future. In short, the financial consequences of IO performance indicators are conditioned in critical ways by institutional relationships of competition and collaboration.

I test the argument using a mixed-methods approach. I begin by examining qualitative evidence on the assessments' financial effects from a selection of primary and secondary sources – most notably interviews with more than 80 IO officials and donor representatives – probing different behavioral as well as non-behavioral implications of the argument. I then conduct statistical tests of the argument based on an original dataset including all six sets of performance indicators issued thus far, which collectively cover 54 IOs spanning a wide range of issue areas. My methodological strategy involves analyzing – in both observational and quasi-experimental settings – the relationship between post-assessment changes in resource flows and multiplicative interaction terms between each set of indicators and the two conditioning variables highlighted by my argument. To gather information on institutional competition, I designed and implemented a survey of officials from all 54 assessed IOs. Data on governance partnerships were collected through a comprehensive mapping exercise covering all forms of substantive collaboration between IOs and non-state actors during five key stages of the international policymaking process.

By theorizing and empirically examining the financial consequences of IO performance indicators, the chapter contributes to our understanding of global assessment power in three ways. First, it draws attention to a substantively significant yet previously neglected area in which GPIs have emerged in recent years. In doing so, it provides a fitting counterpoint to the other contributions to this volume, most of which examine GPIs that evaluate states and are developed by IOs.[3] Second, it presents the first systematic evidence that GPIs can influence resource allocation decisions by public actors, extending recent analyses in the economics and management literatures demonstrating their impact on the behavior of private investors.[4] Such evidence, moreover,

---

[3] See Bisbee et al.; Kelley, Simmons, and Doshi, and Morse, this volume.

[4] Aaron, McMillan, and Cline 2012; Brammer, Brooks, and Pavelin 2009; Murguia and Lence 2015.

comes from an area in which the material stakes are high: the 54 assessed IOs have jointly received more than half a trillion dollars in contributions over the past decade. Third, and most significantly from a theoretical perspective, it sheds new light on *when* and *why* – and not just whether – GPIs matter in world politics by examining the conditions under which they exert social influence. My argument complements existing analyses of GPI scope conditions (in this volume as well as in fields such as anthropology and international law), which mostly focus on characteristics of GPIs and their creators, by highlighting how the broader relational context in which assessed entities operate mediates their effects.[5] It thus enhances our analytical understanding of the mechanisms by which shared information and knowledge can become a source of power in the contemporary international system – and, equally important, the limits of such power.

The chapter also makes contributions to a number of other emerging areas of research in international relations. First, it complements recent work on institutional choice and organizational ecology in global governance by showing how institutional environments influence the effects of common information and knowledge as well as patterns of long-run institutional change.[6] Second, and relatedly, it joins a growing number of studies in investigating the consequences of institutional competition at the global level, an issue that has traditionally received little attention in the international relations literature.[7] Unlike previous scholarship, however, it examines the material as well as political ramifications of competition and gathers systematic data on the variable covering a diverse sample of institutions. Third, it extends recent research on the phenomenon of IO orchestration by drawing attention to the critical role of governance partnerships in conditioning the financial effects of IO performance indicators.[8] Finally, as suggested above, it contributes to the burgeoning literature on delegation and principal-agent theory by showing – contrary to the conventional wisdom – that state principals only financially reward and sanction IO agents in response to performance information under certain relational conditions.[9]

IO PERFORMANCE ASSESSMENTS: OVERVIEW AND PUZZLE

To illustrate the puzzling variation in the relationship between IO performance indicators and resource flows, I begin with a brief overview of the assessments. As summarized in Table 10.1, since 2008 indicators have been

---

[5] See Cooley and Snyder 2015; Davis, Merry, and Kingsbury 2015; Davis et al. 2012; Kelley and Simmons; Lee and Matanock, this volume. Note that Bisbee et al. argue that GPA effects are mediated by characteristics of assessed entities themselves (namely, democratic accountability and transparency).
[6] Abbott, Green, and Keohane 2016; Jupille, Mattli, and Snidal 2013.
[7] Abbott, Green, and Keohane 2016; Alter and Meunier 2009; Frey 2008; Lipscy 2015.
[8] Abbott et al. 2015; Mattli and Seddon 2015.
[9] See, for instance, Hawkins et al. 2006; Nielson and Tierney 2003; Pollack 1997.

TABLE 10.1. *Summary of IO performance assessments*

| | Assessment | | | | | | MOPAN | |
	Australia	United Kingdom	Denmark	Netherlands	Sweden		Survey	Review
Year(s)	2012	2011, 2016	2012	2011, 2013, 2015	2008–2011		2010–2014	
IOs	41	41	17	31	23		16	
Main data sources		Stakeholder consultations, written submissions; field visits; MOPAN and Paris Aid surveys; other GPIs, e.g. QuODA, Publish What You Fund ATI, COMPAS indicators	MOPAN surveys; ratings from British assessment	IO documents; internal/external evaluations; audits; feedback from overseas missions; MOPAN surveys	IO documents; feedback from overseas missions		Cross-national survey of public and private stakeholders	IO documents (analyzed by two consulting firms)
Indicators		Delivery of results; contribution to international community's objectives; cost consciousness; financial management; transparency and accountability; strategic/performance management	One overall measure	Results control, strategy, focus on core mandate, effective governance, policy evaluation, human resources policy, financial management, anti-corruption policy	Internal and external effectiveness		Providing direction for results; corporate, country focus on results; thematic priorities; resource allocation; performance-oriented allocation, programming, financial accountability; using, presenting performance information; managing human resources; evaluating results; learning lessons	

Assessment

	Australia	United Kingdom	Denmark	Netherlands	Sweden	MOPAN Survey	MOPAN Review
Year(s)	2012	2011, 2016	2012	2011, 2013, 2015	2008–2011	2010–2014	
IOs	41	41	17	31	23	16	
Scale	Numerical (1–4)	Numerical (1–4)	Numerical (3.2–4.8)	Numerical (1–4)	Categorical (6 groups)	Numerical (1–6)	
r within assessment	0.49	0.57	–	0.40	0.89	0.67	0.23
r across assessments	0.60	0.58	0.31	0.44	0.32	0.31	0.36

Abbreviations: MOPAN = Multilateral Organisation Performance Assessment Network; QuODA = Quality of Official Development Assistance; ATI = Aid Transparency Index; COMPAS = Common Performance Assessment System.

produced by five states – Australia, Denmark, the Netherlands, Sweden, and the United Kingdom – and the Multilateral Organization Performance Assessment Network (MOPAN), a group comprising 17 of the largest donor countries (including all of the previous five) that seeks to enhance knowledge of IO effectiveness.[10] Four of the six sets of indicators have been issued more than once, with the Australian and Danish assessments still awaiting their first update. The indicators are based on a mixture of new and existing data sources, including cross-national surveys, stakeholder consultations, feedback from diplomatic missions, and other GPIs such as the Quality of Official Development Assistance (QuODA) Assessment and the Publish What You Fund Aid Transparency Index (ATI).[11] As mentioned earlier, they collectively cover 54 IOs – a full list is provided in the chapter appendix – that span a diverse range of issue areas, including agriculture, development, the environment, human rights, public health, and trade. The Australian and British assessments have the widest organizational coverage (41 IOs each), while the MOPAN assessment has the narrowest (16 IOs).

International organizations are assessed on six distinct dimensions of institutional performance: (1) delivery of results; (2) cost and value consciousness; (3) resource management; (4) accountability and transparency; (5) strategic management; and (6) knowledge management.[12] The Australian, British, and Dutch assessments include between six and eight discrete numerical indicators of these dimensions ranging from 1 ("Weak"/"Unsatisfactory") to 4 ("Very Strong"/"Strong"). The MOPAN assessment contains 14 numerical indicators measuring the third, fifth, and sixth dimensions. The IOs are assigned two scores from 1 to 6 on each indicator, one based on a multicountry stakeholder survey (a continuous scale) and other based on a review of organizational documents by two consulting firms (a discrete scale). The Swedish assessment contains two categorical indicators, "internal effectiveness" and "external effectiveness," on which IOs are ranked in six classes spanning from "Very Low" to "Very High."[13] Finally, the Danish assessment contains just one overall performance measure, a continuous numerical scale from 3.2 to 4.8.

---

[10] The documents comprising each set of ratings can be found at the following links (all accessed February 21, 2015): http://dfat.gov.au/about-us/publications/Pages/australian-multilateral-assessment-ama-full-report.aspx (Australia); http://www.ft.dk/samling/20111/almdel/uru/bilag/245/1153552.pdf (Denmark); http://www.mopanonline.org/Assessments/ (MOPAN); https://www.rijksoverheid.nl/zoeken?trefwoord=scorecard (Netherlands); http://www.government.se/search/?query=%22swedish+assessment%22 (Sweden); https://www.gov.uk/government/collections/multilateral-aid-review (United Kingdom).

[11] On the ATI, see Honig and Weaver this volume.

[12] All six correspond to one of the three dimensions of institutional performance traditionally emphasized in the organizational theory and public administration literatures on the concept: (1) the achievement of stated objectives; (2) cost-effectiveness; and (3) responsiveness to a wide range of stakeholders. See Cameron 1978; Etzioni 1964; and Price 1972. Some assessments include additional indicators that do not correspond to any of these dimensions and are thus excluded from consideration.

[13] I convert these categories into a 1–6 numerical scale in the subsequent analyses.

Within the five assessments that contain multiple performance indicators, there is a strong positive correlation among ratings. That is, IOs with higher (or lower) ratings on some dimensions of performance also tend to have higher (or lower) ratings on others. As shown in Table 10.1, the mean correlation among indicator scores from each wave of a given assessment *a* between its initial release (*year t_a*) and 2015 is $r = 0.53$ (more than four-fifths of the 532 individual coefficients are positive and statistically significant at the 10 percent level). Interestingly, ratings are also strongly and positively correlated *across* assessments. The mean correlation between averages of each set of indicator scores in the period from year t_a to 2015 is $r = 0.42$ (17 of the 21 coefficients are positive and significant). In other words, there is a high degree of consensus among the assessments about which IOs are performing well and which are performing poorly.

Figure 10.1 provides a graphical overview of the relationship between performance ratings and over-time changes in resource flows to assessed IOs.

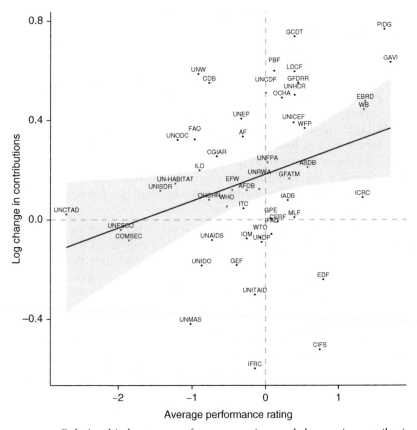

FIGURE 10.1. Relationship between performance ratings and changes in contributions.

The x-axis measures the standardized mean of an IO's indicator scores from all assessments averaged over the period from the release of its first set of ratings (year u_{IO}) to 2015. The y-axis measures the log ratio of an IO's average annual contributions since financial year $(FY)u_{IO}$ to its contributions in the previous FY $u_{IO} - 1$:

$$y = ln\left(\frac{\frac{\sum_{i=0}^{n} CONTRIBUTIONS_{u_{IO}+i}}{n}}{CONTRIBUTIONS_{u_{IO}-1}}\right)$$

Data on contributions, which were collected from IO financial statements and annual reports (acquired online and in some cases through personal communications with officials), are all converted into millions of United States dollars at contemporary exchange rates and adjusted for inflation using the Bureau of Labor Statistics' Consumer Price Index (with 2003 as the base year).

The scatterplot reveals striking variation in post-assessment funding trends among both high- and low-rated IOs. For approximately half of the sample, trends are consistent with a straightforward "GPA influence hypothesis": IOs with higher ratings have received proportionally larger increases in contributions since FY u_{IO} (roughly the lower-left and upper-right quadrants of the graph). For the remaining institutions, however, trends provide little support for the hypothesis: IOs with below-average ratings have received disproportionately large increases in funding (upper-left quadrant), while IOs with above-average ratings have seen either disproportionately small increases or absolute decreases (lower-right quadrant). The upshot of these differences is that the overall relationship between x and y is positive but relatively weak, with only 16 of the 54 IOs falling inside the shaded 95 percent confidence interval around the regression line.

Figures 10.2 and 10.3 provide a micro-level view of such variation by displaying time-series data on resource flows to 12 individual IOs.[14] For the six institutions in Figure 10.2, funding patterns are consistent with the GPA influence hypothesis: the first three (reading from left to right) have received high ratings and enjoyed robust growth in contributions since FY u_{IO}; the last three have received low ratings and experienced weak or negative growth. Visual analysis of the timing of these changes provides prima facie evidence that they were a direct response to the ratings rather than a product of broader (exogenous) shifts in funding. The six institutions in Figure 10.3 display the opposite patterns: the first three have received high ratings, but subsequently suffered a

---

[14] I return to a number of these institutions in the fourth section, providing qualitative evidence on the factors shaping their funding trends.

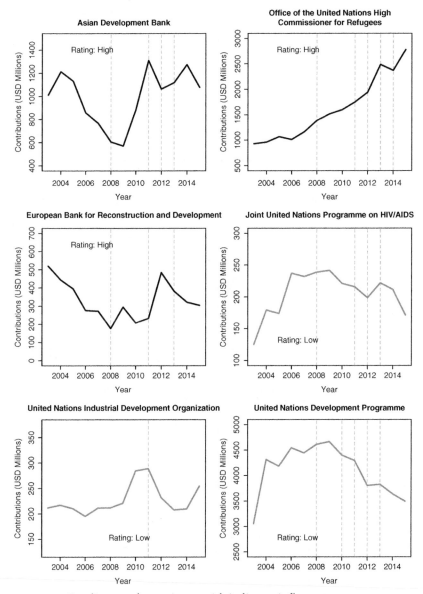

FIGURE 10.2. Funding trends consistent with indicator influence.
Note: The dotted lines indicate the years in which an IO has been assessed.

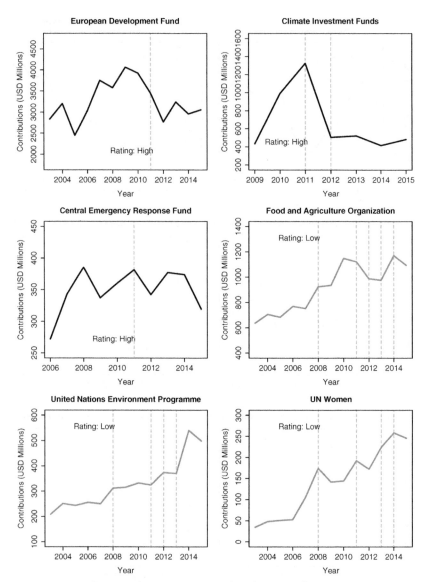

FIGURE 10.3. Funding trends inconsistent with indicator influence.
Note: The dotted lines indicate the years in which an IO has been assessed.

stagnation or decline in contributions; the last three have received low ratings, but seen strong growth. Unlike before, visual analysis of these trends suggests that they were largely unaffected by ratings. In short, in line with the evidence presented in Figure 10.1, only in a *subset* of assessed IOs do resource flows appear to have been responsive to performance indicators.

A RELATIONAL THEORY OF ASSESSMENT POWER

The IO performance indicators constitute a form of social knowledge produced by a set of respected actors whose authority stems from their institutional expertise, bureaucratic capacity, and central position in the "network" of multilateral donors. By defining and setting standards for institutional performance, they highlight, frame, and instill meaning in the behavior and effects of IOs. They thus not only increase the salience of institutional performance as a metric by which IOs are judged but also clarify and crystallize shared understandings of the concept. In doing so, they alter the material and normative calculus by which donors allocate resources to IOs, incentivizing them to place greater weight on performance considerations as a means of both maximizing the "return" on their contributions and enhancing their status and reputation in the donor community.[15] Other things equal, therefore, the creation of IO performance indicators should bring about an increase in funding for high-rated institutions and a reduction for low-rated ones.

Yet other things are not always equal. IOs exist not in a vacuum but in a distinct transnational policy space populated by diverse actors from different institutional levels (subnational, national, and supranational) and sites of authority (public, private, and hybrid). What distinguishes these actors as inhabitants of a common policy space is that they seek to shape substantive outcomes in the same issue area, whether by performing, supporting, or influencing the exercise of governance functions. The central claim of my argument is that the financial consequences of IO performance indicators are contingent upon the *relationship* between these institutions and other actors within their policy space. Only under particular relational conditions do ratings affect resource flows to IOs through the three pathways of GPA influence delineated by Kelley and Simmons, that is, domestic politics, elite response, and transnational mobilization. I highlight two such conditions, the first mediating the elite pathway and the second mediating the domestic and transnational pathways: (1) IOs are subject to a high level of institutional competition; and (2) IOs possess robust governance partnerships with non-state actors.

Institutional Competition

The degree of institutional competition faced by IOs is a function of the number of institutions within their policy space that exercise similar governance functions to them. In most instances, these institutions are themselves IOs. While other types of institutions – such as treaties, agreements, and laws – often address similar policy problems to IOs, their lack of a permanent secretariat prevents them from performing many of the latter's distinctive

---

[15] In this way, reputational concerns can affect how actors linked to assessed entities – and not just assessed entities themselves – respond to GPIs.

governance functions, such as gathering and providing information, resolving disputes, allocating pooled resources, identifying emerging transnational problems, and formulating rules and standards.[16]

The political implications of competition among IOs have received surprisingly little attention from scholars of such institutions, a possible reflection of the traditional dominance of functionalist approaches to analyzing international cooperation, which imply that intense competition is unlikely to arise because overlap in governance functions is inefficient as well as redundant (since only one institution is needed to perform a given function).[17] In reality, as recent studies have pointed out, there is substantial *variation* in the degree of competition experienced by IOs.[18] Some policy spaces are indeed sparsely populated with functionally similar IOs, ensuring that each enjoys a monopoly or quasi-monopoly over governance functions. In other policy spaces, however, IOs share authority with a sizable population of competitors, each of which makes only a marginal contribution to the aggregate supply of institutional goods.

These differences are primarily a function of two issue-specific characteristics. The first is the presence of barriers to entry into the policy space, i.e. costs incurred in the exercise of governance functions that prevent IOs from establishing themselves as "suppliers." A major barrier to entry in the mostly low-politics issue areas covered by IO performance indicators is the need for technical knowledge in the policymaking process.[19] Such expertise is costly to acquire because it requires IOs to recruit staff with specialized qualifications – which may be in short supply and command a wage premium – and often to provide them with years of additional training and practical experience related to their specific tasks. The second characteristic is the existence of economies of scale in the provision of governance functions, i.e. declines in the average cost of provision as output increases. Perhaps the most common source of scale economies in low-politics domains is the occurrence of "network effects," whereby the marginal utility of participating in an IO's activities rises with the number of participants. This is because many IOs in such domains perform standard-setting functions, which give rise to network effects because each adoption of a given standard yields coordination benefits for all previous adopters.

How do differences in these characteristics across policy spaces mediate the financial effects of IO performance indicators? In policy spaces characterized by high barriers to entry or economies of scale, IOs have few or no close substitutes to which donors can reallocate resources. Given the high transaction

---

[16] Abbott and Snidal 1998; and Pevehouse, Nordstrom, and Warnke 2004.

[17] It may also reflect the field's focus on a relatively small number of IOs that *do* face little competition, such as the International Monetary Fund (IMF) and the World Trade Organization (WTO).

[18] Abbott, Green, and Keohane 2016; Frey 2008; Jupille, Mattli, and Snidal 2013; Lipscy 2015.

[19] Lipscy 2015.

costs and uncertain distributional consequences of creating new institutions, donors are thus likely to refrain from imposing major financial sanctions on IOs receiving low performance ratings for fear of jeopardizing the supply of institutional goods in the policy space.[20] That is, material and social incentives to withdraw support from ineffective IOs are likely to be trumped by concerns about squandering *all* the benefits of institutionalized cooperation, blocking the elite response pathway of GPA influence. Nor, conversely, will donors have incentives to provide increased contributions to IOs receiving high ratings: since they cannot credibly threaten to punish such institutions for suboptimal performance in the future, rewards are unlikely to have their desired effect of incentivizing continued effectiveness.

In policy spaces characterized by low barriers to entry or diseconomies of scale, by contrast, IOs have a sizable pool of close substitutes. In accordance with the elite response pathway, therefore, donors can sanction low-rated IOs without fear of compromising the supply of institutional goods in the policy space. In addition, they have incentives to provide additional contributions to high-rated IOs: because the threat of sanctioning poor performance is now credible, rewards *are* likely to have their intended effect of incentivizing such institutions to continue performing effectively. In sum, I hypothesize that only a high degree of institutional competition will result in a strong positive relationship between performance indicators and resource flows.

Governance Partnerships

Governance partnerships are relational arrangements between IOs and actors above and below the state – including non-governmental organizations (NGOs), businesses, transgovernmental networks, and other IOs – involving voluntary and sustained collaboration in the exercise of governance functions.[21] Such arrangements are based on a convergence of both goals and interests. IOs often lack the informational, epistemic, administrative, and logistical resources to successfully fulfill their mandates – a consequence of the ambitious nature of such mandates as well as the limited support they receive from their members – and enlist partners as a means of addressing these capacity deficits. Partners are willing to provide assistance because they share organizational objectives, perceive potential synergies in combining their capabilities with those of IOs, and derive considerable non-material benefits from collaboration, including access to contacts and networks, normative guidance, and the legitimacy that comes with endorsement by a multilateral institution.[22]

---

[20] Jupille, Mattli, and Snidal 2013.
[21] Closely related concepts include "joint governance," "multi-stakeholder partnerships," and "orchestration." I follow Mattli and Seddon 2015 in using "governance partnerships" as an umbrella term for these various arrangements.
[22] See Abbott and Snidal 1998; and Abbott et al. 2015.

While many IOs have established governance partnerships in recent years, there is substantial variation in the *robustness* of such arrangements. I define robustness as an increasing function of three factors. The first is the depth of cooperation between IOs and partners. Upon closer inspection, many partnerships turn out to be purely symbolic arrangements formed in order to satisfy external pressures for stakeholder engagement. I only consider partnerships to be robust if they involve substantive collaboration at one of the five principal stages of the IO policymaking process: agenda setting, formulation, monitoring, implementation, and enforcement. The second factor is the degree of alignment between the policy preferences of IOs and partners. Although partners share the broad objectives of IOs, their views about the specific policies needed to advance such objectives often conflict with those of IO officials. Misalignment is particularly common when there are differences in the geographical scope and range of issue areas covered by partners and IOs. The third factor is the level of complementarity between the capabilities of IO and partners. Naturally, partners with ample (material and non-material) resources are better able to remedy IO capacity deficits. Yet since the size of such deficits depends on an IO's own level of resources, complementarity increases not with the *absolute* level of partner resources but with the *ratio* of partner to IO resources.

Robust governance partnerships create incentives for non-state actors to behave in ways that enhance the sensitivity of resource flows to IO performance indicators. When an IO receives high ratings, the logic is straightforward: due to their close operational ties with the institution, support for its policies, and sizable resource base, partners are both willing and able to assist it in mobilizing additional contributions. Such assistance can take several forms, including lobbying governments and other donors at the domestic level; publicizing and disseminating information about the assessments; identifying and targeting potential new donors; and increasing their own contributions to the IO.[23] When robustness is low, partners are unlikely to invest in these mobilization strategies for want of both incentives (they have weak operational ties with the IO and non-aligned policy preferences) and means (they possess limited resources).[24] That is, the domestic and transnational pathways of GPA influence are unlikely to operate as specified.

When an IO receives low ratings, the effects of variation in partnership robustness are less clear. It may appear that when robustness is high, partners will seek to protect the IO from financial sanctions using the mobilization strategies mentioned above, mitigating the ratings' impact on resource flows. I argue, however, that they are more likely to respond in ways that *increase* the size of such sanctions. This is because the gains they derive from continued

---

[23] For examples of these strategies, see Broz and Hawes 2006; Busby 2007; and Lavelle 2011.
[24] Similarly, non-state actors who are not part of governance partnerships will often lack a sufficiently large stake in the IO's success to be willing to incur these costs.

collaboration will tend to be outweighed by (1) the reputational costs of association with a low-rated IO (which can include a reduction in their own funding) and (2) the opportunity costs of foregoing collaboration with more effective IOs (which can include reputational gains and an enhanced capacity to achieve their objectives). Partners thus have incentives to scale down or withdraw their support for the IO (including on the financial front) and establish ties with higher-rated institutions. Such actions, in turn, exacerbate the reputational damage suffered by the IO and raise concerns that it may exhibit even worse performance in the future. The upshot is likely to be a further intensification of sanctions. When partnerships are weak, this sequence of events is unlikely to transpire: since cooperation involves no meaningful exchange of resources or services, partners neither incur major (reputational or opportunity) costs from maintaining the relationship nor inflict major (reputational or operational) damage on the IO by withdrawing their support. In sum, my first hypothesis is that only a high degree of institutional competition will result in a strong positive relationship between performance indicators and resource flows.[25]

QUALITATIVE EVIDENCE

How much support is there for these hypotheses? I begin my empirical investigation by examining a range of primary and secondary qualitative sources on the financial effects of IO performance indicators, including policy statements and budgetary documents from donor governments, media reports, and information from more than 80 interviews with IO officials and donor representatives conducted between 2012 and 2016.[26] In addition to providing a preliminary test of the hypotheses, this examination sheds light on the argument's posited causal mechanisms – both behavioral and non-behavioral – and offers concrete illustrations of how such mechanisms have shaped funding trends in individual institutions (including several of those featured in Figures 10.2 and 10.3).

The most direct evidence that IO performance indicators have influenced resource flows comes from the states that developed them. All five governments

---

[25] Note that both hypotheses imply a weak relationship between the conditioning variable and performance indicators. Indeed, there are obvious reasons why competition and partnerships are likely to have mixed effects on ratings. While competition puts pressure on IOs to perform well to secure funding, for instance, it can also lead to institutional overlap and "crowding out" that undermines effectiveness. Similarly, while robust partnerships may enhance the ability of IOs to perform governance functions, they can also dilute the influence of member states and thus facilitate shirking and slippage.

[26] The interviews were conducted in four waves: the first in Washington, DC, in spring 2012; the second in Geneva in summer 2012; the third in London in summer 2014; and the fourth in Rome in winter 2015. Additional interviews were conducted via telephone throughout the period.

that have conducted individual assessments have explicitly indicated that their findings have informed subsequent multilateral funding decisions.[27] In addition, a recent survey of MOPAN's 17 member nations – a group that accounts for 95 percent of the world's multilateral development assistance – revealed that all but two have used its evaluations to "decide on funding allocations about multilateral organizations."[28] The only public time-series data on such allocations, which come from the British government, suggest that the assessments' impact has been significant.[29] As a direct result of its first set of ratings in 2011, the government eliminated its assessed funding for four low-rated IOs – the International Labour Organization (ILO), the UN Human Settlements Programme (UN-Habitat), the UN International Strategy for Disaster Reduction (UNISDR), and the UN Industrial Development Organization (UNIDO) – and more than doubled contributions to 11 high-rated IOs. Media reports suggest that a recent update of the ratings, released in December 2016, will result in a further £180m of cuts to poorly rated UN agencies – most notably the UN Educational, Scientific, and Cultural Organization (UNESCO) – causing them to lose almost all of their assessed British contributions.[30]

Interviews with IO officials and representatives of donor states provide further evidence of such influence. Several of the latter described "triangulating" between different assessments in determining allocations – a feat rendered easier by the high correlation between them – with some even referring to them as the "single most salient" factor in the decision-making process. Interestingly, in line with the argument's emphasis on framing and meaning making, some interviewees also noted that the assessments have altered the official discourse around multilateral funding. According to an employee of the Swiss Agency for Development and Cooperation (SDC),

"The evaluations have changed how governments talk about and justify supporting IOs, causing them to frame funding decisions in terms of 'efficiency' and 'value for money' rather than the protection of national interests. Since the ratings effectively

[27] Ministry for Foreign Affairs (Sweden) 2011; Department for International Development (United Kingdom) 2013; Department of Foreign Affairs and Trade (Australia) 2013; Ministerie van Buitenlandse Zaken (Netherlands) 2013; and Ministry for Foreign Affairs (Denmark) 2013.

[28] Multilateral Organisation Performance Assessment Network 2015, 19.

[29] Statistics on International Development, Department for International Development (United Kingdom). Available at https://www.gov.uk/government/organisations/department-for-international-development/about/statistics, accessed December 14, 2016. Where possible, I supplement this source with data from the government's Development Tracker database (https://devtracker.dfid.gov.uk/, accessed December 14, 2015) and IO annual reports and financial statements. All figures are converted into millions of British pounds at contemporary exchange rates and adjusted for inflation (using 2000 as the base year).

[30] "'Wasteful' UNESCO targeted as Britain makes £180m funding cuts." *The Sunday Times*, April 17, 2016, 20.

quantify and compare these characteristics across IOs, they have created a competitive dynamic among donors whereby supporting weakly rated IOs can lead to reputational damage."[31]

The IO staff similarly attested to the assessments' impact on funding decisions. Division heads in both UNAIDS and the United Nations Development Programme (UNDP), for instance, cited the combination of low ratings and intense competition from similar IOs as the primary reason for their institutions' recent decline in contributions.[32] The UNAIDS official also highlighted the ratings' non-behavioral effects – effects strikingly parallel to those mentioned above – observing that "being directly compared with peers" had made UNAIDS's "entire organizational culture more efficiency- and results-oriented" and heightened "internal awareness about our relative status and reputation."[33]

Is there other evidence that the financial effects of the assessments have been mediated by institutional competition and governance partnerships? Consistent with the evidence presented in the second section, not all IOs that received low ratings in the first British assessment have been financially sanctioned by the country, while not all IOs that received high ratings have been rewarded. A closer look at the "anomalous" cases suggests that resource flows have been less responsive to ratings when IOs are subject to limited competition and possess weak partnerships. Of the eight low-rated IOs placed in the lowest summary category "poor value for money," for example, the only two that have avoided funding cuts are the UN Entity for Gender Equality and the Empowerment of Women (UN Women), the sole IGO (intergovernmental organization) with a mandate to promote women's rights; and the Food and Agriculture Organization (FAO), which, in addition to being the only IGO responsible for monitoring food security and setting agricultural standards at the global level, has a notoriously poor reputation for collaborating with non-state actors.[34] Similarly, of the nine IOs in the highest "very good value for money" category, the only one that has failed to receive additional contributions is the EDF, a poverty reduction fund known to possess weak partnerships due to its distinctive "joint ownership" governance model, which allows recipient country governments – but not non-state actors – to play a direct role in designing and implementing development projects.[35]

---

[31] Author interview with employee of Swiss Agency for Development and Cooperation, June 9, 2012, Geneva.

[32] Author interview with UNAIDS division director, June 12, 2012, Geneva; and author telephone interview with UNDP division director, May 21, 2018.

[33] Author interview with UNAIDS division director, June 12, 2012, Geneva.

[34] The World Food Programme (WFP) also operates in the realm of global food security, but performs the very different function of delivering emergency food aid on the ground. On the FAO's weak partnerships, see Food and Agriculture Organization 2007.

[35] See Gavas 2012.

Interviews provide further evidence of the conditioning effects of competition and partnerships. Donor representatives frequently expressed concerns that sanctioning low-rated IOs with a dearth of close substitutes could jeopardize key global public goods and thus undermine foreign policy goals. As a senior bureaucrat in Italy's Ministry of Foreign Affairs explained, "While [ratings] do guide our funding decisions, it is not always in our interest to follow them. For instance, if we stop financing UNEP because it is poorly rated, who will lead the global response to global warming?"[36] Such concerns were also recognized by low-rated IOs themselves, with one UNEP official even suggesting that the agency had been "saved from life-threatening funding cuts" by its "unique niche in coordinating national efforts to address climate change."[37] A number of officials in high-rated IOs, meanwhile, highlighted how low levels of competition had weakened incentives for donors to reward them. One economist in the Multilateral Fund (MLF) for the Implementation of the Montreal Protocol, for instance, complained that the institution's strong ratings had not led to increased funding because "we're the only source of funding for mitigating ozone depletion, which makes it difficult for states to pull the plug if we perform badly in the future – and, as economists know, rewards don't work without a credible threat of sanctions."[38]

Interviewees also drew attention to the key role of partnerships in shaping how donors respond to ratings. A recurring theme was the importance of robust partnerships – particularly those characterized by high levels of complementarity – in providing high-rated IOs with the political and organizational support necessary to mobilize additional funds. The following view, expressed by a financial officer in UNHCR, was typical:

"We've received consistently high scores in the evaluations, but wouldn't have received such a large increase in funding if it hadn't been for our major NGO partners, such as the International Rescue Committee, Save the Children, and the Scandinavian Refugee Councils... They've been incredibly effective in using their campaigning infrastructure to raise public awareness about the ratings and their political contacts to lobby wealthy donor governments – in particular the US – for increased contributions."[39]

Government officials also acknowledged the influence of partners in their decision to reward high-rated IOs. One employee of the United States Agency for International Development (USAID), for instance, noted that its near threefold increase in annual contributions to UNHCR since 2009 is "in part the result of an aggressive ratings-focused lobbying drive by the agency's most well-resourced civil society partners."[40] Staff in low-rated IOs, by contrast, lamented

---

[36] Author interview with employee of Italy's Ministry of Foreign Affairs and International Cooperation, January 23, 2015, Rome.

[37] Author telephone interview with UNEP program officer, December 2, 2013.

[38] Author interview with MLF staff economist, July 14, 2018, Washington, DC.

[39] Author interview with UNHCR financial officer, June 6, 2012, Geneva.

[40] Author interview with employee of USAID, May 8, 2012, Washington, DC.

the unexpected tendency of robust partnerships to exacerbate the financial damage caused by the assessments. In the words of a partnerships coordinator in the Commonwealth, "Instead of using their clout with donors to protect us against funding cuts [resulting from low ratings], many of our most important civil society partners have weakened or severed ties with us, causing even greater alarm among donors. Unfortunately, the result has been yet deeper cuts."[41]

STATISTICAL ANALYSIS

In this section, I subject the argument to a series of observational and quasi-experimental statistical tests based on a new panel dataset, part of which was introduced in the second section. This analysis complements the qualitative examination both by providing systematic cross-organizational data on the dependent and explanatory variables and by showing that the earlier findings are generalizable to a larger and more representative population of IOs. I begin by describing the contents of the dataset, before outlining my methodological strategy and presenting the results.

The main dependent variable $\Delta CONTRIBUTIONS_a$, which is similar to y in Figure 10.1, is the log ratio of an IO's contributions in each FY since the release of a given assessment a (FYv_{IO}) to its contributions in the FY preceding this date ($FYv_{IO} - 1$):

$$\Delta CONTRIBUTIONS_a = ln\left(\frac{CONTRIBUTIONS_{vIO+i}}{CONTRIBUTIONS_{vIO-1}}\right)$$

$RATING_a$ is the standardized mean of an IO's indicator scores from the most recent wave of an assessment a in $FYv_{IO} + i$. To maximize the sample size and capture the possibility that donors are "triangulating" between different sets of ratings, I supplement this measure with an aggregate index ($RATING_{avg}$) that averages its value across all assessments (similarly to x in Figure 10.1). As discussed below, in separate analyses I also disaggregate indicator scores within each assessment to examine whether resource flows are more responsive to information about some dimensions of performance than others.

Institutional competition is measured using responses to an original online survey of IO head officials conducted between September 2013 and January 2015.[42] Participants were asked the following question for a selection of recent years:

[41] Author interview with Commonwealth Secretariat partnerships coordinator, July 6, 2014, London.

[42] The survey, which was implemented using the Qualtrics Survey Software, was sent to participants via an emailed link. In most cases, 2–3 reminder messages were sent before the response was submitted. In five cases, participants preferred to provide their responses either verbally (during a telephone interview) or in writing. To check the reliability of responses, in 20 percent of cases the survey was sent to another senior official (usually a division or department head). In no instances were there discrepancies between the two sets of answers, indicating a high degree of reliability.

"*How many international organizations perform a similar function to your organization and thus might be seen to compete with it?*" Five response options were provided: (1) "Zero"; (2) "Between 1 and 5"; (3) "Between 5 and 10"; (4) "Between 10 and 20"; and (5) "More than 20." COMPETITION is constructed by converting responses for the year $(FY v_{IO} - 1)$: into a five-point scale ranging from 0 (corresponding to option 1) to 4 (corresponding to option 5).[43] I later experiment with alternative (non-survey-based) measures, some of which capture the issue-specific determinants of competition discussed in the third section.

PARTNERSHIPS is an additive index of four indicators measuring the three dimensions of governance partnership robustness outlined earlier. All indicators are measured as of FY $v_{IO} - 1$ using information from IO websites, most of which have a section devoted specifically to partnerships.[44] The first indicator measures the depth of cooperation between IOs and partners. IOs receive a score between 0 and 1 reflecting the proportion of partnerships that involve substantive collaboration at the agenda-setting, formulation, monitoring, implementation, or enforcement stage of the policymaking process (as opposed to a purely symbolic affiliation). The second and third indicators measure policy preference alignment. IOs are assigned a score from 0 to 1 based on the proportion of partners that share their geographical scope (second indicator) and range of issue areas (third indicator).[45] The fourth indicator measures complementarity in capabilities, taking a value of 1 if the ratio of combined partner-to-IO expenditures exceeds 10 and 0 otherwise. IOs that have no listed partnerships are assigned a score of 0 on each indicator.

I control for four financial variables that are likely to affect how resource flows respond to ratings. TREND_a is the average log ratio of an IO's contributions in FY $v_{IO} - j$ to its contributions in the previous FY $v_{IO} - j - 1$ during the five-year period before the release of an assessment a:

$$\text{TREND}_a = \frac{\sum_{k=0}^{5} ln\left(\frac{\text{CONTRIBUTIONS}_{v_{IO}-j}}{\text{CONTRIBUTIONS}_{v_{IO}-j-1}} \right)}{5}$$

CONTRIBUTIONS is an IO's log contributions in FY $u_{IO} - 1$. VOLUNTARY is the proportion of an IO's contributions in FY $u_{IO} - 1$ that are voluntary rather than assessed (i.e. not paid as a condition of IO membership). INDEPENDENT is the proportion of an IO's total income in FY $u_{IO} - 1$ that is composed of independently earned revenue – for instance, from investments, interest charges, and fees for services rendered – as opposed to contributions.

---

[43] Responses varied little across years, perhaps reflecting that the fact that competition is primarily a function of issue-specific characteristics that tend to change slowly over time.

[44] To access older versions of these websites, I used the Internet Archive's Wayback Machine. Available at https://archive.org/web/, accessed February 21, 2016.

[45] I distinguish between three levels of geographical focus – global, regional, and national – and 25 issue areas based on a list compiled by Hooghe et al. 2017.

Baseline Model and Results

Given the conditional nature of the argument, I estimate a linear multiplicative interaction model, clustering robust standard errors by IO to address potential cross-sectional dependence. In light of the relatively small sample size (due to the recent emergence of the assessments), I begin by testing the two hypotheses separately:

$$\Delta \text{CONTRIBUTIONS}_a = \beta_0 + \beta_1 \text{RATING}_a + \beta_2 \text{COMPETITION}$$

$$+ \beta_3 \text{RATING}_a \times \text{COMPETITION} + \beta_4 \text{TREND}_a + \beta_5 \text{CONTRIBUTIONS}$$

$$+ \beta_6 \text{VOLUNTARY} + \beta_7 \text{INDEPENDENT} + \varepsilon \tag{10.1}$$

$$\Delta \text{CONTRIBUTIONS}_a = \beta_0 + \beta_1 \text{RATING}_a + \beta_2 \text{PARTNERSHIPS}$$

$$+ \beta_3 \text{RATING}_a \times \text{PARTNERSHIPS} + \beta_4 \text{TREND}_a$$

$$+ \beta_5 \text{CONTRIBUTIONS} + \beta_6 \text{VOLUNTARY}_a$$

$$+ \beta_7 \text{INDEPENDENT}_a + \varepsilon \tag{10.2}$$

The argument has two key empirical implications, both of which concern the marginal effect of RATING_a on $\Delta \text{CONTRIBUTIONS}_a$. This is equal to $\beta_1 + \beta_3$ COMPETITION in Equation (10.1) and $\beta_1 + \beta_3$ PARTNERSHIPS in Equation (10.2), which entails that β_1 represents the marginal effect when COMPETITION = 0 in Equation (10.1) and PARTNERSHIPS = 0 in Equation (10.2). Since the argument posits that ratings do not influence resource flows when IOs are subject to little competition or possess weak partnerships, we should expect β_1 to be zero in both equations. The argument also implies that the marginal effect will become positive as COMPETITION and PARTNERSHIPS increase. Given that these variables are non-negative and RATING_a has a mean of zero (because it is standardized), IOs with below-average ratings have negative interaction term values that decrease with the variables, while IOs with above-average ratings have positive values that increase with them. Thus, the second implication is that β_3 will be positive in both equations.

Table 10.2 reports the results for Equation (10.1). In line with the argument, the coefficient on RATING_a is statistically significant at the 10 percent level in only one of the eight models, whereas the coefficient on $\text{RATING}_a \times$ COMPETITION is positive and significant in seven. The latter's lack of significance in Model (5) may be a consequence of the relatively late release of the Danish ratings (in 2012), which could result in attenuated estimates because resource flows in FY $v_{IO} - 1$ were already influenced by earlier assessments. As suggested in the introduction, however, they may also stem from characteristics of the ratings themselves or their creator (for instance, Denmark may have less credibility or influence in the donor community than

TABLE 10.2. *Effect of performance ratings on changes in contributions as mediated by institutional competition (Equation 10.1)*

	Dependent Variable: ΔCONTRIBUTIONS$_a$ (log)							
	(1) UK	(2) AUS	(3) NET	(4) SWE	(5) DEN	(6) MOP(S)	(7) MOP(R)	(8) AVG
RATING$_{UK}$	0.05 (0.05)							
RATING$_{AUS}$		0.14 (0.12)						
RATING$_{NET}$			-0.02 (0.05)					
RATING$_{SWE}$				0.13*** (0.04)				
RATING$_{DEN}$					0.06 (0.07)			
RATING$_{MOP(S)}$						-0.06 (0.06)		
RATING$_{MOP(R)}$							-0.09 (0.06)	
RATING$_{AVG}$								-0.002 (0.06)
COMPETITION	-0.07 (0.05)	-0.11 (0.08)	0.01 (0.04)	-0.08** (0.03)	-0.04 (0.04)	-0.08 (0.05)	0.02 (0.05)	-0.01 (0.03)
TREND$_a$	-0.67* (0.37)	-1.47* (0.80)	-1.18 (0.91)	-0.02 (0.45)	0.15 (1.34)	-0.35 (0.79)	0.1 (0.53)	-0.41** (0.21)

Dependent Variable: ΔCONTRIBUTIONS$_a$ (log)

	(1) UK	(2) AUS	(3) NET	(4) SWE	(5) DEN	(6) MOP(S)	(7) MOP(R)	(8) AVG
CONTRIBUTIONS (log)	-0.03 (0.05)	-0.08 (0.06)	-0.06 (0.04)	-0.06*** (0.02)	-0.02 (0.06)	-0.03 (0.05)	0.01 (0.04)	-0.05** (0.02)
VOLUNTARY	0.003** (0.00)	0.0003 (0.00)	0.003* (0.00)	0.002 (0.00)	0.003 (0.00)	0.002 (0.00)	0.003*** (0.00)	0.002** (0.00)
INDEPENDENT	0.001 (0.00)	-0.01 (0.01)	0.001 (0.00)	-0.002* (0.00)	-0.001 (0.00)	0.002 (0.00)	0.0001 (0.00)	0.001 (0.00)
RATING$_{UK}$ × COMPETITION	0.11*** (0.03)							
RATING$_{AUS}$ × COMPETITION		0.07** (0.03)						
RATING$_{NET}$ × COMPETITION			0.12*** (0.05)					
RATING$_{SWE}$ × COMPETITION				0.05* (0.03)				
RATING$_{DEN}$ × COMPETITION					-0.04 (0.06)			
RATING$_{MOP(S)}$ × COMPETITION						0.13* (0.07)		
RATING$_{MOP(R)}$ × COMPETITION							0.13** (0.06)	
RATING$_{AVG}$ × COMPETITION								0.11*** (0.03)

Dependent Variable: ΔCONTRIBUTIONS$_a$ (log)

	(1) UK	(2) AUS	(3) NET	(4) SWE	(5) DEN	(6) MOP(S)	(7) MOP(R)	(8) AVG
Constant	0.1 (0.37)	0.82** (0.40)	0.3 (0.22)	0.57*** (0.12)	0.03 (0.32)	0.08 (0.37)	-0.26 (0.27)	0.3 (0.18)
Observations	192	160	127	167	68	62	62	308
R^2	0.33	0.35	0.36	0.3	0.14	0.24	0.3	0.26
Adjusted R^2	0.3	0.32	0.32	0.26	0.04	0.14	0.21	0.24

*** $p < 0.01$, ** $p < 0.05$, * $p < 0.1$.

Notes: Ordinary least squares regressions with robust standard errors clustered by IO in parentheses.

the other assessor states). Encouragingly, the coefficient has the largest size and lowest *p*-value in the model with the aggregate index RATING$_{avg}$ (Model 8) – that is, the model with the highest sample size – providing evidence of the "triangulation" behavior described earlier.

The left panel of Figure 10.4 plots the estimated marginal effect of RATING$_{avg}$ on ΔCONTRIBUTIONS$_a$ at different levels of COMPETITION. When IOs are subject to no competition, the effect is statistically indistinguishable from zero (as indicated by the intersection of $y = 0$ with the 90 percent confidence interval). As competition increases, however, it becomes positive and significant. More importantly, it becomes *substantively* significant: on average, a one-point increase in RATING$_{avg}$ (which ranges from −2.83 to 2.28) is associated with roughly a 25 percent rise in contributions when IOs have 5–10 competitors; a 35 percent rise when IOs have 10–20 competitors; and a 45 percent rise when IOs have more than 20 competitors.

The results for Equation (10.2), shown in Table 10.3, provide similarly strong support for the argument. The coefficient on RATING$_a$ fails to reach significance in all eight models, whereas the coefficient on RATING$_a \times$ PARTNERSHIPS is positive and significant in six. Similarly to before, the latter is non-significant only in Models (2) and (5) – in which ratings were first released in 2012 – and has the largest size and lowest *p*-value in Model (8). The right panel of Figure 10.4 displays the equivalent of the previous marginal effect plot for Model (8). As predicted, when partnerships are weak or non-existent (PARTNERSHIPS < 1.5 on a scale of 0 to 3.98), the estimated marginal effect of RATING$_{avg}$ on ΔCONTRIBUTIONS$_a$ is indistinguishable from zero

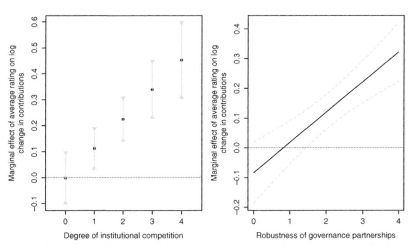

FIGURE 10.4. Marginal effects of average ratings on changes in contributions at different levels of institutional competition and partnership robustness.
Notes: The graphs are based on the results of Model (8) in Tables 10.2 (left graph) and 10.3 (right graph). The light gray lines represent 90 percent confidence intervals.

TABLE 10.3. *Effect of performance ratings on changes in contributions as mediated by governance partnerships (Equation 10.2)*

Dependent Variable: ΔCONTRIBUTIONS$_a$ (log)

	(1) UK	(2) AUS	(3) NET	(4) SWE	(5) DEN	(6) MOP(S)	(7) MOP(R)	(8) AVG
RATING$_{UK}$	-0.04 (0.09)							
RATING$_{AUS}$		0.2 (0.17)						
RATING$_{NET}$			-0.23 (0.16)					
RATING$_{SWE}$				0.06 (0.07)				
RATING$_{DEN}$					0.04 (0.07)			
RATING$_{MOP(S)}$						-0.09 (0.06)		
RATING$_{MOP(R)}$							-0.15 (0.09)	
RATING$_{AVG}$								-0.08 (0.06)
PARTNERSHIPS	0.05 (0.04)	0.05 (0.06)	0.05 (0.04)	-0.01 (0.03)	0.01 (0.03)	0.02 (0.04)	0.04 (0.03)	0.03 (0.02)
TREND$_a$	-0.59 (0.36)	-1.42 (0.87)	-0.72 (0.74)	-0.2 (0.38)	0.27 (1.45)	-0.47 (0.76)	0.09 (0.61)	-0.41 (0.25)
CONTRIBUTIONS (*log*)	-0.04 (0.05)	-0.06 (0.06)	-0.04 (0.04)	-0.07*** (0.02)	-0.03 (0.08)	-0.07 (0.05)	-0.02 (0.03)	-0.04** (0.02)
VOLUNTARY	0.001 (0.00)	-0.002 (0.00)	0.002 (0.00)	0.002 (0.00)	0.003 (0.00)	0.002** (0.00)	0.004*** (0.00)	0.001 (0.00)
INDEPENDENT	0.0001 (0.00)	-0.01 (0.01)	0.002 (0.00)	-0.002* (0.00)	-0.0003 (0.00)	0.001 (0.00)	-0.001 (0.00)	0.0004 (0.00)

Dependent Variable: ΔCONTRIBUTIONS$_a$ (log)

	(1) UK	(2) AUS	(3) NET	(4) SWE	(5) DEN	(6) MOP(S)	(7) MOP(R)	(8) AVG
RATING$_{UK}$ × PARTNERSHIPS	0.08** (0.03)							
RATING$_{AUS}$ × PARTNERSHIPS		−0.02 (0.08)						
RATING$_{NET}$ × PARTNERSHIPS			0.12* (0.06)					
RATING$_{SWE}$ × PARTNERSHIPS				0.04* (0.02)				
RATING$_{DEN}$ × PARTNERSHIPS					−0.02 (0.02)			
RATING$_{MOP(S)}$ × PARTNERSHIPS						0.05** (0.03)		
RATING$_{MOP(R)}$ × PARTNERSHIPS							0.07* (0.04)	
RATING$_{AVG}$ × PARTNERSHIPS								0.10*** (0.03)
Constant	0.17 (0.37)	0.69 (0.45)	0.09 (0.22)	0.61*** (0.16)	0.01 (0.34)	0.29 (0.33)	−0.15 (0.21)	0.32* (0.17)
Observations	192	160	127	167	68	62	62	308
R^2	0.3	0.32	0.36	0.27	0.1	0.19	0.23	0.22
Adjusted R^2	0.28	0.29	0.32	0.24	−0.002	0.09	0.13	0.21

*** $p < 0.01$, ** $p < 0.05$, * $p < 0.1$.

Notes: Ordinary least squares regressions with robust standard errors clustered by IO in parentheses.

(the lower 90 percent confidence bound intersects $y = 0$). When partnerships are robust, however, it is positive, significant, and substantively sizable. For IOs whose partnerships are in the upper quartile of the robustness distribution ($3.35 \leq$ PARTNERSHIPS ≤ 3.98), for instance, a one-point increase in RATING$_{avg}$ is associated with an average rise in contributions of roughly 25–30 percent. This is an impressive 35–40 percent higher than the corresponding figure when partnerships are at the bottom end of the distribution.

Tables A1–A12 in the online appendix display the results when the baseline equations are re-estimated with disaggregated standardized indicator scores from each assessment. Seventy-five of the 100 individual coefficients on the interaction terms are positive, of which one third are significant (only nine coefficients on RATING$_a$ are positive and significant). There is little evidence that lower p-values are clustered in any of the six dimensions of performance listed in the second section, though (perhaps unsurprisingly) a higher proportion of the significant coefficients involve indicators of resource management and cost and value consciousness. In general, the fact that the results are stronger at the aggregate than at the indicator level suggests donors may be "triangulating" between different types of performance information *within* as well as *across* assessments.

Distinguishing Performance from Performance Indicators

One potential concern about the baseline models is that they fail to distinguish the effect of IO performance indicators from the effect of IO performance itself. It is conceivable, for instance, that the interaction-term coefficients are positive because ratings are capturing recent shifts in performance that have yet to influence resource flows or because performance has moved in the same direction as ratings since their release.

To address the first possibility, I employ a quasi-experimental design that involves expanding the sample to include unassessed IOs as a "control group." I select such institutions by exploiting a sharp discontinuity in the rule determining the eligibility of IOs for inclusion in the United Kingdom's assessment, namely, they must have received an average of at least one million British pounds in annual funding from the country's Department for International Development (DFID) in the decade prior to the release of the first set of ratings in 2011.[46] Since IOs near each side of this threshold have similar characteristics, but varying levels of the treatment (see Tables A14–A16 for balance statistics), we can isolate the effect of performance ratings by restricting the sample to these institutions and estimating the following regression discontinuity (RD) models:

---

[46] Data on DFID funding come from the sources cited in fn. 33. The Australian government employs a similar threshold but does not disclose contributions to individual institutions. For a similar approach to distinguishing the effects of GPIs from the effects of underlying performance, see Roberts and Tellez this volume.

$$\Delta \text{CONTRIBUTIONS}_{UK} = \beta_0 + \beta_1 \text{POOLED}_{UK} + \beta_2 \text{COMPETITION}$$

$$+ \beta_3 \text{AUTHENTIC} + \beta_4 \text{POOLED}_{UK} \times \text{COMPETITION} + \beta_5 \text{POOLED}_{UK}$$

$$\times \text{ AUTHENTIC} + \beta_6 \text{COMPETITION} \times \text{AUTHENTIC} + \beta_7 \text{POOLED}_{UK}$$

$$\times \text{ COMPETITION} \times \text{AUTHENTIC} + \beta_8 \text{DFIDFUNDING}$$

$$+ \beta_9 \text{DFIDFUNDING}^2 + \beta_{10} \text{DFIDFUNDING}^3 + \varepsilon \qquad (10.3)$$

$$\Delta \text{CONTRIBUTIONS}_{UK} = \beta_0 + \beta_1 \text{POOLED}_{UK}$$

$$+ \beta_2 \text{PARTNERSHIPS} + \beta_3 \text{AUTHENTIC} + \beta_4 \text{POOLED}_{UK}$$

$$\times \text{ PARTNERSHIPS} + \beta_5 \text{POOLED}_{UK} \times \text{AUTHENTIC}$$

$$+ \beta_6 \text{PARTNERSHIPS} \times \text{AUTHENTIC} + \beta_7 \text{POOLED}_{UK}$$

$$\times \text{ PARTNERSHIPS} \times \text{AUTHENTIC} + \beta_8 \text{DFIDFUNDING}$$

$$+ \beta_9 \text{DFIDFUNDING}^2 + \beta_{10} \text{DFIDFUNDING}^3 + \varepsilon \qquad (10.4)$$

where POOLED_{UK} is a combined ratings measure equal to RATING_{UK} for the assessed IOs and a predicted rating based on the four control variables (which are strong predictors of RATING_{UK}) for the unassessed IOs;[47] AUTHENTIC is a dummy for whether an IO has been assessed; and DFIDFUNDING, the forcing variable, is an IO's average annual contributions from DFID over the period 2002–11 in millions of pounds (the polynomial terms address the possibility of a nonlinear relationship with the dependent variable). For the unassessed IOs, PARTNERSHIPS is measured in the same way as for the assessed IOs, while COMPETITION is measured by converting the number of IOs in the *Yearbook of International Organizations* database that share their "subject of activity" into the five-point scale described earlier.[48] If the authentic ratings have an independent conditional effect on resource flows – an effect distinct from that of IO performance itself – we should expect β_7, the coefficient on the triple interaction term in each equation, to be positive; and β_4, the marginal effect of the interaction between POOLED_{UK} and each conditioning variable on Δ CONTRIBUTIONS$_{UK}$ when AUTHENTIC = 0, to be zero.

Table 10.4 presents the results for three different bandwidths: (1) IOs with a DFIDFUNDING value of less than 3.5 (the smallest bandwidth at which

---

[47] In a regression of RATING_{UK} on the controls, three of the four coefficients are significant at the 1 percent level (the other has a *p*-value of 0.24).

[48] *The Yearbook of International Organizations Online.* Available at https://www.uia.org/yearbook, accessed December 14, 2015. Both variables are measured as of 2010 (i.e. FY v_{10-1}). If an IO's subject of activity does not match one of the *Yearbook*'s near-thousand categories, COMPETITION takes a score of 0.

TABLE 10.4. *Effect of pooled British ratings on changes in contributions as mediated by institutional competition and governance partnerships (Equations 10.3 and 10.4)*

	Cubic RD		Matching		Cubic RD		Matching	
	(1) DFIDFUND < 3.5	(2) DFIDFUND < 5	(3) Full Sample	(4) Full Sample	(5) DFIDFUND < 3.5	(6) DFIDFUND < 5	(7) Full Sample	(8) Full Sample
			Dependent Variable: $\Delta CONTRIBUTIONS_{UK}$ (log)					
$POOLED_{UK}$	0.31 (0.28)	0.31 (0.27)	0.31 (0.26)	0.34 (0.29)	0.71 (0.49)	0.69 (0.49)	0.57 (0.42)	0.32 (0.35)
COMPETITION	−0.24 (0.19)	−0.24 (0.19)	−0.25 (0.19)	−0.27 (0.20)				
PARTNERSHIPS					−0.43 (0.29)	−0.41 (0.29)	−0.35 (0.25)	−0.14 (0.17)
AUTHENTIC	−0.48 (0.52)	−0.31 (0.54)	−0.33 (0.41)	−0.36 (0.44)	−4.36** (1.68)	−0.74 (0.97)	−0.53 (0.60)	−0.12 (0.42)
DFIDFUNDING	0.52 (0.45)	0.61 (0.39)	−0.0003 (0.01)		0.4 (0.41)	0.97** (0.44)	−0.001 (0.01)	
DFIDFUNDING^2	−0.34 (0.34)	−0.44** (0.18)	0 (0.00)		0.42** (0.21)	−0.55*** (0.20)	0 (0.00)	
DFIDFUNDING^3	0.06 (0.08)	0.07*** (0.03)	0 (0.00)		−0.15*** (0.04)	0.08*** (0.03)	0 (0.00)	
$POOLED_{UK}$ × COMPETITION	−0.17 (0.13)	−0.17 (0.13)	−0.17 (0.13)	−0.21 (0.14)				
$POOLED_{UK}$ × PARTNERSHIPS					−0.35 (0.22)	−0.34 (0.22)	−0.29 (0.19)	−0.25 (0.16)

Dependent Variable: ΔCONTRIBUTIONS$_{UK}$ (log)

	Cubic RD		Matching		Cubic RD		Matching	
	(1) DFIDFUND < 3.5	(2) DFIDFUND < 5	(3) Full Sample	(4) Full Sample	(5) DFIDFUND < 3.5	(6) DFIDFUND < 5	(7) Full Sample	(8) Full Sample
POOLED$_{UK}$ × AUTHENTIC	−0.28 (0.28)	−0.34 (0.29)	−0.23 (0.27)	−0.27 (0.30)	−2.39*** (0.91)	−0.6 (0.53)	−0.56 (0.43)	−0.33 (0.35)
COMPETITION× AUTHENTIC	0.16 (0.20)	0.21 (0.20)	0.23 (0.20)	0.27 (0.21)				
POOLED$_{UK}$ × COMPETITION × AUTHENTIC	0.62*** (0.17)	0.29* (0.15)	0.23* (0.13)	0.24* (0.14)				
PARTNERSHIPS × AUTHENTIC					1.24** (0.49)	0.34 (0.30)	0.35 (0.26)	0.13 (0.17)
POOLED$_{UK}$ × PARTNERSHIPS × AUTHENTIC					0.82** (0.32)	0.33 (0.23)	0.37* (0.19)	0.22* (0.13)
Constant	0.39 (0.41)	0.38 (0.41)	0.48 (0.40)	0.48 (0.43)	0.77 (0.62)	0.69 (0.62)	0.69 (0.58)	0.25 (0.42)
Observations	200	225	357	517	200	225	357	517
R^2	0.09	0.1	0.12	0.09	0.13	0.13	0.14	0.09
Adjusted R^2	0.04	0.06	0.09	0.08	0.08	0.09	0.12	0.08

*** $p < 0.01$, ** $p < 0.05$, * $p < 0.1$.

Notes: Robust standard errors clustered by IO in parentheses. In Models (4) and (8), assessed (AUTHENTIC = 1) and unassessed (AUTHENTIC = 0) observations are genetically matched on the conditioning and control variables, with missing values (which are not permitted) filled in using multiple imputation.

there are enough assessed observations to estimate the equations); (2) IOs with a DFIDFUNDING value of less than 5; and (3) the full sample.[49] In addition, it reports the results of an alternative strategy for improving balance across the treated and control groups, namely, matching assessed and unassessed observations on the conditioning and control variables.[50] Consistent with expectations, seven of the eight coefficients on the triple interaction terms are positive and significant, with the lowest p-values in the models with the smallest bandwidth (Models 1 and 5), in which the assessed and unassessed IOs are most similar. By contrast, every coefficient on $POOLED_{UK} \times COMPETITION$ and $POOLED_{UK} \times PARTNERSHIPS$ is nonsignificant and negative.[51] Comparing the estimated marginal effect of $POOLED_{UK}$ on $\Delta CONTRIBUTIONS_{tIK}$ at different levels of the conditioning variables for assessed and unassessed IOs in the DFIDFUNDING < 3.5 bandwidth indicates that the treatment makes a major substantive difference: contributions rise by roughly 45 percent for assessed IOs versus –15 percent for unassessed IOs with each one-point increase in COMPETITION; and 45 percent versus –35 percent with each one-point increase in PARTNERSHIPS.

The second possibility mentioned above – that performance has moved in the same direction as ratings since their release – is difficult to address directly. However, it can be substantially mitigated by making a small adjustment to the dependent variable, namely, restricting the post-assessment period to FY v_{IO} (i.e. changing the variable's numerator to $CONTRIBUTIONS_{v_{IO}}$). This is because performance exhibits relatively little change from year to year, and it is unlikely that a high proportion of IOs would coincidentally experience shifts in the same direction as ratings during the year of the latter's release. The results of the modified baseline equations, shown in Tables A21 and A22, continue to support the argument, though are marginally weaker than those in Tables 10.2 and 10.3 – as should be expected, given the smaller sample size and the fact that many donors are likely to be either unaware of or unable to respond to ratings during FY v_{IO}.[52]

Additional Robustness Checks

The findings remained consistent with the argument throughout a number of alternative specifications of the baseline models, the results of which are also

---

[49] Table A13 provides a list of the unassessed IOs – which exclude those that have been rated in any of the other assessments – and their values of DFIDFUNDING. The third column of the list of assessed IOs in the chapter appendix shows their DFIDFUNDING values, which range from 1.19 to 78,018.13 and have a mean of 1,880.16.

[50] I employ genetic matching, filling in missing values – which are not permitted – using multiple imputation. Tables A17 and A18 display post-matching balance statistics.

[51] As shown in Tables A19 and A20, these results are robust to the use of lower order polynomials.

[52] Importantly, the results are stronger in the models with larger sample sizes (in particular Model 8).

reported in the online appendix.[53] First, I included FY $v_{IO} + i$ fixed effects to address temporal heterogeneity, a serious possibility given that the dataset covers the financially turbulent period following the global economic crisis (Tables A23 and A24). Second, I controlled for four additional variables: AGE, an IO's log age in FY $v_{IO} - 1$; SCOPE, the number of issue areas in which an IO operates in FY $v_{IO} - 1$; REGIONAL, a dummy for whether an IO has a regional focus in FY $v_{IO} - 1$; and DIVERGENCE, the variance of an IO's standardized mean indicator scores in each assessment (since resource flows may be more responsive to ratings when there is greater agreement among assessors) (Tables A25 and A26). Third, I included both sets of conditioning variables and interaction terms in the same equation (Table A27). Fourth, I excluded influential observations from the analyses, which were identified using the widely used Cook's Distance metric (Tables A28 and A29).[54]

A final set of checks involved experimenting with alternative measures of key variables in the analysis. To address the possibility that resource flows in FY $v_{IO} - 1$ are anomalous relative to general pre-assessment funding levels, I constructed modified measures of the dependent variable in which the denominator is changed to $\Sigma_{j=1}^{3} \text{CONTRIBUTIONS}_{v_{IO}-j}/3$ (Tables A30 and A31) and $\Sigma_{j=1}^{5} \text{CONTRIBUTIONS}_{v_{IO}-j}/3$ (Tables A32 and A33), i.e. the pre-assessment period is expanded to three and five FYs, respectively. In addition, I employed three different measures of institutional competition, the first two based on the issue-specific determinants of the variable discussed in the third section and the third based on the measure developed for unassessed IOs in the previous subsection: (1) a proxy for expertise-based barriers to entry that measures whether an IO performs specialized technical assistance functions for its members in FY $v_{IO} - 1$ (EXPERTISE) (Table A34); (2) a proxy for network effects-based economies of scale that measures whether an IO engages in standard-setting activities in FY $v_{IO} - 1$ (STANDARDS) (Table A35); and (3) the log number of IOs in the *Yearbook of International Organizations* database that share an IO's subject of activity in FY $v_{IO} - 1$ (SHARED) (Table A36).[55]

CONCLUSION

As a form of social knowledge produced by respected and authoritative actors, IO performance indicators highlight and shape shared understandings of the

---

[53] The interaction-term coefficients marginally exceeded the p 0.1 significance threshold in some models with lower sample sizes and observation-to-variable ratios.

[54] Observations were excluded if their Cook's Distance exceeded $4/n$ (where n is the analysis sample size).

[55] The interaction-term coefficients in Tables A33 and A34 are negative because barriers to entry and economies of scale are inversely related to competition. The results of these models provide stronger support for the unconditional GPA influence hypothesis, but should be treated with some caution because EXPERTISE and STANDARDS are less direct measures of competition.

behavior and impact of such institutions, enhancing the salience of performance as a basis for making multilateral funding decisions. I have argued, however, that performance ratings do not influence resource flows to IOs under all circumstances; rather, their impact is conditional on the nature of the relationship between IOs and other actors within their policy space. Specifically, they only exert influence when IOs (1) are subject to a high degree of institutional competition and (2) possess robust governance partnerships with non-state actors. A combination of qualitative and quantitative evidence from a variety of original sources has provided consistent empirical support for the argument.

In addition to furthering our understanding of the sources – and limits – of assessment power in world politics, the findings have implications for other kinds of GPIs with the potential to influence material resource flows to target entities, such as indicators of democracy, governance, corruption, and business conditions.[56] They suggest, for instance, that such GPIs will have a greater impact on resource flows when there is a sizable pool of target entities that possess similar characteristics and could thus serve as substitutes for one another. Thus, we might expect assessments of a state's business conditions or governance to be less likely to affect foreign direct investment (FDI) inflows if it possesses a particularly rare natural resource or large internal market. The argument also implies that GPIs will have stronger material effects when assessed entities have close operational ties with actors capable of influencing resource holders – or with resource holders themselves. Economies that are highly integrated with the home countries of foreign investors, for example, may be more likely to receive a boost in FDI inflows when their political or business climate receives a positive assessment.

The findings also have implications for understanding the *non-material* effects of GPIs. In addition to funding levels, IO performance indicators are likely to influence outcomes such as the size of an IO's membership, the degree of (state and non-state) compliance with its policies, and the extent of its soft power and informal influence in the international system. If my argument is correct, we should expect these variables to be more responsive to performance ratings when IOs face few competitors and have powerful allies above and below the state. By a similar logic, we might expect assessments of a state's level of democracy or internal security to have a weaker impact on outcomes such as its ability to form alliances and engage in institutionalized cooperation when it occupies a strategically important position in the international system (for instance, due to its geographical location or capabilities) and has close political, economic, and social ties with potential cooperators. These and the above possibilities point to relational analyses of the material and non-material effects of GPIs as a fruitful area for further research.

---

[56] See Kelley, Simmons, and Doshi; Lee and Matanock; Morse; and Roberts and Tellez, this volume.

Another promising research avenue concerns the sources of variation in governance partnerships. While my argument sheds light on the factors affecting institutional competition, it does not directly address the question of why some IOs are able to form more robust partnerships than others. A comprehensive answer to this question is beyond the scope of this chapter, though a few possibilities are worth mentioning. First, some policy spaces are simply populated by fewer non-state actors than others, for instance, because the issue in question has little popular resonance or is associated with severe collective action problems.[57] Second, partnership formation may be influenced by the openness of an IO's policymaking process to external actors (in part a function of institutional design), which affects its opportunities to identify and interact with potential partners.[58] Finally, non-state actors sometimes play an important role in the establishment of IOs, forging informal ties with such institutions that may provide the basis for future operational collaboration.[59] In other words, variation in partnership robustness may reflect historical legacies of institutional creation. Developing and testing a full theory of partnership formation is an important task for future research.

References

Aaron, Joshua R., Amy McMillan, and Brandon N. Cline. 2012. Investor Reaction to Firm Environmental Management Reputation. *Corporate Reputation Review* 15 (4):304–18.

Abbott, Kenneth W., Philipp Genschel, Duncan Snidal, and Bernhard Zangl, eds. 2015. *International Organizations as Orchestrators*. Cambridge: Cambridge University Press.

Abbott, Kenneth W., Jessica F. Green, and Robert O. Keohane. 2016. Organizational Ecology and Institutional Change in Global Governance. *International Organization* 70 (2):247–77.

Abbott, Kenneth W., and Duncan Snidal. 1998. Why States Act through Formal International Organizations. *Journal of Conflict Resolution* 42 (1):3–32.

Ackrill, Robert, and Adrian Kay. 2006. Historical-Institutionalist Perspectives on the Development of the EU Budget System. *Journal of European Public Policy* 13 (1):113–33.

Alter, Karen J., and Sophie Meunier. 2009. The Politics of International Regime Complexity. *Perspectives on Politics* 7 (1):13–24.

[57] Abbott et al. 2015 make a similar conjecture. In addition, they posit that partnerships are more likely to be formed when IOs lack the capabilities to achieve their goals, occupy a focal institutional position in their issue area, have entrepreneurial cultures, and are subject to weak oversight by states.

[58] See Tallberg et al. 2013.

[59] Johnson 2014.

Bisbee, James H., James R. Hollyer, B. Peter Rosendorff, and James Raymond
    Vreeland. this volume. The Millennium Development Goals and
    Education: Accountability and Substitution in Global Indicators. In *The
    Power of Global Performance Indicators*, edited by Judith Kelley and
    Beth A. Simmons. New York: Cambridge University Press.
Brammer, Stephen, Chris Brooks, and Stephen Pavelin. 2009. The Stock
    Performance of America's 100 Best Corporate Citizens. *The Quarterly
    Review of Economics and Finance* 49 (3):1065–80.
Broz, J. Lawrence, and Michael B. Hawes. 2006. Congressional Politics of
    Financing the International Monetary Fund. *International Organization*
    60 (2):367–99.
Busby, Joshua William. 2007. Bono Made Jesse Helms Cry: Jubilee 2000, Debt
    Relief, and Moral Action in International Politics. *International Studies
    Quarterly* 51 (2):247–75.
Cameron, Kim S. 1978. Measuring Organizational Effectiveness in Institutions
    of Higher Education. *Administrative Science Quarterly* 23 (4):604–32.
Cooley, Alexander, and Jack Snyder, eds. 2015. *Ranking the World: Grading States
    as a Tool of Global Governance*. Cambridge: Cambridge University Press.
Davis, Kevin E., Angelina Fisher, Benedict Kingsbury, and Sally Engle Merry.
    2012. *Governance by Indicators: Global Power through Classification
    and Rankings*. Oxford: Oxford University Press.
Department for International Development (United Kingdom). 2013.
    Multilateral Aid Review Update. London: DFID.
Department of Foreign Affairs and Trade (Australia). 2013. Australia's
    International Development Assistance Program 2013–14. Statement by
    Senator the Hon. Bob Carr, Minister for Foreign Affairs, May 14, 2013,
    Canberra.
Etzioni, A. 1964. *Modern Organizations*. Englewood Cliffs, NJ: Prentice-Hill.
Food and Agriculture Organization. 2007. *Report of the Independent
    External Evaluation of the Food and Agriculture Organization of the
    United Nations (FAO)*. Conference document C 2007/7A.1-Rev.1, 34th
    Session. Rome.
Frey, Bruno S. 2008. Outside and Inside Competition for International
    Organizations – From Analysis to Innovations. *The Review of
    International Organizations* 3 (4):335–50.
Gavas, Mikaela. 2012. Reviewing the Evidence: How Well Does the European
    Development Fund Perform? ODI Discussion Paper. London: Overseas
    Development Institute.
Hawkins, Darren G., David A. Lake, Daniel L. Nielson, and Michael J. Tierney,
    eds. 2006. *Delegation and Agency in International Organizations*.
    Cambridge: Cambridge University Press.
Honig, Dan, and Catherine Weaver. this volume. A Race to the Top?: The Aid
    Transparency Index and the Normative Power of Global Performance
    Indicators. *Annual Meeting of the American Political Science Association*.
Hooghe, Liesbet, Gary Marks, Tobias Lenz, Jeanine Bezuijen, Besir Ceka, and
    Svet Derderyan. 2017. *Measuring International Authority: A Postfunctionalist
    Theory of Governance, Volume III*. Oxford: Oxford University Press.
Hoole, Francis W., David H. Handley, and Charles W. Ostrom. 1979. Policy-
    Making Models, Budgets and International Organizations. *The Journal of
    Politics* 41 (3):923–32.

Hoole, Francis W., Brian L. Job, and Harvey J. Tucker. 1976. Incremental Budgeting and International Organizations. *American Journal of Political Science* 20 (2):273–301.

Johnson, Tana. 2014. *Organizational Progeny: Why Governments Are Losing Control over the Proliferating Structures of Global Governance.* Oxford: Oxford University Press.

Jupille, Joseph, Walter Mattli, and Duncan Snidal. 2013. *Institutional Choice and Global Commerce.* Cambridge: Cambridge University Press.

Kelley, Judith G., and Beth A. Simmons. this volume. Introduction: The Power of Global Performance Indicators. Chapter 1 in *The Power of Global Performance Indicators.*

Kelley, Judith G., Beth A. Simmons, and Rush Doshi. this volume. The Power of Ranking: The Ease of Doing Business and Global Regulatory Behavior. Chapter 2 in *The Power of Global Performance Indicators.*

Lavelle, Kathryn C. 2011. Multilateral Cooperation and Congress: The Legislative Process of Securing Funding for the World Bank. *International Studies Quarterly* 55 (1):199–222.

Lee, Melissa M., and Aila M. Matanock. this volume. Third Party Policymakers and the Limits of the Influence of Indicators. Chapter 11 in *The Power of Global Performance Indicators.* Cambridge: Cambridge University Press.

Lipscy, Phillip Y. 2015. Explaining Institutional Change: Policy Areas, Outside Options, and the Bretton Woods Institutions. *American Journal of Political Science* 59 (2):341–56.

Mattli, Walter, and Jack Seddon. 2015. Orchestration along the Pareto frontier: winners and losers. In *International Organizations as Orchestrators,* edited by Kenneth W. Abbott, Philipp Genschel, Duncan Snidal, and Bernhard Zangl. Cambridge: Cambridge University Press.

Merry, Sally Engle, Kevin E. Davis, and Benedict Kingsbury, eds. 2015. *The Quiet Power of Indicators: Measuring Governance, Corruption, and Rule of Law.* Cambridge: Cambridge University Press.

Ministerie van Buitenlandse Zaken (Netherlands). 2013. Kamerbrief over scorecards internationale organisaties. Den Haag.

Ministry for Foreign Affairs (Denmark). 2013. Danish Multilateral Development Cooperation Analysis: An Assessment of Denmark's Multilateral Engagement in Light of the Right to a Better Life, the Strategy for Danish Development Cooperation. Copenhagen.

Ministry for Foreign Affairs (Sweden). 2011. Swedish Assessment of Multilateral Organisations: Summary 2011. Stockholm.

Morse, Julia C. this volume. Blacklists, Market Enforcement, and the Global Regime to Combat Terrorist Financing. *Annual Meeting of the American Political Science Association.*

Multilateral Organization Performance Assessment Network. 2015. Annual Report 2014. Paris.

Murguia, Juan M., and Sergio H. Lence. 2015. Investors' Reaction to Environmental Performance: A Global Perspective of the Newsweek's "Green Rankings." *Environmental and Resource Economics* 60 (4):583–605.

Nielson, Daniel, and Michael J. Tierney. 2003. Delegation to International Organizations: Agency Theory and World Bank Environmental Reform. *International Organization* 57 (2):241–76.

Pevehouse, Jon, Timothy Nordstrom, and Kevin Warnke. 2004. The
    Correlates of War 2 International Governmental Organizations Data
    Version 2.0. *Conflict Management and Peace Science* 21 (2):101–19.
Pollack, Mark A. 1997. Delegation, Agency, and Agenda Setting in the
    European Community. *International Organization* 51 (1):99–134.
Price, James L. 1972. The Study of Organizational Effectiveness. *The
    Sociological Quarterly* 13 (1):3–15.
Roberts, Jordan, and Roberts Fernando Tellez. this volume. Freedom House's
    Scarlet Letter: Assessment Power through Transnational Pressure.
Singer, J. David. 1961. *Financing International Organization: The United
    Nations Budget Process.* The Hague: Nijhoff.
Tallberg, Jonas, Thomas Sommerer, Theresa Squatrito, and Christer Jönsson.
    2013. *The Opening Up of International Organizations: Transnational
    Access in Global Governance.* Cambridge: Cambridge University Press.

PART IV

SKEPTICAL VOICES

Null Results, Unintended Consequences

11

Third-Party Policymakers and the Limits of the Influence of Indicators

Melissa M. Lee and Aila M. Matanock

Rating and ranking states are increasingly common tools of global governance.[1] Global performance indicators (GPIs), defined as "regularized, public reporting routines that states, intergovernmental organizations (IGOs), nongovernmental organizations (NGOs), or private actors use to attract attention to the performance of countries or other organizations,"[2] can provoke action on the issues they raise. The creators of GPIs often explicitly intend for GPIs to serve a multitude of policy purposes, including the transformation of societies or policies through the identification and provision of information on offenders. The "recurring monitoring and comparative grading of countries" is an exercise of power to influence behavior by states and other actors.[3] But through what mechanisms do GPIs work?

Existing scholarship, including the contributions to this volume, has largely focused on a social rather than material mechanism, and persuasive rather than coercive power. International relations scholars have long been interested in power, with realists focusing more on material power and constructivists focusing more on social power, though both forms can be used to coerce and persuade. Studies on GPIs posit social channels of influence primarily from bottom-up domestic political pressure or domestic elite response in rated states, wherein GPIs act as symbols that shape perceptions

---

[1] Broome, Homolar, and Kranke 2018; Broome and Quirk 2015; Cooley and Snyder 2015; Davis, Kingsbury, and Merry 2012; Davis et al. 2012; Fisher 2012; Fukuda-Parr 2014; Hansen and Porter 2012; Kelley and Simmons 2015; Masaki and Parks 2019; Merry, Davis, and Kingsbury 2015; Radaelli 2018; Rottenburg, Merry, Park et al. 2015; Sharman 2009; Shore and Wright 2015.
[2] Kelley and Simmons 2017, 5.
[3] Kelley and Simmons 2015.

and reputational concerns.[4] This pathbreaking work, however, downplays or ignores the possibility of a material-external mechanism.[5] In international relations, external material power remains a potent instrument for influencing other states. It may be the only option for altering state behavior in the "hardest" cases resistant to social pressure and with little possibility for domestic reform.

This chapter explores whether GPIs prompt the exercise of material power from policymakers in third-party states and international financial institutions (IFIs).[6] These third-party policymakers control important material resources like foreign aid. When conditioned on ratings, this material pressure can change rated states' actions. We investigate the first essential step in the causal chain: whether GPIs influence policymakers. We theorize that GPIs can act as focal points that transform the discourse about policy decisions, set agendas and norms about that policy, and, in doing so, create political cover for policy actions. These channels of influence are tied to GPI structure and authority, as the quantitative ranking of countries and the identification of extreme cases can serve as an informational shortcut and a strong signal of consensus about the worst of the worst. Focal effects then increase the likelihood that third-party policymakers respond to GPIs by pressuring poorly performing states using the levers of material power.

We test our arguments about GPI influence using Transparency International's Corruption Perceptions Index (CPI). The CPI is a prominent GPI that assigns quantitative ratings and rankings to states on their perceived levels of corruption, an important issue area in the discourse on good governance, statebuilding, and development.

We use the case of the CPI to evaluate two implications from our theory. First, we investigate whether the CPI attracts attention. We conduct a systematic review of media coverage of the CPI for six major English-language news outlets, and we also assess whether policymakers discuss the CPI, including systematically in their policy briefings with the media.

Second, we assess whether the CPI increases the likelihood that third parties punish corruption offenders by reducing foreign aid or altering the composition of foreign aid prone to capture to types less prone to capture. We focus on foreign aid because it is an important instrument of material power

---

[4] Honig and Weaver this volume; Kelley and Simmons 2015; Masaki and Parks 2019; Morse this volume; Sharman 2009; Sundstrom and Henry 2017.

[5] Studies often suggest it is too rare to be effective: for example, examining human trafficking, Kelley mentions fear of material repercussions, but submits that these are uncommon in the cases. See Kelley 2017, 91. Outside the domain of state behavior, Jensen and Malesky find that the OECD's Anti-Bribery Convention, whose peer review mechanism exemplifies a broader category of global performance *assessment*, reduced bribery from firms facing material punishments in signatory countries. See Jensen and Malesky 2018.

[6] Our chapter complements Roberts and Tellez, who show in this volume that countries rated poorly in one domain face non-material penalties in other domains.

and thus a channel of influence that has received less attention in the scholarship on GPIs. We test whether a country's CPI rank or score influences the amount and type of aid that a country receives. We also test whether third party donors treat the ten worst corruption offenders – a group that receives outsized scrutiny – systematically differently than the next ten corruption offenders. In keeping with our interest in assessing the influence of corruption *indicators* rather than corruption itself, an important feature of our research design is our effort to hold constant the level of corruption while exploiting variation in the assessment of corruption.

This research design reflects our view that the external-material pathway is a "less likely" mechanism of GPI influence. The multiple empirical approaches and the selection of an "easy" case – corruption and the CPI – gives us the best opportunity to uncover evidence in favor of this "hard" mechanism. Even so, we uncover remarkably little evidence that the CPI influences third-party actors. While we find that the CPI does attract attention from the media, it does not attract similar attention from policymakers, suggesting that it does not have all the effects that its creators seek – a mechanism that could pressure states resistant to social shaming. Nor do we find statistical evidence that the CPI induces policymakers to punish corruption offenders using foreign aid.

These results are theoretically and substantively important. Our null finding is strikingly consistent across multiple models and third-party responses, but this does not mean that the CPI exercises no influence. Whereas other contributions in this volume demonstrate that GPIs exercise considerable influence on state behavior, this chapter suggests limits to that influence. The CPI garners the lion's share of media coverage, which demonstrates the CPI's success in publicizing and framing understandings of corruption. However, our findings cast doubt on the material-external pathway in this issue area. This chapter therefore raises important theoretical questions about the conditions under which GPIs affect policy in rated states through the transnational politics channel, and implies limits to the influence of indicators as a tool of global governance. We take up that discussion in the conclusion of this chapter.

GPIs AS FOCAL POINTS

Scholars increasingly recognize global performance indicators (GPIs) as important instruments through which international actors shape behavior. The GPIs are simplifications of complex reality.[7] They take the form of grades that indicate performance or rankings or ratings that compare performance between actors. As such, GPIs constitute a form of monitoring. Importantly, GPIs are purposive: the organizations creating them seek to change policy through pressure and strategically package them to achieve these aims.[8]

---

[7] Espeland and Sauder 2012.
[8] Kelley 2017; Kelley and Simmons 2015.

The creators of GPIs often explicitly seek to influence state behavior, and much of the existing evidence shows that GPIs do so directly via social means through the channels of bottom-up domestic politics or domestic elite responses in the rated states (what we call the "social-domestic pathway"). The use of rating or rankings is a particularly potent way to elicit reputational concerns. Grades, too, are powerful symbols that shape perceptions about the performance of the graded.[9] Indeed, most of the extant examinations of the power of GPIs, including many of the contributions in this volume, focuses on this social-domestic pathway.[10]

Considering the pathways of power in international relations, however, the scholarly attention paid to social and persuasive mechanisms leaves unexplored an important means through which GPIs may in influence behavior: coercion through material incentives.[11] We therefore complement the existing work on social influence by investigating whether GPIs also influence state behavior through a "material-external pathway" that runs through third-party policymakers. Third-party states and intergovernmental organizations are important because they wield instruments of material power like foreign aid or economic sanctions that can be brought to bear on poorly performing rated states, which in turn can change behavior or policy in the rated states. This "long" transnational pathway of GPI influence thus resembles an inverse boomerang effect. Unlike the traditional boomerang effect, where domestic actors solicit the help of international actors to pressure target governments, the inverse boomerang effect operates where the international producers of GPIs seek to coordinate with third-party state policymakers to pressure governments.[12]

Many of the existing theorized effects of GPIs in the literature only peripherally involve international third parties.[13] For example, Kelley argues that GPIs can work through a cycle wherein NGOs shape perceptions through information provision, and the NGOs in turn receive third-party resources to advance their missions.[14] She shows this process in the case of the annual Trafficking in Persons (TIP) reports, which resulted in rated countries responding to the GPI by changing their human tracking laws to increase criminalization.

---

[9] Kelley and Simmons 2015.

[10] Honig and Weaver this volume; Kelley 2017; Kelley and Simmons this volume; Kijima and Lipscy this volume; Masaki and Parks 2019; Morse this volume; Schueth 2015; Sundstrom and Henry 2017.

[11] The notable exception is Chapter 8 in this volume by Roberts and Tellez, which examines outside-domain effects and shows that poorly rated countries in a particular domain face state-imposed penalties across domains other than the issue area. Our chapter differs in that we explore within-domain effects, or how third parties treat the rated with respect to the issue area in question. See Roberts and Tellez this volume.

[12] Keck and Sikkink 1998.

[13] In contrast, there is a large literature about the role of third parties in international politics more generally, particularly in the domain of human rights and in NGO activism.

[14] Kelley 2017, 96.

In that case, US involvement was limited to providing resources for NGOs, rather than pressuring the rated states with its material resources directly. The scholarship has also uncovered some evidence of third-party state-to-state routes, but primarily focused on social mechanisms like non-coercive forms of diplomacy.[15] To the extent that these studies note the possibility of a material-external pathway of influence, they have asserted that it is rare.[16]

Our work builds on existing scholarship and the logic of this inverse boomerang effect. We investigate whether GPIs influence third-party states to wield material pressure, the crucial first step in the material-external pathway of change. We argue that GPIs are most likely to exercise influence through the production of focal points. Focal points, devices that coordinate multiple actors' attention, increase the ability of actors to collectively observe and effectively respond to information and set standards.[17] Two aspects of GPIs as focal points are important for influencing policymaker behavior, and they may change behavior either by encouraging different action or providing cover for what some seek to do anyway.

First, GPIs provide new and digestible information to reduce complexity around issues like corruption.[18] Quantifying complex concepts facilitates comparisons between countries and over time, which allows policymakers to more easily interpret differences across contexts as well as improvements or backsliding. Such information may be wholly new to policymakers, or, more likely, it may be presented in an easily digestible and comparable form that reduces complexity of inherently difficult concepts.[19] Consider an example from the crusade against corruption, an important issue area in the realm of good governance. The US government may wish to avoid giving development aid to the egregiously corrupt, but identifying corruption is an inherently laborious task that requires difficult to obtain data as well as knowledge of the context. These challenges arise because corruption is a complex phenomenon that takes many forms and is based on culturally relativistic understandings.[20] Corruption also raises the problem of observation and detection, since those engaged in corruption often seek to hide their illicit activities.

Another example comes from the domain of environmental conservation. The Environmental Performance Index gathers a large number of easily understandable and comparable indicators and country rankings on different dimensions of environmental health and ecosystem vitality. A common feature of these domains is their highly complex and technical nature, and the use of jargon and concepts

---

[15] Broome and Quirk 2015; Davis et al. 2012; Kelley and Simmons this volume.
[16] For instance, in her examination of human tracking, Kelley acknowledges the possibility of sanctions and the fear of material repercussions, but notes that states rarely impose these punishments in the cases. See Kelley 2017.
[17] Schelling 1960, 54–58.
[18] Kelley and Simmons this volume; Sinclair 2005.
[19] Fisher 2012; Kelley and Simmons this volume.
[20] Bukovansky 2015, 61.

that are only accessible to trained specialists in that field. Since policymakers are unlikely to possess that kind of technical expertise, but may nonetheless care about these issues, GPIs play an important role by providing information in a form that increases lay accessibility and permits quick comparisons.

Second, GPIs set and reinforce standards of appropriateness and inappropriateness. Put differently, GPIs transform the discourse around the issue area and shape the agendas of other actors, and in turn they alter how policymakers think about global performance issues or their own policy priorities. Setting standards increases policymakers' ability to collectively observe and effectively respond to violations of set standards, while coordinating actors increases the chances that behavior will be appropriately rewarded and punished.[21]

Consider an example of agenda setting. The issue of government transparency likely owes some of its current status as a Western cause célèbre to the efforts of international organizations and their GPIs. The International Budget Partnership, which operates a flagship GPI, the Open Budget Survey, explicitly states that a core area of its work is to establish global norms around open, transparent government. Or consider an example of shaping current understandings of a complex concept. Freedom House and its annual *Freedom in the World* report define democracy in terms of political rights and civil liberties. By defining democracy as *liberal* democracy in its GPI and its advocacy work, Freedom House has transformed how other actors understand the concept itself. These "knowledge effects" can influence how various actors think about issues and then the choices they make based on that thinking.[22]

By providing information and establishing standards of behavior, GPIs influence policymakers in two ways. They encourage policymakers to take different actions, and they provide political cover for domestic or international actors whose authority is lacking or contested but who still wish to make changes. By clearly delineating a standard of appropriate behavior around which other actors have coordinated, GPIs equip policymakers with ammunition to justify decisions.[23] This cover can reduce the downside of punishing violations, which can either change the calculation on a policy or simply make the policy planned less costly. Though the latter is difficult to observe, we present some qualitative evidence later that addresses the possibility. Importantly, however, only changing policy would engage the material-external pathway that we explore in this chapter.

The structure and authority of GPIs enhance these potential channels of influence. Quantitative GPIs are especially useful for providing cover, since they carry the veneer of objectivity and scientific fact.[24] These features of

---

[21] Fearon 2011, 1662.

[22] Merry, Davis, and Kingsbury 2015.

[23] Lebovic and Voeten 2006.

[24] We do not claim that quantitative data are always objective; the CPI itself is a subjective indicator based on several subjective inputs. Rather, the claim is that others perceive quantitative data to be more objective than qualitative data.

GPIs could change decisions or justifications for decisions on the basis of "data," which may be useful for disarming criticisms about bias, or political and geostrategic considerations, including from rated states. For example, on the domestic front, the authority and quantitative structure of GPIs allows bureaucrats and policymakers to defend their recommendations to principals. In this way, GPIs play a similar role as international law in providing cover for certain kinds of domestic actors.[25] On the international front, GPIs play an important role by providing "data" and "evidence" to which external actors can appeal when criticizing states in politically sensitive domains.

In addition to producing quantitative data, many GPIs explicitly rank and then list especially problematic states. Identifying the extremes can channel attention and mobilize pressure for action against these worst offenders, augmented by consensus.[26] Extreme cases are often perceived in terms of the "bottom ten," an example of a well-documented cognitive preference for base ten numbers.[27] Scholars have shown that creating thresholds below which units are identified as needing improvement has especially profound effects on performance in subsequent periods.[28] Others have shown that identifying extreme cases in blacklists or watch lists provides "bright lines," indicating where sanctions should be applied.[29] The organizations producing GPIs identify these worst cases and often highlight them through an "alert." Identifying the extremes channels attention and mobilizes pressure for action against these worst offenders.[30] The extreme cases also reflect consensus about the best and worst cases.

Rankings and the identification of extremes are particularly likely to garner media coverage. According to interviews they conducted, Kelley and Simmons (this volume) concluded that "the media is particularly fond of indices." Given the existence of the base-ten bias, we also expect that media reporting on indices to focus disproportionately on groups of ten, particularly on such groups in the extreme values of the indices. Indeed, many news outlets build top ten or bottom ten lists around GPIs.

This media coverage amplifies GPIs and the information they convey in two ways. First, traditional and social media alike facilitate the spread of information and knowledge to mass and elite audiences. By reaching larger and more diverse audiences, the media increases the likelihood that those audiences internalize the importance of the issue area or communicate to policymakers the need for action on some issue. In this case, amplification occurs through audience expansion. Second, in issue areas where multiple GPIs compete, media coverage can also arbitrate which GPIs rise to greater prominence, as coverage

---

[25] Huth, Croco, and Appel 2011.
[26] Pratto and John 1991.
[27] "Base-ten bias." See Lynn, Flynn, and Helion 2013; Pope and Simonsohn 2011; Rosch 1975; Schlenker and Scorse 2017; Sonnemans 2006.
[28] Callen, Gulzar, Hasanain et al. 2016; Kelley and Simmons 2017; Schlenker and Scorse 2017.
[29] Kelley and Simmons 2015, 57.
[30] Pratto and John 1991.

explicitly or implicitly reflects a judgment about what matters more. In this case, amplification occurs through more intense coverage. Both pathways may directly or indirectly affect third-party policymakers.

Our theory about GPIs as focal points implies two main propositions that we test in the remainder of this chapter. First, we should see actors responding to the release of GPIs. In particular, our arguments about the structure of GPIs, base-ten bias, and the identification of extremes suggests that the top ten and bottom ten ranked states will be the subject of significant media exposure and policymaker attention. Second, we expect that the wielders of material power will also respond to GPIs. If GPIs successfully set focal points and coordinate coercive action among third-party states, we anticipate that we will observe this effect through the application of economic pressure: third-party states should increase economic pressure based on the information contained in GPIs.

CASE SELECTION: CORRUPTION AND THE CPI

We test our hypotheses about the influence of GPIs on third-party policy-makers on corruption. An important assumption underpinning any external pathway of GPI influence is that third-party policymakers find an issue area sufficiently compelling that they respond to the information and standards in GPIs. Corruption has become such an issue area. The post-Cold War period saw the rise of the good governance agenda and increasing concern among intergovernmental organizations, non-governmental organizations, and powerful Western states about the role of corruption in development.[31] In part due to the work of GPI creators and this good governance agenda, aid donors began paying more attention to issues surrounding corruption.[32] The International Monetary Fund (IMF) declared good governance to be an essential ingredient for economic success, while the World Bank points to the pernicious effects of corruption on human and economic development.[33] Donors consider good governance factors like corruption when making allocation decisions; they give less aid and different kinds of aid to poorly governed states.[34] Because policymakers see corruption as a pressing issue, there is an opportunity for

---

[31] Dunning 2004; Weaver 2008. An important study by Alesina and Weder 2002 finds no effect of corruption on aid allocation. However, their data cover the period 1975–1994, which precedes the era in which corruption became a central piece of the discussion on good governance and indeed the era in which good governance became a crucial consideration in aid allocation. Recent scholarship in contrast shows that corruption does influence foreign aid decision-making (see Dietrich 2013; Winters 2010), which lays an important foundation for our effort to study the effect of corruption *indicators* on foreign aid allocations.

[32] Bukovansky 2002; Charron 2011; Goldsmith 2001; Hjertholm and White 2000; Sandholtz and Gray 2003; Weaver 2008.

[33] International Monetary Fund 2017.

[34] Bermeo 2017; Claessens, Cassimon, and Van Campenhout 2009; Clist 2011; Dietrich 2013, 2016; Winters 2010; Winters and Martinez 2015.

corruption GPIs to influence discourse and policy decisions. We therefore consider corruption to be an easy case within the otherwise difficult material-external pathway of GPI influence.

Within the issue area of corruption, we look for evidence of GPI influence in the specific case of Transparency International's Corruption Perceptions Index. Transparency International (TI) explicitly seeks to force policymakers to pay attention:[35] the CPI "sends a powerful message" to make policymakers and others "notice and act."[36] The CPI is one of the best-known GPIs on corruption. Transparency International has produced it annually since 1995, and explicitly designates the bottom ten countries.[37]

We select the CPI from among the corruption GPIs for both theoretical and practical reasons. From a theoretical standpoint, the CPI exemplifies all five characteristics of GPIs identified in Kelley and Simmons (this volume). The reports are released regularly on an annual basis. The rankings, scores, and methodology are publicly accessible. The CPI is also inclusive in scope, growing from 45 countries in coverage in its first year to now more than 160 states (Figure 11.1). It facilitates comparisons between rated countries. The CPI is also purposive.[38] Transparency International is explicit in its mission to reduce corruption in the world by influencing policy; forcing policymakers to pay attention to corruption is central to the CPI's description.[39] Transparency International's website states that the CPI "has been widely credited with putting the issue of corruption on the international policy agenda," and asserts that the CPI "sends a powerful message and governments have been forced to take notice and act."[40]

The CPI also has practical advantages for our analysis. The CPI ranks countries and permits the identification of a "bottom ten" list that contains the most egregiously corrupt countries. Transparency International itself sometimes treats the top ten least corrupt countries and the bottom ten most corrupt countries as special categories of interest in its reports on the CPI. It is likely that users of the CPI also perceive the extreme cases as the ten countries ranked closest to the bottom in the index, rather than some other number of countries (the bottom seven or bottom thirteen, for example), especially given the broader literature on tens discussed in the theory above. As also noted above, news media may make particular use

---

[35] Wang and Rosenau 2001.

[36] Transparency International 2016.

[37] The CPI is a composite index that scores the perceived amount of corruption in countries' public sectors. It aggregates surveys and expert assessments from independent institutions. Higher ranks indicate more corruption.

[38] Wang and Rosenau 2001.

[39] A drawback of using an NGO-produced GPI rather than an IGO-produced GPI is that the NGO's GPI is less "institutionalized" both in its composition and its use in official policy-making processes. Our analyses therefore also examine the World Bank Institute's corruption GPI.

[40] Transparency International 2016.

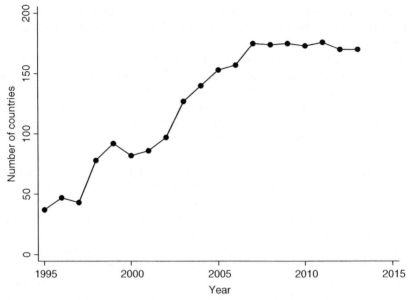

FIGURE 11.1. Number of countries in the Corruption Perceptions Index.

of these top ten or bottom ten lists as they report on these countries. We therefore expect the CPI to be especially effective at garnering coverage for these states that are identified as at the extreme end of the spectrum (which is also an intermediary step in the mechanism that we examine in the next section).

DOES THE CPI ATTRACT ATTENTION?

The first theoretical implication that we test is whether the CPI attracts media and policymaker attention. If GPIs such as the CPI have focal effects, then they should attract attention to an issue area, and we expect to see this attention in the form of extensive coverage of the CPI in the media. Moreover, if the identification of extreme cases is important, then we should also see the media disproportionately covering extreme cases. We look for similar evidence among policymakers by assessing whether policymakers discuss the CPI in media briefings and disproportionately accord attention to the extreme cases.

Media Coverage of the CPI

Next, To test our theory's implications about media coverage, we conduct a systematic review of reporting on the CPI in six major news outlets. The CPI's influence is evident in the media coverage surrounding the annual release of

TABLE 11.1. *Media coverage of the CPI, 1995–2014*

Media Outlet	CPIs Covered
New York Times	15
The Washington Post	8
The Associated Press	16
Reuters	19
The Economist	16
CNN	8

index since its inception in 1995. As shown in Table 11.1, the CPI attracts considerable attention from the media. *Reuters* has reported on the most editions of the CPI (19 out of 21 possible). *CNN* has reported on the fewest editions, but still covered eight releases.

In terms of content, media reports almost always focus on the countries that TI identifies as the most and least corrupt in the world. Some media reports about the annual CPI release list the countries in the top ten and bottom ten positions, while others only name a few countries from those groups.[41] Other reports mirror the content of the TI press releases, which can vary considerably in which countries are shamed or praised. Besides reporting on the countries that occupy the extreme positions on the CPI, media reports also highlight the scores and ranks of major powers, such as the United States, China, and Russia. Our review of media coverage suggests that countries that do not fall into one of these two categories largely escape media scrutiny during the annual release of the CPI. As shown in Figure 11.2, the bottom ten countries (most corrupt) receive much more media coverage than the next ten countries: 2.39 mentions on average, compared to just 0.23 mentions.[42]

The CPI's influence in the news media is also evident in the way the media reports on corruption in any country. If a corruption GPI is mentioned at all, it tends to be the CPI. For example, when the *New York Times* covered efforts by Mikheil Saakashvili, former president of Georgia and then governor of Ukraine's Odessa region, to clean up corruption in Ukraine, the news article referenced that country's poor performance on the CPI.[43] A BBC story on Hong Kong's integration into China observed that, unlike mainland China, the city had a reputation for being "clean" according to the 2012 CPI.[44]

---

[41] See for example Jolly 2011 and Nienaber 2014 compared to the Associated Press 2014 and *The Economist* 2014.

[42] The difference is statistically significant. The fact that the latter differs from zero at all is likely driven by occasional coverage of ties, which we discuss further in the section below.

[43] Kramer 2016.

[44] Yip 2013.

Melissa M. Lee and Aila M. Matanock

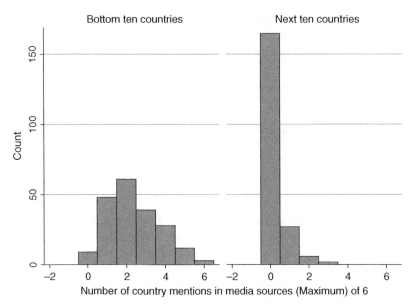

FIGURE 11.2. Media coverage of the Corruption Perceptions Index (bottom ten countries compared to the next ten countries).
Sources: Associated Press, CNN, The Economist, New York Times, The Washington Post, Reuters. Years surveyed: 1995–2014.

The Washington Post contextualized its story on Afghan President Ashraf Ghani's call for a "holy war" against corruption by noting that Afghanistan ranked near the bottom of the CPI in 2014.[45] These are just a few of many references to the CPI in corruption stories, especially for the countries with the worst rankings. Indeed, *The Economist* has called the CPI the "most-quoted league table of graft."[46]

While other corruption indicators exist, their comparative lack of coverage suggests that the CPI exercises outsized influence in the business of reporting about corruption. The CPI draws on a number of different sources on perceptions of corruption. Of the other open sources, most received an average of zero media mentions. The only other source that received some coverage was the World Economic Forum's Global Competitiveness Report. Though this GPI had 36 mentions in the media (compared to the CPI's 80), most mentions were not actually related to corruption. We also compared media coverage of the CPI with the control of corruption measure from the Worldwide Governance Indicator (WGI), which is affiliated with the World Bank Institute. Comparing the bottom ten percent of countries to the next

[45] Holley 2015.
[46] *The Economist* 2014.

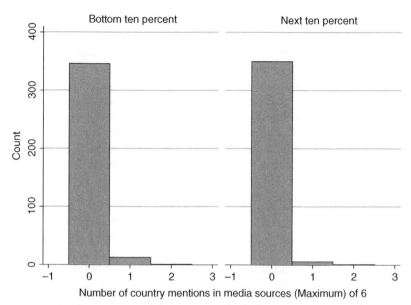

FIGURE 11.3. Media coverage of the WGI's control of corruption (bottom ten percent of all countries compared to the next ten percent).
Sources: Associated Press, CNN, The Economist, New York Times, The Washington Post, Reuters. Years surveyed: 1996–2015.

ten percent, we found very few media mentions of countries in either category, and very little difference between the categories.[47] As shown in Figure 11.3, the bottom ten percent of countries (most corrupt) receive 0.04 mentions on average, while the next ten percent receive 0.02.[48]

The evidence thus supports our conjecture that the CPI acts like a focal point in the domain of corruption. The CPI attracts considerable attention from the media, which amplifies the informational and standard-setting features of index. This media attention is also consistent with our argument that GPIs that take the form of ranking systems are especially likely to serve as focal points. Both the CPI and the WGI assign corruption scores to countries, but only the CPI assigns ranks in the commonly understood sense of the word (ranks as integers). In contrast, the WGI assigns percentile ranks. For example, the CPI ranked Equatorial Guinea 168th least corrupt out of 179 total countries evaluated in 2007, whereas the WGI's calculations assigned that country a

---

[47] The WGI, unlike the CPI, does not rank countries, so the percentages are more comparable. Using percentages produces a larger number of countries. Even then, we still see less coverage in absolute terms.

[48] The difference is not statistically significant, unless using a one-tailed test, then it is at the 0.10 level.

percentile rank of 2.43. The more straightforward nature of the CPI's rankings likely enhance its ability to serve as a focal point and garner media attention.

The media's coverage of extreme cases in the CPI also suggests a potential intermediary step between the CPI and third-party policymakers who might use reputational and material instruments of power to compel rated states to change their behavior. Media coverage amplifies the focal effects of GPIs like the CPI, which in turn elevates the issue area of corruption – and the CPI itself – in policy decisions. We would therefore expect to observe not only the CPI playing a role in policy decisions toward rated countries, but also countries that are the subject of media attention to be disproportionately affected as a result.

Policymaker Attention to the CPI

Our preceding analysis suggests that the CPI attracts attention from the media. Does it also attract attention from policymakers in powerful third-party states? To test this proposition, we examine the policymaking process in the United States using interview evidence. We also analyze whether policymakers discuss the CPI in their policy briefings with the media, and we look for evidence that policymakers accord extra attention to the bottom ten most corrupt countries. This attention is a form of naming and shaming, an important instrument of social power. In this reputational variant of the external pressure channel, naming and shaming is a form of social opprobrium rather than material coercion.[49]

Before turning to our analysis of naming and shaming, we present preliminary evidence that the CPI appears to play a focal role in some domains of foreign policy related to the good governance agenda for third-party policymakers. The Millennium Challenge Corporation, a US foreign aid agency, consults the CPI and other GPIs to help make allocation decisions. The CPI is also a component of the Standard Foreign Assistance Indicators, a set of indicators that the US Department of State and the US Agency for International Development (USAID) use to measure the impact of foreign assistance. The United Kingdom's Department for International Development's (DFID) 2013 series of anti-corruption strategy policy papers included a CPI score for each country receiving DFID funds.[50] Similarly, a USAID analysis of its anti-corruption programming also included CPI scores for countries implementing anti-corruption projects.[51] The USAID and DFID also consult the CPI and other GPIs when preparing budget justification reports for country foreign aid packages. This evidence suggests that the CPI may work in the ways hypothesized above to provide information to third-party policymakers who control foreign aid. Even if

---

[49] Found, for instance, in some human rights contexts; see Lebovic and Voeten 2006; Nielsen and Simmons 2015.

[50] DFID's anti-corruption strategy policy papers can be found at https://www.gov.uk/government/collections/anti-corruption-strategies-by-country.

[51] Winbourne and Spector 2014.

civil servants in aid agencies have access to the full ranking of countries and do not themselves rely on the extreme cases as informational shortcuts, bureaucrats respond to politicians who may be more inclined than the bureaucrats to use such shortcuts.

Qualitative evidence also indicates that the CPI provides cover for bureaucrats, an important channel through which focal points matter for policy. For example, when requesting more information about countries from aid agencies, Senate staffers use these indicators as justification for their requests.[52] In addition, aid agencies also use the CPI to explain programming or write reports. The CPI appears in the United Kingdom's DFID 2013 anti-corruption strategy and USAID's anti-corruption programming analysis.[53] This preliminary evidence suggests that if a GPI can influence third-party policymakers to change their aid allocation, we should detect it in this case. But the role of the CPI even in providing cover does not appear to extend much further, as we show in the rest of the tests, suggesting policymakers use the CPI to justify particular decision they would have made anyway but that it does not actually change their decisions.

THIRD-PARTY NAMING AND SHAMING

We analyze whether policymakers shame poorly ranked states. Verbal shaming occurs when politicians or other official domestic elites issue on-the-record statements about corruption in some target state. Shaming is an example of a "softer" kind of power that nonetheless could induce policy changes in the target if the shamed state cares about status or approval from other states – or sees shaming as a signal of potential future sanctions.[54] Shaming may therefore constitute more than just cheap talk. It is also a policy response most likely to be under the direct control of politicians as opposed to civil servants. We compare countries in the CPI's bottom ten and next ten.

We use *announcement periods* – the 30 days following the annual announcement of the CPI – as our unit of analysis. The short announcement period reflects our interest in linking shaming directly to TI's announcement, rather than to the behavior of the rated state. We compare shaming in the announcement periods among states in the bottom ten to those in the next ten. We assess whether a simple discussion of corruption, or verbal shaming and condemnation are systematically more likely among the former, which would be consistent with the theorized effect of the CPI.

Drawing on data from Nielsen and Simmons, we examine EU press releases published between 1995 and 2010 on political topics and US State Department daily press briefings between 1995 and 2008 to understand (1) if discussion of

---

[52] Author interview, April 13, 2017.
[53] See https://www.gov.uk/government/collections/anti-corruption-strategies-by-country) and Winbourne and Spector 2014, respectively.
[54] DeMeritt 2012; Hafner-Burton 2008; Hendrix and Wong 2013; Krain 2012.

TABLE 11.2. *Naming and shaming results*

		Bottom Ten	Next Ten
United States	Discussed	6 percent (8)	4 percent (5)
	Not discussed	94 percent (132)	96 percent (135)
		Pearson chi2(1) = 0.73 Pr = 0.39	
	Shamed	0 percent (0)	1 percent (1)
	Not shamed	100 percent (140)	99 percent (139)
		Pearson chi2(1) = 1.00 Pr = 0.32	
Europe	Discussed	1 percent (2)	2 percent (3)
	Not Discussed	99 percent (158)	98 percent (157)
		Pearson chi2(1) = 0.20 Pr = 0.65	
	Discussed	1 percent (1)	0 percent (0)
	Not Discussed	99 percent (140)	100 percent (139)
		Pearson chi2(1) = 1.00 Pr = 0.32	

Note: The sample contains briefings (USA) or press releases (Europe) that mention the word corruption. Numbers in parentheses refer to the number of cases.

corruption is more likely on the bottom ten cases than the next ten cases, and (2) if shaming is also systematically different.[55] The US State Department daily press briefings also include discussion with reporters, so if the media is reporting more on the bottom ten cases than the next ten cases, we would expect to see differences in this measure. In this way, on this measure, our analysis is similar in spirit to Roberts and Tellez (this volume), who examine whether countries systematically treat countries rated poorly in Freedom House's *Freedom in the World* in worse ways than those rated less poorly.

As Table 11.2 shows, we do not detect any meaningful difference in even the amount of discussion of those countries that are in the bottom ten compared to the next ten. When we examined each statement's content, we also rarely encountered shaming. Overall, there was no evidence of any systematic effect of CPI treatment on this outcome. This result is surprising in light of our media results. Shaming is a low-cost response to a problem that many would acknowledge as normatively desirable to condemn, yet we see little evidence that the most odious corruption offenders draw attention in press briefings and press releases. Additionally, the discussions with reporters in the case of the US State Department do not seem to reflect the same level of interest that we saw in our earlier media analysis, even though the reporters have the opportunity to ask questions of the press briefer.[56]

[55] Nielsen and Simmons 2015.

[56] Furthermore, although we do not find any evidence of shaming, Roberts and Tellez (this volume) demonstrate that Freedom House, a democracy GPI, influences verbal treatment of rated states. Their work suggests that there could something particular about the CPI as a GPI or the corruption issue area that might explain the different results, a proposition we return to later in this chapter.

DOES THE CPI ELICIT MATERIAL PRESSURE?

Though the results so far are mixed, we now assess the second implication from our theory, which holds that third-party states will respond to the focal nature of GPIs by applying material pressure to poorly performing states. We assess this proposition by examining the CPI's influence on an important lever of material pressure: official development aid. Development aid is an important instrument of state policy. For recipient countries, it provides a source of capital that can be used to undertake development projects or programs that would otherwise be difficult to finance given their fiscal constraints. For donors, for whom aid is a discretionary budget item, foreign aid can be used as a form of coercive pressure. Reducing foreign aid flows can impose costs on recalcitrant states, while increasing foreign aid can reward states that make improvements in development or good governance outcomes. Aid has been an especially important level of foreign policy influence in the domain of governance standards since the end of the Cold War.[57]

Donors can respond to the CPI by adjusting their aid packages in two ways. First, they can penalize corruption offenders by reducing the overall (aggregate) level of foreign aid. Following the large scholarship on foreign aid, we operationalize aggregate aid as logged aid. Since heterogeneous effects between donors are possible (e.g. political cover may apply most to IFIs),[58] we also recognize heterogeneity among donors by calculating aggregate aid and sectoral aid separately for major donors: the United States, the United Kingdom, Germany, three Scandinavian countries as a group (Norway, Sweden, and Denmark), and two IFIs as a group (the IMF and World Bank).[59] States and IFIs themselves have linked corruption with aggregate foreign aid. For example, the World Bank during Paul Wolfowitz's presidency canceled or suspended loans to at least nine countries on the basis of corruption.[60]

Second, donors can shift the composition of aid across sectors in response to the CPI by decreasing aid more susceptible to capture, what we call "capture-prone" aid, but substituting aid less susceptible, which we call "non-capture-prone" aid.[61] Capture is especially important in countries with high degrees of corruption, since aid is a resource that leaders can divert or abuse. While all aid is fungible to some extent, certain kinds of aid are more likely to be captured than others. We argue that aid allocated to human development sectors is less prone to capture, while aid with a more discretionary character will be more prone to capture. To see this intuition, consider health aid, a form of non-capture-prone aid. Donors may feel pressure from domestic populations or non-governmental organizations to give health aid regardless of

---

[57] Dunning 2004.
[58] Lebovic and Voeten 2006.
[59] Tierney, Nielson, Hawkins et al. 2011.
[60] Weaver 2008, 131.
[61] Bermeo 2017.

recipient state characteristics unrelated to health, since health aid can directly affect human well-being. We would not expect similar pressure in the case of construction aid, a form of capture-prone aid, where the linkages to human wellbeing are less direct, less clear, and less likely to be the subject of activism. Indeed, a 2006 speech by Hilary Benn, UK Secretary of State for International Development, illustrates this logic:

> When problems arise, some people argue that we should suspend our aid or withdraw it completely. I don't agree. Why should a child be denied education? Why should a mother be denied healthcare? Or an H.I.V.-positive person AIDS treatment, just because someone or something in their government is corrupt?[62]

We use aid sector codes available from the AidData project to assign aid to the "capture-prone" category and "non-capture-prone" category.[63] Aid prone to capture includes budget support, infrastructure aid, industry aid, and construction aid. Aid less prone to capture includes aid for corruption reform, civil society, public financial management, legal assistance, and social infrastructure, which includes health and education.[64]

To assess whether the CPI spurs third parties to wield material power, we take a twofold empirical strategy. First, we conduct observational analyses in which we look for evidence of a simple relationship between the CPI's evaluation of a country and the amount of economic aid it receives. This first cut ignores the inferential challenges inherent in identifying an effect of the CPI. We expect a positive relationship if the CPI overall shapes the policymaking process. Second, we build on our arguments about GPI structure and the identification of extreme cases. Recall that extreme cases may be especially likely to become the focus of policymaker action because of the greater consensus about the extremes and the psychological threshold effects of being in the bottom ten or top ten. We assess whether policymakers behave differently toward the bottom ten countries than the next ten countries ranked in the CPI. Both groups have similar levels of corruption, but differ in that the bottom ten attracts more attention, at least from the media. This cut better tackles inferential challenges although remains less perfect than an experiment (which was not possible for us to conduct in this context). Because the CPI's structure allows for improvements in corruption to be quantified, we estimate models examining linear changes in ranks and "large improvers" in ranks. The latter test allows for the possibility that large changes might be especially informative.

Our flexibility in empirical approach, model specification, and donor identity reflects theoretical and methodological considerations. First, our

---

[62] Cited in Weaver 2008, 55.
[63] Tierney, Nielson, Hawkins et al. 2011. Of course, these are rhetorical shorthands for ease of exposition, since there is no foolproof guarantee against capture.
[64] See the online appendix Table A1 for the list of sector codes.

arguments about political cover and focal points imply different processes of influence, which necessitate different tests. Second, our approach "builds in" robustness checks to ensure our findings are not an artifact of sampling or specification decisions. Third, multiple tests also give the material-external channel the best chance for finding an effect.

The CPI and Aid Allocation across All Recipients

Our first statistical test investigates whether CPI rank or score influences aid allocations by country. We control for a battery of common covariates found in existing literature to shape aid, including GDP and population, as well as dyad-specific arms buys, trade, and UN voting similarity, democracy, civil war occurrence, and logged number of natural disaster deaths.[65] We lag all predictors by one year following this literature. The sample includes all countries that are not members of the Organization for Economic Co-operation and Development, 1996–2013.

We calculate a first difference model to assess whether an increase (improvement) in lagged recipient score or rank results in an increase in foreign aid (conversely: whether a worsening of corruption as determined by the CPI results in penalty in the form of aid reduction). For robustness, we also estimate aid in levels as an alternative to the first difference approach. We specify the levels models in three ways: pooled ordinary least squares, country fixed effects, and country and year fixed effects. For parsimonious presentation of the results across two independent variables and five donors, we graph the point estimates and 95 percent confidence interviews for rank and score. We also standardize all variables except the CPI score and rank measures to have mean 0 and standard deviation 1, which allows us to compare effect sizes.

Figures 11.4 and 11.5 display the first-difference and levels results, respectively. Across these models, we find remarkably little evidence third-party policymakers allocate aggregate aid on the basis of the CPI. The theory expected a positive coefficient on our score and rank variables, but the point estimates are inconsistent and often effectively zero in terms of their magnitude. So few models reach statistical significance that we regard those that do as the result of random chance. Neither the differences nor levels approach uncovers evidence IFIs are different from other donors, either, which casts doubt on the arguments about political cover.

Next, we assess whether donors respond to the CPI by altering aid composition. Sectoral aid introduces additional empirical challenges for our analysis because not all countries receive capture-prone aid in each year. In other words, the decision to give, say, infrastructure aid (the selection stage) is independent from the decision of how much infrastructure aid to give (the allocation stage). Recent scholarship accounts for the independence of the two

[65] Bermeo 2017; Dietrich 2013.

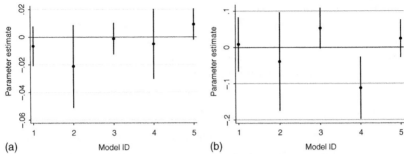

(a)   Model ID   (b)   Model ID

FIGURE 11.4. CPI: First differences results. (a) Δ CPI rank and (b) Δ CPI score.
Notes: First differences regression results. The dependent variable is logged aid and
is standardized to have mean 0 and standard deviation 1. Because the effect sizes
differ depending on whether the predictor is CPI rank or score, the subfigures use
differently scaled y-axes. Across the board, the effect sizes are substantively close to 0
and statistically indistinguishable from 0.

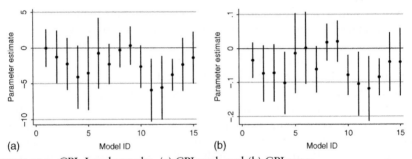

(a)   Model ID   (b)   Model ID

FIGURE 11.5. CPI: Levels results. (a) CPI rank and (b) CPI score.
Note: OLS regression results. The dependent variable is logged aid and is standardized
to have mean 0 and standard deviation 1. Because the effect sizes differ depending
on whether the predictor is CPI rank or score, the subfigures use differently scaled
y-axes. The models that reach statistical significance use logged aid as the dependent
variable and exclude controls for GDP and population size. In the case of the score
variable, the substantive effect remains close to 0.

stages selection typically using at least one of three approaches: a Tobit regression model that explicitly takes into account the censored nature of the data,
a "two part" model, and a Heckman selection model.[66] The two part and
Heckman approaches are similar in that they first model the selection stage as
a binary decision and then model the allocation stage as a linear model using
only the positive observations for aid. They differ in that Heckman explicitly uses information from the first stage in the computation of the second
stage, but requires very strong assumptions. Below, we present results using

---

[66] Bermeo 2018; Berthélemy 2006; Cingranelli and Pasquarello 1985; Clist 2011; Fariss 2010;
Fleck and Kilby 2010; Meernik, Krueger, and Poe 1998.

the Tobit approach and report results from the two part and Heckman procedures in the online appendix.[67]

We expect that if the CPI influences donors, donors should respond to poorly rated countries by decreasing aid prone to capture, increase aid not prone to capture, or both. Figure 11.6 reports the results separated by type of aid and whether we measure the CPI's effect as changes in rank or changes in score. Overall, the results are consistent with prior models: little evidence indicates CPI influence.[68]

The CPI, Extreme Focal Points, and the Bottom Ten

The previous analyses looked for evidence of a simple relationship between the CPI and aid allocation across all recipient states, but found no support for our argument that the CPI operates through a material-external pathway. We argued previously that the CPI might be especially likely to focus policymaker attention on a subset of states: those that fall into the bottom ten in the rankings. We found mixed support of our conjecture that GPIs like the CPI draw attention to countries below the base-ten threshold. Though we did not observe policymakers responding to this focal aspect of the CPI through verbal shaming or public discussion, it is still possible that they apply material pressure against the world's worst corruption offenders.

Besides suggesting a more likely place to uncover evidence of the CPI's influence, the threshold effect has the attractive feature of mitigating an important inferential problem. The primary empirical challenge we confront in detecting an effect of the CPI on foreign aid is identifying whether third parties respond to the CPI's ranking and evaluation of that country, or to the underlying conditions in the country itself that presumably drive the CPI. For example, donors may punish Turkmenistan not because the CPI ranks Turkmenistan among the most corrupt countries in the world but rather because Turkmenistan is in fact a highly corrupt country. Although our failure to find evidence in the observational analyses would ordinarily suggest

---

[67] To be clear, these approaches only address the issue of independence of the selection and allocation stages. Only the Heckman also addresses issues of endogeneity – but only when researchers can identify an "instrument" that passes the exclusion restriction. Because few plausible instruments exist, recent foreign aid articles by Bermeo and others favor the Tobit and two part approaches. We are skeptical that such an instrument exists for aid prone to capture and aid not prone to capture, and while we are less concerned with causal identification given our robust null results, we still attempt to find a suitable instrument. See the online appendix for further discussion.

[68] Recent work in the foreign aid literature has shown that donors may adjust for governance problems in recipient states in other ways. Our results notwithstanding, future research might fruitfully explore these potential adjustments in the distribution of aid. See Dietrich 2013; Winters 2010.

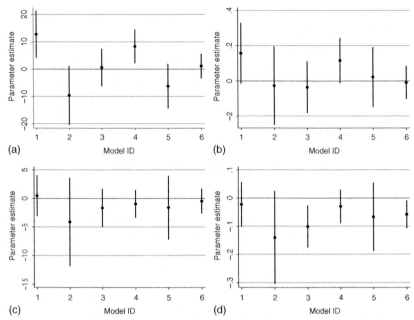

FIGURE 11.6. CPI: Sectoral aid results. (a) Aid prone to capture, CPI rank, (b) Aid prone to capture, CPI score, (c) Aid not prone to capture, CPI rank, and (d) Aid not prone to capture, CPI score.

Note: Tobit regression. The dependent variables are logged aid prone to capture and logged aid not prone to capture, and are standardized to have mean 0 and standard deviation 1. Aid prone to capture includes budget support, infrastructure aid, industry aid, and construction aid. Aid not prone to capture includes aid for corruption reform, civil society, public financial management, legal assistance, and social infrastructure, which includes health and education. See the online appendix for the list of sector codes.

that careful attention to causal inference may not be warranted (since we have not even uncovered a robust correlation), we take advantage of this opportunity to improve inference.

Our empirical strategy with respect to the extreme cases in the CPI compares the ten states that TI identifies as the most corrupt in the world, which tend to appear in media reports about corruption, with the next ten TI identifies, which are largely absent from media coverage. We assume that there is some element of randomness in the assignment of cases into the bottom ten group and the next ten group. Three facts support this assumption.

First, a country can enter or leave the bottom ten or next ten groups for reasons independent of their assessed level of corruption in the CPI. A country might change ranks despite having the same CPI score because other countries saw their scores change or new countries have been added to the index. For example, Nigeria had a corruption score of 2.2 out of 10 in both 2006 and 2007, but was ranked 18th most corrupt in 2006 and 32nd in 2007. Second, the CPI is the product of many inputs, not all of which are available in every iteration and which sometimes diverge considerably in their assessments of corruption. Its ratings are therefore prone to significant measurement error.[69] Third, countries that are tied in score might fall into the bottom ten or next ten group by virtue of where their names appear in the alphabet. In 2012, for example, this resulted in *CNN* highlighting Haiti's presence among the bottom ten countries in terms of corruption but not Burundi or Chad, even though all three countries were tied (each scoring 19). Together, these factors point to an interpretation that the assignment to the bottom ten or next ten is as-if random.[70]

We build on these insights about the bottom ten and next ten in two ways. First, in what we call the "rank change" approach, we investigate whether countries that *entered* the bottom ten are subsequently penalized more by policymakers in donor states than countries that entered the next ten. The media scrutiny accorded to countries in the bottom ten suggests that we should observe a greater penalty for the bottom ten group. Most countries experience only relatively small changes in their ranks, with a mean and median change of about five positions.[71] The sample consists of countries in the bottom ten or next ten in year *t*, respectively, but not in that group in year *t–1*. This approach treats CPI movement linearly (Figure 11.7).

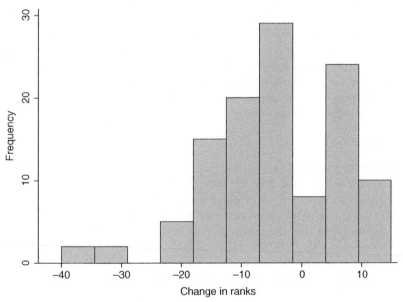

FIGURE 11.7. Histogram of change in ranks.

[69] Hough 2017.
[70] For more details, see the online appendix.
[71] For robustness we drop the outlier countries that experience large changes in ranks.

Second, in what we call the "big improvers" approach, we compare whether countries moving out of the bottom ten and next ten between consecutive CPI releases receive rewards. If the media spotlight that accompanies assignment in the bottom ten amplifies the CPI and thereby increases the likelihood that donors impose negative consequences on offending states, then countries that start in the bottom ten and improve considerably in the next edition of the CPI should experience greater rewards than countries that start in the next ten and see similarly large improvements. In other words, the benefits in terms of aid to leaving the bottom ten should be greater than the benefits of leaving the next ten, a group that may not provide the same focal aspects. The sample is comprised of countries that started in the bottom ten or next ten and experienced improvement by at least ten ranks.

The independent variable is logged aid. The independent variable, bottom ten, is an indicator coded 1 if a country is the bottom ten and 0 in the next ten. We expect a negative coefficient on this variable in the rank change approach (since countries entering the bottom ten should experience a greater penalty than those entering the next ten), and a positive coefficient in the big improvements approach (since those beginning in the bottom ten should experience greater reward for their "improvements"). Constraining comparisons to the bottom and next ten substantially reduces our sample size, so we run models with and without controls for GDP and population.

Figures 11.8 and 11.9 display the point estimates and 95 percent confidence intervals for the rank change and big improvements results, respectively. Once again, there is no evidence that countries entering the bottom ten were more penalized than those entering the next ten. Similarly, we find no evidence that bottom ten countries whose CPI ranking improved considerably received greater reward than next ten countries with similar improvements. In both cases, almost all estimates are statistically indistinguishable from zero.

Discussion

Our findings provided mixed evidence that the CPI acts as a focal point. To the extent that this GPI does produce focal effects, they appear to be limited to drawing attention of some third-party actors and potentially serving to provide some cover for policymakers on decisions they are likely to make anyway, meaning that they do appear to be coordinating material coercion.[72] Our work about the CPI's inability to elicit such responses sets this chapter apart from others in this volume that demonstrate the influence of GPIs in a variety of ways. Before addressing what our findings mean for understanding the promise and limits of GPIs to effect change in rated states, it is first useful to consider why the CPI attracts attention, but does not shape the behavior of third-party policymakers. We discuss three potential explanations.

[72] Our interviews are our only evidence of this, but we suggest this may be a valuable area for future study.

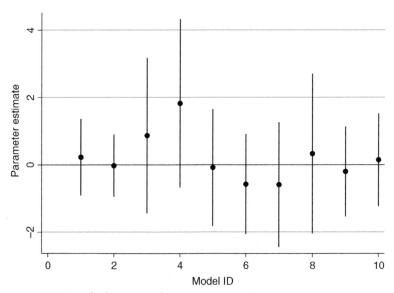

FIGURE 11.8. CPI rank change results.
Note: OLS regression results. The dependent variable is logged aid and is standardized to have mean 0 and standard deviation 1. The independent variable is a binary indicator coded 1 if a country is in the bottom ten and 0 in the next ten.

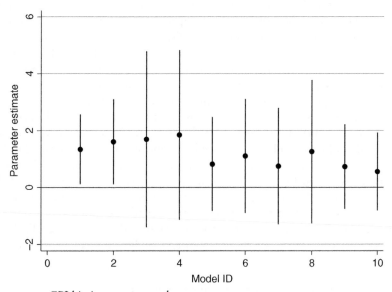

FIGURE 11.9. CPI big improvers results.
Note: OLS regression results. The dependent variable is logged aid and is standardized to have mean 0 and standard deviation 1. The independent variable is a binary indicator coded 1 if a country is in the bottom ten and 0 in the next ten.

One explanation is that GPIs do influence policymaker behavior, but that this effect is confined only to GPIs created by states and intergovernmental organizations.[73] Perhaps we find no effect of the CPI on third-party policymakers because its creator, Transparency International, is a non-governmental actor, rather than a state actor or intergovernmental organization.[74]

Could creator identity explain why third-party policymakers do not accord the same attention to these rankings as the media? In theory, this explanation is plausible. First, Any organization that creates a GPI signals that it believes the issue is important. When governments create GPIs, unilaterally or multilaterally, they voluntarily participate in creating the focal point. Consider the Millennium Development Goals (MDGs) as an example. The MDGs were drawn from the United Nations Millennium Declaration, a document signed by the leaders of 189 states. The MDGs represent a highly visible and public voluntary commitment by states to reach specific public goods targets.[75] In contrast, non-governmental creators of ratings and rankings must work to convince other actors to care about the issue. Second, governments can directly couple material resources and institutional muscle with their GPIs. Even if non-governmental organizations convince other actors to care about the issue, they then also have to convince them to take action.

We assess whether the CPI's non-governmental origins may explain our null findings for foreign aid and do not find supporting evidence. We replicate our analysis with a corruption GPI produced by an intergovernmental organization: the Worldwide Governance Indicators "control of corruption" measure. However, the results do not appreciably differ from those using the CPI. These results are also consistent with work by Sending and Lie, who find that the World Bank's own GPI, the Country Policy and Institutional Assessment, does not influence World Bank allocations in Malawi or Ethiopia.[76] Consequently, we are not convinced by explanation of our null findings.

A second explanation for our results is that GPIs might act as focal points in terms of setting agendas and defining issue areas, but they do not otherwise provide additional information through rankings and ratings. In other words, GPIs like the CPI have elevated corruption to the top of the good governance agenda, such that policymakers care about corruption, but not as measured by GPIs. Our media results underscore the power of the CPI in attracting attention and shaping discourse about corruption. But the irony of the CPI's success is that policymakers may already be mobilized around corruption. The CPI has been part of the governance discourse since TI debuted the index in the 1990s. In an environment of heightened awareness about

---

[73] Bush makes this argument about other ratings. See Bush 2017.

[74] Note that Büthe 2012 identifies rule-makers, rule-demanders, users of rankings, and targets as potentially separate actors. Their configuration may have consequences for effectiveness.

[75] Bisbee et al. this volume.

[76] Sending and Lie 2015.

the importance of corruption, observers may not be surprised to find that Somalia, Sudan, Iraq, and Afghanistan fare poorly in terms of their perceived level of corruption, blunting the focal power of "extremes" as ranked in the CPI. Counterintuitively, the CPI's own success may be the cause of its failure to induce third-party state actors to punish corruption.

We assess this explanation through a series of interviews with US policymakers. We found that policymakers know what the "clear" cases of corruption are, and they are made aware of "crises" independently of GPIs. Senators hear about these cases from hearings, the news media breaking a story, or even constituent calls.[77] Those at USAID also reported that they directly see challenges with monitoring in cases of corruption or hear about scandals from the media ("if *The Washington Post* has reported that money has been lost").[78] When needed, these policymakers seek more information from country experts, recognizing that there are subtle distinctions in corruption such as between ministries in particular countries.[79] USAID also undertakes its own study of the country public financial management system when deciding how to give aid.[80] When requesting more information about these cases from USAID or another agencies, Senate staffers may then point to indicators for justification – a related function hypothesized about GPIs' authority – but the CPI and related indicators did not provide the basis for rare action on corruption.[81] Indeed, there is some role for indicators in these formal processes of requesting information between organizations, and on dimensions where statutory requirements exist.[82] Even then, they do not seem to be providing new information to motivate decisions about aid allocation.

A third explanation for our results holds that policymakers do not even account for corruption when they allocate foreign aid. Scholars and policymakers working on the issue of good governance may find our results surprising given the prominence of the good governance agenda in the development community, though some existing scholarly studies of the topic come to some of the same conclusions. Foreign aid is a valuable instrument of statecraft, and third-party policymakers often have other priorities that override the effect of corruption, but potentially also GPIs generally.[83] Our interview evidence corroborates our quantitative analyses about the lack of importance of corruption in aid allocation despite the lip service paid to good governance. In our interviews of aid officials about the aid allocation process, no one

---

[77] Author interview, April 13, 2017.
[78] A USAID officer, author interview, April 17, 2017.
[79] A USAID officer, author interview, April 17, 2017.
[80] Senior aid official, author interview, May 10, 2017.
[81] Author interview, April 13, 2017.
[82] Former USAID official, author interview, April 13, 2017.
[83] Alesina and Dollar 2000; Alesina and Weder 2002; Baccini and Urpelainen 2012; Bermeo and Leblang 2015; Boutton and Carter 2014.

mentioned corruption on their own. When prompted, these officials occasionally noted that corruption had little role in decisions concerning the amount of aid allocated.[84]

This evidence does not mean that corruption does not matter at all in allocation decisions. Recent scholarship shows that states do account for corruption and adjust their foreign aid policies accordingly, which updates earlier work that finds no overall effects in allocation.[85] However, corruption may only matter at the margins, and perhaps mainly in cases where the GPIs provide surprising information about a country. Our observational analyses shed some light on the plausibility of this explanation that foreign aid is usually used for purposes aside from changing state behavior on corruption or other governance indicators. We found little evidence that donors responded to changes in the recipient states' corruption rankings or scores. The absence of even a simple correlation between GPI rank or score and foreign aid is consistent with this intuition: third-party policymakers care about other factors more than corruption.[86]

These findings likely to apply to most GPIs beyond the CPI. Many of the issue areas in which NGOs create GPIs are not pressing strategic priorities for third-party policymakers – and, indeed, that is why these organizations seek to draw attention to them. For example, recent work on GPIs focuses on the domains of education, labor, human trafficking, and forest conservation.[87] In fact, as we describe, the mere fact that policymakers pay lip service to corruption makes it an easier case than many of the other issues on which GPIs focus. Our non-findings thus suggest that the material-external pathway of GPI influence is unlikely. Further work in other issue areas, though, would be nice extensions of this chapter.

Taken together, these findings therefore suggest that GPIs may raise awareness of an issue but do not then provide new actionable information to third-party policymakers in the issue area of corruption.

THE PROMISE AND LIMITS OF GPIs

Global performance indicators have pervaded the landscape of global governance. States, intergovernmental organizations, and non-governmental organizations have all joined the rankings and ratings craze, seeking to define issue areas, simplify information, and ultimately alter behavior. Existing political science scholarship shows that GPIs are an important tool for changing beliefs and

---

[84] For example, author interview, May 10, 2017.

[85] Contrast Dietrich 2013; Winters 2010 with Alesina and Weder 2002; Neumayer 2003.

[86] Dietrich 2013, 2016; Winters 2010. An additional explanation is possible: aid organizations suffer from organizational hypocrisy, and are unable or unwilling to adjust their operations to match the rhetoric accorded to the good governance agenda. See Weaver 2008.

[87] Kelley and Simmons 2015; Kijima and Lipscy this volume; Koliev et al. this volume; Sundstrom and Henry 2017.

inducing compliance, and that they exercise this influence through social power. This chapter implies that this influence is confined to these channels alone.

Our analysis uncovered focal effects, but little evidence the CPI prompted third-party policymakers to wield material forms of coercion against corruption offenders. While the CPI attracts attention and is part of the policy-making process, it does not appear to change the amount or composition of aid. This null finding is strikingly robust, persisting across several empirical approaches and a multiplicity of model specifications and donors.

Although we are careful not to overgeneralize a null result, this chapter sounds a word of caution by suggesting possible limits to the power of indicators as tools of global governance. GPIs seek to affect hard-to-change policy areas. This is especially true in the realm of good governance. Existing research on GPI effectiveness finds convincing evidence GPIs influence states through a social-domestic channel. But the worst corruption offenders often lack the conditions needed for the social-domestic channel to operate. The material-external channel is then the only viable pathway for influence. Yet, we find no evidence of a GPI inducing third-party policymakers to activate material pressure in a likely case, casting doubt on the ability of external actors to bring about good governance reforms in states resistant to social pressure. Future research should continue to explore the pathways and domains of GPI influence beyond corruption and good governance.

These findings thus constitute an important addendum to the burgeoning literature on GPI effectiveness and to this volume in particular. Since the material pathway is an important channel for effecting reform in states resistant to social forms of influence, our results suggest that GPIs may only exercise influence among states predisposed toward responsiveness. Given the continued proliferation of GPIs, it is clear that quantitative rankings and ratings will remain a part of the toolkit of global governance. As with many instruments of international influence, however, GPIs are not one-size-fits-all tools of power.

References

Alesina, Alberto, and David Dollar. 2000. Who Gives Foreign Aid to Whom and Why? *Journal of Economic Growth* 5 (1):33–63.

Alesina, Alberto, and Beatrice Weder. 2002. Do Corrupt Governments Receive Less Foreign Aid? *American Economic Review* 92 (4):1126–37.

Baccini, Leonardo, and Johannes Urpelainen. 2012. Strategic Side Payments: Preferential Trading Agreements, Economic Reform, and Foreign Aid. *The Journal of Politics* 74 (4):932–49.

Bermeo, Sarah Blodgett. 2017. Aid Allocation and Targeted Development in an Increasingly Connected World. *International Organization* 71 (4):735–66.

2018. *Targeted Development: Industrialized Country Strategy in a Globalizing World.* New York: Oxford University Press.

Bermeo, Sarah Blodgett, and David Leblang. 2015. Migration and Foreign Aid. *International Organization* 69 (3):627–57.

Berthélemy, Jean-Claude. 2006. Bilateral Donors Interest vs. Recipients
    Development Motives in Aid Allocation: Do All Donors Behave the Same?
    Review of Development Economics 10 (2):179–94.
Bisbee, James H., James R. Hollyer, B. Peter Rosendorff, and James Raymond
    Vreeland. this volume. The Millennium Development Goals and
    Education: Accountability and Substitution in Global Indicators.
    In *The Power of Global Performance Indicators*, edited by Judith Kelley
    and Beth A. Simmons. New York: Cambridge University Press.
Boutton, Andrew, and David B. Carter. 2014. Fair-Weather Allies? Terrorism
    and the Allocation of US Foreign Aid. *Journal of Conflict Resolution* 58
    (7):1144–73.
Broome, André, and Joel Quirk. 2015. Governing the World at a Distance:
    The Practice of Global Benchmarking. *Review of International Studies* 41
    (5):819–41.
Broome, André, Alexandra Homolar, and Matthias Kranke. 2018. Bad
    Science: International Organizations and the Indirect Power of Global
    Benchmarking. *European Journal of International Relations* 24 (3):
    514–39.
Bukovansky, Mlada. 2002. Corruption Is Bad: Normative Dimensions of
    the Anti-Corruption Movement. Working Paper no. 2002/5, Australian
    National University. https://openresearch-repository.anu.edu.au/
    bitstream/1885/40136/3/02-5.pdf.
    2015. Corruption Rankings: Constructing and Contesting the Global Anti-
    Corruption Agenda. In *Ranking the World: Grading States as a Tool of
    Global Governance*, edited by Alexander Cooley and Jack Snyder, 60–84.
    New York: Cambridge University Press.
Bush, Sarah Sunn. 2017. The Politics of Rating Freedom: Ideological Affinity,
    Private Authority, and the Freedom in the World Ratings. *Perspectives on
    Politics* 15 (3):711–31.
Büthe, Tim. 2012. Beyond Supply and Demand: A Political-Economic
    Conceptual Model. In *Governance by Indicators: Global Power Through
    Quantification and Rankings*, edited by Kevin Davis, Angelina Fisher,
    Benedict Kingsbury, and Sally Engle Merry, 29–51. New York: Oxford
    University Press.
Callen, Michael, Saad Gulzar, Ali Hasanain, and Yasir Khan. 2016. The
    Political Economy of Public Sector Absence: Experimental Evidence from
    Pakistan. NBER Working Paper. http://www.nber.org/papers/w22340.pdf.
Charron, Nicholas. 2011. Exploring the Impact of Foreign Aid on Corruption:
    Has the "Anti-Corruption Movement" Been Effective? *The Developing
    Economies* 49 (1):66–88.
Cingranelli, David L., and Thomas E. Pasquarello. 1985. Human Rights
    Practices and the Distribution of U.S. Foreign Aid to Latin American
    Countries. *American Journal of Political Science* 29 (3):539–63.
Claessens, Stijn, Danny Cassimon, and Bjorn Van Campenhout. 2009.
    Evidence on Changes in Aid Allocation Criteria. *World Bank Economic
    Review* 23 (2):185–208.
Clist, Paul. 2011. 25 Years of Aid Allocation Practice: Whither Selectivity?
    World Development 39 (10):1724–34.

Cooley, Alexander, and Jack Snyder. 2015. Conclusion - Rating the Ratings
    Craze: From ConsumerChoice to Public Policy Outcomes. In *Ranking
    the World: Grading States as a Tool of Global Governance*, edited by
    Alexander Cooley and Jack Snyder, 178–93. New York: Cambridge
    University Press.
Davis, Kevin E., Angelina Fisher, Benedict Kingsbury, and Sally Engle
    Merry, eds. 2012. *Governance by Indicators: Global Power Through
    Quantification and Rankings*. New York: Oxford University Press.
Davis, Kevin E., Benedict Kingsbury, and Sally Engle Merry. 2012. Indicators as
    a Technology of Global Governance. *Law & Society Review* 46 (1):71–104.
DeMeritt, Jacqueline H.R. 2012. International Organizations and Government
    Killing: Does Naming and Shaming Save Lives? *International Interactions*
    38 (5):597–621.
Dietrich, Simone. 2013. Bypass or Engage? Explaining Donor Delivery Tactics in
    Foreign Aid Allocation. *International Studies Quarterly* 57 (4):698–712.
    2016. Donor Political Economies and the Pursuit of Aid Effectiveness.
    International Organization 70 (1):65–102.
Dunning, Thad. 2004. Conditioning the Effects of Aid: Cold War Politics,
    Donor Credibility, and Democracy in Africa. *International Organization*
    58 (2):409–23.
Espeland, Wendy Nelson, and Michael Sauder. 2012. The Dynamism
    of Indicators. In *Governance by Indicators: Global Power through
    Qunatification and Rankings*, edited by Kevin Davis, Angelina Fisher,
    Benedict Kingsbury, and Sally Engle Merry, 86–109. New York: Oxford
    University Press.
Fariss, Christopher J. 2010. The Strategic Substitution of United States Foreign
    Aid. *Foreign Policy Analysis* 6 (2):107–31.
Fearon, James D. 2011. Self-Enforcing Democracy. *Quarterly Journal of
    Economics* 126 (4):1661–708.
Fisher, Angelina. 2012. From Diagnosing Under-immunization to Evaluating
    Health Care Systems: Immunization Coverage Indicators as a Technology
    of Global Governance. In *Governance by Indicators: Global Power
    through Quantification and Rankings*, edited by Kevin Davis, Angelina
    Fisher, Benedict Kingsbury, and Sally Engle Merry, 217–46. New York:
    Oxford University Press.
Fleck, Robert K., and Christopher Kilby. 2010. Changing Aid Regimes?
    US Foreign Aid from the Cold War to the War on Terror. *Journal of
    Development Economics* 91 (2):185–97.
Fukuda-Parr, Sakiko. 2014. Global Goals as a Policy Tool: Intended and
    Unintended Consequences. *Journal of Human Development and
    Capabilities* 15 (2–3):118–31.
Goldsmith, Arthur A. 2001. Foreign Aid and Statehood in Africa.
    International Organization 55 (1):123–48.
Hafner-Burton, Emilie M. 2008. Sticks and Stones: Naming and Shaming
    the Human Rights Enforcement Problem. *International Organization*
    62:689–716.
Hansen, Hans Krause, and Tony Porter. 2012. What Do Numbers Do in
    Transnational Governance? *International Political Sociology* 6 (4):409–26.

Hendrix, Cullen S., and Wendy H. Wong. 2013. When Is the Pen Truly Mighty? Regime Type and the Efficacy of Naming and Shaming in Curbing Human Rights Abuses. *British Journal of Political Science* 43 (3):651–72.

Hjertholm, Peter, and Howard White. 2000. Survey of Foreign Aid: History, Trends, and Allocation. Working Paper, University of Copenhagen and University of Sussex. http://www.economics.ku.dk/research/publications/wp/2000/0004.pdf.

Holley, Peter. 2015. Afghan President Calls for a "Holy War" Against His Country's Greatest Enemy- Corruption. *The Washington Post*, September 1.

Honig, Dan, and Catherine Weaver. this volume. A Race to the Top?: The Aid Transparency Index and the Normative Power of Global Performance Indicators. *Annual Meeting of the American Political Science Association.*

Hough, Dan. 2017. *Analyzing Corruption*. Newcastle upon Tyne: Agenda.

Huth, Paul K., Sarah E. Croco, and Benjamin J. Appel. 2011. Does International Law Promote the Peaceful Settlement of International Disputes? Evidence from the Study of Territorial Conflicts since 1945. *American Political Science Review* 105 (2):415–36.

International Monetary Fund. 2017. *The Role of the Fund in Governance Issues - Review of the Guidance Note - Preliminary Considerations.* Washington, DC: International Monetary Fund.

Jensen, Nathan M., and Edmund J. Malesky. 2018. Nonstate Actors and Compliance with International Agreements: An Empirical Analysis of the OECD Anti-Bribery Convention. *International Organization* 72 (1):33–69.

Jolly, David. 2011. New Zealand Has World's Cleanest Government, Survey Finds. *New York Times*, November 30.

Keck, Margaret E., and Kathryn Sikkink. 1998. *Activists Beyond Borders: Advocacy Networks in International Politics.* Ithaca, NY: Cornell University Press.

Kelley, Judith G. 2017. *Scorecard Diplomacy: Grading States to Influence their Reputation and Behavior.* New York: Cambridge University Press.

Kelley, Judith G., and Beth A. Simmons. 2015. Politics by Number: Indicators as Social Pressure in International Relations. *American Journal of Political Science* 59 (1):55–70.

  this volume. Introduction: The Power of Global Performance Indicators. Chapter 1 in *The Power of Global Performance Indicators.*

Kijima, Rie and Phillip Y. Lipscy. this volume. International Assessments and Education Policy: Evidence from an Elite Survey.

Koliev, Faraj, Thomas, Sommerer, and Jonas Tallberg. this volume. Reporting Matters: Performance Assessment and Compliance in the ILO. *The Power of Global Performance Indicators.* New York: Cambridge University Press.

Krain, Matthew. 2012. J'accuse! Does Naming and Shaming Perpetrators Reduce the Severity of Genocides or Politicides? *International Studies Quarterly* 56 (3):574–589.

Kramer, Andrew E. 2016. Railing Against Graft, a Georgian Leads Call for a Cleanup in Ukraine. *New York Times*, February 3.

Lebovic, James H., and Erik Voeten. 2006. The Politics of Shame: The Condemnation of Country Human Rights Practices in the UNCHR. *International Studies Quarterly* 50 (4):861–88.

Lynn, Michael, Sean Masaki Flynn, and Chelsea Helion. 2013. Do Consumers Prefer Round Prices? Evidence from Pay-What-You-Want Decisions and Self-Pumped Gasoline Purchases. *Journal of Economic Psychology* 35:96–102.

Masaki, Takaaki, and Bradley C. Parks. 2019. When Do Performance Assessments Influence Policy Behavior? Micro-evidence from the 2014 Reform Efforts Survey. *The Review of International Organizations*. [forthcoming]

Meernik, James, Eric L. Krueger, and Steven C. Poe. 1998. Testing Models of US Foreign Policy: Foreign Aid During and After the Cold War. *The Journal of Politics* 60 (1):63–85.

Merry, Sally Engle, Kevin Davis, and Benedict Kingsbury, eds. 2015. *The Quiet Power of Indicators: Measuring Governance, Corruption, and the Rule of Law*. New York: Cambridge University Press.

Morse, Julia C. this volume. Blacklists, Market Enforcement, and the Global Regime to Combat Terrorist Financing. *Annual Meeting of the American Political Science Association*.

Neumayer, Eric. 2003. The Determinants of Aid Allocation by Regional Multilateral Development Nanks and United Nations Agencies. *International Studies Quarterly* 47 (1):101–22.

Nielsen, Richard A., and Beth A. Simmons. 2015. Rewards for Ratification: Payoffs for Participating in the International Human Rights Regime? *International Studies Quarterly* 59:197–208.

Nienaber, Michael. 2014. The Most and Least Corrupt Countries in the World. *Reuters*, December 2.

Pope, Devin, and Uri Simonsohn. 2011. Round Numbers as Goals: Evidence From Baseball, SAT Takers, and the Lab. *Psychological Science* 22:71–9.

Pratto, Felicia, and Oliver P. John. 1991. Automatic Vigilance: The Attention-Grabbing Power of Negative Social Information. *Journal of Personality and Social Psychology* 61 (3):380–91.

Radaelli, Claudio M. 2018. Regulatory Indicators in the European Union and the Organization for Economic Cooperation and Development: Performance Assessment, Organizational Processes, and Learning. *Public Policy and Administration*. [forthcoming, online first]

Roberts, Jordan, and Roberts Fernando Tellez. this volume. Freedom House's Scarlet Letter: Assessment Power through Transnational Pressure.

Rosch, Eleanor. 1975. Cognitive Reference Points. *Cognitive Psychology* 7:532–47.

Rottenburg, Richard, Sally Engle Merry, Sung-Joon Park, and Johanna Mugler, eds. 2015. *The World of Indicators: The Making of Governmental Knowledge through Quantification*. New York: Cambridge University Press.

Sandholtz, Wayne, and Mark M. Gray. 2003. International Integration and National Corruption. *International Organization* 57 (4):761–800.

Schelling, Thomas C. 1960. *The Strategy of Conflict*. Cambridge, MA: Harvard University Press.

Schlenker, Wolfram, and Jason Scorse. 2017. Does Being a "Top 10" Worst Polluter Affect Environmental Releases? Evidence from the U.S. Toxic Release Inventory. Working Paper, Columbia University, NBER, and Monterey Institute of International Studies. https://cenrep.ncsu.edu/cenrep/wp-content/uploads/2015/07/SchlenkerScorse.pdf.

Schueth, Sam. 2015. Winning the Ranking Game: The Republic of Georgia, USAID, and the Doing Business Project. In *Ranking the World: Grading States as a Tool of Global Governance*, edited by Alexander Cooley and Jack Snyder, 151–77. New York: Cambridge University Press.

Sending, Ole Jacob, and Jon Harald Sande Lie. 2015. The Limits of Global Authority: World Bank Benchmarks in Ethiopia and Malawi. *Review of International Studies* 41 (5):993–1010.

Sharman, Jason C. 2009. The Bark Is the Bite: International Organizations and Blacklisting. *Review of International Political Economy* 16 (4):573–96.

Shore, Cris, and Susan Wright. 2015. Governing by Numbers: Audit Culture, Rankings and the New World Order. *Social Anthropology* 23 (1):22–8.

Sinclair, Timothy. 2005. *The New Masters of Capital: American Bond Rating Agencies and the Politics of Creditworthiness*. Ithaca, NY: Cornell University Press.

Sonnemans, Joep. 2006. Price Clustering and Natural Resistance Points in the Dutch Stock Market: A Natural Experiment. *European Economic Review* 50:1937–50.

Sundstrom, Lisa McIntosh, and Laura A. Henry. 2017. Private Forest Governance, Public Policy Impacts: The Forest Stewardship Council in Russia and Brazil. *Forests* 8 (11):445.

The Associated Press. 2014. China, Turkey, Angola Slip in Global Graft Index. *The Associated Press*, December 3.

The Economist. 2014. Transparency International: A More Combative Approach? *The Economist*, October 16.

Tierney, Michael J., Daniel L. Nielson, Darren G. Hawkins, J. Timmons Roberts, Michael G. Findley, Ryan M. Powers, Bradley Parks, Sven E. Wilson, and Robert L. Hicks. 2011. More Dollars than Sense: Refining Our Knowledge of Development Finance Using AidData. *World Development* 39 (11):1891–906.

Transparency International. 2016. Research - CPI - Overview. http://www.transparency.org/ research/cpi/overview.

Wang, Hongying, and James N. Rosenau. 2001. Transparency International and Corruption as an Issue of Global Governance. *Global Governance* 7 (25):25–49.

Weaver, Catherine. 2008. *Hypocrisy Trap: The World Bank and the Poverty of Reform*. Princeton, NJ: Princeton University Press.

Winbourne, Svetlana, and Bertram I. Spector. 2014. *Analysis of USAID Anticorruption Programming Worldwide (2007–2013)*. Washington, DC: United States Agency for International Development and Management Systems International.

Winters, Matthew S. 2010. Choosing to Target: What Types of Countries Get Different Types of World Bank Projects. *World Politics* 62 (3):422–58.

Winters, Matthew S., and Gina Martinez. 2015. The Role of Governance in Determining Foreign Aid Flow Composition. *World Development* 66:516–31.

Yip, Martin. 2013. Can Hong Kong Stay Corruption-Free Under China? *BBC News*, July 11.

12

The Millennium Development Goals and Education

Accountability and Substitution in Global Indicators

James H. Bisbee, James R. Hollyer, B. Peter Rosendorff, and
James Raymond Vreeland

> Not everything that can be counted counts, and not everything that counts can
> be counted.
>
> William Bruce Cameron, *Informal Sociology: A Casual*
> *Introduction to Sociological Thinking*, p. 13

INTRODUCTION

Quantifiable targets shape incentives. Indeed, the idea that global performance
indicators (GPIs) represent attempts to influence governments is a central tenet
of this volume. When economic development organizations and the foreign aid
ministries of states deploy performance assessment metrics, they stimulate the
governments of developing countries to meet and surpass those quantified goals.[1]

Other chapters in this volume corroborate this hypothesis. Doshi, Kelley,
and Simmons document the *reactivity* of states to the World Bank's *Ease of
Doing Business Indicators*, as they take policy steps to attempt to climb in
the rankings.[2] Measurable targets can also influence aid donors – Honig and
Weaver demonstrate that even a small organization can influence aid agencies
to publish the outcomes of development projects simply by promising to report
on the publication.[3] Failure to achieve measurement targets can also influence
market actors. Julia Morse finds that being labeled as non-compliant by the
Financial Action Task Force induces private sector investors to avoid a given
country.[4]

The upshot of these studies is that GPIs can serve as effective incentives
for governments by either directly influencing elite behavior or by indirectly

[1] Kelley and Simmons 2020.
[2] Kelley, Simmons, and Doshi 2020.
[3] Honig and Weaver 2020.
[4] Morse 2020.

impacting third parties. Precisely because of their effectiveness, however, we explore the unintended consequences of quantified targets. As suggested by the epigraph above, when an organization sets a quantified target, they explicitly inform developing countries that some outcomes count – but they also implicitly convey that other outcomes do not count. As a result, governments have an incentive to substitute resources and effort toward outcomes that are counted and away from those that are not. This unintended effect of assessment is implicitly noted by others in this volume. In our study of the Millennium Development Goals, we formalize the mechanism by which assessments can lead to unintended outcomes and find empirical evidence consistent with our model.

The Millennium Development Goals (MDGs) were the product of the Millennium Summit of the UN General Assembly in September of 2000. At this meeting, members committed to "… spare no effort to free our fellow men, women, and children from the abject and dehumanizing conditions of extreme poverty, to which more than a billion of them are currently subjected."[5] To this end, the Declaration advanced resolutions to achieve key numeric targets which evolved into the Millennium Development Goals.[6] Specific targets applied to eight areas: the eradication of extreme poverty and hunger, the achievement of universal primary education, the promotion of gender equality, the reduction of child mortality, the improvement of maternal health, combating HIV and malaria, the promotion of environmental sustainability, and the creation of a global partnership for development.[7]

We focus on the key educational measures of primary and secondary enrollment rates and how they respond to GPIs in equilibrium. Our GPI of interest is the Millennium Development Goal targeting universal primary education. Note that secondary education is not targeted by the MDGs, but may be influenced by them in unintended or unanticipated ways.

A rich literature on the relative importance of these public goods to long-run development outcomes motivates our focus on the relative provision of primary and secondary education. Writ large, education's impact has been charted directly (skill development, social network access, etc.) and indirectly (character traits such as motivation and self-discipline) which are crucial for social and economic outcomes.[8]

Evidence of unintended consequences of assessment in education reform at the micro level is ample. In the United States, policies such as No Child Left Behind (NCLB) and North Carolina's ABCs programs have been shown to diminish education outcomes for groups not included in assessment measures.

---

5 United Nations Millennium Declaration, A/RES/55/2, §11, September 18, 2000. http://www.un.org/millennium/declaration/ares552e.pdf, accessed April 18, 2016.
6 Hulme 2009.
7 See http://www.un.org/millenniumgoals/bkgd.shtml, accessed April 18, 2016.
8 See Heckman, Stixrud, and Urzua 2006.

Fuller and Ladd find that elementary schools transferred higher quality teachers from lower (non-evaluated) grades to higher (evaluated) grades in response to NCLB in order to improve their accountability metrics.[9] Similarly, Hugh Macartney identifies a ratchet effect when accountability reforms are conditioned on prior student test scores, as teachers reduce contemporary effort in order to ensure room for improvement in the following year.[10]

Studies have also found more general evidence of unintended consequences of quantifiable goals. In sociology, the connection between evaluation and perverse outcomes is so widespread as to be labeled a "law."[11] Le and Malesky demonstrate that provincial governments respond to performance ratings, they also find that these governments "teach to the test."[12] Doshi, Kelley, and Simmons recount interviews with World Bank staff who describe the strategic responses to the Ease of Doing Business indicator, specifically optimizing their response to "score well" as evidenced by the negative relationship between regulatory "distance" and the number of reforms pursued.[13] In this case, governments devote effort to reforms that lead to the greatest changes in rankings, for minimal effort, rather than those that necessarily have the largest economic impact. The literature on government accountability has documented related behavior, in which democratic governments focus their efforts on the provision of readily observable public goods in an attempt to claim credit,[14] a tendency that has been particularly documented in the provision of education.[15] In this chapter, we formalize our intuition with a simple model of government accountability in the absence and presence of a GPI. This framework generates empirical propositions that we take to the data, exploring whether the tendency to focus on achieving measured targets induces governments to substitute effort, attention, and resources away from the provision of unmeasured public goods. Specifically, we examine cross national patterns in the provision of (assessed) primary and (unassessed) secondary education enrollment rates following the passage of the MDGs.

The most direct mechanism connecting GPIs to substitution of resources is via directed aid flows. The Millennium Development Goals and the rich metrics associated with them are used by international actors to inform where to donate aid. Kijima and Lipscy show that participation in cross-national assessments of education influences flows of education aid.[16] These flows of

---

[9] Fuller and Ladd 2013.

[10] Macartney 2016.

[11] See Campbell 1979. Academia itself is replete with examples of sub-optimal equilibria as PhD students and tenure-track professors react to evaluation systems such as publications and cites (Edwards and Roy 2017).

[12] Le and Malesky 2019.

[13] Kelley, Simmons, and Doshi 2020, p. 35.

[14] Mani and Mukand 2007.

[15] See Harding and Stasavage 2014. For a model that documents such distortions with regard to a very different policy area, see Bueno de Mesquita 2007.

[16] Kijima and Lipscy 2020.

aid can yield substitution effects through the expansion of state budgets or via the incentives they carry for policymakers, although their results suggest that foreign aid inflows are not meaningfully associated with higher net secondary enrollment. Other channels of influence theorized to matter in global assessment elsewhere in this volume (i.e. Hawthorn effects, activated civil society) can also pertain. We test competing channels of influence via mediation and moderation analyses, finding no evidence of a foreign aid channel and suggestive support for a role played by domestic politics.

We further argue that both the direct effect of international assessment (the promotion of primary education) and the indirect effect on the relationship between primary and secondary education will be moderated by the characteristics of targeted states. To be more precise, both effects should diminish as domestic accountability rises. In states with accountable governments – i.e. in democracies with high levels of government transparency – the composition of public goods should reflect the desires of the electorate, at least to a greater extent than in autocracies or opaque states. Accountable states thus have both less need, and less ability, to alter their menu of service provision in response to international pressure.

Our analysis stimulates what we believe are interesting questions about not just the MDGs, but GPIs more generally. On the one hand, we find evidence suggesting that states with healthier civil society and transparency are less susceptible to the substitution incentives associated with monitoring and assessment. However, we also find that these countries are less responsive to the stated goal of the GPI – the explicit incentives are also weaker. Our contribution is located at the end of the theoretical framework encompassing this volume, reproduced in Figure 12.1. Our formal model is agnostic to the specific mechanisms by which GPIs induce policy change. We use mediation analysis on our data to test whether foreign aid plays a meaningful role in the context of MDG adoption.

Our contribution also poses questions about the rarity of these mechanisms and the associated normative implications. While we believe unintended consequences are common, if not a foregone conclusion when dealing with strategic actors, its unclear whether they always subvert the implicit goals of the GPI. All governments are resource constrained, and all allocate these resources in a manner to maximize political support at minimal cost.[17] Any increase in the political returns for the provision of a particular good will imply that the relative incentive to provide another will decline. The normative effects of such substitution, however, need not be negative. Governments' political incentives may induce them to focus on the provision of public goods valued most highly by a narrow elite, in the absence of external pressure. And spillovers in the production of public goods – e.g. the expansion of primary education opens access to further schooling to a broader array of students – may imply

[17] Bueno de Mesquita et al. 2003.

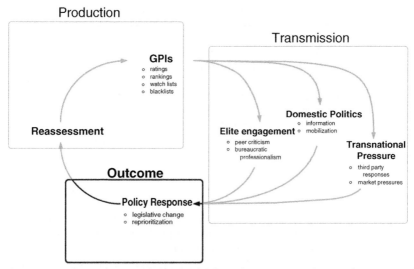

FIGURE 12.1. The pathways of GPIs to policy change. Our chapter focuses on the unintended consequences reprioritization can have on state behavior (highlighted in black).

that a shift in resources is positive for total social welfare. In this chapter, we bracket such critical welfare concerns to focus on the strategic incentives of governments facing GPIs. We acknowledge that such normative conclusions are crucial to the future research on GPIs, and are raised by other works in this volume and in the ground-breaking research on this topic by Judith Kelley and Beth Simmons.[18]

THE MILLENNIUM DEVELOPMENT GOALS

The MDGs consist of eight goals (see Table 12.1) which were promulgated by the UN, agreed to by such international financial institutions as the World Bank, and adopted by a variety of bilateral aid organizations. Each goal is mapped into one or more "targets," which, in turn, is mapped into several numerical indicators which serve as a basis for assessment of progress. For instance, the goal we examine here – (2) universal primary education – is mapped into the task of "ensur[ing] that, by 2015, children everywhere... will be able to complete a full course of primary schooling." Progress toward this target is assessed by primary education enrollment and completion rates, as well as the literacy rate of 15–24 year olds, broken down by gender.[19]

[18] Kelley and Simmons 2015.
[19] UN Official List of MDG Indicators, January 15, 2008. http://mdgs.un.org/unsd/mdg/ Host.aspx?Content=Indicators/OfficialList.htm, accessed April 18, 2016.

TABLE 12.1. *Millennium Development Goals*

(1) Eradicate extreme poverty and hunger
(2) Achieve universal primary education
(3) Promote gender equality and empower women
(4) Reduce child mortality
(5) Improve maternal health
(6) Combat HIV/AIDS, malaria and other diseases
(7) Ensure environmental sustainability
(8) Develop a global partnership for development

Many of these goals were drawn directly from the UN's Millennium Declaration, which the General Assembly issued and approved as the culmination of the Millennium Summit, held in September of 2000.[20] The more precise indicators, and several of the more general goals, were only agreed upon during a World Bank conference, "From Consensus to Action: a Seminar on the International Development Goals," held in 2001.[21] The agenda for both the World Bank conference, and the UN Summit, however, was determined by a pre-existing set of development targets – the International Development Goals (IDGs).

The IDGs were originally promulgated by the OECD in 1996 as part of an effort to shape the aid policies of member-states. In content, they were very nearly identical to the MDGs. The targets were set by rich world donors, with fairly minimal input from aid recipients, and were constructed to appeal to domestic audiences in the developed world.[22] In particular, the goals were intended to focus on concrete measures that appealed to a broad audience (e.g. poverty reduction through economic growth, gender equality). Moreover, these goals were thought to advance a degree of *accountability* on the part of recipient states.[23] The aim of such precise numeric targets was explicitly to increase accountability, particularly for states that received development aid. (Only indicators for Goal 8, the "global partnership for development," included measures of donor generosity.) In laying out these goals, the Secretary General's report noted: "In order to help focus national and international priority-setting, goals and targets should be limited in number, be stable over time and communicate clearly to a broad

---

[20] http://www.un.org/millennium/declaration/ares552e.pdf.
[21] Hulme 2009.
[22] Hulme 2009.
[23] Hulme 2009.

audience. Clear and stable numerical targets can help to trigger action and promote new alliances for development."[24]

We examine the effects of the MDGs through the lens of existing theories of political accountability. We focus on the goal pertaining to primary education, in part because the mapping between this goal and a numeric indicator was particularly precise, and in part because measures of closely related public goods (secondary and tertiary enrollment rates) were *not* targeted by the MDGs.

GLOBAL ASSESSMENT POWER AND PUBLIC GOODS PRODUCTION

The MDGs represented a public international commitment by governments to achieve gains in the provision of *specific* public goods. They increased the incentives of government to provide these goods. Governments, therefore, would be likely to devote greater personnel, material resources, and effort toward providing these specific public goods once the MDGs were in effect. However, these incentives have a secondary effect – governments are likely to divert resources from the production of other public goods in order to achieve MDG goals.

First, consider the effect of the MDGs on government incentives. Kelley and Simmons argue that the dissemination of international standards may exert social pressure on governments to achieve certain policy outcomes, and that such standards are particularly likely to do so if "they are based on systematic monitoring, are comparative (and especially quantitative), are wielded by a respected actor or group/organization of actors, and are widely disseminated."[25] Perhaps no set of international standards meet these criteria as well as the MDGs. These standards were (1) explicitly linked to precise statistical targets;[26] (2) subject to annual monitoring by the UN and other donor organizations; (3) initially linked to the Millennium Declaration, and thus approved by the UN General Assembly and its constituent member states, and subsequently promulgated jointly by the World Bank, IMF, and OECD;[27] and (4) widely disseminated through public statements by these agencies as well as bilateral lenders.

As visualized in Figure 12.1 above, international standards like the MDGs may affect government behavior through a variety of channels, including international actors, domestic politics, and the personal or reputational concerns of individual leaders. Global standards may alter behaviors in the

---

[24] Annex to "Road Map Towards the Implementation of the United Nations Millennium Development Declaration," Report of the Secretary General. A/56/326, September 6, 2001, p. 56, §3. http://www.un.org/millenniumgoals/sgreport2001.pdf, accessed April 18, 2016.
[25] Kelley and Simmons 2015, p. 55.
[26] See http://mdgs.un.org/unsd/mdg/Host.aspx?Content=Indicators/OfficialList.htm, accessed April 18, 2016.
[27] Hulme 2009.

international or intergovernmental realm. The creation of a common set of international standards may facilitate decentralized enforcement through bilateral sanctioning or a withdrawal of bilateral benefits.[28] This was a particular risk with regard to the MDGs, given that the Goals were explicitly endorsed by most bilateral development agencies soon after their promulgation – with the US as a notable hold-out.[29] Alternatively, standards may be enforced through material sanctions (or withdrawal of benefits) by international bodies. Lebovic and Voeten, for instance, demonstrate that the World Bank enforced international standards of human rights, and was less willing to lend to countries that had been "shamed" by the UN's High Commissioner for Refugees (UNCHR).[30] This danger, again, would seem particularly acute for governments that failed to make progress on the MDGs, given the central role both the World Bank and IMF played in the construction of the Goals.

Global indicators may also serve to inform residents of monitored states, in a readily digestible manner, of the quality of their government's performance with respect to certain policy goals. Individuals within these states might use such information to discipline government behavior either through the ballot box,[31] or through protest or collective action.[32] A well-developed literature finds that such information enables citizens to hold their leaders accountable for public goods provision,[33] which, in turn, induces leaders to more actively provide public goods.[34] Hence, government leaders should face greater domestic pressure to achieve specific public goods targets once the MDGs are promulgated.

Finally, international standards may alter government incentives by generating global norms of acceptable behavior.[35] In defining basic standards of "development," the MDGs may have altered leaders' notions of what constitutes "success" and "failure." Such definitions may shape leaders' primitive preferences over public goods allocations – or shift their strategies for regime legitimation.[36] Focusing on the MDG targeting maternal health and its impact in Zambia, Alice Evans documents extensive evidence of norm-adjustment among elites as the primary mechanism by which this particular GPI influenced policy.[37]

---

[28] Johns 2012; Milgrom and North 1990.

[29] Hulme 2009.

[30] Lebovic and Voeten 2009.

[31] Besley and Burgess 2002.

[32] Hollyer, Rosendorff, and Vreeland 2015.

[33] See, for instance, Di Tella and Schargrodsky 2003; Ferraz and Finan 2008; Peters and Welch 1980.

[34] See, for instance, Adserà, Boix, and Payne 2003; Besley and Burgess 2002; Glaeser and Goldin 2006; Hollyer, Rosendorff, and Vreeland 2014; Reinikka and Svensson 2003. Though, Chong et al. 2010 introduce a cautionary note as to these effects.

[35] Risse and Sikkink 1999.

[36] Kapuściński 1989 is instructive on Emperor Haile Selassie's obsession with a nebulously defined notion of "economic development."

[37] Evans 2017.

It is our contention that the MDGs had the effect of increasing the incentive to provide the specific public goods delineated in the Goals. Any or all of these mechanisms may be effective, and other, unlisted, mechanisms may also be at work. Although our main focus in this chapter is on the equilibrium provision of targeted and non-targeted public goods, we are able to test some channels of influence, including foreign aid and domestic politics. Our findings relate to similar work by Helena Skagerlind who conducts a detailed process tracing of the effects of the MDG with regard to the empowerment of women.[38] She finds some evidence that all three of these causal channels were in operation with the strongest results for aid conditionality and the socialization of government elites. Our findings for education indicate alternative channels of influence, highlighting the heterogeneity of these mechanisms across targets.

While we contend that the MDGs had the intended effect of increasing government incentives to provide specific public goods, we further contend that they had the unintended effect of causing governments to substitute away from efforts *not* delineated by the UN. As is argued by Holmstsrom and Milgrom, when a given agent is faced with a multiplicity of tasks, some of which are monitored and others of which are not, the agent will rationally devote a disproportional level of effort to those goals which are subject to monitoring.[39] We therefore focus on government's tendency to provide a public good listed in the MDGs – i.e. primary education – relative to its tendency to provide a public good that is not so-listed – i.e. secondary education. We argue that MDGs alter the relative provision of primary and secondary education, boosting the former relative to the latter. This tendency may be somewhat offset to the extent that various public goods are complements in production. For instance, increasing primary enrollment and completion rates perforce increases the pool of students eligible for secondary education. However, the substitution effect should dominate provided these complementarities in production are not too large.

Ironically, the very characteristics that make the MDGs valuable in terms of increasing accountability also render them particularly prone to this substitution effect. Because they focus on precisely defined quantitative metrics of performance, with regard to very specific public goods, they are particularly vulnerable to "gaming." More nebulous or qualitative goals, which are less susceptible to monitoring and less useful for the types of comparisons that give global indicators their power,[40] are also likely to be less prone to substitution effects. However, such weak assessments are also less likely to alter government behavior at all.

---

[38] Skagerlind 2020.
[39] Holmstrom and Milgrom 1991.
[40] Kelley and Simmons 2020.

THE MODERATING ROLE OF INFORMATION AND INSTITUTIONS

We expect that the intuition described above may vary by context. Government institutions and the domestic informational environment moderate the effects of global assessment – both the direct effects on the provision of specific services and the indirect substitution effects on the provision of unassessed public goods. To be more precise, both effects are weakened in instances where governments are highly accountable to domestic audiences. Highly transparent states and democracies are less prone to alter the menu of public goods delivered by the government in response to global indicators than opaque autocracies.

The rationale for this contention is twofold: First, and most directly, domestic and international accountability are substitutes. Recall that one of the mechanisms though which global indicators might induce policy change works through such indicators' effect on domestic politics. Global monitoring may serve to inform domestic interests of their government's performance with regard to a particular policy area, inducing domestic demands for improved performance.[41] Naturally, however, if the domestic information environment is relatively rich, such information is superfluous. Citizens are *already* aware of their government's performance and any pressure to change policy as a result is likely to have already made itself manifest. Moreover, if the issue area in question is one of high public salience, or has important implications for domestic welfare, governments are likely to be induced to disclose information in response to electoral pressures in democratic political systems.[42] Precisely because accountable governments face a strong domestic pressure to provide public goods, increased international demands are likely to have minor effects.

The second reason we expect global indicators to have a relatively minor effect on governments with a high level of domestic accountability is more subtle. Any shift in the composition of public goods in such regimes is likely to be politically costly. Governments in such states are *already* providing levels of public goods provision, in keeping with the demands of large swaths of the population, to stay in power. Any change in the composition of these public goods is likely to be politically costly, more so than for comparable autocracies, who rely less on public goods provision to retain power. Moreover, because accountable states provide higher levels of public goods than autocratic states,[43] they will need alter service provision less to satisfy international demands even in the instances in which they choose to so comply with the MDGs.

[41] Kelley and Simmons 2020.
[42] Hollyer, Rosendorff, and Vreeland 2011.
[43] Bueno de Mesquita et al. 2003.

MODEL

In what follows, we illustrate our claims formally. To do so, we adapt a variant of the selectorate model of Bueno de Mesquita et al.[44] We compare two game forms: one with and one without the MDGs. The model demonstrates that (1) the MDGs (weakly) increase the provision of primary education and (2) that wherever this increase is strictly positive there is a substitution away from secondary education provision. The formalization further demonstrates that the effects are more likely to be present in unaccountable (autocratic, opaque) than accountable (democratic, transparent) states.

Model without MDGs

Consider an infinite horizon discrete time interaction between a leader L and her selectorate. Normalize the size of the selectorate to one. In each period of play, L will face a challenger C.[45] To maintain her hold on power, L must maintain the support of a share $\omega \in \left(0, \frac{1}{2}\right]$ of her selectors – a "winning coalition." We conceive of ω as capturing the degree of accountability of L to the selectorate – the probability that L is accountable to (requires the support of) an individual selector randomly selected from the set of selectors.[46] We map the term ω into empirical measures of democracy, government transparency, and their interaction. All actors share a common discount factor, δ.

In each period, the leader and challenger make a simultaneous offers of public goods – here consisting of primary (p) and higher/secondary (h) education; they may also offer private transfers (t) to each member of the (potential or actual) winning coalition. A representative member of the selectorate has preferences across p, h, t, according to the additively separable utility function $U(p,h,t) = U_p(p) + U_h(h) + U_t(t)$, with the standard assumptions: $U_k' > 0$, $U_k'' < 0$, $U_k(0) = 0$, $U_k'(0) = \infty$, $U_k'(\infty) = 0$, $k \in \{p,h,t\}$.

L and C make a decision about how to allocate a budget of size $B > 0$ between p, h, and t. If in power, her utility is defined as the residual sum left over after this provision is made. If not in power, her utility is normalized to zero.

---

[44] Bueno de Mesquita et al. 2003.

[45] Throughout, we will adopt feminine pronouns for L and selectors. C will be given a masculine pronoun.

[46] Membership in L's winning coalition is fixed and common knowledge. Formally, denote $\sigma_{i,\tau} \in \{0,1\}$ as an indicator function of such membership, where i indexes selectors and τ indexes time. L has lexicographic preferences for distributing private transfers to members of her winning coalition over any alternative selectors. In the event L is displaced, new values of $\sigma_{i,\tau+1}$ are drawn for all i, in which all selectors are equally likely to enter the new winning coalition. If L is retained in power, $\sigma_{i,\tau+1} = \sigma_{i,\tau} \forall i$. Values of $\sigma_{i,\tau}$ are common knowledge in each period τ and all actors condition their strategies on the realization of this value.

$$U_j(p,h,t) = \begin{cases} B - p - h - \omega t & \text{if in power} \\ 0 & \text{otherwise.} \end{cases} \quad \text{for } j \in \{L,C\}$$

At the start of each period of play, L and C make their offers of p, h, and t. Then there is an election – a decision is made by members of winning coalition whether to retain the leader L. To remain in power, L must retain the support of a share ω of the selectors.

> **Definition 1.** *Define an equilibrium to this game as the pair of triples $\left(p_C^*, h_C^*, t_C^*\right)$ for the challenger and $\left(p^*, h^*, t^*\right)$ for the leader. Define*
> $$U_C^* = U_p\left(p_C^*\right) + U_h\left(h_C^*\right) + U_t\left(t_C^*\right).$$

In equilibrium, C will tailor his offer to buy off members of the winning coalition – his entire budget will be devoted to this task. L will address this threat by offering a menu of public goods provision and transfers that guarantees members of the winning coalition a continuation value at least as high as that from backing C. This is feasible for the incumbent, because she can credibly commit to provide private transfers t to members of the winning coalition into the future. The offers of the challenger lack future credibility, and are discounted accordingly. The incumbent thus always retains her office.

In the appendix, we offer a model extension that relaxes the assumption that L's promises are perfectly credible. We assume that members of her winning coalition may be replaced by members of the wider selectorate with a fixed probability in each period of play – though, the probability of being removed by the incumbent is less than the probability of losing one's place in the winning coalition if the incumbent is removed and the regime toppled. Our comparative statics are qualitatively unchanged by this model extension.

> **Lemma 1.** *In any (Markov Perfect) equilibrium to this (no MDG) game, the fraction p^*/t^* is rising in ω.*[47]

> **Lemma 2.** *Comparative statics: p^* rises and t^* falls with ω.*

As is standard in these games,[48] greater domestic accountability leads to greater public goods provision. This is true both relative to the amount of private transfers provided, and in absolute amounts. Having established these preliminaries and laid out the basic game form, we can now turn to the central question: How does the existence of the MDGs affect this domestic equilibrium?

Model with MDGs

To capture the role of the MDGs, we consider a model isomorphic to the one above. The only difference lies in L's utility function. We now assume that the

---

[47] All proofs are presented in the appendix, available here: https://www.cambridge.org/core/journals/international-organization/article/millennium-development-goals-and-education-accountability-and-substitution-in-global-assessment/.

[48] Bueno de Mesquita et al. 2003.

international community offers the leader a benefit for exceeding a certain threshold of primary education, as is specified by the MDGs. (We remain agnostic as to which of the theorized transmission mechanisms diagrammed in Figure 12.1 are at play. In our empirical results, we test the role of foreign aid via mediation analysis.) Let $\beta > 0$ denote this benefit and $\bar{p}$ denote the exogenously imposed threshold from the international community. We can then redefine the utility of the leader:

$$U_L(p,h,t) = \begin{cases} B - p - h - \omega t + \beta I(p) \text{ if in power} \\ 0 \text{ otherwise.} \end{cases}$$

where

$$I(p) = \begin{cases} 1 \text{ if } p \geq \bar{p} \\ 0 \text{ otherwise.} \end{cases}$$

As before, the incumbent leader will always successfully buy-off her winning coalition and remain in power. Our focus is on her equilibrium offer of primary and secondary education levels, which we will denote p^{**} and h^{**}, respectively. Denote the equilibrium transfer to a given member of the winning coalition as t^{**}.

Before we can proceed further, we require some definitions. Recall that U_C^*, p^*, h^* and t^* are defined in Definition 1 and $\bar{p}$ is the exogenous MDG threshold. The choice of the triple (p, h, t) is endogenous.

Definition 2.

1. *Define the* **retention constraint** *as* $U_h(h) + \left[1 + \dfrac{\delta}{1-\delta}(1-\omega)\right] U_t(t) \geq U_C^* - U_p(p)$.

2. *Define the* **residual constraint** *as* $h + \omega t \leq B + \beta - p$.

3. *Define the* **participation constraint** *as* $h + \omega t \leq h^* + p^* - \bar{p} + \omega t^* + \beta$.

4. *Define the set* $\Theta(\omega, \bar{p}, \beta, B)$ *as the set of triples* (p,h,t) *that satisfy these three constraints. That is*

$$\Theta(\omega,\bar{p},\beta,B) = \left\{(p,h,t) \in \mathbb{R}_+^3 \mid U_h(h) + \left[1 + \dfrac{\delta}{1-\delta}(1-\omega)\right] U_t(t) \geq U_C^* - U_p(p) \text{ and} \right.$$

$$\left. h + \omega t \leq +B + \beta - p \text{ and } h + \omega t \leq h^* + p^* - \bar{p} + \omega t^* + \beta \right\}.$$

Note that this set is parameterized by the exogenous variables, including $\bar{p}$.

5. *Let* $\hat{p}$ *be the largest value of p among all the triples in* $\Theta(\omega, \bar{p}, \beta, B)$. *That is* $\hat{p} = \sup\{p \mid (p,h,t) \in \Theta(\omega, \bar{p}, \beta, B)\}$.

The retention constraint is, as its name suggests, a restriction on the values of the menu of goods offered to the selectorate which must be satisfied by the incumbent if she is to retain office. In particular the benefits to the selectorate must be larger than those on offer from the challenger. The residual constraint requires the leader to offer a menu that spends no more than the available budget. The participation constraint recognizes that the leader's decision to adopt the MDGs is voluntary, in the sense that the leader pockets a (weakly) larger residual after adopting the MDG $\bar{p}$ and receiving the bonus β than was the case absent the MDG (and choosing p^*, h^*, t^*). The set of all possible triples (p, h, t) that satisfy all three of these constraints is denoted $\Theta(\cdot)$, and is parameterized by the exogenous variables of the model.

If the benefits the international community offers for attaining the MDG goals are not too large, there is a maximal target the international community can set and expect compliance. If this target for primary education provision $\bar{p}$ is set too high, L will recognize that she cannot possibly satisfy international demands, her residual and participation constraints, and the need to stay in power. We define this value of the MDG goal as $\hat{p}$.

This of course holds for "modest" values of the international reward β. If the international reward is large enough, then the leader can buy off the winning coalition, and satisfy the international community and have plenty left over. In order to ensure that the equilibrium to MDG game is not degenerate – in the sense that the parameter space where the MDGs can potentially affect behavior is not empty—we adopt the following restriction:

Lemma 3. *A sufficient condition for $\Theta(\omega, \bar{p}, \beta, B)$ to be non-empty is $\beta \geq \bar{p} - p^*$.*

Given that the feasible set $\Theta(\cdot)$ is not empty (and convex), we can find the element in this set (the optimal choice of t and h) that maximizes the leader's utility in the case that the leader chooses to adopt the MDG, $\bar{p}$:

Definition 3. *For any exogenous $\bar{p}$, define the triple*

$$(\bar{p}, \bar{h}, \bar{t}) = argmax_{(\bar{p},h,t) \in \Theta(\omega,\bar{p},\beta,B)} B + \beta - \bar{p} - h - \omega t$$

We are now ready to characterize the equilibrium to the MDG game. Let the equilibrium to the MDG game be denoted $\{(p_C^{**}, h_C^{**}, t_C^{**}); (p^{**}, h^{**}, t^{**})\}$. Recall the equilibrium to the No MDG game is denoted $\{(p_C^*, h_C^*, t_C^*); (p^*, h^*, t^*)\}$.

Proposition 1. *Given an exogenous MDG goal of $\bar{p}$, the equilibrium to the MDG game is:*

For C, $(p_C^{**}, h_C^{**}, t_C^{**}) = (p_C^*, h_C^*, t_C^*)$. For L,

$$\left(p^{**}, h^{**}, t^{**}\right) = \begin{cases} \left(p^*, h^*, t^*\right) \text{ if } \bar{p} \leq p^* \\ \left(\bar{p}, \bar{h}, \bar{t}\right) \text{ if } \bar{p} \in (p^*, \hat{p}) \\ \left(p^*, h^*, t^*\right) \text{ if } \bar{p} \geq \hat{p} \end{cases}$$

The promulgation of the MDGs thus can affect primary education provision, but will only do so for certain configurations of parameter values. Straightforwardly, if the government were already meeting the international community's demand that primary education exceed a certain threshold, the MDGs will have no effect on state behavior. Compliance was given *ex ante*. Contrastingly, if international standards are too high, the government will find it impossible to comply while simultaneously meeting her domestic constraints. Since failing to satisfy these domestic considerations will entail a loss of office, the government will disregard the international target.

But, for intermediate values of $\bar{p}$ – those that exceed the prior provision of primary education, but are not so onerous that they inhibit the government's ability to satisfy domestic audiences, the MDGs induce a change in behavior. The government will meet the international community's demand and set $p^{**} = \bar{p}$.

Comparison across the Two Cases

We are now in a position to compare the equilibrium provision of primary and secondary education under the two different equilibria, which we interpret as the effect of the MDGs. Specifically, we will examine how this effect is moderated by the level of domestic accountability – i.e. how this effect varies with ω.

While the MDG level $\bar{p}$ is exogenous with respect to the game form above, we should bear in mind that the level is in fact set by the international community. It would make little sense for the community to set an MDG level that is in fact out of reach of the very countries and leaders that it is designed to incentivize. That is for the low ω countries, it makes little practical sense to consider any $\bar{p} > \hat{p}$. In what follows we make the following assumption:

Assumption 1. $\bar{p} \leq \hat{p} \,\forall\, \omega$.

Intuitively, this means that the MDGs are attainable for all countries (given the size of the reward, β) without causing failure in office.[49] For any country, if β is large enough, Assumption 1 is satisfied.

Let us begin by looking at the direct effect of the MDGs – the effect on primary education provision. Formally, this is defined as the difference in the equilibrium primary education provision across the two models $p^{**} - p^*$.

---

[49] Substantively, we believe this restriction on the parameter space to be reasonable. While the goals ($\bar{p}$) specified by the MDGs (universal primary education) applied to all states, the material benefits β used to achieve these goals vary across countries. Given the backing of major multilateral and bilateral development agencies, resources could be expected to be allocated such that the MDGs were achievable for all states. Theoretically, we put this restriction in place because the sign of $\frac{\partial \hat{p}}{\partial \omega}$ is ambiguous, limiting our ability to make predictions outside the portion of the parameter space defined by Assumption 1. More definitively pinning down predictions for this term would require stricter functional form restrictions on $U_k(\cdot), k \in \{p, h, t\}$.

Proposition 2. *The MDGs weakly increase the provision of primary education:* $p^{**} - p^* \geq 0$. *The size of this effect is (weakly) decreasing in domestic accountability* ω.

The provision of primary education is weakly higher when the MDGs are present relative to when they are absent. Some polities increase their provision up to the standard set by the international community $(\bar{p})$. Others leave their level of primary education unchanged.

Systematically, the effect of the introduction of the MDGs is smaller in more accountable (higher ω) states. Primary education provision is higher in states with greater domestic accountability *ex ante*. Some such states will meet international standards with or without the MDGs, and so the introduction of global performance indicators will have no effect. Other accountable governments may fall a little short of international standards, but they will do so by less than their less accountable contemporaries. Meeting the goals set by the international community requires less of such states.

We can now turn our attention to the substitution effect. We begin by documenting that, whenever the effect of the MDGs on primary education is strictly positive (i.e., where the effect is non-zero), their effect on the provision of secondary education is negative. When governments respond to the MDGs they do so by increasing primary, and reducing secondary, education provision. Everywhere else, the MDGs have no effect on public goods provision.

Proposition 3. *In all instances where the MDGs increase primary education* $(p^{**} > p^*)$, *equilibrium levels of secondary education provision fall* $(h^{**} < h^*)$. *We term this the* **substitution effect**.

We can go further and characterize the circumstances under which the substitution effect is likely to emerge. Systematically, less accountable states are more likely to experience substitution than more accountable states.[50] Recall from Proposition 2 that polities with higher levels of domestic accountability are less responsive to the MDGs with regard to primary education provision. When there is no direct effect of the MDGs on primary education, there can be no substitution effect on secondary education. By contrast, less accountable states have greater leeway to respond to international incentives. Because their provision of primary education is more responsive to the MDGs, they are more inclined to engage in substitution.

---

[50] This is not equivalent to stating that everywhere the magnitude of the substitution effect $h^* - h^{**}$ is falling in ω. There are two competing effects here: First, less accountable states must boost primary education provision by more to meet international standards. This would tend to increase substitution. Second, and contrastingly, secondary education provision is lower *ex ante* in less accountable states than in more. The concavity of $U_h(\cdot)$ then implies that cutting secondary education provision reduces the utility of members of the winning coalition by more as ω falls, making substitution more costly. We loosely say that an increase in ω diminishes the size of the substitution effect so long as $U_h(\cdot)$ is not "too concave." More formally, if we let $U_h(h) = h^{\alpha}$, $\alpha \in (0,1)$, then in the limit as $\alpha \to 1$ the substitution effect is falling in ω for all parameter values.

Lemma 4. *For any value of $\bar{p}$ that satisfies Assumption 1, there exists a corresponding threshold $\hat{\omega}$ such that the substitution effect is present for $\omega < \hat{\omega}$ and absent for values of $\omega \geq \hat{\omega}$*

In what follows, we empirically test Propositions 2 and 3 and Lemma 4. We anticipate that MDG adoption increased the provision of primary education, and this effect was most evident in the least domestically accountable states (autocracies with low levels of transparency). This effect should be smallest in more accountable polities (democracies with high government transparency). We further test the existence of a substitution effect – a decline in the relative provision of secondary education following the promulgation of the MDGs. This substitution effect should likewise be most evident in the least accountable states.

EMPIRICS

We test our formal intuition on a cross-national panel of country-level primary and secondary enrollment rates measured between 1980 and 2010. Our empirical tests of the relationship between MDG adoption and enrollment use several methods to reduce bias and spurious associations, including country and year random effects, county-specific time trends, and first-differenced and lagged measures of our dependent variables. Nevertheless, our empirical approach relies on documenting evidence consistent with our theoretical predictions, and not making causal claims about MDG adoption.

Data

We draw our definitions of primary and secondary enrollment rates from the UNESCO Institute of Statistics.[51] Primary enrollment rates are defined as the total number of children of official primary school age who are enrolled in primary education divided by the total population of official primary school age. Secondary and tertiary enrollment rates are defined analogously and are combined in our data (and our analysis). The UNESCO data contain a nontrivial number of missing observations. We drop country panels with fewer than 10 years of data and impute missing values for the remaining country panels using the Amelia II package for R. We implement multiple imputation techniques to account for uncertainty across imputed datasets.[52]

After dropping countries with fewer than 10 years of data, we are left with 114 countries with data from 1980 to 2010. We merge this dataset with the HRV index of transparency from Hollyer, Rosendorff, and Vreeland[53] which

---

[51] See http://www.uis.unesco.org/Pages/default.aspx, accessed March 1, 2016.
[52] Honaker et al. 2011.
[53] Hollyer, Rosendorff, and Vreeland 2014, 2018.

includes additional information – importantly the annual change in real GDP –drawn originally from the Penn World Table version 6.3[54] – and a measure of democracy – drawn originally from Cheibub, Gandhi, and Vreeland.[55] The democracy measure extends only through 2008, so we impute the values for 2009 and 2010 from this value for each country. We also include a measure of per capita GDP (current USD) from the World Bank[56] as well as three different measures of aid: total aid, aid targeting primary education, and aid targeting secondary education. All measures of aid are transformed to reflect logged *per capita* estimates. Table 12.2 presents summary statistics of our key variables, separated by the full sample, countries with GDP per capita in 2000 under $1000, and those with GDP per capita in 2000 under $13,000.

One issue with both the primary and secondary enrollment rate data is that they are subject to ceiling effects. While neither enrollment figure is strictly bounded above by 100 percent – if, for instance, children enroll in primary education at ages below 6 years, the primary enrollment figure may exceed 100 percent – in practice, neither figure can substantially exceed 100 percent. To diminish the risk that ceiling effects may produce nonlinearities in our relationships of interest, we first scale all enrollment figures relative to their maximum values (such that all fall on the [0, 1] interval) and then apply a logistic transformation to these data.[57] We apply this transformation to all enrollment figures in our dataset.

To measure government accountability, we rely on two measures. The first of these captures political institutions, namely democracy. We draw our measure of democracy from the *Democracy and Development Revisited* dataset,[58] which codes a binary indicator *democracy* $\in$ {0, 1} equal to one if both legislative and executive posts are filled by meaningful elections.

Our second measure of accountability measures the informational environment of a given country-year. Our measure of this concept is the HRV index of government transparency.[59] The HRV index is a continuous measure, derived from an item-response model of data missingness. It captures the tendency of the government to disclose credible information, pertinent to economics and citizen welfare, to the public.[60]

---

[54] Heston, Summers, and Aten 2009.

[55] Cheibub, Gandhi, and Vreeland 2010.

[56] http://data.worldbank.org/indicator/NY.GDP.PCAP.CD, accessed April 14, 2016.

[57] Denote $p \in [0, 1]$ as the rescaled enrollment figure. We transform this measure by $\ln\left(\frac{p}{1-p}\right)$.

[58] Cheibub, Gandhi, and Vreeland 2010.

[59] Hollyer, Rosendorff, and Vreeland 2014, 2018.

[60] Note that we use a narrow measure of a specific facet of transparency: The dissemination of data. We view this measure as most appropriate for this study, given that MDGs are measured by some of the very same variables used to construct the HRV index. That said, we acknowledge that in other theoretical settings, measures that capture alternative facets of transparency may be more appropriate (see e.g. Adserà, Boix, and Payne 2003; Berliner and Erlich 2015; Berliner 2014; Besley and Burgess 2002; Bremmer 2006; Broz 2002; Brunetti and Weder 2003; Copelovitch, Gandrud, and Hallerberg 2018; Djankov et al. 2003; Grief 2006; Habyarimana et al. 2009; Islam 2006; Kosack and Fung 2014).

TABLE 12.2. *Summary statistics for pre- and post-millennium declaration by sample*

	Full Sample		GDP$_{2000}$ ≤ $1000		GDP$_{2000}$ ≤ $13,000	
	Pre-MDG	Post-MDG	Pre-MDG	Post-MDG	Pre-MDG	Post-MDG
Primary Enrollment	96.09	102.64	80.66	95.54	94.95	102.35
(% of Eligible)	(22.80)	(15.48)	(29.40)	(21.71)	(24.88)	(16.93)
Sec./Ter. Enrollment	58.74	72.24	31.70	43.43	50.55	64.72
(% of Eligible)	(33.01)	(31.14)	(27.67)	(26.74)	(30.17)	(28.95)
GDP	4789	9853	1233	2701	2411	5199
(2000 USD pc)	(7,278)	(13,029)	(2,963)	(4,471)	(3,525)	(5,400)
Transparency Index	0.86	2.01	−0.04	0.55	0.54	1.61
	(1.73)	(2.20)	(1.22)	(1.40)	(1.53)	(1.99)
Democracy	0.46	0.58	0.24	0.42	0.38	0.52
	(0.44)	(0.43)	(0.37)	(0.45)	(0.42)	(0.44)
Total Aid	48.91	53.18	51.74	53.39	53.74	62.11
(2011 USD pc)	(109.03)	(131.93)	(70.25)	(63.03)	(81.95)	(121.33)
Primary Educ. Aid	0.48	0.79	0.66	1.27	0.59	0.97
(2011 USD pc)	(3.40)	(2.80)	(4.04)	(3.41)	(3.76)	(3.08)
Secondary Educ. Aid	0.24	0.20	0.28	0.19	0.26	0.25
(2011 USD pc)	(1.91)	(1.46)	(1.92)	(0.63)	(1.99)	(1.62)
N	3300	1815	1120	616	2680	1474

Estimating the Direct Effect of the MDGs

We begin by estimating the direct effect of the MDGs on primary enrollment rates. That is, we start by parsing the evidence that the MDGs increased the growth rate of primary enrollment across countries. Proposition 2 contends that the effect of the MDGs should be positive, and should be larger in unaccountable states. To conduct this estimation, we estimate a varying intercepts multi-level model of the following form:

$$\Delta P_{i,t} = \alpha_i + \beta_1 \text{Transparency}_{i,t} + \beta_2 \text{Democracy}_{i,t}$$

$$+ I(t \geq 2000)[\gamma_1 + \gamma_2 \text{Transparency}_{i,t} + \gamma_3 \text{Democracy}_{i,t}] \qquad (12.1)$$

$$+ \beta_3 \Delta r \text{GDP}_{i,t} + \beta_4 \text{Aid}_{i,t-1} + \tau_t + \varepsilon_{i,t}$$

where

$$\alpha_i \sim N(\mu_\alpha, \sigma_\alpha)$$
$$\tau_t \sim N(\mu_\tau, \sigma_\tau)$$

where Δ denotes the difference operator, i indexes country, and t indexes year. By first differencing the outcome term, we eliminate country-specific factors that drive the level of primary education as potential confounds from the specification. In controlling for country (α_i) and year (τ_t) random effects, we help to adjust for random variations in the growth rate in enrollment figures across countries and time. Our results are robust to the inclusion of linear and quadratic time trends.

Our hypotheses are reflected in the γ_j coefficients. Proposition 2 holds that $\gamma_1 > 0$. Our moderating hypotheses, also from Proposition 2 – that any such effect of the MDGs should diminish in transparent and democratic polities – imply that γ_2, $\gamma_3 < 0$. Results from the model specified in Equation 12.1 are presented in Table 12.3.

Table 12.3 reveals that coefficients on the MDG indicator are consistently positive and statistically significant at conventional levels. Descriptively, these results indicate that the change in primary enrollment rates was, year-on-year, consistently more positive following the Millennium Declaration, conditioning on countries, years, and country-specific cubic trends. However, our motivating theory would posit that, failing to control for the confounding effects of transparency and electoral accountability, our estimating equation is inaccurate.

Column 2 updates the specification with these controls. Specifically, we control for transparency and accountability linearly, along with the change in real GDP per capita (not shown) as well as measures of aid, including total aid received, and aid targeting primary and secondary education. The resulting estimate on the MDG indicator maintains its significance and magnitude. However, we still are not properly specifying a linear model in line with our

TABLE 12.3. *The relationship between the Millennium Declaration and the primary school enrollment rate*

	Dependent Variable				
	Δ Primary Enrollment				
	(1)	(2)	(3)	(4)	(5)
MDG	0.069***	0.073***	0.094***	0.067***	0.084***
	(0.013)	(0.014)	(0.017)	(0.011)	(0.016)
Trans		−0.025***	−0.024***	−0.014*	−0.018**
		(0.007)	(0.007)	(0.008)	(0.009)
Dem		0.055***	0.077***	0.071***	0.083***
		(0.015)	(0.019)	(0.017)	(0.019)
Total Aid		−0.003	−0.003	−0.017*	−0.017*
		(0.009)	(0.009)	(0.009)	(0.009)
Aid Primary		0.008*	0.008*	0.009*	0.009*
		(0.005)	(0.005)	(0.005)	(0.005)
Aid Secondary		0.001	0.001	0.0003	0.0003
		(0.004)	(0.004)	(0.004)	(0.004)
MDG*Trans				−0.030***	−0.023**
				(0.009)	(0.010)
MDG*Dem			−0.045**		−0.034
			(0.021)		(0.023)
Constant	−0.074***	−0.111***	−0.124***	−0.111***	−0.118***
	(0.018)	(0.020)	(0.021)	(0.018)	(0.019)
Observations	4950	4950	4950	4950	4950

*$p < 0.10$; **$p < 0.05$; ***$p < 0.01$.
Notes: Multi-level model analysis allowing for random effects by country and year. Lagged primary enrollment rate and country-specific time trends not shown. Standard errors in parentheses.

theoretical motivation. To accurately reflect our intuition, we turn to interaction effects, as displayed in columns 3 through 5.

Here we see suggestive evidence supporting our theoretical framework. Namely, across specifications the MDG indicator is significant and positive. We further note that the conditional effect of MDGs declines with both accountability and transparency. Figure 12.2 displays the marginal effects associated with the relationship between the Millennium Declaration and primary enrollment rates over different values of transparency and among democracies and non-democracies. Column 5 combines the specifications and finds statistically significant relationships only for transparency.

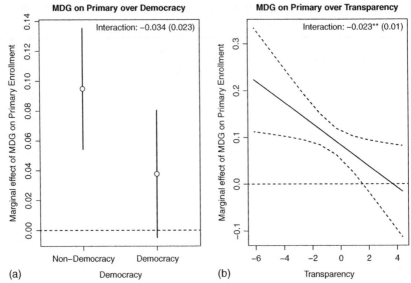

FIGURE 12.2. Linear marginal effects plots characterizing heterogeneity in effect of MDG on primary enrollment rates over values of democracy (a) and transparency index (b).

Results from Equation 12.1 are thus consistent with our Proposition 2: (1) The MDGs are associated with an increase in primary enrollment rates, and (2) this effect is diminished in accountable (and particularly in transparent) states.

As an additional test, we replicate the model specified in Equation 12.1, substituting secondary and tertiary enrollment rates for primary. These results offer some preliminary evidence as to Proposition 3 and Lemma 4. Table 12.4 presents the results, with no evidence of a relationship between enrollment rates at higher levels of education and MDG adoption after controlling for aid flows.

The coefficient on MDGs is noisily estimated, but commensurate in magnitude to the coefficient from the primary enrollment rate regression. Interestingly, we still see negative coefficients on the interaction terms with transparency although these are marginally significant and only half the size of the primary enrollment results.

Although these results are consistent with our theoretical expectations, they do not demonstrate that the *same* countries that increase their primary enrollment rates post-2000 also increase their secondary enrollment rates. To test this relationship, we turn to characterizing the country-level substitution from secondary enrollment to primary in our data.

TABLE 12.4. *The relationship between the Millennium Declaration and the secondary school enrollment rate*

	Dependent Variable				
	Δ Secondary Enrollment				
	(1)	(2)	(3)	(4)	(5)
MDG	0.005**	0.007	0.010	0.011	0.011
	(0.002)	(0.010)	(0.010)	(0.010)	(0.010)
Trans		0.002	0.003	0.005**	0.005**
		(0.002)	(0.002)	(0.002)	(0.002)
Dem		0.006**	0.008***	0.006**	0.007*
		(0.003)	(0.003)	(0.003)	(0.003)
Total Aid		−0.003	−0.003	−0.004	−0.004
		(0.003)	(0.003)	(0.004)	(0.004)
Aid Primary		0.00003	−0.00001	−0.00003	−0.00003
		(0.001)	(0.001)	(0.001)	(0.001)
Aid Secondary		0.0003	0.0003	0.0003	0.0003
		(0.001)	(0.001)	(0.001)	(0.001)
MDG*Trans				−0.005**	−0.005**
				(0.002)	(0.003)
MDG*Dem			−0.006		−0.0004
			(0.004)		(0.005)
Constant	0.020***	0.039	0.038	0.054	0.054
	(0.003)	(0.043)	(0.042)	(0.048)	(0.048)
Observations	4950	4950	4950	4950	4950

$*p < 0.10; **p < 0.05; ***p < 0.01$.
Notes: Multi-level model analysis allowing for random effects by country and year. Lagged secondary enrollment rate and country-specific time trends not shown. Standard errors in parentheses.

Estimating the Substitution Effect of the MDGs

Method 1: Estimating the Difference between Primary and Secondary Enrollment Rates

We begin our analysis of substitution by employing a simple measure of the relationship between primary and secondary education within a given country-year: the difference between secondary and primary enrollment rates ($P_{i,t} - S_{i,t}$). If our substitution claim is correct, this measure should increase following the promulgation of the MDGs – i.e. the primary enrollment rate should increase relative to the secondary enrollment rate.

We thus estimate a model of the form:

$$(P_{i,t} - S_{i,t}) = \alpha_i + I(\text{year} \geq 2000)[\gamma_1 + \gamma_2 \text{Transparency}_{i,t}$$

$$+ \gamma_3 \text{Democracy}_{i,t}] + \mathbf{X}_{i,t}\boldsymbol{\beta} + \varepsilon_{i,t} \tag{12.2}$$

where i denotes country, t year, α_i is a country random effect, and $\mathbf{X}_{i,t}\boldsymbol{\beta}$ is a data vector and associated coefficients. Included as controls are the transparency and democracy measures, GDP *per capita*, and the aforementioned measures of aid.

Our hypotheses hold that $\gamma_1 > 0$, and $\gamma_2, \gamma_3 < 0$. We present results from the model specified in Equation 12.2 in Table 12.5.

Consistent with our theoretical expectations, γ_1 is positive across all specifications and significant at conventional thresholds, indicating that MDG adoption is associated with an increase in the enrollment rates separating primary and secondary students.

Unlike the results presented for primary enrollment in isolation, we note that the transparency index interaction is no longer significant while democracy appears as a highly significant moderator when estimated in the fully-interacted specification (column 6). Aid for primary education is also significant and positive while the estimate for secondary education aid is a precisely estimated zero.

However, the use of the difference between primary and secondary enrollment as an outcome measure induces considerable loss of information. We are unable to tell, for instance, whether the changes in the measure are driven by an absolute decline in secondary rates, by a surge in primary enrollment rates, or some combination of the two factors.

Given these concerns, we turn to two alternative specifications: the first is an error correction model presented below and the second is a vector autoregression discussed in our appendix.

Method 2: Error Correction Specification

First, we turn to an error correction model (ECM). Developed to deal with co-integrated time-series, ECMs postulate a long-term equilibrium relationship between covariates – here primary and secondary education.[61] We are interested in changes in this long-term equilibrium. Specifically, we estimate a model of the form:

$$\Delta P_{i,M,t} = \gamma[P_{i,M,t-1} - \beta_{i,M}S_{i,M,t-1}] + \delta_{i,M}\Delta S_{i,M,t-1} + \varepsilon_{i,M,t} \qquad (12.3)$$

where, as in Equation (12.1), Δ is the difference operator, i denotes country, t denotes year, P is the primary enrollment rate, and S the secondary. $M \in \{0, 1\}$ is an indicator taking the value 1 after the year 2000.

The expression $P_{i,M,t-1} - \beta_{i,M}S_{i,M,t-1}$ denotes the equilibrium relationship between primary and secondary education. When $P_{i,M,t-1} = \beta_{i,M}S_{i,M,t-1}$, the system is in equilibrium, and primary enrollment rates will not tend to adjust. Given $\gamma < 0$ (which is the case in all estimates), when primary education exceeds its equilibrium target $\left(P_{i,M,t-1} > \beta_{i,M}S_{i,M,t-1}\right)$ it will tend to decline. By contrast,

---

[61] Beck and Katz 2011.

TABLE 12.5. *Coefficients relating the Millennium Declaration to the difference between primary and secondary enrollment rates across countries*

| | Dependent Variable | | | | | |
| | Primary – Secondary | | | | | |
	(1)	(2)	(3)	(4)	(5)	(6)
MDG	1.882**	2.517***	2.120***	2.512***	4.433***	4.785***
	(0.743)	(0.700)	(0.710)	(0.720)	(0.951)	(0.871)
Trans		-2.995***	-3.092***	-2.273***	-2.993***	-3.109***
		(0.613)	(0.624)	(0.747)	(0.622)	(0.406)
Dem		4.224***	3.700***	3.712***	5.144***	5.312***
		(0.951)	(1.001)	(0.992)	(1.044)	(0.816)
Total Aid			2.647***	2.543***	2.519***	2.623***
			(0.554)	(0.552)	(0.551)	(0.535)
Aid Primary			1.154***	1.087***	1.138***	1.124***
			(0.231)	(0.231)	(0.230)	(0.218)
Aid Secondary			0.123	0.117	0.123	0.153
			(0.208)	(0.208)	(0.208)	(0.193)
MDG*Trans				-1.536***		-0.723
				(0.557)		(0.465)
MDG*Dem					-4.161***	-4.046***
					(1.035)	(1.042)
Constant	49.995***	46.114***	45.823***	45.687***	44.808***	44.127***
	(1.911)	(2.000)	(1.972)	(1.987)	(2.023)	(1.947)
Observations	4950	4950	4950	4950	4950	4950

* $p < 0.10$; ** $p < 0.05$; *** $p < 0.01$.
Notes: Multi-level model analysis allowing for random effects by country and year. Change in real GDP per capita and country-specific time trends not shown. Standard errors in parentheses.

when primary education falls below its equilibrium level $\left(P_{i,M,t-1} < \beta_{i,M} S_{i,M,t-1} \right)$, primary enrollment rates will tend to rise.

Since we are interested in changes in the equilibrium relationship between primary and secondary education, we examine changes in the $\beta_{i,M}$ parameter before and after the introduction of the MDGs, and variation in this term across countries, as given by:[62]

$$\beta_{i,M} = \alpha + \pi_1 \text{Trans}_i + \pi_2 \text{Dem}_i + \pi_3 \text{Trans}_i \times \text{Dem}_i$$

$$+ I(\text{year} \geq 2000)[\omega_1 + \omega_2 \text{Trans}_i + \omega_3 \text{Dem}_i]$$

$$+ \ln(\text{GDP}_{pc2000})_i + \eta_{i,M} \tag{12.5}$$

Proposition 3 holds that $\omega_1 > 0$, implying that the equilibrium level of secondary education, relative to primary, declines once the MDGs go into effect. Lemma 4 holds that $\omega_j, j \in \{2, 3\} < 0$ – the substitution effect is diminished in accountable polities. Estimates from Equation 12.5 are presented in Table 12.6.

As suggested by Table 12.6, the Millennium Declaration corresponds to a divergence of primary and secondary enrollment rates, suggesting a substitution effect (as indicated by the statistically significant coefficient in column 1).

However, this substitution effect is mitigated by democratic accountability, with the interaction term in column 2 entering negative and marginally significant. A similar effect is documented with transparency, where the substitution effect is reduced in countries with higher levels of transparency. Interestingly, the coefficient on the transparency term is positive, indicating that, before the MDGs, transparent governments had a higher equilibrium level of primary relative to secondary education than unaccountable states. This is consistent with existing claims, notably by David Stasavage.[63] Combining these specifications suggests that the moderating effect is driven primarily by transparency, not electoral accountability.

ECM models, however, impose strong parametric assumptions. We merely posit that primary and secondary enrollment rates exhibit a long-term structural relationship of the form documented by Equation 12.3, and rely heavily on this equilibrium in our interpretation. In particular, Grant and Lebo argue that such general error correction models will be biased if the respective

---

[62] We do so via a two-stage process. First, we estimate an untransformed version of Equation 12.3 given by:

$$\Delta P_{i,M,t} = \gamma P_{i,M,t-1} + \zeta_{i,M} S_{i,M,t-1} + \delta_{i,M} \Delta S_{i,M,t-1} + \varepsilon_{i,M,t}$$

$$\zeta_{i,M} = \omega_{0,i} + \omega_{1,i} M_i + E_i \tag{12.4}$$

where,

$$\omega_{0,i} \sim N(\alpha_{0,i}, U_{0,i})$$

$$\omega_{1,i} \sim N(\alpha_{1,i}, U_{1,i})$$

which gives us estimated values of $\beta_{i,M}$. We then regress these parameters as described in Equation 12.5.

[63] Stasavage 2005.

TABLE 12.6. *β substitution tests for equilibrium levels of secondary and primary education*

	Dependent Variable			
	β_i, M			
	(1)	(2)	(3)	(4)
MDG	0.080***	0.130***	0.136***	0.145***
	(0.026)	(0.030)	(0.037)	(0.033)
Trans			0.013*	0.011
			(0.007)	(0.008)
Dem		0.043**		0.014
		(0.021)		(0.025)
Total Aid	0.016	0.014	0.009	0.009
	(0.016)	(0.016)	(0.016)	(0.016)
Aid Primary	−0.014	−0.015	−0.009	−0.010
	(0.016)	(0.016)	(0.015)	(0.016)
Aid Secondary	−0.004	−0.002	−0.002	−0.002
	(0.020)	(0.020)	(0.019)	(0.018)
MDG*Trans			−0.028***	−0.026***
			(0.007)	(0.009)
MDG*Dem		−0.087***		−0.023
		(0.029)		(0.037)
Constant	0.066	0.040	0.021	0.017
	(0.216)	(0.214)	(0.208)	(0.204)
Observations	228	228	228	228

*$p < 0.10$; **$p < 0.05$; ***$p < 0.01$.
Notes: Multi-level model analysis allowing for random effects by country and year. Change in real GDP per capita and country-specific time trends not shown. Standard errors presented in parentheses.

time-series – here primary and secondary enrollment rates – are either not co-integrated, or are co-integrated of different orders.[64] The coefficient γ, in that instance, will be inconsistent – hence, so too will our parameters of interest β.

To address this concern, we first examine the co-integration of these two time series. While the series appear co-integrated in global tests, running these tests country-by-country only supports co-integration in roughly half our sample of states. We therefore re-estimate our models, restricting our sample only to those states where the evidence clearly indicates that primary and secondary enrollment are co-integrated. Results are substantively similar to those in the full sample.

Mechanisms

Thus far we have developed a model which predicts GPIs can lead to unintended substitution behavior and have presented empirical evidence consistent

[64] Grant and Lebo 2016.

with our predictions. First, we have shown that MDG adoption prompted an increase in primary school enrollment as was its intention, but that the magnitude of this relationship is strongest in the least accountable polities in our data. Second, we have shown that this increase in primary enrollment was accompanied by a decline in secondary enrollment, consistent with our theoretical prediction for substitution effects. Again, evidence of this substitution effect is strongest in the least accountable polities.

However, our formal model is agnostic with respect to the specific mechanisms by which GPIs operate (see Figure 12.1). We are uncertain as to whether these results arise due to the budgetary impacts of foreign aid and investment which may respond to GPIs ("transnational pressures"), due to the activation of civil society ("domestic politics"), or due to a direct effect on policymakers themselves ("elite shaming"). The moderating effects of accountability documented above suggest a possible channel via domestic politics. In the following section, we test whether a transnational pressure channel via foreign aid also operates.

To conduct this analysis, we treat foreign aid as a mediating variable and use a two-stage regression framework as in Baron and Kenny.[65] The first stage predicts changes in foreign aid flows as a function of MDG adoption, given in Equation 12.6. We interact MDG adoption with the primary enrollment rate in the year 2000, reflecting the intuition that performance assessments like the Millennium Development Goals impact aid flows specifically for under-performers.

$$\Delta\text{Aid}_{i,t} = \alpha_i + \beta_1\text{Primary}_{i,2000}$$
$$+ I(t \geq 2000)[\rho_1 + \rho_2\text{Primary}_{i,2000}]$$
$$+ \beta_1\Delta r\text{GDP}_{i,t} + \beta_2\text{GDP}_{i,2000} + \beta_3\text{Transparency}_{i,t}$$
$$+ \beta_4\text{Democracy}_{i,t} + \tau_t + \varepsilon_{i,t} \tag{12.6}$$

where
$$\alpha_i \sim N(\mu_\alpha, \sigma_\alpha)$$
$$\tau_t \sim N(\mu_\tau, \sigma_\tau)$$

We save the coefficient on MDG adoption (ρ_1) for use in our second stage analysis. We test a number of different measures of foreign aid, plotted in the left panel of Figure 12.3. As illustrated, aid targeting primary education increases following MDG adoption, particularly toward countries with low initial primary enrollment rates. This first-stage pattern is consistent with the theorized mechanism of "transnational pressures" discussed in the introduction to this volume and illustrated in Figure 12.1 – aid flows do respond to the MDGs.

In the second stage, we regress the change in primary enrollment on MDG adoption and the same aid measure, replicating the specification described above

[65] Baron and Kenny 1986.

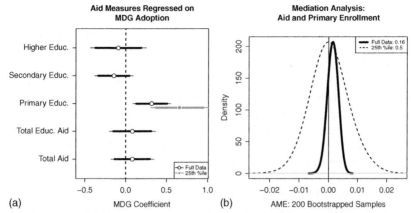

FIGURE 12.3. First stage (a) and overall (b) results from mediation analysis on the mechanism of foreign aid. The first stage results show that foreign aid for primary education increases following MDG adoption, particularly for countries in the bottom quartile of primary enrollment rates. However, the overall results are only marginally significant (pseudo p-values presented in the legend) and represent a small fraction of the overall relationship, suggesting that this mechanism is inactive.

in Equation 12.1 and saving the β_4 coefficient. Under restrictive assumptions,[66] the product of these coefficients captures the average mediation effect between MDG adoption and primary enrollment rates that travels via changes in aid flows. To accommodate the multiply-imputed data, we bootstrap these estimates and plot the distribution of the results in the right panel of Figure 12.3. Pseudo p-values are calculated as the share of bootstrapped estimates greater than zero.

As illustrated, mediation analysis offers no robust support for the theorized mechanism of foreign aid, despite the first-stage channel being active. While foreign aid targeting primary enrollment does respond to the assessments provided by the MDGs (left panel of Figure 12.3), there is no evidence that this is the mechanism by which policymakers reallocate resources. The magnitude of the average mediation effect (AME) is only a fraction of the overall coefficient and is only marginally significant for the full data. Our null finding is consistent with the results of Kijima and Lipscy who also find that, while assessment participation is associated with higher foreign aid inflows, these sources of aid are not meaningfully associated with higher net secondary enrollment.[67] As such, we conclude that – in the context of education and the MDGs – transnational pressures are not the primary mechanism by which this particular GPI induces change.

---

[66] Our empirical endeavor is purely observational and we make no causal claims that would necessitate more sophisticated causal mediation methods such as those pioneered by Imai, Keele, and Yamamoto 2010.

[67] Kijima and Lipscy 2020.

CONCLUSION

To what extent can international initiatives alter country behavior? This volume addresses the topic holistically, starting with how GPIs are produced, charting the mechanisms, and assesses their impact. Our contribution expands our understanding of how GPIs influence state behavior by exploring how these initiatives impact not just their specific target but the larger equilibrium levels of public goods provision. We argue that countries with finite resources must trade-off between different public goods and that their ability to do so is constrained by their institutions. We develop a formal model expressing our argument and take the comparative statics it generates to the data.

In our empirical context, we document evidence of a substitution effect between secondary and primary education in response to the Millennium Development Goals targeting universal primary enrollment. We further find that this substitution effect is stronger in less accountable countries. We argue that our findings support the simple premise that resource-constrained governments (1) do respond to international initiatives, but (2) may do so by reallocating away from other, potentially desirable, outcomes.

Our moderation results highlight an important role played by domestic society. We find that both the direct and substitution effects of MDGs are strongest in less accountable polities. Contrastingly, our mediation analysis suggests a limited role for international actors directly influencing government decision-making through aid allocation. The robustness of our results using the HRV index of transparency, particularly when compared to the weak findings for democracy, suggest that GPIs like the Millennium Development Goals are most effective as information conduits.

Neither of these findings precludes other mechanisms, such as the reputational concerns documented in Zambia by Alice Evans or other types of international actors beyond donors.[68] Further research is required to identify the mechanisms connecting the MDGs to increasing primary enrollment rates and substitution between secondary and primary outcomes.

Our findings offer a mixed take-away for policymakers: On the one hand, we find evidence that global assessment can alter government behavior, and particularly increase the provision of public goods (i.e. primary education). Moreover, these effects are likely to be strongest in the countries that need it most – opaque autocracies which under-provide public goods absent international pressure. However, we also find that global accountability can have unintended second-order effects: Resource constrained leaders, intent on their own political survival, will diminish the provision of goods and services for which the international community does not hold them accountable, even as they increase those emphasized through global assessment programs.

[68] Evans 2017.

We are careful, however, not to draw broader normative conclusions from our analysis. Although the counter-factual conclusion is that secondary enrollment would have been even higher in the absence of the MDGs, this ignores the positive spillovers between primary and secondary enrollment.

Our findings connect with the special issue by expanding the range of outcome behavior to include non-targeted public goods. By accounting for strategic trade-offs and equilibrium behavior, we present a more rounded view of the effects of GPIs, both intended and not. Our findings echo educational program evaluation elsewhere, in which targeted schools make trade-offs in order to attain desired metrics.[69] While our results do not identify the specific mechanisms by which these trade-offs occur, they highlight a fruitful area for research on GPIs writ large and MDGs specifically.

References

Adserà, Alícia, Carles Boix, and Mark Payne. 2003. Are You Being Served? Political Accountability and Quality of Government. *Journal of Law, Economics & Organization* 19 (2):445–90.

Baron, Reuben M., and David A. Kenny. 1986. The Moderator–Mediator Variable Distinction in Social Psychological Research: Conceptual, Strategic, and Statistical Considerations. *Journal of Personality and Social Psychology* 51 (6):1173.

Beck, Nathaniel, and Jonathan N. Katz. 2011. Modeling Dynamics in Time-Series-Cross-Section Political Economy Data. *Annual Review of Political Science* 14:331–52.

Berliner, Daniel. 2014. The Political Origins of Transparency. *Journal of Politics* 76 (2):479–91.

Berliner, Daniel, and Aaron Erlich. 2015. Competing for Transparency: Political Competition and Institutional Reform in Mexican States. *American Political Science Review* 109 (1):110–28.

Besley, Timothy, and Robin Burgess. 2002. The Political Economy of Government Responsiveness: Theory and Evidence from India. *Quarterly Journal of Economics* 117 (4):1415–51.

Bremmer, Ian. 2006. *The J Curve: A New Way to Understand Why Nations Rise and Fall*. New York: Simon and Schuster.

Broz, J. Lawrence. 2002. Political System Transparency and Monetary Commitment Regimes. *International Organization* 56 (4):861–87.

Brunetti, Aymo, and Beatrice Weder. 2003. A Free Press Is Bad News for Corruption. *Journal of Public Economics* 87:1801–24.

Bueno de Mesquita, Bruce, Alastair Smith, Randolph M. Siverson, and James D. Morrow. 2003. *The Logic of Political Survival*. Cambridge, MA: The MIT Press.

Bueno de Mesquita, Ethan. 2007. Politics and the Suboptimal Provision of Counterterror. *International Organization* 61:9–36.

Cameron, William Bruce. 1963. *Informal Sociology: A Casual Introduction to Sociological Thinking*, vol. 21. Random House.

[69] See Fuller and Ladd 2013; Macartney 2016.

Campbell, Donald T. 1979. Assessing the Impact of Planned Social Change. *Evaluation and Program Planning* 2 (1):67–90.

Cheibub, José Antonio, Jennifer Gandhi, and James Raymond Vreeland. 2010. Democracy and Dictatorship Revisited. *Public Choice* 143:67–101.

Chong, Alberto, Ana L. De La O, Dean Karlan, and Leonard Wantchekon. 2010. *Information Dissemination and Local Governments' Electoral Returns: Evidence from a Field Experiment in Mexico.* 106th Annual Meeting of the American Political Science Association, Seattle, March 2010.

Di Tella, Rafael, and Ernesto Schargrodsky. 2003. The Role of Wages and Auditing during a Crackdown on Corruption in the City of Buenos Aires. *Journal of Law, Economics & Organization* 269:269–92.

Djankov, Simeon, Caralee McLiesh, Tatiana Nenova, and Andrei Shleifer. 2003. Who Owns the Media? *Journal of Law and Economics* 46 (2):341–81.

Edwards, Marc A., and Siddhartha Roy. 2017. Academic Research in the 21st Century: Maintaining Scientific Integrity in a Climate of Perverse Incentives and Hypercompetition. *Environmental Engineering Science* 34 (1):51–61.

Evans, Alice. 2017. Amplifying Accountability by Benchmarking Results at District and National Levels. *Development Policy Review* 36 (2):221–40.

Ferraz, Claudio, and Frederico Finan. 2008. Exposing Corrupt Politicians: The Effects of Brazil's Publically Released Audits on Electoral Outcomes. *Quarterly Journal of Economics* 123 (2):703–45.

Fuller, Sarah C., and Helen F. Ladd. 2013. School-Based Accountability and the Distribution of Teacher Quality across Grades in Elementary School. *Education* 8 (4):528–59.

Glaeser, Edward L., and Claudia Goldin, eds. 2006. *Corruption and Reform: Lessons from America's Economic History.* Chicago, IL: The University of Chicago Press.

Grant, Taylor, and Matthew J. Lebo. 2016. Error Correction Methods with Political Time Series. *Political Analysis* 24 (1):3–30.

Grief, Avner. 2006. Institutions and the Path to the Modern Economy: Lessons from Medieval Trade. Cambridge: Cambridge University Press.

Habyarimana, James, Macartan Humphreys, Daniel N. Posner, and Jeremy M. Weinstein. 2009. *Coethnicity: Diversity and the Dilemmas of Collective Action.* New York: Russell Sage Foundation.

Harding, Robin, and David Stasavage. 2014. What Democracy Does (and Doesn't Do) for Basic Services: School Fees, School Inputs, and African Elections. *Journal of Politics* 76 (1):229–45.

Heckman, James J., Jora Stixrud, and Sergio Urzua. 2006. The Effects of Cognitive and Noncognitive Abilities on Labor Market Outcomes and Social Behavior. *Journal of Labor Economics* 24 (3):411–82.

Heston, Alan, Robert Summers, and Bettina Aten. 2009. Penn World Table Version 6.3. Technical Report, Center of International Comparisons at the University of Pennsylvania.

Hollyer, James R., B. Peter Rosendorff, and James Raymond Vreeland. 2011. Democracy and Transparency. *Journal of Politics* 73 (4):1–15.

——— 2014. Measuring Transparency. *Political Analysis* 22 (4):413–34.

2015. Transparency, Protest and Autocratic Instability. *American Political Science Review* 109 (4):764–84.

2018. *Information, Democracy and Autocracy: Economic Transparency and Political (In)Stability*, New York: Cambridge University Press.

Holmstrom, Bengt, and Paul Milgrom. 1991. Multitask Principal-Agent Analyses: Incentive Contracts, Asset Ownership, and Job Design. *Journal of Law, Economics and Organization* 7:24–52.

Honaker, James, Gary King, Matthew Blackwell, et al. 2011. Amelia II: A Program for Missing Data. *Journal of Statistical Software* 45 (7):1–47.

Honig, Dan, and Catherine Weaver. 2020. A Race to the Top? The Aid Transparency Index and the Normative Power of Global Performance Assessments. The Power of Global Performance Indicators. New York: Cambridge University Press.

Hulme, David. 2009. *The Millennium Development Goals (MDGs): A Short History of the World's Biggest Promise*. Brooks World Poverty Institute Working Paper 100.

Imai, Kosuke, Luke Keele, and Teppei Yamamoto. 2010. Identification, Inference and Sensitivity Analysis for Causal Mediation Effects. *Statistical Science* 25 (1):51–71.

Islam, Roumeen. 2006. Does More Transparency Go Along with Better Governance? *Economics and Politics* 18 (2):121–67.

Johns, Leslie. 2012. Courts as Coordinators: Endogenous Enforcement and Jurisdiction in International Adjudication. *Journal of Conflict Resolution* 56 (2):257–89.

Kapuściński, Ryszard. 1989. *The Emperor: Downfall of an Autocrat*. New York: Vintage.

Kelley, Judith G., and Beth A. Simmons. 2015. Politics by Number: Indicators as Social Pressure in International Relations. *American Journal of Political Science* 59 (1):55–70.

2020. *Global Assessment Power in the Twenty-First Century*. The Power of Global Performance Indicators. New York: Cambridge University Press.

Kelley, Judith G., Beth A. Simmons, and Rush Doshi. 2020. *The Power of Ranking: The Ease of Doing Business Indicator as a Form of Social Pressure*. The Power of Global Performance Indicators. New York: Cambridge University Press.

Kijima, Rie, and Phillip Lipscy. 2019. The Politics of International Testing. The Power of Global Performance Indicators. New York: Cambridge University Press.

Kosack, Stephen, and Archon Fung. 2014. Does Transparency Improve Governance? *Annual Review of Political Science* 17:65–87.

Le, Ahn, and Edmund Malesky. 2020. *Do Subnational Assessments (SPAs) Lead to Improved Governance? Evidence from a Field Experiment in Vietnam*. The Power of Global Performance Indicators. New York: Cambridge University Press.

Lebovic, James H., and Erik Voeten. 2009. The Cost of Shame: International Organizations and Foreign Aid in the Punishing of Human Rights Violations. *Journal of Peace Research* 46 (1):79–97.

Macartney, Hugh. 2016. The Dynamic Effects of Educational Accountability. *Journal of Labor Economics* 34 (1):1–28.

Mani, Anandi, and Sharun Mukand. 2007. Democracy, Visibility and Public
    Good Provision. *Journal of Development Economics* 83 (2):506–29.
Mark Copelovitch, Christopher Gandrud, Mark Hallerberg. 2018. Financial
    Data Transparency, International Institutions, and Sovereign Borrowing
    Costs, International Studies Quarterly, 62(1):Pages 23–41.
Milgrom, Paul R., and Douglass C. North. 1990. The Role of Institutions
    in the Revival of Trade: The Law Merchant, Private Judges, and the
    Champaign Fairs. *Economics & Politics* 2 (1):1–23.
Morse, Julia C. 2020. *Blacklists, Market Enforcement, and the Global
    Regime to Combat Terrorist Financing.* The Power of Global Performance
    Indicators. New York: Cambridge University Press.
Peters, John G., and Susan Welch. 1980. The Effects of Charges of Corruption
    on Voting Behavior in Congressional Elections. *American Political
    Science Review* 74:697–708.
Reinikka, Ritva, and Jakob Svensson. 2003. *The Power of Information:
    Evidence from a Newspaper Campaign to Reduce Capture.* Working
    Paper: Institute for International Economic Studies, Stockholm University.
Risse, Thomas, and Kathryn Sikkink. 1999. The Socialization of International
    Human Rights Norms into Domestic Practices: Introduction. In *The
    Power of Human Rights: International Norms and Domestic Change,*
    edited by Thomas Risse, Kathryn Sikkink, and Stephen C. Ropp, 1–38.
    Cambridge: Cambridge University Press.
Skagerlind, Helena Hede. 2020. *The Power of Indicators in Global
    Development Policy: The Millennium Development Goals.* The Power of
    Global Performance Indicators. New York: Cambridge University Press.
Stasavage, David. 2005. Democracy and Education Spending in Africa.
    American Journal of Political Science 49 (2):343–58.

13

Global Performance Indicators: Themes, Findings, and an Agenda for Future Research

Judith G. Kelley and Beth A. Simmons

Globalization, accountability, and technology are changing important aspects of global governance. While coercion, enforcement, and material sanctions have often taken pride of place as major movers of interstate relations, scholars and policy agents alike have come to appreciate the multifaceted nature of power exerted more subtly and gradually.[1]

The proliferation of global performance indicators (GPIs) is one example of such power. They contain ideas and worldviews, and they attempt to "regulate" through non-coercive but nonetheless powerful means. They do not merely measure qualities and practices in order to understand or inform, they pressure their targets to *per*form and *con*form. In wielding such tools, a diverse set of actors insert themselves in the governing process, in some cases even shifting policy parameters. When promulgated by authoritative actors, GPIs can name and categorize information in new ways and have what anthropologists like Merry and others have referred to as "knowledge effects," or the ability to influence how people think about socially legitimate or best practice. Their proliferation and evolution define and contest what is worth knowing, measuring and achieving.

This volume has systematically explored the broad consequences of GPI proliferation. We have argued that by gathering data, monitoring targets, framing issues, transmitting information, and stimulating competitive or reputational concerns, GPIs can engage and influence actors at various levels. They may attract media attention and inspire domestic audiences to mobilize around low ratings to pressure governments for policy reform. They may engage elites directly through learning or by instigating bureaucratic processes that

---

[1] Barnett and Duvall 2005. Baldwin discusses the many scholars who have advanced a view of power as multidimensional. Baldwin 2016.

focus attention on the issue. They may trigger transnational actors criticisms, potentially leading to tangible consequences, especially when the assessment is thought to affect business or aid decisions.

While not all GPIs matter, the contributions to this volume show that some GPIs influence norms and behaviors across a wide range of issues and actors. GPIs are therefore worth paying attention to, as are wider questions of how they might affect the power balance between states and the nature of accountability in global governance. Below, we summarize the main findings of the contributions in this volume, discuss of some broader questions that the findings raise, and suggest avenues for future research.

WHY GPIs MATTER: EFFECTS ON NORMS AND POLICIES

The central question of this book has been whether and how GPIs can exert social pressure on decisionmakers to alter their policies and practices. We have shown that GPIs can influence how an issue is discussed and understood and that some GPIs have ultimately altered the content or speed of reforms in the policy areas targeted, perhaps even in unanticipated ways.

That GPIs can diffuse norms is evident in several cases. Honig and Weaver show that the small non-governmental organization (NGO), Publish What You Fund, who produces the *Aid Transparency Index*, has influenced the meaning of what it is to be a "good" aid agency and thus a "good" aid professional. As a result, aid agencies are much more likely to respond to the *Index* than agencies for whom aid is not the primary mission. Similarly, Kijima and Lipscy find that the testing for the Program for International Student Assessment (PISA) rankings, which require extensive elite interaction with authoritative agencies and experts, provides considerable scope for technical transfers, learning, and socialization. A Honduran delegate noted that the rankings have shaped a "big debate about what quality of education means."

Precisely because GPIs are influential, they have been a lively site of contestation. Kijima and Lipscy note that some critics see the rankings as "educational colonialism" by unaccountable Western technocrats. Over half of developing country respondents question the substance of the PISA testing. The *Ease of Doing Business Index* by the World Bank has been similarly controversial, as discussed by Doshi, Kelley, and Simmons. Indeed, the labor subcomponents of the *Index* were so controversial that they were eventually removed. And when the World Bank finally added measures to account for the freedom of women to start a business, Saudi Arabia protested vehemently as the new criteria challenged its values and caused its ranking to plummet. Contestation of norms are also evident in Skagerlind's study of gender policies in response to the Millennium Development Goals (MDGs). Sometimes the MDG gender norms conflicted directly with local norms, for example around the goal of increasing women's representation in decision-making bodies.

Jo, Phillips, and Alley note that even the designation of a terrorist list highlights the authority relationships and contestation in world politics.

Perhaps even more consequential than their effects on norms and contestation, several of the contributions examined effects on the policies of targeted entities, and found some evidence of GPI influence. Bisbee et al. rely on interrupted time series analysis to show that the MDGs have boosted primary school enrollments as intended. The change in enrollment growth occurs just when the MDGs are introduced, an effect that is not entirely explained by increases in foreign aid. Kijima and Lipscy also show that countries improve their secondary school enrollment after they are included in the PISA rankings, controlling for confounding factors such as pre-PISA commitments to domestic education reform. Likewise, Koliev, Sommerer, and Tallberg find that ILO assessments and reporting significantly and durably affect state respect for labor rights, especially in severe cases of non-compliance.

Sometimes specific laws and practices change as a result of GPIs. Morse shows that countries that are included on the Financial Action Task Force (FATF) list of uncooperative jurisdictions criminalize money laundering and terrorist financing faster than those that are not listed as uncooperative. This is true even after she accounts for countries' prior efforts to pass criminal legislation and other factors that may drive the FATF decision to list countries in the first place. This finding, which is further supported though a case study of Thailand, is consistent with other research that shows that monitoring and reporting hasten criminalization of human trafficking in target countries.[2] Similarly, Hoenig and Weaver found that aid agencies drastically increased their transparency after inclusion in the *Aid Transparency Index*, a finding that is also supported by a wealth of qualitative evidence. Skagerlind, similarly, finds that there has been a significant policy adjustment to MDG 3 across a broad range of countries. Finally, Doshi, Kelley, and Simmons's research on the *Ease of Doing Business Index* found that several of the sub-indicators have improved since the introduction of the *Doing Business Report*, and support a causal interpretation of this evidence with an analysis of official statements in the media that directly reference the rankings as a motivator.

Collectively, the contributions to this volume have provided significant evidence that GPIs affect standards, discourse, and often targeted policies. Several contributors, however, discovered that assessments and public rankings also can have *unintended* consequences. The pressure to score well does not always lead to effective policy. Some of the unintended effects discussed in this volume include hasty implementation, choosing the most low-hanging fruit, and even substituting policies to meet targets. For example, key informants pointed out that the pressures induced by the *Aid Transparency Index* sometimes led organizations to adopt inefficient data collection and reporting systems. Likewise, interviews revealed that states sometimes adopt reforms just to move up in the

[2] Kelley 2017; Kelley and Simmons 2015.

Bank's Doing Business rankings, but that those reforms were not always meaningful on the ground. Bisbee et al. identify a substitution effect, uncovering evidence that countries diverted spending from secondary education to bolster primary education enrollment in response to the MDG goals.

Both intended and unintended policy outputs testify to the fact that actors care about and respond to assessment regimes, both in word and in deed. The contributions to this volume have thus made a solid case for the fact that GPIs have observable consequences for both policies and discussion around norms.

HOW GPIs WORK: TRANSNATIONAL, ELITE, AND OTHER DOMESTIC ACTORS

Transnational Pressures

How and why do GPIs influence specific targets? If target states believe third parties – such as aid donors or investors – are aware of and care about how the target measures up, that matters. Transnational third-party pressures feature especially highly in most accounts of GPI influence. Indeed, this is the only pathway that is discussed across all the contributions to this volume (Introduction, Table 1.1). Several chapters show GPIs influence resource flows. For example, Lall's research on state ratings of the performance of international organizations demonstrates that donors reward organizations that rank as more effective and efficient with greater contributions and that such contributions do not merely reflect underlying IO performance. Skagerlind's study similarly points out that the MDG country reports on gender policy were used as leverage in aid negotiations. In the area of education, GPIs are also associated with foreign aid flows, but, interestingly, Bisbee et al. show that these aid flows are only part of the story and that other domestic political mechanisms are more important. Kijima and Lipscy furthermore note that despite their effects, the PISA scores were never intended to influence aid.

These findings highlight two important points. First, a GPI creator need not possess significant material power of its own, if markets or other actors see it as credible. Secondly, it's not all about money. The effects of the MDGs surpassed what could be explained by changes in aid flows. Third, propagators cannot easily control the end use of their assessments. Social knowledge is necessarily public knowledge. There are no guarantees that these exercises will be strictly limited to achieving the purposes for which they were designed. All in all, GPIs sometimes affect aid, even if the creator possesses no material power on their own. And yet, these linkages to foreign aid, even when at work, do not tell the entire story about GPI influence.

Clearly, for GPIs to matter, important actors must care about what is being measured. Lee and Matanock find that, despite its long-running salience, Transparency International's *Corruptions Perception Index* fails to move aid donors to change their aid giving or even to shame the worst offenders, even though they get more media coverage. Perhaps aid donors are rigidly committed to recipient countries regardless of how corrupt they are perceived to be.

Several contributions also explore effects on investors. Doshi, Kelley, and Simmons present a survey experiment that shows that seasoned investors say they are keener to invest in a country with better rankings in the *Ease of Doing Business Index* than a country with lower ratings, even when other economic conditions are held constant. This aligns with what leaders believe as well. For example, Serbia's Prime Minister explicitly aimed "to enter the top 30 countries...because the better positioned we are, the more we will be able to attract foreign and domestic investors." Relatedly, Morse argues that the effects of the FATF on terrorist financing laws works through interest rates, because international banks and investors shift resources away from listed, non-compliant states. As evidence, she finds that the speed with which countries criminalize terrorist financing is greater for countries that sell sovereign debt and that – in line with this logic – investors demand higher relative yields on sovereign debt for listed countries. Similarly, Jo, Phillips, and Alley find that the terrorism watch lists alter flows of financial support to terrorist groups. Sometimes what matters is simply that targets *believe* that GPIs *could* affect investors. For example, Kijima and Lipscy find that it was sufficient that Malaysia's government *perceived* that foreign investment decisions were tied to assessment performance, though there is no evidence that they are.

Finally, transnational actors may exert pressure in subtler ways. Most GPIs glean media coverage at their release, a relationship that Matanock and Lee document systematically surrounding the *Corruptions Perception Index*. More importantly, GPIs can also stimulate public diplomatic pressure. Tellez and Roberts show that that Freedom House's *Freedom in the World* reports function like a "Scarlet Letter" in that democracies criticize countries barely rated "not free" more and across a range of topics – not just their (un)democratic behavior – even though their performance is practically indistinguishable from countries barely rated "partly free." Apparently, being listed as undemocratic matters above and beyond the otherwise observable behavior. In this way, Freedom House shapes the normative milieu in which states and their officials operate. By highlighting the relative performance and labeling offenders, Freedom House thus increases social opprobrium.

Bottom Up: Domestic Politics

Several contributions illustrate how GPIs resonate in domestic politics, creating new demands on governments. Kijima and Lipscy described how domestic protesters in Chile used low educational rankings to push the government for change. Hungary's poor PISA performance "ignited" protests, "calls for the resignation of government ministers" and demands to centralize the educational system. Bisbee et al. also argued that the extra scrutiny associated with the MDGs criteria encourages greater domestic political attention to those criteria, creating demands for more investment in public goods that improve performance on the MDGs.

Pressure can also come from domestic business. Morse described how a Thai chief bank executive urged the government to modify its laws on money laundering and terrorist financing to improve the image of the country's financial system. Her research illustrates how a GPI can shape a domestic agenda, drawing attention to policy issues that might otherwise have been entirely disconnected from domestic preferences.

GPIs often provide focal information around which domestic civil society organizations find it possible to mobilize. Skagerlind reports that civil society organizations (CSOs) helped monitor MDG performance on gender policies with shadow progress reports highlighting government performance in national and international fora. This was particularly the case in Kenya where CSOs received funding and an increased ability to organize to demand policy progress. And, in a twist, Doshi, Kelley, and Simmons show how President Modi used the *Ease of Doing Business Index* to provoke domestic awareness and pressure on his own bureaucrats and provincial governments to move business deregulation along, effectively becoming an ally of the World Bank's agenda.

Finally, Hoenig and Weaver find that reform proponents use poor ratings from the *Aid Transparency Index* to create pressure. Legislatures may use the information to argue their points, or the NGO community may use the index to lobby officials, as noted by staff in the US House Foreign Affairs Committee and the US Senate Foreign Relations Committee.

If bottom-up politics is less prevalent than transnational pressure, it is worth noting that sometimes the mere *anticipation* of such pressure might matter, as noted by staff at the US General Accounting Office regarding aid transparency. Indeed, General Accounting Office (GAO) staff expressed concern that the *Aid Transparency Index* score would influence the future appropriation of funds toward USAID. Such an implicit constraining role is also what Bisbee et al. contend is at work in more transparent societies, which are less likely to shift their education spending in response to the MDGs.

Elite Politics

Used in conjunction with monitoring, GPIs often directly engage the reputations for competence and effectiveness of specific officials and their agencies. When GPIs target policies for which specific ministries are directly responsible, officials are incentivized to initiate policy change to deflect criticism that could damage their reputations.[3] Several chapters in this volume illustrate this dynamic and the conditions under which it is likely to occur. Morse notes that in the case of the FATF and combating the financing of terrorism, such

---

[3] This theme was evident in a series of 10 interviews with GPI creators conducted by the authors in Washington, DC, August 12–14, 2014.

engagement has resulted in the creation of action plans. In the case of gender policies, bureaucracies formulated policy goals in response to the MDG reports, according to Skagerlind. Many states even create or designate special bureaucracies to implement recommendations from the World Bank's *Doing Business Report* and these teams collaborate closely with the Bank, often producing plans that prioritize implementing outcomes the indicators measure.

In some cases, the process of assessment leads to learning and professionalization. Honig and Weaver find that elites responded to the *Aid Transparency Index (ATI)* by inter- and intra-organizational learning, adopting its norms, and professionalizing aid staff and management around the specific standards of transparency that the index promotes. Staff that work in aid organizations say that they learn from the ATI what other organizations are doing and follow specific recommendations from Publish What You Fund, the NGO that publishes the *Index*. In this way, the authors argue that the ATI shapes donor behavior primarily via the diffusion of professional norms, organizational learning, and horizontal accountability or peer pressure. This contrasts with conventional arguments, particularly those embedded in principal-agent frameworks, that locate the ATI's power over donor agencies in the index's reduction of information asymmetries and the triggering of vertical accountability through political authorizers' oversight and control. As such, the ATI's pathways to influence are also rooted in normative and practical, rather than merely material, power.

Similarly, as many as three-quarters of the elites Kijima and Lipscy surveyed reported that their PISA engagement facilitates learning and exchange of information, with a Chilean official emphasizing that the government regularly sends "a large delegation to the Organization for Economic Cooperation and Development (OECD) for consultations, information exchange, and training."[4] These findings lend support to the argument that GPIs do not merely report behaviors that would have otherwise occurred, but also behaviors that are direct responses to GPI monitoring and engagement. Evidence points clearly to bureaucratic changes in priorities and structures to address performance assessments. Sometimes the consequences are salutary, but not necessarily.

It is difficult to generalize about the desirability of using GPIs to influence elite priorities, because it is hard for GPI creators to know how their assessments will be used once they are public. Some elites use GPIs for their own political purposes. India's President Modi clearly used the *Ease of Doing Business Index* to advance his political agenda, motivate reforms, denigrate opposition, and set visible goals. Indeed, the media analysis shows that many government officials strategically use the *Index* to boast or signal their policy plans to domestic audiences. It is worth noting that not only are GPI creators

---

[4] Kijima and Lipscy this volume, p. 205.

trying to influence targets; targets themselves may seize upon ratings and rankings for their own purposes.

Elites apparently find the competitive and comparative dynamics of rankings hard to resist. About half of the public statements about the *Ease of Doing Business Index* were about officials committing to improve their rankings per se. Doshi, Kelley, and Simmons have excavated a trove of media evidence demonstrating their allure. Indonesian President Jokowi announced "a policy intended to improve Indonesia's position in the World Bank's Ease of Doing Business rankings from 109 to 40."[5] Furthermore, 14 percent of the officials explicitly compare their countries to others, such as the undersecretary to Cyprus' president, who heads the president's administrative reform unit. Underscoring the interesting point that that countries select their own comparison groups, he noted that Cyprus ranked 25th of 28 EU states and that "our performance there is not good."[6] Thus, GPIs may generate discontent and competitive spirits in even well-performing target countries if they fare poorly relative to their peers, a dynamic also observed in other GPIs such as the US Trafficking in Persons Report.[7] The comparative dynamic sparked by FATF was also apparent. For example, Antigua and Barbuda fretted about the reputational impact of being grouped with Nigeria, Sudan, Ukraine, and Myanmar on the FATF's list of high-risk countries with respect to combating the financing of terrorism.

Such comparisons are often rooted in concerns about reputation and status. For example, elites in international organizations admit being concerned that low effectiveness rankings cause reputational damage with their partners, and officials in Vietnam used strong PISA scores to increase their status in the international community. Indeed, although many of their countries fare poorly in the rankings, well over half of the elites surveyed by Kijima and Lipscy thought that their participation in the PISA rankings "improves our reputation/status in the international community." As our own interviews with multiple creators of various GPIs revealed, this type of attitude is one of the main concerns GPIs aim to engender.[8]

Scope Conditions

Our framework suggests some important scope conditions, which themselves should be the subject of future research. First, domestic governance structure matters; clearly not every government reacts in the same way to rankings. Regime type, the density of civil society actors and the information environment are all likely to shape GPI effects. Democratic states may be more

---

[5] Kelley, Simmons, and Doshi, this volume, p. 35.
[6] Kelley, Simmons, and Doshi, this volume, p. 36.
[7] Kelley 2017.
[8] Author interviews with GPI creators, in Washington, DC, August 12–14, 2014.

responsive to certain kinds of assessments, as Koliev, Tallberg, and Sommerer note in their study of the ILO. They stress that reporting improves labor rights more when the target states are democratic and have the resource capacity to correct violations. Transparency matters as well; it may help to mitigate some of the most flagrant strategic behavior. This is one reasonable interpretation of Bisbee et al.'s finding that substitution among educational levels in response to MDG goals is mitigated as government transparency rises.

Second, GPI influence will also vary based on local values. Although GPIs have strong agenda-setting powers, they cannot be expected to force action to which local elites are utterly opposed or where the message does not resonate at all locally. Skagerlind speaks to this issue of local norms in her study of gender policies, noting that while the MDGs may be propelling policy changes, implementation falls far short where there is a conflict with local values.

Third, GPIs are limited by the capacity of the rated entities to respond. A range of conditions can undermine state capacity, from pervasive political violence to corruption to severe resource shortages. Relatedly, GPIs will not matter if important political audiences or actors are not motivated to act on them or face conflicts in doing so. This was plausibly the case with the *Corruptions Perceptions Index*: aid donors seem locked-in to their aid practices, which, as Lee and Matanock find, are surprisingly non-responsive to corruption rankings.

As a corollary, GPIs are more likely to be influential when they are actionable. It is considerably easier for all countries to change a fee or repeal a regulation, for example, than it is to quickly improve child mortality or perceptions about corruption. It is evident, for example, that some subcomponents of the *Ease of Doing Business Index* are hard to move, while others are more malleable. This need for actionability likely explains the near absence of GPIs focused on military issues. The security-related indices that do exist resemble what we might think of as "data," without ambitious statements that they intend to influence state policies. Perhaps relatedly, there is more evidence of policy effects when the creators of GPIs engage extensively with elites and broaden the opportunities for the transfer of ideas and usable information as in the case of the *Ease of Doing Business Index* or the *Aid Transparency Index*.

Fourth, when the creator lacks social importance to the target, GPIs are easily ignored. Thus, criminal networks do not care whether the United States list a terrorist group on its official list, because they have no respect whatsoever for the United States or its law. Again, this insight suggests a corollary: social isolates, such as North Korea, are inherently weak candidates for GPI influence. As with many forms of external pressure, there may be a sweet spot for maximal GPI impact centering on transitioning democracies, the middle-income countries and/or emerging markets.

In addition, while it is reasonable to hypothesize that, all things equal, material leverage or predominant power increase GPI influence, the chapters show that it is not necessary for the creators to possess these traits. Our framework proposes – and the empirical research shows – that GPIs work primarily through reputational concerns sparked by comparative information. Apparently, it is the case that material opportunities and vulnerabilities shape responses. Lall for example shows that funding vulnerability makes some intergovernmental organizations more responsive to effectiveness ratings than others, just as Jo, Alley, and Phillips demonstrate funding source conditions organizations' response to a terrorist designation. But even in the case of the FATF blacklist, which relies primarily on markets to incentivize policy change, Morse finds that officials profess to be more motivated by a desire for a clean international reputation than a specific market reaction. The chapters in this book thus consolidate prior claims that GPIs are strongly driven by reputational concerns while allowing that material leverage and reputation-engaging information likely interact.

GPIs AND GLOBAL GOVERNANCE

Important decisions ride on global performance indicators, from significant changes in the criminal code, increased aid transparency, business deregulation, allocation of school funding, aid flows, contributions to international organizations, and more. The cases in this book show that that GPIs are indeed powerful, their influence may work through but is not isomorphic with material resources, and their influence operates across a wider set of actors and issues than previously demonstrated.

The consequences of GPIs across a variety of issues and entities raises questions about how we understand contemporary global governance when an increasingly diverse set of actors seek to exert power through a wider array of tools. We have characterized GPIs as a form of social pressure, which, to paraphrase Kofi Annan, amplify the effect of their promulgators' own moral, institutional, and material resources.[9] The GPIs studied in this volume suggest that they can be influential across a range of issues, and that they can impact the framing of issues and the behavior of targeted actors, often precisely because they are thought to affect the actions and reactions of others. In addition, several contributions highlight the strong possibility of unintended consequences. One lesson for governance is how to select index measures wisely so that they are not easily gamed or measured in a shallow way.

At a deeper level, such wisdom itself is contestable. It is difficult to generalize about the normative value of the influences of rating and ranking processes. It is not possible to say GPIs generally have salutary consequences any more than it is possible to claim that "information," "influence," and "social pressure" are per se positive or negative. We have argued that though they appear objective, all ranking systems are inherently value-laden, even those

[9] Annan 1998.

that can make a reasonable claim to accuracy. Moreover, the very appearance of objectivity is what makes such systems attractive. International organizations are likely therefore to find them attractive when they come under fire for more coercive or intrusive forms of governance. Thus, the World Bank more legitimately ranks states on their ease of doing business than writing loan contracts conditional on reducing inspections or requiring capital for new businesses to be established. The latter seems an unjustified intrusion on state sovereignty. But ranking the ease of doing business allows for "hands-free" guidance – and lets markets do the enforcement. We suspect this is why international organizations from the United Nations to the European Union have deployed ranking systems. It gives the appearance of global governance without coercion. At a time when such organizations grapple with the problem of legitimacy, "information" is a better output than directives.

While the contributions of this book concentrate on the more immediate consequences of GPIs, this volume hints at an even more profound issue: the impact of GPIs on the asymmetry of power and worldwide authority relationships more generally.[10] If actors can unilaterally use a GPI to yield influence in a given area, then GPIs will potentially empower new actors in ways that change relative power and influence in global governance. Global performance indicators wield influence partly because so many organizations – states, intergovernmental organizations, NGOs, business firms – rely on transnational flows of resources that are tied to their perceived performance. In a dense information environment, creators of GPIs have an outsized opportunity to impact these perceptions of performance. States are therefore being held "accountable" through rankings, but the ranking propagators and transnational pressure that incentivize competition and conformity may have little to do with the will of the people to whom states are ultimately accountable. While the domestic politics channel we have described may preserve local input, the quality of accountability through rankings is hardly assured.

If the creators of GPIs can unilaterally seize agenda setting and normative authority, how might this shift affect who holds power in international relations? On the one hand, the evidence shows that rich states and wealthy people tend to do the rating, while poor countries are often the assessed. In the database explored in the introductory chapter, nearly half of GPIs are promulgated by US-based organizations, while less than 5 percent are headquartered in the Global South, suggesting that GPIs entrench global power imbalances. One potential consequence is a concentration of power in the Global North. On the other hand, GPIs reflect a great diversification of actors and institutions contesting social knowledge and attempting to influence discourse, agendas and, ultimately, outcomes.[11] This suggests that they could also contribute to

---

[10] For interesting discussions see Büthe 2012; Davis, Kingsbury, and Merry 2012; Halliday 2012; Kelley and Simmons 2015; Löwenheim 2008.

[11] Avant, Finnemore, and Sell 2010; Hale and Held 2011; Hale and Roger 2014.

a dispersion of power across different types of actors. Certainly, the evidence and narratives revealed by these chapters is not exclusively about powerful states. Several of our contributions examine GPIs created by IGOs with varying degrees of leverage: The United Nations, while comprehensive, is often considered rather toothless; the World Bank has considerable economic leverage, but claims to maintain a firewall between lending and ranking decisions; and the FATF is a standard-setting body without enforcement powers.

Furthermore, GPIs are not just for those who dominate resources. Even governments' decisions about education spending do not appear to depend exclusively on how the MDGs affect foreign aid flows. Some evidence points more toward the domestic information effects and elite bureaucratic channels of the MDGs. Sometimes even poorly resourced NGOs such as Publish What You Fund can leverage GPIs. Empirical evidence across different types of actors thus shows that it is not necessary that the GPI creator be an already-powerful state or IGO.

Still, it is too early to be sure about how GPIs affect power relationships in the aggregate. We suspect GPIs are potentially more useful for nudging policy change than traditional coercive power resources, like economic and military sanctions, which are generally too blunt to address the kinds of issues discussed in these pages. They do effectively supplement other sources of leverage under the control of developed countries. Some evidence suggests their creators realize this and do not squander perceptions of GPI legitimacy with overt political or economic pressure, as the intentional firewalling of the Ease of Doing Business (EDB) office from the loan office at the World Bank suggests. The FATF does not sanction non-compliant jurisdictions and does not require or even urge its membership to do so. These powerful actors – *who could in theory choose otherwise* – prefer to stage competition and engage reputations rather than threaten sanctions or exert political pressure. Yet, to date, the authority to define the game and to keep score rather firmly resides with existing centers of global power.

Can GPIs work in the face of disagreement on what constitutes appropriate policy, or do they primarily nudge states in directions that reflect broad social consensus? Again, the contributions in this book suggest some answers. The World Bank's focus on business deregulation has sparked massive pushback from environmental and labor groups and major powers such as China. Yet despite these dissenters, numerous governments try to climb the ranking in the belief that a poor ranking is bad for their perceived investment climate. The MDGs' focus on education enrollment, which critics have long argued fails to capture the quality of education, is also controversial as is the MDGs' frequent lack of coherence with local norms. Even a topic as seemingly innocuous as aid transparency has stoked debate about whether this focus is productive. Lack of consensus often spurs GPI promulgation in the first place. Thus, consensus is not a necessary condition for GPI success, although we would expect rankings to have even more clout when they reinforce broadly held social values.

This success of the World Bank and others in using a GPI to set policy agendas also raises questions of accountability of GPI creators themselves.[12] If specific authority in a given area is not expressly delegated by states, but international organizations or other actors can nonetheless create some authority through their own initiative, it will be important to pay attention to who supervises and assesses the exertion of such authority. If no consensus has been derived through interstate negotiations about the underlying values of a GPI, then there may not be anyone to ensure that the values and norms being promulgated align with other international norms and expectations. This is especially relevant in a world of growing contention around facts and concerted production of disinformation.[13] If those who administer a given GPI have no reporting relationship to anyone, then there may be no one outside the creator's own organization to maintain any quality control, or identify any excess or abuse of power. *Ad hoc* criticisms that target states may not carry much weight as this can be dismissed as a purely defensive tactic. In today's rapidly changing information environment, the influence of GPIs on global governance is not likely merely to be more of the same. They have the potential to empower actors in new ways that deserve the attention of scholars and practitioners alike.

AN AGENDA FOR RESEARCH

The proliferation of GPIs is one example of increasingly sophisticated information power. They contain ideas and worldviews, and they attempt to "regulate" through non-coercive means. When promulgated by authoritative actors, GPIs may have direct, indirect, and even unintended effects. Establishing causality is challenging, but the chapters in this volume present corroborating evidence to establish highly plausible channels of GPI influence.

Future research should prioritize several issues in addition to the scope conditions discussed above. First, primary research informed by psychology and sociology should investigate what makes ratings and rankings – and the information on which they are based – believable. Second, more research can be done on the information milieu in which GPIs compete. The chapters in this book are clear about the information ecology of their specific GPI, but it would be useful to know much more about whether and how GPIs compete with other forms of information and misinformation. Relatedly, it would be useful to know not only why some GPIs seem to succeed but also why others gain no traction at all. This would require further investigation of first mover advantages, the authority of the promulgator, and the marketing of ideas in the form of comparative data globally. Third, we envision more intensive

[12] Grant and Keohane 2005.
[13] Cooke 2017.

research on informational contestation. We have provided a flavor of that contestation, but much more can be done to theorize the politics of information gathering and deployment globally. Fourth, scholars should explore how non-state actors develop sophisticated information campaigns. While shaming has taken center stage in the study of global advocacy groups, less attention has been given to advocates' capacity to develop and deploy methodologically transparent performance measures. At most, "shaming" in this context is subtle and indirect; indeed, in many cases, it has developed as an alternative to more aggressive forms of social opprobrium. Fifth, as with any policy instrument, future research should focus not only on whether GPIs obtain their objectives but also at what possible costs, including possible unintended consequences. It will be important to focus research on understanding not just outputs, but also outcomes, intended and unintended. As this volume demonstrates, that is a task not just for bureaucrats but for social scientists as well. Sixth, while we have shown that an array of different types of actors use GPIs with success, future research should test the limits of the claim that GPIs can disperse influence beyond traditional power centers. Seventh, our contribution has found a strong role for reputation, yet we also recognize the link with material leverage. Future research should continue to investigate the interactive consequences of material leverage and reputation-engaging information. For example, are these tools of influence complements or substitutes?

Finally, it would be useful to link research on GPIs as social knowledge and social pressure with other new forms of global governance. GPIs are unique in their iterated, public, and comparative nature. They are potentially useful as a contemporary "hybrid" governance tool, along with other methods of external influence, such as public-private partnerships,[14] experimental governance,[15] report-and-review treaty implementation regimes,[16] and multi-stakeholder initiatives.[17] Now may be the time to think creatively about how GPIs support or undermine governance in the presence of what Michael Zürn refers to as growing global governance dilemmas.[18] As the increasing prevalence of interstate efforts to manipulate social media and other information flows shows, strategic use of information is rapidly becoming an ever more potent tool of influence. Addressing GPI impact on discourse, governance, and global and local power relations is an ambitious research agenda, but the ideas in this book provide a strong start.

---

[14] Börzel and Risse 2005; Osborne 2002; Schäferhoff, Campe, and Kaan 2009.
[15] De Búrca, Keohane, and Sabel 2014; Szyszczak 2006.
[16] Creamer and Simmons forthcoming; Creamer and Simmons 2018.
[17] Bäckstrand 2006; O'Rourke 2006.
[18] Zürn 2018.

References

Annan, Kofi. 1998. The Quiet Revolution. *Global Governance* 4 (2):123–38.

Avant, Deborah D., Martha Finnemore, and Susan K. Sell, eds. 2010. Who Governs the Globe? *Cambridge Studies in International Relations; 114.* New York: Cambridge University Press.

Bäckstrand, Karin. 2006. Multi-Stakeholder Partnerships for Sustainable Development: Rethinking Legitimacy, Accountability and Effectiveness. *European Environment* 16 (5):290–306.

Baldwin, David A. 2016. *Power and International Relations: A Conceptual Approach.* Princeton, NJ: Princeton University Press.

Barnett, Michael, and Raymond Duvall. 2005. Power in International Politics. *International Organization* 59 (1):39–75.

Börzel, Tanja, and Thomas Risse. 2005. Public-Private Partnerships: Effective and Legitimate Tools of International Governance. In *Complex Sovereignty*, edited by Lou Pauly and Edgar Grande, 195–216. Toronto: University of Toronto Press.

Büthe, Tim. 2012. Beyond Supply and Demand: A Political-Economic Conceptual Model. In *Governance by Indicators: Global Power Through Classification and Rankings*, edited by Kevin Davis, Angelina Fisher, Benedict Kingsbury and Sally Engle Merry. Oxford: Oxford University Press, 29–51.

Creamer, Cosette D., and Beth A. Simmons. 2018. The Dynamic Impact of Periodic Review on Women's Rights. *Law and Contemporary Problems* 81 (4):31–72.

Creamer, Cosette D., and Beth A. Simmons. forthcoming, 2020. Do Self-Reporting Regimes Matter? Evidence from the Convention Against Torture. *International Studies Quarterly*.

Davis, Kevin E., Benedict Kingsbury, and Sally Engle Merry. 2012. Indicators as a Technology of Global Governance. *Law & Society Review* 46 (1):71–104.

De Búrca, Gráinne, Robert O. Keohane, and Charles Sabel. 2014. Global Experimentalist Governance. *British Journal of Political Science* 44 (3):477–86.

Grant, Ruth W., and Robert O. Keohane. 2005. Accountability and Abuses of Power in World Politics. *American Political Science Review* 99 (1):29–43.

Hale, Thomas, and David Held. 2011. *Handbook of Transnational Governance.* Cambridge: Polity.

Hale, Thomas, and Charles Roger. 2014. Orchestration and Transnational Climate Governance. *The Review of International Organizations* 9 (1):59–82.

Halliday, Terence C. 2012. Legal Yardsticks: International Financial Institutions as Diagnosticians and Designers of the Laws of Nations. In *Governance by Indicators: Global Power Through Quantification and Rankings*, edited by Kevin E. Davis, Fisher Angelina, Benedict Kingsbury, and Sally Engle Merry. New York: Oxford University Press.

Kelley, Judith. 2017. *Scorecard Diplomacy: Grading States to Influence their Reputation and Behavior.* Cambridge: Cambridge University Press.

Kelley, Judith, and Beth A. Simmons. 2015. Politics by Number: Indicators as Social Pressure in International Relations. *American Journal of Political Science* 59 (1):1146–61.

Kelley, Judith G., Beth A. Simmons, and Rush Doshi. this volume. The Power of Ranking: The Ease of Doing Business and Global Regulatory Behavior. Chapter 2 in *The Power of Global Performance Indicators*.

Kijima, Rie and Phillip Y. Lipscy. this volume. International Assessments and Education Policy: Evidence from an Elite Survey.

Löwenheim, Oded. 2008. Examining the State: A Foucauldian Perspective on International "Governance Indicators". *Third World Quarterly* 29 (2):255–74.

O'Rourke, Dara. 2006. Multi-Stakeholder Regulation: Privatizing or Socializing Global Labor Standards? *World Development* 34 (5):899–918.

Osborne, Stephen. 2002. *Public-Private Partnerships: Theory and Practice in International Perspective*. London: Routledge.

Schäferhoff, Marco, Sabine Campe, and Christopher Kaan. 2009. Transnational Public-Private Partnerships in International Relations: Making Sense of Concepts, Research Frameworks, and Results. *International Studies Review* 11 (3):451–74.

Szyszczak, Erika. 2006. Experimental Governance: The Open Method of Coordination. *European Law Journal* 12 (4):486–502.

Zürn, Michael. 2018. *A Theory of Global Governance: Authority, Legitimacy, and Contestation*. New York: Oxford University Press.

Index